Military of Ancient Rome
753 BC - 476 AD

Compiled by
Jann Tibbetts

Scribbles

Year of Publication 2018

ISBN : 9789352979165

Book Published by

Scribbles

(An Imprint of Alpha Editions)

email - alphaedis@gmail.com

Produced by: PediaPress GmbH
Limburg an der Lahn
Germany
http://pediapress.com/

The content within this book was generated collaboratively by volunteers. Please be advised that nothing found here has necessarily been reviewed by people with the expertise required to provide you with complete, accurate or reliable information. Some information in this book may be misleading or simply wrong. Alpha Editions and PediaPress does not guarantee the validity of the information found here. If you need specific advice (for example, medical, legal, financial, or risk management) please seek a professional who is licensed or knowledgeable in that area.

Sources, licenses and contributors of the articles and images are listed in the section entitled "References". Parts of the books may be licensed under the GNU Free Documentation License. A copy of this license is included in the section entitled "GNU Free Documentation License"

The views and characters expressed in the book are those of the contributors and his/her imagination and do not represent the views of the Publisher.

Contents

Articles 1

Introduction 1
Military of ancient Rome 1

Structure 21
Structural history of the Roman military 21
Roman army 47
List of Roman army unit types 66
Roman military decorations and punishments 71
List of Roman legions 77
Auxilia 90
List of Roman generals 127

Navy 135
Roman navy 135

Campaigns 165
Campaign history of the Roman military 165
List of Roman wars and battles 206

Technology — 231

- Technological history of the Roman military 231
- Castra 235
- Roman siege engines 259
- List of Roman triumphal arches 273
- Roman roads 279

Strategy — 311

- Strategy of the Roman military 311
- Roman infantry tactics 316

Fortification — 361

- Roman military frontiers and fortifications 361

Appendix — 369

- References 369
- Article Sources and Contributors 394
- Image Sources, Licenses and Contributors 396

Article Licenses — 401

Index — 403

Introduction

Military of ancient Rome

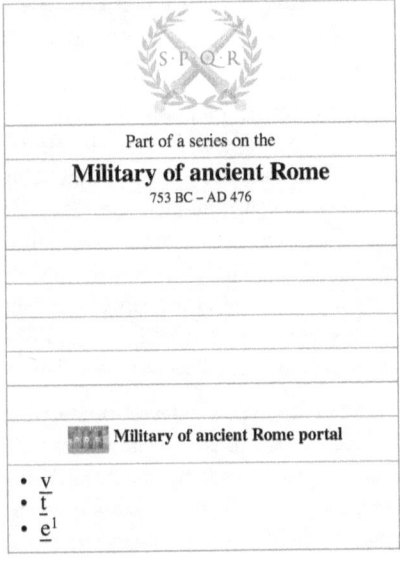

The **military of ancient Rome**, according to Titus Livius, one of the more illustrious historians of Rome over the centuries, was a key element in the rise of Rome over "above seven hundred years"[2] from a small settlement in Latium to the capital of an empire governing a wide region around the shores of the Mediterranean, or, as the Romans themselves said, "mare nostrum", "our sea." Livy asserts

> "... if any people ought to be allowed to consecrate their origins and refer them to a divine source, so great is the military glory of the Roman People that when they profess that their Father and the Father of their Founder

was none other than Mars, the nations of the earth may well submit to this also with as good a grace as they submit to Rome's dominion."

Titus Flavius Josephus, a contemporary historian, sometime high-ranking officer in the Roman army, and commander of the rebels in the Jewish revolt, describes the Roman people as if they were "born ready armed."[3] At the time of the two historians, Roman society had already evolved an effective military and had used it to defend itself against the Etruscans, the Italics, the Greeks, the Gauls, the maritime empire of Carthage, and the Macedonian kingdoms. In each war it acquired more territory until, when civil war ended the Roman Republic, nothing was left for the first emperor, Augustus, to do except declare it an empire and defend it.

The role and structure of the military was then altered during the empire. It became less Roman, the duties of border protection and territorial administration being more and more taken by foreign mercenaries officered by Romans. When they divided at last into warring factions the empire fell, unable to keep out invading armies.

" - an agency designated by 'SPQR' on public inscriptions. Its main body was the senate, which met in a building still extant in the forum of Rome. Its decrees were handed off to the two chief officers of the state, the consuls. They could levy from the citizens whatever military force they judged was necessary to execute such decree. This conscription was executed through a draft of male citizens assembled by age class. The officers of the legion were tasked with selecting men for the ranks. The will of the SPQR was binding on the consuls and the men, with the death penalty often assigned for disobedience or failure. The men were under a rigorous code, known now for its punitive crucifixion.

The consular duties were of any type whatever: military defense, police work, public hygiene, assistance in civil disaster, health work, agriculture, and especially construction of public roads, bridges, aqueducts, buildings, and the maintenance of such. The soldiers were kept busy doing whatever service needed to be done: soldiering, manning vessels, carpentry, blacksmithing, clerking, etc. They were trained as required, but also previous skills, such as a trade, were exploited. They brought to the task and were protected by the authority of the state.

The military's campaign history stretched over 1300 years and saw Roman armies campaigning as far east as *Parthia* (modern-day Iran), as far south as *Africa* (modern-day Tunisia) and *Aegyptus* (modern-day Egypt) and as far north as *Britannia* (modern-day England, south Scotland, and Wales). The makeup of the Roman military changed substantially over its history, from its early history as an unsalaried citizen militia to a later professional force, the Imperial Roman army. The equipment used by the military altered greatly

Figure 1: *Roman soldiers on the cast of Trajan's Column in the Victoria and Albert museum, London.*

in type over time, though there were very few technological improvements in weapons manufacture, in common with the rest of the classical world. For much of its history, the vast majority of Rome's forces were maintained at or beyond the limits of its territory, in order to either expand Rome's domain, or protect its existing borders. Expansions were infrequent, as the emperors, adopting a strategy of fixed lines of defense, had determined to maintain existing borders. For that purpose they constructed extensive walls and created permanent stations that became cities.

Personnel

Population base of the early empire

At its territorial height, the Roman Empire may have contained between 45 million and 120 million people.[4] Historian Edward Gibbon estimated that the size of the Roman army "most probably formed a standing force of three hundred and seventy-five thousand men"[5] at the Empire's territorial peak in the time of the Roman Emperor Hadrian (117 – 138CE). This estimate probably included only legionary and auxiliary troops of the Roman army. However, Gibbon states that it is "not... easy to define *the size of the Roman military*

Figure 2: *Relief scene of Roman legionaries marching, from the Column of Marcus Aurelius, Rome, Italy, 2nd century AD.*

with any tolerable accuracy." In the late Imperial period, when vast numbers of foederati were employed by the Romans, Antonio Santosuosso estimated the combined number of men in arms of the two Roman empires numbered closer to 700,000 in total (not all members of a standing army), drawing on data from the *Notitia Dignitatum*. However, he notes that these figures were probably subject to inflation due to the practice of leaving dead soldiers "on the books" in order to continue to draw their wage and ration. Furthermore, it is irrespective of whether the troops were raised by the Romans or simply hired by them to fight on their behalf.[6]

Recruitment

Initially, Rome's military consisted of an annual citizen levy performing military service as part of their duty to the state. During this period, the Roman army would prosecute seasonal campaigns against largely local adversaries. As the extent of the territories falling under Roman suzerainty expanded, and the size of the city's forces increased, the soldiery of ancient Rome became increasingly professional and salaried. As a consequence, military service at the lower (non-staff) levels became progressively longer-term. Roman military units of the period were largely homogeneous and highly regulated. The army consisted of units of citizen infantry known as legions (Latin: *legiones*) as well as non-legionary allied troops known as *auxilia*. The latter were most commonly called upon to provide light infantry or cavalry support.

Military service in the later empire continued to be salaried yearly and professionally for Rome's regular troops. However, the trend of employing allied or mercenary troops was expanded such that these troops came to represent a substantial proportion of Rome's forces. At the same time, the uniformity of structure found in Rome's earlier military forces disappeared. Soldiery of the era ranged from lightly armed mounted archers to heavy infantry, in regiments of varying size and quality. This was accompanied by a trend in the late empire of an increasing predominance of cavalry rather than infantry troops, as well as an emphasis of more mobile operations.

Military subculture

The British historian Peter Heather describes Roman military culture as being "just like the Marines, but much nastier".[7] The army did not provide much social mobility, and it also took quite some time to complete one's service. The pay was not the best for the time, but could be remedied by advance in rank, loot from wars, and additional pay from emperors. Also, the army did provide a guaranteed supply of food (many times soldiers had to pay for food and supplies), doctors, and stability. In the legions of the Republic, discipline was fierce and training harsh, all intended to instill a group cohesion or *esprit de corps* that could bind the men together into effective fighting units. Unlike opponents such as the Gauls, who were fierce individual warriors, Roman military training concentrated on instilling teamwork and maintaining a level head over individual bravery – troops were to maintain exact formations in battle and "despise wild swinging blows"[8] in favor of sheltering behind one's shield and delivering efficient stabs when an opponent made himself vulnerable.

Loyalty was to the Roman state but pride was based in the soldier's unit, to which was attached a military standard – in the case of the legions a legionary eagle. Successful units were awarded with accolades that became part of their official name, such as the 20th legion, which became the *XX Valeria Victrix* (the "Valiant and Victorious 20th").

Of the martial culture of less valued units such as sailors, and light infantry, less is known, but it is doubtful that its training was as intense or its *esprit de corps* as strong as in the legions.

Literacy was highly valued in the Roman military, and literacy rates in the military far exceeded that of the Roman society as a whole.

Figure 3: *Roman coins grew gradually more debased due to the demands placed on the treasury of the Roman state by the military.*

Funding and expenditures

Private funding

Although early in its history, troops were expected to provide much of their own equipment, eventually, the Roman military became almost entirely funded by the state. Since soldiers of the early Republican armies were also unpaid citizens, the financial burden of the army on the state was minimal. However, since the Roman state did not provide services such as housing, health, education, social security and public transport that are part and parcel of modern states, the military always represented by far the greatest expenditure of the state.[9]

Plunder economy

During the time of expansion in the Republic and early Empire, Roman armies had acted as a source of revenue for the Roman state, plundering conquered territories, displaying the massive wealth in triumphs upon their return and fueling the economy[10] to the extent that historians such as Toynbee and Burke believe that the Roman economy was essentially a plunder economy. However, after the Empire had stopped expanding in the 2nd century CE, this source of revenue dried up; by the end of the 3rd century CE, Rome had "ceased to vanquish."[11] As tax revenue was plagued by corruption and hyperinflation during the Crisis of the Third Century, military expenditures began to become a "crushing burden"[12] on the finances of the Roman state.[13] It now highlighted weaknesses that earlier expansion had disguised. By 440 CE, an imperial law frankly states that the Roman state has insufficient tax revenue to fund an army of a size required by the demands placed upon it.[14]

Several additional factors bloated the military expenditure of the Roman Empire. First, substantial rewards were paid to "barbarian" chieftains for their good conduct in the form of negotiated subsidies and for the provision of allied troops.[15] Secondly, the military boosted its numbers, possibly by one third in a single century. Third, the military increasingly relied on a higher ratio of cavalry units in the late Empire, which were many times more expensive to maintain than infantry units.[16]

Taxation

As military size and costs increased, new taxes were introduced or existing tax laws reformed in the late Empire to finance it, even though more inhabitants were available within the borders of the late Empire, reducing the per capita costs for an increased standing army was impractical. A large number of the population could not be taxed because they were slaves or held Roman citizenship, both of which exempted them from taxation.[17] Of the remaining, a large number were already impoverished by centuries of warfare and weakened by chronic malnutrition. Still, they had to handle an increasing tax rate[18] and so they often abandoned their lands to survive in a city.[19]

Of the Western Empire's taxable population, a larger number than in the East could not be taxed because they were "primitive subsistence peasant[s]" and did not produce a great deal of goods beyond agricultural products. Plunder was still made from suppressing insurgencies within the Empire and on limited incursions into enemy land. Legally, much of it should have returned to the Imperial purse, but these goods were simply kept by the common soldiers, who demanded it of their commanders as a right. Given the low wages and high inflation in the later Empire, the soldiers felt that they had a right to acquire plunder.[20,21]

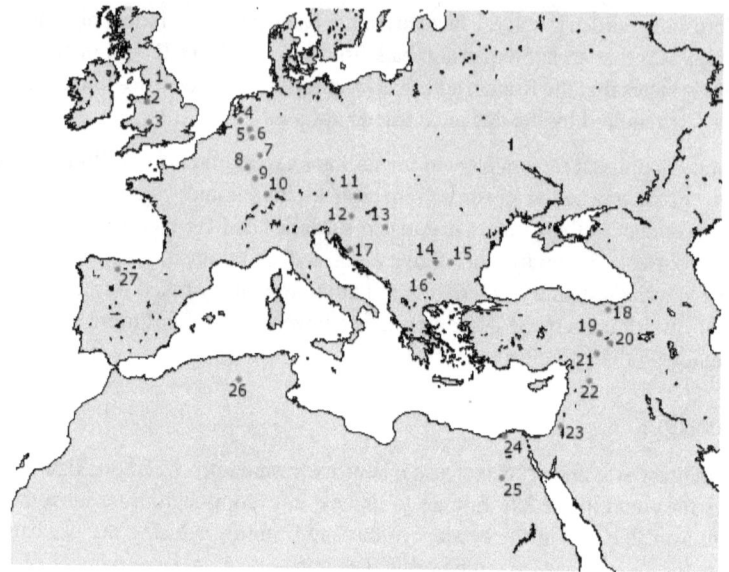

Figure 4: *Locations of Roman legions, 80 CE.*

Capabilities

Readiness and disposition

The military capability of Rome – its preparedness or readiness – was always primarily based upon the maintenance of an active fighting force acting either at or beyond its military frontiers, something that historian Luttwak refers to as a "thin linear perimeter."[22] This is best illustrated by showing the dispositions of the Roman legions, the backbone of the Roman army. (see right). Because of these deployments, the Roman military kept a central strategic reserve after the Social War. Such reserves were only re-established during the late Empire, when the army was split into a border defense force and mobile response field units.

Power projection

The Roman military was keen on the doctrine of power projection – it frequently removed foreign rulers by force or intimidation and replaced them with puppets. This was facilitated by the maintenance, for at least part of its history, of a series of client states and other subjugate and buffer entities beyond its official borders, although over which Rome extended massive political and military control. On the other hand, this also could mean the payment of immense subsidies to foreign powers and opened the possibility of extortion in case military means were insufficient.

Sustainability

The Empire's system of building an extensive and well-maintained road network, as well as its absolute command of the Mediterranean for much of its history, enabled a primitive form of rapid reaction, also stressed in modern military doctrine, although because there was no real strategic reserve, this often entailed the raising of fresh troops or the withdrawing of troops from other parts of the border. However, border troops were usually very capable of handling enemies before they could penetrate far into the Roman hinterland.

The Roman military had an extensive logistical supply chain. There was no specialised branch of the military devoted to logistics and transportation, although this was to a great extent carried out by the Roman Navy due to the ease and low costs of transporting goods via sea and river compared to over land.[23] There is archaeological evidence that Roman armies campaigning in Germania were supplied by a logistical supply chain beginning in Italy and Gaul, then transported by sea to the northern coast of Germania, and finally penetrating into Germania via barges on inland waterways. Forces were routinely supplied via fixed supply chains, and although Roman armies in enemy territory would often supplement or replace this by foraging for food or purchasing food locally, this was often insufficient for their needs: Heather states that a single legion would have required 13.5 tonnes of food per month, and that it would have proved impossible to source this locally.[24]

Policing

For the most part, Roman cities had a civil guard used for maintaining the peace. Due to fear of rebellions and other uprisings, they were forbidden to be armed at militia levels. Policing was split between the civil guard for low-level affairs and the Roman legions and auxilia for suppressing higher-level rioting and rebellion. This civil guard created a limited strategic reserve, one that fared poorly in actual warfare.

Engineering

The military engineering of Ancient Rome's armed forces was of a scale and frequency far beyond that of any of its contemporaries. Indeed, military engineering was in many ways institutionally endemic in Roman military culture, as demonstrated by the fact that each Roman legionary had as part of his equipment a shovel, alongside his *gladius* (sword) and *pila* (spears). Heather writes

Figure 5: *The massive earthen ramp at Masada, designed by the Roman army to breach the fortress' walls.*

that "Learning to build, and build quickly, was a standard element of training".[25]

This engineering prowess was, however, only evident during the peak of Roman military prowess from the mid-Republic to the mid-Empire. Prior to the mid-Republic period there is little evidence of protracted or exceptional military engineering, and in the late Empire likewise there is little sign of the kind of engineering feats that were regularly carried out in the earlier Empire.

Roman military engineering took both routine and extraordinary forms, the former a proactive part of standard military procedure, and the latter of an extraordinary or reactionary nature. Proactive military engineering took the form of the regular construction of fortified camps, in road-building, and in the construction of siege engines. The knowledge and experience learned through such routine engineering lent itself readily to any extraordinary engineering projects required by the army, such as the circumvallations constructed at Alesia and the earthen ramp constructed at Masada.

This engineering expertise practiced in daily routines also served in the construction of siege equipment such as ballistae, onagers and siege towers, as well as allowing the troops to construct roads, bridges and fortified camps.

Figure 6: *Third-century Roman soldiers battling barbarian troops on the Ludovisi Battle sarcophagus (250-260).*

All of these led to strategic capabilities, allowing Roman troops to, respectively, assault besieged settlements, move more rapidly to wherever they were needed, cross rivers to reduce march times and surprise enemies, and to camp in relative security even in enemy territory.

International stance

Rome was established as a nation by making aggressive use of its high military potential. From very early on in its history, it would raise two armies annually to campaign abroad. The Roman military was far from being solely a defence force. For much of its history, it was a tool of aggressive expansion. The Roman army had derived from a militia of mainly farmers and gain of new farm lands for the growing population or later retiring soldiers was often one of the campaign's chief objectives. Only in the late Empire did the preservation of control over Rome's territories become the Roman military's primary role. The remaining major powers confronting Rome were the Kingdom of Aksum, Parthia and the Hunnic Empire. Knowledge of China, the Han dynasty at the times of Mani, existed and it is believed that Rome and China swapped embassies about 170 CE.[26]

Figure 7: *Bas relief of a Roman ballista*

Grand strategy

In its purest form, the concept of strategy deals solely with military issues. However, Rome is offered by Edward Luttwak and others as an early example of a state that possessed a grand strategy which encompassed the management of the resources of an entire nation in the conduct of warfare. Up to half of the funds raised by the Roman state were spent on its military, and the Romans displayed a strategy that was clearly more complicated than simple knee-jerk strategic or tactical responses to individual threats. Rome's strategy changed over time, implementing different systems to meet different challenges that reflected changing internal priorities. Elements of Rome's strategy included the use of client states, the deterrent of armed response in parallel with manipulative diplomacy, and a fixed system of troop deployments and road networks. Luttwak states that there are "instructive similarities" between Roman and modern military strategy.[27]

Rome would rely on brute force and sheer numbers when in doubt. The soldiers were trained to memorize every step in battle, so discipline and order could not break down into chaos. They were largely successful because of this.

Equipment

Although Roman iron-working was enhanced by a process known as carburization, the Romans are not thought to have developed true steel production. From the earliest history of the Roman state to its downfall, Roman arms were therefore uniformly produced from either bronze or, later, iron. As a result, the 1300 years of Roman military technology saw little radical change in technological level. Within the bounds of classical military technology, however, Roman arms and armor was developed, discarded, and adopted from other peoples based on changing methods of engagement. It included at various times stabbing daggers and swords, stabbing or thrusting swords, long thrusting spears or pikes, lances, light throwing javelins and darts, slings, and bow and arrows.[28]

Roman military personal equipment was produced in large numbers to established patterns and used in an established way. It therefore varied little in design and quality within each historical period. According to Hugh Elton, Roman equipment[29] (especially armor) gave them "a distinct advantage over their barbarian enemies."[30] who were often, as Germanic tribesmen, completely unarmoured. However, Luttwak points out that whilst the uniform possession of armour gave Rome an advantage, the actual standard of each item of Roman equipment was of no better quality than that used by the majority of its adversaries.[31] The relatively low quality of Roman weaponry was primarily a function of its large-scale production, and later factors such as governmental price fixing for certain items, which gave no allowance for quality, and incentivised cheap, poor-quality goods.

The Roman military readily adopted types of arms and armour that were effectively used against them by their enemies. Initially Roman troops were armed after Greek and Etruscan models, using large oval shields and long pikes. On encountering the Celts they adopted much Celtic equipment and again later adopted items such as the *gladius* from Iberian peoples. Later in Rome's history, it adopted practices such as arming its cavalry with bows in the Parthian style, and even experimented briefly with niche weaponry such as elephants and camel-troops.

Besides personal weaponry, the Roman military adopted team weaponry such as the ballista and developed a naval weapon known as the corvus, a spiked plank used for affixing and boarding enemy ships.

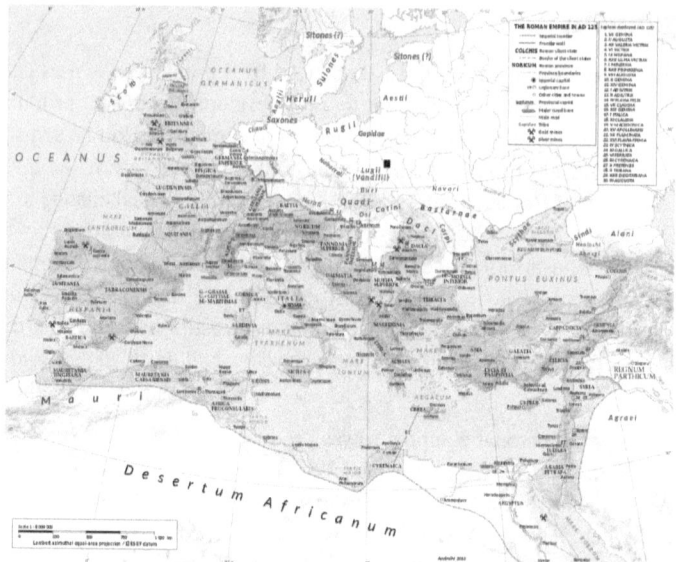

Figure 8: *Showing the vast amount of land held by the Romans.*

Medicine

Need for specialized care

The expansion of the Roman Empire was achieved through military force in nearly every case. Roman culture as a whole revolved around its military for both expansion and protection. Geographic areas on the outskirts of the Empire were prone to attack and required heavy military presence. The constant barrage of attacks and the increase of expansion caused casualties. Due to attack there was a need for specialized medical care for these armies in order to keep them in operational status. The specialized form of care however, was not created until the time of Augustus (31BC-14AD). Prior to this there is little information about the care of soldiers. It is assumed soldiers were self-reliant, treating their own wounds and caring for other ailments encountered. They would also turn to civilians for help throughout the villages they would come across. This was considered a custom of the time, and was quite common for households to take in wounded soldiers and tend to them. As time progressed, there was an increase in care for the wounded as hospitals appeared. The idea was held by the Romans that a healed soldier was better than a dead one and a healed veteran was better than a new recruit.

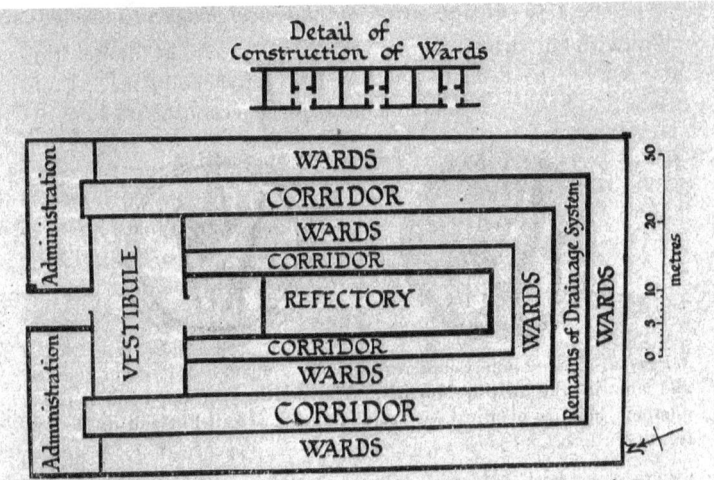

Figure 9: *General set up of Ancient Roman Military Hospital.*

Roman hospitals

With the need for soldier health a growing concern, places for the sick to go in the army were starting to show up. Dates ranged from AD 9 to AD 50, but this is when the first evidence of hospitals was seen in archeological remains. These hospitals were specific places for only military members to go to if they were injured or fell ill. Similar hospitals were set up for slaves in areas where slaves were used in large numbers. Military hospitals were permanent structures set up in forts. These buildings had clear patient rooms and were designed to accommodate large numbers of soldiers. The size of these hospitals varied based on their location. Some of the large facilities, such as the hospital in Hod Hill England, was large enough to accommodate roughly 12% of the force within the hospital. In more stable areas such as Inchtuthil in Scotland, there was room for as little as 2% of the force within the hospital. In areas with more conflict there were larger medical facilities as they saw more casualties. These hospitals were solely designed for the use of the military. If a civilian fell ill or needed surgery they would likely go to the physician's home and stay, not a hospital. Prior to these permanent structures there were tents set up as mobile field hospitals. Soldiers suffering from severe wounds were brought to these for treatment. These were quickly assembled and disassembled as the army moved. The tents served as a precursor for the permanent structured hospitals.

These permanent hospitals and mobile treatment centers were a relatively new concept in this time period.

Physicians

Doctors serving in the army were considered to be a member of the military. Just like everyone else they would take the military oath and be bound by the military law. They would also start among the lower fighting ranks. Even though they took the military oath and were among the lower ranks it did not mean they would be fighting among the masses. These doctors were not always professionals or career physicians. Oftentimes they were slaves who were forced into that career. The Medici was also a group that treated wounded soldiers on the battlefield. These men were not trained physicians even though they played the role of one. Typically they were soldiers who demonstrated they had knowledge in wound treatment and even simple surgical techniques. These men were used before the actual trained doctors were largely implemented. Physicians got their knowledge from experience and information being passed down from person to person. Likely they never used medical texts, as it was not common place even in the civilian field. Generals and Emperors were exceptions, as they would typically have their own personal physician with them. This was a common occurrence as Emperors such as Julian employed famous physicians such as Galen. There were also physicians among the ranks of the Roman soldiers.

Distinctions in practice

With any large number of people being in close quarters there was a constant threat of disease. When one individual in a large group gets sick with a communicable disease, it spreads to others very quickly. This premise remains true even today in the modern military. The Romans recognized the difference between disease and wounds, each requiring separate treatment. Drainage of excess water and waste were common practices in camps as well as the permanent medical structures, which come at a later date. As the medical corps grew in size there was also specialization evolving. Physicians surfaced that specialized in disease, surgery, wound dressing and even veterinary medicine. Veterinary physicians were there to tend to livestock for agricultural purposes as well as combat purposes. The Cavalry was known for their use of horses in combat and scouting purposes. Because of the type of injuries that would have been commonly seen, surgery was a somewhat common occurrence. Tools such as scissors, knives and arrow extractors have been found in remains. In fact, Roman surgery was quite intuitive, in contrast to common thought of ancient surgery. The Roman military surgeons used a cocktail of plants, which created a sedative similar to modern anesthesia. Written documentation also showed surgeons would use oxidation from metal such as copper and scrape it into wounds, which provided an antibacterial effect; however, this method was most likely more toxic than providing an actual benefit. Doctors had the knowledge to clean their surgical instruments with hot water after each use. Wounds were dressed, and dead tissue was removed when bandages were changed. Honey and cobwebs were items used to cover wounds, and have even been shown today to increase healing. Because of the wide array of cases, it was not uncommon for surgeons to begin their careers in the army to learn their trade. Physicians such as Galen and Dioscorides served in the military. Most major advancements in knowledge and technique came from the military rather than civil practice.

Diet

Diet was an issue that is often discussed through this time, as an aspect of medical care. Since our idea of modern technology did not exist, diet was a simple way for Romans to attain a healthy life. This remains true in the Roman Military as the soldiers required appropriate nutrition in order to function at high activity levels. Because of the number of the people requiring food, there were unique circumstances in the acquisition of food. During a campaign the soldiers would often forage food from their enemies land. In fact as part of the standard kit, Roman soldiers would carry a sickle, which would be used to forage food. They would carry a three-day ration of food in case they were in a situation where foraging was not available. This would largely consist of items such as wheat and barley. During a time of peace, the Roman Army would have had a typical diet consisting of bacon, cheese, vegetables, and beer to drink. Corn is mentioned in their works as well, however; this was a common term that was applied to their use of grain. The Roman use of the term corn is not to be confused with maize, which did not come to Europe until the discovery of the New World. Items such as poultry and fish were also likely part of the standard diet. The soldier was given a ration, which was taken from his pay. This shows that the soldiers were well fed in times of peace. If the soldiers were well fed, they were healthier and able to maintain a high level of physical activity, as well as stave off disease. Disease is something that is easier to prevent rather than treat. This idea holds true in the event a fort was under siege; certain food items were rationed such as poultry. The reasoning behind this was that poultry was very inexpensive to maintain and in the event of a siege it did not require a lot of resources to maintain. It was also noted that poultry had benefits for those who were sick. This demonstrates the idea was present that the army needed to maintain the health of its members regardless of circumstances. These discoveries were made while looking at the remains of Roman military sites. By excavating these sites and looking at fecal matter found, scientists were able to determine what was eaten. It is a simple fact that

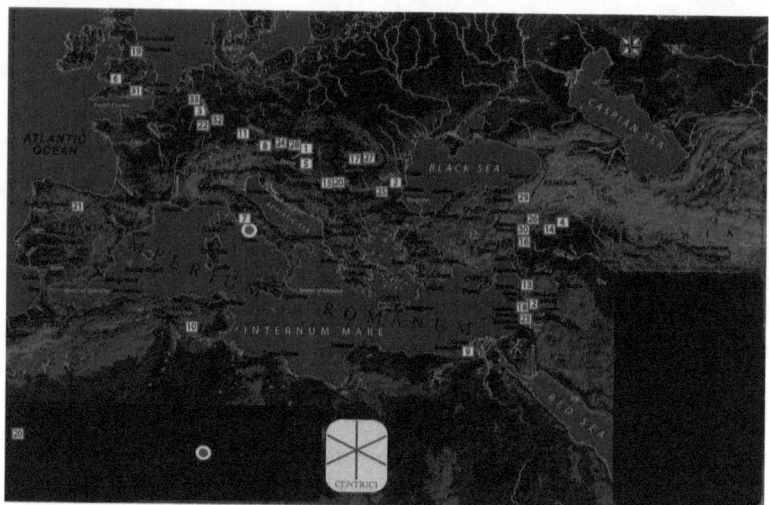

Figure 10: *Shows where various Roman Legions were stationed*

poor diet negatively affects a military's combat readiness. The variety of food found shows the Romans were not focused on just caloric intake, as they knew a variety of food was important to health.

Scale

By the time of Trajan (53AD-117AD), the medical corps was well on the way to being an organized machine. At this time, Physicians were attached to nearly every Army and Navy Unit in all the Roman Military. By this time the Army was massive, consisting of twenty five to thirty legions, each of which contained nearly 6,000 men. Each one included both soldiers and physicians. Despite these massive numbers there was still no formal requirements for being a physician. At this point all physicians were either self-taught or learned their trade through an apprenticeship. Despite this, there was an attempt at organization, as the army did have a medical manual that was passed out to its physicians. The Medici were used on both the front line as emergency care providers and in the rear as the main physicians. The Capsarii were mainly used as the front line care providers and bandagers, but also assisted the Medici behind the lines.

Source of knowledge

Romans received their medical knowledge largely from the Greeks that came before them. As Rome started to expand, it slowly embraced the Greek culture, causing an influx of medicinal information in Roman society. Because of this influx, it allowed this knowledge to become the foundation of all western medical tradition. The Greek theories were kept alive and their practices continued well into the future. This knowledge was also the foundation used in the military medicine since it contained the overarching ideas of their medical knowledge. As time progressed these medical texts would be translated into Arabic and then back into Latin as the flow of information changed. Based on this, we can presume that some of the information in these texts has been lost in translation. Despite this, we are still able to illustrate a clear picture of what military medicine was like during the reign of the Roman Empire.

References

Citations

Library resources about
Military of ancient Rome

- Online books[32]
- Resources in your library[33]
- Resources in other libraries[34]

Bibliography

<templatestyles src="Template:Refbegin/styles.css" />

Primary sources

- Livy, From the Founding of the City on Wikisource (print: *Book 1 as The Rise of Rome, Oxford University Press, 1998, ISBN 0-19-282296-9*).
- Polybius: The Rise of the Roman Empire[35] at LacusCurtius (print: Harvard University Press, 1927. (Translation by W. R. Paton).
- Tacitus: The Annals.

Secondary sources

- Edward Gibbon: The Decline and Fall of the Roman Empire[36] (print: *Penguin Books, 1985, ISBN 0-14-043189-6*).
- Peter Connolly, *Greece and Rome at War*, Greenhill Books, 1998, ISBN 978-1-85367-303-0.
- Adrian Goldsworthy, *In the Name of Rome: The Men Who Won the Roman Empire*, Weidenfeld & Nicolson, 2003, ISBN 0-297-84666-3.
- Michael Grant, *The History of Rome*, Faber and Faber, 1993, ISBN 0-571-11461-X.
- Peter Heather, *The Fall of the Roman Empire: A New History*, Macmillan Publishers, 2005, ISBN 0-330-49136-9.
- Arnold Hugh Martin Jones, *The Later Roman Empire*, Johns Hopkins University Press, 1964, ISBN 0-8018-3285-3.
- Robin Lane Fox, *The Classical World*, Penguin Books, 2005, ISBN 0-14-102141-1
- Edward Luttwak, *The Grand Strategy of the Roman Empire*, Johns Hopkins University Press, ISBN 0-8018-2158-4.
- Philip Matyszak, *The Enemies of Rome*, Thames and Hudson, 2004, ISBN 0-500-25124-X.
- Antonio Santosuosso, *Storming the Heavens: Soldiers, Emperors and Civilians in the Roman Empire*, Westview Press, 2001, ISBN 0-8133-3523-X.

External links

 Wikisourcehas the text of a 1911 *Encyclopædia Britannica*article about *Military of ancient Rome*.

- *Roman soldier reenactment*[37]Wikipedia:Link rot

Structure

Structural history of the Roman military

<indicator name="featured-star"> ⭐ </indicator>

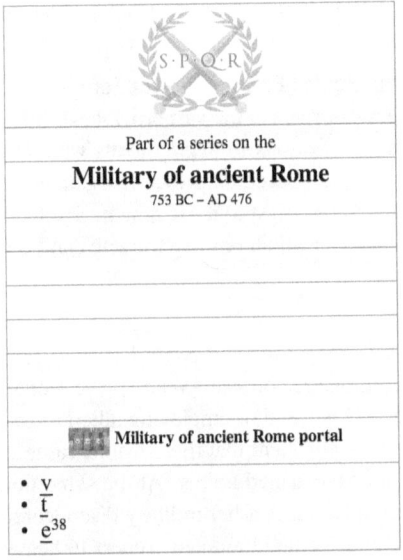

The **structural history of the Roman military** concerns the major transformations in the organization and constitution of ancient Rome's armed forces, "the most effective and long-lived military institution known to history."[39] From its origins around 800 BC to its final dissolution in AD 476 with the demise of the Western Roman Empire, Rome's military organization underwent substantial structural change. At the highest level of structure, the forces were split into the Roman army and the Roman navy, although these two branches were less distinct than in many modern national defense forces. Within the top levels of both army and navy, structural changes occurred as a result of both positive military reform and organic structural evolution. These changes can be divided into four distinct phases.

Phase I
The army was derived from obligatory annual military service levied on the citizenry, as part of their duty to the state. During this period, the Roman army would wage seasonal campaigns against largely local adversaries.

Phase II
As the extent of the territories falling under Roman control expanded and the size of the forces increased, the soldiery gradually became salaried professionals. As a consequence, military service at the lower (non-salaried) levels became progressively longer-term. Roman military units of the period were largely homogeneous and highly regulated. The army consisted of units of citizen infantry known as legions (Latin: *legiones*) as well as non-legionary allied troops known as *auxilia*. The latter were most commonly called upon to provide light infantry, logistical, or cavalry support.

Phase III
At the height of the Roman Empire's power, forces were tasked with manning and securing the borders of the vast provinces which had been brought under Roman control. Serious strategic threats were less common in this period and emphasis was placed on preserving gained territory. The army underwent changes in response to these new needs and became more dependent on fixed garrisons than on march-camps and continuous field operations.

Phase IV
As Rome began to struggle to keep control over its sprawling territories, military service continued to be salaried and professional for Rome's regular troops. However, the trend of employing allied or mercenary elements was expanded to such an extent that these troops came to represent a substantial proportion of the armed forces. At the same time, the uniformity of structure found in Rome's earlier military disappeared. Soldiery of the era ranged from lightly armed mounted archers to heavy infantry, in regiments of varying size and quality. This was accompanied by a trend in the late empire of an increasing predominance of cavalry rather than infantry troops, as well as a requirement for more mobile operations. In this period there was more focus (on all frontiers but the east) on smaller units of independently-operating troops, engaging less in set-piece battles and more in low-intensity, guerilla actions.

Tribal forces (c. 753 BC – c. 578 BC)

According to the historians Livy and Dionysius of Halicarnassus, writing at a far later date, the earliest Roman army existed in the 8th century BC. During this period Rome itself was probably little more than a fortified hilltop settlement and its army a relatively small force, whose activities were limited "mainly [to] raiding and cattle rustling with the occasional skirmish-like battle".[40] Historian Theodor Mommsen referred to it as Rome's *curiate* army, named for its presumed subdivision along the boundaries of Rome's three founding tribes (Latin: *curiae*), the Ramnians, Tities and Luceres.[41] This army's exact structure is not known, but it is probable that it loosely resembled a warrior band or group of bodyguards led by a chieftain or king.[42] Mommsen believes that Roman military organization of this period was regimented by the "Laws of [the apocryphal] King [V]Italus"[43] but these laws, though referred to by Aristotle, have been lost.

The army (Latin: *legio*) consisted, according to Livy, of exactly 3,000 infantry and 300 horsemen, one third from each of Rome's three founding tribes.[44] Warriors served under six "leaders of division" (Latin: *tribuni*) who in turn served under a general, usually in the person of the reigning King. Mommsen uses philological arguments and references from Livy and others to suggest that the greater mass of foot-soldiers probably consisted of *pilumni* (javelin-throwers), with a smaller number possibly serving as *arquites* (archers).[45] The cavalry was far smaller in number and probably consisted solely of the town's richest citizens.[46] The army may also have contained the earliest form of chariots,[47] hinted at by references to the *flexuntes* ("the wheelers").[48]

By the beginning of the 7th century BC, the Iron-Age Etruscan civilization (Latin: *Etrusci*) was dominant in the region.[49] Like most of the other peoples in the region, the Romans warred against the Etruscans. By the close of the century, the Romans had lost their struggle for independence, and the Etruscans had conquered Rome, establishing a military dictatorship, or kingdom, in the city.

Etruscan-model hoplites (578 BC – c. 315 BC)

Although several Roman sources including Livy and Polybius talk extensively about the Roman army of the Roman Kingdom period that followed the Etruscan capture of the city, no contemporary accounts survive. Polybius, for example, was writing some 300 years after the events in question, and Livy some 500 years later. Additionally, what records were kept by the Romans at this time were later destroyed when the city was sacked. The sources for this period cannot therefore be seen as reliable, as they can be for later military history, e.g. from the First Punic War onwards.

Figure 11: *Ancient Greek sculpture of a hoplite (c. 5th century BC, Archæological Museum of Sparti), on which Rome's first class of infantry was based.*

According to our surviving narratives, the three kings of Rome during the Etruscan occupation were Tarquinius Priscus, Servius Tullius, and Tarquinius Superbus. During this period the army underwent a reformation into a *centurial* army based on socio-economic class.[50] This reformation is traditionally attributed to Servius Tullius, the second of the Etruscan kings. Tullius had earlier carried out the first Roman census of all citizens.[51] Livy tells us that Tullius reformed the army by transplanting onto it the structure derived originally for civil life as a result of this census. At all levels, military service was, at this time, considered to be a civic responsibility and a way of advancing one's status within society.[52]

However, Rome's social classes were qualified rather than created by the census. It is perhaps more accurate to say therefore that the army's structure was slightly refined during this period rather than radically reformed. Prior to these reforms, the infantry was divided into the *classis* of rich citizens and the *infra classem* of poorer citizens. The latter were excluded from the regular line of battle on the basis that their equipment was of poor quality. During the reforms, this crude division of poorer and richer citizens was further stratified. The army thereafter consisted of a number of troop types based upon the social class of proppertied citizens, collectively known as *adsidui*. From the poorest in the "fifth class" to the richest in the "first class" and the equestrians above them, military service was compulsory for all.[53] However, Roman citizens at this time generally viewed military service as a proper undertaking of duty to the state, in contrast to later views of military service as an unwelcome and unpleasant burden.[54] Whereas there are accounts of Romans in the late empire mutilating their own bodies in order to exempt themselves from military service,[55] there seems to have been no such reluctance to serve in the military of early Rome. This may in part be due to the generally lower intensity of conflict in this era; to the fact that men were fighting close to and often in protection of their own homes, or due to—as posited by later Roman writers—a greater martial spirit in antiquity.[56]

The equestrians, the highest social class of all, served in mounted units known as *equites*. The first class of the richest citizens served as heavy infantry with swords and long spears (resembling hoplites), and provided the first line of the battle formation. The second class were armed similarly to the first class, but without a breastplate for protection, and with an oblong rather than a round shield. The second class stood immediately behind the first class when the army was drawn up in battle formation. The third and fourth classes were more lightly armed and carried a thrusting-spear and javelins. The third class stood behind the second class in battle formation, normally providing javelin support. The poorest of the propertied men of the city comprised the fifth class. They were generally too poor to afford much equipment at all and were armed as skirmishers with slings and stones. They were deployed in a screen in front of the main army, covering its approach and masking its manoeuvres.

Men without property, who were thereby excluded from the qualifying social classes of the *adsidui*, were exempted from military service on the grounds that they were too poor to provide themselves with any arms whatsoever. However, in the most pressing circumstances, even these *proletarii* were pressed into service,[57] though their military worth was probably questionable. Troops in all of these classes would fight together on the battlefield, with the exception of the most senior troops, who were expected to guard the city.

The army is said to have increased from 3,000 to 4,000 men in the 5th century BC, and then again from 4,000 to 6,000 men sometime before 400 BC. This later army of 6,000 men were then divided into 60 *centuries* of 100 men each.[58] According to Historian P. Fraccaro's hypothesisWikipedia:Please clarify, when the Roman monarchy was replaced by two *praetores* in c. 500 BC, the royal legion was divided into two (one for each *praetor*), each legion comprising 3,000 hoplites. The *velites* and cavalry were also split equally (1,200 *velites* and 300 cavalry each), for a total of 4,500 men.[59] This remained the normal size of a Republican legion until the end of the Social War (88 BC). However, Livy states that a legion at the time of Marcus Furius Camillus (early 4th century BC) consisted of only 3,000 infantry and 300 cavalry.[60]

Figure 12: *Altar of Domitius Ahenobarbus, c. 122 BC; the altar shows two Roman infantrymen equipped with long scuta and a cavalryman with his horse. All are shown wearing chain mail armour.*

Manipular legion (315 BC – 107 BC)

The army of the early Republic continued to evolve, and although there was a tendency among Romans to attribute such changes to great reformers, it is more likely that changes were the product of slow evolution rather than singular and deliberate policy of reform.[61] The manipular formation was probably copied from Rome's Samnite enemies to the south, perhaps as a result of Roman defeats in the Second Samnite War.[62,63]

During this period, a military formation of around 5,000 men was known as a legion (Latin: *legio*). However, in contrast to later legionary formations of exclusively heavy infantry, the legions of the early and middle Republic consisted of both light and heavy infantry. The term *manipular legion*, a legion based on units called maniples (Latin *manipulus* singular, *manipuli* plural, from *manus*, "the hand"), is therefore used to contrast the later *cohortal* legion of the Empire that was based around a system of *cohort* units. The manipular legion was based partially upon social class and partially upon age and military experience.[64] It therefore represents a theoretical compromise between the earlier class-based army and the class-free armies of later years. In practice, even slaves were at one time pressed into the army of the Republic out of necessity.[65] Normally a single legion was raised each year, but in 366 BC two legions were raised in a single year for the first time.

Maniples were units of 120 men each drawn from a single infantry class. The maniples were small enough to permit tactical movement of individual infantry units on the battlefield within the framework of the greater army. The maniples were typically deployed into three discrete lines (Latin: *triplex acies*) based on the three heavy infantry types of *hastati*, *principes* and *triarii*.[66] The first type, the *hastati*, typically formed the first rank in battle formation. They typically wore a brass chest plate (though some could afford mail), a helmet called a galea, and occasionally, greaves (shin guards). They carried an iron bossed wooden shield, 120 cm (4 ft) tall and rectangular in shape with a curved front to partially protect the sides. Traditionally they were armed with a sword known as a *gladius* and two throwing spears known as *pila*: one the heavy *pilum* of popular imagination and one a slender javelin.[67] However the exact introduction of the Gladius and the replacement of the spear with the sword as the primary weapon of the Roman Legions is uncertain, and it's possible that the early manipular legions still fought with the Hastati and Principes wielding the Hasta or Spear.

> "the Romans ... habitually enroll four legions each year, each consisting of about four thousand foot and two hundred horse; and when any unusual necessity arises, they raise the number of foot to five thousand and of the horse to three hundred. Of allies, the number in each legion is the same as that of the citizens, but of the horse three times as great"
>
> Polybius, The Histories, *1:268–70*

The second type, the *principes*, typically formed the second rank of soldiers back from the front of a battle line. They were heavy infantry soldiers armed and armoured as per the hastati. The *triarii*, who typically formed the third rank when the army was arrayed for battle, were the last remnant of hoplite-style troops in the Roman army. They were armed and armoured as per the *principes*, with the exception that they carried a pike rather than two *pila*. A 600-man triarii maniple was divided into two formations each six men across by 10 men deep.[68] A manipular legion typically contained between 1,200-2400 *hastati*, 1,200-2400 *principes* and 600-1200 *triarii*.[69] The three classes of unit may have retained some slight parallel to social divisions within Roman society, but at least officially the three lines were based upon age and experience rather than social class. Young, unproven men would serve as *hastati*, older men with some military experience as *principes*, and veteran troops of advanced age and experience as *triarii*.

The heavy infantry of the maniples were supported by a number of light infantry (Latin: *velites*) and cavalry (Latin: *equites*) troops, typically 300 horsemen per manipular legion. The cavalry was drawn primarily from the richest class of equestrians, but additional cavalry and light infantry were drawn at times from the socii and Latini of the Italian mainland. The *equites* were still drawn from the wealthier classes in Roman society. There was an additional class of troops (Latin: *accensi*, also *adscripticii* and later *supernumerarii*) who followed the army without specific martial roles and were deployed to the rear of the *triarii*. Their role in accompanying the army was primarily to supply any vacancies that might occur in the maniples, but they also seem to have acted occasionally as orderlies to the officers.

The light infantry of 1,200 *velites* consisted of unarmoured skirmishing troops drawn from the youngest and lower social classes. They were armed with a sword and buckler (90 cm (3 ft) diameter), as well as several light javelins, each with a 90 cm (3 ft) wooden shaft the diameter of a finger, with a c. 25 cm (10 in) narrow metal point. Their numbers were swollen by the addition of allied light infantry and irregular *rorarii*.

The Roman levy of 403 BC was the first to be requested to campaign for longer than a single season,[70] and from this point on such a practice became gradually more common, if still not typical.

A small navy had operated at a fairly low level after the Second Samnite War, but it was massively upgraded during this period, expanding from a few primarily river- and coastal-based patrol craft to a full maritime unit. After a period of frenetic construction, the navy mushroomed to a size of more than 400 ships on the Carthaginian pattern. Once completed, it could accommodate up to 100,000 sailors and embarked troops for battle. The navy thereafter declined in size. This was partially because a pacified Roman Mediterranean called for little naval policing, and partially because the Romans chose to rely during this period on ships provided by Greek cities, whose peoples had greater maritime experience.[71]

Proletarianisation of the infantry (217 BC – 107 BC)

The extraordinary demands of the Punic Wars, in addition to a shortage of manpower, exposed the tactical weaknesses of the manipular legion, at least in the short term.[72] In 217 BC, Rome was forced to effectively ignore its long-standing principle that its soldiers must be both citizens and property owners when slaves were pressed into naval service; around 213 BC, the property requirement was reduced from 11,000 to 4,000 asses. Since the Romans are unlikely to have preferred to employ slaves over poor citizens in their armies, it must be assumed that, at this point, the *proletarii* of the poorest citizens must also have been pressed into service despite their lack of legal qualification. By 123 BC, the financial requirement for military service was slashed again from 4,000 asses to just 1,500 asses.[73] By this time, therefore, it is clear that many of the property-less former *proletarii* had been nominally admitted into the *adsidui*.

During the 2nd century BC, Roman territory saw an overall decline in population,[74] partially due to the huge losses incurred during various wars. This was accompanied by severe social stresses and the greater collapse of the middle classes into lower classes of the census and the *proletarii*. As a result, both the Roman society and its military became increasingly proletarianised. The Roman state was forced to arm its soldiers at the expense of the state, since many of the soldiers who made up its lower classes were now impoverished *proletarii* in all but name, and were too poor to afford their own equipment.

The distinction between the heavy infantry types of *hastati*, *principes* and *triarii* began to blur, perhaps because the state was now assuming the responsibility of providing standard-issue equipment to all but the first class of troops, who alone were able to afford their own equipment. By the time of Polybius, the *triarii* or their successors still represented a distinct heavy infantry type armed with a unique style of cuirass, but the *hastati* and *principes* had become indistinguishable.

In addition, the shortage of available manpower led to a greater burden being placed upon its allies (*socii*) for the provision of allied troops.[75] Where accepted allies could not provide the required force types, the Romans were not averse during this period to hiring mercenaries to fight alongside the legions.[76]

Marian legion (107 BC – 27 BC)

In a process known as the Marian reforms, Roman consul Gaius Marius carried out a programme of reform of the Roman military. In 107 BC, all citizens, regardless of their wealth or social class, were made eligible for entry into the Roman army.[77] This move formalised and concluded a gradual process that had been growing for centuries, of removing property requirements for military service.[78] The distinction between *hastati*, *principes* and *triarii*, which had already become blurred, was officially removed,[79] and the legionary infantry of popular imagination was created. Legionary infantry formed a homogeneous force of heavy infantry. These legionaries were drawn from citizen stock; by this time, Roman or Latin citizenship had been regionally expanded over much of ancient Italy and Cisalpine Gaul.[80] Lighter citizen infantry, such as the *velites* and *equites*, were replaced by non-citizen *auxilia* that could consist of foreign mercenaries.[81] Due to the concentration of the citizen legions into a force of heavy infantry Rome's armies depended on auxiliary cavalry attachments for support. As a tactical necessity, legions were almost always accompanied by an equal or greater number of lighter auxiliary troops,[82] which

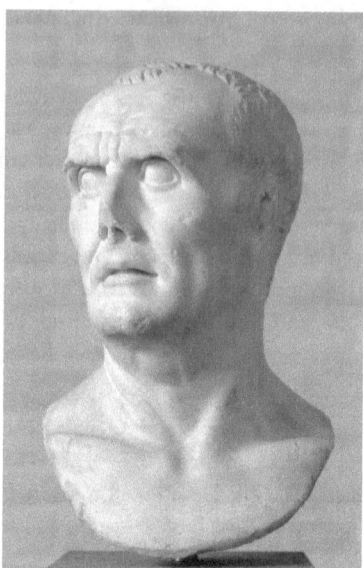

Figure 13: *Bust of Marius, instigator of the Marian reforms*

were drawn from the non-citizens of the Empire's territories. One known exception of legions being formed from non-citizen provinces during this period was the legion that was raised in the province of Galatia.

After Marius, the legions were drawn largely from volunteer citizens rather than citizens conscripted for duty.[83] Volunteers came forward and were accepted not from citizens of the city of Rome itself but from the surrounding countryside and smaller towns falling under Roman control.[84] Whereas some long-term military professionals were classed as veterans, they were outnumbered by civilians with limited military experience who were in active service perhaps only for a few campaigns.[85] The legions of the late Republic remained, unlike the legions of the later Empire, predominantly Roman in origin, although some small number of ex-auxiliary troops were probably incorporated.[86] The army's higher-level officers and commanders were still drawn exclusively from the Roman aristocracy.

Unlike earlier in the Republic, legionaries were no longer fighting on a seasonal basis to protect their land. Instead, they received standard pay, and were employed by the state on a fixed-term basis. As a consequence, military duty began to appeal most to the poorest sections of society, to whom a guaranteed salary was attractive.[87] The army therefore consisted of a far higher proportion of the poor—particularly the rural poor—than it had previously.[88] A destabilising consequence of this development was that the proletariat "acquired a stronger and more elevated position" within the state. This professionalisation of the military was necessary to provide permanent garrisons for newly acquired and distant territories such as Hispania, something not possible under an army of seasonal citizen militia.

Historian R. E. Smith notes that there was a need to raise additional legions in an emergency to repel specific strategic threats. He argues that this may have resulted in two types of legion.[89] Long-standing legions deployed overseas were probably professional troops forming a standing army. Quickly-formed new legions, in contrast, consisted of younger men, perhaps with little or no military experience, who hoped for adventure and plunder. However, no distinction in basic pay, discipline or armour is known of between the two types of legion. The practice of veteran troops signing up again voluntarily into newly raised legions must have meant that no one army conformed exactly to one or other of these theoretical archetypes.

The legions of the late Republic were, structurally, almost entirely heavy infantry. The legion's main sub-unit was called a *cohort* and consisted of approximately 480 infantrymen.[90] The cohort was therefore a much larger unit than the earlier *maniple* sub-unit, and was divided into six centuriae of 80 men each. Each centuria was separated further into 10 "tent groups" (Latin: *contubernia*) of 8 men each. Legions additionally consisted of a small body, typically 120 men, of Roman legionary cavalry (Latin: *equites legionis*). The *equites* were used as scouts and dispatch riders rather than battlefield cavalry.[91] Legions also contained a dedicated artillery crew of perhaps 60 men, who would operate devices such as *ballistae*.

Each legion was normally partnered with an approximately equal number of allied (non-Roman) *auxiliae* troops.[92] The addition of allied troops to the Roman army was a formalisation of the earlier arrangement of using light troops from the Socii and Latini, who had received Roman citizenship after the Social War.[93] Auxiliary troops could be formed from either auxiliary light cavalry known as *alae*, auxiliary light infantry known as *cohors auxiliae*, or a flexible mixture of the two known as *cohors equitata*. Cavalry types included mounted archers (Latin: *sagittarii*) and heavy shock cavalry (Latin: *cataphracti* or *clibanarii*). Infantry could be armed with bows, slings, throwing spears, long swords, or thrusting spears. Auxiliary units were originally led by their own chiefs, and, in this period, their internal organisation was left to their commanders.[94]

However, "the most obvious deficiency" of the Roman army remained its shortage of cavalry, especially heavy cavalry;[95] even auxiliary troops were predominantly infantry. Luttwak argues that auxiliary forces largely consisted of Cretan archers, Balearic slingers and Numidian infantry, all of whom fought on foot.[96] As Rome's borders expanded and its adversaries changed from largely infantry-based to largely cavalry-based troops, the infantry-based Roman army began to find itself at a tactical disadvantage, particularly in the East.

After having declined in size following the subjugation of the Mediterranean, the Roman navy underwent short-term upgrading and revitalisation in the late Republic to meet several new demands. Under Caesar, an invasion fleet was assembled in the English Channel to allow the invasion of Britain; under Pompey, a large fleet was raised in the Mediterranean Sea to clear the sea of Cilician pirates. During the civil war that followed, as many as a thousand ships were either constructed or pressed into service from Greek cities.

Non-citizen recruitment (49 BC – 27 BC)

By the time of Julius Caesar in 54 BC, regular legionary units were supplemented by *exploratores*, a body of scouts, and *speculatores*, spies who infiltrated enemy camps.[97] Due to the demands of the civil war, the extraordinary measure of recruiting legions from non-citizens was taken by Caesar in Transalpine Gaul (Latin: *Gallia Transalpina*), by Brutus in Macedonia, and by Pompey in Pharsalus.[98] This irregular and extraordinary recruitment was not, however, typical of recruitment during this period, and Roman law still officially required that legions were recruited from Roman citizens only.

Imperial legions and reformation of the auxilia (27 BC – 117 AD)

By the turn of the millennium, Emperor Augustus' primary military concern was to prevent Roman generals from further usurping the imperial throne.[99] The experience of Caesar and, earlier, Marius and Sulla, had demonstrated the willingness of "emergency" (re-activated previously decommissioned) legions containing troops keen for plunder to follow their generals against the state. Augustus therefore removed the need for such emergency armies by increasing the size of the standing armies to a size sufficient to provide territorial defence on their own.[100] Perhaps due to similar concerns, the legions and auxiliaries of the army were supplemented under the Emperor Augustus by an elite formation of guards dedicated to the protection of the Emperor. The first such unit was based in Rome and were known as the Praetorian Guard, and a second similar formation were known as the Cohortes urbanae.[101]

The legions, which had been a mix of life professionals and civilian campaigners, was altered into a standing army of professionals only.[102] The actual structure of the cohort army remained much the same as in the late Republic, although around the 1st century AD the first cohort of each legion was increased in size to a total of 800 soldiers.[103] However, while the structure of the

Figure 14: *Bas-relief carving of a Roman legionary out of battle dress, c. 1st century AD (Pergamon Museum, Berlin)*

legions remained much the same, their make-up gradually changed. Whereas early Republican legions had been raised by a draft from eligible Roman citizens, imperial legions were recruited solely on a voluntary basis and from a much wider base of manpower. Likewise, whereas Republican legions had been recruited almost exclusively in Italy, early Imperial legions drew most of their recruits from Roman colonies in the provinces from 68 AD onwards. One estimate places the proportion of Italian troops at 65% under Augustus in c. 1 AD, falling to around 49% by the end of Nero's reign.[104]

Since the legions were officially open only to Roman citizens, Max Cary and Howard Hayes Scullard argue that at least in some provinces at this time "many provincials must have been recruited who lacked any genuine claim to Roman citizenship but received it unofficially on enlistment,"[105] a practice that was to increase in the 2nd century.[106] This is most likely in those provinces where the pool of Roman citizens was not large enough to fulfill the provincial army's recruitment needs. One possible example is Britain, where one estimate puts the citizen pool in the 1st century at only 50,000 out of a total provincial population of around two million.[107]

At the same time as the legions underwent these transformations, the *auxilia* were reorganized and a number of allied troops were formalised into standing units similar to legions. Rather than being raised re-actively when required, the process of raising auxiliary troops was carried out in advance of conflicts according to annual targets.[108] Whereas the internal organisation of the *auxilia* had previously been left up to their commanders, in the early empire they were organised into standardised units known as *turmae* (for cavalry *alae*) and *centuriae* (for infantry *cohortes*). Although never becoming as standardised in their equipment as the legions,[109] and often retaining some national flavour, the size of the units at least was standardised to some degree. Cavalry were formed into either an *ala quingenaria* of 512 horsemen, or an *ala millaria* of 1,000 horsemen. Likewise, infantry auxilia could be formed into a *cohors quingenaria* of 500 men or a *cohors millaria* of 1,000 men. Mixed cavalry/infantry auxiliaries were typically formed with a larger proportion of foot than horse troops: the *cohors equitata quingenaria* consisted of 380 foot and 120 horsemen, and the *cohors equitata millaria* consisted of 760 foot and 240 horsemen.

The vitality of the empire at this point was such that the use of native *auxilia* in the Roman army did not apparently barbarise the military as some scholars claim was to happen in the late empire.[110] On the contrary, those serving in the *auxilia* during this period frequently strove to Romanise themselves. They were granted Roman citizenship on retirement, granting them several social advantages, and their sons became eligible for service in the legions.[111]

As with the army, many non-Italians were recruited into the Roman Navy, partly because the Romans had never readily taken to the sea. It appears that the navy was considered to be slightly less prestigious than the *auxilia* but, like the *auxilia*, troops could gain citizenship on discharge upon retirement. In terms of structure, each ship was staffed by a group of men approximately equivalent to a century, with ten ships forming a naval squadron.[112]

Introduction of vexillationes (76 AD – 117 AD)

Through the final years of the 1st century AD, the legions remained the backbone of the Roman army, although the *auxilia* in fact outnumbered them by up to half as much again.[113] Within the legions, the proportion of troops recruited from within Italy fell gradually after 70 AD.[114] By the close of the 1st century, this proportion had fallen to as low as 22 percent, with the remainder drawn from conquered provinces. Since technically only citizens were allowed to enlist in the legions, where recruits did not possess citizenship then, at least in some instances, citizenship "was simply given [to] them on enlistment".[115] During this time, the borders of the Empire had remained relatively fixed to the extent originally reached under the Emperor Trajan. Because of this, the army was increasingly responsible for protecting existing frontiers rather than expanding into foreign territory, the latter of which had characterised the army's

Figure 15: *Roman soldiers of around 101 AD from a cast of Trajan's column, c. 113 AD (Victoria and Albert Museum, London)*

earlier existence.[116] As a result, legions became stationed in largely fixed locations. Although entire legions were occasionally transferred into theatres of war, they remained largely rooted in one or more legionary bases in a province, detaching into smaller bodies of troops (Latin: *vexillationes*) on demand.[117] This policy eventually led to a split of the military's land-based forces into mobile and fixed troops in the later Empire. In general, the best troops were dispatched as *vexillationes*, and the remainder left to guard border defences were of lower quality, perhaps those with injuries or near retirement.[118]

Barbarisation of the army (117 AD – 253 AD)

By the time of the emperor Hadrian the proportion of Italians in the legions had fallen to just ten percent and provincial citizens now dominated. This low figure is probably a direct result of the changing needs of military staffing: a system of fixed border defences (Latin: *limes*) were established around the Empire's periphery under Hadrian, consolidating Trajan's territorial gains. These called for troops to be stationed permanently in the provinces, a prospect more attractive to locally raised rather than Italian troops. The higher prestige and pay to be found in the Italian dominated Praetorian Guard must also have played a role. The majority of the troops in the legions at the start of the 3rd

Figure 16: *Battle with Germanic troops, on the Portonaccio sarcophagus (190-200)*

century AD were from the more Romanised (though non-Italian) provinces, especially Illyria.[119] As the century progressed, more and more barbarians (Latin: *barbari*) were permitted to settle inside of, and tasked with aiding in the defence of, Rome's borders.[120] As a result, greater numbers of barbarous and semi-barbarous peoples were gradually admitted to the army.

However, whether this regionalisation of the legions was partnered by a drop in the professionalism of the troops is contested. Antonio Santosuosso argues that the strict discipline and high motivation of the days of Marius had lapsed,[121] but Andrew Alfoldi states that the Illyrian troops were both valiant and warlike, and Tacitus described German recruits as being natural mercenaries (Latin: *vivi ad arma nati*).[122] It seems that discipline in the legions did slacken, with soldiers granted permission to live with wives outside of military lodgings and permitted to adopt a more lavish and comfortable lifestyle, in contrast to the strict military regimen of earlier years. However, it is by no means certain that this led to any reduction in the effectiveness of the legions, due to the greater ferocity and stature of the *barbari* recruits. The flavour of the Roman military, however, was now dictated by the increasing number of regional recruits, leading to a partial barbarisation of Rome's military forces beginning in this period.[123] The barbarisation of the lower ranks was paralleled by a concurrent barbarisation of its command structure, with the Roman

Structural history of the Roman military 37

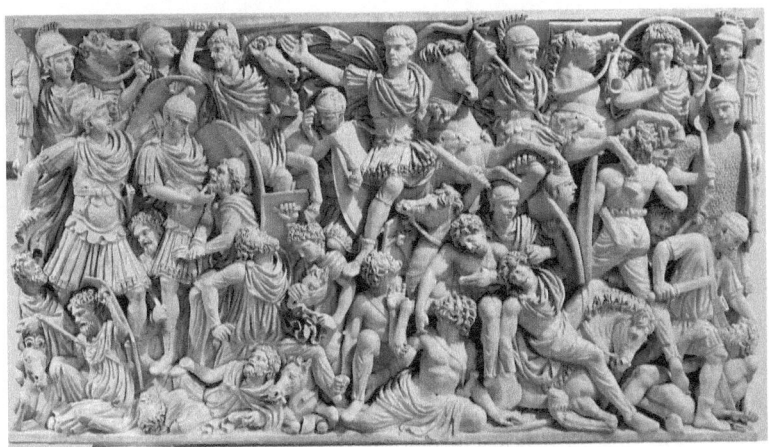

Figure 17: *3rd-century Roman soldiers battling barbarian troops on the Ludovisi Battle sarcophagus (250-260)*

senators who had traditionally provided its commanders becoming entirely excluded from the army. By 235 AD the Emperor himself, the figurehead of the entire military, was a man born outside of Italy to non-Italian parents.[124]

> "A young nobleman, strong of hand and quick of mind and far more intelligent than your average barbarian ... the ardour of his face and eyes showed the burning spirit within. He had fought on our side in previous campaigns and earned the right to become a Roman citizen; indeed, he was even elevated to the rank of Equestrian."
>
> *Velleius Paterculus,* Roman History, *2.108*

Figure 18: *A 6th-century carving of a Sassanid armoured knight, the model for the Roman catafractarii*

The gradual inclusion of greater numbers of non-citizen troops into the military was taken a further step by the creation under Hadrian of a new type of force in addition to the legions and *auxilia*, known as *numeri*. Formed in bodies of around 300 irregular troops, the *numeri* were drawn from subjugate provinces and peoples of client-states or even from beyond the borders of the empire. They were both less regimented and less Romanised than auxiliary troops, with a "pronounced national character,"[125] including native dress and native war cries. The introduction of the *numeri* was a response to the need for cheap troops, who were nevertheless fierce and provided a force balance of light infantry and cavalry.[126] They were therefore largely less well armed and less well trained than *auxilia* or legions, although more prestigious elite irregular native troops were also utilised.[127] However, the legions still made up around one half of the Roman army at this point.

Successive crises (238 AD– 359 AD)

By the late Empire, enemy forces in both the East and West were "sufficiently mobile and sufficiently strong to pierce [the Roman] defensive perimeter on any selected axis of penetration";[128] from the 3rd century onwards, both Germanic tribes and Persian armies pierced the frontiers of the Roman Empire.[129]

In response, the Roman army underwent a series of changes, more organic and evolutionary than the deliberate military reforms of the Republic and early Empire. A stronger emphasis was placed upon ranged combat ability of all types, such as field artillery, hand-held *ballistae*, archery and darts. Roman forces also gradually became more mobile, with one cavalryman for every three infantryman, compared to one in forty in the early Empire.[130] Additionally, the Emperor Gallienus took the revolutionary step of forming an entirely cavalry field army, which was kept as a mobile reserve at the city of Milan in northern Italy. It is believed that Gallienus facilitated this concentration of cavalry by stripping the legions of their integral mounted element.[131] A diverse range of cavalry regiments existed, including *catafractarii* or *clibanarii*, *scutarii*, and legionary cavalry known as *promoti*. Collectively, these regiments were known as *equites*. Around 275 AD, the proportion of *catafractarii* was also increased. There is some disagreement over exactly when the relative proportion of cavalry increased, whether Gallienus' reforms occurred contemporaneously with an increased reliance on cavalry, or whether these are two distinct events. Alfoldi appears to believe that Gallienus' reforms were contemporaneous with an increase in cavalry numbers. He argues that, by 258, Gallienus had made cavalry the predominant troop type in the Roman army in place of heavy infantry, which dominated earlier armies. According to Warren Treadgold, however, the proportion of cavalry did not change between the early 3rd and early 4th centuries.[132]

Larger groups of *barbari* began to settle in Rome's territories around this time, and the troops they were contracted to provide to the Roman army were no longer organised as *numeri* but rather were the forerunners of the later rented native armies known as federated troops (Latin: *foederati*).[133] Though they served under Roman officers, the troops of these units were far more barbarised than the *numeri*, lacked Romanisation of either military structure or personal ideology, and were ineligible for Roman citizenship upon discharge. These native troops were not permitted to fight in native war bands under their own leaders, unlike the later *foederati*; instead, these troops were split into small groups attached to other Roman units.[134] They existed therefore as a halfway house between *numeri*, who were encouraged to be Romanised, and the *foederati*, who raised officers from their own ranks and were almost entirely self-dependent.

Comitatenses and limitanei (284 AD – 395 AD)

A distinction between frontier guard troops and more mobile reserve forces had emerged with the use of certain troops to permanently man frontiers such as Hadrian's Wall in *Britannia* in the 2nd century AD. The competing demands

Figure 19: *Bearded Roman troops as pictured on a triumphal arch, c. 312 AD, however, the sculptured panels were re-used from earlier monuments of Trajanic date.*

of manned frontiers and strategic reserve forces had led to the division of the military into four types of troops by the early 4th century:

- The *limitanei* or *riparienses* patrolled the border and defended the border fortifications. According to some older theories, the *limitanei* were "settled and hereditary" militia that were "tied to their posts."[135] But according to most recent research, the *limitanei* were originally regular soldiers, including infantry, cavalry, and river flotillas,[136,137,138] although they eventually became settled militia.[139,140] According to Luttwak, the *cunei* of cavalry, and *auxilia* of infantry alone by this time, were local provincial reserves that may have evolved from earlier auxiliary units.[141] Wikipedia:Please clarify According to Pat Southern and Karen Dixon, the *legiones*, *auxilia*, and *cunei* of the border armies were part of the *limitanei*, but higher-status than the older *cohortes* and *alae* in the same armies.
- The *comitatenses*, and later the *palatini* were strategic reserves, usually in the rear.[142] After their division into *palatini* and *comitatenses*, the latter were usually associated with the praesental armies, and the former were usually associated with the regional armies, but both types could be moved between the two.

- The emperor Constantine I created the *scholae* to replace the old praetorian guard. The scholae were his personal guard, and were mainly equipped as cavalry. Vogt suggests that the *scholae* formed two small central reserves (Latin: *scholae*) held to the strategic rear even of the *comitatenses*, one each in the presence of the emperors of West and East respectively.[143]

The permanent field armies of the *palatini* and *comitatenses* ultimately derived from the temporary field armies of the earlier *sacer comitatus*.

Created and expanded from the core troops of the Emperor's personal bodyguards,Wikipedia:Please clarify the central field armies by 295 AD seem to have been too large to be accounted for as simple bodyguard forces, but were still too small to be able to campaign independently of legionary or vexillation support.Wikipedia:Please clarify[144]

Of the four troop types, the *limitanei* (border guards) were once considered to have been of the lowest quality,[145] consisting largely of peasant-soldiers that were both "grossly inferior" to the earlier legions and inferior also to their counterparts in the mobile field armies.[146] However, more recent work establishes that the *limitanei* were regular soldiers.[136,137]

While the *limitanei* were supposed to deal with policing actions and low-intensity incursions, the duty of responding to more serious incidents fell upon the provincial troops.Category:Articles contradicting other articles The countering of the very largest scale incursions on a strategic scale was the task of the *comitatenses* and *palatini* or mobile field troops, possibly accompanied by the emperor's *scholae*. Both border and field armies consisted of a mix of infantry and cavalry units[147] although the weight of cavalry was, according to some authorities, greater in the mobile field armies. Overall, approximately one quarter of the army consisted of cavalry troops[148] but their importance is uncertain. Older works such as the Eleventh Edition of the *Encyclopædia Britannica* (1911) state that the Roman military of the late Empire was "marked by that predominance of the horseman which characterised the earlier centuries of the Middle Ages," but many more recent authors believe that the infantry remained predominant.[149]

There is some dispute about whether this new military structure was put into place under the Emperor Diocletian or Constantine since both reorganised the Roman Army in the late 3rd and early 4th centuries to some degree.[150] Both Diocletian and even his predecessor of thirty years Gallienus may already have controlled mobile strategic reserves to assist the empire's border forces;[151] either Diocletian or Constantine expanded this nascent force into permanent field armies.[152]

Recruitment from amongst Roman citizens had become greatly curtailed as a consequence of a declining population,[153] "cripplingly numerous" categories of those exempted from military service and the spread of Christianity with its pacifist message.[154] Together, these factors culminated in "the withdrawal of the urban class from all forms of military activity."[155] In their place, much of Rome's military were now recruited from non-Italian peoples living within the empire's borders. Many of these people were barbarians or semi-barbarians recently settled from lands beyond the empire,[156] including several colonies of *Carpi*, *Bastarnae* and *Sarmatians*.[157]

Although units described as *legiones* existed as late as the 5th century in both the border and field armies,[158] the legionary system was very different from that of the principate and early empire. Since the term legion continued to be used, it is unclear exactly when the structure and role of the legions changed. In the 3rd or 4th century, however, the legions' role as elite heavy infantry was substantially reduced[159] and may have evaporated entirely.[160] Instead, those "legions" that remained were no longer drawn exclusively (and perhaps hardly at all) from Roman citizens. Either Diocletian[161] or Constantine reorganised the legions into smaller infantry units who, according to some sources, were more lightly armoured than their forebears. Their lighter armament may have been either because they "would not consent to wear the same weight of body armour as the legionaries of old"[162] or, as in at least one documented instance, because they were prohibited from wearing heavy armour by their general in order to increase their mobility.[163] 4th-century legions were at times only one sixth the size of early imperial legions, and they were armed with some combination of spears, bows, slings, darts and swords, reflecting a greater contemporary emphasis on ranged fighting.[164] The *auxilia* and *numeri* had also largely disappeared.[165] Constantine further increased the proportion of German troops in the regular army;[166] their cultural impact was so great that even legionaries began wearing German dress. At the start of Diocletian's reign, the Roman army numbered about 390,000 men, but by the end of his reign he successfully increased the number to 581,000 men.[167]

Adoption of barbarian allies (358 AD – 395 AD)

By the late 4th century, the Empire had become chronically deficient in raising sufficient troops from amongst its own population.[168] As an alternative, taxation raised internally was increasingly used to subsidise growing numbers of barbarian recruits. The Romans had, for some time, recruited individual non-Roman soldiers into regular military units. In 358 AD, this practice was accelerated by the wholescale adoption of the entire Salian Franks people into the Empire, providing a ready pool of such recruits. In return for being allowed to settle as *foederatii* in northern *Gallia* on the near side of the Rhine, the Franks were expected to defend the Empire's borders in their territory and provide troops to serve in Roman units.

In 376, a large band of Goths asked Emperor Valens for permission to settle on the southern bank of the Danube River on terms similar to the Franks. The Goths were also accepted into the empire as *foederati*; however, they rebelled later that year and defeated the Romans at the Battle of Adrianople. The heavy losses that the Roman military suffered during this defeat ironically forced the Roman Empire to rely still further on such *foederati* troops to supplement its forces.[169] In 382, the practice was radically extended when federated troops were signed up *en masse* as allied contingents of *laeti* and *foederatii* troops separate from existing Roman units. Near-constant civil wars during the period 408 and 433 between various Roman usurpers, emperors and their supposed deputies such as Constantine III, Constantius III, Aetius and Bonifacius resulted in further losses, necessitating the handing over of more taxable land to foederati.

The size and composition of these allied forces remains in dispute. Santosuosso argues that *foederati* regiments consisted mostly of cavalry[170] that were raised both as a temporary levy for a specific campaign need and, in some cases, as a permanent addition to the army. Hugh Elton believes that the importance of *foederati* has been overstated in traditional accounts by historians such as A.H.M. Jones. Elton argues that the majority of soldiers were probably non-Italian Roman citizens,[171] while Santosuosso believes that the majority of troops were almost certainly non-citizen *barbari*.[172]

Collapse in the West and survival in the East (395 AD – 476 AD)

The non-federated mobile field army, known as the *comitatenses*, was eventually split into a number of smaller field armies: a central field army under the emperor's direct control, known as the *comitatensis palatina* or *praesentalis*, and several regional field armies. Historians Santosuosso and Vogt agree that the latter gradually degraded into low-quality garrison units similar to the *limitanei* that they either supplemented or replaced. By the 5th century, a significant portion of Western Rome's main military strength lay in rented barbarian mercenaries known as *foederati*.

As the 5th century progressed, many of the Empire's original borders had been either wholly or partially denuded of troops to support the central field army.[173] In 395, the Western Roman Empire had several regional field armies in Italy, Illyricum, Gallia, Britannia and Africa, and about twelve border armies. By about 430, two more field armies were established in Hispania and Tingitania

Figure 20: *Mosaic of what is presumed to be a Gothic war leader. The Goths were employed as foederati by the Romans in the 5th century*

but the central government had lost control of Britannia as well as much of Gaul, Hispania, and Africa. In the same period, the Eastern Roman Empire had two palatine field armies (at Constantinople), three regional field armies (in the East, in Thrace, and in Illyricum) and fifteen frontier armies.[174]

> "We received a terrible rumour about events in the West. They told us that Rome was under siege, and the only safety for its citizens was that which they could buy with gold, and when that had been stripped from them, they were besieged again, so that they lost not only their possessions, but also their lives. Our messenger gave the news in a faltering voice, and could hardly speak for sobbing. The city which had captured the world was now itself captured"
>
> *Jerome,* Letters, *127*

As Roman troops were spread increasingly thin over its long border, the Empire's territory continued to dwindle in size as the population of the empire declined.[175] Barbarian war bands increasingly began to penetrate the Empire's vulnerable borders, both as settlers and invaders. In 451, the Romans defeated Attila the Hun, but only with assistance from a confederation of *foederatii* troops, which included Visigoths, Franks and Alans. As barbarian incursions continued, some advancing as far as the heart of Italy, Rome's borders began to collapse, with frontier forces swiftly finding themselves cut off deep in the enemy's rear.[176]

Simultaneously, barbarian troops in Rome's pay came to be "in a condition of almost perpetual turbulence and revolt"[177] from 409 onwards. In 476 these troops finally unseated the last emperor of the Western Roman Empire.[178] The Eastern Roman forces continued to defend the Eastern Roman (Byzantine) Empire until its fall in 1453.[179]

The former Oxford University historian Adrian Goldsworthy has argued that the cause of the fall of the Roman Empire in the West should not be blamed on barbarization of the late Roman Army, but on its recurrent civil wars, which led to its inability to repel or defeat invasions from outside its frontiers. The East Roman or Byzantine empire on the other hand had fewer civil wars to contend with in the late fourth and early fifth centuries, or in the years from 383-432 A.D.[180]

References

Explanatory notes

Citations

Bibliography

Primary sources

- Livy, *From the Founding of the City* on Wikisource (print: *Book 1 as The Rise of Rome*, Oxford University Press, 1998, ISBN 0-19-282296-9)
- Ammianus Marcellinus, *Res Gestae a Fine Corneli Taciti*[181] on The Latin Library.
- *Notitia Dignitatum*[182]
- Polybius: The Rise of the Roman Empire[183] at LacusCurtius print: Harvard University Press, 1927. (Translation by W. R. Paton).
- Tacitus: The Annals.

Secondary and tertiary sources

- Alfoldi, Andrew, *The Crisis of the Empire (AD 249–270)*, in S A Cook et al. (eds.), *The Cambridge Ancient History*, Vol. XII: The Imperial Crisis and Recovery (AD 193–324), pp. 208ff., ISBN 0-521-30199-8.
- Boak, Arthur, *A History of Rome to 565 A.D.*, The MacMillan Company, 1957, ISBN unknown
- Campbell, Brian, *The Army*, in *The Crisis of Empire, AD 193–337*, in *The Cambridge Ancient History*, Second Edition, Vol. XII, ISBN 0-521-30199-8.
- Cary, Max; Scullard, Howard, *A History of Rome*, The MacMillan Press Ltd, 1979, ISBN 0-333-27830-5.
- Elton, Hugh, *Warfare in Roman Europe AD 350–425*, Oxford University Press, 1996, ISBN 0-19-815241-8.
- Gabba, Emilio, *Republican Rome, The Army and The Allies*, University of California Press, 1976, ISBN 0-520-03259-4.
- Gibbon, Edward: *The Decline and Fall of the Roman Empire*[184] (print: *Penguin Books, 1985, ISBN 0-14-043189-6*).
- Goldsworthy, Adrian, *In the Name of Rome: The Men Who Won the Roman Empire*, Weidenfeld and Nicholson, 2003, ISBN 0-297-84666-3.
- Grant, Michael, *The History of Rome*, Faber and Faber, 1993, ISBN 0-571-11461-X.
- Hassall, Mark, *The Army*, in *The High Empire, AD 70–192*, in *The Cambridge Ancient History*, Second Edition, Vol. XI, ISBN 0-521-26335-2.
- Heather, Peter, *The Fall of the Roman Empire: A New History*, Macmillan Publishers, 2005, ISBN 0-330-49136-9.
- Jones, Arnold, *The Later Roman Empire*, Johns Hopkins University Press, 1964, ISBN 0-8018-3285-3.
- Keppie, Lawrence, *The Making of the Roman Army*, Barnes & Noble Books, 1984, ISBN 978-0-389-20447-3.
- Luttwak, Edward, *The Grand Strategy of the Roman Empire*, Johns Hopkins University Press, ISBN 0-8018-2158-4.
- Mattingly, David, *An Imperial Possession-Britain in the Roman Empire*, Allen Lane, 2006, ISBN 0-14-014822-1.
- Matyszak, Philip, *The Enemies of Rome*, Thames and Hudson, 2004, ISBN 0-500-25124-X.
- Theodor Mommsen, *The History of Rome*, Indypublish.com, 2008, ISBN 1-4142-7314-2
- Pallottino, Massimo, *The Etruscans*. Penguin Books. 1975, ISBN 0-253-32080-1.
- Runciman, Steven, *The Fall of Constantinople: 1453*. Cambridge University Press, 1965, ISBN 0-521-39832-0.
- Santosusso, Antonio, *Storming the Heavens: Soldiers, Emperors and Civilians in the Roman Empire*, Westview Press, 2001, ISBN 0-8133-

3523-X.
- Smith, Richard, *Service in the Post-Marian Roman Army*, Manchester University Press, 1958, ASIN B0000CK67F.
- Southern, Pat; Dixon, Karen, *The Late Roman Army*, 1996, ISBN 0-415-22296-6.
- Treadgold, Warren, *Byzantium and its Army*, Stanford University Press, 1995, ISBN 0-8047-3163-2.
- Vogt, Joseph, *The Decline of Rome*, Weidenfeld, 1993, ISBN 0-297-81392-7.
- Graham Webster, *The Roman Imperial Army*, Barnes and Noble Books, 1969, ISBN 0-7136-0934-6.

Roman army

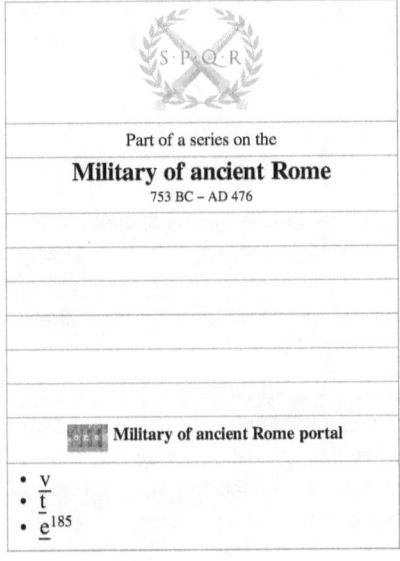

Part of a series on the
Military of ancient Rome
753 BC – AD 476

Military of ancient Rome portal

- v
- t
- e[185]

The **Roman army** (Latin: *exercitus Romanus*) is a term that can in general be applied to the terrestrial armed forces deployed by the Romans throughout the duration of Ancient Rome, from the Roman Kingdom (to c. 500 BC) to the Roman Republic (500–31 BC) and the Roman Empire (31 BC – 395), and its medieval continuation the Eastern Roman Empire. It is thus a term that may span approximately 2,206 years (753 BC to 1453 AD), during which the Roman armed forces underwent numerous permutations in composition, organisation, equipment and tactics, while conserving a core of lasting traditions.[186,187,188]

Figure 21: *Coin showing (obverse) head of the late Roman emperor Julian (ruled 361–363 AD) wearing diadem and (reverse) soldier bearing standard holding kneeling barbarian captive by the hair, legend and Myth VIRTUS EXERCITUS ROMANORUM ("Valour of Roman army"). Gold solidus. Sirmium mint.*

Historical overview

Early Roman army (c. 500 BC to c. 300 BC)

The Early Roman army of the Roman Kingdom and of the early Republic (to c. 300 BC). During this period, when warfare chiefly consisted of small-scale plundering raids, it has been suggested that the Roman Army followed Etruscan or Greek models of organisation and equipment. The early Roman army was based on an annual levy.

The infantry ranks were filled with the lower classes while the cavalry (*equites* or *celeres*) were left to the patricians, because the wealthier could afford horses. Moreover, the commanding authority during the regal period was the high king. Until the establishment of the Republic and the office of consul, the king assumed the role of commander-in-chief.[189] However, from about 508 BC Rome no longer had a king. The commanding position of the army was given to the consuls, "who were charged both singly and jointly to take care to preserve the Republic from danger".[190]

The term legion is derived from the Latin word *legio*; which ultimately means draft or levy. At first there were only four legions. These legions were numbered "I" to "IIII", with the fourth being written as such and not "IV". The first legion was seen as the most prestigious. The bulk of the army was made up of citizens. These citizens could not choose the legion to which they were allocated. Any man "from ages 16–46 were selected by ballot" and assigned to a legion.[191]

Until the Roman military disaster of 390 BC at the Battle of the Allia, Rome's army was organised similarly to the Greek phalanx. This was due to Greek influence in Italy "by way of their colonies". Patricia Southern quotes ancient historians Livy and Dionysius in saying that the "phalanx consisted of 3,000 infantry and 300 cavalry".[192] Each man had to provide his equipment in battle; the military equipment which he could afford determined which position he took in the battle. Politically they shared the same ranking system in the Comitia Centuriata; which ultimately vis-à-vis placed the men on the battlefield.Wikipedia:Please clarify

Roman army of the mid-Republic (c. 300–88 BC)

The Roman army of the mid-Republic was also known as the "manipular army" or the "Polybian army" after the Greek historian Polybius, who provides the most detailed extant description of this phase. The Roman army started to have a full-time army of 150,000 at all times and 3/4 of the rest were levied.

During this period, the Romans, while maintaining the levy system, adopted the Samnite manipular organisation for their legions and also bound all the other peninsular Italian states into a permanent military alliance (see *Socii*). The latter were required to supply (collectively) roughly the same number of troops to joint forces as the Romans to serve under Roman command. Legions in this phase were always accompanied on campaign by the same number of allied *alae*, units of roughly the same size as legions.

After the 2nd Punic War (218–201 BC), the Romans acquired an overseas empire, which necessitated standing forces to fight lengthy wars of conquest and to garrison the newly gained provinces. Thus the army's character mutated from a temporary force based entirely on short-term conscription to a standing army in which the conscripts were supplemented by a large number of volunteers willing to serve for much longer than the legal six-year limit. These volunteers were mainly from the poorest social class, who did not have plots to tend at home and were attracted by the modest military pay and the prospect of a share of war booty. The minimum property requirement for service in the legions, which had been suspended during the 2nd Punic War, was effectively ignored from 201 BC onward in order to recruit sufficient volunteers. Between 150-100 BC, the manipular structure was gradually phased out, and the much larger cohort became the main tactical unit. In addition, from the 2nd Punic War onward, Roman armies were always accompanied by units of non-Italian mercenaries, such as Numidian light cavalry, Cretan archers, and Balearic slingers, who provided specialist functions that Roman armies had previously lacked.

Figure 22: *Imperial Roman legionaries in tight formation, a relief from Glanum, a Roman town in what is now southern France that was inhabited from 27 BC to 260 AD (when it was sacked by invading Alemanni)*

Roman army of the late Republic (88–30 BC)

The Roman army of the late Republic (88–30 BC) marks the continued transition between the conscription-based citizen-levy of the mid-Republic and the mainly volunteer, professional standing forces of the imperial era. The main literary sources for the army's organisation and tactics in this phase are the works of Julius Caesar, the most notable of a series of warlords who contested for power in this period. As a result of the Social War (91–88 BC), all Italians were granted Roman citizenship, the old allied *alae* were abolished and their members integrated into the legions. Regular annual conscription remained in force and continued to provide the core of legionary recruitment, but an ever-increasing proportion of recruits were volunteers, who signed up for 16-year terms as opposed to the maximum 6 years for conscripts. The loss of *ala* cavalry reduced Roman/Italian cavalry by 75%, and legions became dependent on allied native horse for cavalry cover. This period saw the large-scale expansion of native forces employed to complement the legions, made up of *numeri* ("units") recruited from tribes within Rome's overseas empire and neighbouring allied tribes. Large numbers of heavy infantry and cavalry were recruited in Spain, Gaul and Thrace, and archers in Thrace, Anatolia and Syria. However, these native units were not integrated with the legions, but retained their own traditional leadership, organisation, armour and weapons.

Imperial Roman army (30 BC – AD 284)

During this period the Republican system of citizen-conscription was replaced by a standing professional army of mainly volunteers serving standard 20-year terms (plus 5 as reservists), although many in the service of the empire would serve as many as 30 to 40 years on active duty, as established by the first Roman emperor, Augustus (sole ruler 30 BC – AD 14).Regular annual conscription of citizens was abandoned and only decreed in emergencies (e.g. during the Illyrian revolt 6–9 AD). Under Augustus there were 28 legions, consisting almost entirely of heavy infantry, with about 5,000 men each (total 125,000). This had increased to a peak of 33 legions of about 5,500 men each (c. 180,000 men in total) by AD 200 under Septimius Severus. Legions continued to recruit Roman citizens, mainly the inhabitants of Italy and Roman colonies, until 212. Legions were flanked by the auxilia, a corps of regular troops recruited mainly from *peregrini*, imperial subjects who did not hold Roman citizenship (the great majority of the empire's inhabitants until 212, when all were granted citizenship). Auxiliaries, who served a minimum term of 25 years, were also mainly volunteers, but regular conscription of *peregrini* was employed for most of the 1st century AD. The *auxilia* consisted, under Augustus, of about 250 regiments of roughly cohort size, that is, about 500 men (in total 125,000 men, or 50% of total army effectives). Under Severus the number of regiments increased to about 400, of which about 13% were double-strength (250,000 men, or 60% of total army). *Auxilia* contained heavy infantry equipped similarly to legionaries, and almost all the army's cavalry (both armoured and light), and archers and slingers.

Later Roman army (284–476 AD) continuing as East Roman army (476–641 AD)

The Later Roman army period stretches from (284–476 AD and its continuation, in the surviving eastern half of the empire, as the East Roman army to 641). In this phase, crystallised by the reforms of the emperor Diocletian (ruled 284–305 AD), the Roman army returned to regular annual conscription of citizens, while admitting large numbers of non-citizen barbarian volunteers. However, soldiers remained 25-year professionals and did not return to the short-term levies of the Republic. The old dual organisation of legions and auxilia was abandoned, with citizens and non-citizens now serving in the same units. The old legions were broken up into cohort or even smaller sizes. At the same time, a substantial proportion of the army's effectives were stationed in the interior of the empire, in the form of *comitatus praesentales*, armies that escorted the emperors.

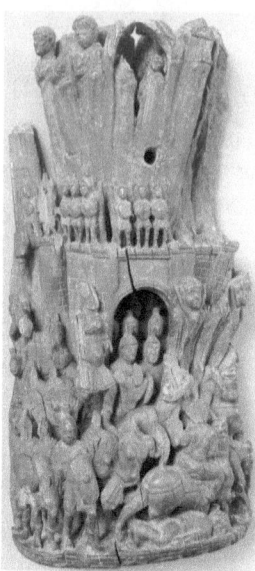

Figure 23: *Stone-carved relief depicting the liberation of a besieged city by a relief force, with those defending the walls making a sortie (i.e. a sudden attack against a besieging enemy from within the besieged town); Western Roman Empire, early 5th Century AD*

Middle Byzantine army (641–1081 AD)

The Middle Byzantine army (641–1081 AD) was the army of the Byzantine state in its classical form (i.e. after the permanent loss of its Near Eastern and North African territories to the Arab conquests after 641 AD). This army was largely composed of semi-professional troops (soldier-farmers) based on the themata military provinces, supplemented by a small core of professional regiments known as the *tagmata* which numbered from 18,000 in 742 to 42,000 in 1025. Ibn al-Fakih estimated the strength of the theme forces in the East c. 902 at 85,000 and Kodama c. 930 at 70,000 Ian Heath and Angus McBride, Byzantine Armies 886-1118,Men-at -Arms Series, 89, 1979, p. 19 ISBN 0 85045 306 2). This structure pertained when the empire was on the defensive, in the 10th century the empire was increasingly involved in territorial expansion, and the themata troops became progressively more irrelevant, being gradually replaced by 'provincial tagmata' units and an increased use of mercenaries.

Komnenian Byzantine army (1081–1204)

The Komnenian Byzantine army was named after the Komnenos dynasty, which ruled from 1081–1185. This was an army built virtually from scratch after the permanent loss of half of Byzantium's traditional main recruiting ground of Anatolia to the Turks following the Battle of Manzikert in 1071, and the destruction of the last regiments of the old army in the wars against the Normans in the early 1080s. It survived until the fall of Constantinople to the Western crusaders in 1204. This army had a large number of mercenary regiments composed of troops of foreign origin such as the Varangian Guard, and the *pronoia* system was introduced.

Palaiologan Byzantine army (1261–1453)

The Palaiologan Byzantine army was named after the Palaiologos dynasty (1261–1453), which ruled Byzantium from the recovery of Constantinople from the Crusaders until its fall to the Turks in 1453. Initially, it continued some practices inherited from the Komnenian era and retained a strong native element until the late 13th century. During the last century of its existence, however, the empire was little more than a city-state that hired foreign mercenary bands for its defence. Thus the Byzantine army finally lost any meaningful connection with the standing imperial Roman army.Wikipedia:Citation needed

This article contains the summaries of the detailed linked articles on the historical phases above, Readers seeking discussion of the Roman army by theme, rather than by chronological phase, should consult the following articles:

History

- Campaign history of the Roman military
- Structural history of the Roman military

Corps

- Praetorian Guard
- Roman legion
- Roman auxiliaries
- Roman cavalry

Strategy and tactics

- Defence-in-depth (Roman military)
- Roman infantry tactics

Equipment & other

- Roman military equipment
- Roman military decorations and punishments

Some of the Roman army's many tactics are still used in modern-day armies today.

Early Roman army (c. 550 to c. 300 BC)

Until c. 550 BC, there was no "national" Roman army, but a series of clan-based war-bands which only coalesced into a united force in periods of serious external threat. Around 550 BC, during the period conventionally known as the rule of king Servius Tullius, it appears that a universal levy of eligible adult male citizens was instituted. This development apparently coincided with the introduction of heavy armour for most of the infantry. Although originally low in numbers the Roman infantry was extremely tactical and developed some of the most influential battle strategies to date.

The early Roman army was based on a compulsory levy from adult male citizens which was held at the start of each campaigning season, in those years that war was declared. There were no standing or professional forces. During the Regal Era (to c. 500 BC), the standard levy was probably of 9,000 men, consisting of 6,000 heavily armed infantry (probably Greek-style hoplites), plus 2,400 light-armed infantry (*rorarii*, later called *velites*) and 600 light cavalry (*equites celeres*). When the kings were replaced by two annually elected *praetores* in c. 500 BC, the standard levy remained of the same size, but was now divided equally between the Praetors, each commanding one legion of 4,500 men.

It is likely that the hoplite element was deployed in a Greek-style phalanx formation in large set-piece battles. However, these were relatively rare, with most fighting consisting of small-scale border-raids and skirmishing. In these, the Romans would fight in their basic tactical unit, the *centuria* of 100 men. In addition, separate clan-based forces remained in existence until c. 450 BC at least, although they would operate under the Praetors' authority, at least nominally.

In 493 BC, shortly after the establishment of the Roman Republic, Rome concluded a perpetual treaty of military alliance (the *foedus Cassianum*), with the combined other Latin city-states. The treaty, probably motivated by the need for the Latins to deploy a united defence against incursions by neighbouring hill-tribes, provided for each party to provide an equal force for campaigns under unified command. It remained in force until 358 BC.

Figure 24: *Levy of the army, detail of the carved relief on the Altar of Domitius Ahenobarbus, 122-115 BC.*

Roman army of the mid-Republic (c. 300 – 107 BC)

The central feature of the Roman army of the mid-Republic, or the Polybian army, was the manipular organization of its battle-line. Instead of a single, large mass (the phalanx) as in the Early Roman army, the Romans now drew up in three lines consisting of small units (maniples) of 120 men, arrayed in chessboard fashion, giving much greater tactical strength and flexibility. This structure was probably introduced in c. 300 BC during the Samnite Wars. Also probably dating from this period was the regular accompaniment of each legion by a non-citizen formation of roughly equal size, the *ala*, recruited from Rome's Italian allies, or *socii*. The latter were c. 150 autonomous states which were bound by a treaty of perpetual military alliance with Rome. Their sole obligation was to supply to the Roman army, on demand, a number of fully equipped troops up to a specified maximum each year.

The Second Punic War (218–201 BC) saw the addition of a third element to the existing dual Roman/Italian structure: non-Italian mercenaries with specialist skills lacking in the legions and *alae*: Numidian light cavalry, Cretan archers, and slingers from the Balearic islands. From this time, these units always accompanied Roman armies.

The Republican army of this period, like its earlier forebear, did not maintain standing or professional military forces, but levied them, by compulsory conscription, as required for each campaigning season and disbanded thereafter (although formations could be kept in being over winter during major wars). The standard levy was doubled during the Samnite Wars to 4 legions (2 per Consul), for a total of c. 18,000 Roman troops and 4 allied *alae* of similar size. Service in the legions was limited to property-owning Roman citizens, normally those known as *iuniores* (age 16–46). The army's senior officers, including its commanders-in-chief, the Roman Consuls, were all elected annually at the People's Assembly. Only *equites* (members of the Roman knightly order) were eligible to serve as senior officers. *Iuniores* of the highest social classes (*equites* and the First Class of commoners) provided the legion's cavalry, the other classes the legionary infantry. The *proletarii* (those assessed at under 400 *drachmae* wealth) were ineligible for legionary service and were assigned to the fleets as oarsmen. Elders, vagrants, freedmen, slaves and convicts were excluded from the military levy, save in emergencies.

The legionary cavalry also changed, probably around 300 BC onwards from the light, unarmoured horse of the early army to a heavy force with metal armour (bronze cuirasses and, later, chain-mail shirts). Contrary to a long-held view, the cavalry of the mid-Republic was a highly effective force that generally prevailed against strong enemy cavalry forces (both Gallic and Greek) until it was decisively beaten by the Carthaginian general Hannibal's horsemen during the second Punic War. This was due to Hannibal's greater operational flexibility owing to his Numidian light cavalry.

The Polybian army's operations during its existence can be divided into three broad phases. (1) The struggle for hegemony over Italy, especially against the Samnite League (338–264 BC); (2) the struggle with Carthage for hegemony in the western Mediterranean Sea (264–201 BC); and (3) the struggle against the Hellenistic monarchies for control of the eastern Mediterranean (201–91 BC). During the earlier phase, the normal size of the levy (including allies) was in the region of 40,000 men (2 consular armies of c. 20,000 men each).

During the latter phase, with lengthy wars of conquest followed by permanent military occupation of overseas provinces, the character of the army necessarily changed from a temporary force based entirely on short-term conscription to a standing army in which the conscripts, whose service was in this period limited by law to 6 consecutive years, were complemented by large numbers of volunteers who were willing to serve for much longer periods. Many of the volunteers were drawn from the poorest social class, which until the 2nd Punic War had been excluded from service in the legions by the minimum property requirement: during that war, extreme manpower needs had forced the army to ignore the requirement, and this practice continued thereafter. Maniples were gradually phased out as the main tactical unit, and replaced by the larger cohorts used in the allied *alae*, a process probably complete by the time the general Marius assumed command in 107 BC. (The "Marian reforms" of the army hypothesised by some scholars are today seen by other scholars as having evolved earlier and more gradually.)

In the period after the defeat of Carthage in 201 BC, the army was campaigning exclusively outside Italy, resulting in its men being away from their home plots of land for many years at a stretch. They were assuaged by the large amounts of booty that they shared after victories in the rich eastern theatre. But in Italy, the ever-increasing concentration of public lands in the hands of big landowners, and the consequent displacement of the soldiers' families, led to great unrest and demands for land redistribution. This was successfully achieved, but resulted in the disaffection of Rome's Italian allies, who as non-citizens were excluded from the redistribution. This led to the mass revolt of the *socii* and the Social War (91-88 BC). The result was the grant of Roman citizenship to all Italians and the end of the Polybian army's dual structure: the *alae* were abolished and the *socii* recruited into the legions.

Imperial Roman army (30 BC – AD 284)

Under the founder–emperor Augustus (ruled 30 BC – 14 AD), the legions, c. 5,000-strong all-heavy infantry formations recruited from Roman citizens only, were transformed from a mixed conscript and volunteer corps serving an average of 10 years, to all-volunteer units of long-term professionals serving a standard 25-year term (conscription was only decreed in emergencies). In the later 1st century, the size of a legion's First Cohort was doubled, increasing legionary personnel to c. 5,500.

Alongside the legions, Augustus established the auxilia, a regular corps of similar numbers to the legions, recruited from the *peregrini* (non-citizen inhabitants of the empire – about 90% of the empire's population in the 1st century). As well as comprising large numbers of extra heavy infantry equipped in a similar manner to legionaries, the auxilia provided virtually all the army's cavalry (heavy and light), light infantry, archers and other specialists. The auxilia were organised in c. 500-strong units called *cohortes* (all-infantry), *alae* (all-cavalry) and *cohortes equitatae* (infantry with a cavalry contingent attached). Around 80 AD, a minority of auxiliary regiments were doubled in size. Until about 68 AD, the auxilia were recruited by a mix of conscription and voluntary enlistment. After that time, the auxilia became largely a volunteer corps, with conscription resorted to only in emergencies. Auxiliaries were required to serve a minimum of 25 years, although many served for longer periods. On

Figure 25: *God Bes as a Roman soldier. Sword in right hand and spear and shield in left hand. Limestone slab, in relief. Roman Period. From Egypt. The Petrie Museum of Egyptian Archaeology, London*

completion of their minimum term, auxiliaries were awarded Roman citizenship, which carried important legal, fiscal and social advantages. Alongside the regular forces, the army of the Principate employed allied native units (called *numeri*) from outside the empire on a mercenary basis. These were led by their own aristocrats and equipped in traditional fashion. Numbers fluctuated according to circumstances and are largely unknown.

As all-citizen formations, and symbolic garantors of the dominance of the Italian "master-nation", legions enjoyed greater social prestige than the auxilia. This was reflected in better pay and benefits. In addition, legionaries were equipped with more expensive and protective armour than auxiliaries. However, in 212, the emperor Caracalla granted Roman citizenship to all the empire's inhabitants. At this point, the distinction between legions and auxilia became moot, the latter becoming all-citizen units also. The change was reflected in the disappearance, during the 3rd century, of legionaries' special equipment, and the progressive break-up of legions into cohort-sized units like the auxilia.

By the end of Augustus' reign, the imperial army numbered some 250,000 men, equally split between legionaries and auxiliaries (25 legions and c. 250

Figure 26: *Recreation of a Roman soldier wearing plate armour (lorica segmentata), National Military Museum, Romania.*

Figure 27: *Roman relief fragment depicting the Praetorian Guard, c. 50 AD*

Figure 28: *Ancient Roman statue fragment of either a general or an emperor wearing a corselet decorated with Selene, and two Nereids. Found at èmegara, dating from 100-130 AD.*

Figure 29: *Relief scene of Roman legionaries marching, from the Column of Marcus Aurelius, Rome, Italy, 2nd century AD*

auxiliary regiments). The numbers grew to a peak of about 450,000 by 211 (33 legions and c. 400 auxiliary regiments). By then, auxiliaries outnumbered legionaries substantially. From the peak, numbers probably underwent a steep decline by 270 due to plague and losses during multiple major barbarian invasions. Numbers were restored to their early 2nd-century level of c. 400,000 (but probably not to their 211 peak) under Diocletian (r. 284–305). After the empire's borders became settled (on the Rhine-Danube line in Europe) by 68, virtually all military units (except the Praetorian Guard) were stationed on or near the borders, in roughly 17 of the 42 provinces of the empire in the reign of Hadrian (r. 117–38).

The military chain of command was relatively uniform across the Empire. In each province, the deployed legions' *legati* (legion commanders, who also controlled the auxiliary regiments attached to their legion) reported to the *legatus Augusti pro praetore* (provincial governor), who also headed the civil administration. The governor in turn reported direct to the emperor in Rome. There was no army general staff in Rome, but the leading *praefectus praetorio* (commander of the Praetorian Guard) often acted as the emperor's *de facto* military chief-of-staff.

Legionary rankers were relatively well-paid, compared to contemporary common labourers. Compared with their subsistence-level peasant families, they enjoyed considerable disposable income, enhanced by periodic cash bonuses on special occasions such as the accession of a new emperor. In addition, on completion of their term of service, they were given a generous discharge bonus equivalent to 13 years' salary. Auxiliaries were paid much less in the early 1st century, but by 100 AD, the differential had virtually disappeared. Similarly, in the earlier period, auxiliaries appear not to have received cash and discharge bonuses, but probably did so from Hadrian onwards. Junior officers (*principales*), the equivalent of non-commissioned officers in modern armies, could expect to earn up to twice basic pay. Legionary centurions, the equivalent of mid-level commissioned officers, were organised in an elaborate hierarchy. Usually risen from the ranks, they commanded the legion's tactical sub-units of *centuriae* (c. 80 men) and cohorts (c. 480 men). They were paid several multiples of basic pay. The most senior centurion, the *primus pilus*, was elevated to equestrian rank upon completion of his single-year term of office. The senior officers of the army, the *legati legionis* (legion commanders), *tribuni militum* (legion staff officers) and the *praefecti* (commanders of auxiliary regiments) were all of at least equestrian rank. In the 1st and early 2nd centuries, they were mainly Italian aristocrats performing the military component of their *cursus honorum* (conventional career-path). Later, provincial career officers became predominant. Senior officers were paid enormous salaries, multiples of at least 50 times basic.

A typical Roman army during this period consisted of five to six legions. One legion was made up of 10 cohorts. The first cohort had five centuria each of 160 soldiers. In the second through tenth cohorts there were six centuria of 80 men each. These do not include archers, cavalry or officers.

Soldiers spent only a fraction of their lives on campaign. Most of their time was spent on routine military duties such as training, patrolling, and maintenance of equipment etc. Soldiers also played an important role outside the military sphere. They performed the function of a provincial governor's police force. As a large, disciplined and skilled force of fit men, they played a crucial role in the construction of a province's Roman military and civil infrastructure: in addition to constructing forts and fortified defences such as Hadrian's Wall, they built roads, bridges, ports, public buildings, entire new cities (Roman colonies), and also engaged in large-scale forest clearance and marsh drainage to expand the province's available arable land.

Soldiers, mostly drawn from polytheistic societies, enjoyed wide freedom of worship in the polytheistic Roman system. They revered their own native deities, Roman deities and the local deities of the provinces in which they served. Only a few religions were banned by the Roman authorities, as being incompatible with the official Roman religion and/or politically subversive, notably Druidism and Christianity. The later Principate saw the rise in popularity among the military of Eastern mystery cults, generally centred on one deity, and involving secret rituals divulged only to initiates. By far the most popular in the army was Mithraism, an apparently syncretist religion which mainly originated in Asia Minor.

Late Roman army/East Roman army (284–641)

The Late Roman army is the term used to denote the military forces of the Roman Empire from the accession of Emperor Diocletian in 284 until the Empire's definitive division into Eastern and Western halves in 395. A few decades afterwards, the Western army disintegrated as the Western empire collapsed. The East Roman army, on the other hand, continued intact and essentially unchanged until its reorganization by themes and transformation into the Byzantine army in the 7th century. The term "late Roman army" is often used to include the East Roman army.

The army of the Principate underwent a significant transformation, as a result of the chaotic 3rd century. Unlike the Principate army, the army of the 4th century was heavily dependent on conscription and its soldiers were more poorly remunerated than in the 2nd century. Barbarians from outside the empire probably supplied a much larger proportion of the late army's recruits than in the army of the 1st and 2nd centuries.

The size of the 4th-century army is controversial. More dated scholars (e.g. A.H.M. Jones, writing in the 1960s) estimated the late army as much larger than the Principate army, half the size again or even as much as twice the size. With the benefit of archaeological discoveries of recent decades, many contemporary historians view the late army as no larger than its predecessor: under Diocletian c. 390,000 (the same as under Hadrian almost two centuries earlier) and under Constantine no greater, and probably somewhat smaller, than the Principate peak of c. 440,000. The main change in structure was the establishment of large armies that accompanied the emperors (*comitatus praesentales*) and were generally based away from the frontiers. Their primary function was to deter usurpations. The legions were split up into smaller units comparable in size to the auxiliary regiments of the Principate. In parallel, legionary armour and equipment were abandoned in favour of auxiliary equipment. Infantry adopted the more protective equipment of the Principate cavalry.

The role of cavalry in the late army does not appear to have been enhanced as compared with the army of the Principate. The evidence is that cavalry was much the same proportion of overall army numbers as in the 2nd century and that its tactical role and prestige remained similar. Indeed, the cavalry acquired a reputation for incompetence and cowardice for their role in three major battles in mid-4th century. In contrast, the infantry retained its traditional reputation for excellence.

The 3rd and 4th centuries saw the upgrading of many existing border forts to make them more defensible, as well as the construction of new forts with much higher defensive specifications. The interpretation of this trend has fuelled an ongoing debate whether the army adopted a defence-in-depth strategy or continued the same posture of "forward defence" as in the early Principate. Many elements of the late army's defence posture were similar to those associated with forward defence, such as a looser forward location of forts, frequent cross-border operations, and external buffer-zones of allied barbarian tribes. Whatever the defence strategy, it was apparently less successful in preventing barbarian incursions than in the 1st and 2nd centuries. This may have been due to heavier barbarian pressure, and/or to the practice of keeping large armies of the best troops in the interior, depriving the border forces of sufficient support.

Komnenian Byzantine army (1081–1204)

The Komnenian period marked a rebirth of the Byzantine army. At the beginning of the Komnenian period in 1081, the Byzantine Empire had been reduced to the smallest territorial extent. Surrounded by enemies, and financially ruined by a long period of civil war, the empire's prospects looked grim.

Figure 30: *Emperor John II Komnenos, the most successful commander of the Komnenian army.*

At the beginning of the Komnenian period, the Byzantine army was reduced to a shadow of its former self: during the 11th century, decades of peace and neglect had reduced the old thematic forces, and the Battle of Manzikert in 1071 had destroyed the professional *tagmata*, the core of the Byzantine army. At Manzikert and later at Dyrrhachium, units tracing their lineage for centuries back to Late Roman army were wiped out, and the subsequent loss of Asia Minor deprived the Empire of its main recruiting ground. In the Balkans, at the same time, the Empire was exposed to invasions by the Norman Kingdom of Sicily, and by Pecheneg raids across the Danube.

The Byzantine army's nadir was reached in 1091, when Alexios I could manage to field only 500 soldiers from the Empire's professional forces. These formed the nucleus of the army, with the addition of the armed retainers of Alexios' relatives and the nobles enrolled in the army and the substantial aid of a large force of allied Cumans, which won the Battle of Levounion against the Pechenegs (Petcheneks or Patzinaks).[193] Yet, through a combination of skill, determination and years of campaigning, Alexios, John and Manuel Komnenos managed to restore the power of the Byzantine Empire by constructing a new army from scratch. This process should not, however, at least in its earlier phases, be seen as a planned exercise in military restructuring. In particular, Alexios I was often reduced to reacting to events rather than controlling them;

the changes he made to the Byzantine army were largely done out of immediate necessity and were pragmatic in nature.

The new force had a core of units which were both professional and disciplined. It contained formidable guards units such as the Varangians, the *Athanatoi*, a unit of heavy cavalry stationed in Constantinople, the *Vardariotai* and the *Archontopouloi*, recruited by Alexios from the sons of dead Byzantine officers, foreign mercenary regiments, and also units of professional soldiers recruited from the provinces. These provincial troops included *kataphraktoi* cavalry from Macedonia, Thessaly and Thrace, and various other provincial forces such as Trebizond Archers from the Black Sea coast of Anatolia. Alongside troops raised and paid for directly by the state the Komnenian army included the armed followers of members of the wider imperial family and its extensive connections. In this can be seen the beginnings of the feudalisation of the Byzantine military. The granting of *pronoia* holdings, where land, or more accurately rights to revenue from land, was held in return for military obligations, was beginning to become a notable element in the military infrastructure towards the end of the Komnenian period, though it became much more important subsequently.

In 1097, the Byzantine army numbered around 70,000 men altogether.[194] By 1180 and the death of Manuel Komnenos, whose frequent campaigns had been on a grand scale, the army was probably considerably larger. During the reign of Alexios I, the field army numbered around 20,000 men which was increased to about 30,000 men in John II's reign.[195] By the end of Manuel I's reign the Byzantine field army had risen to 40,000 men.

Palaiologan Byzantine army (1261–1453)

The Palaiologan army refers to the military forces of the Byzantine Empire from the late 13th century to its final collapse in the mid 15th century, under the House of the Palaiologoi. The army was a direct continuation of the forces of the Nicaean army, which itself was a fractured component of the formidable Komnenian army. Under the first Palaiologan emperor, Michael VIII, the army's role took an increasingly offensive role whilst the naval forces of the Empire, weakened since the days of Andronikos I Komnenos, were boosted to include thousands of skilled sailors and some 80 ships. Due to the lack of land to support the army, the Empire required the use of large numbers of mercenaries.

After Andronikos II took to the throne, the army fell apart and the Byzantines suffered regular defeats at the hands of their eastern opponents, although they would continue to enjoy success against the crusader territories in Greece. By c. 1350, following a destructive civil war and the outbreak of the Black Death, the Empire was no longer capable of raising troops and the supplies to maintain them. The Empire came to rely upon troops provided by Serbs, Bulgarians, Venetians, Latins, Genoans and Ottoman Turks to fight the civil wars that lasted for the greater part of the 14th century, with the latter foe being the most successful in establishing a foothold in Thrace. The Ottomans swiftly expanded through the Balkans and cut off Constantinople, the capital of the Byzantine Empire, from the surrounding land. The last decisive battle was fought by the Palaiologan army in 1453, when Constantinople was besieged and fell on 29 May. The last isolated remnants of the Byzantine state were conquered by 1461.

External links

- Legions and Legionaries in the Age of Augustus[196]
- The Roman Centurion[197]
- Roman Warriors: The Myth of the Military Machine[198]
- Roman Cavalry[199]
- Protecting the Emperor: The Praetorian Guard[200]
- Diocletian and the Roman Army[201]
- The Last Legion[202]
- Life of Roman legionary[203]

List of Roman army unit types

This is a list of Roman army unit types.

- *Actarius* – A military or camp clerk.
- *Adiutor* – A camp or headquarters adjutant or assistant.
- *Aeneator* – Military musician such as a bugler.
- *Agrimensor* – A surveyor (a type of *immunes*).
- *Aquilifer* – Bearer of the legionary eagle.
- *Alaris* – A cavalryman serving in an *ala*.
- *Architecti* – An engineer or artillery constructor.
- *Armicustos* – A soldier tasked with the administration and supply of weapons and equipment. A quartermaster.
- *Ballistarius* – An artillery operator (a type of *immunes*).
- *Beneficiarius* – A soldier performing an extraordinary task such as military policing or a special assignment.
- *Bucinator* – A trumpeter or bugler.
- *Cacula* – Servant or slave of a soldier.
- *Capsarior* – A medical orderly.
- *Causarius* – A soldier discharged for wounds or other medical reasons.

- *Centurion* – Officer rank, generally one per 80 soldiers, in charge of a *centuria*.
- *Clinicus* – A medic.
- *Cornicen* – Bugler.
- *Doctor* – A trainer, subdivisions for everything from weapons to horn-blowing.
- *Draconarius* – Bearer of a cavalry standard.
- *Decurion* – Leader of a troop of cavalry (14-30 men). Often confused with *decanus*.
- *Decanus* – Leader of a *contubernium* (a legionary tent group of 8 men).
- *Discens* – *Miles* in training for an *immunis* position.
- *Dux* – A general in charge of two or more legions. In the Third Century AD, an officer with a regional command transcending provincial boundaries, responsible directly to the emperor alone, usually appointed on a temporary basis in a grave emergency. In the fourth century AD, an officer in charge of a section of the frontier answering to the *Magister Militum*.
- *Equites singulares Augusti* – Elite cavalry unit tasked to guard the Roman Emperors. Usually commanded by a *tribunus* of praetorian rank.
- *Evocatus* – A soldier who had served out his time and obtained his discharge (*missio*), but had voluntarily enlisted again at the invitation of the consul or other commander.
- Frumentarii – Officials of the Roman Empire during the 2nd and 3rd era. Often used as a Secret Service, mostly operating in uniform.
- *Hastatus* – The youngest of the heavy infantry in the pre-Marian armies, who were less well-equipped than the older *Principes* and *Triarii*. These formed the first line of battle in front of the *Principes*.
- *Hastatus Prior* – A centurion commanding a *manipulus* or *centuria* of *hastati*. A high-ranking officer within a *manipulus* or *centuria*.
- *Hastatus Posterior* – A deputy to the *hastatus prior*
- *Hastiliarius* – a weapons instructor.
- *Imaginifer* – A standard-bearer carrying the imago – the standard which bore a likeness of the emperor, and, at later dates, his family.
- *Immunes* – Soldiers who were "immune" from combat duty and fatigues through having a more specialist role within the army.
- *Legatus legionis* – A legion commander of senatorial rank; literally the "deputy" of the emperor, who was the titular commander-in-chief.
- *Legatus pro praetore* – Provincial governor of senatorial rank with multiple legions under his command.
- *Legionary* – The heavy infantry that was the basic military force of the ancient Roman army in the period of the late Roman Republic and the Roman Empire.

- *Medicus* – Physician or combat medic. Specializations included surgery (*medicus vulnerarius*), ophthalmology (*medicus ocularius*), and also veterinary (*medicus veterinarius*). At least some held rank equivalent to a centurion.
- *Miles* or *Miles Gregarius* – The basic private level foot soldier.
- *Numerus* – A unit of barbarian allies not integrated into the regular army structure. Later, a unit of border forces.
- *Optio* – One per century as second-in-command to the centurion. Could also fill several other specialized roles on an *ad hoc* basis.
- *Pedites* – The infantry of the early army of the Roman kingdom. The majority of the army in this period.
- *Peditatus* – A term referring to any infantryman in the Roman Empire.
- *Pilus Prior* – Senior centurion of a cohort.
- *Pilus Posterior* – Deputy to the *pilus prior*.
- *Praefectus Castrorum* – Camp prefect, third-in-command of the legion, also responsible for maintaining the camp, equipment, and supplies. Usually a former *primus pilus*.
- *Praefectus Cohortis* - Commander of a cohort.
- *Praefectus legionis agens vice legati* – Equestrian officer given the command of a legion in the absence of a senatorial *legatus*. After the removal of senators from military command, the title of a legionary commander. ("...*agens vice legati*, dropped in later Third Century")
- *Praetorians* – A special force of bodyguards used by Roman Emperors.
- *Primus Ordinis* – The commanding officer of each *centuria* in the first cohort with the exception of the first *centuria* of the cohort.
- *Primus Pilus* (literally 'first file', not spear) – The centurion commanding the first cohort and the senior centurion of the entire Legion.
- *Princeps* – Pre-Marian soldier, initially equipped with the *Hasta* spear, but later with the *pilum*, these men formed the second line of battle behind the *Hastati* in the pre-Marian armies. They were also chieftains in Briton like Dumnorix of the Regneses (he was killed by Gaius Salvius Liberalis' soldiers).
- *Princeps Prior* – A centurion commanding a *century* of *principes*.
- *Princeps Posterior* – A deputy to the *princeps prior*.
- *Principales* – A group of ranks, including *aquilifer*, *signifer*, *optio*, and *tesserarius*. Similar to modern NCOs (Non-commissioned officers).
- *Protectores Augusti Nostri* (a.k.a. *Protectores Divini Lateris*) - honorific title for senior officers singled out for their loyalty to the Emperor and soldierly qualities. The *protectores* were an order of honor rather than a military unit. The order first appeared in the mid-200s AD.
- *Quaestionarius* – An interrogator or torturer.
- *Retentus* – A soldier kept in service after serving required term.

- *Rorarii* – The final line, or reserve, in the ancient pre-Marius Roman army. These were removed even before the Marian reforms, as the *Triarii* provided a very sturdy anchor.
- *Sagittarii* – Archers, including horse-riding auxiliary archers recruited mainly in the Eastern Empire and Africa.
- *Salararius* – A soldier enjoying special service conditions or hired as a mercenary.
- *Scholae Palatinae* – An elite troop of soldiers created by the Emperor Constantine the Great to provide personal protection of the Emperor and his immediate family.
- *Scorpionarius* – An artilleryman operating a *scorpio* artillery piece.
- *Signifer* – Standard bearer of the Roman Legion.
- *Socii* – Troops from allied states in the pre-Marian army before the Social War (91–88 BC).
- *Speculatores* and Exploratores – The scouts and reconnaissance element of the Roman army.
- *Supernumerarii* – Supernumerary soldiers who served to fill the places of those who were killed or disabled by their wounds.
- *Tablifer* – A guard cavalry standard-bearer
- *Tesserarius* – Guard commander, one per *centuria*.
- *Tirones* – A basic trainee.
- *Triarii* – Spearmen of the pre-Marian armies, equipped with the Hasta, who formed the third line of battle behind the *Principes*.
- *Tribuni militum angusticlavii* or military tribune – Military tribune of equestrian rank, five of whom were assigned to each legion.
- *Tribunus militum laticlavius* – Military tribune of senatorial rank. Second in command of a legion. Appointments to this rank seem to have ceased during the sole reign of Gallienus as part of a policy of excluding senators from military commands.
- *Tubicen* – A trumpeter.
- *Urbanae* - A special police force of Rome, created to counterbalance the Praetorians.
- *Velites* – A class of light infantry in the army of the Roman Republic.
- *Venator* – A hunter (a type of *immunes*).
- *Vexillarius* – Bearer of a *vexillum* (standard).

Sub-units of the Roman legion

Before the Marian reforms of 107 BC the structure of the legions was as follows:

- *Contubernium* – The smallest organized unit of soldiers in the Roman Army. It was composed of eight legionaries led by a *decanus*. When on

the march a Legion would often march *contubernium*-abreast (8-abreast). In the Imperial Legion, ten *contubernia* formed a *centuria*.
- Maniple (*Manipulus*) – The pre-Marian sub-unit of the Roman Legions, consisting of 120 men (60 for the *Triarii*).
- *Legio* (Republic) – A legion in the pre-Marian armies consisted of 60 *manipuli* of infantry and 10 *turmae* of cavalry. By 250 BC, there would be four Legions, two commanded by each Consul: two Roman legions which would be accompanied by an additional two allied Legions of similar strength and structure. For every Roman Legion there would be an allied Legion.
- *Turma* – A unit of cavalry in the pre-Marian army, which usually consisted of 32 horsemen.

After the reforms of Gaius Marius, the organisation of the legions became standardised as follows:

- *Contubernium* – The smallest organized unit of soldiers in the Roman Army. It was composed of eight legionaries led by a *decanus*. Ten *contubernia* formed a *centuria*.
- *Centuria* – 80 men under the command of a *centurion* and his *optio*. Six *centuriae* formed a *cohors*.
- *Cohors* (cohort) – A *cohors* consisted of 480 men. The most senior ranking *centurion* of the six *centuriae* commanded the entire *cohors*.
- First Cohort (*Cohors Prima*) – The first cohort was a double strength cohort (consisting of five double-strength *centuriae*), numbering 800 men (excluding officers). The centurion of its first *centuria*, the *Primus Pilus*, commanded the first cohort and was also the most senior centurion in the legion.
- Legio (Imperial) – A legion was composed of nine cohorts and one first cohort. The legion's overall commander was the *legatus legionis*, assisted by the *praefectus castrorum* and other senior officers.
- *Vexillatio* – A temporary task force of one or more *centuriae* detached from the legion for a specific purpose. A *vexillatio* was commanded by an officer appointed by the *Legatus*.

Roman military decorations and punishments

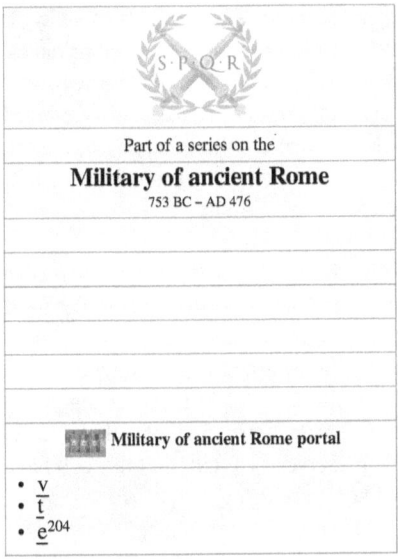

Part of a series on the
Military of ancient Rome
753 BC – AD 476

Military of ancient Rome portal

- v
- t
- e[204]

As with most other military forces the **Roman military** adopted an extensive list of **decorations** for military gallantry and likewise a range of **punishments** for military transgressions.

Decorations, awards and victory titles

Crowns

- Grass crown – (Latin: *corona obsidionalis* or *corona graminea*), was the highest and rarest of all military decorations. It was presented only to a general, commander, or officer whose actions saved the legion or the entire army.
- Civic crown – (Latin: *corona civica*), was a chaplet of common oak leaves woven to form a crown. During the Roman Republic, and the subsequent Principate, it was regarded as the second highest military decoration a citizen could aspire to (the Grass Crown being held in higher regard).
- Naval crown – (Latin: *corona navalis*), was a gold crown awarded to the first man who boarded an enemy ship during a naval engagement. In style, the crown was made of gold and surmounted with the beaks of ships.

- Gold crown – (Latin: *corona aurea*), Awarded to both Centurions and apparently some principales, for killing an enemy in single combat and holding the ground to the end of the battle.
- Battlement crowns – These were made of gold and decorated with the uprights (*valli*) of an entrenchment or turrets of a city. It was awarded to the first soldier or Centurion to mount the wall or palisade of an enemy town or camp.[205]
  - Mural crown – (Latin: *corona muralis*), Also referred to as the "walled crown", this was a golden crown, or circle of gold intended to resemble a battlement, bestowed upon the first soldier who climbed the wall of a besieged city and to successfully place the standard of the attacking army upon it.
  - Camp crown – (Latin: *corona vallaris* or *corona castrensis*), A golden crown which was ornamented with the palisades used in forming an entrenchment.
- Crown of the Preserver – awarded to "those who have shielded and saved any of the citizens or allies" – Polybius relates that the crown is presented by those civilians the soldier saved and adds that "the man thus preserved also reverences his preserver as a father all through his life, and must treat him in every way like a parent.".

Imperial titles

Synonyms for "Emperor"

- Augustus (also "Αὔγουστος" or "Σεβαστός"), "Majestic" or "Venerable"; an honorific cognomen exclusive to the emperor
  - Αὐτοκράτωρ, (lit. "Self-ruler"); Greek title equivalent to imperator i.e. Commander-in-Chief
  - Βασιλεύς (*Basileus*), Greek title meaning sovereign, popularly used in the east to refer to the emperor; a formal title of the Roman emperor beginning with Heraclius
- Caesar (also "Καίσαρ" or "Nobilissimus Caesar"), "Caesar" or "Most Noble Caesar"; an honorific name later used to identify an Emperor-designate
- Censor, a Republican office with a five-year term and one coequal officeholder
- Consul, the highest magistracy of the Roman republic with a one-year term and one coequal officeholder
- Dominus, "Lord" or "Master"; an honorific title popular in the Empire's middle history
- Imperator, "Commander" or "Commander-in-Chief"; a victory title taken on accession to the purple and after a major military victory; the praenomen of most Roman emperors

- Imperator Destinatus, "Destined to be Emperor"; heir apparent, used by Septimius Severus for Caracalla.
- *Imperium maius*, "greater *imperium*"; absolute power to a degree greater than any other, including power of enacting capital punishment
- Invictus, "Unconquered"; an honorific title
- Pater Patriae, "Father of the Fatherland"; an honorific title
- Pius Felix, "Pious and Blessed" (lit. "Dutiful and Happy"); an honorific title
- Pontifex Maximus, "Supreme Pontiff" or "Chief Priest" (lit. "Greatest Bridgemaker"); a title and office of Republican origin – could not be used by Christian Emperors, while by that time only the pope had a claim on the title of highest religious authority.
- Princeps, "First Citizen" or "Leading Citizen"; an honorific title denoting the status of the emperor as first among equals
- Princeps Iuventatis, "First of Youth"; an honorific title awarded to a presumptive Emperor-designate
- Princeps Senatus, "First Man of the Senate" a Republican office with a five-year term
- *Tribunicia potestas*, "tribunician power"; the powers of a tribune of the people including sacrosanctity and the veto

Victory titles

Victory titles were treated as Latin *cognomina* and were usually the name of the enemy defeated by the commander. Hence, names like Africanus ("the African"), Numidicus ("the Numidian"), Isauricus ("the Isaurian"), Creticus ("the Cretan"), Gothicus ("the Goth"), Germanicus ("the German") and Parthicus ("the Parthian"), seemingly out of place for ardently patriotic Romans, are in fact expressions of Roman superiority over these peoples. The most famous grantee of Republican victory title was Publius Cornelius Scipio, who for his great victories in the Second Punic War was awarded by the Roman Senate the title "Africanus" and is thus known to history as "Scipio Africanus".

The practice continued in the Roman Empire, although it was subsequently amended by some Roman Emperors who desired to emphasise the totality of their victories by adding Maximus ("the Greatest") to the victory title (e.g., Parthicus Maximus, "the Greatest Parthian").

Decorations (medal equivalents)

Polybius writes that "After a battle in which some of them have distinguished themselves, the general calls an assembly of the troops, and bringing forward those whom he considers to have displayed conspicuous valour, first of all speaks in laudatory terms of the courageous deeds of each and of anything else in their previous conduct which deserves commendation". Only after this are the military decorations presented:

- *Torc* – gold necklet
- *armillae* – gold armbands
- *phalerae* – gold, silver, or bronze sculpted disks worn on the breastplate during parades
- *hasta pura* or Arrow without a Head- a ceremonial silver spear awarded to "the man who has wounded an enemy". The use of this decoration is not clear.[206]
- a small silver replica of a standard or flag (the vexillum).
- a cup – presented to an infantryman "who has slain and stripped an enemy" not in the normal melee of battle but voluntarily in single combat after throwing themselves into danger
- "horse trappings" – presented to a cavalryman "who has slain and stripped an enemy" not in the normal melee of battle but voluntarily in single combat after throwing themselves into danger

Financial awards

- monetary bonuses
- part of the loot and spoils after a conquest including slaves

Service awards

- *missio honesta* – honorable discharge

Imperial parades

- Ovation – a less-honored form of the Roman triumph. Ovations were granted when war was not declared between enemies on the level of states, when an enemy was considered basely inferior (slaves, pirates), and when the general conflict was resolved with little to no bloodshed or danger to the army itself.
- Triumph – a civil ceremony and religious rite of ancient Rome, held to publicly honour the military commander (dux) of a notably successful foreign war or campaign and to display the glories of Roman victory.

Punishments

When the Roman soldier enrolled in service to the state, he swore a military oath known as the *sacramentum*: originally to the Senate and Roman People, later to the general and the emperor. The *sacramentum* stated that he would fulfill his conditions of service on pain of punishment up to and inclusive of death. Discipline in the army was extremely rigorous by modern standards, and the general had the power to summarily execute any soldier under his command.

Polybius divides the punishments inflicted by a commander on one or more troops into punishments for military crimes, and punishments for "unmanly acts", although there seems to be little difference in the harsh nature of the punishment between the two classes.

Punishments for crimes

- *Fustuarium* or *bastinado* — Following a court-martial sentence for desertion or dereliction of duty, the soldier would be stoned, or beaten to death by cudgels, in front of the assembled troops, by his fellow soldiers, whose lives had been put in danger. Soldiers under sentence of *fustuarium* who escaped were not pursued, but lived under sentence of banishment from Rome.[207] Polybius writes that the *fustuarium* is "also inflicted on those who steal anything from the camp; on those who give false evidence; on young men who have abused their persons; and finally on anyone who has been punished thrice for the same fault."
- *Pecunaria multa* – fines or deductions from the pay allowance.
- Flogging in front of the century, cohort or legion.
- "demanding sureties", including the re-taking of the military oath known as the sacramentum.
- For treason or theft, the punishment would most probably be being placed in a sack of snakes and thrown into a nearby river or lake.

Another punishment in the Roman Military only applied to people involved in the prison system; this rule was that if a prisoner died due to the punishment inflicted by Roman legionaries, unless he was given the death penalty, then the leader of the troops would be given the same punishment.Wikipedia:Citation needed

It would seem that in the later Empire independent commanders were given considerable latitude in the crimes they chose to punish and the penalties they inflicted. According to the Historia Augusta[208] the future Emperor Aurelian once ordered a man who was convicted of raping the wife of the man on whom he had been billeted to be attached to two trees drawn together so that when the restraining ropes were cut, they sprang apart and the unfortunate victim was torn asunder. The author of the Vita Aureliani comments that Aurelian rarely punished twice for the same offence. However, even by Roman standards his justice was considered particularly harsh. As always with the Historia Augusta, one takes this story with a pinch of salt and either wonders what fourth century point the author was attempting to make of a third-century incident or whether he merely attributed to Aurelian a good story that seemed appropriate to that man's reputation. On the other hand, the imposition of cruel and unusual penalties to maintain discipline among the brutalised soldiery in the chaotic conditions of the north European provinces in the mid-third century was a necessity for the maintenance of effective command.[209]

Punishments for unmanly acts

- *Decimatio* – a form of extreme military discipline used by officers in the Roman Army to punish mutinous or cowardly soldiers in exceptional cases. A cohort selected for punishment by decimation was divided into groups of ten; each group cast lots, and the soldier on whom the lot fell was executed by his nine comrades, often by stoning or clubbing. The remaining soldiers were given rations of barley instead of wheat and forced to sleep outside of the Roman encampment. This punishment was forgotten over time since the early Republic, but the ancient punishment was resurrected by Marcus Crassus during the Spartacus gladiator rebellion in 72 BC, when two of his legions disobeyed his direct orders not to engage the enemy. As a result, they suffered a terrible defeat. Crassus's response to the disobedience was brutal. He assembled the two legions and pulled out every 10th man as he walked across the ranks. Each man who was pulled out was to be beaten to death by his preceding nine comrades. Some scholars say that Julius Caesar joined these two legions to form his legendary "Legio X Equitata".

  According to Cassius Dio as re-told by Matthew Dennison, the newly-appointed emperor Galba revived this punishment to deal with a contingent of rebellious soldiers who confronted him as he entered Rome at the Milvian Bridge in autumn of 68 AD.[210] Dio states that Galba ordered this punishment because "he did not believe that an emperor should submit to compulsion in anything."[211]

- *Castigatio* – being hit by the centurion with his staff or *animadversio fustium*
- **Reduction of rations**, or to be forced to eat barley instead of the usual grain ration
- Whipping with the *flagrum* (*flagellum, flagella*), or "short whip" — a much more brutal punishment than simple flogging. The "short whip" was used for slave volunteers, *volones*.

- *gradus deiectio* – a reduction in rank
- Loss of advantages gained from length of service.
- *militiae mutatio* – relegation to inferior service or duties.
- Summary execution.
- *munerum indictio* – additional duties

List of Roman legions

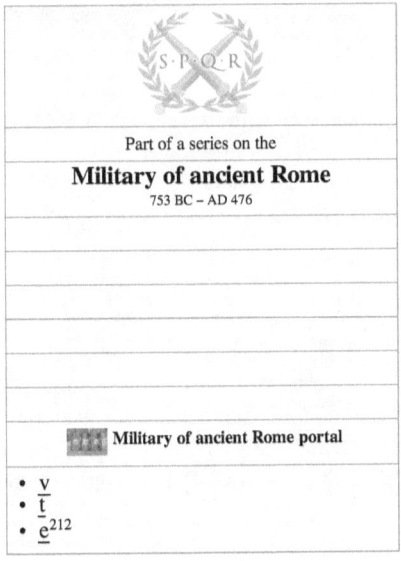

Part of a series on the
Military of ancient Rome
753 BC – AD 476

Military of ancient Rome portal

- v
- t
- e²¹²

This is a **list of Roman legions**, including key facts about each legion, primarily focusing on the Principate (early Empire, 27 BC – 284 AD) legions, for which there exists substantial literary, epigraphic and archaeological evidence.

When Augustus became sole ruler in 31 BC, he disbanded about half of the over 50 legions then in existence. The remaining 28 legions became the core of the early Imperial army of the Principate (27 BC – 284 AD), most lasting over three centuries. Augustus and his immediate successors transformed legions into permanent units, staffed by entirely career soldiers on standard 25-year terms.

During the Dominate period (near the end Empire, 284–476), legions were also professional, but are little understood due to scarcity of evidence compared to the Principate. What is clear is that late legions were radically different in size, structure, and tactical role from their predecessors, despite several retaining early period names. This was the result of the military reforms of

Figure 31: *Nero, Sestertius with countermark "X" of Legio X Gemina. Obv: Laureate bust right. Rev: Nero riding horse right, holding spear, DECVRSIO in exergue; S C across fields.*

Emperors Diocletian and Constantine I, and of further developments during the 4th century.

The legions were identified by Roman numerals, though the spelling sometimes differed from the modern "standard". For example, in addition to the spellings "IV", "IX", "XIV", "XVIII" and "XIX", the respective spellings "IIII", "VIIII", "XIIII", "XIIX" and "XVIIII" were commonly used.

Late Republican legions

Until the Marian reforms of 107 BC, the Republican legions were formed by compulsory levy of Roman citizens (who met a minimum property qualification) and raised whenever it was necessary. Usually they were authorized by the Roman Senate, and were later disbanded.

Gaius Marius' reforms transformed legions into standing units, which could remain in being for several years, or even decades. This became necessary to garrison the Republic's now far-flung territories. Legionaries started large-scale recruiting of volunteer soldiers enlisted for a minimum term of six years and a fixed salary, although conscription was still practiced. The property requirements were abolished by Marius, so that the bulk of recruits were henceforth from the landless citizens, who would be most attracted to the paid employment and land offered after their service.

In the last century of the Republic, proconsuls governing frontier provinces became increasingly powerful. Their command of standing legions in distant and arduous military campaigns resulted in the allegiance of those units transferring from the Roman state to themselves. These *imperatores* (lit: victorious generals, from the title imperator they were hailed with by their troops) frequently fell out with each other and started civil wars to seize control of the state. e.g. Sulla, Caesar, Pompey, Crassus, Mark Antony and Octavian (later Augustus, the first Emperor himself). In this context, the *imperatores* raised many legions that were not authorised by the Senate, sometimes having to use their own resources. As civil wars were resolved, many of these "private" units would be disbanded, only for more to be raised to fight the next civil war. By the time Augustus emerged as sole ruler of Rome in 31BC, over 50 legions were in existence, many of which were disbanded.

The legions included in the following list had a long enough history to be somehow remarkable. Most of them were levied by Julius Caesar and later included into Octavian's army, some of them were levied by Marc Antony.

- Legio I *Germanica* (*Germanic*): 48 BC–70 (Revolt of the Batavi), Julius Caesar
- Legio II *Sabina* (*Sabine*): 43 BC to circa 9 AD, early name of the Legio II *Augusta*
- Legio III *Cyrenaica* (*from Cyrene*): probably around 36 BC to (at least) 5th century, Mark Antony
- Legio III *Gallica* (*Gallic*): around 49 BC to at least early 4th century, Julius Caesar (emblem: bull)
- Legio IV *Macedonica* (*Macedonian*): 48 BC–70 (disbanded by Vespasian), Julius Caesar (emblem: bull, capricorn)
- Legio IV *Scythica* (*from Scythia*): around 42 BC to at least early 5th century, Mark Antony (emblem: capricorn)
- Legio V *Alaudae* (*Larks*): 52 BC–86 (destroyed by the Dacians in the first Battle of Tapae), Julius Caesar (emblem: elephant)
- Legio VI *Ferrata* (*Ironclad*): 52 BC to after 250, Julius Caesar (emblem: bull, she-wolf and Romulus and Remus); twin legion of Legio VI *Victrix*
- Legio VI *Victrix* (*Victorious*): 41 BC to after 402, Octavian (emblem: bull)
- Legio VII *Claudia Pia Fidelis* (*loyal and faithful to Claudius*): 51 BC–44 BC, Julius Caesar; disbanded and re-formed by Vespasian as Legio VII *Gemina*
- Legio VIII *Augusta*: 59 BC–48 BC, Julius Caesar, disbanded and re-enlisted by Augustus as Legio VIII *Augusta*
- Legio IX *Hispana Triumphalis* (*Triumphant*): 59 BC–48 BC, Julius Caesar, disbanded and re-enlisted by Augustus as Legio IX *Hispana*
- Legio X *Fretensis* (*of the sea strait*): levied by Augustus in 41/40 BC
- Legio X *Equestris* (*Equestrian*): before 58 BC–45 BC, Julius Caesar's personal legion

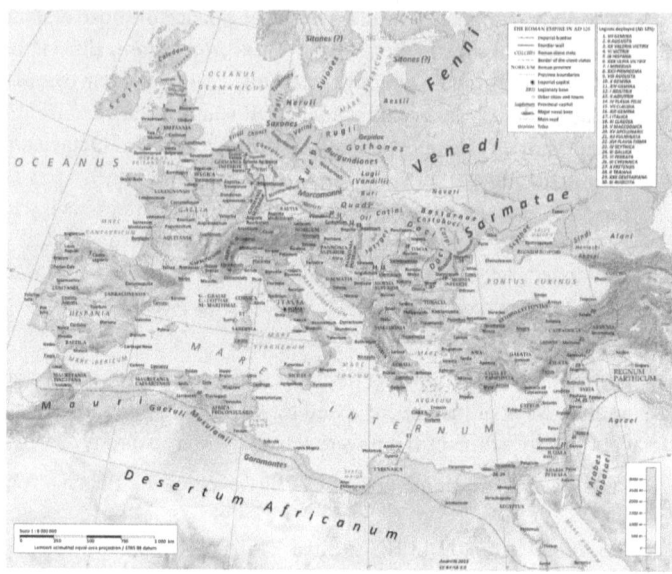

Figure 32: *The Roman empire and legions deployed in 125 AD, in the time of emperor Hadrian.*

- Legio XI Claudia: 58 BC–45 BC, Julius Caesar (emblem: Neptune), disbanded, reconstituted by Augustus
- Legio XII *Victrix* (*Victorious*): 57 BC–45, Julius Caesar
- Legio XII *Fulminata* (*Thunderbolt*): after being renamed by Augustus, first reconstituted by Lepidus in 43 BC, named by Mark Antony as Legio XII *Antiqua* (*Ancient*)
- Legio XIII *Gemina* (*Twin*): 57 BC–45 BC: Julius Caesar, later (41 BC) reconstituted by Augustus
- Legio XIV *Gemina* (*Twin*): 57 BC–48 BC: Julius Caesar, destroyed and reconstituted in 53 BC. Reconstituted by Augustus after 41 BC
- Legio XVIII *Libyca* (*from Libya*): disbanded 31 BC, Mark Antony
- Legio XXX *Classica* (*Naval*): 48 BC–41 BC, Julius Caesar

Early Empire legions

Code for Roman provinces in the table:

- AEG Aegyptus (*Egypt*)
- AFR Africa (*Tunisia/Western Libya*)
- AQ Aquitania (*SW France*)
- AR Arabia Petraea (*Jordan/Sinai*)

List of Roman legions

- BRIT Britannia (*England/Wales*)
- CAP Cappadocia (*Central/Eastern Turkey*)
- DC Dacia (*Romania/Serbia*)
- DLM Dalmatia (*Croatia/Bosnia/Serbia*)
- GAL Galatia (*Central Turkey*)
- GI Germania Inferior (*Netherlands/Rhineland*)
- GS Germania Superior (*Alsace-Lorraine/Rhineland*)
- HISP Hispania Tarraconensis (*Central Spain*)
- IT Italia (*Italy*)
- JUD Judaea (*Israel*)
- MAUR Mauretania (*Western Maghreb*)
- MCD Macedonia (*Southern Balkans*-Greece)
- MI Moesia Inferior (*Romania/Bulgaria*)
- MS Moesia Superior (*Serbia*)
- NR Noricum (*Austria*)
- PAN Pannonia (*Hungary/Croatia/Slovenia*)
- RT Raetia (*Switzerland/Germany*)
- SYR Syria (*Syria/Lebanon*)

Legion no. and title (cognomen)	Main legionary base	Emblem	Date founded/ founder	Date disbanded	Castra legionaria (legion bases) * = main base. Start date 31BC if unspecified	Notes
I Adiutrix	Szőny, Hungary	Capricorn	68 Nero	444	70-86 Moguntiacum (GS); 86-mid-5th century Brigetio* (PAN)	"1st Auxiliary". Was *I classica* (raised from marines)
I Germanica	Bonn, Germany	Bull	48 BC Caesar	70 **DD**	to 16 BC HISP; c.5 BC-70 AD Bonna* (GI)	Disbanded for cowardice in Batavi revolt
I Italica	Svishtov, Bulgaria	Boar	66 Nero	post 400	70-early 5th century Novae* (MI)	*prima Italica*:raised for aborted Caucasus war
I Macriana			68 Macer	69 **DD**	(Raised for mutiny against Nero by Macer, gov of AFR)	*liberatrix*: "Liberator 1st". Disbanded by Galba
I Minervia	Bonn, Germany	Minerva	82 Domitian	post 300	82-4th century Bonna* (GI)	"Minerva-revering 1st"
I Parthica	Sinjar, Iraq	Centaur	197 S. Severus	post 400	197-early 5th century Nisibis* (SYR)	Raised for Severus' Parthian campaign in 197

Legion	Main base	Emblem	Date founded/founder	Date disbanded	Castra legionaria (legion bases)	Notes
II Adiutrix	Budapest, Hungary	Capricorn	70 Vespasian	269+	70-87 BRIT; 87-106 MS; 106-min269 Aquincum* (PAN)	"2nd Auxiliary." Ex-naval legion.
II Augusta	Caerleon, Wales	Capricorn	pre 9 BC Augustus	post 300	to c.9 AD HISP; 43-74 BRIT; 74-min255 Isca Augusta* (BRIT)	Failed to engage Boudica 60. c.395 at Rutupiae (BRIT)
II Italica	Enns, Austria	She-Wolf	165 M Aurelius	post 400	180-c.400 Lauriacum* (NR)	Capitoline Wolf Rome's national emblem
II Parthica	Castra Albana, Italy	Centaur	197 S. Severus	post 350	197-218 Castra Albana (IT); 218-34 Apamea (SYR); 238-c.300 Castra Albana(IT)	4th century recorded at Bezabde (SYR)
II Traiana	Alexandria, Egypt	Hercules	105 Trajan	post 400	125-5th century Nicopolis* (AEG)	*secunda fortis* "Trajan's valliant 2nd"
III Augusta	Batna, Algeria	Pegasus	43 BC Augustus	post 350	to 20 AD AFR; 20-75 Ammaedara 74-350+ Lambaesis* (MAUR)	Decimated for cowardice in Mauri war (18 AD)
III Cyrenaica	Busra, Syria		36 BC M Antony	post 400	to 35 AD Thebes 35-125 Alexandria AEG; 125-5th century Bostra* AR	"3rd from Cyrene"
III Gallica	Abila, Jordan	Two Bulls	49 BC Caesar	post 300	31 BC-4th century Raphana* (SYR)	*tertia Gallica*: "3rd from Gaul"
III Italica	Regensburg, Germany	Stork	165 M Aurelius	post 300	165-4th century Castra Regina* (RT)	Raised for war on Marcomanni
III Parthica	Ra's al-'Ayn, Syria	Bull	197 S. Severus	post 400	197-4th century Resaena* (SYR)	Raised for Severus' Parthian campaign in 197

I+Roman legions of the early Empire (units founded between 59 BC and 250 AD)

Legion no. and title (cognomen)	Main legionary base	Emblem	Date founded/ founder	Date disbanded	Castra legionaria (legion bases) * = main base. Start date 31BC if unspecified	Notes
IV Flavia Felix	Belgrade, Serbia	Lion	70 Vespasian	pre 400	86-4th century Singidunum* (MS)	Vespasian's lucky 4th. Reformed *IV Macedon*

List of Roman legions

IV Macedonica	Mainz, Germany	Bull	48 BC Caesar	70 **DD**	to 43 AD HISP; 43-70 Moguntiacum* (GS)	Disbanded in Batavi revolt
IV Scythica	Gaziantep, Turkey	Capricorn	42 BC M Antony	post 400	to 58 AD MS; 68-5th century Zeugma* (SYR)	*quarta scythica*: "Scythian-conquering 4th"
V Alaudae	Xanten, Germany	Elephant	52 BC Caesar	87 **XX**	to 19 BC HISP; c.10 BC-70 AD Castra Vetera* (GI)	"Larks 5th" Feathers in helmet? XX by Dacians
V Macedonica	Turda, Romania	Eagle	43 BC Augustus	post 500	6-101 Oescus, 107-61 Troesmis (MI); 166-274 Potaissa* (DC)	*quinta macedonica*: "5th from Macedonia"
VI Ferrata	Galilee, Israel	She-Wolf	58 BC Caesar	250+ UF	to 71 AD Raphana (SYR); 135-250+ Caparcotna* (JUD)	"Ironclad 6th". XX at Battle of Edessa 260?
VI Hispana			post 212	250+ UF	unknown	Only 1 record. XX at Battle of Abrittus 251?
VI Victrix	York, England	Bull	41 BC Augustus	post 400	to 70 AD Leon HISP; 71-122 GI; 122-c.400 Eburacum* BRIT	"Victorious 6th" built Hadrian's Wall 122-32
VII Claudia	Kostolac, Serbia	Bull	58 BC Caesar	c.400	to 9 AD GAL; 9-58 DLM; 58-c.400 Viminacium* (MS)	*septima Claudia*: title for crushing mutiny 42
VII Gemina	León, Spain		68 Galba	c.400	75-c.400 Castra Legionis* HISP	Raised in Hispania by Galba for march on Rome
VIII Augusta	Strasbourg, France	Bull	59 BC Caesar	post 371	45-69AD Novae MI; 69-86 Mirebeau-sur-Bèze GS; 86-371+ Argentorate* GS	*octava Augusta*:
IX Hispana	York, England	Bull	41 BC Augustus	132? 161?	to 13 BC HISP; 9-43 PAN?; 71-121 Eburacum* BRIT; 121-130 Nijmegen GI?	*nona Hispana*: XX in Judaea (132)? XX by Parthians in Armenia (161)
X Fretensis	Jerusalem	Boar	40 BC Augustus	post 400	to 25 BC JUD; 25 BC-66 AD SYR; 73-c.400+ Hierosolyma*	*fretum* = Strait of Otranto, Naulochus 36 BC

Legion no. and title (cognomen)	Main legion base	Emblem	Date founded/ founder	Date disband	Castra legionaria (legion bases) * = main base. Start date 31 BC if unspecified	Notes
X Gemina	Vienna, Austria	Bull	42 BC Lepidus	post 400	30BC-63AD Petavonium HISP; 63-68 Carnuntum PAN; Petavonium 68-71 HISP; 71-103 Noviomagus GI; 103-c.400 Vindobona* PAN	Was X Equestris, Caesar's "mounted" legion
XI Claudia	Silistra, Bulgaria	Neptune	42 BC Augustus	post 400	to 71 AD DLM; 71-104 Vindonissa RT; 104-c.400 Durostorum* MI	*undecima Claudia*: honoured by Claudius
XII Fulminata	Malatya, Turkey	Thunderbolt	43 BC Lepidus	post 400	to 14 AD AEG; 14-71 Raphana (SYR); 71-c.400 Melitene* (CAP)	Thunderbolt 12th lost aquila in 1st Jewish War

Legion no. and title (cognomen)	Main legion base	Emblem	Date founded/ founder	Date disband	Castra legionaria (legion bases) * = main base. Start date 31 BC if unspecified	Notes
XIII Gemina	Alba Iulia, Romania	Lion	57 BC Caesar	post 400	45-106 Poetovio PAN 106-270 Apulum* DC 270-400 MI	"Twinned 13th". Crossed Rubicon with Caesar 49 BC
XIV Gemina	Petronell, Austria	Capricorn	57 BC Caesar	post 400	9-43 Moguntiacum GS; 43-58 Mancetter BRIT; 58-67 Wroxeter BRIT; 67-89 Balkans; 92-106 Vindobona PAN; 106-c.400 Carnuntum*	Defeated Boudica's Britons at Watling Street (60 AD)
XV Apollinaris	Saddagh, Turkey	Apollo	41 BC Augustus	post 400	14-62 Carnuntum PAN; 62-73 SYR 71-115 Carnuntum PAN; 115-c.400 Satala* CAP	"Apollo-revering 15th". Fought in First Jewish War
XV Primigenia	Xanten, Germany	Fortuna	39 Caligula	70 XX	39-43 Moguntiacum (GS); 43-70 Castra Vetera* (GI)	Primigenia goddess of Fate. XX in Batavi revolt
XVI Flavia Firma	Samsat, Turkey	Lion	70 Vespasian	post 300	70-117 Satala (CAP); 117-300+ Samosata* SYR	"Vespasian's steadfast 16th". Reformed *XVI Gallica*
XVI Gallica	Mainz, Germany	Lion	41 BC Augustus	70 DD	to 43AD Moguntiacum* (GS); 43-70 Novaesium* (GI)	Disbanded for cowardice in Batavi revolt
XVII	Xanten, Germany		41 BC Augustus	9 XX	to 15 BC AQ?; 15 BC-9 AD Castra Vetera* (GI)	Destroyed in Teutoburg Forest, lost aquila standard, never rebuilt

XVIII	Xanten, Germany		41 BC Augustus	9 XX	to 15 BC AQ?; 15 BC-9 AD Castra Vetera* (GI)	Destroyed in Teutoburg Forest, lost aquila standard, never rebuilt
XIX	Xanten, Germany		41 BC Augustus	9 XX	to 15 BC unknown; 15 BC-9 AD somewhere in GI	Destroyed in Teutoburg Forest, lost aquila standard, never rebuilt
XX Valeria Victrix	Chester, England	Boar	31 BC Augustus	250+ UF	to 9 AD Burnum DLM; 9-43 Oppidum Ubiorum GI; 43-55 Camulodunum* BRIT; 55-66 Burrium* BRIT; 66-78 Viroconium* BRIT; 78-88 Inchtuthil* BRIT; 88-250+ Deva* BRIT	*vigesima* named for Messalla? XX in Allectus' fall 296?
XXI Rapax	Windisch, Switzerland	Capricorn	31 BC Augustus	92 XX	9-43 GI; 43-70 Vindonissa* (RT); 70-89 GI; 89-92 PAN	"Predator 21st". XX by Roxolani Sarmatian tribe PAN
XXII Deiotariana	Alexandria, Egypt		48 BC	132? 161? XX	to c.8 BC GAL; 8 BC-123 AD+ Alexandria* (AEG)	GAL king "Deiotarus's 22nd". XX by Jewish rebels in 132? or by Parthians in Armenia in 161?
XXII Primigenia	Mainz, Germany	Hercules	39 Caligula	post 300	39-c.300 Moguntiacum* (GS)	Raised for Caligula's German war
XXX Ulpia Victrix	Xanten, Germany	Jupiter	105 Trajan	post 400	105-22 DC; 122-c.400 Castra Vetera* (GI)	"Trajan's victorious 30th" (M Ulpius Traianus)

Legend

- **Legion number and title (cognomen)**

The numbering of the legions is confusing, since several legions shared the same number with others. Augustus numbered the legions he founded himself from I, but also inherited numbers from his predecessors. Each emperor normally numbered the legions he raised himself starting from I. However, even this practice was not consistently followed. For example, Vespasian kept the same numbers as before for legions he raised from disbanded units. Trajan's first legion was numbered XXX because there were 29 other legions in existence at the time it was raised; but the second Trajanic legion was given the sequential number II. XVII, XVIII and XIX, the numbers of the legions annihilated in the Teutoburg Forest, were never used again. (These three legions are without titles, suggesting that in disgrace their titles may have been deliberately forgotten or left unmentioned.) As a result of this somewhat chaotic evolution, the legion's title became necessary to distinguish between legions with the same number.

Legions often carried several titles, awarded after successive campaigns, normally by the ruling emperor e.g. XII Fulminata was also awarded: *paterna* (fatherly), *victrix* (victorious), *antiqua* (venerable), *certa constans* (reliable, steadfast) and *Galliena* (Gallienus '). *Pia fidelis* (loyal and faithful), *fidelis constans* and others were titles awarded to several legions, sometimes several times to the same legion. Only the most established, commonly used titles are displayed on this table.

The geographical titles indicate
(a) the country a legion was originally recruited e.g. *Italica* = from Italy or
(b) peoples the legion has vanquished e.g.*Parthica* = victorious over the Parthians

Legions bearing the personal name of an emperor, or of his *gens* (clan) (e.g. *Augusta, Flavia*) were either founded by that Emperor or awarded the name as a mark of special favour.

The title GEMINA means that two diminished legions have been combined to make one new one.

- **Main legionary base**

This shows the *castra* (base) where the legion spent the longest period during the Principate. Legions often shared the same base with other legions. Detachments of legions were often seconded for lengthy periods to other bases and provinces, as operational needs demanded.

- **Emblem**

Legions often sported more than one emblem at the same time, and occasionally changed them. Legions raised by Caesar mostly carried a bull emblem originally; those of Augustus mostly a Capricorn

- **Date disbanded**

For legions that are documented into the 4th century and beyond, we do not know when or how they were terminated. For legions disappearing from the record before 284, the reason (certain or likely) is given as:
XX = annihilated in battle
DD = disbanded in disgrace
UF = unknown fate

- **Castra legionaria**

Figure 33: *Shield pattern of the palatina legion of the Ioviani seniores, according to the Notitia Dignitatum.*

Indicates the bases (*castra*) and/or provinces where the legion was based during its history, with dates.

- **Notes**

Contains points of note, including explanation of titles and details of a legion's fate.

Province names and borders are assumed throughout the Principate period as at 107 AD, during the rule of Trajan, and after the annexation of Dacia and Arabia Petraea. The map above shows provinces at the end of Trajan's reign, 117 AD. They are the same as in 107, except that Armenia and Mesopotamia have been annexed (they were abandoned soon after Trajan's death); and Pannonia has been split into two (the split occurred c. 107). In reality provincial borders were modified several times during the period 30 BC-284 AD: this explains any discrepancy with other sources, as to a legion's location at a particular date

Late Empire legions

Diocletian reorganized the Roman army, in order to better counter the threat of the Germanic peoples of northern Europe as well as that of the Persians from the East. The army was formed by *border* and *field* units.

The *border* (*limitanei*) units were to occupy the limes, the structured border fortifications, and were formed by professional soldiers with an inferior training.

The *field* units were to stay well behind the border, and to move quickly where they were needed, with both offensive and defensive roles. Field units were formed by elite soldiers with high-level training and weapons. They were further divided into:

1. *Scholae*: the personal guard of the Emperor, created by Constantine I to replace the Praetorian Guard;
2. *Palatinae*: "palace troops" were the highest ranked units, created by Constantine I after he disbanded the Praetorian Guard, it was comprised originally of former guardsmen;
3. *Comitatenses*: regular field units, some were newly formed, others were descended from Early-Empire legions;
4. *Pseudocomitatenses*: these were *limitanei* units diverted into the field army and often kept there; some Early Empire legions became *pseudocomitatenses* units.

These units usually numbered between 300 and 2000 soldiers and some of them kept their original numbering schemes. The primary source for the legions of this era is the *Notitia Dignitatum*, a late 4th-century document containing all the civil and military offices of both halves of the Roman Empire (revised in ca. 420 for the Western Empire).

- Legio I
  - I *Armeniaca*
  - I *Flavia Constantia* (*reliable Flavian*): *comitatensis* unit under the command of the *Magister militum per Orientis*
  - I *Flavia Gallicana Constantia* (*reliable Flavian legion from Gallia*): *pseudocomitatensis* under the command of the *Magister Peditum per Gallias*
  - I *Flavia Martis* (*Flavian legion devoted to Mars*): *pseudocomitatensis*
  - I *Flavia Pacis* (*Flavian legion of peace*): *comitatensis* under the command of the *Magister Peditum*
  - I *Flavia Theodosiana*: *comitatensis*
  - I *Illyricorum* (*of the Illyrians*): stationed at the Camp of Diocletian in Palmyra
  - I *Iovia* (*devoted to Jupiter*): levied by Diocletian, stationed in Scythia Minor
  - I *Isaura Sagittaria* (*archers from Isauria*): *pseudocomitatensis* under the command of the *Magister militum per Orientis*
  - I *Iulia Alpina*: *pseudocomitatensis* under the command of the *Magister Peditum* in Italy

- I *Martia* possibly based near modern Kaiseraugst
- I *Maximiana Thaebanorum* (*the Thebans of Maximianus*): *comitatensis* unit stationed near Thebes, Egypt, and probably fighting in the battle of Adrianople
- I *Noricorum* (*of the Noricans*): stationed in Noricum
- I *Pontica*
- Legio II
  - II *Armeniaca*
  - II *Britannica*: *comitatensis* under *Magister Peditum*
  - II *Flavia Constantia:* comitatensis *under the command of the* Magister Peditum
  - II *Flavia Virtutis*: *comitatensis* under the command of the *Magister Peditum*
  - II *Herculia* (*devoted to Hercules*): levied by Diocletian, stationed in Scythia Minor
  - II *Isaura*
  - II *Iulia Alpina*: *pseudocomitatensis* under the command of the *Magister Peditum*, in *Comes Illyricum* command
  - II *Felix Valentis Thebaeorum*: *comitatensis*
- Legio III
  - III *Diocletiana*
  - III *Flavia Salutis*: *comitatensis* under the command of the *Magister Peditum*
  - III *Herculea*: *comitatensis* under the command of the *Comes Illyricum*
  - III *Isaura*
  - III *Iulia Alpina*: *comitatensis* under the command of the *Magister Peditum* command in Italy
- Legio IV
  - IV *Italica*
  - IV *Martia*
  - IV *Parthica*
- Legio V
  - V *Iovia* (maybe the *Jovians*)
  - V *Parthica*
- Legio VI
  - VI *Gemella*
  - VI *Gallicana*
  - VI *Herculia* (maybe the Herculians)
  - VI *Hispana*
  - VI *Parthica*
- Legio XII
  - XII *Victrix*

References

Primary sources

- *Notitia Dignitatum* reports the military units and their locations at the beginning of the 5th century.

Secondary sources

- *Oxford Classical Dictionary*
- Keppie, Lawrence. *The Making of the Roman Army*, 1984 pp. 205–215
- Stephen Dando-Collins "Legions Of Rome"

External links

- Legio X[213] - Legio X Gemina (Equites) - "Viri Clarissimi"
- Livius.org: List of Roman legions[214]
- A catalogue of Roman legions[215]
- Legio V Living History Group in Tennessee[216]
- Roman legions from Dacia (KML file)[217]

Auxilia

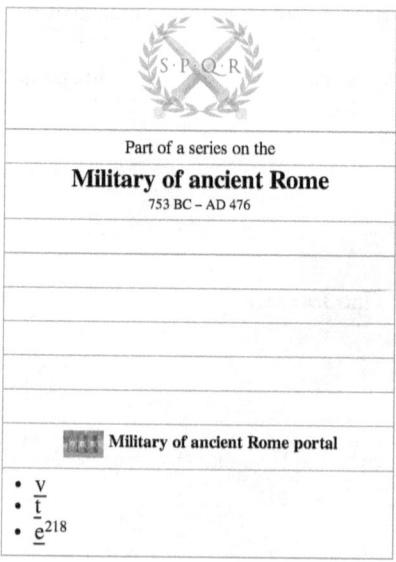

Part of a series on the
Military of ancient Rome
753 BC – AD 476

Military of ancient Rome portal

- v
- t
- e[218]

Figure 34: *Roman auxiliary infantry crossing a river, Danube, the emperor Trajan's Dacian Wars (AD 101–106). They can be distinguished by the oval shield (clipeus) they were equipped with, in contrast to the rectangular scutum carried by legionaries. Panel from Trajan's Column, Rome*

The **Auxilia** (Latin, lit. "auxiliaries") constituted the standing non-citizen corps of the Imperial Roman army during the Principate era (30 BC–284 AD), alongside the citizen legions. By the 2nd century, the Auxilia contained the same number of infantry as the legions and, in addition, provided almost all of the Roman army's cavalry (especially light cavalry and archers) and more specialised troops. The *auxilia* thus represented three-fifths of Rome's regular land forces at that time. Like their legionary counterparts, auxiliary recruits were mostly volunteers, not conscripts.

The Auxilia were mainly recruited from the *peregrini*, free provincial subjects who did not hold Roman citizenship and constituted the vast majority of the population in the 1st and 2nd centuries (c. 90% in the early 1st century). In contrast to the legions, which only admitted Roman citizens, members of the Auxilia could be recruited from territories outside of Roman control.

Reliance on the various contingents of non-Italic troops, especially cavalry, increased when the Roman Republic employed them in increasing numbers to support its legions after 200 BC. The Julio-Claudian period (30 BC–68 AD) saw the transformation of the Auxilia from motley levies to a standing corps

Figure 35: *Etruscan funerary urn crowned with the sculpture of a woman and a front-panel relief showing two warriors fighting, polychrome terracotta, c. 150 BC*

with standardised structure, equipment and conditions of service. By the end of the period, there were no significant differences between legionaries and auxiliaries in terms of training, and thus, combat capability.

Auxiliary regiments were often stationed in provinces other than that in which they were originally raised, for reasons of security and to foster the process of Romanisation in the provinces. The regimental names of many auxiliary units persisted into the 4th century, but by then the units in question were different in size, structure, and quality from their predecessors.

Historical development

Background: Roman Republic (to 30 BC)

The mainstay of the Roman republic's war machine was the manipular legion, a heavy infantry unit suitable for close-quarter engagements on more or less any terrain, which was probably adopted sometime during the Samnite Wars (343–290 BC).[219] Despite its formidable strength, the legion had a number of deficiencies, especially a lack of cavalry. Around 200 BC, a legion of 4,200 infantry had a cavalry arm of only 300 horse (just 7% of the total force).[220] This was because the class of citizens who could afford to pay for their own horse and equipment – the equestrian order, the second rank in Roman society, after the senatorial order – was relatively small. In addition, the legion lacked missile forces such as slingers and archers.[221] Until 200 BC, the bulk of a Roman army's cavalry was provided by Rome's regular Italian allies (*socii*), commonly known as the "Latin" allies, which made up the Roman military confederation. This was Rome's defence system until the Social War of 91–88 BC. The Italian forces were organised into *alae* (literally: "wings", because they were generally posted on the flanks of the Roman line of battle). An allied *ala*, commanded by 3 Roman *praefecti sociorum*, was similar or slightly larger in infantry size (4–5,000 men) to a legion, but contained a more substantial cavalry contingent: 900 horse, three times the legionary contingent. Since a pre-Social War consular army always contained an equal number of legions and *alae*, 75% of its cavalry was provided by the Latin allies. The overall cavalry element, c. 12% of the total force (2,400 out of a normal consular army of approximately 20,000 total effectives), was greater than in most peninsular Italian forces, but well below the overall 21% cavalry component that was typical of the Principate army (80,000 cavalry out of 380,000 total effectives in the early 2nd century).[222,223]

The Roman/Latin cavalry was sufficient while Rome was in conflict with other states in the mountainous Italian peninsula, which also disposed of limited cavalry resources. But, as Rome was confronted by external enemies that deployed far more powerful cavalry elements, such as the Gauls and the Carthaginians, the Roman deficiency in cavalry numbers could be a serious liability, which in the Second Punic War (218–202 BC) resulted in crushing defeats. Hannibal's major victories at the Trebia and at Cannae, were owed to his Spanish and Gallic heavy cavalry, which far outnumbered the Roman and Latin levies, and to his Numidians, light, fast cavalry which the Romans wholly lacked.[224] The decisive Roman victory at Zama in 202 BC, which ended the war, owed much to the Numidian cavalry provided by king Massinissa, which outnumbered the Roman/Latin cavalry fielded by 2 to 1.[225] From then, Roman armies were always accompanied by large numbers of non-Italian cavalry: Numidian light cavalry and, later, Gallic heavy cavalry. For example, Caesar relied heavily on Gallic and German cavalry for his Conquest of Gaul (58–51 BC).[226]

As the role of native cavalry grew, that of Roman/Latin cavalry diminished. In the early 1st century BC, Roman cavalry was phased out altogether. After the Social War, the *socii* were all granted Roman citizenship, the Latin *alae* abolished, and the *socii* recruited into the legions.[227] Furthermore, Roman equestrians were no longer required to perform cavalry service after this time.[228] The late Republican legion was thus probably bereft of cavalry (a tiny cavalry force of 120 men was probably added back to the legion under Augustus).[229]

Figure 36: *Slingers from the cast of Trajan's Column in the Victoria and Albert Museum, London, 2nd century AD*

By the outbreak of the Second Punic War, the Romans were remedying the legions' other deficiencies by using non-Italian specialised troops. Livy reports Hiero of Syracuse offering to supply Rome with archers and slingers in 217 BC.[230] From 200 BC onwards, specialist troops were hired as mercenaries on a regular basis: *sagittarii* (archers) from Crete, and *funditores* (slingers) from the Balearic Isles almost always accompanied Roman legions in campaigns all over the Mediterranean.[231]

The other main sources of non-Italian troops in the late Republic were subject provincials, allied cities and Rome's *amici* (satellite kings). During the late Republic, non-Italian units were led by their own native chiefs, and their internal organisation was left to their own commanders. The units varied widely in dress, equipment, and weapons. They were normally raised for specific campaigns and often disbanded soon afterwards, in a similar manner to the earlier *socii* militia legions.[232]

Foundation of the auxilia under Augustus (30 BC–14 AD)

It appears that not all indigenous units were disbanded at the end of the civil war period (31 BC). Some of the more experienced units were kept in existence to complement the legions, and became the core of the standing auxiliary forces that developed in the Julio-Claudian period.[233] During the early part of Augustus' rule (27 BC onwards), the corps of regular Auxilia was created. It was clearly inspired by the Latin forces of the pre-Social War Republic, as a corps of non-citizen troops parallel to the legions. But there were fundamental differences, the same as between Republican and Augustan legions. The Latin forces of the Republic were made up of part-time conscripts in units that would be raised and disbanded for and after particular campaigns. The Augustan Auxilia were mainly volunteer professionals serving in permanent units.

The unit structure of the Auxilia also differed from the Latin *alae*, which were like legions with a larger cavalry arm. However, Augustus organised the Auxilia into regiments the size of cohorts (a tenth the size of legions), due to the much greater flexibility of the smaller unit size. Further, the regiments were of three types: *ala* (cavalry), *cohors (peditata)* (infantry) and *cohors equitata* (mixed cavalry/infantry).[234]

The evidence for the size of the Augustus' new units is not clearcut, with our most precise evidence dating to the 2nd century, by which time the unit strengths may have changed. *Cohortes* were likely modelled on legionary cohorts i.e. six *centuriae* of about 80 men each (total about 480 men).[235] *Alae* were divided into *turmae* (squadrons) of 30 (or 32) men, each under a *decurio* (literally: "leader of ten").[236] This title derives from the old Roman cavalry of the pre-Social War republic, in which each *turma* was under the command of three *decuriones*.[237] *Cohortes equitatae* were infantry *cohortes* with a cavalry contingent of four *turmae* attached.[238]

Auxiliary regiments were now led by a *praefectus* (prefect), who could be either a native nobleman, who would probably be granted Roman citizenship for the purpose (e.g. the famous German war leader Arminius gained Roman citizenship probably by serving as an auxiliary prefect before turning against Rome); or a Roman, either of knightly rank, or a senior centurion.[239]

At the start of Augustus' sole rule (30 BC), the original core auxiliary units in the West were composed of warlike tribesmen from the Gallic provinces (especially Gallia Belgica, which then included the regions later separated to form the provinces Germania Inferior and Germania Superior), and from the Balkan provinces (Dalmatia and Illyricum). By 19 BC, the Cantabrian and Asturian Wars were concluded, leading to the annexation of northern Hispania and Lusitania. Judging by the names of attested auxiliary regiments, these parts of the

Iberian peninsula soon became a major source of recruits. Then the Danubian regions were annexed: Raetia (annexed 15 BC), Noricum (16 BC), Pannonia (9 BC) and Moesia (6 AD), becoming, with Illyricum, the Principate's most important source of auxiliary recruits for its entire duration. In the East, where the Syrians already provided the bulk of the Roman army's archers, Augustus annexed Galatia (25 BC) and Judaea: the former, a region in central Anatolia with a Celtic-speaking people, became an important source of recruits. In N. Africa, Egypt, Cyrene, and Numidia (25 BC) were added to the empire. Numidia (modern day Eastern Algeria) was home to the Numidians/Moors, the ancestors of today's Berber people. Their light cavalry (*equites Maurorum*) was highly prized and had alternately fought and assisted the Romans for well over two centuries: they now started to be recruited into the regular Auxilia. Even more Mauri units were formed after the annexation of Mauretania (NW Algeria, Morocco), the rest of the Berber homeland, in 44 AD by emperor Claudius (ruled 41–54).[240]

Recruitment was thus heavy throughout the Augustan period, with a steady increase in the number of units formed. By AD 23, the Roman historian Tacitus records that there were roughly the same numbers of auxiliaries in service as there were legionaries.[241] Since at this time there were 25 legions of c. 5,000 men each, the Auxilia thus amounted to c. 125,000 men, implying c. 250 auxiliary regiments.[242]

Illyrian revolt (6–9 AD)

During the early Julio-Claudian period, many auxiliary regiments raised in frontier provinces were stationed in or near their home provinces, except during periods of major crises such as the Cantabrian Wars, when they were deployed temporarily in theatre. This carried the obvious risk if their own tribe or ethnic group rebelled against Rome (or attacked the Roman frontier from outside the Empire), auxiliary troops could be tempted to make common cause with them. The Romans would then be faced by an enemy that included units fully equipped and trained by themselves, thus losing their usual tactical advantages over tribal foes.[243]

The German leader Arminius is the classic example at an individual level: after several years of serving in Rome's forces as prefect of an auxiliary unit, he used the military training and experience he had gained to lead a confederacy of German tribes against Rome, culminating in the destruction of three Roman legions in the Teutoberg Forest in 9 AD, and the abandonment of Augustus' strategy of annexing Germany as far as the Elbe river. (This strategy was never revived by later emperors).[244]

At a collective level, the risk was even greater, as the hugely dangerous Illyrian revolt proved. The central Illyrian tribes were tough and spartan shepherds of the Bosnian mountains and excellent soldier-material. Their territory formed part of the strategic province of Illyricum, recently expanded to include the territory of the Pannonii, Celticised Illyrian tribes based on the west bank of the Danube who were subjugated by Rome in 12–9 BC (the *Bellum Pannonicum*). By the start of the Common Era, they were an important recruitment base for the auxilia.[245] But discontent was festering among the Illyrian tribes, largely due to what they saw as the rapacity of Roman tax officials.[246] In AD 6, several regiments of Dalmatae, a warlike Illyrian tribe, were ordered to report to a designated location to prepare to join Augustus' stepson and senior military commander Tiberius in a war against the Germans. Instead, they mutinied at the assembly point, and defeated a Roman force sent against them.[247] The Dalmatae were soon joined by the Breuci, another Illyrian tribe that supplied several auxiliary regiments. They gave battle to a second Roman force from Moesia. They lost, but inflicted heavy casualties.[248] The rebels were now joined by a large number of other Illyrian tribes. The Dalmatae attacked the port of Salona and overran the Adriatic coast, defeating a Roman force and exposing the Roman heartland of Italy to the fear of a rebel invasion.[249]

Augustus ordered Tiberius to break off operations in Germany and move his main army to Illyricum.[250] When it became clear that even Tiberius' forces were insufficient, Augustus was obliged to raise a second task force under Tiberius' nephew Germanicus, resorting to the compulsory purchase and emancipation of thousands of slaves to find enough troops, for the first time since the aftermath of the Battle of Cannae over two centuries earlier.[251] The Romans had now deployed no less than 15 legions and an equivalent number of auxilia.[252] This amounts to a total of c. 150,000 men, including at least 50 auxiliary cohorts composed, exceptionally, of Roman citizens. These were men whose status or background was regarded by Augustus as unsuitable for recruitment into the legions: either natural-born citizens of the lowest category, including vagrants and convicted criminals, or the freed slaves (Roman law accorded citizenship to the freed slaves of Roman citizens). These special units were accorded the title *civium Romanorum* ("of Roman citizens"), or *c.R.* for short. After the Illyrian revolt, these cohorts remained in being and recruited non-citizens like other auxiliary units, but retained their prestigious *c.R.* title.[253] In addition, the regular forces were assisted by a large number of allied troops from neighbouring Thrace deployed by their king Rhoemetalces I, a Roman *amicus* (puppet king).[254]

The Romans faced further reverses on the battlefield and a savage guerrilla war in the Bosnian mountains.[255] It took them three years of hard fighting to quell the revolt, which was described by the Roman historian Suetonius, writing in c. AD 100, as the most difficult conflict faced by Rome since the Punic Wars over two centuries earlier. Tiberius finally succeeded in quelling the revolt in 9 AD.

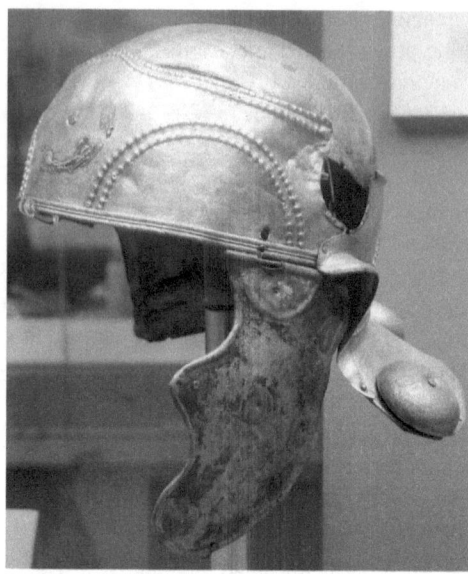

Figure 37: *The cavalry Witcham Gravel helmet from Cambridgeshire (England), 1st century AD*

This was apparently lucky timing for the Romans: that same year Arminius destroyed Varus' three legions in Germany. The Roman high command had no doubt that Arminius would have formed a grand alliance with the Illyrians.[256]

Despite the gravity of this rebellion, the Illyrians went on, alongside their neighbours the Thracians, to become the backbone of the Roman army. By the 2nd century, with roughly half the Roman army deployed on the Danube frontier, the auxilia and legions alike were dominated by Illyrian recruits. In the 3rd century, Illyrians largely replaced Italians in the senior officer echelons of *praefecti* of auxiliary regiments and *tribuni militum* of legions. Finally, from AD 268 to 379, virtually all emperors, including Diocletian and Constantine the Great were Romanised Illyrians from the provinces of Dalmatia, Moesia Superior and Pannonia. These were members of a military aristocracy, outstanding soldiers who saved the empire from collapse in the turbulent late 3rd century.[257]

Later Julio-Claudians (14–68 AD)

Significant development of the Auxilia appears to have taken place during the rule of the emperor Claudius (41–54 AD).

A minimum term of service of 25 years was established, at the end of which the retiring auxiliary soldier, and all his children, were awarded Roman citizenship.[258] This is deduced from the fact that the first known Roman military diplomas date from the time of Claudius. This was a folding bronze tablet engraved with the details of the soldier's service record, which he could use to prove his citizenship.[259] Claudius also decreed that prefects of auxiliary regiments must all be of equestrian rank, thus excluding centurions from such commands. The fact that auxiliary commanders were now all of the same social rank as most *tribuni militum*, (military tribunes, a legion's senior staff officers, all of whom only one, the *tribunus laticlavius*, was of the higher senatorial rank), probably indicates that auxilia now enjoyed greater prestige. Indigenous chiefs continued to command some auxiliary regiments, and were probably granted equestrian rank for the purpose. It is also likely that auxiliary pay was standardised at this time, but we only have estimates for the Julio-Claudian period.

Auxiliary uniform, armour, weapons and equipment were probably standardised by the end of the Julio-Claudian period. Auxiliary equipment was broadly similar to that of the legions (see Section 2.1 below for possible differences in armour). By 68 AD, there was little difference between most auxiliary infantry and their legionary counterparts in equipment, training and fighting capability. The main difference was that auxilia contained combat cavalry, both heavy and light, and other specialized units that legions lacked.[260]

Claudius annexed to the empire three regions that became important sources of auxiliary recruits: Britannia (43 AD), and the former client kingdoms of Mauretania (44) and Thracia (46). The latter became as important as Illyria as a source of auxiliary recruits, especially cavalry and archers. Britain in mid-2nd century contained the largest number of auxiliary regiments in any single province: about 60 out of about 400 (15%). By the rule of Nero (54–68), auxiliary numbers may have reached, by one estimate, about 200,000 men, implying about 400 regiments.

Revolt of the Batavi (69–70 AD)

The Batavi, a Germanic tribe, inhabited the region today known as Gelderland (Netherlands), in the Rhine river delta, then known as the *Insula Batavorum* ("Island of the Batavi", because surrounded by branches of the Rhine), part of the Roman province of Germania Inferior.[261] They were a warlike people, skilled horsemen, boatmen and swimmers. In return for the unusual privilege of exemption from *tributum* (direct taxes on land and heads normally exacted from *peregrini*), they supplied a disproportionate number of recruits to the Julio-Claudian auxilia: one *ala* and eight *cohortes*.[262] They also provided most of Augustus' elite personal bodyguard unit (the *Germani corpore custodes*),

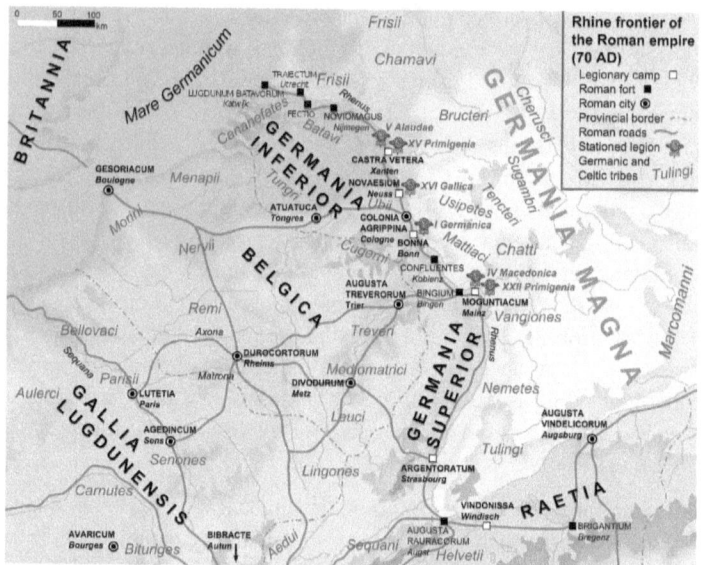

Figure 38: *Rhine frontier of the Roman empire, 70 AD, showing the location of the Batavi in the Rhine delta region. Roman territory is shaded dark. Their homeland was called the Insula Batavorum by the Romans and corresponded roughly with modern Gelderland province, Neth. Their chief town was Noviomagus (Nijmegen, Neth.), a strategic prominence in an otherwise flat and waterlogged land that became the site of a Roman legionary fortress (housing the legion X Gemina) after the Batavi revolt ended in 70 AD. The name is of Celtic origin, meaning "new market", suggesting that the Germanic Batavi either displaced or subjugated an indigenous Gallic tribe*

which continued in service until 68 AD. The Batavi auxilia amounted to about 5,000 men, implying that during the entire Julio-Claudian period, over 50% of all Batavi males reaching military age (16 years) may have enlisted in the auxilia.[263] Thus the Batavi, although just 0.05% of the total population of the empire of c. 70 million in 23 AD,[264] supplied about 4% of the total auxilia i.e. 80 times their proportionate share. They were regarded by the Romans as the very best (*fortissimi, validissimi*) of their auxiliary, and indeed all, their forces.[265] In Roman service, both their cavalry and infantry had perfected a technique for swimming across rivers wearing full armour and weapons.[266,267]

Julius Civilis (literally: "Julius the Citizen", clearly a Latin name adopted on gaining Roman citizenship, not his native one) was a hereditary prince of the Batavi and the prefect of a Batavi cohort. A veteran of 25 years' service, he had distinguished himself by service in Britain, where he and the eight Batavi cohorts had played a crucial role in both the Roman invasion in 43 AD and the subsequent subjugation of southern Britain.[268]

By 69, however, Civilis, the Batavi regiments and the Batavi people had become utterly disaffected with Rome. After the Batavi regiments were withdrawn from Britain to Italy in 66, Civilis and his brother (also a prefect) were arrested by the governor of Germania Inferior on a fabricated accusation of sedition. The governor ordered his brother's execution, while Civilis, who as a Roman citizen had the right to appeal to the emperor, was sent to Rome in chains for judgement by Nero.[269] He was released by Nero's overthrower and successor, Galba, but the latter also disbanded the imperial bodyguard unit for their loyalty to Nero. This alienated several hundred crack Batavi troops, and indeed the whole Batavi nation who regarded it as a grave insult.[270] At the same time, relations collapsed between the Batavi cohorts and the legion to which they had been attached since the invasion of Britain 25 years earlier (*XIV Gemina*). Their mutual hatred erupted in open fighting on at least two occasions.[271]

At this juncture, the Roman empire was convulsed by its first major civil war since the Battle of Actium exactly a century earlier: the Year of the Four Emperors (69–70 AD). The governor of Germania Inferior, ordered to raise more troops, outraged the Batavi by attempting to conscript more Batavi than the maximum stipulated in their treaty. The brutality and corruption of the Roman recruiting-centurions (including incidents of sexual assault on Batavi young men) brought already deep discontent in the Batavi homeland to the boil.[272]

Civilis now led his people in open revolt. Initially, he claimed he was supporting the bid for power of Vespasian, the general in command of the legions in Syria, whom Civilis had probably befriended when both were involved in the Roman invasion of Britain 25 years earlier (Vespasian was then commander of the legion *II Augusta*).[273] But the uprising soon became a bid for independence.[274] Civilis exploited the fact that some legions were absent from the Rhine area due to the civil war, and the rest under-strength. In addition, the Roman commanders and their rank-and-file soldiers were divided by loyalty to rival emperors.[275] Civilis quickly won the support of the Batavi's neighbours and kinsmen, the Cananefates, who in turn won over the Frisii. First the rebel allies captured two Roman forts in their territory, and a cohort of Tungri defected to Civilis.[276] Then two legions sent against Civilis were defeated when their companion Batavi *ala* defected to his side. The *Classis Germanica* (Rhine flotilla), largely manned by Batavi, was seized by Civilis.[277] Most importantly, the 8 Batavi cohorts stationed at Mainz with *XIV Gemina* mutinied and joined him, defeating at Bonn a Roman force that attempted to block their return to their homeland.[278] By now, Civilis commanded at least 12 regiments (6,000 men) of Roman-trained and equipped auxiliary troops, as well as a much larger number of tribal levies. A number of German tribes from beyond the Rhine joined his cause.[279] Several other German and Gallic units sent against him deserted, as the revolt spread to the rest of Gallia Belgica, including the Tungri, Lingones and Treviri tribes.[280] He was able to destroy the two remaining legions in Germania Inferior, (*V Alaudae* and *XV Primigenia*).[281]

By this stage, Rome's entire position on the Rhine and even in Gaul was imperiled. Their civil war over, the Romans mustered a huge task force of eight legions (five dispatched from Italy, two from Spain and one from Britain) to deal with Civilis.[282] Its commander Petillius Cerialis had to fight two difficult battles, at Trier and Xanten, before he could overrun the Batavi's homeland.[283] Tacitus' surviving narrative breaks off as he describes a meeting on an island in the Rhine delta between Civilis and Cerialis to discuss peace terms.[284] We do not know the outcome of this meeting or Civilis' ultimate fate. But, in view of his former friendship with Vespasian, who had already offered him a pardon, and the fact that the Romans still needed the Batavi levies, it is likely that the terms were lenient by Roman standards.[285]

Petilius Cerialis took a number of reconstituted Batavi units with him to Britain, and the Batavi regiments continued to serve with special distinction in Britain and elsewhere for the rest of the 1st century and beyond.[286] Even as late as 395, units with the Batavi name, although long since composed of recruits from all over the empire, were still classified as elite *palatini*, e.g. the *equites Batavi seniores* (cavalry) and *auxilium Batavi seniores* (infantry).[287]

Flavian era (69–96 AD)

The revolt of the Batavi appears to have led to a significant change in the Roman government's policy on deployment of Auxilia. The revolt proved that in times of civil strife, when legions were far from their bases campaigning for rival claimants to the imperial throne, it was dangerous to leave provinces exclusively in the hands of auxiliary regiments recruited from the indigenous nation. During the Julio-Claudian period, auxiliary regiments had often been deployed away from their original home province. But in the Flavian period (69–96), this appears to have become standard policy. Thus in AD 70, five reconstituted Batavi regiments (one *ala* and four *cohortes*) were transferred to Britain under Petillius Cerialis, who had suppressed the Civilis revolt and then embarked on the governorship of the island.[288] The great majority of regiments probably founded in the 1st century were stationed away from their province of origin in the second e.g. of 13 British regiments recorded in the mid-2nd century, none were stationed in Britain.[289] Furthermore, it appears

Figure 39: *Tombstone of the Flavian-era eques alaris (ala cavalryman)* **Titus Flavius Bassus**, *son of Mucala. A Dansala, (i.e. member of the Thracian Dentheletae tribe), he belonged to the* **Ala Noricorum** *(originally raised from the Taurisci tribe of Noricum). He died at age 46 after 26 years' service, not having advanced beyond the lowest rank. Bassus' adopted Roman names, Titus Flavius, indicate that he had gained Roman citizenship, doubtless by serving the required 25 years in the auxilia. The names adopted would normally be those of the emperor ruling at the time of the citizenship award. In this case, they could refer to any of the 3 emperors of the Flavian dynasty (ruled 69–96), Vespasian and his two sons, Titus and Domitian, all of whom carried the same names. The arrangement of the scene, a rider spearing a man (the motif of the Thracian Hero), indicates that Bassus was a Thracian, as does his father's name. Date: late 1st century. Römisch-Germanisches Museum, Cologne, Germany*

that in the Flavian era native noblemen were no longer permitted to command auxiliary units from their own tribe.[290]

After a prolonged period in a foreign province a regiment would become assimilated, since the majority of its new recruits would be drawn from the province in which it was stationed, or neighbouring provinces. Those same "British" units, mostly based on the Danube frontier, would by c. 150, after almost a century away from their home island, be largely composed of Illyrian, Thracian and Dacian recruits. However, there is evidence that a few regiments

Figure 40: *Roman cavalry spatha, a longer sword (median blade length: 780 mm [30.7 in]), designed to give the rider a longer reach than the gladius*[293]

at least continued to draw some recruits from their original home provinces in the 2nd century e.g. Batavi units stationed in Britain.[291]

The Flavian period also saw the first formation of large, double-size units, both infantry and cavalry, of a nominal strength of 1,000 men (*cohors/ala milliaria*), though they were actually mostly smaller (720 for an *ala milliaria* and 800 for a *cohors milliaria*). These were the mirror image of the double-strength first cohorts of legions also introduced at this time. Such units remained a minority of the Auxilia: in the mid-2nd century, they constituted 13% of units, containing 20% of total manpower.[292]

Later Principate (97–284)

In 106 AD, emperor Trajan finally defeated the Dacian kingdom of Decebalus and annexed it as the Roman province of Dacia Traiana. By the mid-2nd century, there were 44 auxiliary regiments stationed there, about 10% of the total auxilia. In Britain, there were 60. Together, these two provinces contained about a quarter of the total auxiliary regiments.

There is considerable scholarly dispute about the precise size of the auxilia during the imperial era, even during the corp's best-documented period, the rule of Trajan's successor, Hadrian (117–138). This is evident if one compares calculations by Spaul (2000) and Holder (2003):

Estimates of Roman auxilia numbers
(units attested in the mid-2nd century)

Author	No. Alae	No. Cohortes	Total no. units	Total cavalry	Total infantry	Total effectives
J. Spaul (2000)[294]	80	247	**327**	56,160	124,640	**180,800**
P. A. Holder (2003)	88	279	**367**	74,624	143,200	**217,624**

NOTE: Manpower figures exclude officers (centurions and decurions), which would have numbered about 3,500 men overall.

In addition, Holder believes that a further 14 *cohortes*, which are attested under Trajan, immediately before Hadrian's rule, but not during or after it, probably continued in existence, giving a total of 381 units and 225,000 effectives. The discrepancy between the two scholars is due to: (i) Interpretation of units with the same name and number, but attested in different provinces in the same period. Spaul tends to take a more cautious approach and to assume such are the same unit moving base frequently, while Holder tends to regard them as separate units which acquired the same number due to duplicated (or even triplicated) seriation. (ii) Assumptions about how many *cohortes* were *equitatae*. Spaul accepts only those *cohortes* specifically attested as *equitatae* i.e., about 40% of recorded units. Holder estimates that at least 70% of *cohortes* contained cavalry contingents by the early 2nd century

Even according to the more conservative estimate, the auxilia were by this time significantly larger than the legions, which contained c. 155,000 effectives (28 legions of 5,500 men each) at this time, of which just 3,360 were cavalry. (For a detailed breakdown, see section 4: Auxilia deployment in the 2nd century, below).

During the second half of the 2nd century, the Roman army underwent considerable further expansion, with the addition of five new legions (27,500 men) to a Principate peak of 33.[295] A matching number of auxilia (i.e. c. 50 regiments, although only the names of around 25–30 have survived in the epigraphic record) were probably added, possibly reaching a peak of c. 440 regiments and around 250,000 effectives by the end of Septimius Severus's rule (211 AD).

The likely growth of the Roman auxilia may be summarised as follows:

Estimated size of Roman army 24–305 AD

Army corps	Tiberius 24 AD	Hadrian c. 130 AD	S. Severus 211 AD	3rd-century crisis c. 270 AD	Diocletian 284–305
LE-GIONS	125,000[296]	155,000[297]	182,000[298]		
AUX-ILIA	125,000[299] Wikipedia:Verifiability	218,000[300]	250,000[301]		
Praetorian Guard	~~5,000[302]	~~8,000[303]	~15,000		
Total Roman Army	255,000[304]	381,000[305]	447,000[306]	290,000?[307]	390,000[308]

NOTE: Regular land forces only. Excludes citizen-militias, barbarian *foederati*, and Roman navy effectives

During the 2nd century, some units with the new names *numerus* ("group") and *vexillatio* ("detachment") appear in the diploma record.[309] Their size is uncertain, but was likely smaller than the regular *alae* and *cohortes*, as originally they were probably detachments from the latter, acquiring independent status after long-term separation. As these units are mentioned in diplomas, they were presumably part of the regular auxiliary organisation.[310] But *numeri* was also a generic term used for barbarian units outside the regular auxilia. (see section 2.4 Irregular units, below).

In 212, the *constitutio Antoniniana* (Antonine decree) of emperor Caracalla granted Roman citizenship to all the free inhabitants of the Empire – the *peregrini* – thus abolishing their second-class status.[311] But there is no evidence that the citizens-only rule for legions was also abolished at this time. The legions simply gained a much wider recruitment base, as they were now able to recruit any male free resident of the empire. Auxiliary units were now recruited mainly from Roman citizens, but probably continued to recruit non-citizen *barbari* from outside the Empire's borders.[312] However, the citizens-only rule for legions appears to have been dropped some time during the 3rd century, as by the 4th-century Romans and barbarians are found serving together in all units.[313]

In the mid to late 3rd century, the army was afflicted by a combination of military disasters and of pestilence, the so-called Crisis of the Third Century. In 251–271, Gaul, the Alpine regions and Italy, the Balkans and the East were simultaneously overrun by Alamanni, Sarmatians, Goths and Persians respectively.[314] At the same time, the Roman army was struggling with the effects of a devastating pandemic, probably of smallpox: the Plague of Cyprian, which began in 251 and was still raging in 270, when it claimed the life of emperor Claudius II Gothicus. The evidence for an earlier pandemic, the Antonine Plague (also smallpox) indicates a mortality of 15–30% in the empire as a whole.[315] The armies would likely have suffered deaths at the top end of the range, due to their close concentration of individuals and frequent movements across the empire.[316] This probably led to a steep decline in military numbers, which only recovered at the end of the century under Diocletian (r. 284–305).[317]

The recruitment shortfall caused by the crisis seems to have led to recruitment of barbarians to the auxilia on a much greater scale than previously. By the 4th century, it has been estimated that some 25% of regular army recruits were barbarian-born. In the elite *palatini* regiments, anywhere between a third and a half of recruits may have been barbarian. This is likely a much greater proportion of foreigners than joined the auxilia in the 1st and 2nd centuries.[318] In the 3rd century, a small number of regular auxiliary units appear in the record that, for the first time, bear the names of barbarian tribes from outside the empire e.g. the *ala I Sarmatarum* attested in 3rd-century Britain.[319] This was probably an offshoot of the 5,500 surrendered Sarmatian horsemen posted on Hadrian's Wall by emperor Marcus Aurelius in c. 175.[320] This unit may be an early example of a novel process whereby irregular units of *barbari* (*foederati*) were transformed into regular auxilia. This process intensified in the 4th century: the *Notitia Dignitatum*, a key document on the late Roman army, lists a large number of regular units with barbarian names.[321]

4th century

In the 4th century, the Roman army underwent a radical restructuring. In the rule of Diocletian (284–305), the traditional Principate formations of *legiones*, *alae* and *cohortes* appear to have been broken up into smaller units, many of which bore a variety of new names.[322] Under Constantine I (r. 312–337) it appears that military units were classified into three grades based on strategic role and to some extent quality: *palatini*, elite units normally part of the *exercitus praesentales* (imperial escort armies); *comitatenses*, higher-grade interception forces based in frontier provinces; and *limitanei*, lower-grade border troops.[323] (See Late Roman army).

The old Principate auxilia regiments provided the basis for units at all three grades. The *Notitia Dignitatum* lists about 70 *alae* and *cohortes* that retained their 2nd-century names, mostly *limitanei*.[324] But traces of other auxilia regiments can be found in the *praesentales* and *comitatenses* armies. For example, many of the new-style *auxilia palatina* infantry regiments, considered among

Figure 41: *Roman cavalry from a mosaic of the Villa Romana del Casale, Sicily, 4th century AD*

the best units in the army, were probably formed from old-style auxiliary *cohortes*, which they appear to closely resemble.[325]

The late 4th-century writer on military affairs Vegetius complains of contemporary young men joining the "auxilia" in preference to the "legions" to avoid the latter's tougher training and duties.[326] But it is unclear what types of units he was referring to. It is possible that those older terms were still popularly used (misleadingly) to mean *limitanei* and *comitatenses* respectively. In any event, his quote in no way describes accurately the Principate auxilia, many of which were of very high quality.

Unit types and structure

Regular unit types

The following table sets out the official, or establishment, strength of auxiliary units in the 2nd century. The real strength of a unit would fluctuate continually, but would likely have been somewhat less than the establishment most of the time.

Roman auxiliary regiments: Type, structure and strength

Unit type	Service	Unit commander	Sub-unit commander	No of sub-units	Sub-unit strength	Unit strength
Ala quingenaria	cavalry	praefectus	decurio	16 *turmae*	30 *(32)*	480 *(512)*
Ala milliaria	cavalry	praefectus	decurio	24 *turmae*	30 *(32)*	720 *(768)*
Cohors quingenaria	infantry	praefectus*	centurio	6 *centuriae*	80	480
Cohors milliaria	infantry	tribunus militum**	centurio	10 *centuriae*	80	800
Cohors equitata quingenaria	infantry plus cavalry contingent	praefectus	centurio (inf) decurio (cav)	6 *centuriae* 4 *turmae*	80 30.	600 (480 inf/120 cav)
Cohors equitata milliaria	infantry plus cavalry contingent	tribunus militum**	centurio (inf) decurio (cav)	10 *centuriae* 8 *turmae*	80 30	1,040 (800 inf/240 cav)

* *tribunus militum* in original c.R. *cohortes*[327]
** *praefectus* in Batavi and Tungri *cohortes milliariae*

NOTE: Opinion is divided about the size of an *ala turma*, between 30 and 32 men. 30 was the size of a *turma* in the Republican cavalry and in the *cohors equitata* of the Principate auxilia. Against this is a statement by Arrian that an *ala* was 512 strong.[328] This would make an ala *turma* 32 men strong.

Cohortes

These all-infantry units were modelled on the cohorts of the legions, with the same officers and sub-units. They were typically considered to be more of a light infantry than proper legionaries. Some auxiliaries may however have been equipped with the *lorica segmentata*, the most sophisticated legionary body-armour, although scholars dispute this.[329,330]

There is no evidence that auxiliary infantry fought in a looser order than legionaries. It appears that in a set-piece battle-line, auxiliary infantry would normally be stationed on the flanks, with legionary infantry holding the centre e.g. as in the Battle of Watling Street (AD 60), the final defeat of the rebel Britons under queen Boudicca.[331] This was a tradition inherited from the Republic, when the precursors of auxiliary *cohortes*, the Latin *alae*, occupied the same position in the line.[332] The flanks of the line required equal, if not greater, skill to hold as the centre.

Alae

During the Principate period of the Roman Empire (30 BC – AD 284), the all-mounted *alae* ("wings") contained the elite cavalry of the army. They were specially trained in elaborate manoeuvres, such as those displayed to the emperor Hadrian during a documented inspection in Numidia. They were best-suited for large-scale operations and battle, during which they acted as the primary cavalry escort for the legions, which had almost no cavalry of their own. Roman alares were normally armoured, with mail or scale body armour, a cavalry version of the infantry helmet (with more protective features, such as completely covered ears) and oval shield or hexagonal. Their weapons could be a lance, javelins, or bow and arrow but all Roman horseman had a sword called a (*spatha*) and the ubiquitous pugio. The elite status of an *alaris* is shown by the fact that he received 20% more pay than his counterpart in an auxiliary cohort or a legionary infantryman.

The favored sources of recruitment for the cavalry of the *auxilia* were Gauls, Germans, Iberians and Thracians. All of these peoples had long-established skills and experience of fighting from horseback – in contrast to the Romans themselves. The *alae* were better paid and mounted than the more numerous horsemen of the *cohortes equitatae* (see below).

Cohortes equitatae

These were *cohortes* with a cavalry contingent attached. There is evidence that their numbers expanded with the passage of time. Only about 40% of attested *cohortes* are specifically attested as *equitatae* in inscriptions, which is probably the original Augustan proportion. A study of units stationed in Syria in the mid-2nd century found that many units that did not carry the *equitata* title did in fact contain cavalrymen e.g. by discovery of a tombstone of a cavalryman attached to the cohort. This implies that by that time, at least 70% of *cohortes* were probably *equitatae*.[333] The addition of cavalry to a cohort obviously enabled it to carry out a wider range of independent operations. A *cohors equitata* was in effect a self-contained mini-army.[334]

The traditional view of *equites cohortales* (the cavalry arm of *cohortes equitatae*), as expounded by G.L. Cheesman, was that they were just a mounted infantry with poor-quality horses. They would use their mounts simply to reach the battlefield and then would dismount to fight.[335] This view is today discredited. Although it is clear that *equites cohortales* did not match *equites alares* (*ala* cavalrymen) in quality (hence their lower pay), the evidence is that they fought as cavalry in the same way as the *alares* and often alongside them. Their armour and weapons were the same as for the *alares*.[336]

Auxilia

Figure 42: *Routed Sarmatian cataphracts (right) flee for their lives from Roman alares (auxiliary cavalrymen), during the Dacian Wars (AD 101–106). Note full-body scalar armour, also armoured caparison for horses (including eye-guards). The Sarmatians' lances (as well as the Romans') have disappeared due to stone erosion, but a sword is still visible, as is a bow carried by one man. It was apparently in the period following this conflict (perhaps as a result of the lessons learnt from it) that the Romans first established their own regular units of cataphracts, and deployed them in the Danubian region. They were most likely equipped as the Sarmatians. Panel from Trajan's Column, Rome*

Nevertheless, non-combat roles of the *equites cohortales* differed significantly from the *alares*. Non-combat roles such as despatch-riders (*dispositi*) were generally filled by cohort cavalry.

Auxiliary specialised units

In the Republican period, the standard trio of specialised auxilia were Balearic slingers, Cretan archers and Numidian light cavalry. These functions, plus some new ones, continued in the 2nd-century auxilia.

Heavily-armoured lancers

Equites cataphractarii, or simply *cataphractarii* for short, were the heavily armoured cavalry of the Roman army. Based on Sarmatian and Parthian models, they were also known as *contarii* and *clibanarii*, although it is unclear whether these terms were interchangeable or whether they denoted variations in equipment or role. Together with new units of light mounted archers, the *cataphractarii* were designed to counter Parthian (and, in Pannonia, Sarmatian) battle

Figure 43: *Roman archers (top left) in action. Note conical helmets, indicating Syrian unit, and recurved bows. Trajan's Column, Rome*

Figure 44: *Roman slingers (funditores) in action in the Dacian Wars. Detail from Trajan's Column, Rome*

tactics. Parthian armies consisted largely of cavalry. Their standard tactic was to use light mounted archers to weaken and break up the Roman infantry line, and then to rout it with a charge by the *cataphractarii* concentrated on the weakest point.[337] The only special heavy cavalry units to appear in the 2nd-century record are: *ala I Ulpia contariorum* and *ala I Gallorum et Pannoniorum cataphractaria* stationed in Pannonia and Moesia Inferior respectively in the 2nd century.[338]

Light cavalry

From the Second Punic War until the 3rd century AD, the bulk of Rome's light cavalry (apart from mounted archers from Syria) was provided by the inhabitants of the Maghrebi provinces of Africa and Mauretania Caesariensis, the Numidae or Mauri (from whom derives the English term "Moors"), who were the ancestors of the Berber people of modern Algeria and Morocco. They were known as the *equites Maurorum* or *Numidarum* ("Moorish or Numidian cavalry"). On Trajan's Column, Mauri horsemen, depicted with long hair in dreadlocks, are shown riding their small but resilient horses bare-back and unbridled, with a simple braided rope round their mount's neck for control. They wear no body or head armour, carrying only a small, round leather shield. Their weaponry cannot be discerned due to stone erosion, but is known from Livy to have consisted of several short javelins.[339,340] Exceptionally fast and maneuverable, Numidian cavalry would harass the enemy by hit-and-run attacks, riding up and loosing volleys of javelins, then scattering faster than any opposing cavalry could pursue. They were superbly suited to scouting, harassment, ambush and pursuit.[341] It is unclear what proportion of the Numidian cavalry were regular auxilia units as opposed to irregular *foederati* units.[342]

In the 3rd century, new formations of light cavalry appear, apparently recruited from the Danubian provinces: the *equites Dalmatae* ("Dalmatian cavalry"). Little is known about these, but they were prominent in the 4th century, with several units listed in the *Notitia Dignitatum*.

Camel troops

A unit of *dromedarii* ("camel-mounted troops") is attested from the 2nd century, the *ala I Ulpia dromedariorum milliaria* in Syria.[343]

Archers

A substantial number of auxiliary regiments (32, or about 1 in 12 in the 2nd century) were denoted *sagittariorum*, or archer-units (from *sagittarii* lit. "arrow-men", from *sagitta* = "arrow"). These 32 units (of which 4 were double-strength) had a total official strength of 17,600 men. All three types of auxiliary regiment (*ala*, *cohors* and *cohors equitata*) could be denoted *sagittariorum*. Although these units evidently specialised in archery, it is uncertain from the available evidence whether all *sagittariorum* personnel were archers, or simply a higher proportion than in ordinary units. At the same time, ordinary regiments probably also possessed some archers, otherwise their capacity for independent operations would have been unduly constrained. Bas-reliefs appear to show personnel in ordinary units employing bows.

From about 218 BC onwards, the archers of the Roman army of the mid-Republic were virtually all mercenaries from the island of Crete, which boasted a long specialist tradition. During the late Republic (88–30 BC) and the Augustan period, Crete was gradually eclipsed by men from other, much more populous, regions subjugated by the Romans with strong archery traditions. These included Thrace, Anatolia and, above all, Syria. Of the 32 *sagittarii* units attested in the mid-2nd century, 13 have Syrian names, 7 Thracian, 5 from Anatolia, 1 from Crete and the remaining 6 of other or uncertain origin.[344]

Three distinct types of archers are shown on Trajan's Column: (a) with scalar cuirass, conical steel helmet and cloak; (b) without armour, with cloth conical cap and long tunic; or (c) equipped in the same way as general auxiliary foot-soldiers (apart from carrying bows instead of javelins). The first type were probably Syrian or Anatolian units; the third type probably Thracian.[345] The standard bow used by Roman auxilia was the recurved composite bow, a sophisticated, compact and powerful weapon.[346]

Slingers

From about 218 BC onwards, the Republican army's slingers were exclusively mercenaries from the Balearic Islands, which had nurtured a strong indigenous tradition of slinging from prehistoric times. As a result, in classical Latin, *Baleares* (literally "inhabitants of the Balearic Islands") became an alternative word for "slingers" (*funditores*, from *funda* = "sling"). Because of this, it is uncertain whether the most of the imperial army's slingers continued to be drawn from the Balearics themselves, or, like archers, derived mainly from other regions.

Independent slinger units are not attested in the epigraphic record of the Principate. However, slingers are portrayed on Trajan's Column. They are shown unarmoured, wearing a short tunic. They carry a cloth bag, slung in front, to hold their shot (*glandes*).

Scouts/numeri

Exploratores ('reconnaissance troops', from *explorare* = "to scout"). Two examples include *numeri exploratorum* attested to in the 3rd century in Britain: *Habitanco* and *Bremenio* (both names of forts).[347] It is possible, however, that more than 20 such units served in Britain.[348] The literal translation of *numeri* is 'numbers' and it was often used in the context of a generic title for any unit that was not of a standard size or structure. From the 2nd century onward they served as frontier guards, often supplied by the Sarmatians and the Germans.[349] Little else is known about such units.

Irregular allied forces

Throughout the Principate period, there is evidence of ethnic units of *barbari* outside the normal auxilia organisation fighting alongside Roman troops. To an extent, these units were simply a continuation of the old client-king levies of the late Republic: *ad hoc* bodies of troops supplied by Rome's puppet petty-kings on the imperial borders for particular campaigns. Some clearly remained in Roman service beyond the campaigns, keeping their own native leadership, attire and equipment and structure. These units were known to the Romans as *socii* ("allies"), *symmachiarii* (from *symmachoi*, Greek for "allies") or *foederati* ("treaty troops" from *foedus*, "treaty"). One estimate puts the number of *foederati* in the time of Trajan at about 11,000, divided into about 40 *numeri* (units) of about 300 men each. The purpose of employing *foederati* units was to use their specialist fighting skills.[350] Many of these would have been troops of Numidian cavalry (see light cavalry above).

The *foederati* make their first official appearance on Trajan's Column, where they are portrayed in a standardised manner, with long hair and beards, barefoot, stripped to the waist, wearing long trousers held up by wide belts and wielding clubs. In reality, several different tribes supported the Romans in the Dacian wars. Their attire and weapons would have varied widely. The Column stereotypes them with the appearance of a single tribe, probably the most outlandish-looking, to differentiate them clearly from the regular auxilia.[351] Judging by the frequency of their appearance in the Column's battle scenes, the *foederati* were important contributors to the Roman operations in Dacia. Another example of *foederati* are the 5,500 captured Sarmatian cavalrymen sent by Emperor Marcus Aurelius (r. 161–180) to garrison a fort on Hadrian's Wall after their defeat in the Marcomannic Wars.[352]

Recruitment, ranks and pay

The evidence for auxiliary ranks and pay is scant: even less exists than the patchy evidence for their legionary counterparts. There seems to be some consensus, however, that the auxiliary was paid one third of what a legionary received: 300 sesterces a year (400 after the reign of the emperor Commodus). Both auxiliaries and seamen received the *viaticum* of 300 sesterces, although the various sources differ as to whether auxiliaries and sailors received the retirement bonus[353] known as the *honesta missio*, or honorable discharge.[354,355]

The available data may be broken down and summarised as follows:

Auxilia ranks and pay (mid-1st century)[356]

Pay scale (as multiple of basic)	Cohors infantry rank (in ascending order)	Amount (denarii)	XXX	Ala rank (in ascending order)	Amount (denarii)
1 (*caligati* = "rankers")	*pedes* (*infantryman*)	188		*gregalis* (*ala* cavalryman)	263
1.5 (*sesquiplicarii* = "one-and-half-pay men")	*tesserarius* (corporal)	282		*sesquiplicarius* (corporal)	395
2 (*duplicarii* = "double-pay men")	*signifer* (*centuria* standard-bearer) *optio* (centurion's deputy) *vexillarius* (cohort standard-bearer)	376		*signifer* (*turma* standard-bearer) *curator*? (decurion's deputy) *vexillarius* (*ala* standard-bearer)	526
Over 5	*centurio* (centurion = *centuria* commander) *centurio princeps* (chief centurion) *beneficiarius*? (deputy cohort commander)	940 +		*decurio* (decurion = *turma* commander) *decurio princeps* (chief decurion) *beneficiarius*? (deputy *ala* commander)	1,315 +
50	*praefectus* or *tribunus* (cohort commander)	9,400		*praefectus* or *tribunus* (*ala* commander)	13,150

Rankers (*caligati*)

At the bottom end of the rank pyramid, rankers were known as *caligati* (lit: "sandal men" from the *caligae* or hob-nailed sandals worn by soldiers). Depending on the type of regiment they belonged to, they held the official ranks of *pedes* (foot soldier in a *cohors*), *eques* (cavalryman in a *cohors equitata*) and *gregalis* (*ala* cavalryman).[357]

During the Principate, recruitment into the legions was restricted to Roman citizens only. This rule, which derived from the pre-Social War Republican

Figure 45: *Tombstone of Marius son of Ructicnus. The inscription states that he was a miles (ranker) of the Alpine infantry regiment* **Cohors I Montanorum**, *who died in his 25th year of service (i.e. in the final year of the minimum term for an auxiliary and just before qualifying for Roman citizenship). His heir, who erected the stone, is named Montanus, the same ethnic name as the regiment's, meaning a native of the eastern Alps, most likely the origin of the deceased. Note (top corners) the Alpine edelweiss flowers, called stella Alpina ("Alpine star") in Latin. These were either a regimental symbol, or a national symbol of the Montani. The crescent moon-and-star motif between the flowers may be either a regimental emblem or a religious symbol. Date: 1st century, probably ante 68. From Carinthia, Austria*

army, was strictly enforced. The few exceptions recorded, such as during emergencies and for the illegitimate sons of legionaries, do not warrant the suggestion that the rule was routinely ignored.[358]

In the 1st century, the vast majority of auxiliary common soldiers were recruited from the Roman *peregrine* (second-class citizens). In the Julio-Claudian era, conscription of *peregrini* seems to have been practiced alongside voluntary recruitment, probably in the form of a fixed proportion of men reaching military age in each tribe being drafted.[359] From the Flavian era onwards, the auxilia were an all-volunteer force.[360] Although recruits as young as 14 are recorded, the majority of recruits (66%) were from the 18–23 age group.[361]

When it was first raised, an auxiliary regiment would have been recruited from the native tribe or people whose name it bore. In the early Julio-Claudian period, it seems that efforts were made to preserve the ethnic integrity of units, even when the regiment was posted in a faraway province. But in the later part of the period, recruitment in the region where the regiment was posted increased and became predominant from the Flavian era onwards. The regiment would thus lose its original ethnic identity. The unit's name would thus become a mere curiosity devoid of meaning, although some of its members might inherit foreign names from their veteran ancestors. This view has to be qualified, however, as evidence from military diplomas and other inscriptions shows that some units continued to recruit in their original home areas e.g. Batavi units stationed in Britain, where some units had an international membership. It also appears that the Danubian provinces (Raetia, Pannonia, Moesia, Dacia) remained key recruiting grounds for units stationed all over the empire.[362,363]

It appears that Roman citizens were also regularly recruited to the auxilia. Most likely, the majority of citizen recruits to auxiliary regiments were the sons of auxiliary veterans who were enfranchised on their fathers' discharge.[364] Many such may have preferred to join their fathers' old regiments, which were a kind of extended family to them, rather than join a much larger, unfamiliar legion. There are also instances of legionaries transferring to the auxilia (to a higher rank).[365] The incidence of citizens in the auxilia would thus have grown steadily over time until, after the grant of citizenship to all *peregrini* in 212, auxiliary regiments became predominantly, if not exclusively, citizen units.

Less clearcut is the question of whether the regular auxilia recruited *barbari* (barbarians, as the Romans called people living outside the empire's borders). Although there is little evidence of it before the 3rd century, the consensus is that auxilia recruited barbarians throughout their history.[366] In the 3rd century, a few auxilia units of clearly barbarian origin start to appear in the record e.g. *Ala I Sarmatarum, cuneus Frisiorum* and *numerus Hnaufridi* in Britain.[367,368]

There existed a hierarchy of pay between types of auxiliary, with cavalry higher paid than infantry. One recent estimate is that in the time of Augustus, the annual pay structure was: *eques alaris* (*gregalis*) 263 *denarii*, *eques cohortalis* 225, and *cohors* infantryman 188.[369] The same differentials (of about 20% between grades) seem to have existed at the time of Domitian (r. 81–96).[370] However, Goldsworthy points out that the common assumption that rates of pay were universal across provinces and units is unproven. Pay may have varied according to the origin of the unit.[371]

The remuneration of an auxiliary *pedes cohortalis* may be compared to a legionary's as follows:

Remuneration of Roman common foot soldiers (about AD 70)[372]

Remuneration item	legionary *pedes*: amount (*denarii*) (annualised)	XXX	auxiliary *pedes* amount (*denarii*) (annualised)
Stipendium (gross salary)	225		188
Less: Food deduction	60		60
Less: Equipment etc. deductions	50		50
Net disposable pay	115		78
Plus: *Donativa* (bonuses) (average: 75 *denarii* every 3 years)	25		none proven
Total disposable income	140		78
Praemia (discharge bonus: 3,000 *denarii*)	120		none proven

Gross salary was subject to deductions for food, clothing, boots and hay (probably for the company mules). It is unclear whether the cost of armour and weapons was also deducted, or borne by the army. Deductions left the soldier with a net salary of 78 *denarii*. This sum was sufficient, on the basis of the food deduction, to amply feed an adult for a year. In 84 AD Domitian increased basic legionary pay by 33% (from 225 to 300 *denarii*): a similar increase was presumably accorded to auxiliaries, boosting their net income to 140 *denarii*, i.e. more than two food allowances.[373] It was entirely disposable, as the soldier was exempt from the poll tax (*capitatio*), did not pay rent (he was housed in fort barracks) and his food, clothing and equipment were already deducted. It should be borne in mind that most recruits came from peasant families living at subsistence level. To such persons, any disposable income would appear attractive.[374] It could be spent on leisure activities, sent to relatives or simply saved for retirement.

There is no evidence that auxiliaries received the substantial cash bonuses (donativum) handed to legionaries on the accession of a new emperor and other occasions.[375] Although irregular, these payments (each worth 75 *denarii* to a common legionary) averaged once every 7.5 years in the early 1st century and every three years later. Duncan-Jones has suggested that *donativa* may have been paid to auxiliaries also from the time of Hadrian onwards, on the grounds that the total amount of donative to the military increased sharply at that time.[376] A very valuable benefit paid to legionaries was the discharge bonus (*praemia*) paid on completion of the full 25 years' service. At 3,000 *denarii*, this was equivalent to ten years' gross salary for a common legionary after the pay increase of 84 AD. It would enable him to purchase a substantial plot of land. Again, there is no indication that auxiliaries were paid a discharge bonus. For auxiliaries, the discharge bonus was the grant of Roman citizenship, which carried important tax exemptions. However, Duncan-Jones argues that the fact that service in the auxilia was competitive with the legions (deduced from the many Roman citizens that joined the auxilia) that a discharge bonus may have been paid.[377]

Junior officers (*principales*)

Below centurion/decurion rank, junior officers in the Roman army were known as *principales*. An auxiliary cohort's ranks appear the same as in a legionary *centuria*. These were, in ascending order: *tesserarius* ("officer of the watch"), *signifer* (standard-bearer for the *centuria*), *optio* (centurion's deputy) and *vexillarius* (standard-bearer for the whole regiment, from *vexillum*). In the *turmae* of *cohortes equitatae* (and of *alae*?), the decurion's second-in-command was probably known as a *curator*, responsible for horses and caparison.[378] As in the legions, the *principales*, together with some regimental specialists, were classified in two pay-scales: *sesquiplicarii* ("one-and-a-half-pay men") and *duplicarii* ("double-pay men"). These ranks are probably most closely resembled by the modern ranks of corporal and sergeant respectively.

Besides combat effectives, regiments also contained specialists, the most senior of whom were *sesquiplicarii* or *duplicarii*, the rest common soldiers with the status of *milities immunes* ("exempt soldiers" i.e. exempt from normal duties). Ranking specialists included the *medicus* (regimental doctor), *veterinarius* (veterinary doctor, in charge of the care of horses, pack animals and livestock), *custos armorum* (keeper of the armoury), and the *cornicularius* (clerk in charge of all the regiment's records and paperwork).[379]

Senior officers

The limited evidence on auxiliary *centuriones* and *decuriones* is that such officers could be directly commissioned as well as promoted from the ranks. Many appear to have come from provincial aristocracies.[380] Those rising from the ranks could be promotions from the legions as well as from the regiment's own ranks. In the Julio-Claudian period auxiliary *centuriones* and *decuriones* were a roughly equal split between citizens and *peregrini*, though later citizens became predominant due to the spread of citizenship among military families. Because *centuriones* and *decuriones* often rose from the ranks, they

Figure 46: *Tombstone of Titus Calidius Severus, a Roman cavalryman. The career summary in the inscription shows that Severus joined the auxiliary regiment **cohors I Alpinorum**, rising from eques (common cavalryman) through optio to decurion. He then switched to a legion (presumably after gaining Roman citizenship after 25 of his 34 years of service) and became a centurion in **Legio XV Apollinaris** (it appears that legion cavalrymen used infantry ranks). He died at age 58, probably a few years after his discharge. Note the portrayal of his chain-mail armour, centurion's transverse-crested helmet and his horse, led by his equerry, probably a slave. This soldier's long career shows that many auxiliaries served longer than the minimum 25 years, and sometimes joined legions. Erected by his brother, Quintus. Dates from ante 117, when XV Apollinaris was transferred from Carnuntum (Austria) to the East*

have often been compared to warrant officers such as sergeants-major in modern armies. However, centurions' social role was much wider than a modern warrant-officer. In addition to their military duties, centurions performed a wide range of administrative tasks, which was necessary in the absence of an adequate bureaucracy to support provincial governors. They were also relatively wealthy, due to their high salaries (see table above).[381] However, most of the surviving evidence concerns legionary centurions and it is uncertain whether their auxiliary counterparts shared their high status and non-military role.

There is little evidence about the pay-scales of auxiliary *centuriones* and *decuriones*, but these are also believed to have amounted to several times that of a *miles*.

Unlike a *legatus legionis* (who had an officer staff of 6 *tribuni militum* and one *praefectus castrorum*), an auxiliary *praefectus* does not appear to have enjoyed the support of purely staff officers. The possible exception is an attested *beneficiarius* ("deputy"), who may have been the praefectus' second-in-command, if this title was a regular rank and not simply an *ad hoc* appointment for a specific task. Also attached to the *praefectus* were the regiment's *vexillarius* (standard-bearer for the whole unit) and *cornucen* (horn-blower).

Commanders

From a survey by Devijver of persons whose origin can be determined, it appears that during the 1st century, the large majority (65%) of auxiliary prefects were of Italian origin. The Italian proportion dropped steadily, to 38% in the 2nd century, and 21% in the 3rd century.[382] From the time of emperor Claudius (r. 41–54) only Roman knights were eligible to hold command of an auxiliary regiment. This status could be obtained either by birth (i.e. if the person was the son of a hereditary Roman knight; or by attaining the property qualification (100,000 *denarii*, the equivalent of 400 years' gross salary for an auxiliary *alaris*); or by military promotion: the latter were the chief centurions of legions (*centurio primus pilus*) who would normally be elevated to equestrian rank by the emperor after completing their single-year term as *primuspilus*.[383]

Equestrians by birth would normally begin their military careers at c. 30 years of age. An axillary had to do 25 years of service before joining the army. Commands were held in a set sequence, each held for 3–4 years: prefect of an auxiliary *cohors*, *tribunus militum* in a legion and finally prefect of an auxiliary *ala*. In Hadrian's time, a fourth command was added, for exceptionally able officers, of prefect of an *ala milliaria*. Like officers senatorial rank, hereditary equestrians held civilian posts before and after their decade of military service, whereas non-hereditary officers tended to remain in the army, commanding various units in various provinces. By the 3rd century, most auxiliary prefects had exclusively military careers.[384]

The pay of a *praefectus* of an auxiliary regiment in the early 2nd century has been estimated at over 50 times that of a *miles* (common soldier). (This compares to a full colonel in the British Army, who is currently paid about five times a private's salary). The reason for the huge gap between the top and the bottom of the pyramid is that Roman society was far more hierarchical than a modern one. A *praefectus* was not just a senior officer. He was also a Roman citizen (which most of his men were not) and, as a member of the equestrian order, an aristocrat. The social gulf between the *praefectus* and a *peregrinus* soldier was thus immense, and the pay differential reflected that fact.

Names, titles and decorations

Regimental names

The nomenclature of the great majority of regiments followed a standard configuration: unit type, followed by serial number, followed by name of the *peregrini* tribe (or nation) from whom the regiment was originally raised, in the genitive plural case e.g. *cohors III Batavorum* ("3rd Cohort of Batavi"); *cohors I Brittonum* ("1st Cohort of Britons"). Some regiments combine the names of two *peregrini* tribes, most likely after the merger of two previously separate regiments e.g. *ala I Pannoniorum et Gallorum* ("1st Wing of Pannonii and Gauls"). A minority of regiments are named after an individual, mostly after the first prefect of the regiment, e.g. *ala Sulpicia* (presumably named after a prefect whose middle (*gens*) name was Sulpicius). The latter is also an example of a regiment that did not have a serial number.[385]

Titles

Regiments were often rewarded for meritorious service by the grant of an honorific title. The most sought-after was the prestigious *c.R.* (*civium Romanorum* = "of Roman citizens") title. In the latter case, all the regiment's members at the time, but not their successors, would be granted Roman citizenship. But the regiment would retain the c.R. title in perpetuity. Another common title was the *gens* name of the emperor making the award (or founding the regiment) e.g. *Ulpia*: the *gens* name of Trajan (Marcus Ulpius Traianus r.98–117). Other titles were similar to those given to the legions e.g. *pia fidelis* (*p.f.* = "dutiful and loyal").[386]

Decorations

The Roman army awarded a variety of individual decorations (*dona*) for valour to its legionaries. *Hasta pura* was a miniature spear; *phalerae* were large medal-like bronze or silver discs worn on the cuirass; *armillae* were bracelets worn on the wrist; and torques were worn round the neck, or on the cuirass. The highest awards were the *coronae* ("crowns"), of which the most prestigious was the *corona civica*, a crown made of oak-leaves awarded for saving the life of a Roman citizen in battle. The most valuable award was the *corona muralis*, a crown made of gold awarded to the first man to scale an enemy rampart. This was awarded rarely, as such a man hardly ever survived.

There is no evidence that auxiliary common soldiers received individual decorations, although auxiliary officers did. Instead, the whole regiment was honoured by a title reflecting the type of award e.g. *torquata* (awarded a torque) or *armillata* (awarded bracelets). Some regiments would, in the course of time, accumulate a long list of titles and decorations e.g. *cohors I Brittonum Ulpia torquata pia fidelis c.R..*

Deployment in the 2nd century

Imperial auxilia: Summary of known deployments c. 130 AD[387]

Province	Approx. modern equivalent	Alae (no. mill.)	Cohortes (no. mill.)	Total aux. units	Auxiliary infantry	Auxiliary cavalry*	Total auxilia
Britannia	England/Wales	11 (1)	45 (6)	56	25,520	10,688	36,208
Rhine Frontier							
Germania Inferior	S Neth/NW Rhineland	6	17	23	8,160	4,512	12,672
Germania Superior	Pfalz/Alsace	3	22 (1)	25	10,880	3,336	14,216
Danube Frontier							
Raetia/-Noricum	S Ger/Switz/-Austria	7 (1)	20 (5)	27	11,220	5,280	16,500
Pannonia (Inf + Sup)	W Hungary/-Slovenia/-Croatia	11 (2)	21 (4)	32	11,360	8,304	19,664
Moesia Superior	Serbia	2	10	12	4,800	1,864	6,664
Moesia Inferior	N Bulgaria/-coastal Rom	5	12	17	5,760	3,520	9,280
Dacia (Inf/-Sup/Poroliss)	Romania	11 (1)	32 (8)	43	17,920	7,328	25,248
Eastern Frontier							
Cappadocia	Central/East Turkey	4	15 (2)	19	7,840	3,368	11,208
Syria (inc Judaea/-Arabia)	Syria/Leb/-Palest/Jordan/-Israel	12 (1)	43 (3)	55	21,600	10,240	31,840
North Africa							
Aegyptus	Egypt	4	11	15	5,280	3,008	8,288

Mauretania (inc Africa)	Tunisia/-Algeria/-Morocco	10 *(1)*	30 *(1)*	40	14,720	7,796	**22,516**
Internal provinces		2	15	17	7,200	2,224	**9,424**
Total Empire		88 *(7)*	293 *(30)*	381	152,260	71,468	**223,728**

Notes: (1) Table excludes about 2,000 officers (centurions and above). (2) Auxiliary cavalry nos. assumes 70% of *cohortes* were *equitatae*

Analysis

1. The table shows the importance of auxiliary troops in the 2nd century, when they outnumbered legionaries by 1.5 to 1.
2. The table shows that legions did not have a standard complement of auxiliary regiments[388] and that there was no fixed ratio of auxiliary regiments to legions in each province. The ratio varied from six regiments per legion in Cappadocia to 40 per legion in Mauretania.
3. Overall, cavalry represented about 20% (including the small contingents of legionary cavalry) of the total army effectives. But there were variations: in Mauretania the cavalry proportion was 28%.
4. The figures show the massive deployments in Britannia and Dacia. Together, these two provinces account for 27% of the total auxilia corps.

References

Ancient

- Arrian *Acies contra Alanos* (early 2nd century)
- Dio Cassius *Roman History* (mid-3rd century)
- Suetonius *De vita Caesarum* (early 2nd century)
- Tacitus *Agricola* (end of 1st century)
- Tacitus *Annales* (end of 1st century)
- Tacitus *Historiae* (end of 1st century)
- Vegetius *De re militari* (late 4th century)

Modern

- Birley, Anthony (2002). *Band of Brothers: Garrison Life at Vindolanda*.
- Burton, G. (1988). The Roman World *(J. Wacher ed.)*.
- Campbell, Brian (2005). *'The Army" in Cambridge Ancient History 2nd Ed Vol XII (The Crisis of Empire 193–337)*.
- Davies, R.W. (1988). *Service in the Roman Army*.

Figure 47: *Roman Empire during Hadrian's reign (AD 125)*

- Devijver, Hubert (1992). *The Equestrian Officers of the Roman Imperial Army.*
- Duncan-Jones, Richard (1990). *Structure and Scale in the Roman Economy.*
- Duncan-Jones, Richard (1994). *Money and Government in the Roman Empire.*
- Elton, Hugh (1996). *Frontiers of the Roman empire.*
- Goldsworthy, Adrian (2000). *Roman Warfare.*
- Goldsworthy, Adrian (2003). *Complete Roman Army.*
- Grant, Michael (1985). *The Roman Emperors.*
- Hassall, Mark (2000). *"The Army" in Cambridge Ancient History 2nd Ed Vol XI (The High Empire 70–192).*
- Holder, Paul (1980). *Studies in the Auxilia of the Roman Army.*
- Holder, Paul (1982). *The Roman Army in Britain.*
- Holder, Paul (2003). *Auxiliary Deployment in the Reign of Hadrian.*
- Holder, Paul (2006). *Roman Military Diplomas V.*
- Keppie, Lawrence (1996). *"The Army and the Navy" in Cambridge Ancient History 2nd Ed Vol X (The Augustan Empire 30BC – 69 AD).*
- Luttwak, Edward (1976). *Grand Strategy of the Roman Empire.*
- Mattingly, David (2006). *An Imperial Possession: Britain in the Roman Empire.*

- Jones, A.H.M. (1964). *The Later Roman Empire*.
- Rossi, L. (1971). *Trajan's Column and the Dacian Wars*.
- Roxan, Margaret (2003). *Roman Military Diplomas IV*.
- Spaul, John (2000). *COHORS2*.

External links

- Roman Military Diplomas Online[389]
- Batavian auxiliaries re-enactors[390]
- List of auxiliary units in Britain[391]
- Vindolanda Tablets Online[392]

List of Roman generals

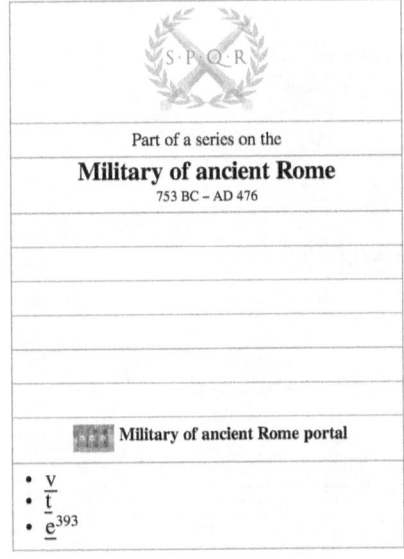

Part of a series on the
Military of ancient Rome
753 BC – AD 476

Military of ancient Rome portal

- v
- t
- e[393]

Roman generals were often career statesmen, remembered by history for reasons other than their service in the Roman Army. This page encompasses men whom history remembers for their accomplishments commanding Roman armies on land and sea.

A

- Manius Acilius Glabrio (consul 67 BC)[394]
- Manius Acilius Glabrio (consul 191 BC)[395]
- Titus Aebutius Elva[396]
- Aegidius
- Lucius Aemilius Barbula
- Marcus Aemilius Lepidus (triumvir)
- Lucius Aemilius Paulus Macedonicus
- Marcus Aemilius Scaurus (praetor 56 BC)
- Marcus Antonius Orator[397]
- Gaius Antonius[398]
- Lucius Antonius (brother of Mark Antony)
- Marcus Antonius Creticus[399]
- Mark Antony
- Manius Aquillius (129 BC)
- Arrian
- Lucius Artorius Castus
- Gaius Asinius Pollio (consul 40 BC)
- Aulus Atilius Calatinus[400]
- Marcus Atilius Regulus[401]
- Publius Attius Varus[402]
- Aureolus[403]
- Graltinus Maximus Aurelius

B

- Lucius Cornelius Balbus (minor) – defeated the Garamantes
- Barbatio
- Lucilius Bassus
- Publius Ventidius Bassus
- Bonifacius
- Bonosus (usurper)
- Decimus Junius Brutus Albinus – commanded Caesar's fleet in the war against the Veneti
- Decimus Junius Brutus Callaicus – led the Roman legions in the conquest of western Iberia
- [Marcus Junius Brutus the Younger]

C

- Quintus Caecilius Metellus[404]
- Aulus Caecina Alienus
- Marcus Calpurnius Bibulus
- Gaius Calpurnius Piso (consul 67 BC)
- Gaius Carrinas (general)
- Gaius Carrinas (consul 43 BC)
- Gaius Cassius Longinus
- Quintus Tullius Cicero
- Gaius Julius Civilis
- Appius Claudius Caudex
- Marcus Claudius Marcellus
- Gaius Claudius Nero
- Claudius Pompeianus
- Publius Claudius Pulcher
- Lucius Clodius Macer
- Gnaeus Domitius Corbulo
- Gaius Marcius Coriolanus
- Lucius Cornelius Cinna
- Gnaeus Cornelius Lentulus Clodianus
- Publius Cornelius Lentulus Spinther
- Lucius Cornelius Lentulus
- Scipio Aemilianus Africanus
- Publius Cornelius Scipio
- Scipio Asiaticus
- Lucius Cornelius Scipio Barbatus
- Publius Cornelius Scipio Nasica[405]

D

- Publius Decius Mus (279 BC) – fought Pyrrhus of Epirus at the Battle of Asculum (279 BC)
- Publius Decius Mus (340 BC) – awarded the Grass Crown during First Samnite War
- Publius Decius Mus (312 BC)
- Dexippus
- Aulus Didius Gallus
- Titus Didius
- Gnaeus Domitius Ahenobarbus (consul 32 BC)
- Gnaeus Domitius Ahenobarbus (consul 122 BC)
- Gnaeus Domitius Calvinus

- Nero Claudius Drusus
- Julius Caesar Drusus
- Gaius Duilius

F

- Quintus Fabius Maximus Rullianus[406]
- Quintus Fabius Maximus Verrusosus[407]
- Fabius Valens
- Gaius Flaminius
- Gaius Flavius Fimbria
- Quintus Fufius Calenus
- Fullofaudes
- Marcus Fulvius Flaccus (consul 125 BC)
- Marcus Fulvius Flaccus (consul 264 BC)
- Quintus Fulvius Flaccus
- Quintus Fulvius Flaccus (consul 179 BC)
- Marcus Fulvius Nobilior
- Marcus Furius Camillus
- Flavius Aetius
- Cornelius Fuscus

G

- Aulus Gabinius[408]
- Gaius Julius Caesar the Elder
- Servius Sulpicius Galba (praetor 54 BC)
- Cestius Gallus
- Lucius Gellius Publicola
- Germanicus
- Gundobad
- Gaius Salvius Liberalis

H

- Gnaeus Hosidius Geta – defeated Sabalus, chief of the Mauri

J

- Lucius Julius Caesar
- Julius Caesar
- Lucius Junius Brutus founder of Roman republic

L

- Gaius Laelius
- Titus Larcius
- Marcus Aemilius Lepidus (consul AD 6)
- Publius Licinius Crassus Dives Mucianus
- Marcus Licinius Crassus
- Lucius Licinius Lucullus
- Litorius
- Lucullus
- Mucianus
- Quintus Ligarius
- Marcus Livius Salinator
- Marcus Lollius
- Quintus Lollius Urbicus
- Lucius Caecilius Metellus Denter
- Lucius Pinarius
- Gaius Lutatius Catulus
- Quintus Lutatius Catulus

M

- Gnaeus Mallius Maximus
- Titus Manlius Torquatus (consul 347 BC)
- Titus Manlius Torquatus (235 BC)
- Lucius Manlius Vulso Longus
- Gaius Marcius Rutilus
- Marcius Turbo
- Gaius Marius – initiated "Marian reforms" of the army
- Gaius Marius the Younger
- Lucius Mummius Achaicus
- Marcus Valerius Maximianus

N

- Tiberius Nero – commanded Caesar's fleet in the Alexandrian War
- Gaius Norbanus Flaccus
- Gaius Norbanus

O

- Gaius Octavius – put down a slave rebellion at Thurii •
- Gnaeus Octavius
- Odaenathus
- Lucius Opimius
- Publius Ostorius Scapula – responsible for the defeat and capture of Caratacus

P

- Gnaeus Papirius Carbo
- Lucius Papirius Cursor
- Tiberius Claudius Paulinus
- Marcus Perperna Vento
- Marcus Perperna
- Quintus Petillius Cerialis
- Publius Petronius Turpilianus
- Lucius Calpurnius Piso (consul 15 BC)
- Aulus Plautius[409]
- Gnaeus Pompeius
- Pompey
- Sextus Pompeius
- Pompeius Strabo
- Pomponius Secundus
- Marcus Popillius Laenas
- Marcus Popillius Laenas (consul 173 BC)
- Lucius Postumius Albinus
- Marcus Antonius Primus
- Publius Cornelius Dolabella (consul 283 BC)
- Marcus Pupius Piso Frugi Calpurnianus

Q

- Lusius Quietus
- Lucius Quinctius Cincinnatus – dictator
- Publius Quinctilius Varus – lost three Roman legions and his own life when attacked by Germanic leader Arminius in the Battle of the Teutoburg Forest
- Titus Quinctius Flamininus
- Quintus Aemilius
- Quintus Pedius

R

- Ricimer
- Marcus Roscius Coelius
- Publius Rutilius Lupus (consul 90 BC)
- Publius Rutilius Rufus

S

- Quintus Salvidienus Rufus
- Gaius Scribonius Curio
- Sejanus
- Tiberius Sempronius Gracchus (consul 238 BC)
- Tiberius Sempronius Gracchus (consul 215 and 213 BC)
- Tiberius Gracchus Major
- Tiberius Sempronius Longus (consul 194 BCE)
- Tiberius Sempronius Longus (consul 218 BC)
- Marcus Sergius
- Quintus Sertorius
- Gaius Servilius Ahala
- Quintus Servilius Caepio
- Gnaeus Servilius Geminus
- Quintus Servilius Caepio the Younger
- Sextus Julius Severus
- Lucius Cornelius Sisenna
- Lucius Flavius Silva
- Gaius Sosius
- Staurakios the eunuch[410]
- Stilicho
- Gaius Suetonius Paulinus[411]
- Faustus (II) Cornelius Sulla

- Publius Cornelius Sulla
- Publius Sulpicius Galba Maximus[412]
- Servius Sulpicius Galba (consul 144 BC)
- Publius Sulpicius Rufus
- Syagrius
- Scipio
- Sextus Calpurnius Classicus (senator and general of Hadrian)

T

- Marcus Terentius Varro Lucullus[413]
- Gaius Terentius Varro
- Titus Vinius
- Trebonius

U

- Ursicinus (Roman general) – Entrusted to suppress the Jewish revolt against Gallus (Constantius Gallus)

V

- Valens (usurper)
- Marcus Valerius Corvus[414]
- Gaius Valerius Flaccus (consul)
- Lucius Valerius Flaccus
- Publius Valerius Laevinus
- M. Valerius Laevinus
- Manius Valerius Maximus Corvinus Messalla
- Marcus Valerius Messalla Corvinus
- Flavius Valila Theodosius
- Marcus Vipsanius Agrippa[415]

Navy

Roman navy

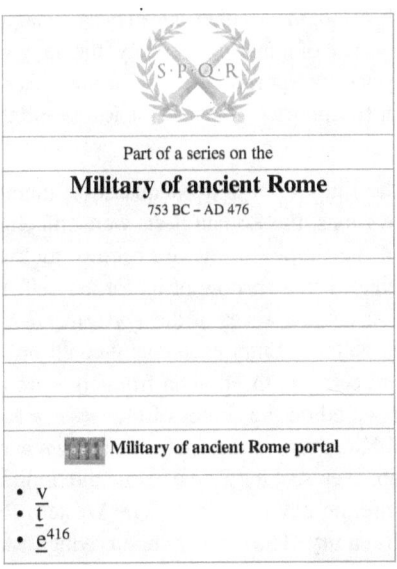

Part of a series on the
Military of ancient Rome
753 BC – AD 476

Military of ancient Rome portal

- v
- t
- e[416]

The **Roman navy** (Latin: *Classis*, lit. "fleet") comprised the naval forces of the Ancient Roman state. The navy was instrumental in the Roman conquest of the Mediterranean basin, but it never enjoyed the prestige of the Roman legions. Throughout their history, the Romans remained a primarily land-based people and relied partially on their more nautically inclined subjects, such as the Greeks and the Egyptians, to build their ships. Because of that, the navy was never completely embraced by the Roman state, and deemed somewhat "un-Roman".

In Antiquity, navies and trading fleets did not have the logistical autonomy that modern ships and fleets possess. Unlike modern naval forces, the Roman navy even at its height never existed as an autonomous service but operated as an adjunct to the Roman army.

During the course of the First Punic War, the Roman navy was massively expanded and played a vital role in the Roman victory and the Roman Republic's eventual ascension to hegemony in the Mediterranean Sea. In the course of the first half of the 2nd century BC, Rome went on to destroy Carthage and subdue the Hellenistic kingdoms of the eastern Mediterranean, achieving complete mastery of the inland sea, which they called *Mare Nostrum*. The Roman fleets were again prominent in the 1st century BC in the wars against the pirates, and in the civil wars that brought down the Republic, whose campaigns ranged across the Mediterranean. In 31 BC, the great naval Battle of Actium ended the civil wars culminating in the final victory of Augustus and the establishment of the Roman Empire.

During the Imperial period, the Mediterranean became largely a peaceful "Roman lake". In the absence of a maritime enemy, the navy was reduced mostly to patrol, anti-piracy and transport duties.[417] The navy also manned and maintained craft on major frontier rivers such as the Rhine and the Danube for supplying the army.

On the fringes of the Empire, in new conquests or, increasingly, in defense against barbarian invasions, the Roman fleets were still engaged in open warfare. The decline of the Empire in the 3rd century took a heavy toll on the navy, which was reduced to a shadow of its former self, both in size and in combat ability. As successive waves of the *Völkerwanderung* crashed on the land frontiers of the battered Empire, the navy could only play a secondary role. In the early 5th century, the Roman frontiers were breached, and barbarian kingdoms appeared on the shores of the western Mediterranean. One of them, the Vandal Kingdom, raised a navy of its own and raided the shores of the Mediterranean, even sacking Rome, while the diminished Roman fleets were incapable of offering any resistance. The Western Roman Empire collapsed in the late 5th century. The navy of the surviving eastern Roman Empire is known as the Byzantine navy.

History

Early Republic

The exact origins of the Roman fleet are obscure. A traditionally agricultural and land-based society, the Romans rarely ventured out to sea, unlike their Etruscan neighbours. There is evidence of Roman warships in the early 4th century BC, such as mention of a warship that carried an embassy to Delphi in 394 BC, but at any rate, the Roman fleet, if it existed, was negligible. The traditional birth date of the Roman navy is set at ca. 311 BC, when, after the conquest of Campania, two new officials, the *duumviri navales classis ornandae reficiendaeque causa*, were tasked with the maintenance of a fleet.[418] As a result, the Republic acquired its first fleet, consisting of 20 ships, most likely triremes, with each *duumvir* commanding a squadron of 10 ships. However, the Republic continued to rely mostly on her legions for expansion in Italy; the navy was most likely geared towards combating piracy and lacked experience in naval warfare, being easily defeated in 282 BC by the Tarentines.

This situation continued until the First Punic War: the main task of the Roman fleet was patrolling along the Italian coast and rivers, protecting seaborne trade from piracy. Whenever larger tasks had to be undertaken, such as the naval blockade of a besieged city, the Romans called on the allied Greek cities of southern Italy, the *socii navales*, to provide ships and crews.[419] It is possible that the supervision of these maritime allies was one of the duties of the four new *praetores classici*, who were established in 267 BC.[420]

First Punic War

The first Roman expedition outside mainland Italy was against the island of Sicily in 265 BC. This led to the outbreak of hostilities with Carthage, which would last until 241 BC. At the time, the Punic city was the unchallenged master of the western Mediterranean, possessing a long maritime and naval experience and a large fleet. Although Rome had relied on her legions for the conquest of Italy, operations in Sicily had to be supported by a fleet, and the ships available by Rome's allies were insufficient. Thus in 261 BC, the Roman Senate set out to construct a fleet of 100 quinqueremes and 20 triremes. According to Polybius, the Romans seized a shipwrecked Carthaginian quinquereme, and used it as a blueprint for their own ships.[421] The new fleets were commanded by the annually elected Roman magistrates, but naval expertise was provided by the lower officers, who continued to be provided by the *socii*, mostly Greeks. This practice was continued until well into the Empire, something also attested by the direct adoption of numerous Greek naval terms.[422]

Figure 48: *Three-banked ("trireme") Roman quinquereme with the corvus boarding bridge. The use of the corvus negated the superior Carthaginian naval expertise, and allowed the Romans to establish their naval superiority in the western Mediterranean.*

Despite the massive buildup, the Roman crews remained inferior in naval experience to the Carthaginians, and could not hope to match them in naval tactics, which required great maneuverability and experience. They therefore employed a novel weapon which transformed sea warfare to their advantage. They equipped their ships with the *corvus*, possibly developed earlier by the Syracusans against the Athenians. This was a long plank with a spike for hooking onto enemy ships. Using it as a boarding bridge, marines were able to board an enemy ship, transforming sea combat into a version of land combat, where the Roman legionaries had the upper hand. However, it is believed that the *corvus*' weight made the ships unstable, and could capsize a ship in rough seas.[423]

Although the first sea engagement of the war, the Battle of the Lipari Islands in 260 BC, was a defeat for Rome, the forces involved were relatively small. Through the use of the *corvus*, the fledgling Roman navy under Gaius Duilius won its first major engagement later that year at the Battle of Mylae. During the course of the war, Rome continued to be victorious at sea: victories at Sulci (258 BC) and Tyndaris (257 BC) were followed by the massive Battle of Cape Ecnomus, where the Roman fleet under the consuls Marcus Atilius Regulus

Figure 49: *Roman as coin of the second half of the 3rd century BC, featuring the prow of a galley, most likely a quinquereme. Several similar issues are known, illustrating the importance of naval power during that period of Rome's history.*

and Lucius Manlius inflicted a severe defeat on the Carthaginians. This string of successes allowed Rome to push the war further across the sea to Africa and Carthage itself. Continued Roman success also meant that their navy gained significant experience, although it also suffered a number of catastrophic losses due to storms, while conversely, the Carthaginian navy suffered from attrition.

The Battle of Drepana in 249 BC resulted in the only major Carthaginian sea victory, forcing the Romans to equip a new fleet from donations by private citizens. In the last battle of the war, at Aegates Islands in 241 BC, the Romans under Gaius Lutatius Catulus displayed superior seamanship to the Carthaginians, notably using their rams rather than the now-abandoned *corvus* to achieve victory.

Illyria and the Second Punic War

After the Roman victory, the balance of naval power in the Western Mediterranean had shifted from Carthage to Rome. This ensured Carthaginian acquiescence to the conquest of Sardinia and Corsica, and also enabled Rome to deal decisively with the threat posed by the Illyrian pirates in the Adriatic. The Illyrian Wars marked Rome's first involvement with the affairs of the Balkan peninsula.[424] Initially, in 229 BC, a fleet of 200 warships was sent against Queen Teuta, and swiftly expelled the Illyrian garrisons from the Greek coastal cities of modern-day Albania. Ten years later, the Romans sent another expedition in the area against Demetrius of Pharos, who had rebuilt the Illyrian navy and engaged in piracy up into the Aegean. Demetrius was supported by Philip V of Macedon, who had grown anxious at the expansion of Roman power in

Illyria. The Romans were again quickly victorious and expanded their Illyrian protectorate, but the beginning of the Second Punic War (218–201 BC) forced them to divert their resources westwards for the next decades.

Due to Rome's command of the seas, Hannibal, Carthage's great general, was forced to eschew a sea-borne invasion, instead choosing to bring the war over land to the Italian peninsula. Unlike the first war, the navy played little role on either side in this war. The only naval encounters occurred in the first years of the war, at Lilybaeum (218 BC) and the Ebro River (217 BC), both resulting Roman victories. Despite an overall numerical parity, for the remainder of the war the Carthaginians did not seriously challenge Roman supremacy. The Roman fleet was hence engaged primarily with raiding the shores of Africa and guarding Italy, a task which included the interception of Carthaginian convoys of supplies and reinforcements for Hannibal's army, as well as keeping an eye on a potential intervention by Carthage's ally, Philip V. The only major action in which the Roman fleet was involved was the siege of Syracuse in 214-212 BC with 130 ships under Marcus Claudius Marcellus. The siege is remembered for the ingenious inventions of Archimedes, such as mirrors that burned ships or the so-called "Claw of Archimedes", which kept the besieging army at bay for two years. A fleet of 160 vessels was assembled to support Scipio Africanus' army in Africa in 202 BC, and, should his expedition fail, evacuate his men. In the event, Scipio achieved a decisive victory at Zama, and the subsequent peace stripped Carthage of its fleet.

Operations in the East

Rome was now the undisputed master of the Western Mediterranean, and turned her gaze from defeated Carthage to the Hellenistic world. Small Roman forces had already been engaged in the First Macedonian War, when, in 214 BC, a fleet under Marcus Valerius Laevinus had successfully thwarted Philip V from invading Illyria with his newly built fleet. The rest of the war was carried out mostly by Rome's allies, the Aetolian League and later the Kingdom of Pergamon, but a combined Roman-Pergamene fleet of ca. 60 ships patrolled the Aegean until the war's end in 205 BC. In this conflict, Rome, still embroiled in the Punic War, was not interested in expanding her possessions, but rather in thwarting the growth of Philip's power in Greece. The war ended in an effective stalemate, and was renewed in 201 BC, when Philip V invaded Asia Minor. A naval battle off Chios ended in a costly victory for the Pergamene-Rhodian alliance, but the Macedonian fleet lost many warships, including its flagship, a *deceres*. Soon after, Pergamon and Rhodes appealed to Rome for help, and the Republic was drawn into the Second Macedonian War. In view of the massive Roman naval superiority, the war was fought on land, with the Macedonian fleet, already weakened at Chios, not daring to venture out of its anchorage at Demetrias. After the crushing Roman victory

Figure 50: *A Roman naval bireme depicted in a relief from the Temple of Fortuna Primigenia in Praeneste (Palastrina),*[425] *which was built c. 120 BC;*[426] *exhibited in the Pius-Clementine Museum (Museo Pio-Clementino) in the Vatican Museums.*

at Cynoscephalae, the terms imposed on Macedon were harsh, and included the complete disbandment of her navy.

Almost immediately following the defeat of Macedon, Rome became embroiled in a war with the Seleucid Empire. This war too was decided mainly on land, although the combined Roman-Rhodian navy also achieved victories over the Seleucids at Myonessus and Eurymedon. These victories, which were invariably concluded with the imposition of peace treaties that prohibited the maintenance of anything but token naval forces, spelled the disappearance of the Hellenistic royal navies, leaving Rome and her allies unchallenged at sea. Coupled with the final destruction of Carthage, and the end of Macedon's independence, by the latter half of the 2nd century BC, Roman control over all of what was later to be dubbed *mare nostrum* ("our sea") had been established. Subsequently, the Roman navy was drastically reduced, depending on its Socii navales.[427]

Figure 51: *Pompey the Great. His swift and decisive campaign against the pirates re-established Rome's control over the Mediterranean sea lanes.*

Late Republic

Mithridates and the pirate threat

In the absence of a strong naval presence however, piracy flourished throughout the Mediterranean, especially in Cilicia, but also in Crete and other places, further reinforced by money and warships supplied by King Mithridates VI of Pontus, who hoped to enlist their aid in his wars against Rome.[428] In the First Mithridatic War (89–85 BC), Sulla had to requisition ships wherever he could find them to counter Mithridates' fleet. Despite the makeshift nature of the Roman fleet however, in 86 BC Lucullus defeated the Pontic navy at Tenedos.[429]

Immediately after the end of the war, a permanent force of ca. 100 vessels was established in the Aegean from the contributions of Rome's allied maritime states. Although sufficient to guard against Mithridates, this force was totally inadequate against the pirates, whose power grew rapidly. Over the next decade, the pirates defeated several Roman commanders, and raided unhindered even to the shores of Italy, reaching Rome's harbor, Ostia.[430] According to the account of Plutarch, "the ships of the pirates numbered more than a thousand, and the cities captured by them four hundred."[431] Their activity posed a growing threat for the Roman economy, and a challenge to Roman power: several prominent Romans, including two praetors with their retinue and the young Julius Caesar, were captured and held for ransom. Perhaps most important of all, the pirates disrupted Rome's vital lifeline, namely the massive shipments of grain and other produce from Africa and Egypt that were needed to sustain the city's population.[432]

The resulting grain shortages were a major political issue, and popular discontent threatened to become explosive. In 74 BC, with the outbreak of the Third Mithridatic War, Marcus Antonius (the father of Mark Antony) was appointed *praetor* with extraordinary *imperium* against the pirate threat, but signally failed in his task: he was defeated off Crete in 72 BC, and died shortly after.[433] Finally, in 67 BC the *Lex Gabinia* was passed in the Plebeian Council, vesting Pompey with unprecedented powers and authorizing him to move against them.[434] In a massive and concerted campaign, Pompey cleared the seas from the pirates in only three months.[427,435] Afterwards, the fleet was reduced again to policing duties against intermittent piracy.

Caesar and the Civil Wars

In 56 BC, for the first time a Roman fleet engaged in battle outside the Mediterranean. This occurred during Julius Caesar's Gallic Wars, when the maritime tribe of the Veneti rebelled against Rome. Against the Veneti, the Romans were at a disadvantage, since they did not know the coast, and were inexperienced in fighting in the open sea with its tides and currents.[436] Furthermore, the Veneti ships were superior to the light Roman galleys. They were built of oak and had no oars, being thus more resistant to ramming. In addition, their greater height gave them an advantage in both missile exchanges and boarding actions.[437] In the event, when the two fleets encountered each other in Quiberon Bay, Caesar's navy, under the command of D. Brutus, resorted to the use of hooks on long poles, which cut the halyards supporting the Veneti sails.[438] Immobile, the Veneti ships were easy prey for the legionaries who boarded them, and fleeing Veneti ships were taken when they became becalmed by a sudden lack of winds.[439] Having thus established his control of the English Channel, in the next years Caesar used this newly built fleet to carry out two invasions of Britain.

The last major campaigns of the Roman navy in the Mediterranean until the late 3rd century AD would be in the civil wars that ended the Republic. In the East, the Republican faction quickly established its control, and Rhodes, the last independent maritime power in the Aegean, was subdued by Gaius Cassius Longinus in 43 BC, after its fleet was defeated off Kos. In the West, against the triumvirs stood Sextus Pompeius, who had been given command of the Italian fleet by the Senate in 43 BC. He took control of Sicily and made it his base, blockading Italy and stopping the politically crucial supply of grain

Figure 52: *Silver denarius struck by Sextus Pompeius in 44–43 BC, featuring a bust of Pompey the Great and a Roman warship.*

Figure 53: *The Battle of Actium, by Laureys a Castro, painted 1672.*

from Africa to Rome. After suffering a defeat from Sextus in 42 BC, Octavian initiated massive naval armaments, aided by his closest associate, Marcus Agrippa: ships were built at Ravenna and Ostia, the new artificial harbor of Portus Julius built at Cumae, and soldiers and rowers levied, including over 20,000 manumitted slaves. Finally, Octavian and Agrippa defeated Sextus in the Battle of Naulochus in 36 BC, putting an end to all Pompeian resistance.

Octavian's power was further enhanced after his victory against the combined fleets of Mark Antony and Cleopatra, Queen of Egypt, in the Battle of Actium in 31 BC, where Antony had assembled 500 ships against Octavian's 400 ships. This last naval battle of the Roman Republic definitively established Octavian as the sole ruler over Rome and the Mediterranean world. In the aftermath of his victory, he formalized the Fleet's structure, establishing several key harbors in the Mediterranean (see below). The now fully professional navy had its main duties consist of protecting against piracy, escorting troops and patrolling the river frontiers of Europe. It remained however engaged in active warfare in the periphery of the Empire.

Principate

Operations under Augustus

Under Augustus and after the conquest of Egypt there were increasing demands from the Roman economy to extend the trade lanes to India. The Arabian control of all sea routes to India was an obstacle. One of the first naval operations under *princeps* Augustus was therefore the preparation for a campaign on the Arabian Peninsula. Aelius Gallus, the prefect of Egypt ordered the construction of 130 transports and subsequently carried 10,000 soldiers to Arabia. But the following march through the desert towards Yemen failed and the plans for control of the Arabian peninsula had to be abandoned.

At the other end of the Empire, in Germania, the navy played an important role in the supply and transport of the legions. In 15 BC an independent fleet was installed at the Lake Constance. Later, the generals Drusus and Tiberius used the Navy extensively, when they tried to extend the Roman frontier to the Elbe. In 12 BC Drusus ordered the construction of a fleet of 1,000 ships and sailed them along the Rhine into the North Sea.[440] The Frisii and Chauci had nothing to oppose the superior numbers, tactics and technology of the Romans. When these entered the river mouths of Weser and Ems, the local tribes had to surrender.

In 5 BC the Roman knowledge concerning the North and Baltic Sea was fairly extended during a campaign by Tiberius, reaching as far as the Elbe: Plinius describes how Roman naval formations came past Heligoland and set sail to the north-eastern coast of Denmark, and Augustus himself boasts in his *Res Gestae*: "My fleet sailed from the mouth of the Rhine eastward as far as the lands of the Cimbri to which, up to that time, no Roman had ever penetrated either by land or by sea...".[441] The multiple naval operations north of Germania had to be abandoned after the battle of the Teutoburg Forest in the year 9 AD.

Julio-Claudian dynasty

In the years 15 and 16, Germanicus carried out several fleet operations along the rivers Rhine and Ems, without permanent results due to grim Germanic resistance and a disastrous storm.[442] By 28, the Romans lost further control of the Rhine mouth in a succession of Frisian insurgencies. From 43 to 85, the Roman navy played an important role in the Roman conquest of Britain. The *classis Germanica* rendered outstanding services in multitudinous landing operations. In 46, a naval expedition made a push deep into the Black Sea region and even travelled on the Tanais. In 47 a revolt by the Chauci, who took to piratical activities along the Gallic coast, was subdued by Gnaeus Domitius Corbulo.[443] By 57 an expeditionary corps reached Chersonesos (see Charax, Crimea).

It seems that under Nero, the navy obtained strategically important positions for trading with India; but there was no known fleet in the Red Sea. Possibly, parts of the Alexandrian fleet were operating as escorts for the Indian trade. In the Jewish revolt, from 66 to 70, the Romans were forced to fight Jewish ships, operating from a harbour in the area of modern Tel Aviv, on Israel's Mediterranean coast. In the meantime several flotilla engagements on the Sea of Galilee took place.

In 68, as his reign became increasingly insecure, Nero raised *legio* I *Adiutrix* from sailors of the praetorian fleets. After Nero's overthrow, in 69, the "Year of the four emperors", the praetorian fleets supported Emperor Otho against the usurper Vitellius,[444] and after his eventual victory, Vespasian formed another legion, *legio* II *Adiutrix*, from their ranks.[445] Only in the Pontus did Anicetus, the commander of the *Classis Pontica*, support Vitellius. He burned the fleet, and sought refuge with the Iberian tribes, engaging in piracy. After a new fleet was built, this revolt was subdued.[446]

Flavian, Antonine and Severan dynasties

During the Batavian rebellion of Gaius Julius Civilis (69-70), the rebels got hold of a squadron of the Rhine fleet by treachery,[447] and the conflict featured frequent use of the Roman Rhine flotilla. In the last phase of the war, the British fleet and *legio* XIV were brought in from Britain to attack the Batavian coast, but the Cananefates, allies of the Batavians, were able to destroy or capture a large part of the fleet.[448] In the meantime, the new Roman commander, Quintus Petillius Cerialis, advanced north and constructed a new fleet. Civilis attempted only a short encounter with his own fleet, but could not hinder the superior Roman force from landing and ravaging the island of the Batavians, leading to the negotiation of a peace soon after.[449]

In the years 82 to 85, the Romans under Gnaeus Julius Agricola launched a campaign against the Caledonians in modern Scotland. In this context the

Figure 54: *Two-banked lburnians of the Danube fleets during Trajan's Dacian Wars. Casts of reliefs from Trajan's Column, Rome.*

Figure 55: *Mosaic of a Roman galley, Bardo Museum, Tunisia, 2nd century AD.*

Roman navy significantly escalated activities on the eastern Scottish coast.[450] Simultaneously multiple expeditions and reconnaissance trips were launched. During these the Romans would capture the Orkney Islands (*Orcades*) for a short period of time and obtained information about the Shetland Islands.[451] There is some speculation about a Roman landing in Ireland, based on Tacitus reports about Agricola contemplating the island's conquest,[452] but no conclusive evidence to support this theory has been found.

Under the Five Good Emperors the navy operated mainly on the rivers; so it played an important role during Trajan's conquest of Dacia and temporarily an independent fleet for the Euphrates and Tigris rivers was founded. Also during the wars against the Marcomanni confederation under Marcus Aurelius several combats took place on the Danube and the Tisza.

Under the aegis of the Severan dynasty, the only known military operations of the navy were carried out under Septimius Severus, using naval assistance on his campaigns along the Euphrates and Tigris, as well as in Scotland. Thereby Roman ships reached *inter alia* the Persian Gulf and the top of the British Isles.

3rd century crisis

As the 3rd century dawned, the Roman Empire was at its peak. In the Mediterranean, peace had reigned for over two centuries, as piracy had been wiped out and no outside naval threats occurred. As a result, complacency had set in: naval tactics and technology were neglected, and the Roman naval system had become moribund.[453] After 230 however and for fifty years, the situation changed dramatically. The so-called "Crisis of the Third Century" ushered a period of internal turmoil, and the same period saw a renewed series of seaborne assaults, which the imperial fleets proved unable to stem.[454] In the West, Picts and Irish ships raided Britain, while the Saxons raided the North Sea, forcing the Romans to abandon Frisia. In the East, the Goths and other tribes from modern Ukraine raided in great numbers over the Black Sea.[455] These invasions began during the rule of Trebonianus Gallus, when for the first time Germanic tribes built up their own powerful fleet in the Black Sea. Via two surprise attacks (256) on Roman naval bases in the Caucasus and near the Danube, numerous ships fell into the hands of the Germans, whereupon the raids were extended as far as the Aegean Sea; Byzantium, Athens, Sparta and other towns were plundered and the responsible provincial fleets were heavily debilitated. It was not until the attackers made a tactical error, that their onrush could be stopped.

In 267–270 another, much fiercer series of attacks took place. A fleet composed of Heruli and other tribes raided the coasts of Thrace and the Pontus. Defeated off Byzantium by general Venerianus,[456] the barbarians fled into the Aegean, and ravaged many islands and coastal cities, including Athens and Corinth. As they retreated northwards over land, they were defeated by Emperor Gallienus at Nestos.[457] However, this was merely the prelude to an even larger invasion that was launched in 268/269: several tribes banded together (the *Historia Augusta* mentions Scythians, Greuthungi, Tervingi, Gepids, Peucini, Celts and Heruli) and allegedly 2,000 ships and 325,000 men strong,[458] raided the Thracian shore, attacked Byzantium and continued raiding the Aegean as far as Crete, while the main force approached Thessalonica. Emperor Claudius II however was able to defeat them at the Battle of Naissus, ending the Gothic threat for the time being.[459]

Barbarian raids also increased along the Rhine frontier and in the North Sea. Eutropius mentions that during the 280s, the sea along the coasts of the provinces of Belgica and Armorica was "infested with Franks and Saxons". To counter them, Maximian appointed Carausius as commander of the British Fleet.[460] However, Carausius rose up in late 286 and seceded from the Empire with Britannia and parts of the northern Gallic coast.[461] With a single blow Roman control of the channel and the North Sea was lost, and emperor Maximinus was forced to create a completely new Northern Fleet, but in lack of training it was almost immediately destroyed in a storm.[462] Only in 293, under *Caesar* Constantius Chlorus did Rome regain the Gallic coast. A new fleet was constructed in order to cross the Channel,[463] and in 296, with a concentric attack on Londinium the insurgent province was retaken.[464]

Late Antiquity

By the end of the 3rd century, the Roman navy had declined dramatically. Although Emperor Diocletian is held to have strengthened the navy, and increased its manpower from 46,000 to 64,000 men,[465] the old standing fleets had all but vanished, and in the civil wars that ended the Tetrarchy, the opposing sides had to mobilize the resources and commandeered the ships of the Eastern Mediterranean port cities. These conflicts thus brought about a renewal of naval activity, culminating in the Battle of the Hellespont in 324 between the forces of Constantine I under Caesar Crispus and the fleet of Licinius, which was the only major naval confrontation of the 4th century. Vegetius, writing at the end of the 4th century, testifies to the disappearance of the old praetorian fleets in Italy, but comments on the continued activity of the Danube fleet.[466] In the 5th century, only the eastern half of the Empire could field an effective fleet, as it could draw upon the maritime resources of Greece and the Levant. Although the *Notitia Dignitatum* still mentions several naval units for the Western Empire, these were apparently too depleted to be able to carry out much more than patrol duties.[467] At any rate, the rise of the naval power of the Vandal Kingdom under Geiseric in North Africa, and its raids in the Western Mediterranean, were practically uncontested. Although there is some

Figure 56: *Roman warship on a denarius of Mark Antony*

evidence of West Roman naval activity in the first half of the 5th century, this is mostly confined to troop transports and minor landing operations. The historian Priscus and Sidonius Apollinaris affirm in their writings that by the mid-5th century, the Western Empire essentially lacked a war navy.[468] Matters became even worse after the disastrous failure of the fleets mobilized against the Vandals in 460 and 468, under the emperors Majorian and Anthemius.

For the West, there would be no recovery, as the last Western Emperor, Romulus Augustulus, was deposed in 476. In the East however, the classical naval tradition survived, and in the 6th century, a standing navy was reformed. The East Roman (Byzantine) navy would remain a formidable force in the Mediterranean until the 11th century.

Organization

Crews

The bulk of a galley's crew was formed by the rowers, the *remiges* (sing. *remex*) or *eretai* (sing. *eretēs*) in Greek. Despite popular perceptions, the Roman fleet, and ancient fleets in general, relied throughout their existence on rowers of free status, and not on galley slaves. Slaves were employed only in times of pressing manpower demands or extreme emergency, and even then, they were freed first.[469] In Imperial times, non-citizen freeborn provincials (*peregrini*), chiefly from nations with a maritime background such as Greeks, Phoenicians, Syrians and Egyptians, formed the bulk of the fleets' crews.[470]

During the early Principate, a ship's crew, regardless of its size, was organized as a *centuria*. Crewmen could sign on as marines (Called Marinus), rowers/seamen, craftsmen and various other jobs, though all personnel serving in the imperial fleet were classed as *milites* ("soldiers"), regardless of their function; only when differentiation with the army was required, were the adjectives *classiarius* or *classicus* added. Along with several other instances of prevalence of army terminology, this testifies to the lower social status of naval personnel, considered inferior to the auxiliaries and the legionaries. Emperor Claudius first gave legal privileges to the navy's crewmen, enabling them to receive Roman citizenship after their period of service. This period was initially set at a minimum of 26 years (one year more than the legions), and was later expanded to 28. Upon honorable discharge (*honesta missio*), the sailors received a sizable cash payment as well.

As in the army, the ship's *centuria* was headed by a centurion with an *optio* as his deputy, while a *beneficiarius* supervised a small administrative staff. Among the crew were also a number of *principales* (junior officers) and *immunes* (specialists exempt from certain duties). Some of these positions, mostly administrative, were identical to those of the army auxiliaries, while some (mostly of Greek provenance) were peculiar to the fleet. An inscription from the island of Cos, dated to the First Mithridatic War, provides us with a list of a ship's officers, the *nautae*: the *gubernator* (*kybernētēs* in Greek) was the helmsman or pilot, the *celeusta* (*keleustēs* in Greek) supervised the rowers, a *proreta* (*prōreus* in Greek) was the look-out stationed at the bow, a *pentacontarchos* was apparently a junior officer, and an *iatros* (Lat. *medicus*), the ship's doctor.

Each ship was commanded by a *trierarchus*, whose exact relationship with the ship's centurion is unclear. Squadrons, most likely of ten ships each, were put under a *nauarchus*, who often appears to have risen from the ranks of the *trierarchi*.[471,472] The post of *nauarchus archigubernes* or *nauarchus princeps* appeared later in the Imperial period, and functioned either as a commander of several squadrons or as an executive officer under a civilian admiral, equivalent to the legionary *primus pilus*.[473] All these were professional officers, usually *peregrini*, who had a status equal to an auxiliary centurion (and were thus increasingly called *centuriones* [*classiarii*] after ca. 70 AD). Until the reign of Antoninus Pius, their careers were restricted to the fleet. Only in the 3rd century were these officers equated to the legionary centurions in status and pay, and could henceforth be transferred to a similar position in the legions.[474]

High Command

During the Republic, command of a fleet was given to a serving magistrate or promagistrate, usually of consular or praetorian rank.[475] In the Punic Wars for instance, one consul would usually command the fleet, and another the army. In the subsequent wars in the Eastern Mediterranean, praetors would assume the command of the fleet. However, since these men were political appointees, the actual handling of the fleets and of separate squadrons was entrusted to their more experienced legates and subordinates. It was therefore during the Punic Wars that the separate position of *praefectus classis* ("fleet prefect") first appeared.[476]

Initially subordinate to the magistrate in command, after the fleet's reorganization by Augustus, the *praefectus classis* became a procuratorial position in charge of each of the permanent fleets. These posts were initially filled either from among the equestrian class, or, especially under Claudius, from the Emperor's freedmen, thus securing imperial control over the fleets.[477] From the period of the Flavian emperors, the status of the *praefectura* was raised, and only equestrians with military experience who had gone through the *militia equestri* were appointed.[478] Nevertheless, the prefects remained largely political appointees, and despite their military experience, usually in command of army auxiliary units, their knowledge of naval matters was minimal, forcing them to rely on their professional subordinates. The difference in importance of the fleets they commanded was also reflected by the rank and the corresponding pay of the commanders. The prefects of the two praetorian fleets were ranked *procuratores ducenarii*, meaning they earned 200,000 sesterces annually, the prefects of the *Classis Germanica*, the *Classis Britannica* and later the *Classis Pontica* were *centenarii* (i.e. earning 100,000 sesterces), while the other fleet prefects were *sexagenarii* (i.e. they received 60,000 sesterces).[479]

Ship types

The generic Roman term for an oar-driven galley warship was "long ship" (Latin: *navis longa*, Greek: *naus makra*), as opposed to the sail-driven *navis oneraria* (from *onus, oneris:* burden), a merchant vessel, or the minor craft (*navigia minora*) like the *scapha*.

The navy consisted of a wide variety of different classes of warships, from heavy polyremes to light raiding and scouting vessels. Unlike the rich Hellenistic Successor kingdoms in the East however, the Romans did not rely on heavy warships, with quinqueremes (Gk. *pentērēs*), and to a lesser extent quadriremes (Gk. *tetrērēs*) and triremes (Gk. *triērēs*) providing the mainstay of the Roman fleets from the Punic Wars to the end of the Civil Wars. The heaviest vessel mentioned in Roman fleets during this period was the hexareme, of which a few were used as flagships. Lighter vessels such as the liburnians and the hemiolia, both swift types invented by pirates, were also adopted as scouts and light transport vessels.

During the final confrontation between Octavian and Mark Antony, Octavian's fleet was composed of quinqueremes, together with some "sixes" and many

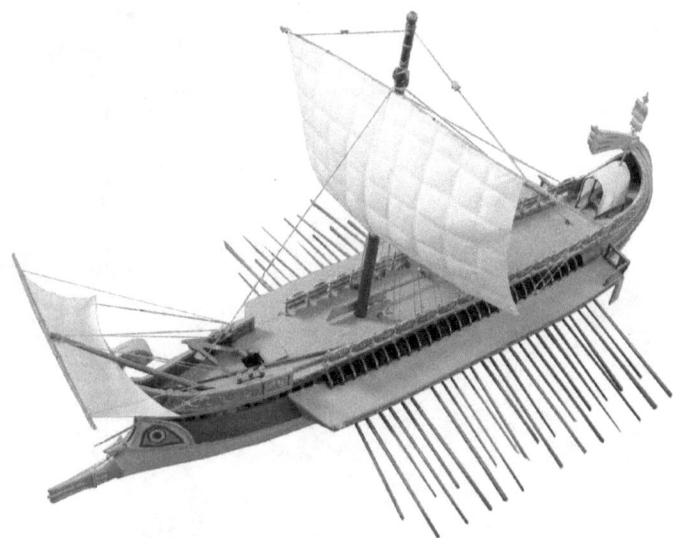

Figure 57: *Model of a Roman bireme*

triremes and liburnians, while Antony, who had the resources of Ptolemaic Egypt to draw upon, fielded a fleet also mostly composed of quinqueremes, but with a sizeable complement of heavier warships, ranging from "sixes" to "tens" (Gk. *dekērēs*).[480] Later historical tradition made much of the prevalence of lighter and swifter vessels in Octavian's fleet,[481] with Vegetius even explicitly ascribing Octavian's victory to the liburnians.[482]

This prominence of lighter craft in the historical narrative is perhaps best explained in light of subsequent developments. After Actium, the operational landscape had changed: for the remainder of the Principate, no opponent existed to challenge Roman naval hegemony, and no massed naval confrontation was likely. The tasks at hand for the Roman navy were now the policing of the Mediterranean waterways and the border rivers, suppression of piracy, and escort duties for the grain shipments to Rome and for imperial army expeditions. Lighter ships were far better suited to these tasks, and after the reorganization of the fleet following Actium, the largest ship kept in service was a hexareme, the flagship of the *Classis Misenensis*. The bulk of the fleets was composed of the lighter triremes and liburnians (Latin: *liburna*, Greek: *libyrnis*), with the latter apparently providing the majority of the provincial fleets.[483] In time, the term "liburnian" came to mean "warship" in a generic sense.[427]

In addition, there were smaller oared vessels, such as the *navis actuaria*, with 30 oars (15 on each bank), a ship primarily used for transport in coastal and

Figure 58: *Reconstruction of a late Roman navis lusoria at Mainz*

fluvial operations, for which its shallow draught and flat keel were ideal. In late Antiquity, it was succeeded in this role by the *navis lusoria* ("playful ship"), which was extensively used for patrols and raids by the legionary flotillas in the Rhine and Danube frontiers.

Roman ships were commonly named after gods (*Mars, Iuppiter, Minerva, Isis*), mythological heroes (*Hercules*), geographical maritime features such as *Rhenus* or *Oceanus*, concepts such as Harmony, Peace, Loyalty, Victory (*Concordia, Pax, Fides, Victoria*) or after important events (*Dacicus* for the Trajan's Dacian Wars or *Salamina* for the Battle of Salamis).[484] They were distinguished by their figurehead (*insigne* or *parasemum*), and, during the Civil Wars at least, by the paint schemes on their turrets, which varied according to each fleet.[485]

Armament and tactics

In Classical Antiquity, a ship's main weapon was the ram (*rostra*, hence the name *navis rostrata* for a warship), which was used to sink or immobilize an enemy ship by holing its hull. Its use, however, required a skilled and experienced crew and a fast and agile ship like a trireme or quinquereme. In the Hellenistic period, the larger navies came instead to rely on greater vessels. This

Figure 59: *Ballistae on a Roman ship*

had several advantages: the heavier and sturdier construction lessened the effects of ramming, and the greater space and stability of the vessels allowed the transport not only of more marines, but also the placement of deck-mounted ballistae and catapults.[486] Although the ram continued to be a standard feature of all warships and ramming the standard mode of attack, these developments transformed the role of a warship: from the old "manned missile", designed to sink enemy ships, they became mobile artillery platforms, which engaged in missile exchange and boarding actions. The Romans in particular, being initially inexperienced at sea combat, relied upon boarding actions through the use of the *corvus*. Although it brought them some decisive losses, it was discontinued because it tended to unbalance the quinqueremes in high seas; two Roman fleets are recorded to have been lost during storms in the First Punic War.[487]

During the Civil Wars, a number of technical innovations, which are attributed to Agrippa,[488] took place: the *harpax*, a catapult-fired grappling hook, which was used to clamp onto an enemy ship, reel it in and board it, in a much more efficient way than with the old *corvus*, and the use of collapsible fighting towers placed one apiece bow and stern, which were used to provide the boarders with supporting fire.[489]

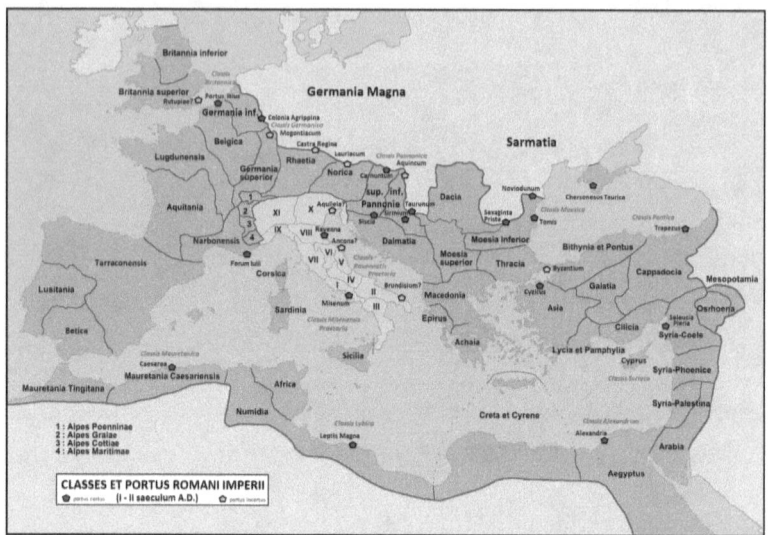

Figure 60: *Map of the Roman fleets and major naval bases during the Principate*

Fleets

Principate period

After the end of the civil wars, Augustus reduced and reorganized the Roman armed forces, including the navy. A large part of the fleet of Mark Antony was burned, and the rest was withdrawn to a new base at Forum Iulii (modern Fréjus),[490] which remained operative until the reign of Claudius. However, the bulk of the fleet was soon subdivided into two praetorian fleets at Misenum and Ravenna, supplemented by a growing number of minor ones in the provinces, which were often created on an *ad hoc* basis for specific campaigns. This organizational structure was maintained almost unchanged until the 4th century.

Praetorian fleets

The two major fleets were stationed in Italy and acted as a central naval reserve, directly available to the Emperor (hence the designation "praetorian"). In the absence of any naval threat, their duties mostly involved patrolling and transport duties. These were not confined to the waters around Italy, but throughout the Mediterranean. There is epigraphic evidence for the presence of sailors of the two praetorian fleets at Piraeus and Syria. These two fleets were:

- The *Classis Misenensis*, established in 27 BC and based at Portus Julius. Later *Classis praetoria Misenesis Pia Vindex*. Detachments of the fleet served at secondary bases, such as Ostia, Puteoli, Centumcellae and other harbors.[491]
- The *Classis Ravennas*, established in 27 BC and based at Ravenna. Later *Classis praetoria Ravennatis Pia Vindex*.

Provincial fleets

The various provincial fleets were smaller than the praetorian fleets and composed mostly of lighter vessels. Nevertheless, it was these fleets that saw action, in full campaigns or raids on the periphery of the Empire.

- The *Classis Africana Commodiana Herculea*, established by Commodus in 186 to secure the grain shipments (*annona*) from North Africa to Italy,[492] after the model of the *Classis Alexandrina*.
- The *Classis Alexandrina*, based in Alexandria, it controlled the eastern part of the Mediterranean sea. It was founded by Augustus around 30 BC, probably from ships that fought at the Battle of Actium and manned mostly by Greeks of the Nile Delta.[493] Having supported emperor Vespasian in the civil war of 69, it was awarded of the *cognomen Augusta*. The fleet was responsible chiefly for the escort of the grain shipments to Rome (and later Constantinople), and also apparently operated the Nile river patrol.
- The *Classis Britannica*, established in 40 or 43 AD at Gesoriacum (Boulogne-sur-Mer).[494] It participated in the Roman invasion of Britain and the subsequent campaigns in the island. The fleet was probably based at Rutupiae (Richborough) until 85 AD, when it was transferred to Dubris (Dover). Other bases were Portus Lemanis (Lympne) and Anderitum (Pevensey), while Gesoriacum on the Gallic coast likely remained active.[495] During the 2nd-3rd centuries, the fleet was chiefly employed in transport of supplies and men across the English Channel. The *Classis Britannica* disappears (at least under that name) from the mid-3rd century, and the sites occupied by it were soon incorporated into the Saxon Shore system.
- The *Classis Germanica* was established in 12 BC by Drusus at Castra Vetera.[496] It controlled the Rhine river, and was mainly a fluvial fleet, although it also operated in the North Sea. It is noteworthy that the Romans' initial lack of experience with the tides of the ocean left Drusus' fleet stranded on the Zuiderzee.[497] After ca. 30 AD, the fleet moved its main base to the *castrum* of Alteburg, some 4 km south of *Colonia Agrippinensis* (modern Cologne).[498] Later granted the honorifics *Augusta Pia Fidelis Domitiana* following the suppression of the Revolt of Saturninus.[499]

- The *Classis nova Libyca*, first mentioned in 180, based most likely at Ptolemais on the Cyrenaica.
- The *Classis Mauretanica*, based at Caesarea Mauretaniae (modern Cherchell), it controlled the African coasts of the western Mediterranean sea. Established on a permanent basis after the raids by the Moors in the early 170s.
- The *Classis Moesica* was established sometime between 20 BC and 10 AD. It was based in Noviodunum and controlled the Lower Danube from the Iron Gates to the northwestern Black Sea as far as the Crimea.[500] The honorific *Flavia*, awarded to it and to the *Classis pannonica*, may indicate its reorganization by Vespasian.[501]
- The *Classis Pannonica*, a fluvial fleet controlling the Upper Danube from Castra Regina in Raetia (modern Regensburg) to Singidunum in Moesia (modern Belgrade). Its exact date of establishment is unknown. Some trace it to Augustus' campaigns in Pannonia in ca. 35 BC, but it was certainly in existence by 45 AD. Its main base was probably Taurunum (modern Zemun) at the confluence of the river Sava with the Danube. Under the Flavian dynasty, it received the *cognomen Flavia*.
- The *Classis Perinthia*, established after the annexation of Thrace in 46 AD and based in Perinthus. Probably based on the indigenous navy, it operated in the Propontis and the Thracian coast. Probably united with the *Classis Pontica* at a later stage.
- The *Classis Pontica*, founded in 64 AD from the Pontic royal fleet,[502] and based in Trapezus, although on occasion it was moved to Byzantium (in ca. 70),[503] and in 170, to Cyzicus.[504] This fleet was used to guard the southern and eastern Black Sea, and the entrance of the Bosporus. According to the historian Josephus, in the latter half of the 1st century, it numbered 40 warships and 3,000 men.[505]
- The *Classis Syriaca*, established probably under Vespasian, and based in Seleucia Pieria (hence the alternative name *Classis Seleucena*)[506] in Syria. This fleet controlled the Eastern Mediterranean and the Aegean sea.

In addition, there is significant archaeological evidence for naval activity by certain legions, which in all likelihood operated their own squadrons: *legio* XXII *Primigenia* in the Upper Rhine and Main rivers, *legio* X *Fretensis* in the Jordan River and the Sea of Galilee, and several legionary squadrons in the Danube frontier.[507]

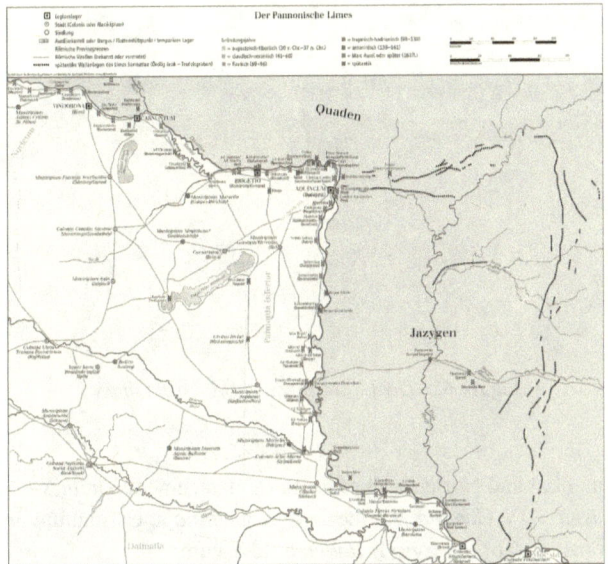

Figure 61: *The Upper Danube (Pannonian) limes*

Dominate period

Our main source for the structure of the late Roman military is the *Notitia Dignitatum*, which corresponds to the situation of the 390s for the Eastern Empire and the 420s for the Western Empire. Notable in the *Notitia* is the large number of smaller squadrons that have been created, most of these fluvial and of a local operational role.

Fleets of the Danube frontier

The *Classis Pannonica* and the *Classis Moesica* were broken up into several smaller squadrons, collectively termed *Classis Histrica*, authority of the frontier commanders (*duces*).[508] with bases at Mursa in Pannonia II,[509] Florentia in Pannonia Valeria,[510] Arruntum in Pannonia I,[511] Viminacium in Moesia I[512] and Aegetae in Dacia ripensis.[513] Smaller fleets are also attested on the tributaries of the Danube: the *Classis Arlapensis et Maginensis* (based at Arelape and Comagena) and the *Classis Lauriacensis* (based at Lauriacum) in Pannonia I, the *Classis Stradensis et Germensis*, based at Margo in Moesia I, and the *Classis Ratianensis*, in Dacia ripensis. The naval units were complemented by port garrisons and marine units, drawn from the army. In the Danube frontier these were:

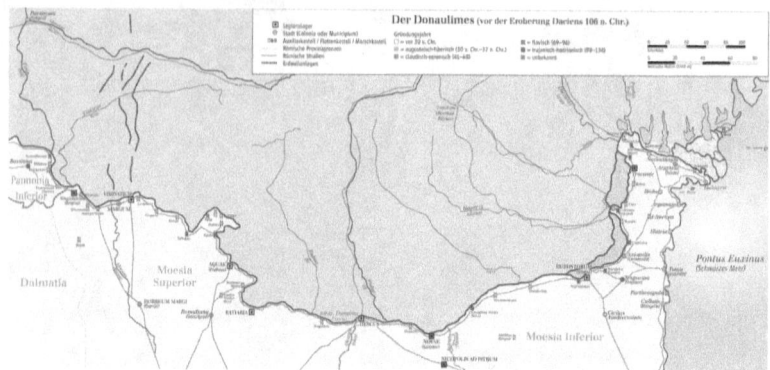

Figure 62: *The Lower Danube (Moesian) limes*

- In Pannonia I and Noricum ripensis, naval detachments (*milites liburnarii*) of the *legio* XIV *Gemina* and the *legio* X *Gemina* at Carnuntum and Arrabonae, and of the *legio* II *Italica* at Ioviacum.
- In Pannonia II, the I *Flavia Augusta* (at Sirmium) and the II *Flavia* are listed under their prefects.
- In Moesia II, two units of sailors (*milites nauclarii*) at Appiaria and Altinum.[514]
- In Scythia Minor, marines (*muscularii*)[515] of *legio* II *Herculia* at Inplateypegiis and sailors (*nauclarii*) at Flaviana.[516]

Fleets in Western Europe

In the West, and in particular in Gaul, several fluvial fleets had been established. These came under the command of the *magister peditum* of the West, and were:[517]

- The *Classis Anderetianorum*, based at Parisii (Paris) and operating in the Seine and Oise rivers.
- The *Classis Ararica*, based at Caballodunum (Chalon-sur-Saône) and operating in the Saône River.
- A *Classis barcariorum*, composed of small vessels, at Eburodunum (modern Yverdon-les-Bains) at Lake Neuchâtel.
- The *Classis Comensis* at Lake Como.
- The old praetorian fleets, the *Classis Misenatis* and the *Classis Ravennatis* are still listed, albeit with no distinction indicating any higher importance than the other fleets. The "praetorian" surname is still attested until the early 4th century, but absent from Vegetius or the *Notitia*.[518]

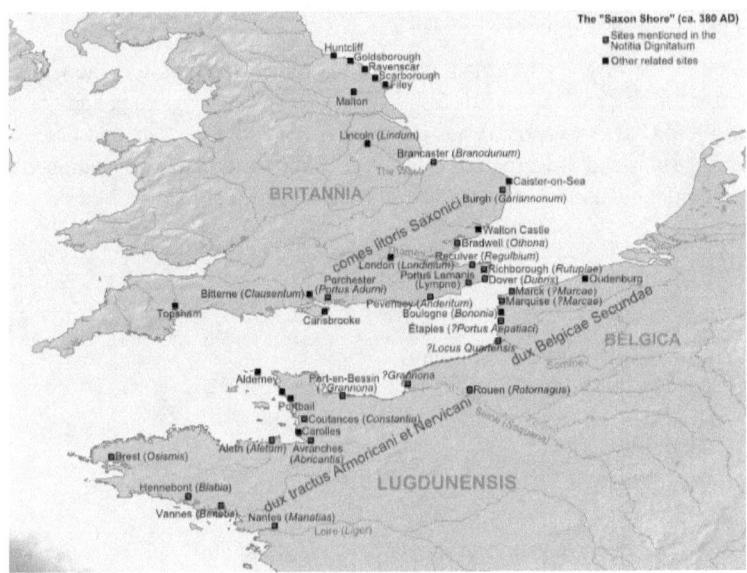

Figure 63: *Bases and command sectors of the Saxon Shore system*

- The *Classis fluminis Rhodani*, based at Arelate and operating in the Rhône River. It was complemented with a marine detachment (*milites muscularii*) based at Marseilles.
- The *Classis Sambrica*, based at Locus Quartensis (unknown location) and operating in the Somme River and the Channel. It came under the command of the *dux Beligae Secundae*.[519]
- The *Classis Venetum*, based at Aquileia and operating in the northern Adriatic Sea. This fleet may have been established to ensure communications with the imperial capitals in the Po Valley (Ravenna and Milan) and with Dalmatia.[520]

It is notable that, with the exception of the praetorian fleets (whose retention in the list does not necessarily signify an active status), the old fleets of the Principate are missing. The *Classis Britannica* vanishes under that name after the mid-3rd century;[521] its remnants were later subsumed in the Saxon Shore system.

By the time of the *Notitia Dignitatum*, the *Classis Germanica* has ceased to exist (it is last mentioned under Julian in 359),[522] most probably due to the collapse of the Rhine frontier after the Crossing of the Rhine by the barbarians in winter 405-406, and the Mauretanian and African fleets had been disbanded or taken over by the Vandals.

Fleets in the Eastern Mediterranean

As far as the East is concerned, we know from legal sources that the *Classis Alexandrina*[523] and the *Classis Seleucena*[524] continued to operate, and that in ca. 400 a *Classis Carpathia* was detached from the Syrian fleet and based at the Aegean island of Karpathos.[525] A fleet is known to have been stationed at Constantinople itself, but no further details are known about it.

Ports

Major Roman ports were:

- Portus Julius, located at Misenum
- Classis, near Ravenna
- Alexandria
- Leptis Magna
- Ostia
- Portus
- Port of Mainz (Mogontiacum, river navy on the Rhine)

References

<templatestyles src="Template:Refbegin/styles.css" />

- Casson, Lionel (1991), *The Ancient Mariners: Seafarers and Sea Fighters of the Mediterranean in Ancient Times*[526], Princeton University Press, ISBN 978-0-691-01477-7
- Casson, Lionel (1995), *Ships and Seamanship in the Ancient World*, Johns Hopkins University Press, ISBN 0-8018-5130-0
- Cleere, Henry (1977), "The Classis Britannica"[527] (PDF), *CBA Research Report* (18): 16–19, retrieved 2008-10-11
- Connolly, Peter (1998), *Greece and Rome at War*, Greenhill
- Gardiner, Robert (Ed.) (2004), *AGE OF THE GALLEY: Mediterranean Oared Vessels since pre-Classical Times*, Conway Maritime Press, ISBN 978-0-85177-955-3
- Goldsworthy, Adrian (2000), *The Fall of Carthage: The Punic Wars 265–146 BC*, Cassell, ISBN 0-304-36642-0
- Goldsworthy, Adrian (2003), *The Complete Roman Army*, Thames & Hudson Ltd., ISBN 0-500-05124-0
- Goldsworthy, Adrian (2007), "A Roman Alexander: Pompey the Great", *In the name of Rome: The men who won the Roman Empire*, Phoenix, ISBN 978-0-7538-1789-6
- Gruen, Erich S. (1984), *The Hellenistic World and the Coming of Rome: Volume II*, University of California Press, ISBN 0-520-04569-6

- Lewis, Archibald Ross; Runyan, Timothy J. (1985), *European Naval and Maritime History, 300-1500*, Indiana University Press, ISBN 0-253-20573-5
- MacGeorge, Penny (2002), "Appendix: Naval Power in the Fifth Century", *Late Roman Warlords*, Oxford University Press, ISBN 978-0-19-925244-2
- Meijer, Fik (1986), *A History of Seafaring in the Classical World*, Routledge, ISBN 978-0-7099-3565-0
- Potter, David (2004), "The Roman Army and Navy", in Flower, Harriet I., *The Cambridge Companion to the Roman Republic*, Cambridge University Press, pp. 66–88, ISBN 978-0-521-00390-2
- Rodgers, William L. (1967), *Naval Warfare Under Oars, 4th to 16th Centuries: A Study of Strategy, Tactics and Ship Design*, Naval Institute Press, ISBN 978-0-87021-487-5
- Rost, Georg Alexander (1968), *Vom Seewesen und Seehandel in der Antike* (in German), John Benjamins Publishing Company, ISBN 90-6032-361-0
- Saddington, D.B. (2007), "*Classes*. The Evolution of the Roman Imperial Fleets", in Erdkamp, Paul, *A Companion to the Roman Army*, Blackwell Publishing Ltd., ISBN 978-1-4051-2153-8
- Starr, Chester G. (1960), *The Roman Imperial Navy: 31 B.C.-A.D. 324 (2nd Edition)*, Cornell University Press
- Starr, Chester G. (1989), *The Influence of Sea Power on Ancient History*, Oxford University Press US, ISBN 978-0-19-505667-9
- Treadgold, Warren T. (1997), *A History of the Byzantine State and Society*, Stanford University Press, ISBN 0-8047-2630-2
- Warry, John (2004), *Warfare in the Classical World*, Salamander Books Ltd., ISBN 0-8061-2794-5
- Webster, Graham; Elton, Hugh (1998), *The Roman Imperial Army of the First and Second Centuries A.D.*, University of Oklahoma Press, ISBN 0-8061-3000-8
- Wesch-Klein, Gabriele (1998), *Soziale Aspekte des römischen Heerwesens in der Kaiserzeit* (in German), Franz Steiner Verlag, ISBN 3-515-07300-0
- Workman-Davies, Bradley (2006), *Corvus: A Review of the Design and Use of the Roman Boarding Bridge During the First Punic War 264 -241 B.C.*[528], Lulu.com, ISBN 978-1-84728-882-0

External links

- (in Italian) The Imperial fleet of Misenum[529]
- The Classis Britannica[530]
- The Roman Fleet[531], *Roman-Empire.net*

- The Roman Navy: Masters of the Mediterranean[532], *HistoryNet.com*
- *Galleria Navale*[533] on Navigare Necesse Est[534]
- *Port of Claudius*[535], the museum of Roman merchant ships found in Fiumicino (Rome)
- *Diana Nemorensis*[536], Caligula's ships in the lake of Nemi.
- *Römisch-Germanisches Zentralmuseum Mainz*: The Fleets and Roman Border Policy[537]
- Forum Navis Romana[538]

Campaigns

Campaign history of the Roman military

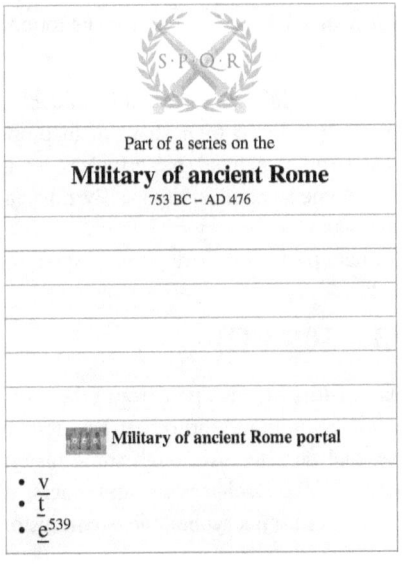

From its origin as a city-state on the peninsula of Italy in the 8th century BC, to its rise as an empire covering much of Southern Europe, Western Europe, Near East and North Africa to its fall in the 5th century AD, the political history of Ancient Rome was closely entwined with its military history. The core of the **campaign history of the Roman military** is an aggregate of different accounts of the Roman military's land battles, from its initial defense against and subsequent conquest of the city's hilltop neighbors on the Italian peninsula, to the ultimate struggle of the Western Roman Empire for its existence against invading Huns, Vandals and Germanic tribes. These accounts were written by various authors throughout and after the history of the Empire. Following the First Punic War, naval battles were less significant than land battles to the military history of Rome due to its encompassment of lands of the periphery and its unchallenged dominance of the Mediterranean Sea.

The Roman army battled first against its tribal neighbours and Etruscan towns within Italy, and later came to dominate the Mediterranean and at its height the provinces of Britannia and Asia Minor. As with most ancient civilizations, Rome's military served the triple purpose of securing its borders, exploiting peripheral areas through measures such as imposing tribute on conquered peoples, and maintaining internal order.[540] From the outset, Rome's military typified this pattern, and the majority of Rome's campaigns were characterised by one of two types. The first is the territorial expansionist campaign, normally begun as a counter-offensive,[541] in which each victory brought subjugation of large areas of territory and allowed Rome to grow from a small town to a population of 55 million in the early empire when expansion was halted.[542] The second is the civil war, which plagued Rome from its foundation to its eventual demise.

Roman armies were not invincible, despite their formidable reputation and host of victories,[543] Romans "produced their share of incompetents"[544] who led Roman armies into catastrophic defeats. Nevertheless, it was generally the fate of even the greatest of Rome's enemies, such as Pyrrhus and Hannibal, to win the battle but lose the war. The history of Rome's campaigning is, if nothing else, a history of obstinate persistence overcoming appalling losses.[545,546]

Kingdom (753 – 509 BC)

Knowledge of Roman history stands apart from other civilizations in the ancient world. Its chronicles, military and otherwise, document the city's very foundation to its eventual demise. Although some histories have been lost, such as Trajan's account of the Dacian Wars, and others, such as Rome's earliest histories, are at least semi-apocryphal, the extant histories of Rome's military history are extensive.

Rome's earliest history, from the time of its founding as a small tribal village,[547] to the downfall of its kings, is the least well preserved. Although the early Romans were literate to some degree,[548] this void may be due to the lack of will to record their history at that time, or such histories as they did record were lost.[549]

Although the Roman historian Livy (59 BC – 17 AD)[550] lists a series of seven kings of early Rome in his work *Ab urbe condita*, from its establishment through its earliest years, the first four kings (Romulus,[551] Numa,[552,553] Tullus Hostilius[554] and Ancus Marcius)[555] may be apocryphal. A number of

Figure 64: *Rape of the Sabine Women, by Nicolas Poussin, Rome, 1637–38 (Louvre Museum)*

points of view have been proposed. Grant and others argue that prior to the establishment of the Etruscan kingdom of Rome under the traditional fifth king, Tarquinius Priscus,[556] Rome would have been led by a religious leader of some sort.[557] Very little is known of Rome's military history from this era, and what history has come down to us is more of a legendary than of factual nature. Traditionally, Romulus, after founding the city, fortified the Palatine Hill, and shortly thereafter, Rome was "*equal to any of the surrounding cities in her prowess in war*".[558]

> "Events before the city was founded or planned, which have been handed down more as pleasing poetic fictions than as reliable records of historical events, I intend neither to affirm nor to refute. To antiquity we grant the indulgence of making the origins of cities more impressive by comingling the human with the divine, and if any people should be permitted to sanctify its inception and reckon the gods as its founders, surely the glory of the Roman people in war is such that, when it boasts Mars in particular as its parent... the nations of the world would as easily acquiesce in this claim as they do in our rule."
>
> *Livy, on Rome's early history*[559]

The first of the campaigns fought by the Romans in this legendary account are the wars with various Latin cities and the Sabines. According to Livy, the Latin village of Caenina responded to the event of the abduction of the Sabine women by invading Roman territory, but were routed and their village captured. The Latins of Antemnae and those of Crustumerium were defeated next in a similar fashion. The remaining main body of the Sabines attacked Rome and briefly captured the citadel, but were then convinced to conclude a treaty with the Romans under which the Sabines became Roman citizens.[560]

There was a further war in the 8th century BC against Fidenae and Veii. In the 7th century BC there was a war with Alba Longa, a second war with Fidenae and Veii and a second Sabine War. Ancus Marcius led Rome to victory against the Latins and, according to the Fasti Triumphales, over the Veientes and Sabines also.

Tarquinius Priscus (Ruled 616–579 BC)

Lucius Tarquinius Priscus' first war was waged against the Latins. Tarquinius took the Latin town of Apiolae by storm and took great booty from there back to Rome.[561] According to the *Fasti Triumphales*, the war occurred prior to 588 BC.

His military ability was tested by an attack from the Sabines. Tarquinius doubled the numbers of equites to help the war effort,[562] and defeat the Sabines. In the peace negotiations that followed, Tarquinius received the town of Collatia and appointed his nephew, Arruns Tarquinius, also known as *Egerius*, as commander of the garrison which he stationed in that city. Tarquinius returned to Rome and celebrated a triumph for his victories that, according to the *Fasti Triumphales*, occurred on 13 September 585 BC.

Subsequently, the Latin cities of Corniculum, old Ficulea, Cameria, Crustumerium, Ameriola, Medullia and Nomentum were subdued and became Roman.[563]

Servius Tullius (Ruled 578–535 BC)

Early in his reign, Servius Tullius warred against Veii and the Etruscans. He is said to have shown valour in the campaign, and to have routed a great army of the enemy. The war helped him to cement his position at Rome.[564] According to the *Fasti Triumphales*, Servius celebrated three triumphs over the Etruscans, including on 25 November 571 BC and 25 May 567 BC (the date of the third triumph is not legible on the *Fasti*).

Tarquinius Superbus (Ruled 535-509 BC)

Early in his reign Tarquinius Superbus, Rome's seventh and final king, called a meeting of the Latin leaders at which he persuaded them to renew their treaty with Rome and become her allies rather than her enemies, and it was agreed that the troops of the Latins would attend at a grove sacred to the goddess Ferentina on an appointed day to form a united military force with the troops of Rome. This was done, and Tarquin formed combined units of Roman and Latin troops.[565]

Tarquin next began a war against the Volsci. He took the wealthy town of Suessa Pometia, with the spoils of which he commenced the erection of the Temple of Jupiter Optimus Maximus which his father had vowed. He also celebrated a triumph for his victory.[566]

He was next engaged in a war with Gabii, one of the Latin cities, which had rejected the Latin treaty with Rome. Unable to take the city by force of arms, Tarquin had his son, Sextus Tarquinius, infiltrate the city, gain the trust of its people and command of its army. In time he killed or exiled the city's leaders, and handed control of the city over to his father.[567]

Tarquin also agreed to a peace with the Aequi, and renewed the treaty of peace between Rome and the Etruscans.[568] According to the Fasti Triumphales, Tarquin also won a victory over the Sabines.

Tarquinius later went to war with the Rutuli. According to Livy, the Rutuli were, at that time, a very wealthy nation. Tarquinius was desirous of obtaining the booty which would come with victory over the Rutuli.[569] Tarquin unsuccessfully sought to take the Rutulian capital, Ardea, by storm, and subsequently began an extensive siege of the city. The war was interrupted by the revolution which overthrew the Roman monarchy. The Roman army, camped outside Ardea, welcomed Lucius Junius Brutus as their new leader, and expelled the king's sons. It is unclear what was the outcome of the siege, or indeed the war.[570]

Republic

Early (509-275 BC)

Early Italian campaigns (509-396 BC)

The first non-apocryphal Roman wars were wars of both expansion and defence, aimed at protecting Rome itself from neighbouring cities and nations and establishing its territory in the region.[571] Florus writes that at this time "their neighbours, on every side, were continually harassing them, as they had no land of their own ... and as they were situated, as it were, at the junction

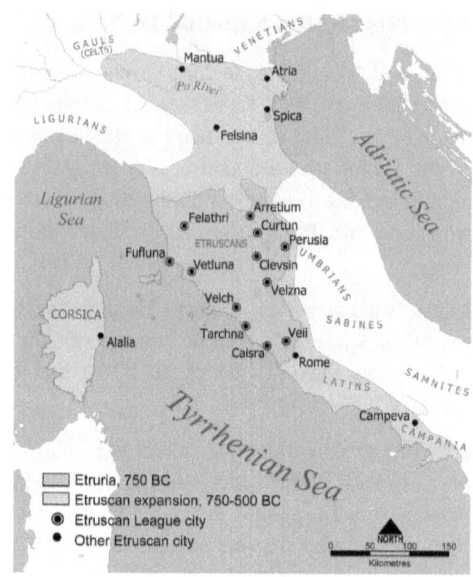

Figure 65: *Map showing Rome's Etruscan neighbours*

of the roads to Latium and Eturia, and, at whatever gate they went out, were sure to meet a foe."

In the semi-legendary period of the early republic, sources record Rome was twice attacked by Etruscan armies. About 509 BC war with Veii and Tarquinii was said to have been instigated by the recently overthrown king Tarquinius Superbus.[572,573] Again in 508 BC Tarquin persuaded the king of Clusium, Lars Porsenna, to wage war on Rome, resulting in a siege of Rome and afterwards a peace treaty.[574,575]

Initially, Rome's immediate neighbours were either Latin towns and villages[576] on a tribal system similar to that of Rome, or else tribal Sabines from the Apennine hills beyond.[577] One by one, Rome defeated both the persistent Sabines and the local cities that were either under Etruscan control or else Latin towns that had cast off their Etruscan rulers, as had Rome. Rome defeated the Lavinii and Tusculi in the Battle of Lake Regillus in 496 BC,[578,579] were defeated by the Veientes in the Battle of the Cremera in 477 BC,[580,581] the Sabines in an unnamed battle in 449 BC, the Aequi in the Battle of Mount Algidus in 458 BC, the Aequi and Volsci in 446 BC,[582,583] in the Battle of Corbio,[584] in 446 BC the Aurunci in the Battle of Aricia,[585] the Capture of Fidenae in 435 BC[586] and the Siege of Veii in 396 BC,[587] and the Capture of Antium in 377 BC.[588]

After defeating the Veientes, the Romans had effectively completed the conquest of their immediate Etruscan neighbours,[589] as well as secured their position against the immediate threat posed by the tribespeople of the Apennine hills.

However, Rome still controlled only a very limited area and the affairs of Rome were minor even to those in Italy and Rome's affairs were only just coming to the attention of the Greeks, the dominant cultural force at the time.[590] At this point the bulk of Italy remained in the hands of Latin, Sabine, Samnite and other peoples in the central part of Italy, Greek colonies to the south, and the Celtic people, including the Gauls, to the north.

Celtic invasion of Italia (390–387 BC)

By 390 BC, several Gallic tribes had begun invading Italy from the north as their culture expanded throughout Europe. Most of this was unknown to the Romans at this time, who still had purely local security concerns, but the Romans were alerted when a particularly warlike tribe,[591] the Senones, invaded the Etruscan province of Siena from the north and attacked the town of Clusium,[592] not far from Rome's sphere of influence. The Clusians, overwhelmed by the size of the enemy in numbers and ferocity, called on Rome for help. Perhaps unintentionally the Romans found themselves not just in conflict with the Senones, but their primary target. The Romans met them in pitched battle at the Battle of the Allia around 390–387 BC. The Gauls, under their chieftain Brennus, defeated the Roman army of around 15,000 troops and proceeded to pursue the fleeing Romans back to Rome itself and partially sacked the town[593,594] before being either driven off[595,596] or bought off.

Now that the Romans and Gauls had blooded one another, intermittent Roman-Gallic wars were to continue between the two in Italy for more than two centuries, including the Battle of Lake Vadimo, the Battle of Faesulae in 225 BC, the Battle of Telamon in 224 BC, the Battle of Clastidium in 222 BC, the Battle of Cremona in 200 BC, the Battle of Mutina in 194 BC, the Battle of Arausio in 105 BC, and the Battle of Vercellae in 101 BC. The Celtic problem would not be resolved for Rome until the final subjugation of all Gaul following the Battle of Alesia in 52 BC.

Expansion into Italia (343–282 BC)

After swiftly recovering from the sack of Rome,[597] the Romans immediately resumed their expansion within Italy. Despite their successes, their mastery of the whole of Italy was by no means assured. The Samnites were a people just as martial[598] and as rich[599] as the Romans and had the objective of their own to secure more lands in the fertile Italian plains on which Rome itself lay.[600] The First Samnite War of between 343 BC and 341 BC that followed widespread

Figure 66: *Apennine hills around Samnium*

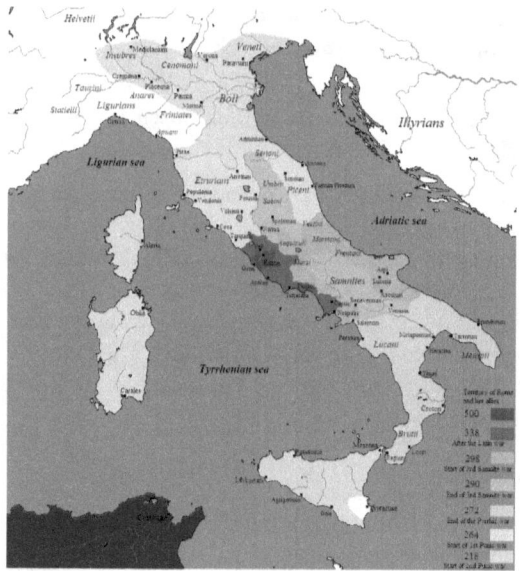

Figure 67: *Map showing Roman expansion in Italy*

Samnite incursions into Rome's territory[601] was a relatively short affair: the Romans beat the Samnites in both the Battle of Mount Gaurus in 342 BC and the Battle of Suessula in 341 BC but were forced to withdraw from the war before they could pursue the conflict further due to the revolt of several of their Latin allies in the Latin War.[602,603]

Rome was therefore forced to contend by around 340 BC against both Samnite incursions into their territory and, simultaneously, in a bitter war against their former allies. Rome bested the Latins in the Battle of Vesuvius and again in the Battle of Trifanum, after which the Latin cities were obliged to submit to Roman rule.[604,605] Perhaps due to Rome's lenient treatment of their defeated foe, the Latins submitted largely amicably to Roman rule for the next 200 years.

The Second Samnite War, from 327 BC to 304 BC, was a much longer and more serious affair for both the Romans and Samnites,[606] running for over twenty years and incorporating twenty-four battles that led to massive casualties on both sides. The fortunes of the two sides fluctuated throughout its course: the Samnites seized Neapolis in the Capture of Neapolis in 327 BC, which the Romans then re-captured before losing at the Battle of the Caudine Forks[607] and the Battle of Lautulae. The Romans then proved victorious at the Battle of Bovianum and the tide turned strongly against the Samnites from 314 BC onwards, leading them to sue for peace with progressively less generous terms. By 304 BC the Romans had effectively annexed the greater degree of the Samnite territory, founding several colonies. This pattern of meeting aggression in force and so inadvertently gaining territory in strategic counterattacks was to become a common feature of Roman military history.

Seven years after their defeat, with Roman dominance of the area looking assured, the Samnites rose again and defeated the Romans at the Battle of Camerinum in 298 BC, to open the Third Samnite War. With this success in hand they managed to bring together a coalition of several previous enemies of Rome, all of whom were probably keen to prevent any one faction dominating the entire region. The army that faced the Romans at the Battle of Sentinum in 295 BC included Samnites, Gauls, Etruscans and Umbrians.[608] When the Roman army won a convincing victory over these combined forces it must have become clear that little could prevent Roman dominance of Italy and in the Battle of Populonia (282 BC) Rome destroyed the last vestiges of Etruscan power in the region.

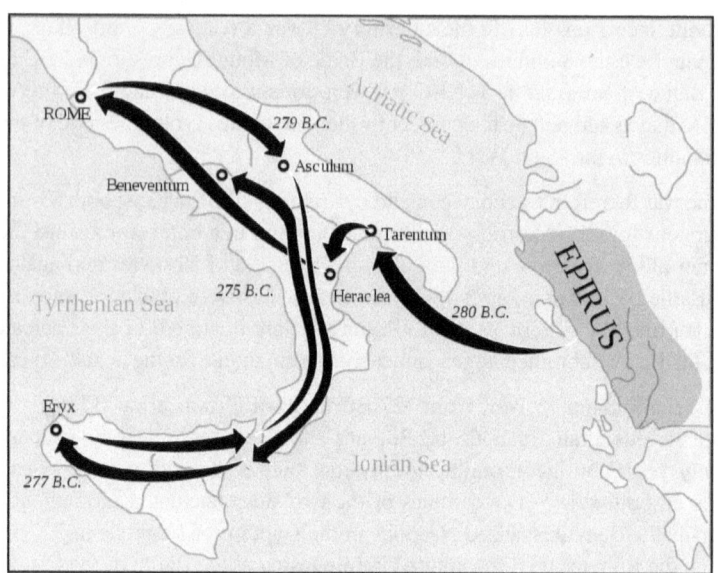

Figure 68: *Route of Pyrrhus of Epirus*

Pyrrhic War (280–275 BC)

By the beginning of the 3rd century, Rome had established itself in 282 BC as a major power on the Italian Peninsula, but had not yet come into conflict with the dominant military powers in the Mediterranean at the time: Carthage and the Greek kingdoms. Rome had all but completely defeated the Samnites, mastered its fellow Latin towns, and greatly reduced Etruscan power in the region. However, the south of Italy was controlled by the Greek colonies of Magna Grecia[609] who had been allied to the Samnites, and continued Roman expansion brought the two into inevitable conflict.[610,611]

In the naval Battle of Thurii, Tarentum appealed for military aid to Pyrrhus, ruler of Epirus.[612] Motivated by his diplomatic obligations to Tarentum, and a personal desire for military accomplishment,[613] Pyrrhus landed a Greek army of some 25,000 men and a contingent of war elephants[614] on Italian soil in 280 BC,[615] where his forces were joined by some Greek colonists and a portion of the Samnites who revolted against Roman control, taking up arms against Rome for the fourth time in seventy years.

The Roman army had not yet seen elephants in battle, and their inexperience turned the tide in Pyrrhus' favour at the Battle of Heraclea in 280 BC,[616] and again at the Battle of Ausculum in 279 BC.[617] Despite these victories, Pyrrhus found his position in Italy untenable. Rome steadfastly refused to negotiate with Pyrrhus as long as his army remained in Italy.[618] Furthermore, Rome entered into a treaty of support with Carthage, and Pyrrhus found that despite his expectations, none of the other Italic peoples would defect to the Greek and Samnite cause.[619] Facing unacceptably heavy losses with each encounter with the Roman army, and failing to find further allies in Italy, Pyrrhus withdrew from the peninsula and campaigned in Sicily against Carthage,[620] abandoning his allies to deal with the Romans.

When his Sicilian campaign was also ultimately a failure, and at the request of his Italian allies, Pyrrhus returned to Italy to face Rome once more. In 275 BC, Pyrrhus again met the Roman army at the Battle of Beneventum. This time the Romans had devised methods to deal with the war elephants, including the use of javelins, fire and, one source claims, simply hitting the elephants heavily on the head. While Beneventum was indecisive, Pyrrhus realised that his army had been exhausted and reduced by years of foreign campaigns, and seeing little hope for further gains, he withdrew completely from Italy.

The conflicts with Pyrrhus would have a great effect on Rome. It had shown that it was capable of pitting its armies successfully against the dominant military powers of the Mediterranean, and further showed that the Greek kingdoms were incapable of defending their colonies in Italy and abroad. Rome quickly moved into southern Italia, subjugating and dividing Magna Grecia.[621] Effectively dominating the Italian peninsula,[622] and with a proven international military reputation,[623] Rome now began to look to expand from the Italian mainland. Since the Alps formed a natural barrier to the north, and Rome was none too keen to meet the fierce Gauls in battle once more, the city's gaze turned to Sicily and the islands of the Mediterranean, a policy that would bring it into direct conflict with its former ally Carthage.[624]

Middle (274-148 BC)

Rome first began to make war outside the Italian peninsula during the Punic wars against Carthage, a former Phoenician colony[625] that had established on the north coast of Africa and developed into a powerful state. These wars, starting in 264 BC[626] were probably the largest conflicts of the ancient world yet[627] and saw Rome become the most powerful state of the Western Mediterranean, with territory in Sicily, North Africa, Iberia, and with the end of the Macedonian wars (which ran concurrently with the Punic wars) Greece as well. After the defeat of the Seleucid Emperor Antiochus III the Great in the Roman-Syrian War (Treaty of Apamea, 188 BC) in the eastern sea, Rome emerged as the dominant Mediterranean power and the most powerful city in the classical world.

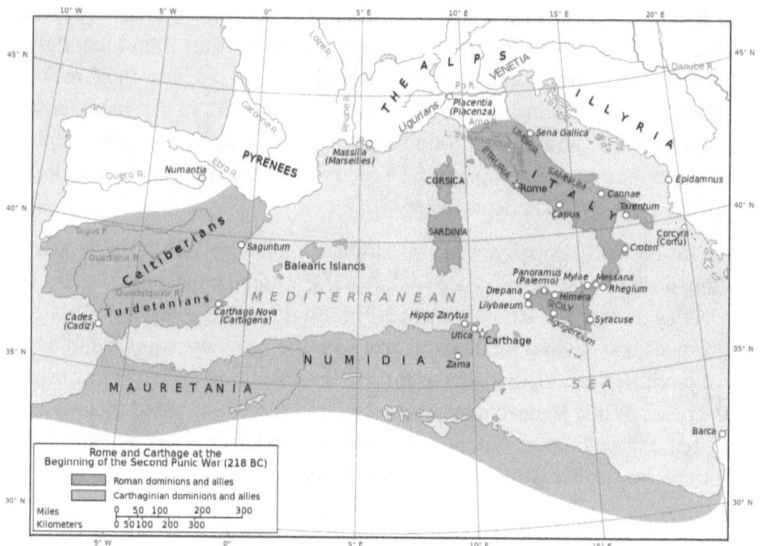

Figure 69: *Theatre of Punic Wars*

Punic Wars (264–146 BC)

The First Punic War began in 264 BC when settlements on Sicily began to appeal to the two powers between which they lay – Rome and Carthage – in order to solve internal conflicts. The willingness of both Rome and Carthage to become embroiled on the soil of a third party may indicate a willingness to test each other's power without wishing to enter a full war of annihilation; certainly there was considerable disagreement within Rome about whether to prosecute the war at all.[628] The war saw land battles in Sicily early on, such as the Battle of Agrigentum, but the theatre shifted to naval battles around Sicily and Africa. For the Romans, naval warfare was a relatively unexplored concept.[629] Before the First Punic War in 264 BC there was no Roman navy to speak of, as all previous Roman wars had been fought on land in Italy. The new war in Sicily against Carthage, a great naval power,[630] forced Rome to quickly build a fleet and train sailors.[631]

Rome took to naval warfare "like a brick to water" and the first few naval battles of the First Punic War such as the Battle of the Lipari Islands were catastrophic disasters for Rome, as might fairly be expected from a city that had no real prior experience of naval warfare. However, after training more sailors and inventing a grappling engine known as a Corvus,[632] a Roman naval force under C. Duillius was able to roundly defeat a Carthaginian fleet at the Battle of Mylae. In just four years, a state without any real naval experience had managed to better a major regional maritime power in battle. Further naval victories followed at the Battle of Tyndaris and the Battle of Cape Ecnomus.[633]

After having won control of the seas, a Roman force landed on the African coast under Marcus Regulus, who was at first victorious, winning the Battle of Adys[634] and forcing Carthage to sue for peace.[635] However, the terms of peace that Rome proposed were so heavy that negotiations failed, and in response, the Carthaginians hired Xanthippus of Carthage, a mercenary from the martial Greek city-state of Sparta, to reorganise and lead their army.[636] Xanthippus managed to cut off the Roman army from its base by re-establishing Carthaginian naval supremacy and then defeated and captured Regulus[637] at the Battle of Tunis.[638]

Despite being defeated on African soil, the Romans with their newfound naval abilities, roundly beat the Carthaginians in naval battle again – largely through the tactical innovations of the Roman fleet – at the Battle of the Aegates Islands. Carthage was left without a fleet or sufficient coin to raise a new one. For a maritime power, the loss of their access to the Mediterranean stung financially and psychologically, and the Carthaginians again sued for peace,[639] during which negotiations, Rome battled the *Ligures* tribe in the Ligurian War[640] and the *Insubres* in the Gallic War.[641]

Continuing distrust led to the renewal of hostilities in the Second Punic War when Hannibal Barca, a member of the Barcid family of Carthaginian nobility, attacked Saguntum,[642,643] a city with diplomatic ties to Rome.[644] Hannibal then raised an army in Iberia and famously crossed the Italian Alps with elephants to invade Italy.[645,646] In the first battle on Italian soil at Ticinus in 218 BC Hannibal defeated the Romans under Scipio the Elder in a small cavalry fight.[647,648] Hannibal's success continued with victories in the Battle of the Trebia,[649] the Battle of Lake Trasimene, where he ambushed an unsuspecting Roman army,[650,651] and the Battle of Cannae,[652,653] in what is considered one of the great masterpieces of tactical art, and for a while "Hannibal seemed invincible", able to beat Roman armies at will.[654]

In the three battles of Nola, Roman general Marcus Claudius Marcellus managed to hold off Hannibal but then Hannibal smashed a succession of Roman consular armies at the First Battle of Capua, the Battle of the Silarus, the Second Battle of Herdonia, the Battle of Numistro and the Battle of Asculum. By this time Hannibal's brother Hasdrubal Barca sought to cross the Alps into Italy and join his brother with a second army. Despite being defeated in Iberia in the Battle of Baecula, Hasdrubal managed to break through into Italy only to be defeated decisively by Gaius Claudius Nero and Marcus Livius Salinator on the Metaurus River.

> "Apart from the romance of Scipio's personality and his political importance as the founder of Rome's world-dominion, his military work has a greater value to modern students of war than that of any other great captain of the past.. His genius revealed to him that peace and war are the two wheels on which the world runs."
>
> BH Liddell Harton Scipio Africanus Major[655]

Unable to defeat Hannibal himself on Italian soil, and with Hannibal savaging the Italian countryside but unwilling or unable to destroy Rome itself, the Romans boldly sent an army to Africa with the intention of threatening the Carthaginian capital.[656] In 203 BC at the Battle of Bagbrades the invading Roman army under Scipio Africanus Major defeated the Carthaginian army of Hasdrubal Gisco and Syphax and Hannibal was recalled to Africa. At the famous Battle of Zama Scipio decisively defeated[657] – perhaps even "annihilated" – Hannibal's army in North Africa, ending the Second Punic War.

Carthage never managed to recover after the Second Punic War[658] and the Third Punic War that followed was in reality a simple punitive mission to raze the city of Carthage to the ground.[659] Carthage was almost defenceless and when besieged offered immediate surrender, conceding to a string of outrageous Roman demands.[660] The Romans refused the surrender, demanding as their further terms of surrender the complete destruction of the city[661] and, seeing little to lose, the Carthaginians prepared to fight. In the Battle of Carthage the city was stormed after a short siege and completely destroyed,[662] its culture "almost totally extinguished".[663]

Conquest of the Iberian peninsula (219–18 BC)

Rome's conflict with the Carthaginians in the Punic Wars led them into expansion in the Iberian peninsula of modern-day Spain and Portugal.[664] The Punic empire of the Carthaginian Barcid family consisted of territories in Iberia, many of which Rome gained control of during the Punic Wars. Italy remained the main theatre of war for much of the Second Punic War, but the Romans also aimed to destroy the Barcid Empire in Iberia and prevent major Punic allies from linking up with forces in Italy.

Over the years, Rome had expanded along the southern Iberian coast until in 211 BC it captured the city of Saguntum. Following two major military expeditions to Iberia, the Romans finally crushed Carthaginian control of the peninsula in 206 BC, at the Battle of Ilipa, and the peninsula became a Roman province known as Hispania. From 206 BC onwards the only opposition to Roman control of the peninsula came from within the native Celtiberian tribes themselves, whose disunity prevented their security from Roman expansion.

Following two small-scale rebellions in 197 BC,[665] in 195–194 BC war broke out between the Romans and the Lusitani people in the Lusitanian War, in modern-day Portugal.[666] By 179 BC, the Romans had mostly succeeded in pacifying the region and bringing it under their control.

About 154 BC, a major revolt was re-ignited in Numantia, which is known as the First Numantine War, and a long war of resistance was fought between the advancing forces of the Roman Republic and the Lusitani tribes of Hispania. The praetor Servius Sulpicius Galba and the proconsul Lucius Licinius Lucullus arrived in 151 BC and began the process of subduing the local population.[667] In 150 BC, Galba betrayed the Lusitani leaders he had invited to peace talks and had them killed, ingloriously ending the first phase of the war.

The Lusitani revolted again in 146 BC under a new leader called Viriathus, invading Turdetania (southern Iberia) in a guerrilla war.[668] The Lusitanians were initially successful, defeating a Roman army at the Battle of Tribola and going on to sack nearby Carpetania,[669] and then besting a second Roman army at the First Battle of Mount Venus in 146 BC, again going on to sack another nearby city. In 144 BC, the general Quintus Fabius Maximus Aemilianus campaigned successfully against the Lusitani, but failed in his attempts to arrest Viriathus.

In 144 BC, Viriathus formed a league against Rome with several Celtiberian tribes[670] and persuaded them to rise against Rome too, in the Second Numantine War.[671] Viriathus' new coalition bested Roman armies at the Second Battle of Mount Venus in 144 BC and again at the failed Siege of Erisone. In 139 BC, Viriathus was finally killed in his sleep by three of his companions who had been promised gifts by Rome.[672] In 136 and 135 BC, more attempts were made to gain complete control of the region of Numantia, but they failed. In 134 BC, the Consul Scipio Aemilianus finally succeeded in suppressing the rebellion following the successful Siege of Numantia.[673]

Since the Roman invasion of the Iberian peninsula had begun in the south in the territories around the Mediterranean controlled by the Barcids, the last region of the peninsula to be subdued lay in the far north. The Cantabrian Wars or Astur-Cantabrian Wars, from 29 BC to 19 BC, occurred during the Roman conquest of these northern provinces of Cantabria and Asturias. Iberia was fully occupied by 25 BC and the last revolt put down by 19 BC[674]

Macedon, the Greek poleis, and Illyria (215–148 BC)

Rome's preoccupation with its war with Carthage provided an opportunity for Philip V of the kingdom of Macedon in northern Greece to attempt to extend his power westward. Philip sent ambassadors to Hannibal's camp in Italy, to negotiate an alliance as common enemies of Rome.[675,676] However, Rome discovered the agreement when Philip's emissaries, along with emissaries from Hannibal, were captured by a Roman fleet. Desiring to prevent Philip from aiding Carthage in Italy and elsewhere, Rome sought out land allies in Greece

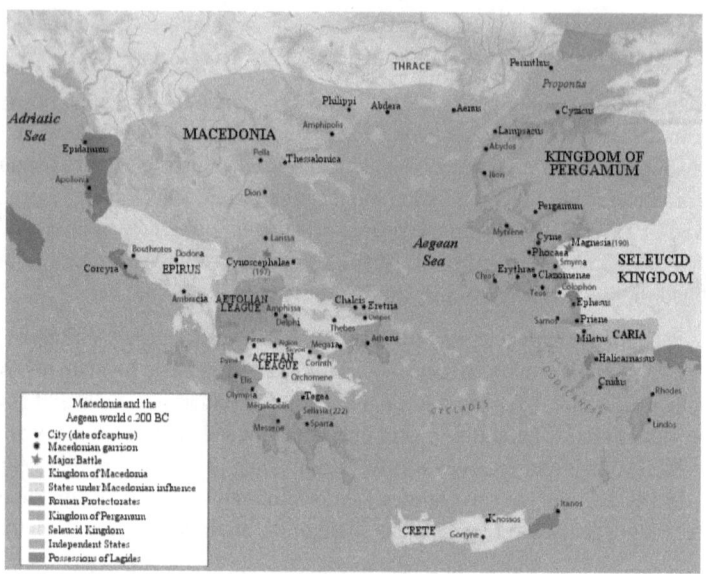

Figure 70: *Greece, Macedonia and their environs. Circa 200 BC.*

to fight a proxy war against Macedon on its behalf and found partners in the Aetolian League of Greek city-states, the Illyrians to the north of Macedon and the kingdom of Pergamon[677] and the city-state of Rhodes, which lay across the Aegean from Macedon.[678]

The First Macedonian War saw the Romans involved directly in only limited land operations. When the Aetolians sued for peace with Philip, Rome's small expeditionary force, with no more allies in Greece, was ready to make peace. Rome had achieved its objective of pre-occupying Philip and preventing him from aiding Hannibal. A treaty was drawn up between Rome and Macedon at Phoenice in 205 BC which promised Rome a small indemnity, formally ending the First Macedonian War.[679]

Macedon began to encroach on territory claimed by several other Greek city states in 200 BC and these pleaded for help from their newfound ally Rome.[680] Rome gave Philip an ultimatum that he must submit Macedonia to being essentially a Roman province. Philip, unsurprisingly, refused and, after initial internal reluctance for further hostilities,[681] Rome declared war against Philip in the Second Macedonian War. In the Battle of the Aous Roman forces under Titus Quinctius Flamininus defeated the Macedonians,[682] and in a second larger battle under the same opposing commanders in 197 BC, in the Battle of Cynoscephalae,[683] Flamininus again beat the Macedonians decisively.[684]

Macedonia was forced to sign the Treaty of Tempea, in which it lost all claim to territory in Greece and Asia, and had to pay a war indemnity to Rome.[685]

Between the second and third Macedonian wars Rome faced further conflict in the region due to a tapestry of shifting rivalries, alliances and leagues all seeking to gain greater influence. After the Macedonians had been defeated in the Second Macedonian War in 197 BC, the Greek city-state of Sparta stepped into the partial power vacuum in Greece. Fearing the Spartans would take increasing control of the region, the Romans drew on help from allies to prosecute the Roman-Spartan War, defeating a Spartan army at the Battle of Gythium in 195 BC. They also fought their former allies the Aetolian League in the Aetolian War,[686] against the Istrians in the Istrian War,[687] against the Illyrians in the Illyrian War,[688] and against Achaia in the Achaean War.[689]

Rome now turned its attentions to Antiochus III of the Seleucid Empire to the east. After campaigns as far abroad as Bactria, India, Persia and Judea, Antiochus moved to Asia Minor and Thrace[690] to secure several coastal towns, a move that brought him into conflict with Roman interests. A Roman force under Manius Acilius Glabrio defeated Antiochus at the Battle of Thermopylae and forced him to evacuate Greece:[691] the Romans then pursued the Seleucids beyond Greece, beating them again in naval battles at the Battle of the Eurymedon and Battle of Myonessus, and finally in a decisive engagement of the Battle of Magnesia.[692]

In 179 BC Philip died[693] and his talented and ambitious son, Perseus of Macedon, took his throne and showed a renewed interest in Greece.[694] He also allied himself with the warlike Bastarnae, and both this and his actions in Greece possibly violated the treaty signed with the Romans by his father or, if not, certainly was not "behaving as [Rome considered] a subordinate ally should". Rome declared war on Macedonia again, starting the Third Macedonian War. Perseus initially had greater military success against the Romans than his father, winning the Battle of Callicinus against a Roman consular army. However, as with all such ventures in this period, Rome responded by simply sending another army. The second consular army duly defeated the Macedonians at the Battle of Pydna in 168 BC[695] and the Macedonians, lacking the reserve of the Romans and with King Perseus captured,[696] duly capitulated, ending the Third Macedonian War.[697]

The Fourth Macedonian War, fought from 150 BC to 148 BC, was the final war between Rome and Macedon and began when Andriscus usurped the Macedonian throne. The Romans raised a consular army under Quintus Caecilius Metellus, who swiftly defeated Andriscus at the Second battle of Pydna.

Under Lucius Mummius, Corinth was destroyed following a siege in 146 BC, leading to the surrender and thus conquest of the Achaean League (see Battle of Corinth).

Late (147–30 BC)

Jugurthine War (112–105 BC)

Rome had, in the earlier Punic Wars, gained large tracts of territory in Africa, which they consolidated in the following centuries.[698] Much of that land had been granted to the kingdom of Numidia, a kingdom on the north African coast approximating to modern Algeria, in return for its past military assistance.[699] The Jugurthine War of 111–104 BC was fought between Rome and Jugurtha of Numidia and constituted the final Roman pacification of Northern Africa,[700] after which Rome largely ceased expansion on the continent after reaching natural barriers of desert and mountain. In response to Jugurtha's usurpation of the Numidian throne,[701] a loyal ally of Rome since the Punic Wars,[702] Rome intervened. Jugurtha impudently bribed the Romans into accepting his usurpation[703,704,705] and was granted half the kingdom. Following further aggression and further bribery attempts, the Romans sent an army to depose him. The Romans were defeated at the Battle of Suthul[706] but fared better at the Battle of the Muthul[707] and finally defeated Jugurtha at the Battle of Thala,[708,709] the Battle of Mulucha,[710] and the Battle of Cirta (104 BC).[711] Jugurtha was finally captured not in battle but by treachery,[712,713] ending the war.[714]

Resurgence of the Celtic threat (121 BC)

Memories of the sack of Rome by Celtic tribes from Gaul in 390/387 BC, had been made into a legendary account that was taught to each generation of Roman youth, were still prominent despite their historical distance. In 121 BC, Rome came into contact with the Celtic tribes of the Allobroges and the Arverni, both of which they defeated with apparent ease in the First Battle of Avignon near the Rhone river and the Second Battle of Avignon, the same year.[715]

New Germanic threat (113–101 BC)

The Cimbrian War (113–101 BC) was a far more serious affair than the earlier clashes of 121 BC. The Germanic tribes of the *Cimbri*[716] and the *Teutons* or *Teutones* migrated from northern Europe into Rome's northern territories,[717] where they clashed with Rome and her allies.[718] The Cimbrian War was the first time since the Second Punic War that Italia and Rome itself had been seriously threatened, and caused great fear in Rome. The opening action of the Cimbrian War, the Battle of Noreia in 112 BC, ended in defeat and near disaster for the Romans. In 105 BC the Romans were defeated at the Battle of Arausio and was the costliest Rome had suffered since the Battle of Cannae. After the Cimbri inadvertently granted the Romans a reprieve by diverting to plunder Iberia,[719] Rome was given the opportunity to carefully prepare for and successfully meet the Cimbri and Teutons in the Battle of Aquae Sextiae (102 BC) and the Battle of Vercellae (101 BC) where both tribes were virtually annihilated, ending the threat.

Internal unrest (135–71 BC)

The extensive campaigning abroad by Rome, and the rewarding of soldiers with plunder from those campaigns, led to the trend of soldiers becoming increasingly loyal to their commanders rather than to the state, and a willingness to follow their generals in battle against the state.[720] Rome was plagued by several slave uprisings during this period, in part because in the past century vast tracts of land had been given to veterans who farmed by use of slaves and who came to greatly outnumber their Roman masters. In the last century BC, at least twelve civil wars and rebellions occurred. This pattern did not break until Octavian (later *Caesar Augustus*) ended it by becoming a successful challenger to the Senate's authority, and was made *princeps* (emperor).

Between 135 BC and 71 BC there were three Servile Wars against the Roman state; the third, and most serious,[721] may have involved the revolution of 120,000[722] to 150,000[723] slaves. Additionally, in 91 BC the Social War broke out between Rome and its former allies in Italy,[724,725] collectively known as the *Socii*, over the grievance that they shared the risk of Rome's military campaigns, but not its rewards.[726,727] Despite defeats such as the Battle of Fucine Lake, Roman troops defeated the Italian militias in decisive engagements, notably the Battle of Asculum. Although they lost militarily, the *Socii* achieved their objectives with the legal proclamations of the *Lex Julia* and *Lex Plautia Papiria*, which granted citizenship to more than 500,000 Italians.

The internal unrest reached its most serious stage in the two civil wars or marches upon Rome by the consul Lucius Cornelius Sulla at the beginning of 82 BC. In the Battle of the Colline Gate at the very door of the city of Rome, a Roman army under Sulla bested an army of the Roman senate and its Samnite allies.[728] Whatever the merits of his grievances against those in power of the state, his actions marked a watershed of the willingness of Roman troops to wage war against one another that was to pave the way for the wars of the triumvirate, the overthrowing of the Senate as the *de facto* head of the Roman state, and the eventual endemic usurpation of power by contenders for the emperor-ship in the later Empire.

Conflicts with Mithridates (89–63 BC)

Mithridates the Great was the ruler of Pontus,[729] a large kingdom in Asia Minor, from 120 to 63 BC. He is remembered as one of Rome's most formidable and successful enemies who engaged three of the most prominent generals of the late Roman Republic: Sulla, Lucullus, and Pompey the Great. In a pattern familiar from the Punic Wars, the Romans came into conflict with him after the two states' spheres of influence began to overlap. Mithridates antagonised Rome by seeking to expand his kingdom, and Rome for her part seemed equally keen for war and the spoils and prestige that it might bring.[730] After conquering western Anatolia (modern Turkey) in 88 BC, Roman sources claim that Mithridates ordered the killing of the majority of the 80,000 Romans living there.[731] In the subsequent First Mithridatic War, the Roman general Lucius Cornelius Sulla forced Mithridates out of Greece proper after the Battle of Chaeronea and later Battle of Orchomenus but then had to return to Italy to answer the internal threat posed by his rival Marius; consequently, Mithridates VI was defeated but not destroyed. A peace was made between Rome and Pontus, but this proved only a temporary lull.

The Second Mithridatic War began when Rome tried to annex Bithynia as a province. In the Third Mithridatic War, first Lucius Licinius Lucullus and then Pompey the Great were sent against Mithridates.[732] Mithridates was finally defeated by Pompey in the night-time Battle of the Lycus.[733] After defeating Mithridates, Pompey invaded Caucacus, subjugated the Kingdom of Iberia and established Roman control over Colchis.

Campaign against the Cilician pirates (67 BC)

The Mediterranean had at this time fallen into the hands of pirates, largely from Cilicia. Rome had destroyed many of the states that had previously policed the Mediterranean with fleets, but had failed to step into the gap created.[734] The pirates had seized the opportunity of a relative power vacuum and had not only strangled shipping lanes but had plundered many cities on the coasts of Greece and Asia,[735] and had even made descents upon Italy itself.[736] After the Roman admiral Marcus Antonius Creticus (father of the triumvir Marcus Antonius) failed to clear the pirates to the satisfaction of the Roman authorities, Pompey was nominated his successor as commander of a special naval task force to campaign against them. It supposedly took Pompey just forty days to clear the western portion of the western Mediterranean of pirates,[737] and restore communication between Iberia, Africa, and Italy. Plutarch describes how Pompey first swept their craft from the Mediterranean in a series of small actions and through the promise of honouring the surrender of cities and craft. He then followed the main body of the pirates to their strongholds on the coast of Cilicia, and destroyed them there in the naval Battle of Korakesion.

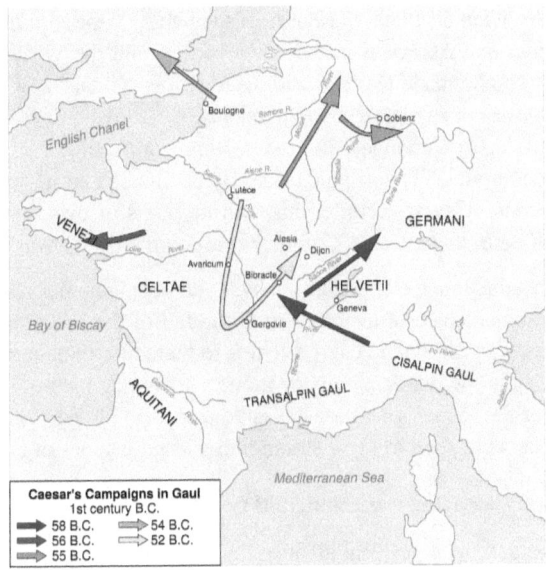

Figure 71: *Map of the Gallic Wars*

Caesar's early campaigns (59–50 BC)

During a term as praetor in Iberia, Pompey's contemporary Julius Caesar of the Roman Julii clan defeated the Calaici and Lusitani in battle.[738] Following a consular term, he was then appointed to a five-year term as Proconsular Governor of Transalpine Gaul (current southern France) and Illyria (the coast of Dalmatia).[739] Not content with an idle governorship, Caesar strove to find reason to invade Gaul, which would give him the dramatic military success he sought.[740] To this end he stirred up popular nightmares of the first sack of Rome by the Gauls and the more recent spectre of the Cimbri and Teutones. When the Helvetii and Tigurini tribes began to migrate on a route that would take them near (not into)[741] the Roman province of Transalpine Gaul, Caesar had the barely sufficient excuse he needed for his Gallic Wars, fought between 58 BC and 49 BC.[742] After slaughtering the Helvetii tribe,[743] Caesar prosecuted a "long, bitter and costly"[744] campaign against other tribes across the breadth of Gaul, many of whom had fought alongside Rome against their common enemy the Helvetii, and annexed their territory to that of Rome. Plutarch claims that the campaign cost a million Gallic lives.[745] Although "fierce and able" the Gauls were handicapped by internal disunity and fell in a series of battles over the course of a decade.[746]

Caesar defeated the *Helvetii* in 58 BC at the Battle of the Arar and Battle of Bibracte,[747] the Belgic confederacy known as the *Belgae* at the Battle of the

Axona, the *Nervii* in 57 BC at the Battle of the Sabis,[748] the *Aquitani*, *Treviri*, *Tencteri*, *Aedui* and *Eburones* in unknown battles, and the *Veneti* in 56 BC. In 55 and 54 BC he made two expeditions to Britain.[749] In 52 BC, following the Siege of Avaricum and a string of inconclusive battles,[750] Caesar defeated a union of Gauls led by Vercingetorix[751] at the Battle of Alesia,[752,753] completing the Roman conquest of Transalpine Gaul. By 50 BC, the entirety of Gaul lay in Roman hands. Caesar recorded his own accounts of these campaigns in *Commentarii de Bello Gallico* ("Commentaries on the Gallic War").

Gaul never regained its Celtic identity, never attempted another nationalist rebellion, and remained loyal to Rome until the fall of the Western Empire in 476 AD. However, although Gaul itself was to thereafter remain loyal, cracks were appearing in the political unity of Rome's governing figures – partly over concerns over the loyalty of Caesar's Gallic troops to his person rather than the state – that were soon to drive Rome into a lengthy series of civil wars.

Triumvirates, Caesarian ascension, and revolt (53–30 BC)

By 59 BC an unofficial political alliance known as the First Triumvirate was formed between Gaius Julius Caesar, Marcus Licinius Crassus, and Gnaeus Pompeius Magnus to share power and influence.[754] It was always an uncomfortable alliance given that Crassus and Pompey intensely disliked one another. In 53 BC, Crassus launched a Roman invasion of the Parthian Empire. After initial successes,[755] he marched his army deep into the desert;[756] but here his army was cut off deep in enemy territory, surrounded and slaughtered at the Battle of Carrhae[757,758] in "the greatest Roman defeat since Hannibal"[759] in which Crassus himself perished.[760] The death of Crassus removed some of the balance in the Triumvirate and, consequently, Caesar and Pompey began to move apart. While Caesar was fighting against Vercingetorix in Gaul, Pompey proceeded with a legislative agenda for Rome that revealed that he was at best ambivalent towards Caesar[761] and perhaps now covertly allied with Caesar's political enemies. In 51 BC, some Roman senators demanded that Caesar would not be permitted to stand for Consul unless he turned over control of his armies to the state, and the same demands were made of Pompey by other factions.[762,763] Relinquishing his army would leave Caesar defenceless before his enemies. Caesar chose Civil War over laying down his command and facing trial. The triumvirate was shattered and conflict was inevitable.

Pompey initially assured Rome and the senate that he could defeat Caesar in battle should he march on Rome.[764,765] However, by the spring of 49 BC, when Caesar crossed the Rubicon river with his invading forces and swept down the Italian peninsula towards Rome, Pompey ordered the abandonment of Rome. Caesar's army was still under-strength, with certain units remaining in Gaul, but on the other hand Pompey himself only had a small force at his command, and that with uncertain loyalty having served under Caesar. Tom Holland attributes Pompey's willingness to abandon Rome to waves of panicking refugees as an attempt to stir ancestral fears of invasions from the north.[766] Pompey's forces retreated south towards Brundisium,[767] and then fled to Greece.[768] Caesar first directed his attention to the Pompeian stronghold of Iberia[769] but following campaigning by Caesar in the Siege of Massilia and Battle of Ilerda he decided to attack Pompey in Greece.[770,771] Pompey initially defeated Caesar at the Battle of Dyrrachium in 48 BC[772] but failed to follow up on the victory. Pompey was decisively defeated in the Battle of Pharsalus in 48 BC[773,774] despite outnumbering Caesar's forces two to one.[775] Pompey fled again, this time to Egypt, where he was murdered[776] in an attempt to ingratiate the country with Caesar and avoid a war with Rome.

Pompey's death did not see the end of the civil wars since initially Caesar's enemies were manifold and Pompey's supporters continued to fight on after his death. In 46 BC Caesar lost perhaps as much as a third of his army when his former commander Titus Labienus, who had defected to the Pompeians several years earlier, defeated him at the Battle of Ruspina. However, after this low point Caesar came back to defeat the Pompeian army of Metellus Scipio in the Battle of Thapsus, after which the Pompeians retreated yet again to Iberia. Caesar defeated the combined forces of Titus Labienus and Gnaeus Pompey the Younger at the Battle of Munda in Iberia. Labienus was killed in the battle and the Younger Pompey captured and executed.

> "The Parthians began to shoot from all sides. They did not pick any particular target since the Romans were so close together that they could hardly miss...If they kept their ranks they were wounded. If they tried to charge the enemy, the enemy did not suffer more and they did not suffer less, because the Parthians could shoot even as they fled...When Publius urged them to charge the enemy's mail-clad horsemen, they showed him that their hands were riveted to their shields and their feet nailed through and through to the ground, so that they were helpless either for flight or for self-defence."
>
> Plutarch on the Battle of Carrhae[777]

Despite his military success, or probably because of it, fear spread of Caesar, now the primary figure of the Roman state, becoming an autocratic ruler and ending the Roman Republic. This fear drove a group of senators naming themselves The Liberators to assassinate him in 44 BC.[778] Further civil war followed between those loyal to Caesar and those who supported the actions of the Liberators. Caesar's supporter Mark Antony condemned Caesar's assassins and war broke out between the two factions. Antony was denounced as a public enemy, and Octavian was entrusted with the command of the war against him. In the Battle of Forum Gallorum Antony, besieging Caesar's assassin Decimus Brutus in Mutina, defeated the forces of the consul Pansa, who was killed, but Antony was then immediately defeated by the army of the other consul, Hirtius. At the Battle of Mutina Antony was again defeated in battle by

Hirtius, who was killed. Although Antony failed to capture Mutina, Decimus Brutus was murdered shortly thereafter.

Octavian betrayed his party, and came to terms with Caesarians Antony and Lepidus and on 26 November 43 BC the Second Triumvirate was formed,[779] this time in an official capacity. In 42 BC Triumvirs Mark Antony and Octavian fought the indecisive Battle of Philippi with Caesar's assassins Marcus Brutus and Cassius. Although Brutus defeated Octavian, Antony defeated Cassius, who committed suicide. Brutus also committed suicide shortly afterwards.

Civil war flared again when the Second Triumvirate of Octavian, Lepidus and Mark Antony failed just as the first had almost as soon as its opponents had been removed. The ambitious Octavian built a power base and then launched a campaign against Mark Antony. Together with Lucius Antonius, Mark Antony's wife Fulvia raised an army in Italy to fight for Antony's rights against Octavian but she was defeated by Octavian at the Battle of Perugia. Her death led to partial reconciliation between Octavian and Antony who went on to crush the army of Sextus Pompeius, the last focus of opposition to the second triumvirate, in the naval Battle of Naulochus.

As before, once opposition to the triumvirate was crushed, it started to tear at itself. The triumvirate expired on the last day of 33 BC and was not renewed in law and in 31 BC, war began again. At the Battle of Actium,[780] Octavian decisively defeated Antony and Cleopatra in a naval battle near Greece, using fire to destroy the enemy fleet.[781]

Octavian went on to become Emperor under the name Augustus and, in the absence of political assassins or usurpers, was able to greatly expand the borders of the Empire.

Empire

Early to Middle (30 BC – 180 AD)

Imperial expansion (40 BC – 117 AD)

Secure from interior enemies, Rome achieved great territorial gains in both the East and the West. In the West, following humiliating defeats at the hands of the Sugambri, Tencteri and Usipetes tribes in 16 BC,[782] Roman armies pushed north and east out of Gaul to subdue much of Germania. The Pannonian revolt in 6 AD forced the Romans to cancel their plan to cement their conquest of Germania.[783,784] Despite the loss of a large army almost to the man of Varus' famous defeat at the hands of the Germanic leader Arminius in the Battle of the Teutoburg Forest in 9 AD,[785,786,787] Rome recovered and continued its expansion up to and beyond the borders of the known world. Roman armies under

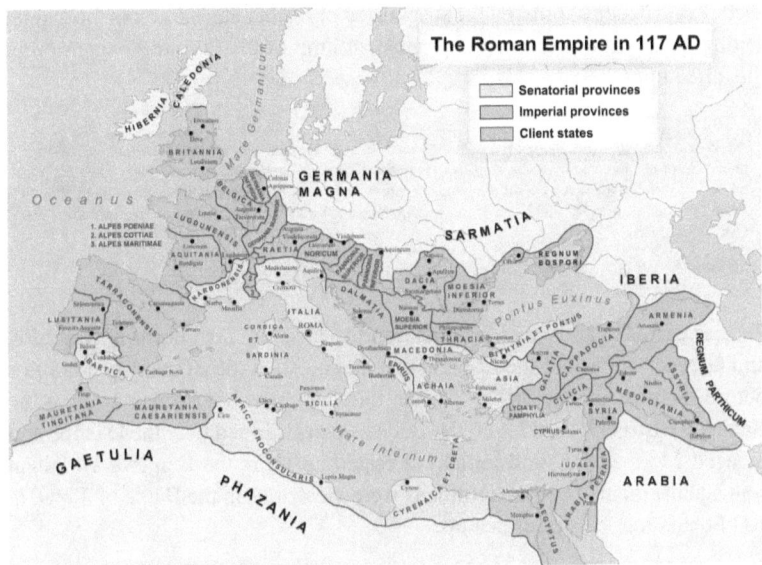

Figure 72: *The Roman Empire at its greatest extent under Trajan in 117 AD*

Germanicus pursued several more campaigns against the Germanic tribes of the Marcomanni, Hermunduri, Chatti,[788] Cherusci,[789] Bructeri, and Marsi.[790] Overcoming several mutinies in the armies along the Rhine,[791] Germanicus defeated the Germanic tribes of Arminius in a series of battles culminating in the Battle of the Weser River.[792]

After Caesar's preliminary low-scale invasions of Britain,[793,794] the Romans invaded in force in 43 AD,[795] forcing their way inland through several battles against British tribes, including the Battle of the Medway, the Battle of the Thames, the Battle of Caer Caradoc and the Battle of Mona.[796] Following a general uprising[797,798] in which the Britons sacked Colchester,[799] St Albans[800] and London,[801] the Romans suppressed the rebellion in the Battle of Watling Street[802,803] and went on to push as far north as central Scotland in the Battle of Mons Graupius.[804,805] Tribes in modern-day Scotland and Northern England repeatedly rebelled against Roman rule and two military bases were established in Britannia to protect against rebellion and incursions from the north, from which Roman troops built and manned Hadrian's Wall.[806]

On the continent, the extension of the Empire's borders beyond the Rhine hung in the balance for some time, with the emperor Caligula apparently poised to invade Germania in 39 AD, and Cnaeus Domitius Corbulo crossing the Rhine in 47 AD and marching into the territory of the Frisii and Chauci.[807] Caligula's successor, Claudius, ordered the suspension of further attacks across the Rhine, setting what was to become the permanent limit of the Empire's expansion in this direction.

> "Never was there slaughter more cruel than took place there in the marshes and woods, never were more intolerable insults inflicted by barbarians, especially those directed against the legal pleaders. They put out the eyes of some of them and cut off the hands of others; they sewed up the mouth of one of them after first cutting out his tongue, which one of the barbarians held in his hand, exclaiming *At last, you viper, you have ceased to hiss!*."
>
> *Florus on the loss of Varus' force*[808]

Further east, Trajan turned his attention to Dacia, an area north of Macedon and Greece and east of the Danube that had been on the Roman agenda since before the days of Caesar[809,810] when they had beaten a Roman army at the Battle of Histria.[811] In 85 AD, the Dacians had swarmed over the Danube and pillaged Moesia[812,813] and initially defeated an army the Emperor Domitian sent against them,[814] but the Romans were victorious in the Battle of Tapae in AD 88 and a truce was drawn up.

Emperor Trajan recommenced hostilities against Dacia and, following an uncertain number of battles,[815] defeated the Dacian general Decebalus in the Second Battle of Tapae in 101 AD.[816] With Trajan's troops pressing towards the Dacian capital Sarmizegethusa, Decebalus once more sought terms.[817] Decebalus rebuilt his power over the following years and attacked Roman garrisons again in 105 AD. In response Trajan again marched into Dacia,[818] besieging the Dacian capital in the Siege of Sarmizethusa, and razing it to the ground.[819] With Dacia quelled, Trajan subsequently invaded the Parthian empire to the east, his conquests taking the Roman Empire to its greatest extent. Rome's borders in the east were indirectly governed through a system of client states for some time, leading to less direct campaigning than in the west in this period.[820]

The Kingdom of Armenia between the Black Sea and Caspian Sea became a focus of contention between Rome and the Parthian Empire, and control of the region was repeatedly gained and lost. The Parthians forced Armenia into submission from 37 AD[821] but in 47 AD the Romans retook control of the kingdom and offered it client kingdom status. Under Nero, the Romans fought a campaign between 55 and 63 AD against the Parthian Empire, which had again invaded Armenia. After gaining Armenia once more in 60 AD and subsequently losing it again in 62 AD, the Romans sent Gnaeus Domitius Corbulo in 63 AD into the territories of Vologases I of Parthia. Corbulo succeeded in returning Armenia to Roman client status, where it remained for the next century.

Year of the Four Emperors (69 AD)

In 69 AD, Marcus Salvius Otho, governor of Lusitania, had the Emperor Galba murdered[822,823] and claimed the throne for himself.[824,825] However, Vitellius, governor of the province of Germania Inferior, had also claimed the throne[826,827] and marched on Rome with his troops. Following an inconclusive battle near Antipolis,[828] Vitellius' troops attacked the city of Placentia in the Assault of Placentia, but were repulsed by the Othonian garrison.[829]

Otho left Rome on March 14, and marched north towards Placentia to meet his challenger. In the Battle of Locus Castorum the Othonians had the better of the fighting,[830] and Vitellius' troops retreated to Cremona. The two armies met again on the Via Postunia, in the First Battle of Bedriacum,[831] after which the Othonian troops fled back to their camp in Bedriacum,[832] and the next day surrendered to the Vitellian forces. Otho decided to commit suicide rather than fight on.[833]

Meanwhile, the forces stationed in the Middle East provinces of Judaea and Syria had acclaimed Vespasian as emperor and the Danubian armies of the provinces of Raetia and Moesia also acclaimed Vespasian as emperor. Vespasian's and Vitellius' armies met in the Second Battle of Bedriacum,[834] after which the Vitellian troops were driven back into their camp outside Cremona, which was taken.[835] Vespasian's troops then attacked Cremona itself,[836] which surrendered.

Under pretence of siding with Vespasian, Civilis of Batavia had taken up arms and induced the inhabitants of his native country to rebel.[837] The rebelling Batavians were immediately joined by several neighbouring German tribes including the Frisii. These forces drove out the Roman garrisons near the Rhine and defeated a Roman army at the Battle of Castra Vetera, after which many Roman troops along the Rhine and in Gaul defected to the Batavian cause. However, disputes soon broke out amongst the different tribes, rendering co-operation impossible; Vespasian, having successfully ended the civil war, called upon Civilis to lay down his arms, and on his refusal his legions met him in force, defeating him in the Battle of Augusta Treverorum.

Jewish revolts (66–135 AD)

The first Jewish-Roman War, sometimes called The Great Revolt, was the first of three major rebellions by the Jews of Judaea Province against the Roman Empire.[838] Judea was already a troubled region with bitter violence among several competing Jewish sects and a long history of rebellion[839] The Jews' anger turned on Rome following robberies from their temples and Roman insensitivity – Tacitus says disgust and repulsion[840] – towards their religion. The Jews began to prepare for armed revolt. Early successes, including the repulse of the First Siege of Jerusalem[841] and the Battle of Beth-Horon, only attracted greater attention from Rome and Emperor Nero appointed general Vespasian to crush the rebellion. Vespasian led his forces in a methodical clearance of the areas in revolt. By the year 68 AD, Jewish resistance in the North had been crushed. A few towns and cities held out for a few years before falling to the Romans, leading to the Siege of Masada in 73 AD[842,843] and the Second Siege of Jerusalem.[844]

In 115 AD, revolt broke out again in the province, leading to the second Jewish-Roman war known as the Kitos War, and again in 132 AD in what is known as Bar Kokhba's revolt. Both were brutally crushed.

Struggle with Parthia (114–217 AD)

By the 2nd century AD the territories of Persia were controlled by the Arsacid dynasty and known as the Parthian Empire. Due in large part to their employment of powerful heavy cavalry and mobile horse archers, Parthia was the most formidable enemy of the Roman Empire in the east. As early as 53 BC, the Roman general Crassus had invaded Parthia, but he was killed and his army was defeated at the Battle of Carrhae. In the years following Carrhae, the Romans were divided in civil war and hence unable to campaign against Parthia. Trajan also campaigned against the Parthians from 114–117 AD and briefly captured their capital Ctesiphon, putting the puppet ruler Parthamaspates on the throne. However, rebellions in Babylonia and the Jewish revolts in Judea made it difficult to maintain the captured province and the territories were abandoned.

A revitalised Parthian Empire renewed its assault in 161 AD, defeating two Roman armies and invading Armenia and Syria. Emperor Lucius Verus and general Gaius Avidius Cassius were sent in 162 AD to counter the resurgent Parthia. In this war, the Parthian city of Seleucia on the Tigris was destroyed and the palace at the capital Ctesiphon was burned to the ground by Avidius Cassius in 164 AD. The Parthians made peace but were forced to cede western Mesopotamia to the Romans.[845]

In 197 AD, Emperor Septimius Severus waged a brief and successful war against the Parthian Empire in retaliation for the support given to a rival for the imperial throne Pescennius Niger. The Parthian capital Ctesiphon was sacked by the Roman army, and the northern half of Mesopotamia was restored to Rome.

Emperor Caracalla, the son of Severus, marched on Parthia in 217 AD from Edessa to begin a war against them, but he was assassinated while on the march.[846] In 224 AD, the Parthian Empire was crushed not by the Romans but by the rebellious Persian vassal king Ardashir I, who revolted, leading to the

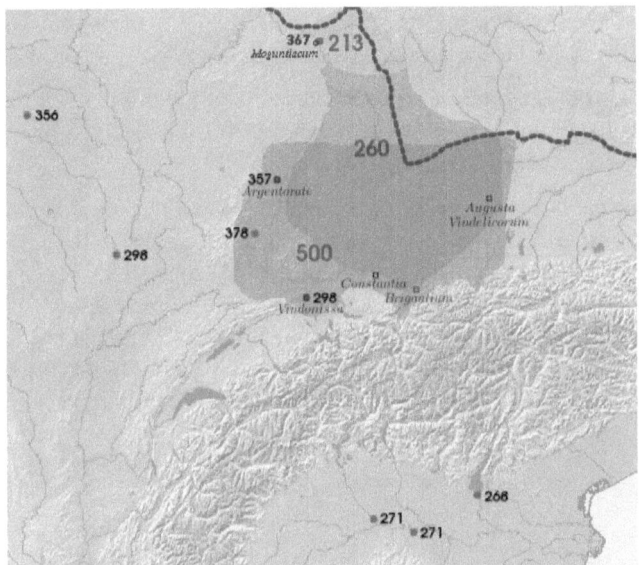

Figure 73: *Area settled by the Alamanni, and sites of Roman-Alamannic battles, 3rd to 6th century*

establishment of Sassanid Empire of Persia, which replaced Parthia as Rome's major rival in the East.

Throughout the Parthian wars, tribal groups along the Rhine and Danube took advantage of Rome's preoccupation with the eastern frontier (and the plague that the Romans suffered from after bringing it back from the east) and launched a series of incursions into Roman territories, including the Marcomannic Wars.

Late (180–476 AD)

Migration period (163–378 AD)

After Varus' defeat in Germania in the 1st century, Rome had adopted a largely defensive strategy along the border with Germania, constructing a line of defences known as *limes* along the Rhine. Although the exact historicity is unclear, since the Romans often assigned one name to several distinct tribal groups, or conversely applied several names to a single group at different times, some mix of Germanic peoples, Celts, and tribes of mixed Celto-Germanic ethnicity were settled in the lands of Germania from the 1st century onwards. The Cherusci, Bructeri, Tencteri, Usipi, Marsi, and Chatti of Varus' time had by the 3rd century either evolved into or been displaced by a confederacy or alliance of Germanic tribes collectively known as the Alamanni,[847] first mentioned by Cassius Dio describing the campaign of Caracalla in 213 AD.

In around 166 AD, several Germanic tribes pushed across the Danube, striking as far as Italy itself in the Siege of Aquileia in 166 AD, and the heartland of Greece in the Sack of Eleusis.

Although the essential problem of large tribal groups on the frontier remained much the same as the situation Rome faced in earlier centuries, the 3rd century saw a marked increase in the overall threat,[848,849] although there is disagreement over whether external pressure increased, or Rome's ability to meet it declined.[850] The Carpi and Sarmatians whom Rome had held at bay were replaced by the Goths and likewise the Quadi and Marcomanni that Rome had defeated were replaced by the greater confederation of the Alamanni.[851]

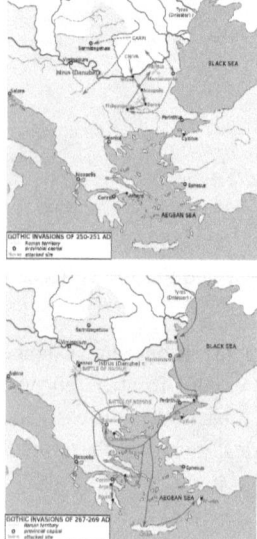

Gothic invasions

The assembled warbands of the Alamanni frequently crossed the *limes*, attacking Germania Superior such that they were almost continually engaged in conflicts with the Roman Empire, whilst Goths attacked across the Danube in battles such as the Battle of Beroa[852] and Battle of Philippopolis in 250 AD and the Battle of Abrittus in 251 AD, and both Goths and Heruli ravaged the Aegean and, later, Greece, Thrace and Macedonia.[853] However, their first major assault deep into Roman territory came in 268 AD. In that year the Romans were forced to denude much of their German frontier of troops in response to a massive invasion by another new Germanic tribal confederacy, the Goths, from the east. The pressure of tribal groups pushing into the Empire was the

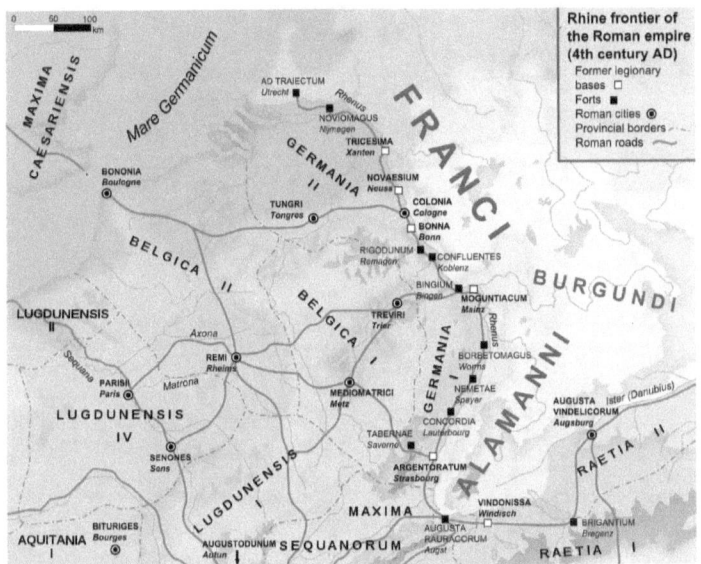

Figure 74: *Northeastern Gaul and the Rhine frontier of the Roman empire in the time of Julian*

end result of a chain of migrations with its roots far to the east:[854] Huns from the Russian steppe attacked the Goths,[855,856,857] who in turn attacked the Dacians, Alans and Sarmatians at or within Rome's borders.[858] The Goths first appeared in history as a distinct people in this invasion of 268 AD when they swarmed over the Balkan peninsula and overran the Roman provinces of Pannonia and Illyricum and even threatened Italia itself.

The Alamanni seized the opportunity to launch a major invasion of Gaul and northern Italy. However, the Visigoths were defeated in battle that summer near the modern Italian-Slovenian border and then routed in the Battle of Naissus[859] that September by Gallienus, Claudius and Aurelian, who then turned and defeated the Alemanni at the Battle of Lake Benacus. Claudius' successor Aurelian defeated the Goths twice more in the Battle of Fanum Fortunae and the Battle of Ticinum. The Goths remained a major threat to the Empire but directed their attacks away from Italy itself for several years after their defeat. By 284 AD, Gothic troops were serving on behalf of the Roman military as federated troops.[860]

The Alamanni on the other hand resumed their drive towards Italy almost immediately. They defeated Aurelian at the Battle of Placentia in 271 AD but were beaten back for a short time after they lost the battles of Fano and Pavia

Figure 75: *The Battle of the Milvian Bridge by Giulio Romano (1499–1546)*

later that year. They were beaten again in 298 AD at the battles of Lingones and Vindonissa but fifty years later they were resurgent again, making incursions in 356 AD at the Battle of Reims,[861] in 357 AD at the Battle of Strasbourg,[862] in 367 AD at the Battle of Solicinium and in 378 AD at Battle of Argentovaria. In the same year the Goths inflicted a crushing defeat on the Eastern Empire at the Battle of Adrianople,[863,864] in which the Eastern Emperor Valens was massacred along with tens of thousands of Roman troops.[865]

At the same time, Franks raided through the North Sea and the English Channel,[866] Vandals pressed across the Rhine, Iuthungi against the Danube, Iazyges, Carpi and Taifali harassed Dacia, and Gepids joined the Goths and Heruli in attacks round the Black Sea.[867] At around the same time, lesser-known tribes such as the Bavares, Baquates and Quinquegentanei raided Africa.

At the start of the 5th century, the pressure on Rome's western borders was growing intense. However, it was not only the western borders that were under threat: Rome was also under threat both internally and on its eastern borders.

Usurpers (193–394 AD)

An army that was often willing to support its general over its emperor, meant that if commanders could establish sole control of their army, they could usurp the imperial throne from that position. The so-called Crisis of the Third Century describes the turmoil of murder, usurpation and in-fighting that followed the murder of the Emperor Alexander Severus in 235 AD.[868] However, Cassius Dio marks the wider imperial decline as beginning in 180 AD with the ascension of Commodus to the throne,[869] a judgement with which Gibbon concurred,[870] and Matyszak states that "the rot ... had become established long before" even that.

Although the crisis of the 3rd century was not the absolute beginning of Rome's decline, it nevertheless did impose a severe strain on the empire as Romans waged war on one another as they had not done since the last days of the Republic. Within the space of a single century, twenty-seven military officers declared themselves emperors and reigned over parts of the empire for months or days, all but two meeting with a violent end.[871] The time was characterized by a Roman army that was as likely to be attacking itself as it was an outside invader, reaching a low point around 258 AD.[872] Ironically, while it was these usurpations that led to the breakup of the Empire during the crisis, it was the strength of several frontier generals that helped reunify the empire through force of arms.

The situation was complex, often with three or more usurpers in existence at once. Septimius Severus and Pescennius Niger, both rebel generals declared to be emperors by the troops they commanded, clashed for the first time in 193 AD at the Battle of Cyzicus, in which Niger was defeated. However, it took two further defeats at the Battle of Nicaea later that year and the Battle of Issus the following year, for Niger to be destroyed. Almost as soon as Niger's userpation had been ended, Severus was forced to deal with another rival for the throne in the person of Clodius Albinus, who had originally been allied to Severus. Albinus was proclaimed emperor by his troops in Britain and, crossing over to Gaul, defeated Severus' general Virius Lupus in battle, before being in turn defeated and killed in the Battle of Lugdunum by Severus himself.

After this turmoil, Severus faced no more internal threats for the rest of his reign,[873] and the reign of his successor Caracalla passed uninterrupted for a while until he was murdered by Macrinus, who proclaimed himself emperor. Despite Macrinus having his position ratified by the Roman senate, the troops of Varius Avitus declared him to be emperor instead, and the two met in battle at the Battle of Antioch in 218 AD, in which Macrinus was defeated.[874] However, Avitus himself, after taking the imperial name Elagabalus, was murdered shortly afterwards and Alexander Severus was proclaimed emperor by both the Praetorian Guard and the senate who, after a short reign, was murdered in turn. His murderers were working on behalf of the army who were unhappy with their lot under his rule and who raised in his place Maximinus Thrax. However, just as he had been raised by the army, Maximinus was also brought down by them and despite winning the Battle of Carthage against the senate's newly proclaimed Gordian II, he too was murdered[875] when it appeared to his forces as though he would not be able to best the next senatorial candidate for the throne, Gordian III.

Gordian III's fate is not certain, although he may have been murdered by his own successor, Philip the Arab, who ruled for only a few years before the army again raised a general, Decius, by their proclamation to emperor, who then defeated Philip in the Battle of Verona.[876] Several succeeding generals avoided battling usurpers for the throne by being murdered by their own troops before battle could commence. The lone exception to this rule was Gallienus, emperor from 260 to 268 AD, who confronted a remarkable array of usurpers, most of whom he defeated in pitched battle. The army was mostly spared further infighting until around 273 AD, when Aurelian defeated the Gallic usurper Tetricus in the Battle of Chalons. The next decade saw an incredible number of usurpers, sometimes three at the same time, all vying for the imperial throne. Most of the battles are not recorded, due primarily to the turmoil of the time, until Diocletian, a usurper himself, defeated Carinus at the Battle of the Margus and become emperor.

Some small measure of stability again returned at this point, with the empire split into a Tetrarchy of two greater and two lesser emperors, a system that staved off civil wars for a short time until 312 AD. In that year, relations between the tetrarchy collapsed for good and Constantine I, Licinius, Maxentius and Maximinus jostled for control of the empire. In the Battle of Turin Constantine defeated Maxentius, and in the Battle of Tzirallum, Licinius defeated Maximinus. From 314 AD onwards, Constantine defeated Licinius in the Battle of Cibalae, then the Battle of Mardia, and then again at the Battle of Adrianople, the Battle of the Hellespont and the Battle of Chrysopolis.

Constantine then turned upon Maxentius, beating him in the Battle of Verona and the Battle of Milvian Bridge in the same year. Constantine's son Constantius II inherited his father's rule and later defeated the usurper Magnentius in first the Battle of Mursa Major and then the Battle of Mons Seleucus.

Successive emperors Valens and Theodosius I also defeated usurpers in, respectively, the Battle of Thyatira, and the battles of the Save and the Frigidus.

Struggle with the Sassanid Empire (230–363 AD)

After overthrowing the Parthian confederacy,[877] the Sassanid Empire that arose from its remains pursued a more aggressive expansionist policy than their predecessors[878,879] and continued to make war against Rome. In 230 AD, the first Sassanid emperor attacked Roman territory first in Armenia and then in Mesopotamia but Roman losses were largely restored by Severus within a few years. In 243 AD, Emperor Gordian III's army retook the Roman cities of Hatra, Nisibis and Carrhae from the Sassanids after defeating the Sassanids at the Battle of Resaena[880] but what happened next is unclear: Persian sources claim that Gordian was defeated and killed in the Battle of Misikhe[881] but Roman sources mention this battle only as an insignificant setback and suggest that Gordian died elsewhere.[882]

Certainly, the Sassanids had not been cowed by the previous battles with Rome and in 253 AD the Sassanids under Shapur I penetrated deeply into Roman territory several times, defeating a Roman force at the Battle of Barbalissos and conquering and plundering Antiochia in 252 AD following the Siege of Antiochia. The Romans recovered Antioch by 253 AD,[883] and Emperor Valerian gathered an army and marched eastward to the Sassanid borders. In 260 AD at the Battle of Edessa the Sassanids defeated the Roman army and captured the Roman Emperor Valerian.

By the late 3rd century, Roman fortunes on the eastern frontier improved dramatically. During a period of civil upheaval in Persia, emperor Carus led a successful campaign into Persia essentially uncontested, sacking Ctesiphon in 283 AD. During the reign of the Tetrarchy, emperors Diocletian and Galerius brought a decisive conclusion to the war, sacking Ctesiphon in 299 AD and expanding the Roman eastern frontier dramatically with the Treaty of Nisibis. The treaty brought lasting peace between Rome and the Sassanids for almost four decades until the end of Constantine the Great's reign. In 337 AD, Shapur II broke the peace and began a 26-year conflict, attempting with little success to conquer Roman fortresses in the region. After early Sassanid successes including the Battle of Amida in 359 AD and the Siege of Pirisabora in 363 AD,[884] Emperor Julian met Shapur in 363 AD in the Battle of Ctesiphon outside the walls of the Persian capital. The Romans were victorious but were unable to take the city, and were forced to retreat due to their vulnerable position in the middle of hostile territory. Julian was killed in the Battle of Samarra during the retreat, possibly by one of his own men.

There were several future wars, although all brief and small-scale, since both the Romans and the Sassanids were forced to deal with threats from other directions during the 5th century. A war against Bahram V in 420 AD over the persecution of the Christians in Persia led to a brief war that was soon concluded by treaty and in 441 AD a war with Yazdegerd II was again swiftly concluded by treaty after both parties battled threats elsewhere.[885]

Figure 76: *Europe in 476, from Muir's Historical Atlas (1911)*

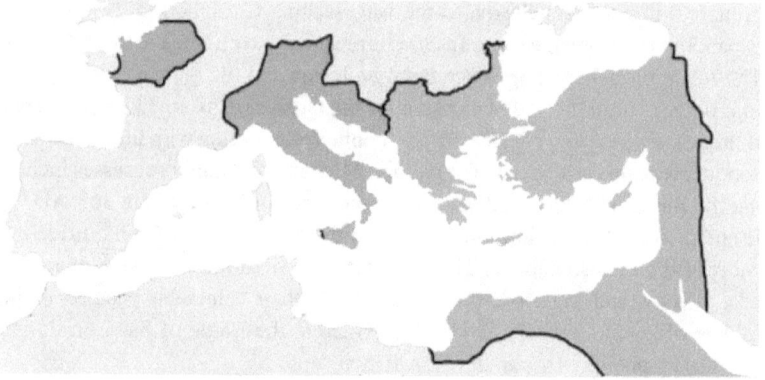

Figure 77: *The Western and Eastern Roman Empires by 476*

Collapse of the Western Empire (402–476 AD)

Many theories have been advanced in way of explanation for decline of the Roman Empire, and many dates given for its fall, from the onset of its decline in the 3rd century[886] to the fall of Constantinople in 1453.[887] Militarily, however, the Empire finally fell after first being overrun by various non-Roman peoples and then having its heart in Italy seized by Germanic troops in a revolt. The historicity and exact dates are uncertain, and some historians do not consider that the Empire fell at this point.

The Empire became gradually less Romanised and increasingly Germanic in nature: although the Empire buckled under Visigothic assault, the overthrow of the last Emperor Romulus Augustus was carried out by federated Germanic troops from within the Roman army rather than by foreign troops. In this sense had Odoacer not renounced the title of Emperor and named himself "King of Italy" instead, the Empire might have continued in name. Its identity, however, was no longer Roman – it was increasingly populated and governed by Germanic peoples long before 476 AD. The Roman people were by the 5th century "bereft of their military ethos"[888] and the Roman army itself a mere supplement to federated troops of Goths, Huns, Franks and others fighting on their behalf.

Rome's last gasp began when the Visigoths revolted around 395 AD.[889] Led by Alaric I,[890] they attempted to seize Constantinople,[891] but were rebuffed and instead plundered much of Thrace in northern Greece.[892] In 402 AD they besieged Mediolanum, the capital of Roman Emperor Honorius, defended by Roman Gothic troops. The arrival of the Roman Stilicho and his army forced Alaric to lift his siege and move his army towards Hasta (modern Asti) in western Italy, where Stilicho attacked it at the Battle of Pollentia,[893,894] capturing Alaric's camp. Stilicho offered to return the prisoners in exchange for the Visigoths returning to Illyricum but upon arriving at Verona, Alaric halted his retreat. Stilicho again attacked at the Battle of Verona[895] and again defeated Alaric,[896] forcing him to withdraw from Italy.

In 405 AD, the Ostrogoths invaded Italy itself, but were defeated. However, in 406 AD an unprecedented number of tribes took advantage of the freezing of the Rhine to cross *en masse*: Vandals, Suevi, Alans and Burgundians swept across the river and met little resistance in the Sack of Moguntiacum and the Sack of Treviri,[897] completely overrunning Gaul. Despite this grave danger, or perhaps because of it, the Roman army continued to be wracked by usurpation, in one of which Stilicho, Rome's foremost defender of the period, was put to death.[898]

It is in this climate that, despite his earlier setback, Alaric returned again in 410 AD and managed to sack Rome.[899,900,901] The Roman capital had by this time moved to the Italian city of Ravenna,[902] but some historians view 410 AD as an alternative date for the true fall of the Roman Empire.[903] Without possession of Rome or many of its former provinces, and increasingly Germanic in nature, the Roman Empire after 410 AD had little in common with the earlier Empire. By 410 AD, Britain had been mostly denuded of Roman troops,[904,905] and by 425 AD was no longer part of the Empire, and much of western Europe was beset "by all kinds of calamities and disasters",[906] coming under barbarian kingdoms ruled by Vandals, Suebians, Visigoths and Burgundians.[907]

> "The fighting became hand-to-hand, fierce, savage, confused and without the slightest respite.... Blood from the bodies of the slain turned a small brook which flowed through the plain into a torrent. Those made desperately thirsty by their injuries drank water so augmented with blood that in their misery it seemed as though they were forced to drink the very blood which had poured from their wounds"
>
> *Jordanes on the Battle of the Catalaunian Plains*[908]

The remainder of Rome's territory—if not its nature—was defended for several decades following 410 AD largely by Flavius Aëtius, who managed to play off each of Rome's barbarian invaders against one another. In 436 AD he led a Hunnic army against the Visigoths at the Battle of Arles, and again in 436 AD at the Battle of Narbonne. In 451 AD he led a combined army, including his former enemy the Visigoths, against the Huns at the Battle of the Catalaunian Plains,[909,910,911] beating them so soundly that although they later sacked Concordia, Altinum, Mediolanum,[912] Ticinum, and Patavium, they never again directly threatened Rome. Despite being the only clear champion of the Empire at this point Aëtius was slain by the Emperor Valentinian III's own hand, leading Sidonius Apollinaris to observe, "I am ignorant, sir, of your motives or provocations; I only know that you have acted like a man who has cut off his right hand with his left".[913]

Carthage, the second largest city in the empire, was lost along with much of North Africa in 439 AD to the Vandals,[914,915] and the fate of Rome seemed sealed. By 476 AD, what remained of the Empire was completely in the hands of federated Germanic troops and when they revolted, led by Odoacer and deposed the Emperor Romulus Augustus[916] there was nobody to stop them. Odoacer happened to hold the part of the Empire around Italy and Rome but other parts of the Empire were ruled by Visigoths, Ostrogoths, Franks, Alans and others. The Empire in the West had fallen, and its remnant in Italy was no longer Roman in nature. The Eastern Roman Empire and the Goths continued to fight over Rome and the surrounding area for many years, though by this point Rome's importance was primarily symbolic.

Bibliography

Primary sources

<templatestyles src="Template:Refbegin/styles.css" />

- Julius Caesar (1869). 🕮 *Commentaries on the Civil War*. Trans. William Alexander McDevitte and W. S. Bohn. New York: Harper & Brothers. Wikisource. (print: *Penguin Books, 1976, (tr. Jane Mitchell), ISBN 0-14-044187-5*)

- Julius Caesar (1869). ⓦ *The Alexandrian War*. Trans. William Alexander McDevitte and W. S. Bohn. New York: Harper & Brothers. Wikisource.
- Julius Caesar (1869). ⓦ *The African War*. Trans. William Alexander McDevitte and W. S. Bohn. New York: Harper & Brothers. Wikisource.
- Julius Caesar (1869). ⓦ *The Spanish War*. Trans. William Alexander McDevitte and W. S. Bohn. New York: Harper & Brothers. Wikisource.
- Cassius Dio. *The Roman History* at Project Gutenberg (print: *Penguin Books, 1987, ISBN 0-14-044448-3*)
- Florus (1889). ⓦ *Epitome of Roman History*. Trans. John Selby Watson. London: George Bell & Sons. Wikisource.
- Livy (1905). ⓦ *From the Founding of the City*. Trans. Canon Roberts. Wikisource. (print: *Book 1 as The Rise of Rome, Oxford University Press, 1998, ISBN 0-19-282296-9*)
- Jordanes. *The Origin and Deeds of the Goths* at Project Gutenberg
- Plutarch. ⓦ *Lives*. Trans. John Dryden. Wikisource. (print: *Jacques Amyot and Thomas North (tr.), Plutarch,* Lives of the Noble Grecians and Romans, *Southern Illinois University Press, 1963, ISBN 0-404-51870-2*)
- Polybius: *The Rise of the Roman Empire*[917] at LacusCurtius (print: Harvard University Press, 1927. (Translation by W. R. Paton), unknown ISBN
- Procopius. ⓦ *History of the Wars*. Trans. Henry Bronson Dewing. Wikisource.
- Sallust. *Conspiracy of Catiline and the Jurgurthine War* at Project Gutenberg (print: *John Carew Rolfe (tr.),* Sallust, *Loeb Classical Library, 1940, ISBN 0-674-99128-1*)
- Tacitus (1876). ⓦ *Annals*. Trans. Alfred John Church & William Jackson Brodribb. New York: Random House, Inc.. Wikisource.
- Tacitus (1876). ⓦ *The Histories*. Trans. Alfred John Church & William Jackson Brodribb. New York: Random House, Inc.. Wikisource. (print: *Penguin Books, 1975, ISBN 0-14-044150-6*)

Secondary and tertiary sources

<templatestyles src="Template:Refbegin/styles.css" />

- John Bagnall Bury: *History of the Later Roman Empire*[918] at LacusCurtius, 1889
- Cantor, Norman. *Antiquity*, Perennial Press, 2004, ISBN 0-06-093098-5
- Chaliand, Gérard. (ed.), *The Art of War in World History*, University of California Press, 1994, ISBN 0-520-07964-7

- Churchill, Winston. *A History of the English-Speaking Peoples*, Cassell, 1998, ISBN 0-304-34912-7
- Clunn, Tony. *In Quest of the Lost Legions*, Arminius Publishing, 1999, ISBN 0-9544190-0-6
- Ferrill, Arther. *The Fall of the Roman Empire: The Military Explanation*, Thames and Hudson, 1988, ISBN 0-500-27495-9
- Fraser, James. *The Roman Conquest Of Scotland: The Battle Of Mons Graupius AD 84*, Tempus Publishing, 2005, ISBN 0-7524-3325-3
- Edward Gibbon. *The Decline and Fall of the Roman Empire* at Project Gutenberg (print: *Penguin Books, 1985, ISBN 0-14-043189-6*)
- Goldsmith, Raymond W (1984). "An Estimate of the Size and Structure of the National Product of the Early Roman Empire"[919] (PDF). *The Review of Income and Wealth*. Series. Journal of the International Association for Research in Income and Wealth. **30**: 263–288. Archived from the original[920] (pdf) on 18 July 2011. Retrieved 3 August 2009.
- Goldsworthy, Adrian (2004). *In the Name of Rome: The Men Who Won the Roman Empire*. London: Weidenfeld & Nicolson. ISBN 0-297-84666-3.
- Goldsworthy, Adrian (2001). *The Punic Wars*. London: Cassell Military. ISBN 0-304-35284-5.
- Goldsworthy, Adrian. *The Complete Roman Army*, Thames and Hudson, 2003, ISBN 0-500-05124-0
- Grant, Michael (1993). *The History of Rome* (Revised ed.). London: Faber.
- Hanson, Victor Davis. *Carnage and Culture*, Hanson Press, 2002, ISBN 0-385-72038-6
- Harkness, Albert. *The Military System Of The Romans*, University Press of the Pacific, 2004, ISBN 1-4102-1153-3
- Heather, Peter. *The Fall of the Roman Empire: A New History*, Macmillan Publishers, 2005, ISBN 0-330-49136-9
- Holland, Tom. *Rubicon*, Little Brown, 2003, ISBN 0-316-86130-8
- Johnson, Boris (2006). *The Dream of Rome*. HarperPress. ISBN 0-00-722441-9.
- Arnold Hugh Martin Jones, *The Later Roman Empire*, Johns Hopkins University Press, 1964, ISBN 0-8018-3285-3
- Robin Lane Fox, *The Classical World*, Penguin Books, 2005, ISBN 0-14-102141-1
- B. H. Liddell Hart, *Scipio Africanus*, Da Capo Press, 1994, ISBN 0-306-80583-9
- Luttwak, Edward (1979). *The grand strategy of the Roman Empire: from the first century A.D. to the third*. Baltimore: Johns Hopkins University Press. ISBN 0-8018-2158-4.

- Philip Matyszak, *The Enemies of Rome*, Thames and Hudson, 2004, ISBN 0-500-25124-X
- Theodor Mommsen. *The History of Rome* at Project Gutenberg
- Pennell, Robert Franklin (2004) [1894]. *Ancient Rome: From the earliest times down to 476 A. D.*[921] (Revised ed.). Boston, Chicago: Allyn and Bacon, Project Gutenberg.
- Rodgers, Nigel. *The Roman Army: Legions, Wars and Campaigns: A Military History of the World's First Superpower From the Rise of the Republic and the Might of the Empire to the Fall of the West*, Southwater, 2005, ISBN 1-84476-210-6
- Henry William Frederick Saggs, *Civilization Before Greece and Rome*, Yale University Press, 1989, ISBN 0-300-05031-3
- Antonio Santosuosso, *Storming the Heavens: Soldiers, Emperors and Civilians in the Roman Empire*, Westview Press, 2001, ISBN 0-8133-3523-X
- Trigger, Bruce G (2003). *Understanding Early Civilizations: A Comparative Study*. Cambridge: Cambridge University Press. ISBN 0-521-82245-9.
- Michael Wood, *In Search of the First Civilizations*, BBC Books, 1992, ISBN 0-563-52266-6
- George Patrick Welch, *Britannia: The Roman Conquest & Occupation of Britain*, Hale, 1963, OCLC 676710326[922]

<indicator name="featured-star"> </indicator>

List of Roman wars and battles

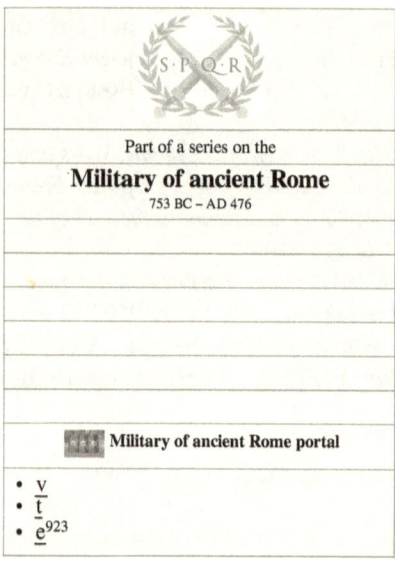

The following is a **List of Roman wars and battles** fought by the ancient Roman Kingdom, Roman Republic and Roman Empire, organized by date.

8th century BC

- Wars with the Latins and the Sabines
- War with Fidenae and Veii

7th century BC

- Second war with Fidenae and Veii
- Second Sabine War
- Roman–Latin wars

6th century BC

- Pometian Revolt (503-502 BC)
    - 502 BC – Battle of Pometia – The Romans put down the revolt of Pometia and Cora.
- Roman-Sabine wars
- Roman-Etruscan wars

List of Roman wars and battles 207

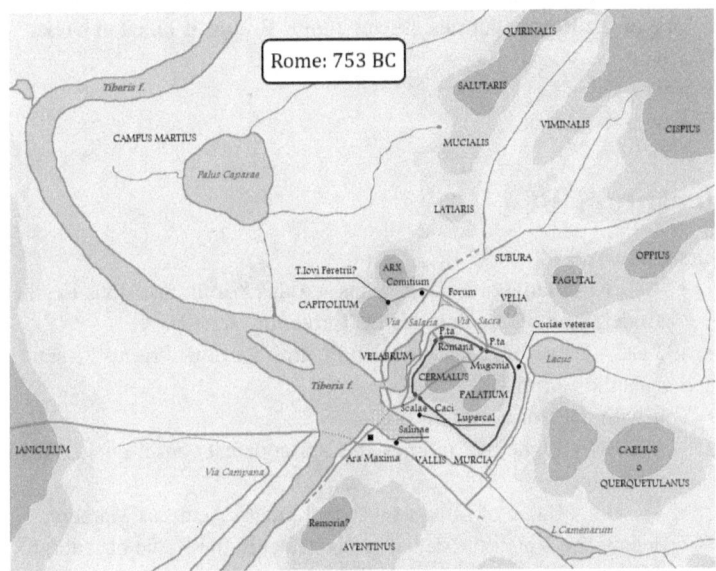

Figure 78: *The city of Rome in 753 BC*

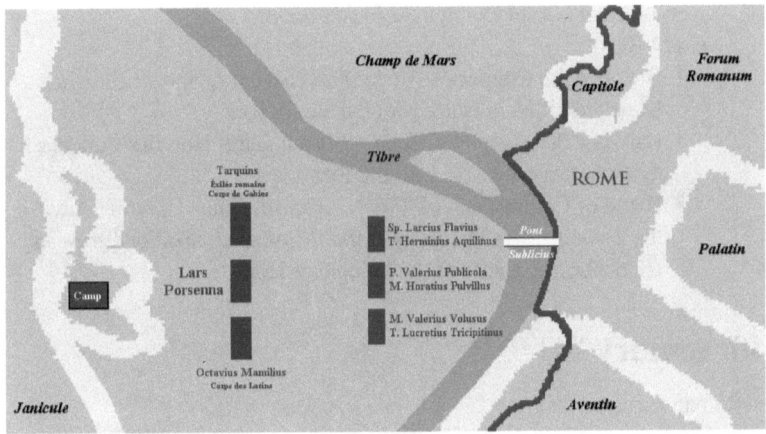

Figure 79: *508 BC Siege by Etruscans (forces in blue) of Rome (forces in red).*

- 509 BC – Battle of Silva Arsia – The Romans defeated the forces of Tarquinii and Veii led by the deposed king Lucius Tarquinius Superbus. One of the Roman consuls, Lucius Junius Brutus, is killed in battle.
- War with the Volsci
- War with Gabii
- War with the Rutuli

5th century BC

- First Latin War (498-493 BC)
    - 497 BC – Battle of Lake Regillus – Aulus Postumius Albus Regillensis defeats the Tarquinii, led by Tarquinius Superbus.
    - 495 BC – Battle of Aricia – consul Publius Servilius Priscus Structus defeats the Aurunci.
- War with the Volsci and the Aequi
    - 482 BC – Battle of Antium – the Volsci defeat consul Lucius Aemilius Mamercus.
    - 482 BC – Battle of Longula – consul Lucius Aemilius Mamercus defeats the Volsci the day after his defeat in the Battle of Antium.
    - 458 BC – Battle of Mount Algidus – Cincinnatus defeats the Aequi.
    - 446 BC – Battle of Corbio – Titus Quinctius Capitolinus Barbatus leads Roman troops to defeat the Aequi and the Volsci.
    - 480 BC – Battle of Veii (480 BC) – Consuls Marcus Fabius Vibulanus and Gnaeus Manlius Cincinnatus win heavy battle against Veians and their Etruscan allies. Consul Gnaeus Manlius Cincinnatus and former consul Quintus Fabius are slain.
    - 477 BC –
        - Battle of the Cremera – All the Fabii except Quintus Fabius Vibulanus are killed in battle with the Veii|Veians
        - Battle of the Temple of Hope – Consul Gaius Horatius Pulvillus fights indecisive battle with the Etruscans
        - Battle of Colline Gate (477 BC) – Consul Gaius Horatius Pulvillus has indecisive victory over the Etruscan civilization|Etruscans soon after the Battle of the Temple of Hope

4th century BC

- Roman-Etruscan Wars
    - 396 BC – Battle of Veii – Romans complete conquest of Etruscans
- Battle of Allia River (390 BC) – Gauls defeat the Romans, then sack Rome.
- First Samnite War (343-341 BC)

- 342 BC – Battle of Mount Gaurus – Roman general Marcus Valerius Corvus defeats the Samnites.
- 341 BC – Battle of Suessula – Roman consul Marcus Valerius Corvus defeats the Samnites once more.
- Latin War (340-338 BC)
  - 339 BC – Battle of Vesuvius – Romans under P. Decius Mus and T. Manlius Imperiosus Torquatus defeat the rebellious Latins.
  - 338 BC – Battle of Trifanum – Roman general T. Manlius Imperiosus Torquatus decisively defeats the Latins.
- Second Samnite War (326-304 BC)
  - 321 BC – Battle of the Caudine Forks – Romans under Spurius Postumius Albinus and T. Verturius Calvinus are defeated by the Samnites under Gaius Pontius.
  - 316 BC – Battle of Lautulae – Romans are defeated by the Samnites.
  - 305 BC – Battle of Bovianum – Roman consuls M. Fulvius and L. Postumius decisively defeat the Samnites.
  - 310 BC – Battle of Lake Vadimo – Romans, led by dictator Lucius Papirius Cursor, defeat the Etruscans.

3rd century BC

- Third Samnite War (298-290 BC)
  - 298 BC – Battle of Camerinum – Samnites defeat the Romans under Lucius Cornelius Scipio Barbatus.
  - 297 BC – Battle of Tifernum – Romans under Quintus Fabius Maximus and Lucius Cornelius Scipio Barbatus defeat the Samnite army led by Gellius Statius.
  - 295 BC – Battle of Sentinum – Romans under Fabius Rullianus and Publius Decimus Mus defeat the Samnites and their Etruscan and Gallic allies, forcing the Etruscans, Gauls, and Umbrians to make peace.
  - 293 BC – Battle of Aquilonia – Romans decisively defeat the Samnites.
- Wars with Gauls and Etruscans (285-282 BC)
  - 284 BC – Battle of Arretium – A Roman army under Lucius Caecilius is destroyed by the Gauls.
  - 283 BC – Battle of Lake Vadimo – A Roman army under P. Cornelius Dolabella defeats the Etruscans and Gauls.
  - 282 BC – Battle of Populonia – Etruscan resistance to Roman domination of Italy is finally crushed.
- Pyrrhic War (280-275 BC)
  - 280 BC – Battle of Heraclea – First engagement of Roman and Greek armies, the latter led by Pyrrhus of Epirus, who is victorious, but at great cost.

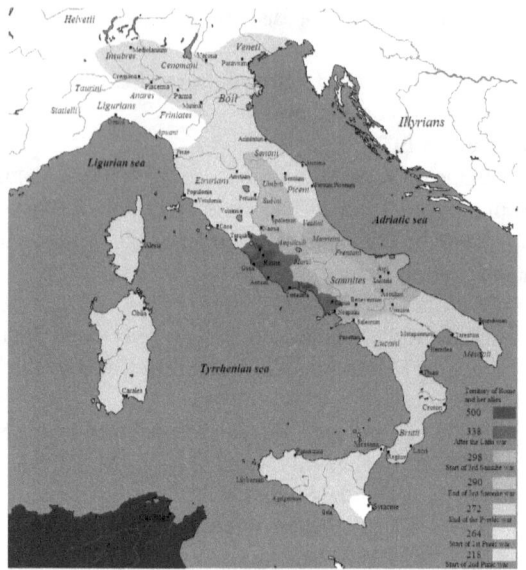

Figure 80: *Roman conquest of Italy through the Latin War (red), Samnite Wars (pink/orange), Pyrrhic War (beige), and Punic Wars (green).*

- 279 BC – Battle of Asculum – Pyrrhus again defeats the Romans but once again suffers significant casualties in the process.
- 275 BC – Battle of Beneventum – Inconclusive encounter between Pyrrhus and the Romans under Manius Curius.
- First Punic War (264-241 BC)
  - 261 BC – Battle of Agrigentum – Carthaginian forces under Hannibal Gisco and Hanno are defeated by the Romans, who attain control of most of Sicily.
  - 260 BC -
    - Battle of the Lipari Islands – A Roman naval force is defeated by the Carthaginians.
    - Battle of Mylae – A Roman naval force under C. Duillius defeats the Carthaginian fleet, giving Rome control of the western Mediterranean.
  - 258 BC – Battle of Sulci – Minor Roman victory against the Carthaginian fleet near Sardinia.
  - 257 BC – Battle of Tyndaris – Naval victory of Rome over Carthage in Sicilian waters.
  - 256 BC –
    - Battle of Cape Ecnomus – A Carthaginian fleet under Hamilcar and

Hanno is defeated in an attempt to stop a Roman invasion of Africa by Marcus Atilius Regulus.
- Battle of Adys – Romans under Regulus defeat the Carthaginians in North Africa
- 255 BC – Battle of Tunis – Carthaginians under Xanthippus, a Greek mercenary, defeat the Romans under Regulus, who is captured.
- 251 BC – Battle of Panormus – Carthaginian forces under Hasdrubal are defeated by the Romans under L. Caecilius Metellus.
- 250 BC - Siege of Lilybaeum - Siege on the Carthaginian city of Lilybaeum by Roman army under Gaius Atilius Regulus Serranus and Lucius Manlius Vulso Longus. Carthaginian victory.
- 249 BC – Battle of Drepana – Carthage under Adherbal defeat the fleet of Roman admiral Publius Claudius Pulcher.
- 242 BC – Battle of the Aegates Islands – Roman sea victory over the Carthaginians.
- First Illyrian War (229-228 BC)
- Second Illyrian War (220-219 BC)
- Second Punic War (218-201 BC)
  - 218 BC –
    - Battle of Lilybaeum – First naval clash between the navies of Carthage and Rome during the Second Punic War.
    - Battle of Cissa – Romans defeat Carthaginians near Tarraco and gain control of the territory north of the Ebro River.
    - Battle of the Ticinus – Hannibal defeats the Romans under Publius Cornelius Scipio the elder in a cavalry fight.
    - Battle of the Trebia – Hannibal defeats the Romans under Tiberius Sempronius Longus with the use of an ambush.
  - 217 BC -
    - Battle of Ebro River – In a surprise attack, Romans defeat and capture the Carthaginian fleet in Hispania.
    - Battle of Lake Trasimene – In another ambush, Hannibal destroys the Roman army of Gaius Flaminius, who is killed.
    - Battle of Ager Falernus – Avoiding destruction with deceit, Hannibal escapes Fabius' trap in this small skirmish.
  - 216 BC –
    - Battle of Cannae – Hannibal destroys the main Roman army of Lucius Aemilius Paulus and Publius Terentius Varro in what is considered one of the great masterpieces of the tactical art.
    - First Battle of Nola – Roman general Marcus Claudius Marcellus holds off an attack by Hannibal.
  - 215 BC – Second Battle of Nola – Marcellus again repulses an attack by Hannibal.

- 214 BC – Third Battle of Nola – Marcellus fights an inconclusive battle with Hannibal.
- 212 BC –
  - First Battle of Capua – Hannibal defeats the consuls Q. Fulvius Flaccus and Appius Claudius, but the Roman army escapes
  - Battle of the Silarus – Hannibal destroys the army of the Roman praetor M. Centenius Penula.
  - Battle of Herdonia – Hannibal destroys the Roman army of the praetor Gnaeus Fulvius.
- 211 BC –
  - Battle of the Upper Baetis – Publius and Gnaeus Cornelius Scipio are killed in battle with the Carthaginians under Hasdrubal Barca
  - Second Battle of Capua – Hannibal is not able to break the Roman siege of the city.
- 210 BC –
  - Second Battle of Herdonia – Hannibal destroys the Roman army of Fulvius Centumalus, who is killed.
  - Battle of Numistro – Hannibal defeats Marcellus once more
- 209 BC – Battle of Asculum – Hannibal once again defeats Marcellus, in an indecisive battle
- 208 BC – Battle of Baecula – Romans in Hispania (Iberia) under P. Cornelius Scipio the Younger defeat Hasdrubal Barca.
- 207 BC –
  - Battle of Grumentum – Roman general Gaius Claudius Nero fights an indecisive battle with Hannibal.
  - Battle of the Metaurus – Hasdrubal is defeated and killed by Nero's Roman army.
  - Battle of Carmona – Romans under Publius Cornelius Scipio besiege the city of Carmona and take it from Hasdrubal Gisco
- 206 BC –
  - Battle of Ilipa – Scipio again decisively defeats the remaining Carthaginian forces in Hispania.
  - Battle of the Guadalquivir – Roman army under Gaius Lucius Marcius Séptimus defeats a Carthaginian army under Hannón at Guadalquivir.
  - Battle of Carteia – Roman fleet under Gaius Laelius defeats a Carthaginian fleet under Adherbal
- 204 BC – Battle of Crotona – Hannibal fights a drawn battle against the Roman general Sempronius in Southern Italy.
- 203 BC – Battle of Bagbrades – Romans under Scipio defeat the Carthaginian army of Hasdrubal Gisco and Syphax. Hannibal is sent to return to Africa.

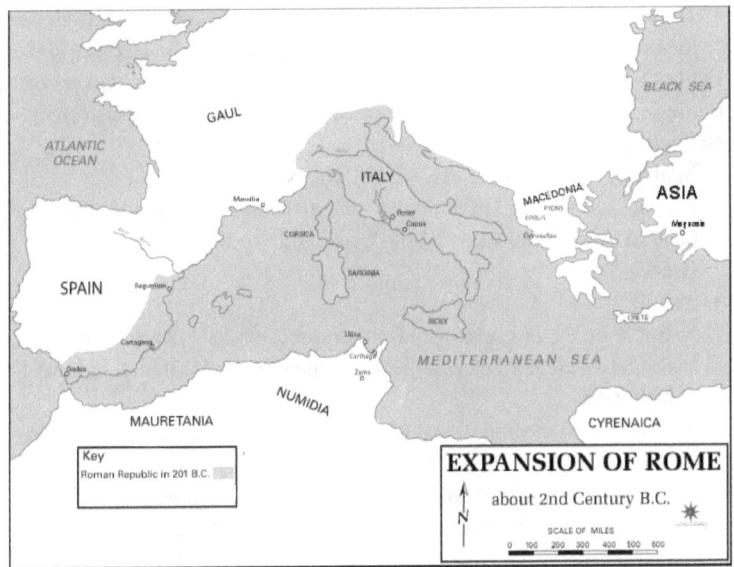

Figure 81: *Expansion of Rome by 200 BC*

- 202 BC, 19 October – Battle of Zama – Scipio Africanus Major decisively defeats Hannibal in North Africa, ending the Second Punic War.
- First Macedonian War (214-205 BC)
- Roman-Gallic wars (225-200 BC)
  - 225 BC – Battle of Faesulae – Romans are defeated by the Gauls of Northern Italy.
  - 224 BC – Battle of Telamon – Romans under Aemilius Papus and Gaius Atilius Regulus defeat the Gauls.
  - 222 BC – Battle of Clastidium – Romans under Marcus Claudius Marcellus defeat the Gauls.
  - 200 BC – Battle of Cremona – Roman forces defeat the Gauls of Cisalpine Gaul

2nd century BC

- Second Macedonian War (200-196 BC)
  - 198 BC – Battle of the Aous – Roman forces under Titus Quinctius Flamininus defeat the Macedonians under Philip V
  - 197 BC – Battle of Cynoscephalae – Romans under Flamininus decisively defeats Philip in Thessaly
- Roman-Spartan War (195 BC)

- 194 BC – Battle of Gythium – With some Roman assistance, Philopoemen of the Achaean League defeats the Spartans under Nabis
- Battle of Placentia (194 BC) – Roman victory over the Boian Gauls
- Battle of Mutina (193 BC) – Roman victory over the Boii, decisively ending the Boian threat.
- Roman-Seleucid War (192 BC - 188 BC)
  - 191 BC – Battle of Thermopylae – Romans under Manius Acilius Glabrio defeat Antiochus III the Great and force him to evacuate Greece
  - 190 BC –
    - Battle of the Eurymedon – Roman forces under Lucius Aemilius Regillus defeat a Seleucid fleet commanded by Hannibal, fighting his last battle.
    - Battle of Myonessus – Another Seleucid fleet is defeated by the Romans
    - December, Battle of Magnesia – (near Smyrna) Romans under Lucius Cornelius Scipio and his brother Scipio Africanus Major defeat Antiochus III the Great in the decisive victory of the war.
- Aetolian War (191-189 BC)
- Galatian War (189 BC)
  - Battle of Mount Olympus – Romans under Gnaeus Manlius Vulso allied with Attalus II of Pergamum deliver a crushing defeat to an army of Galatian Gauls
  - Battle of Ancyra – Gnaeus Manlius Vulso and Attalus II defeat the Galatian Gauls again before Ancyra, in what was an almost identical repeat of the Battle of Mount Olympus.
- First Celtiberian War (181-179 BC)
  - 181 BC – Battle of Manlian Pass – Romans under Fulvius Flaccus defeat an army of Celtiberians.
- Third Macedonian War (171-168 BC)
  - 171 BC – Battle of Callicinus – Perseus of Macedon defeats a Roman army under Publius Licinius Crassus.
  - 168 BC, 22 June – Battle of Pydna – Romans under Lucius Aemilius Paullus Macedonicus defeat and capture Macedonian King Perseus.
- Third Illyrian War (169-167 BC)
- Lusitanian War (155-139 BC)
- Numentine\Second Celtiberian War (154-133 BC)
  - 134 BC - Siege of Numantia - Roman forces under Scipio Aemilianus Africanus defeat and raze the Celtiberian city of Numantia.
- Fourth Macedonian War (150-148 BC)
  - 148 BC – Second battle of Pydna – The forces of the Macedonian pretender Andriscus are defeated by the Romans under Quintus Caecilius

Metellus Macedonicus.
- Third Punic War (149-146 BC)
  - 147 BC -
    - Battle of the Port of Carthage - Roman forces under Lucius Hostilius Mancinus are defeated by the Carthaginians.
    - Second Battle of Neferis - Roman forces under Scipio Aemilianus win a decisive victory against Carthage marking the turning point in the Third Punic War.
  - 146 BC – Battle of Carthage ends: Scipio Africanus Minor captures and destroys Carthage.
- Achaean War (146 BC)
  - 146 BC – Battle of Corinth – Romans under Lucius Mummius defeat the Achaean League forces of Critolaus, who is killed. Corinth is destroyed and Greece comes under direct Roman rule.
- First Servile War (135-132 BC)
- Cimbrian War (113-101 BC)
  - 112 BC - Battle of Noreia - Roman force under Gnaeus Papirius Carbo are defeated by the Cimbri
  - 109 BC – Battle of the Rhone River – Roman force under Marcus Junius Silanus are defeated by the Helvetii
  - 107 BC – Battle of Burdigala – Roman forces under Lucius Cassius Longinus are defeated by the Helvetii
  - 105 BC, 6 October – Battle of Arausio – Cimbri inflict a major defeat on the Roman army of Gnaeus Mallius Maximus
  - 102 BC - Battle of Aquae Sextiae - Romans under Gaius Marius defeat Teutons, with mass suicides among the captured women.
  - 101 BC - Battle of Vercellae – Romans under Gaius Marius defeat the Cimbri, who are entirely annihilated.
- Jugurthine War (112-105 BC)
  - 108 BC – Battle of the Muthul – Roman forces under Caecilius Metellus fight indecisively against the forces of Jugurtha of Numidia
- Second Servile War (104-103 BC)

1st century BC

- Social War (90-88 BC)
  - 89 BC – Battle of Fucine Lake – Roman forces under Lucius Porcius Cato are defeated by the Italian rebels.
  - 89 BC – Battle of Asculum – Roman army of C. Pompeius Strabo decisively defeats the rebels.
- First Mithridatic War (90-85 BC)

Figure 82: *Expansion of Rome from 200 BC (green) to 100 BC (orange).*

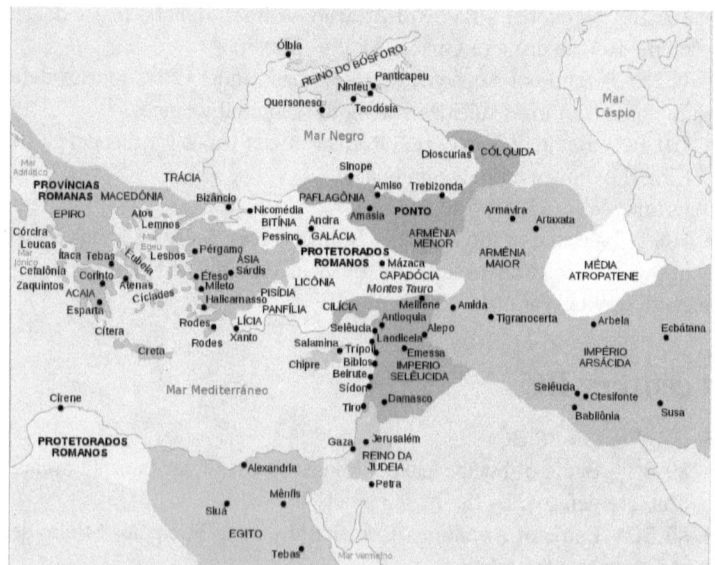

Figure 83: *Roman holdings in the East (red), clients (pink), and other nations.*

- 87 BC - 86 BC - Siege of Athens and Piraeus - Siege of Athens, which had sided with the Pontic invaders during the First Mithridatic War by Lucius Cornelius Sulla. Roman victory.
- 86 BC – Battle of Chaeronea – Roman forces of Lucius Cornelius Sulla defeat the Pontic forces of Archelaus in the First Mithridatic War
- 85 BC – Battle of Orchomenus – Sulla again defeats Archelaus in the decisive battle of the First Mithridatic War.
- First Marian-Sullan Civil War (88-87 BC)
  - 83 BC – Battle of Mount Tifata – Sulla defeats the popular forces of Caius Norbanus.
- Second Mithridatic War (83-82 BC)
- Sertorian War (83-81 BC)
  - 80 BC – Battle of the Baetis River – Rebel forces under Quintus Sertorius defeat the legal Roman forces of Lucius Fulfidias in Hispania.
- Second Marian-Sullan Civil War (82-81 BC)
  - 82 BC –
    - Battle of the Asio River – Quintus Caecilius Metellus Pius defeats a Popular army under Gaius Carrinas.
    - Battle of Sacriporto – Fought between the Optimates under Lucius Cornelius Sulla Felix and the Populares under Gaius Marius the Younger, Optimate victory.
    - First Battle of Clusium – Fought between the Optimates under Lucius Cornelius Sulla Felix and the Populares under Gnaeus Papirius Carbo, Popular victory.
    - Battle of Faventia – Fought between the Optimates under Quintus Caecilius Metellus Pius and the Populares under Gaius Norbanus Balbus, Optimate victory.
    - Battle of Fidentia – Fought between the Optimates under Marcus Terentius Varro Lucullus and the Populares under Lucius Quincius, Optimate victory.
    - Second Battle of Clusium – Pompei Magnus defeats a numerically superior Populares army under Gaius Carrinas and Gaius Marcius Censorinus.
    - Battle of Colline Gate – Sulla defeats Samnites allied to the popular party in Rome in the decisive battle of the Civil War.
- Third Mithridatic War (73-63 BC)
  - 73 BC – Battle of Cyzicus – Roman forces under Lucius Lucullus defeat the forces of Mithridates VI of Pontus
  - 72 BC – Battle of Cabira or the Rhyndacus – Lucullus defeats the retreating forces of Mithridates, opening way to Pontus
  - 69 BC – Battle of Tigranocerta – Lucullus defeats the army of Tigranes II of Armenia, who was harbouring his father-in-law Mithridates VI of

- Pontus
  - 68 BC – Battle of Artaxata – Lucullus again defeats Tigranes.
  - 66 BC – Battle of the Lycus – Pompey the Great decisively defeats Mithridates VI, effectively ending the Third Mithridatic War
- Third Servile War (73-71 BC)
  - 73 BC – Battle of Mount Vesuvius – Spartacus defeats Gaius Claudius Glaber
  - 72 BC – Battle of Picenum – Slave Revolt led by Spartacus defeat a Roman army led by Gellius Publicola and Gnaeus Cornelius Lentulus Clodianus
  - 72 BC – Battle of Mutina I – Slave Revolt led by Spartacus defeat another army of Romans.
  - 71 BC –
    - Battle of Campania – Slave Revolt led by Spartacus defeat a Roman army.
    - Battle of Campania II – a Roman army under Marcus Crassus defeats Spartacus's army of slaves.
    - Battle of the Siler River – Marcus Crassus defeats the army of Spartacus.
- Pompey's Georgian campaign (65 BC)
- Catilinarian Civil War (63-62 BC)
  - 62 BC, January – Battle of Pistoria – The forces of the conspirator Catiline are defeated by the loyal Roman armies under Gaius Antonius.
- Gallic Wars (59-51 BC)
  - 58 BC –
    - June – Battle of the Arar (Saône) – Caesar defeats the migrating Helvetii
    - July – Battle of Bibracte – Caesar again defeats the Helvetians, this time decisively.
    - September – Caesar decisively defeats the forces of the Germanic chieftain Ariovistus near modern Belfort
  - 57 BC –
    - Battle of the Axona (Aisne) – Caesar defeats the forces of the Belgae under King Galba of Suessiones.
    - Battle of the Sabis (Sambre) – Caesar defeats the Nervii.
    - Battle of Octodurus (Martigny) – Servius Galba defeats the Seduni and Veragri.
  - 52 BC – Battle of Alesia – Caesar defeats the Gallic rebel Vercingetorix, completing the Roman conquest of Gallia Comata.
- War with the Parthian Empire (53 BC)
  - 53 BC - Battle of Carrhae – Roman triumvir Crassus is disastrously

List of Roman wars and battles

Figure 84: *The extent of the Roman Republic in 40 BC after Caesar's conquests.*

defeated and killed by the Parthians. Crassus has molten gold poured down his throat by his captors.
- Caesar's Civil War (49-45 BC)
  - 49 BC, June – Battle of Ilerda – Caesar's army surround Pompeian forces and cause them to surrender.
  - 49 BC, 24 August – Battle of the Bagradas River – Caesar's general Gaius Curio is defeated in North Africa by the Pompeians under Attius Varus and King Juba I of Numidia. Curio commits suicide.
  - 48 BC, 10 July – Battle of Dyrrhachium – Caesar barely avoids a catastrophic defeat by Pompey in Macedonia
  - 48 BC, 9 August – Battle of Pharsalus – Caesar decisively defeats Pompey, who flees to Egypt
  - 47 BC, February – Battle of the Nile – Caesar defeats the forces of the Egyptian king Ptolemy XIII
  - 46 BC, 4 January – Battle of Ruspina – Caesar loses perhaps as much as a third of his army to Titus Labienus
  - 46 BC, 6 February – Battle of Thapsus – Caesar defeats the Pompeian army of Metellus Scipio in North Africa.
  - 45 BC, 17 March – Battle of Munda – In his last victory, Caesar defeats the Pompeian forces of Titus Labienus and Gnaeus Pompey the Younger in Hispania. Labienus is killed in the battle and the Younger Pompey captured and executed.
- War with Pontus

- 47 BC, May – Battle of Zela – Caesar defeats Pharnaces II of Pontus. This is the battle where he famously said *Veni, vidi, vici*. (I came, I saw, I conquered.)
- Liberators' civil war (44-42 BC)
  - 43 BC, 14 April – Battle of Forum Gallorum – Antony, besieging Caesar's assassin Decimus Brutus in Mutina, defeats the forces of the consul Pansa, who is killed, but is then immediately defeated by the army of the other consul, Hirtius
  - 43 BC, 21 April – Battle of Mutina – Antony is again defeated in battle by Hirtius, who is killed. Although Antony fails to capture Mutina, Decimus Brutus is murdered shortly thereafter.
  - 42 BC, 3 October – First Battle of Philippi – Triumvirs Mark Antony and Octavian fight an indecisive battle with Caesar's assassins Marcus Brutus and Cassius. Although Brutus defeats Octavian, Antony defeats Cassius, who commits suicide.
  - 42 BC, 23 October – Second Battle of Philippi – Brutus's army is decisively defeated by Antony and Octavian. Brutus escapes, but commits suicide soon after.
- Sicilian revolt (44-36 BC)
  - 36 BC – Battle of Naulochus – Octavian's fleet, under the command of Marcus Vipsanius Agrippa defeats the forces of the rebel Sextus Pompeius.
- Fulvia's civil war (Perusine War) (41-40 BC)
  - 41 BC – Battle of Perugia – Mark Antony's brother Lucius Antonius and his wife Fulvia are defeated by Octavian.
- Final War of the Roman Republic (32-30 BC)
  - 31 BC, 2 September – Battle of Actium – Octavian decisively defeats Antony and Cleopatra in a naval battle near Greece.
- Cantabrian Wars (29-19 BC)
  - 25 BC - Battle of Vellica - Roman forces under Augustus against the Cantabri people, Roman victory.
  - 25 BC - Siege of Aracillum - Roman forces under Gaius Antistius Vetus against the Cantabri people, Roman victory.
- Germanic Battles (16-11 BC)
  - Clades Lolliana (16 BC) – The troops of Consul Marcus Lollius Paulinus are defeated by West Germanic warriors in Gaul.
  - Battle of the Lupia River (11 BC) – Roman forces under Augustus's stepson Drusus win a victory in Germany.

List of Roman wars and battles 221

Figure 85: *The Roman Empire under Augustus: The Republic in 31 BC (yellow) and Augustus's conquests (shades of green). Client states are in pink.*

1st century

- Battle of the Teutoburg Forest (9) – German leader Arminius ambushes three Roman legions under Publius Quinctilius Varus.
- Battle of the Weser River (16) - Legions under Germanicus defeat German tribes of Arminius.
- Roman conquest of Britain (43-96)
  - 43 – Battle of the Medway – Claudius and general Aulus Plautius defeat a confederation of British Celtic tribes. Roman invasion of Britain begins
  - 50 – Battle of Caer Caradoc – British chieftain Caractacus is defeated and captured by the Romans under Ostorius Scapula.
  - 71 - Battle of Scotch Corner
  - 84 – Battle of Mons Graupius. Romans under Gnaeus Julius Agricola defeat the Caledonians.
- Roman–Parthian War of 58–63
  - 58 – Sack of Artaxata by Gnaeus Domitius Corbulo during the Roman–Parthian War over Armenia
  - 49 – The Siege of Uspe – Roman auxiliaries under Julius Aquila and King Cotys besiege the rebel forces of Siraces and Mithridates
  - 59 – Capture of Tigranocerta by Corbulo.

- 62 – Battle of Rhandeia – Romans under Lucius Caesennius Paetus are defeated by a Parthian-Armenian army under King Tiridates of Parthia.
- Boudica's uprising (60-61)
  - 60 – Battle of Camulodunum – Boudica begins her uprising against the Romans by capturing and then sacking Camulodunum then moves on Londinium.
  - 61 – Battle of Watling Street – Boudica is defeated by Suetonius Paullinus
- First Jewish–Roman War (66-73)
  - 66 - Battle of Beth-Horon – Jewish forces led by Eleazar ben Simon defeat a Roman punitive force led by Cestius Gallus, Governor of Syria
  - 73 – Battle of Masada
- Roman Civil War of 68-69 AD
  - 69 –
    - Winter – Battle of 'Forum Julii' Othonian forces defeat a small group of Vitellianist auxiliaries in Gallia Narbonensis
    - 14 April – Battle of Bedriacum – Vitellius, commander of the Rhine armies, defeats Emperor Otho and seizes the throne.
    - 24 October – Second Battle of Bedriacum – Forces under Antonius Primus, the commander of the Danube armies, loyal to Vespasian, defeat the forces of Emperor Vitellius.
- Domitian's Dacian War (87-88)
  - 87 – Dacian King Decebalus crushes the Roman army at Tapae (today Transylvania, Romania), Legio V Alaudae and general Cornelius Fuscus perish in battle.
  - 88 – the Romans return and obtain a victory in the same battleground

2nd century

- First Dacian War (101-102)
  - 101 – Second Battle of Tapae – Trajan defeats Decebalus, with heavy losses.
  - 102 – Battle of Adamclisi - Roman forces led by Trajan annihilate a mixed Dacian-Roxolano-Sarmatae army, with heavy casualties on the Roman side.
- Second Dacian War (105-106)
  - 106 – Battle of Sarmisegetusa – A Roman army led by Trajan conquers and destroys the Dacian capital. Part of Dacia is annexed to the Roman Empire.
- Roman-Persian Wars
  - 114-117 – Trajan invades Parthia and occupies Ctesiphon.

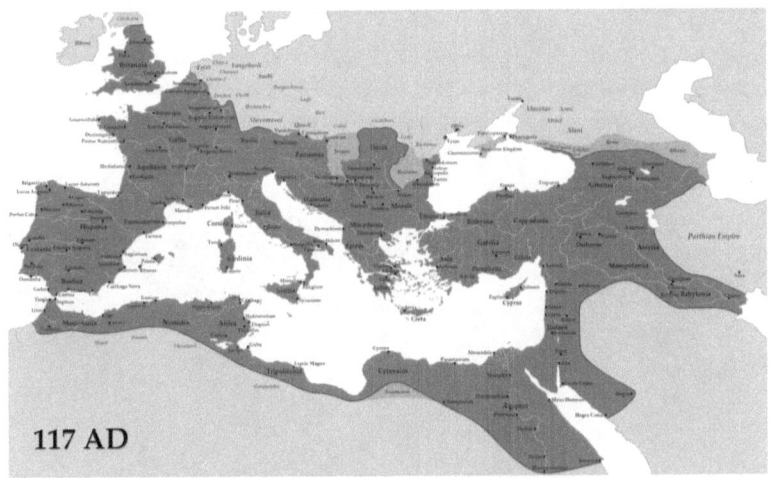

Figure 86: *The extent of the Roman Empire under Trajan (117) The Empire is in red and dependencies are in pink.*[924]

- 161-165 – Roman–Parthian War — Vologases IV invades Armenia, but is pushed back and Ctesiphon is sacked.
- 195-197 – Septimus Severus invades, sacks Ctesiphon, and acquires northern Mesopotamia.
- Kitos War (115-117)
- Second Jewish Revolt (132-135)
- Marcomannic Wars (166-180)
  - 170 – Battle of Carnuntum – Marcomannic King Ballomar defeats the Roman Army and invade Italy.
  - 178-179 – Praetorian Prefect Teratenius Paternus defeats the Quadi.
  - 179 or 180 – Battle of Laugaricio – Marcus Valerius Maximianus defeats the Quadi in Slovakia.
- Roman Civil War of 193-197 AD
  - 193 – Battle of Cyzicus – Septimius Severus, the new Emperor, defeats his eastern rival Pescennius Niger
  - 193 – Battle of Nicaea – Severus again defeats Niger
  - 194 – Battle of Issus – Severus finally defeats Niger.
  - 197, 17 February – Battle of Lugdunum – Emperor Septimius Severus defeats and kills his rival Clodius Albinus, securing full control over the Empire.

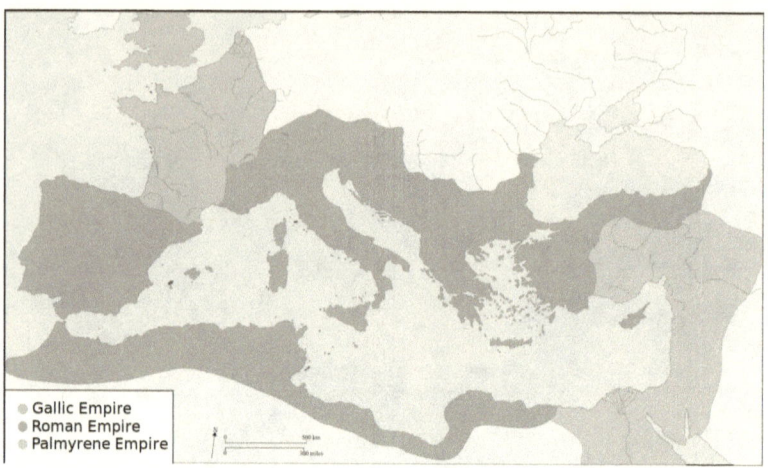

Figure 87: *The Empires of Gaul (green), Rome (red), and Palmyra (yellow) in 271.*

3rd century

See Crisis of the Third Century

- Persian wars
  - 217 – Battle of Nisibis – Bloody stalemate between the Parthians and the Roman army under Emperor Macrinus.
  - 243 – Battle of Resaena – Roman forces under Gordian III defeat the Persians under Shapur I.
  - 260 – Battle of Edessa – Emperor Shapur I of Persia defeats and captures the Roman Emperor Valerian
  - 296 – Battle of Callinicum – Romans under the Caesar Galerius are defeated by the Persians under Narseh.
- Civil wars
  - 218, 18 June – Battle of Antioch – Varius Avitus defeats Emperor Macrinus to claim the throne under the name Elagabalus.
  - 238 – Battle of Carthage – Troops loyal to the Roman Emperor Maximinus Thrax defeat and kill his successor Gordian II.
  - 274 – Battle of Châlons (274) – Aurelian defeats the Gallic usurper Tetricus, reestablishing central control of the whole empire.
  - 285 – Battle of the Margus – The usurper Diocletian defeats the army of the Emperor Carinus, who is killed.
- Gothic and Alamannic wars
  - 235 - late in the winter time - Battle of Harzhorn - Small Roman army defeats a German army while retreating back to Roman territory.

- 250 – Battle of Philippopolis – King Cuiva of the Goths defeats a Roman army.
- 251, 1 July – Battle of Abrittus – Goths defeat and kill the Roman Emperors Decius and Herennius Etruscus
- 259 – Battle of Mediolanum – Emperor Gallienus decisively defeats the Alemanni that invaded Italy
- 268 – Battle of Naissus – Emperor Gallienus and his generals Claudius and Aurelian decisively defeat the Goths.
- 268 – Battle of Lake Benacus – Romans under Emperor Claudius II defeat the Alemanni
- 271 – Battle of Placentia – Emperor Aurelian is defeated by the Alemanni forces invading Italy
- 271 –Battle of Fano – Aurelian defeats the Alamanni, who begin to retreat from Italy
- 271 –Battle of Pavia – Aurelian destroys the retreating Alemanni army.
- 298 –Battle of Lingones – Caesar Constantius Chlorus defeats the Alemanni
- 298 –Battle of Vindonissa – Constantius again defeats the Alamanni
- Palmyrene war
    - 272 –Battle of Immae – Aurelian defeats the army of Zenobia of Palmyra
    - 272 – Battle of Emesa – Aurelian decisively defeats Zenobia.

4th century

The 4th century begins with civil war resulting in the ascendancy of Constantine I, then, after his death, wars with Persia and Germanic tribes, punctuated frequently with more civil wars.

- Civil Wars of the Tetrarchy (306-324)
    - 312 –
        - Battle of Turin – Constantine I defeats forces loyal to Maxentius.
        - Battle of Verona – Constantine I defeats more forces loyal to Maxentius.
        - 28 October – Battle of Milvian Bridge – Constantine I defeats Maxentius and takes control of Italy.
    - 313, 30 October – Battle of Tzirallum – In the eastern part of the Empire, the forces of Licinius defeat Maximinus.
    - 314, 8 October – Battle of Cibalae – Constantine defeats Licinius
    - 316 – Battle of Mardia – Constantine again defeats Licinius, who cedes Illyricum to Constantine.
    - 324 –

Figure 88: *The Roman Empire under the Tetrarchy, with the territory of Constantius (yellow), Maximian (green), Galerius (pink), and Diocletian (purple)*

Figure 89: *The Roman Empire in 337, showing the Empire under Constantine (shaded purple) and other Roman dependencies (light purple).*

- 3 July – Battle of Adrianople – Constantine defeats Licinius, who flees to Byzantium
- July – Battle of the Hellespont – Flavius Julius Crispus, son of Constantine, defeats the naval forces of Licinius
- 18 September – Battle of Chrysopolis – Constantine decisively defeats Licinius, establishing his sole control over the empire.
- Wars with Persia (344-363)
  - c. 344 – Battle of Singara – Emperor Constantius II fights an indecisive battle against King Shapur II of Persia
  - 359 – Battle of Amida – Sassanids capture Amida from Romans
  - 363 – Battle of Ctesiphon – Emperor Julian defeats Shapur II of Persia outside the walls of the Persian capital, but is unable to take the city, and his death leads to an ultimate disaster on the retreat back to Roman territory.
- Civil War (350-351)
  - 351 – Battle of Mursa Major – Emperor Constantius II defeats the usurper Magnentius
  - 353 – Battle of Mons Seleucus – Final defeat of Magnentius by Constantius II
- Wars with Alemanni (356-367)
  - 356 – Battle of Reims – Caesar Julian is defeated by the Alamanni
  - 357 – Battle of Strasbourg – Julian expels the Alamanni from the Rhineland
  - 367 – Battle of Solicinium – Romans under Emperor Valentinian I defeat yet another Alamanni incursion.
- Civil War – 366 – Battle of Thyatira – The army of the Roman emperor Valens defeats the usurper Procopius.
- Gothic War (376-382)
  - 377 – Battle of the Willows – Roman troops fight an inconclusive battle against the Goths
  - 378 –
    - Battle of Argentovaria – Western Emperor Gratianus is victorious over the Alamanni, yet again.
    - 9 August – Battle of Adrianople – Thervings under Fritigern defeat and kill the Eastern Emperor Valens
  - 380 – Battle of Thessalonica – The new Eastern Emperor, Theodosius I, is also defeated by the Thervings under Fritigern.
- Civil War – 388 – Battle of the Save – Emperor Theodosius I defeats the usurper Magnus Maximus.
- Civil War – 394 – Battle of the Frigidus – Theodosius I defeats and kills the usurper Eugenius and his Frankish *magister militum* Arbogast.

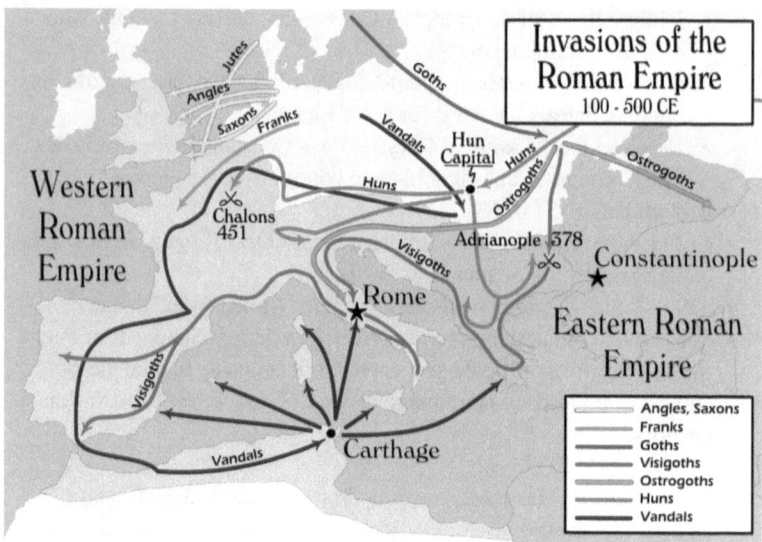

Figure 90: *Map showing the paths of invasion by various groups into Eastern and Western Roman territory*

5th century

The 5th century involves the final fall of the Western Roman Empire to Goths, Vandals, Alans, Huns, and Franks.

- Wars with Gothic Tribes (402-419)
    - 402 –
        - Battle of Pollentia – Stilicho defeats the Visigoths under Alaric.
        - Battle of Verona – Stilicho defeats Alaric, who withdraws from Italy.
    - 406 – Battle of Mainz – Franks lose to Vandals, Suebi and Alans.
    - 410 – Sack of Rome – Visigoths under Alaric sack Rome.
    - 419 – Battle of the Nervasos Mountains – Romans and Suebi defeat Vandals and Alans.
    - 468 – Battle of Cap Bon - Failure of the invasion of the kingdom of the Vandals by the Western and Eastern Roman Empires
- Civil War – 432 – Battle of Ravenna – Bonifacius defeats rival Roman general Flavius Aetius, but is mortally wounded in the process.
- War with Visigoths – 436 – Battle of Narbonne – Flavius Aetius again defeats the Visigoths led by Theodoric.
- War with the Huns (447-451)

- 447 – Battle of the Utus – The Romans in the East fight an indecisive battle with Huns led by Attila.
- 451 – Battle of the Catalaunian Plains – The Romans with Flavius Aetius and the Visigoths with Theodoric, defend against Attila the Hun.
- Fall of the West (450-493)
  - 455 – Sack of Rome by Geiseric, King of the Vandals
  - 463 – Battle of Orleans – Gallo-Roman and Salian Frank forces under the command of Aegidius defeat a force of Visigoths at Orleans.
  - 476 – Odoacer defeats the remnants of the Western Roman army, exiles emperor Romulus Augustulus, and declares himself King of Italy
  - 486 – Battle of Soissons – Clovis I defeats Syagrius, last Roman commander in Gaul, and annexes the Roman rump state into the Frankish realm.
  - 493 – Battle of Mons Badonicus – Romano-British under Ambrosius Aurelianus defeat Anglo-Saxons.

Sources

- Jones, Jim, (2013). Roman History Timeline. West Chester University of Pennsylvania. http://courses.wcupa.edu/jones/Roman History Timeline[925].

External links

- Elton, Hugh and Christos Nüssli, " *Imperial Battle Map Index*[926]". An Online Encyclopedia of Roman Emperors.
- "Roman Battles" map, platial.com[927]

Technology

Technological history of the Roman military

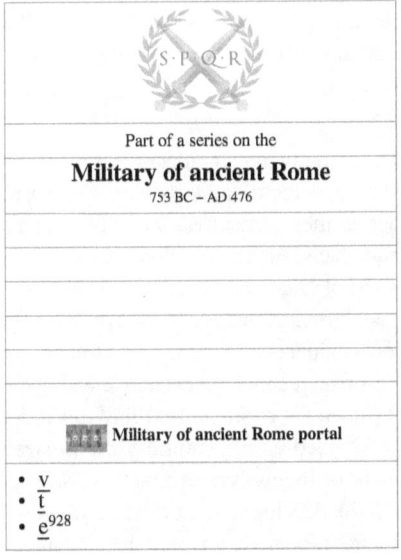

Part of a series on the
Military of ancient Rome
753 BC – AD 476

Military of ancient Rome portal

- v
- t
- e[928]

The technology history of the Roman military covers the development of and application of technologies for use in the armies and navies of Rome from the Roman Republic to the fall of the Western Roman Empire. The rise of Hellenism and the Roman Republic are generally seen as signalling the end of the Iron Age in the Mediterranean. Roman iron-working was enhanced by a process known as carburization. The Romans used the better properties in their armaments, and the 1,300 years of Roman military technology saw radical changes. The Roman armies of the early empire were much better equipped than early republican armies. Metals used for arms and armor primarily included iron, bronze, and brass. For construction, the army used wood, earth, and stone. The later use of concrete in architecture was widely mirrored in Roman military technology, especially in the application of a military workforce to civilian construction projects.[929]

Origins and development

Much of what is described as typically Roman technology, as opposed to that of the Greeks, comes directly from the Etruscan civilization, which was thriving to the North when Rome was just a small kingdom. The Etruscans had invented the stone arch, and used it in bridges as well as buildings. Some later Roman technologies were taken directly from Greek civilization.

After the absorption of the ancient Greek city states into the Roman Republic in 146 BC, the highly advanced Greek technology began to spread across many areas of Roman influence and supplement the Empire. This included the military advances that the Greeks had made, as well as all the scientific, mathematical, political and artistic developments.

New materials

However, the Romans made many significant technological advances, such as the invention of hydraulic cement and concrete. They used such new materials to great advantage in their structures, many of which survive to this day, like their masonry aqueducts, such as the Pont du Gard, and buildings, such as the Pantheon and Baths of Diocletian in Rome. Their methods were recorded by such luminaries as Vitruvius and Frontinus for example, who wrote handbooks to advise fellow engineers and architects. Romans knew enough history to be aware that widespread technological change had occurred in the past and brought benefits, as shown for example by Pliny the Elder's Naturalis Historia. That tradition continued as the empire grew in size and absorbed new ideas. Romans thought of themselves as practical, so small-scale innovation was common (such as the development of the ballista into the polybolos or repeating ballista). The traditional view is that their reliance on a plentiful slave labour force and a lack of a patent or copyright system have both been cited as reasons that there was little social or financial pressure to automate or reduce manual tasks. However, this view is being challenged by new research that shows they did indeed innovate, and on a wide scale. Thus the watermill had been known to the Greeks, but it was the Romans who developed their efficient utilisation. The set of mills at Barbegal in southern France were worked by a single aqueduct, which drove no fewer than 16 overshot mills built into the side of a hill. They probably were built by the army and supplied flour to a wide region. Floating mills were also used to exploit fast flowing rivers.

Figure 91: *Pont du Gard*

Mining

The Romans also used water power in an unexpected way during mining operations. It's known from the writings of Pliny the Elder that they exploited the alluvial gold deposits of north-west Spain soon after the conquest of the region in 25 BC using large-scale hydraulic mining methods. The spectacular gold mine at Las Medulas was worked by no fewer than seven long aqueducts cut into the surrounding mountains, the water being played directly onto the soft auriferous ore.

The outflow was channelled into sluice boxes, and the heavier gold collected on rough pavements. They also developed many deep mines, such as those for copper at Rio Tinto, where Victorian mining developments exposed the much earlier workings. Dewatering machines, such as Archimedean screws and reverse overshot water wheels, were found *in situ*, one of which is on show at the British Museum. Another fragmentary example was recovered from the Roman gold mine at Dolaucothi in west Wales, and is preserved at the National Museum of Wales in Cardiff. The army were at the forefront of development of gold mines, since the metal was imperial property, and developed the Dolaucothi mines from the outset by establishing a fort there that was known as Luentinum. They had the expertise to build the infrastructure of aqueducts and reservoirs, as well as control production.

Figure 92: *Panoramic view of Las Médulas*

The period in which technological progress was fastest and greatest was during the 2nd century and 1st century BC, which was the period in which Roman political and economic power greatly increased. By the 2nd century, Roman technology appears to have peaked.

Roman implementation of technology

The Romans advanced military technology significantly, and implemented it on a massive scale. From a few early models of ballista from Greek city-states the Romans adopted and improved the design, eventually issuing one to every century in the legions.

To facilitate this organization, an engineering corps was developed. An officer of engineers, or praefectus fabrum, is referenced in armies of the Late Republic, but this post is not verifiable in all accounts and may have simply been a military advisor on the personal staff of a commanding officer.[930] There were legion architects (whose rank is yet unknown), who were responsible for the construction of war machines. Ensuring that constructions were level was the job of the libratores, who would also launch missiles and other projectiles (on occasion) during battle.[931] The engineering corps was in charge of massive production, frequently prefabricating artillery and siege equipment to facilitate its transportation[932]

References

Primary sources

- Frontinus
- Pliny the elder
- Vitruvius

External links

- Roman Swords in the Republic and After,[933]

Castra

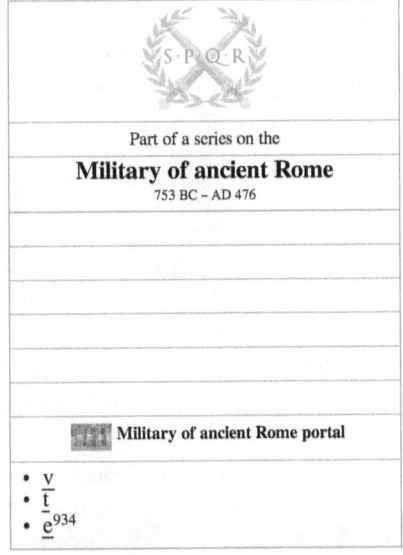

Part of a series on the
Military of ancient Rome
753 BC – AD 476

Military of ancient Rome portal

- v
- t
- e[934]

In the Roman Republic and the Roman Empire, the Latin word **castrum**[935] (plural **castra**) was a building, or plot of land, used as a fortified military camp.

Castrum was the term used for different sizes of camps including a large legionary fortress, smaller *auxiliary* forts, temporary encampments, and "marching" forts. The diminutive form *castellum* was used for fortlets,[936] typically occupied by a detachment of a *cohort* or a *century*.

In English, the terms *Roman fortress*, *Roman fort*, and *Roman camp* are commonly used for *castrum*. However, scholastic convention tends toward the use of the words *camp*, *marching camp*, and *fortress* as a translation of *castrum*.[937]

For a list of known castra see *List of castra*.

Figure 93: *Templeborough Roman Fort visualised 3D fly-through, produced for Rotherham Museums and Archives.*

Etymology

The etymology, or origin, of a word frequently reveals its deepest level of meaning, associating it with the ancient culture from which it came. Historical linguists resort to the concept of linguistic archaeology, uncovering layers of meaning through linguistic change. Latin is undisputedly one of the Italic languages, a group within the Indo-European languages. The fact that forms of *castrum* also appear in Oscan and Umbrian, two other Italic languages, suggests an origin at least as old as Proto-Italic language.

Julius Pokorny (major Indo-Europeanist of the 20th century) in his encyclopedia of Indo-European roots, traces a probable derivation from *k̂es-, *schneiden* ("cut") in *k̂es-tro-m, *Schneidewerkzeug* ("cutting tool"). The k̂ is not a letter or an IPA symbol. Called the circumflex k, it began as a symbol to transliterate Ka (Cyrillic) into Latin script in the Scientific transliteration of Cyrillic. More recently the latter was incorporated into ISO 9.[938]

The k̂ is one of a group of sounds called on the one hand dorsal consonants because articulated by constricting the back of the tongue, or dorsum, against the roof of the mouth, and on the other are subclassified by the exact point on the roof of the mouth, of interest here mainly the velars, which use the velum, and the palatals, which use the hard palate. The IPA classification offers a different point of view on the palatals, that they are formed from the other dorsals by moving the point of contact up to the palate, a supposed process called palatalization. The IPA symbol for the k̑ is therefore kʲ, where the superscript j represents the supposed palatalization. In more ordinary terms, the k sound can be articulated either up on the palate or down on the velum.

To the etymologists, Proto-Indo-European is conceived to have contained a group of words that began with palatals and another that began with velars. After this proto phase; that is, after the formation of the major language groups, the palatal group changed according to one of two different phonetic destinies, one termed centumization and the other satemization, to create the Centum and satem languages. In centumization the k̑ changed to k, merging the group with the velar group. The Italic languages are centum. *k̑estrom therefore became *kastrom in the Italic languages, but there was a change in meaning as well.

These Italic reflexes based on *kastrom include Oscan *castrous* (genitive case) and Umbrian *castruo, kastruvuf* (accusative case). They have the same meaning, says Pokorny, as Latin *fundus*, an estate, or tract of land. This is not any land, but is a prepared or cultivated tract, such as a farm enclosed by a fence or a wooden or stone wall of some kind. Cornelius Nepos uses Latin *castrum* in that sense: when Alcibiades deserts to the Persians, Pharnabazus gives him an estate (*castrum*) worth 500 talents in tax revenues. This is a change of meaning from the reflexes in other languages, which still mean some sort of knife, axe, or spear. Pokorny explains it as *'Lager' als 'abgeschnittenes Stück Land'*, "a lager, as a cut-off piece of land."

If this is the civilian interpretation, the military version must be "military reservation," a piece of land cut off from the common land around it and modified for military use. All castra must be defended by works, often no more than a stockade, for which the soldiers carried stakes, and a ditch. The *castra* could be prepared under attack within a hollow square or behind a battle line. Considering that the earliest military shelters were tents made of hide or cloth, and all but the most permanent bases housed the men in tents placed in quadrangles and separated by numbered streets, one *castrum* may well have acquired the connotation of tent.[939]

Linguistic development of the military castra

The commonest Latin syntagmata (here phrases) for the term *castra* are:

castra stativa
  Permanent camp/fortresses

castra aestiva
  Summer camp/fortresses

castra hiberna
Winter camp/fortresses

castra navalia or castra nautica
Navy camp/fortresses

In Latin the term *castrum* is much more frequently used as a proper name for geographical locations: e.g., Castrum Album, Castrum Inui, Castrum Novum, Castrum Truentinum, Castrum Vergium. The plural was also used as a place name, as Castra Cornelia, and from this come the Welsh place name prefix *caer-* and English suffixes *-caster* and *-chester*; e.g., Winchester, Lancaster.

Castrorum Filius, "son of the camps," was one of the names used by the emperor Caligula and then also by other emperors.

Castro, also derived from *Castrum*, is a common Spanish family name as well as toponym in Italy, the Balkans and Spain and other Hispanophone countries, either by itself or in various compounds such as the World Heritage Site of Gjirokastër (earlier *Argurokastro*).

The terms **stratopedon** (*army camp*) and **phrourion** (*fortification*) were used by Greek language authors to translate *castrum* and *castellum*, respectively.

Description

A *castrum* was designed to house and protect the soldiers, their equipment and supplies when they were not fighting or marching.

This most detailed description that survives about Roman military camps is *De Munitionibus Castrorum*, a manuscript of 11 pages that dates most probably from the late 1st to early 2nd century AD.[940]

Regulations required a major unit in the field to retire to a properly constructed camp every day. "... as soon as they have marched into an enemy's land, they do not begin to fight until they have walled their camp about; nor is the fence they raise rashly made, or uneven; nor do they all abide ill it, nor do those that are in it take their places at random; but if it happens that the ground is uneven, it is first levelled: their camp is also four-square by measure, and carpenters are ready, in great numbers, with their tools, to erect their buildings for them."[941] To this end a marching column ported the equipment needed to build and stock the camp in a baggage train of wagons and on the backs of the soldiers.

Camps were the responsibility of engineering units to which specialists of many types belonged, officered by *architecti*, "chief engineers", who requisitioned manual labor from the soldiers at large as required. They could throw up a camp under enemy attack in as little as a few hours. Judging from the names, they probably used a repertory of camp plans, selecting the one appropriate to

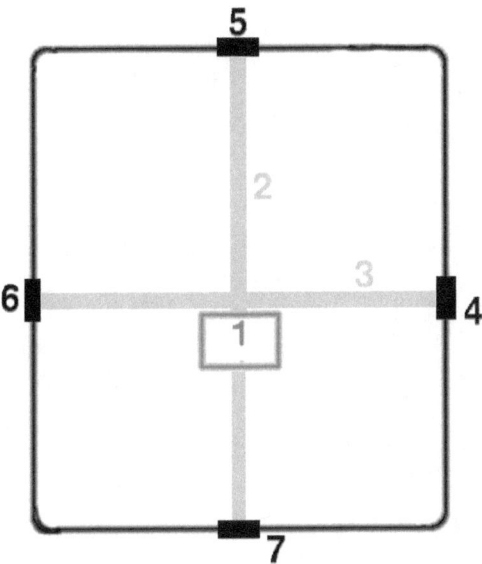

Figure 94: *Basic ideal plan of a Roman castrum. (1) Principia; (2) Via Praetoria; (3) Via Principalis; (4) Porta Principalis Dextra; (5) Porta Praetoria (main gate); (6) Porta Principalis Sinistra; (7) Porta Decumana (back gate).*

the length of time a legion would spend in it: *tertia castra, quarta castra*, etc. (*a camp of three days, four days*, etc.).[942]

More permanent camps were *castra stativa* (*standing camps*). The least permanent of these were *castra aestiva* or *aestivalia*, "summer camps", in which the soldiers were housed *sub pellibus* or *sub tentoriis*, "under tents".[943] Summer was the campaign season. For the winter the soldiers retired to *castra hiberna* containing barracks and other buildings of more solid materials, with timber construction gradually being replaced by stone.[944]

The camp allowed the Romans to keep a rested and supplied army in the field. Neither the Celtic nor Germanic armies had this capability: they found it necessary to disperse after only a few days.

The largest castra were *legionary fortresses* built as bases for one or more whole legions.[945,946]

From the time of Augustus more permanent castra with wooden or stone buildings and walls were introduced as the distant and hard-won boundaries of the expanding empire required permanent garrisons to control local and external threats from war-like tribes. Previously, legions were raised for specific military campaigns and subsequently disbanded, requiring only temporary castra.

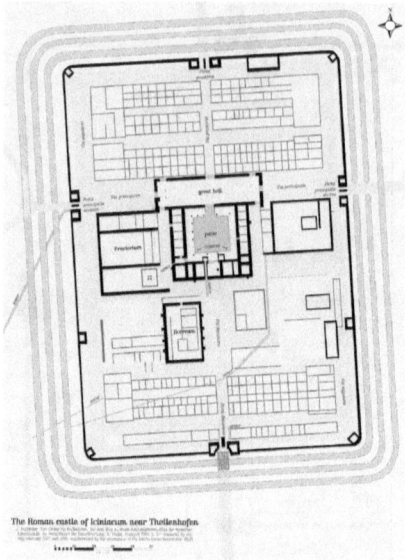

Figure 95: *Plan of a typical Roman fort.*

From then on many castra of various sizes were established many of which became permanent settlements.

Plan of forts

Sources and origins

From the most ancient times Roman camps were constructed according to a certain ideal pattern, formally described in two main sources, the *De Munitionibus Castrorum* and the works of Polybius.[948] P. Fl. Vegetius Renatus has a small section on entrenched camps as well. The terminology varies but the basic plan is the same.[949] The hypothesis of an Etruscan origin is a viable alternative.[950]

Layout

The ideal enforced a linear plan for a camp or fort: a square for camps to contain one legion or smaller unit, a rectangle for two legions, each legion being placed back-to-back with headquarters next to each other. Laying it out was a geometric exercise conducted by experienced officers called *metatores*, who used graduated measuring rods called *decempedae* ("10-footers") and *gromatici* who used a groma, a sighting device consisting of a vertical

Figure 96: *Reconstructed gateway of a Castrum Stativum. Note the battlements, the Roman arches, the turres.*

staff with horizontal cross pieces and vertical plumb-lines. Ideally the process started in the centre of the planned camp at the site of the headquarters tent or building (principia). Streets and other features were marked with coloured pennants or rods.

The street plans of various present-day cities still retain traces of a Roman camp, for example Marsala in Sicily, the ancient Lilybaeum, where the name of the main street, the Cassaro, perpetuates the name "castrum".

Wall and ditch

The Castrum's special structure also defended from attacks.

The base (*munimentum*, "fortification") was placed entirely within the *vallum* ("wall"), which could be constructed under the protection of the legion in battle formation if necessary. The *vallum* was quadrangular aligned on the cardinal points of the compass. The construction crews dug a trench (*fossa*), throwing the excavated material inward, to be formed into the rampart (*agger*). On top of this a palisade of stakes (*sudes* or *valli*) was erected. The soldiers had to carry these stakes on the march.[951] Over the course of time, the palisade might be replaced by a fine brick or stone wall, and the ditch serve also as a moat. A legion-sized camp always placed towers at intervals along the wall with positions between for the division artillery.

Figure 97: *Reconstruction of the specula or vigilarium (Germanic burgus), "watchtower", a type of castrum, of Fectio. An ancient watchtower would have been surrounded by wall and ditch.*[947]

Figure 98: *The reconstructed porta praetoria of Castrum Pfünz, Germany, near the Rhaetian Limes.*

Figure 99: *Castrum at Masada. Note the classical "playing-card" layout.*

Interval

Around the inside periphery of the *vallum* was a clear space, the *intervallum*, which served to catch enemy missiles, as an access route to the *vallum* and as a storage space for cattle (*capita*) and plunder (*praeda*). Legionaries were quartered in a peripheral zone inside the *intervallum*, which they could rapidly cross to take up position on the *vallum*. Inside of the legionary quarters was a peripheral road, the *Via Sagularis*, probably a type of "service road", as the *sagum*, a kind of cloak, was the garment of soldiers.

Streets, gates and central plaza

Every camp included "main street", which ran unimpeded through the camp in a north-south direction and was very wide. The names of streets in many cities formerly occupied by the Romans suggest that the street was called *cardo* or *cardus maximus*. This name applies more to cities than it does to ancient camps.[952]

Typically "main street" was the *via principalis*. The central portion was used as a parade ground and headquarters area. The "headquarters" building was called the *praetorium* because it housed the *praetor* or base commander ("first officer"), and his staff. In the camp of a full legion he held the rank of *consul* or *proconsul* but officers of lesser ranks might command.

Figure 100: *Reconstructed east gate of a Castrum Stativum, a more permanent base.*

Figure 101: *Porta called Savoia, Susa, Piedmont, 275-290 BC.*

Figure 102: *Porta Decumana at Weißenburg, Bavaria, Germany*

On one side of the *praetorium* was the *quaestorium*, the building of the *quaestor* (supply officer). On the other side was the *forum*, a small duplicate of an urban forum, where public business could be conducted. Along the *Via Principalis* were the homes or tents of the several tribunes in front of the barracks of the units they commanded.

The *Via Principalis* went through the *vallum* in the *Porta Principalis Dextra* ("right principal gate") and *Porta Principalis Sinistra* ("left, etc."), which were gates fortified with *turres* ("towers"). Which was on the north and which on the south depends on whether the praetorium faced east or west, which remains unknown.

The central region of the *Via Principalis* with the buildings for the command staff was called the *Principia* (plural of *principium*). It was actually a square, as across this at right angles to the *Via Principalis* was the *Via Praetoria*, so called because the *praetorium* interrupted it. The *Via Principalis* and the *Via Praetoria* offered another division of the camp into four quarters.

Across the central plaza (*principia*) to the east or west was the main gate, the *Porta Praetoria*. Marching through it and down "headquarters street" a unit ended up in formation in front of the headquarters. The standards of the legion were located on display there, very much like the flag of modern camps.

On the other side of the praetorium the *Via Praetoria* continued to the wall, where it went through the *Porta Decumana*. In theory this was the back gate.

Figure 103: *Plan of the legionary fortress of Deva (Chester) in Britannia (reconstruction).*

Supplies were supposed to come in through it and so it was also called, descriptively, the *Porta Quaestoria*. The term Decumena, "of the 10th", came from the arranging of *manipuli* or *turmae* from the first to the 10th, such that the 10th was near the *intervallum* on that side. The *Via Praetoria* on that side might take the name *Via Decumena* or the entire *Via Praetoria* be replaced with *Decumanus Maximus*.[953]

Canteen

In peaceful times the camp set up a marketplace with the natives in the area. They were allowed into the camp as far as the units numbered 5 (half-way to the praetorium). There another street crossed the camp at right angles to the *Via Decumana*, called the *Via Quintana*, "5th street". If the camp needed more gates, one or two of the *Porta Quintana* were built, presumably named *dextra* and *sinistra*. If the gates were not built, the *Porta Decumana* also became the *Porta Quintana*. At "5th street" a public market was allowed.Wikipedia:Citation needed

Major buildings

The *Via Quintana* and the *Via Principalis* divided the camp into three districts: the *Latera Praetorii*, the *Praetentura* and the *Retentura*. In the *latera* ("sides") were the *Arae* (sacrificial altars), the *Auguratorium* (for auspices), the *Tribunal*, where courts martial and arbitrations were conducted (it had a raised platform), the guardhouse, the quarters of various kinds of staff and the storehouses for grain (*horrea*) or meat (*carnarea*). Sometimes the *horrea* were located near the barracks and the meat was stored on the hoof. Analysis

Figure 104: *Not much remains of these horrea (granaries) at Arbeia, but the longitudinal supports for the floor can be seen.*

of sewage from latrines indicates the legionary diet was mainly grain. Also located in the *Latera* was the *Armamentarium*, a long shed containing any heavy weapons and artillery not on the wall.

The *Praetentura* ("stretching to the front") contained the *Scamnum Legatorum*, the quarters of officers who were below general but higher than company commanders (*Legati*).[954] Near the *Principia* were the *Valetudinarium* (hospital), *Veterinarium* (for horses), *Fabrica* ("workshop", metals and wood), and further to the front the quarters of special forces. These included *Classici* ("marines", as most European camps were on rivers and contained a river naval command), *Equites* ("cavalry"), *Exploratores* ("scouts"), and *Vexillarii* (carriers of vexillae, the official pennants of the legion and its units). Troops who did not fit elsewhere also were there.

The part of the *Retentura* ("stretching to the rear") closest to the *Principia* contained the *Quaestorium*. By the late empire it had developed also into a safekeep for plunder and a prison for hostages and high-ranking enemy captives. Near the *Quaestorium* were the quarters of the headquarters guard (*Statores*), who amounted to two centuries (companies). If the *Imperator* was present they served as his bodyguard.

Figure 105: *Roman artillery piece (Onager)*

Barracks

Further from the *Quaestorium* were the tents of the *Nationes* ("natives"), who were auxiliaries of foreign troops, and the legionaries themselves in double rows of tents or barracks (*Strigae*). One *Striga* was as long as required and 18 m wide. In it were two *Hemistrigia* of facing tents centered in its 9 m strip. Arms could be stacked before the tents and baggage carts kept there as well. Space on the other side of the tent was for passage.

In the northern places like Britain, where it got cold in the winter, they would make wood or stone barracks. The Romans would also put a fireplace in the barracks. They had about three bunk beds in it. They had a small room beside it where they put their armour; it was as big as the tents. They would also make these barracks if the fort they had was going to stay there for good.[955]

A tent was 3 by 3.5 metres (0.6 m for the aisle), ten men per tent. Ideally a company took 10 tents, arranged in a line of 10 companies, with the 10th near the *Porta Decumana*. Of the c. 9.2 square metres of bunk space each man received 0.9, or about 0.6 by 1.5 m, which was only practical if they slept with heads to the aisle. The single tent with its men was called *contubernium*, also used for "squad". A squad during some periods was 8 men or fewer.

The *Centurion*, or company commander, had a double-sized tent for his quarters, which served also as official company area. Other than there, the men had

Figure 106: *A sanitary channel at Potaissa, Dacia (modern Romania). It is placed cross-slope with a slight decline and then exits down-slope.*

to find other places to be. To avoid mutiny, it became extremely important for the officers to keep them busy.

A covered portico might protect the walkway along the tents. If barracks had been constructed, one company was housed in one barracks building, with the arms at one end and the common area at the other. The company area was used for cooking and recreation, such as gaming. The army provisioned the men and had their bread (*panis militaris*) baked in outdoor ovens, but the men were responsible for cooking and serving themselves. They could buy meals or supplementary foods at the canteen. The officers were allowed servants.

Sanitation

For sanitary facilities, a camp had both public and private latrines. A public latrine consisted of a bank of seats situated over a channel of running water. One of the major considerations for selecting the site of a camp was the presence of running water, which the engineers diverted into the sanitary channels. Drinking water came from wells; however, the larger and more permanent bases featured the *aqueduct*, a structure running a stream captured from high ground (sometimes miles away) into the camp. The praetorium had its own latrine,

Figure 107: *Reconstructed barracks of a Castra Hiberna, or "winter camp". Each doorway provides entry to a large room, the sleeping quarters of one contubernium, or "squad" of about 10 men.*

and probably the quarters of the high-ranking officers. In or near the *intervallum*, where they could easily be accessed, were the latrines of the soldiers. A public bathhouse for the soldiers, also containing a latrine, was located near or on the *Via Principalis*.

Territory

The influence of a base extended far beyond its walls. The total land required for the maintenance of a permanent base was called its *territoria*. In it were located all the resources of nature and the terrain required by the base: pastures, woodlots, water sources, stone quarries, mines, exercise fields and attached villages. The central castra might also support various fortified adjuncts to the main base, which were not in themselves self-sustaining (as was the base). In this category were *speculae*, "watchtowers", *castella*, "small camps", and naval bases.

All the major bases near rivers featured some sort of fortified naval installation, one side of which was formed by the river or lake. The other sides were formed by a polygonal wall and ditch constructed in the usual way, with gates and watchtowers. The main internal features were the boat sheds and the docks.

When not in use, the boats were drawn up into the sheds for maintenance and protection. Since the camp was placed to best advantage on a hill or slope near the river, the naval base was usually outside its walls. The *classici* and the *optiones* of the naval installation relied on the camp for its permanent defense. Naval personnel generally enjoyed better quarters and facilities. Many were civilians working for the military.

Modifications in practice

This ideal was always modified to suit the terrain and the circumstances. Each camp discovered by archaeology has its own specific layout and architectural features, which makes sense from a military point of view.

If, for example, the camp was built on an outcrop, it followed the lines of the outcrop. The terrain for which it was best suited and for which it was probably designed in distant prehistoric times was the rolling plain. The camp was best placed on the summit and along the side of a low hill, with spring water running in rivulets through the camp (*aquatio*) and pastureland to provide grazing (*pabulatio*) for the animals. In case of attack, arrows, javelins and sling missiles could be fired down at an enemy tiring himself to come up. For defence troops could be formed in an *acies*, or "battle-line", outside the gates, where they could be easily resupplied and replenished, as well as being supported by archery from the palisade.

The streets, gates and buildings present depended on the requirements and resources of the camp. The gates might vary from two to six and not be centred on the sides. Not all the streets and buildings might be present.

Quadrangular camps in later times

Many settlements in Europe originated as Roman military camps and still show traces of their original pattern (e.g. Castres in France, Barcelona in Spain).[956] The pattern was also used by Spanish colonizers in America following strict rules by the Spanish monarchy for founding new cities in the New World.

Many of the towns of England still retain forms of the word *castra* in their names, usually as the suffixes "-caster" or "-chester" – Lancaster, Colchester, Tadcaster, Chester, Manchester, Mancetter, Uttoxeter and Ribchester, for example. Castle has the same derivation, from the diminutive *castellum* or "little fort", but does not always indicate a former Roman camp.

Figure 108: *The pillars supported a raised floor to keep food dry and free from vermin in this granary at Housesteads Roman Fort (Vercovicium)*

Camp life

Activities conducted in a castra can be divided into ordinary and "the duty" or "the watch". Ordinary activity was performed during regular working hours. The duty was associated with operating the installation as a military facility. For example, none of the soldiers were required to man the walls all the time, but round-the clock duty always required a portion of the soldiers to be on duty at any time.

Duty time was divided into *vigilia*, the eight watches into which the 24-hour day was divided so they stood guard for 3 hours that day.[957] The Romans used signals on brass instruments to mark time. These were mainly the *buccina* or *bucina*, the *cornu* and the *tuba*. As they did not possess valves for regulating the pitch, the range of these instruments was somewhat limited. Nevertheless, the musicians (*Aenatores*, "brassmen") managed to define enough signals for issuing commands. The instrument used to mark the passage of a watch was the *buccina*, from which the trumpet derives. It was sounded by a *buccinator*.

Ordinary life

Ordinary camp life began with a *buccina* call at daybreak, the first watch of the day. The soldiers arose at this time and shortly after collected in the company area for breakfast and assembly. The centurions were up before them and off to the *principia* where they and the *equites* were required to assemble. The regimental commanders, the tribunes, were already converging on the *praetorium*. There the general staff was busily at work planning the day. At a staff meeting the *Tribunes* received the password and the orders of the day. They brought those back to the *centuriones*, who returned to their company areas to instruct the men.

For soldiers, the main item of the agenda was a vigorous training session lasting about a watch long. Recruits received two, one in the morning and one in the afternoon.[958] Planning and supervision of training were under a general staff officer, who might manage training at several camps. According to Vegetius, the men might take a 32 kilometres (20 mi) hike or a 6–8 kilometres (3.7–5.0 mi) jog under full pack, or swim a river. Marching drill was always in order.

Each soldier was taught the use of every weapon and also was taught to ride. Seamanship was taught at naval bases. Soldiers were generalists in the military and construction arts. They practiced archery, spear-throwing and above all swordsmanship against posts (*pali*) fixed in the ground. Training was taken very seriously and was democratic. Ordinary soldiers would see all the officers training with them including the *praetor*, or the Emperor, if he was in camp.

Swordsmanship lessons and use of the shooting range probably took place on the *campus*, a "field" outside the *castra*, from which English camp derives. Its surface could be lightly paved. Winter curtailed outdoor training. The general might in that case have sheds constructed, which served as field houses for training. There is archaeological evidence in one case of an indoor equestrian ring.

Apart from the training, each soldier had a regular job on the base, of which there were a large variety from the various kinds of clerks to the craftsmen. Soldiers changed jobs frequently. The commander's policy was to have all the soldiers skilled in all the arts and crafts so that they could be as interchangeable as possible. Even then the goal was not entirely achievable. The gap was bridged by the specialists, the *optiones* or "chosen men", of which there were many different kinds. For example, a skilled artisan might be chosen to superintend a workshop.

The supply administration was run as a business using money as the medium of exchange.[959] The aureus was the preferred coin of the late republic and early empire; in the late empire the solidus came into use. The larger bases, such as *Moguntiacum*, minted their own coins. As does any business, the base quaestorium required careful record keeping, performed mainly by the optiones. A chance cache of tablets from Vindolanda in Britain gives us a

Figure 109: *An aureus of the late republic*

glimpse of some supply transactions. They record, among other things, the purchase of consumables and raw supplies, the storage and repair of clothing and other items, and the sale of items, including foodstuffs, to achieve an income. Vindolanda traded vigorously with the surrounding natives.[960]

Another feature of the camp was the military hospital (*valetudinarium*, later *hospitium*). Augustus instituted the first permanent medical corps in the Roman army. Its physicians, the *medici ordinarii*,[961] had to be qualified physicians. They were allowed medical students, practitioners and whatever orderlies they needed; i.e., the military hospitals were medical schools and places of residency as well.[962]

Officers were allowed to marry and to reside with their families on base. The army did not extend the same privileges to the men, who were not allowed to marry.[963] However, they often kept common law families off base in communities nearby. The communities might be native, as the tribesmen tended to build around a permanent base for purposes of trade, but also the base sponsored villages (*vici*) of dependents and businessmen. Dependants were not allowed to follow an army on the march into hostile territory.

Military service was for about 25 years. At the end of that time, the veteran was given a certificate of honorable discharge (*honesta missio*). Some of these have survived engraved on stone. Typically they certify that the veteran, his wife (one per veteran) and children or his sweetheart were now Roman citizens, which is a good indication that troops, which were used chiefly on the frontier, were from peoples elsewhere on the frontier who wished to earn Roman citizenship. However, under Antoninus Pius, citizenship was no longer granted to the children of rank-and-file veterans, the privilege becoming restricted only to officers.[964]

Figure 110: *The remains of a granary at Housesteads Roman Fort on Hadrian's Wall.*

Veterans often went into business in the communities near a base.⁹⁶⁵ They became permanent members of the community and would stay on after the troops were withdrawn, as in the notable case of Saint Patrick's family.

Duties

Conducted in parallel with the ordinary activities was "the duty", the official chores required by the camp under strict military discipline. The *Legate* was ultimately responsible for them as he was for the entire camp, but he delegated the duty to a tribune chosen as officer of the day. The line *Tribunes* were commanders of *Cohortes* and were approximately the equivalent of colonels. The 6 tribunes were divided into units of two, with each unit being responsible for filling the position of officer of the day for two months. The two men of a unit decided among themselves who would take what day. They could alternate days or each take a month. One filled in for the other in case of illness. On his day, the tribune effectively commanded the camp and was even respected as such by the *Legate*.

The equivalent concept of the duties performed in modern camps is roughly the detail. The responsibilities (*curae*) of the many kinds of detail were distributed to the men by all the methods considered fair and democratic: lot, rotation and negotiation. Certain kinds of *cura* were assigned certain classes or types of troops; for example, wall sentries were chosen only from *Velites*. Soldiers could be temporarily or permanently exempted: the *immunes*. For example, a Triarius was *immunis* from the *curae* of the Hastati.

The duty year was divided into time slices, typically one or two months, which were apportioned to units, typically maniples or centuries. They were always allowed to negotiate who took the duty and when. The most common kind of *cura* were the posts of the sentinels, called the *excubiae* by day and the *vigilae* at night. Wall posts were *praesidia*, gate posts, *custodiae*, advance positions before the gates, *stationes*.

In addition were special guards and details. One post was typically filled by four men, one sentinel and the others at ease until a situation arose or it was their turn to be sentinel. Some of the details were:

- guarding, cleaning and maintaining the *principia*.
- guarding and maintaining the quarters of each tribune.
- tending the horses of each cavalry *turma*.
- guarding the *praetorium*.[966]

References

Primary sources

- Josephus. *The War of the Jews*. Trans. William Whiston. Wikisource.
- Population of Vindolanda (100 AD). "(the Tablets)"[967] (shtml). *Vindolanda Tablets Online: The Roman Army: Activities*. Centre for the Study of Ancient Documents, Academic Computing Development Team at Oxford University.
- pseudo-Hyginus. "De Munitionibus Castrorum"[968]. *The Latin Library*. Ad fontes Academy. (Latin text.)
- Polybius. "The Histories (English translation) Book VI"[969]. *The Loeb Classical Library, Volume III Section VI*. Web publication on Bill Thayer's *Polybius* site.
- Roman government (160 AD). "(Military Diploma)"[970]. *Military Diploma of Discharge and Roman Citizenship*. Metz, George W. Legion xxiv website.
- Unknown inscriber (3rd century AD). "(the Tombstone)"[971]. *Tombstone of Anicius Ingenuus, Museum of Antiquities Website*. Newcastle University. Archived from the original[972] on 2006-08-25.
- Vegetius. "Flavius Vegetius Renatus Epitoma Rei Militaris Book I"[973]. Armamentarium. Archived from the original[974] on 2006-06-18. Selections, Latin and English juxtaposed by paragraph. Translator unknown.

- Publius Flavius Vegetius Renatus (2001). "The Military Institutions of the Romans (De Re Militari)"[975]. *Digital Attic 2.0.* Clarke, Lieutenant John (translator); unknown editor. Brevik, Mads. Books I-III only. The unknown editor altered the translation "to conform to modern usage" and abbreviated the text. Access is by subtitle. Search only within subsection.

Secondary sources

- Bishop, M.C. (2012). *Handbook to Roman Legionary Fortresses.* Barnsley: Pen and Sword. ISBN 978-1-84884-138-3.
- Campbell, Duncan B. (2009). *Roman Auxiliary Forts 27 BC-AD 378.* Oxford: Osprey Publishing. ISBN 978-1-84603-380-3.
- Johnson, Anne (1983). *Roman Forts of the 1st and 2nd centuries AD in Britain and the German Provinces,.* London: Adam & Charles Black. ISBN 0-7136-2223-7.
- Keppie, Lawrence (1994). *The Making of the Roman Army from Republic to Empire.* New York: Barnes and Noble Books. ISBN 1-56619-359-1.
- Roby, Henry John (1872). *A Grammar of the Latin Language from Plautus to Suetonius: Second Edition*[976]. London: Macmillan. p. 453.

External links

Wikimedia Commons has media related to *Castra*.

Below are a number of links to sites reporting or summarizing current research or thinking. Many are reprints of articles made available to the public at no charge. The historical researcher will find their bibliographies of great interest.

General

- "Fortress Study Group"[977]. *Study Group devoted to the knowledge of Forts and Fortifications of all times and Greek and Roman ones: with a Journal* Fort *and a newsletter* Casemate. Fortress Study Group.
- "Army Picture Index"[978]. *Illustrated History of the Roman Empire.* roman-empire.net.
- Bell, Anders (2001). "Castra et urbs romana: An Examination of the Common Features of Roman Settlements in Italy and the Empire and a System to aid in the Discovery of their Origins"[979]. *CAC Undergraduate Essay Contest for 2000-2001.* Classical Association of Canada.
- Lewis, Charlton T.; Short, Charles. "Castrum/Castra"[980]. *A Latin Dictionary.* The Perseus Digital Library.

- Ramsay, William (1875). "Castra"[981]. *William Smith A Dictionary of Greek and Roman Antiquities*. John Murray, republished on Bill Thayer's LacusCurtius site.
- "The Roman Military in Britain"[982]. roman-britain.org. Links to a Glossary.
- The Romans in Britain, Glossary of Military terms[983]. Note that both Latin and Greek terms with the same meaning are included.

Forts and fortifications

- "Antonine Wall Fort: Bearsden, New Kilpatrick, Strathclyde"[984]. roman-britain.org.
- Hanson, W.S.; Friel, J.G.P. (1995). "Westerton: A Roman Watchtower on the Gask Frontier"[985] (PDF). *Proceedings of the Society of Antiquaries of Scotland*. **125**: 499–519.
- "Iron-Age Hillfort, Roman Stores Depot Brandon Camp, Leintwardine Herefordshire"[986]. roman-britain.org.
- Lendering, Jona. "Haltern"[987]. *Livius articles on ancient history*. livius.org.
- "Nidum: Roman Auxiliary Fort: Neath, West Glamorgan"[988]. roman-britain.org.
- "Pinnata Castra: Roman Legionary Fortress & Marching Camps: Inchtuthill, Tayside"[989]. roman-britain.org.
- "Roman Fortress"[990]. *Time trail*. Exeter City Council. Archived from the original[991] on 2006-06-12.
- Smith, William (1875). "Vallum"[992]. *A Dictionary of Greek and Roman Antiquities*. London: John Murray. p. 1183.. Article republished on Bill Thayer's LacusCurtius site, which has the advantage of linking to ancient texts cited by Smith.
- Tribus. "The Roman Camp in Bonn"[993]. Eduvinet Services.
- "The Roman Camp Sostra"[994]. bulgariancastles.com. Archived from the original[995] on 2008-07-24.

Camp life

- Campbell, Duncan B. (2010). "Women in Roman forts: Residents, visitors or barred from entry?". *Ancient Warfare*. **IV** (6): 48–53.
- Miranda, Frank (2002). "Castra et Coloniae: The Role of the Roman Army in the Romanization and Urbanization of Spain"[996] (PDF). *Quaestio: The UCLA Undergraduate History Journal*. Phi Alpha Theta: History Honors Society, UCLA Theta Upsilon Chapter, UCLA Department of History. Archived from the original[997] (pdf) on 2006-09-13.

- Scheidel, Walter (November 2005). "Marriage, Families and Survival in the Roman Imperial Army: Demographic Aspects"[998] (pdf). *Princeton/Stanford Working Papers in Classics*. Princeton University.
- Verboven, Koenraad (2007). "Good for Business. The Roman Army and the Emergence of a 'Business Class' in the Northwestern Provinces of the Roman Empire (1st century BCE - 3rd century CE)"[999] (PDF). In Lukas, De Blois; Elio, Lo Cascio. *The Impact of the Roman Army (200 BC - AD 476). Economic, Social, Political, Religious and Cultural Aspects*. Leiden & Boston: Brill. pp. 295–314. ISBN 90-04-16044-2.

Roman siege engines

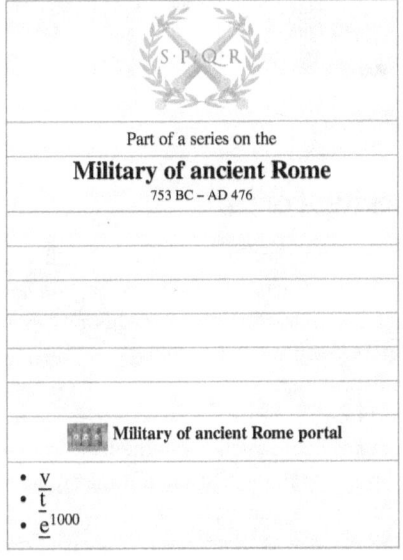

Part of a series on the
Military of ancient Rome
753 BC – AD 476

Military of ancient Rome portal

- v
- t
- e[1000]

Roman siege engines were, for the most part, adapted from Hellenistic siege technology. Relatively small efforts were made to develop the technology; however, the Romans brought an unrelentingly aggressive style to siege warfare[1001] that brought them repeated success. Up to the 1st century BC the Romans utilized siege weapons only as required and relied for the most part on ladders, towers and rams to assault a fortified town. Ballistae were also employed, but held no permanent place within a legion's roster, until later in the Republic, and were used sparingly. Julius Caesar took great interest in the integration of advanced siege engines, organizing their use for optimal battlefield efficiency.[1002]

Figure 111: *Roman springald.*

Army engineering corps

To facilitate this organization and the army's self-sufficiency, an engineering corps was developed. An officer of engineers, or *praefectus fabrum*, is referenced in armies of the Late Republic, but this post is not verifiable in all accounts and may have simply been a military advisor on the personal staff of a commanding officer. There were legion architects (whose rank is yet unknown) who were responsible for the construction of war machines who would also assure that all artillery constructions in the field were level. Ensuring that constructions were level was the job of the *libratores*, who would also launch missiles and other projectiles (on occasion) during battle (Le Bohec 1994: 52). The engineering corps was in charge of massive production, frequently prefabricating artillery and siege equipment to facilitate its transportation.

Artillery

Roman artillery was very efficient at that time, and during a siege the Romans would attack the weakest area of their enemy's defenses and attempt to breach the walls at that point. To support this effort, artillery fire would commence, with three main objectives:[1003] to cause damage to defenses, casualties among the opposing army, and loss of enemy morale. It would also provide cover fire for troops building siege ramps or those in siege towers. There were machines called *tormenta*, which would launch (sometimes incendiary) projectiles such

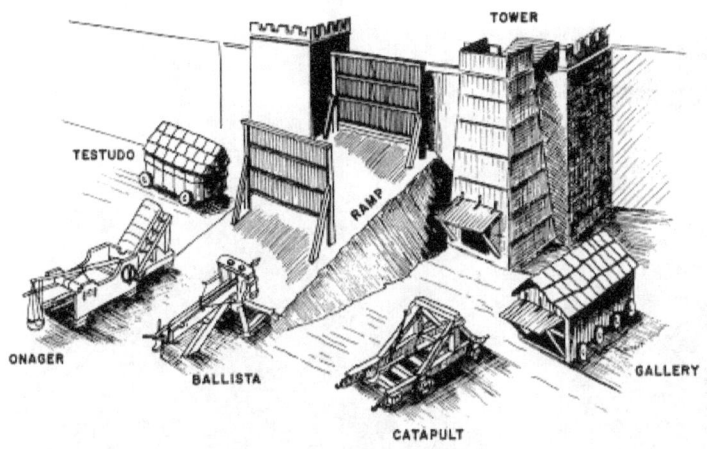

ROMAN SIEGECRAFT AND WORKS

Figure 112: *Roman siege engines*

as javelins, arrows, rocks, or beams. These devices were on wheeled platforms to follow the line's advance. All were "predicated on a principle of physics: a lever was inserted into a skein of twisted horsehair to increase torsion, and when the arm was released, a considerable amount of energy was thus freed". It was later stated that sinew, instead of twisted hair, provided a better "spring." These weapons were high-maintenance devices and vulnerable to having their leather, sinew, or hemp skeins affected by wet or even damp, which would cause them to slacken and lose tension, rendering the engine useless.[1004]

It is somewhat difficult to clearly define and describe Roman artillery, as names are easily confused and historians still do not agree on all definitions. Perhaps best known are the *ballista*, the *onager*, and the *scorpio*.

Ballista

After the absorption of the Ancient Greek City states into the Roman Republic in 146 BC, some advanced Greek technology began to spread across many areas of Roman influence. This included the hugely advantageous military advances the Greeks had made (most notably by Dionysus of Syracuse), as well as all the scientific, mathematical, political and artistic developments.

The Romans 'inherited' the torsion powered Ballistae which had by now spread to several cities around the Mediterranean, all of which became Roman spoils of war in time, including one from Pergamum, which was depicted among a pile of 'trophy' weapons in relief on a balustrade.

Figure 113: *Roman arrow machine.*

Rome ballista of 1 talent caliber

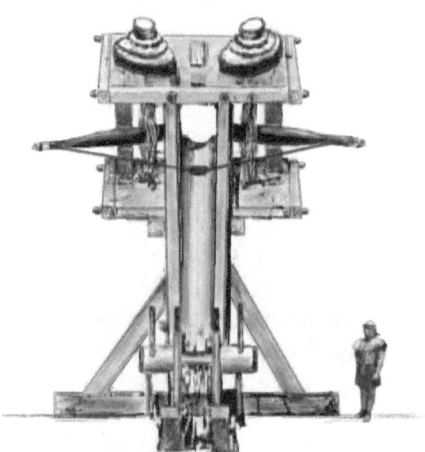

Figure 114: *One talent ballista (26 kg weight projectile). The heaviest versions could shoot up to three talents (78 kg), possibly much more.*[1005]

Roman siege engines

Figure 115: *A ballista.*

The torsion ballista, developed by Alexander, was a far more complicated weapon than its predecessor, and the Romans developed it even further.

Vitruvius, in his *De Architectura* Book X, describes the construction and tuning of Ballistae.

Every century (group of 60-100 men) in the Roman army had a *ballista* by the 1st century AD.[1006] It was the command of the chief of the *ballista*, under whom were the artillery experts, or *doctores ballistarum* and finally, the artillerymen, or *ballistarii*.[1007] *Ballistae* were heavy missile weapons, hurling large rocks great distances to damage rampart walls. They resembled large crossbows, rather than catapults. They were powered by two horizontal like arms, which were inserted into two vertical and tightly wound "skein" springs contained in a rectangular frame structure making up the head or principal part of the weapon. The arms were drawn rearward with a winch lever to further twist the skeins and thus gain the torsion power to cast a projectile. It has been said that the whirring sound of a ballista-fired stone struck fear and dread into the hearts of those inside the walls of besieged cities. The stones chosen to be used in the *ballista* had to be a particular sort. According to Vegetius river stones were best, since they are round, smooth, and dense. Ballista stones found at the site of Masada were chiseled to make them as round as possible.[1008]

Figure 116: *Roman 'catapult-nest' on Trajan's Column*

Early Roman ballista

The early Roman *ballistae* were made of wood, and held together with iron plates around the frames and iron nails in the stand. The main stand had a slider on the top, into which were loaded the bolts or stone 'shot'. Attached to this, at the back, was a pair of winches and a claw, used to ratchet the bowstring back to the armed firing position. A slider passed through the field frames of the weapon, in which were located the torsion springs (rope made of animal sinew), which were twisted around the bow arms, which in turn were attached to the bowstring.

Drawing the bowstring back with the winches twisted the already taut springs, storing the energy to fire the projectiles.

The ballista was a highly accurate weapon (there are many accounts right from its early history of single soldiers being picked off by the operators), but some design aspects meant it could compromise its accuracy for range. The lightweight bolts could not gain the high momentum of the stones over the same distance as those thrown by the later onagers, trebuchets, or mangonels; these could be as heavy as 90-135 kg (200-300 pounds).

The Romans continued the development of the Ballista, and it became a highly prized and valued weapon in the army of the Roman Empire.

Figure 117: *Ballista, military equipment of ancient Rome.*

It was used, just before the start of the Empire, by Julius Caesar during his conquest of Gaul and on both of his expeditions to Britain. Both attempted invasions of Britain and the siege of Alesia are recorded in his own *Commentarii* (journal), *The Gallic Wars* (*De Bello Gallico*). It was also used in the Roman siege of Masada.

First invasion of Britain

The first invasion of Britain took place in 55 BC, after a rapid and successful initial conquest of Gaul, in part as an exploratory expedition, and more practically to try to put an end to the re-enforcements sent by the native Britons to fight the Romans in Gaul.

A total of eighty transports, carrying two legions, attempted to land on the British shore, only to be driven back by the many British warriors assembled along the shoreline. The ships had to unload their troops on the beach, as it was the only one suitable for many kilometers, yet the massed ranks of British charioteers and javeliners were making it impossible.

> *Seeing this, Caesar ordered the warships – which were swifter and easier to handle than the transports, and likely to impress the natives more by their unfamiliar appearance – to be removed a short distance from the others, and then be rowed hard and run ashore on the enemy's right flank,*

Figure 118: *Sketch of an Onager, from Antique technology by Diels*

from which position the slings, bows and artillery could be used by men on deck to drive them back. This manoeuvre was highly successful. Scared by the strange shape of the warships, the motion of the oars, and the unfamiliar machines, the natives halted and then retreated a little. (Caesar, The Conquest of Gaul, p. 99)

Siege of Alesia

In Gaul, the stronghold of Alesia was under a Roman siege in 52 BC, and surrounded by Roman fortifications. As was standard siege technique at the time, ballistae were placed up in the towers with other soldiers armed with either bows or slings.

Onager

The **onager** was a post-classical Roman siege engine, which derived its name from the kicking action of the machine, similar to that of an onager (wild ass). It is a type of catapult that uses torsional pressure, generally from twisted rope, to store energy for the shot.

The onager consisted of a frame placed on the ground to whose front end a vertical frame of solid timber was rigidly fixed; through the vertical frame ran an axle, which had a single stout spoke. On the extremity of the spoke was a sling used to launch a projectile.

Roman siege engines

Figure 119: *Modern reconstruction of a Scorpio*

In action the spoke was forced down, against the tension of twisted ropes or other springs, by a windlass, and then suddenly released. The spoke thus kicked the crosspiece of the vertical frame, and the projectile at its extreme end was shot forward.

The onagers of the Roman Empire were mainly used for besieging forts or settlements. They would often be loaded with large stones or rocks that could be covered with a flammable substance and set alight.

In the Middle Ages (recorded from around 1200 A.D.) a less powerful version of the onager was used that employed a fixed bowl rather than a sling, so that many small projectiles could be thrown, as opposed to a single large one. This engine was sometimes called the *mangonel*, although the same name may have been used for a variety of siege engines.

Scorpio

The *scorpio* was a crossbow-like device that fired smaller arrows with deadly accuracy used both in the field and in sieges. They were so-named for their deadly, armor-piercing sting and could be operated by just one or two men. Scorpios were meant to kill and injure enemy troops, rather than break down enemy fortifications. Thanks to their smaller size, they could be mounted on or in siege towers. During the Siege of Amida, a scorpion-fired arrow killed

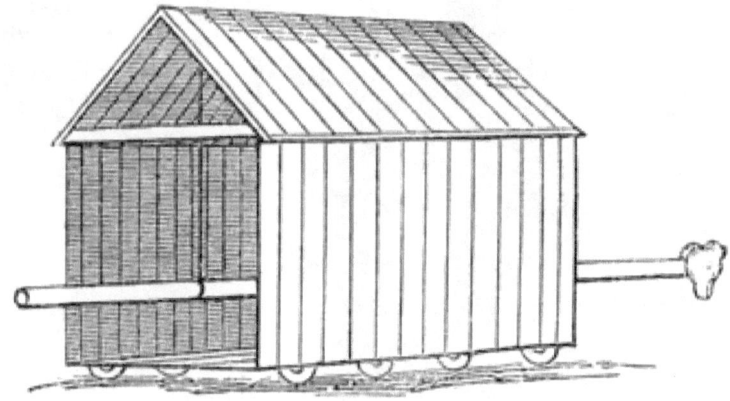

Figure 120: *Roman battering ram.*

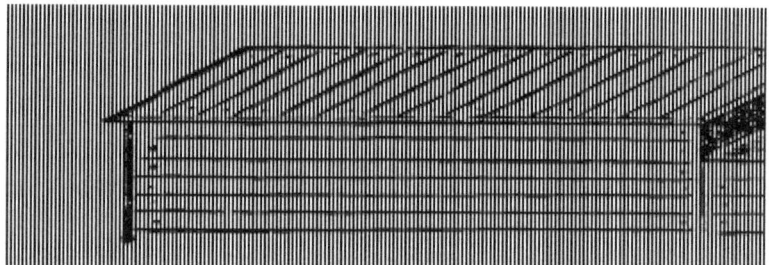

Figure 121: *A battering ram (aries) with a shed (testudo). After a relief on Septimius Severus' triumphal arc in Rome.*

the son of Grumbate, king of the Chionitae, when he was approaching the city to surrender.[1009]

There has been some research done into the existence of the self-loading, serial-fire *scorpio* or polybolos. Legionaries either side would continuously keep turning cranks which turned a chain, which operated the various mechanisms to load and fire the catapult. All that was needed was for another soldier to keep feeding in more arrows.[1010]

Figure 122: *The remains of the Roman siege-ramp at Masada*

Breaking the walls

Battering ram

Roman battering rams, or *aries*, were an effective weapon for breaking down an enemy's walls, as well as their morale. Under Roman law, any defenders who failed to surrender before the first ram touched their wall were denied any rights.[1011] The moment they heard the ram hit the wall, those inside the city knew that the siege proper had begun and there was no turning back.[1012]

Josephus describes the battering ram used at Jotapata thus:[1013]

> *It is an immense beam, similar to a ship's mast, with one end covered with iron shaped into a ram's head; hence its name. It is suspended from another beam like a balance arm by cables around its middle, and this in turn is supported at both ends by posts fixed in the ground. It is drawn back by a huge number of men who then push it forward in unison with all their might so that it hits the wall with its iron head. There is no tower strong enough nor any wall thick enough to withstand repeated blows of this kind, and many cannot resist the first shock.*

Vitruvius in *De Architectura* Book X describes the construction and use of battering rams.

Figure 123: *Siege Machine.*

For protection, a battering ram was suspended in a mobile shelter called a tortoise, or *testudo*. According to Vegetius, it was given this name because the ram would swing out of the shelter much like a tortoise's head comes out of its shell. Such shelters would provide the men within protection against missiles and incendiary devices. They were constructed from a framework of strong timbers with planks and wicker hurdles on the sides. The entire shelter would then be covered with a fireproof material such as uncured hides.[1014] According to Apollodorus of Damascus, the shelter should be fixed to the ground while the ram was being used to both prevent skidding and strain on the axles from the weight of the moving apparatus. This would also increase the strength of the impact on the walls.[1015]

Siege tower

According to Josephus, the Roman siege towers at Jotapata were 50 feet high and iron-plated to protect them from fire; those at Masada were reported to be 75 feet high. It was possible to have many different devices on siege towers, such as artillery, draw bridges and rams. Those at the top of the tower were to keep defenders off the walls while those below them attempted to breach the wall using ramps. In the battle of Jerusalem in 70 AD the Romans began assault on the third defensive wall within Jerusalem, the tower stood 75ft tall and was compromised when the Jewish resistance tunneled underneath the tower leading it to collapse.[1016] Following a basic design, details of tower construction varied from siege to siege and there is no known treatise which specifies at which level siege equipment should be placed. Vegetius noted that, "besiegers sometimes built a tower with another turret inside it that could suddenly be raised by ropes and pulleys to over-top the wall".[1017]

Mine

Mines could be dug under city walls as a means of entering a city secretly and capturing it but were more frequently constructed to weaken city walls. Once dug, sappers would underpin the walls with wood and cause the walls to collapse by firing the supports with resin, sulfur and other incendiary materials.[1018]

Corvus

In chapter 1.22 "The Victory of Mylae" of his *History*, Polybius writes:

> "Now their ships were badly fitted out and not easy to manage, and so some one suggested to them as likely to serve their turn in a fight the construction of what were afterwards called "crows""[1019].

Corvus means "Crow" or "Raven" in Latin and was the name given to a Roman boarding device first documented during the First Punic War against Carthage. Polybius goes on to describe this siege engine as a bridge used to span the distance between two ships in battle. The device was a plank, 4ft wide and 36ft long, affixed to the Roman vessel around a poll. This construction allowed the bridge to be swung port to starboard and therefore used on either side of the ship. A pulley at the top of the poll allowed the planks to be raised and lowered on command. At the end of the bridge there was a heavy metal spike that when dropped on the deck of an enemy ship would, with the aid of gravity, become imbedded in the deck. By connecting the two ships in such a way, Roman soldiers could gain access to the deck of the enemy ship and engage in a more hand to hand based combat styles instead of depending on naval combat styles. Polybius also includes an insight on how these siege engines would have practically functioned in battle:

> "And as soon as the "crows" were fixed in the planks of the decks and grappled the ships together, if the ships were alongside of each other, the men leaped on board anywhere along the side, but if they were prow to prow, they used the "crow" itself for boarding, and advanced over it two abreast. The first two protected their front by holding up before them their shields, while those who came after them secured their sides by placing the rims of their shields upon the top of the railing. Such were the preparations

which they made; and having completed them they watched an opportunity of engaging at sea."

Based on this historical description the Corvus used some mechanisms seen in the more complex siege towers or the sheds constructed around battering rams. They protected, to an extent, the Roman soldiers as they gained entry to the enemy's space where they could engage in combat.

Notes

References

<templatestyles src="Template:Refbegin/styles.css" />

- James V. Garrison (1997). "Casting stones: ballista, stones as weapons, and death by stoning". *Brigham Young University Studies*. **36** (3): 351–352.
- Gilliver, C.M. (1999). *The Roman Art of War*. Charleston, SC: Tempus. ISBN 0-7524-1939-0.
- Goldsworthy, Adrian (2000). *Roman Warfare*. London: Cassell. ISBN 0-304-35265-9.
- Keppie, Lawrence (1984). *The Making of the Roman Army from Empire to Republic*. Totowa, NJ: Barnes & Noble Books. ISBN 0-389-20447-1.
- Le Bohec, Yann (1994). *The Imperial Roman Army*. London: B.T. Batsford Ltd. ISBN 0-7134-7166-2.

Shuckburgh, Evelyn S. (1962). *Translation of "The Histories" by Polybius*. Bloomington. p. 1.22.

List of Roman triumphal arches

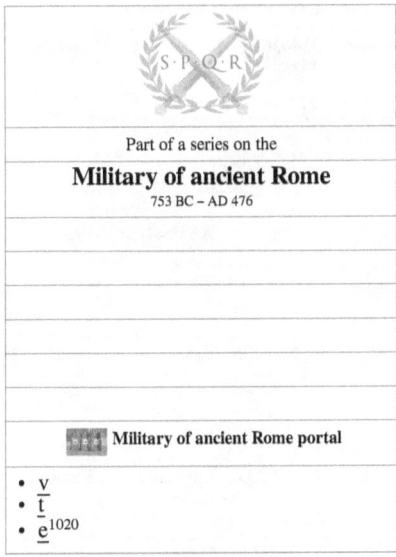

Part of a series on the
Military of ancient Rome
753 BC – AD 476

Military of ancient Rome portal

- v
- t
- e[1020]

For the history of triumphal arches, see Triumphal arch.

For post-Roman triumphal arches, see List of post-Roman triumphal arches.

This is a **list of Roman triumphal arches**. All currently surviving Roman arches date from the imperial period (1st century BC onwards). They were preceded by honorific arches set up under the Roman Republic, none of which survive. Triumphal arches were constructed across the Roman Empire and remain one of the most iconic examples of Roman architecture.

List

Image	Name	Date	Modern city	Modern country	Ancient name
	Arch of Caracalla	216 AD	Djémila	Algeria	Cuicul, Curculum
	Arch of Caracalla	211–214 AD	Tébessa	Algeria	Theveste

	Arch of Trajan	c. 2nd or 3rd centuries AD	Timgad	Algeria	Marciana Traiana Thamugadi
	Heidentor (Pagan gate)	354–361 AD	Petronell-Carnuntum	Austria	Carnuntum
	Arch of the Sergii	29–27 BC	Pula	Croatia	Colonia Pietas Iulia Pola Pollentia Herculanea
	Arch of Campanus	1st century AD	Aix-les-Bains	France	Aquae Gratianae
	Porte Noire	c. 171–175 AD	Besançon	France	Vesontio
	Arch of Carpentras	18–19 AD	Carpentras	France	Carpentoracte Meminorum, Forum Neronis
	Triumphal Arch of Orange	c. 20–27 AD	Orange	France	Colonia Julia Firma Secundanorum Arausio
	Porte Mars	3rd century AD	Reims	France	Durocortorum
	Pont Flavien	c. 12 BC	Saint-Chamas	France	n/a
	Arch of Glanum	10–25 AD	Saint-Rémy-de-Provence	France	Glanum
	Arch of Germanicus	18–19 AD	Saintes	France	Mediolanum Santonum
	Hadrian's Arch	131–132 AD	Athens	Greece	Athína, Athenae
	Arch of Galerius	298–299 AD	Thessaloniki	Greece	Thessaloníkē
	Arch of Trajan	113 AD	Ancona	Italy	Ancona
	Arch of Augustus	25 BC	Aosta	Italy	Augusta Praetoria Salassorum

List of Roman triumphal arches

	Arch of Mark Antony	113 AD	Aquino	Italy	Aquinum
	Arch of Trajan	114–117 AD	Benevento	Italy	Maleventum, Beneventum
	Arch of Trajan	c. 109 AD	Canosa di Puglia	Italy	Canusium
	Arch of Augustus	9 AD	Fano	Italy	Fanum Fortunae
	Triumphal Arch	18–19 AD	Pompei	Italy	Pompeii
	Arch of Augustus	27 BC	Rimini	Italy	Ariminium
	Arch of Constantine	312–315 AD	Rome	Italy	Roma
	Arch of Drusus	9 BC	Rome	Italy	Roma
	Arch of Gallienus	262 AD	Rome	Italy	Roma
	Arch of Septimius Severus	203 AD	Rome	Italy	Roma
	Arch of Titus	82 AD	Rome	Italy	Roma
	Arch of Janus	4th century AD	Rome	Italy	Roma
	Arch of Malborghetto	c. 315 AD	Rome	Italy	Roma
	Arch of Hadrian	c. 1st or 2nd centuries AD	Capua	Italy	Capuae

	Arch of Drusus	14–37 AD	Spoleto	Italy	Spoletium
	Arch of Augustus	8 BC	Susa	Italy	Segusio
	Arco di Riccardo	33 BC	Trieste	Italy	Tergeste, Tergestum
	Arco dei Gavi	c. 50 AD	Verona	Italy	Verona
	Arch of Hadrian	129–130 AD	Jerash	Jordan	Gerasa
	Triumphal Arch		Tyre	Lebanon	Tyros, Tyrus
	Arch of Tiberius	35 AD	Khoms	Libya	Leptis Magna
	Arch of Trajan	109–110 AD	Khoms	Libya	Leptis Magna
	Arch of Septimius Severus	146–211 AD	Khoms	Libya	Leptis Magna
	Arch of Marcus Aurelius	165 AD	Tripoli	Libya	Oea
	Arch of Caracalla	217 AD	Volubilis	Morocco	Volubilis
	Arch of Cabanes	c. 2nd century AD	Castellón de la Plana	Spain	n/a
	Arco de Medinaceli	c. 1st century BC	Medinaceli	Spain	Occilis, Okilis
	Arc de Berà	c. 13 BC	Roda de Barà	Spain	n/a
	Latakia Tetraporticus (Arch of Septimius Severus)	183 AD	Latakia	Syria	Laodicea ad Mare

List of Roman triumphal arches

Image	Name	Date	Modern city	Modern country	Notes
	Arch of Alexander Severus	228 AD	Dougga	Tunisia	Colonia Licinia Septimia Aurelia Alexandriana Thuggensis
	Arch of Septimius Severus	205 AD	Dougga	Tunisia	Colonia Licinia Septimia Aurelia Alexandriana Thuggensis
	Triumphal Arch of the Tetrarchy	~300 AD	Sbeitla	Tunisia	Sufetula
	South Gate		Anazarbus	Turkey	Anazarbos
	Hadrian's Gate	2nd century AD	Antalya	Turkey	Attaleia

Destroyed Roman arches

- Note: MUR stands for the 12th century Mirabilia Urbis Romae

Image	Name	Date of construction	Date destroyed	Modern city	Modern country	Notes	Citation
	Arch of Arcadius, Honorius and Theodosius	405 AD	1362–1370	Rome	Italy		MUR, p. 10.
	Arch of Augustus	29 BC		Rome	Italy	Some fragments survive	
	Arch of Claudius	51–52 AD		Rome	Italy	Some fragments survive	MUR, p. 12.
	Arch of Faustinus		After 12th century	Rome	Italy		MUR, p. 13.
	Arch of Gratian, Valentinian and Theodosius	379–383 AD	c. 13th century	Rome	Italy		MUR, p. 10.
	Arch of Lentulus and Crispinus	2nd century AD	15th century	Rome	Italy		
	Arch Manus Carnae (Hand of Flesh)		After 12th century	Rome	Italy		MUR, p. 13.

	Arch of Nero	58–62 AD	c. 1st century AD	Rome	Italy		
	Arcus Novus	293–304 AD	1491	Rome	Italy	Some reliefs survive	
	Arch of Octavian or Marcus Aurelius		After 12th century	Rome	Italy		MUR, p. 12.
	Arch of Octavius	c. 28 BC		Rome	Italy		
	Arch Panis Aurei or Aureus (Golden)		After 12th century	Rome	Italy		MUR, p. 13.
	Arch of Pietas		After 12th century	Rome	Italy		MUR, p. 13.
	Arch of Portugal	c. 3rd century AD	1662	Rome	Italy	Some reliefs preserved at the Capitoline Museums	MUR, p. 10.
	Arch of Tiberius	16 AD		Rome	Italy	Some foundations still survive	
	Arch of Titus	81 AD	After 15th century	Rome	Italy	Some fragments still survive	MUR, p. 11.
	Monumental Arch	3rd century AD	October 2015	Palmyra	Syria	Most of the stonework is still intact	
	Arch of Theodosius	393 AD	6th–8th centuries	Istanbul	Turkey	Some fragments still survive	
	Arch at Richborough Castle	c. 1st century AD		Richborough	United Kingdom	Foundations and mound still visible	

Sources

- Anonymous (1889). English Translation of 12th century Text; Translation by Francis Morgan Nichols, ed. Mirabilia Urbis Romae *or* Marvels of Rome or a Picture of the Golden City[1021]. Ellis and Elvey, London; Spithoever, Rome.

Roman roads

Roman roads (Latin: *viae Romanae*; singular: *via Romana* meaning "Roman way") were physical infrastructure vital to the maintenance and development of the Roman state, and were built from about 300 BC through the expansion and consolidation of the Roman Republic and the Roman Empire. They provided efficient means for the overland movement of armies, officials, and civilians, and the inland carriage of official communications and trade goods.[1022] Roman roads were of several kinds, ranging from small local roads to broad, long-distance highways built to connect cities, major towns and military bases. These major roads were often stone-paved and metaled, cambered for drainage, and were flanked by footpaths, bridleways and drainage ditches. They were laid along accurately surveyed courses, and some were cut through hills, or conducted over rivers and ravines on bridgework. Sections could be supported over marshy ground on rafted or piled foundations.[1023]

At the peak of Rome's development, no fewer than 29 great military highways radiated from the capital, and the late Empire's 113 provinces were interconnected by 372 great roads.[1024] The whole comprised more than 400,000 kilometres (250,000 miles) of roads, of which over 80,500 kilometres (50,000 mi) were stone-paved.[1025,1026] In Gaul alone, no less than 21,000 kilometres (13,000 mi) of roadways are said to have been improved, and in Britain at least 4,000 kilometres (2,500 mi). The courses (and sometimes the surfaces) of many Roman roads survived for millennia; some are overlaid by modern roads.

Roman systems

Dionysius of Halicarnassus, *Ant. Rom. 3.67.5*[1027]

Livy mentions some of the most familiar roads near Rome, and the milestones on them, at times long before the first paved road—the Appian Way. Unless these allusions are just simple anachronisms, the roads referred to were probably at the time little more than levelled earthen tracks. Thus, the Via Gabina (during the time of Porsena) is mentioned in about 500 BC; the Via Latina (during the time of Coriolanus) in about 490 BC; the Via Nomentana (also known as "Via Ficulensis"), in 449 BC; the Via Labicana in 421 BC; and the Via Salaria in 361 BC.[1028]

In the Itinerary of Antoninus, the description of the road system, after the death of Julius Caesar and during the tenure of Augustus, is as follows:

> "With the exception of some outlying portions, such as Britain north of the Wall, Dacia, and certain provinces east of the Euphrates, the whole

Figure 124: *A Roman street in Pompeii*

Empire was penetrated by these itinera (plural of iter). There is hardly a district to which we might expect a Roman official to be sent, on service either civil or military, where we do not find roads. They reach the Wall in Britain; run along the Rhine, the Danube, and the Euphrates; and cover, as with a network, the interior provinces of the Empire."

A road map of the empire reveals that it was generally laced with a dense network of prepared *viae*. Beyond its borders there were no paved roads; however, it can be supposed that footpaths and dirt roads allowed some transport. There were, for instance, some pre-Roman ancient trackways in Britain, such as the Ridgeway and the Icknield Way.[1029]

For specific roads, see Roman road locations *below.*

Laws and traditions

The Laws of the Twelve Tables, dated to about 450 BC, required that any public road (Latin *via*) be 8 Roman feet (perhaps about 2.37 m) wide where straight and twice that width where curved. These were probably the minimum widths for a *via*; in the later Republic, widths of around 12 Roman feet were common for public roads in rural regions, permitting the passing of two carts of

Figure 125: *Old Roman Road, leading from Jerusalem to Beit Gubrin, adjacent to regional hwy 375 in Israel*

standard (4 foot) width without interference to pedestrian traffic. Actual practices varied from this standard. The Tables command Romans to build public roads and give wayfarers the right to pass over private land where the road is in disrepair. Building roads that would not need frequent repair therefore became an ideological objective, as well as building them as straight as possible in order to build the narrowest roads possible, and thus save on material.

Roman law defined the right to use a road as a *servitus*, or liability. The *ius eundi* ("right of going") established a claim to use an *iter*, or footpath, across private land; the *ius agendi* ("right of driving"), an *actus*, or carriage track. A *via* combined both types of *servitutes*, provided it was of the proper width, which was determined by an *arbiter*. The default width was the *latitudo legitima* of 8 feet.

Roman law and tradition forbade the use of vehicles in urban areas, except in certain cases. Married women and government officials on business could ride. The *Lex Iulia Municipalis* restricted commercial carts to night-time access in the city within the walls and within a mile outside the walls.

Figure 126: *The central road of Aeclanum.*

Types

Roman roads varied from simple corduroy roads to paved roads using deep roadbeds of tamped rubble as an underlying layer to ensure that they kept dry, as the water would flow out from between the stones and fragments of rubble, instead of becoming mud in clay soils. According to Ulpian, there were three types of roads:

1. *Viae publicae, consulares, praetoriae* or *militares*
2. *Viae privatae, rusticae, glareae* or *agrariae*
3. *Viae vicinales*

Viae publicae, consulares, praetoriae **and** *militares*

The first type of road included public high or main roads, constructed and maintained at the public expense, and with their soil vested in the state. Such roads led either to the sea, or to a town, or to a public river (one with a constant flow), or to another public road. Siculus Flaccus, who lived under Trajan (98-117), calls them *viae publicae regalesque*, and describes their characteristics as follows:

1. They are placed under *curatores* (commissioners), and repaired by *redemptores* (contractors) at the public expense; a fixed contribution, however, being levied from the neighboring landowners.

2. These roads bear the names of their constructors (e.g. Via Appia, Cassia, Flaminia).

Roman roads were named after the censor who had ordered their construction or reconstruction. The same person often served afterwards as consul, but the road name is dated to his term as censor. If the road was older than the office of censor or was of unknown origin, it took the name of its destination or of the region through which it mainly passed. A road was renamed if the censor ordered major work on it, such as paving, repaving, or rerouting. With the term *viae regales* compare the roads of the Persian kings (who probably organized the first system of public roads) and the King's highway. With the term *viae militariae* compare the Icknield Way (e.g., Icen-hilde-weg, or "War-way of the Iceni").

However, there were many other people, besides special officials, who from time to time, and for a variety of reasons, sought to connect their names with a great public service like that of the roads. Gaius Gracchus, when Tribune of the People (123-122 BC), paved or gravelled many of the public roads, and provided them with milestones and mounting-blocks for riders. Again, Gaius Scribonius Curio, when Tribune (50 BC), sought popularity by introducing a Lex Viaria, under which he was to be chief inspector or commissioner for five years. Dio Cassius mentions as one of the forcible acts of the triumvirs of 43 BC (Octavianus, Antony, and Lepidus), that they obliged the senators to repair the public roads at their own expense.

Viae privatae, rusticae, glareae and *agrariae*

The second category included private or country roads, originally constructed by private individuals, in whom their soil was vested, and who had the power to dedicate them to the public use. Such roads benefited from a right of way, in favor either of the public or of the owner of a particular estate. Under the heading of *viae privatae* were also included roads leading from the public or high roads to particular estates or settlements. These Ulpian considers to be public roads in themselves.

Features off the *via* were connected to the *via* by *viae rusticae*, or secondary roads. Both main or secondary roads might either be paved, or left unpaved, with a gravel surface, as they were in North Africa. These prepared but unpaved roads were *viae glareae* or *sternendae* ("to be strewn"). Beyond the secondary roads were the *viae terrenae*, "dirt roads".

Viae vicinales

The third category comprised roads at or in villages, districts, or crossroads, leading through or towards a *vicus* or village. Such roads ran either into a high road, or into other *viae vicinales*, without any direct communication with a high road. They were considered public or private, according to the fact of their original construction out of public or private funds or materials. Such a road, though privately constructed, became a public road when the memory of its private constructors had perished.

Siculus Flaccus describes *viae vicinales* as roads "*de publicis quae divertunt in agros et saepe ad alteras publicas perveniunt*" (which turn off the public roads into fields, and often reach to other public roads). The repairing authorities, in this case, were the *magistri pagorum* or magistrates of the cantons. They could require the neighboring landowners either to furnish laborers for the general repair of the *viae vicinales*, or to keep in repair, at their own expense, a certain length of road passing through their respective properties.

Governance and financing

With the conquest of Italy, prepared *viae* were extended from Rome and its vicinity to outlying municipalities, sometimes overlying earlier roads. Building *viae* was a military responsibility and thus came under the jurisdiction of a consul. The process had a military name, *viam munire*, as though the *via* were a fortification. Municipalities, however, were responsible for their own roads, which the Romans called *viae vicinales*. The beauty and grandeur of the roads might tempt us to believe that any Roman citizen could use them for free, but this was not the case. Tolls abounded, especially at bridges. Often they were collected at the city gate. Freight costs were made heavier still by import and export taxes. These were only the charges for using the roads. Costs of services on the journey went up from there.

Financing road building was a Roman government responsibility. Maintenance, however, was generally left to the province. The officials tasked with fund-raising were the *curatores viarum*. They had a number of methods available to them. Private citizens with an interest in the road could be asked to contribute to its repair. High officials might distribute largesse to be used for roads. Censors, who were in charge of public morals and public works, were expected to fund repairs *suâ pecuniâ* (with their own money). Beyond those means, taxes were required.

A *via* connected two cities. *Viae* were generally centrally placed in the countryside.Wikipedia:Please clarify The construction and care of the public roads, whether in Rome, in Italy, or in the provinces, was, at all periods of Roman history, considered to be a function of the greatest weight and importance.

This is clearly shown by the fact that the censors, in some respects the most venerable of Roman magistrates, had the earliest paramount authority to construct and repair all roads and streets. Indeed, all the various functionaries, not excluding the emperors themselves, who succeeded the censors in this portion of their duties, may be said to have exercised a devolved censorial jurisdiction.

Costs and civic responsibilities

The devolution to the censorial jurisdictions soon became a practical necessity, resulting from the growth of the Roman dominions and the diverse labors which detained the censors in the capital city. Certain *ad hoc* official bodies successively acted as constructing and repairing authorities. In Italy, the censorial responsibility passed to the commanders of the Roman armies, and later to special commissioners – and in some cases perhaps to the local magistrates. In the provinces, the consul or praetor and his legates received authority to deal directly with the contractor.

The care of the streets and roads within the Roman territory was committed in the earliest times to the censors. They eventually made contracts for paving the street inside Rome, including the Clivus Capitolinus, with lava, and for laying down the roads outside the city with gravel. Sidewalks were also provided. The aediles, probably by virtue of their responsibility for the freedom of traffic and policing the streets, co-operated with the censors and the bodies that succeeded them.

It would seem that in the reign of Claudius (AD 41-54) the quaestors had become responsible for the paving of the streets of Rome, or at least shared that responsibility with the quattuorviri viarum. It has been suggested that the quaestors were obliged to buy their right to an official career by personal outlay on the streets. There was certainly no lack of precedents for this enforced liberality, and the change made by Claudius may have been a mere change in the nature of the expenditure imposed on the quaestors.

Official bodies

The official bodies which first succeeded the censors in the care of the streets and roads were two in number. They were:

1. *Quattuorviri viis in urbe purgandis*, with jurisdiction inside the walls of Rome;
2. *Duoviri viis extra urbem purgandis*, with jurisdiction outside the walls.

Both these bodies were probably of ancient origin, but the true year of their institution is unknown. Little reliance can be placed on Pomponius, who states that the *quattuorviri* were instituted *eodem tempore* (at the same time) as the *praetor peregrinus* (i.e. about 242 BC) and the *Decemviri litibus iudicandis*[1030] (time unknown). The first mention of either body occurs in the *Lex Julia Municipalis* of 45 BC. The quattuorviri were afterwards called *Quattuorviri viarum curandarum*. The extent of jurisdiction of the Duoviri is derived from their full title as *Duoviri viis extra propiusve urbem Romam passus mille purgandis*.[1031] Their authority extended over all roads between their respective gates of issue in the city wall and the first milestone beyond.

In case of an emergency in the condition of a particular road, men of influence and liberality were appointed, or voluntarily acted, as *curatores* or temporary commissioners to superintend the work of repair. The dignity attached to such a curatorship is attested by a passage of Cicero. Among those who performed this duty in connection with particular roads was Julius Caesar, who became *curator* (67 BC) of the Via Appia, and spent his own money liberally upon it. Certain persons appear also to have acted alone and taken responsibility for certain roads.

In the country districts, as has been stated, the magistri pagorum had authority to maintain the *viae vicinales*. In Rome itself each householder was legally responsible for the repairs to that portion of the street which passed his own house. It was the duty of the aediles to enforce this responsibility. The portion of any street which passed a temple or public building was repaired by the aediles at the public expense. When a street passed between a public building or temple and a private house, the public treasury and the private owner shared the expense equally. No doubtWikipedia:Cleanup, if only to secure uniformity, the personal liability of householders to execute repairs of the streets was commuted for a paving rate payable to the public authorities who were responsible from time to time.

Augustus' changes

The governing structure was changed by Augustus. In the course of his reconstitution of the urban administration he created new offices in connection with the public works, streets, and aqueducts of Rome. He foundWikipedia:Please clarify the *quattuorviri* and *duoviri* forming part of the body of magistrates known as vigintisexviri. These he reduced from 26 to 20 members (vigintiviri), but retained the *quattuorviri* among them. The latter were certainly still in existence under Hadrian (117-138). Augustus abolished the *duoviri*, no doubt because the time had come to deal comprehensively with the superintendence of the roads which connected Rome with Italy and the provinces.

Dio Cassius relates that Augustus personally accepted the post of superintendent. In this capacity he represented the paramount authority which belonged originally to the censors. Moreover, he appointed men of praetorian rank to be road-makers, assigning to each of them two lictors. He also made the office of curator of each of the great public roads a perpetual magistracy, instead of a special and temporary commission, as had been the case hitherto.

In Augustus' capacity as supreme head of the public road system, he converted the temporary *cura* of each of the great roads into a permanent magistracy. The persons appointed under the new system were of senatorial or equestrian rank, according to the relative importance of the roads respectively assigned to them. It was the duty of each curator to issue contracts for the maintenance and repairs of his road, and to see that the contractor who undertook the work performed it faithfully, as to both quantity and quality. Moreover, he authorized the construction of sewers and removed obstructions to traffic, as the aediles did in Rome. It was in the character of an imperial curator, though probably of one armed with extraordinary powers, that Corbulo (as has been already mentioned) denounced the *magistratus* and *mancipes* of the Italian roads to Tiberius. He pursued them and their families with fines and imprisonment for 18 years (AD 21-39), and was rewarded with a consulship by Caligula, who was himself in the habit of condemning well-born citizens to work on the roads. It is noticeable that Claudius brought Corbulo to justice, and repaid the money which had been extorted from his victims.

Other *curatores*

Special *curatores* for a term seem to have been appointed on occasion, even after the institution of the permanent magistrates bearing that title. The Emperors who succeeded Augustus exercised a vigilant control over the condition of the public highways. Their names occur frequently in the inscriptions to restorers of roads and bridges. Thus, Vespasian, Titus, Domitian, Trajan, and Septimius Severus were commemorated in this capacity at Emérita. The Itinerary of Antoninus, which was probably a work of much earlier date, republished in an improved and enlarged form, under one of the Antonine emperors, remains as standing evidence of the minute care which was bestowed on the service of the public roads.

Construction and engineering

Ancient Rome boasted impressive technological feats, using many advances that would be lost in the Middle Ages. These accomplishments would not be rivaled until the Modern Age. Many practical Roman innovations were adopted from earlier designs. Some of the common, earlier designs incorporated arches.

Figure 127: *Road construction on Trajan's Column*

Practices and terminology

Roman road builders aimed at a regulation width (see Laws and traditions above), but actual widths have been measured at between 3.6 feet (1.1 metres) and more than 23 feet (7.0 metres). Today, the concrete has worn from the spaces around the stones, giving the impression of a very bumpy road, but the original practice was to produce a surface that was no doubt much closer to being flat. Many roads were built to resist rain, freezing and flooding. They were constructed to need as little repair as possible.

Roman construction took a directional straightness. Many long sections are ruler-straight, but it should not be thought that all of them were. Some links in the network were as long as 55 miles (89 km). Gradients of 10%–12% are known in ordinary terrain, 15%–20% in mountainous country. The Roman emphasis on constructing straight roads often resulted in steep slopes relatively impractical for most commercial traffic; over the years the Romans themselves realized this and built longer, but more manageable, alternatives to existing roads. Roman roads generally went straight up and down hills, rather than in a serpentine pattern.

As to the standard Imperial terminology that was used, the words were localized for different elements used in construction and varied from region to region. Also, in the course of time, the terms *via munita* and *vía publica* became identical.

Materials and methods

Viae were distinguished not only according to their public or private character, but according to the materials employed and the methods followed in their construction. Ulpian divided them up in the following fashion:

1. *Via terrena*: A plain road of leveled earth.
2. *Via glareata*:[1032] An earthed road with a graveled surface.
3. *Via munita*:[1033] A regular built road, paved with rectangular blocks of the stone of the country, or with polygonal blocks of lava.

The Romans, though certainly inheriting some of the art of road construction from the Etruscans, borrowed the knowledge of construction of *viae munitae* from the Carthaginians according to Isidore of Sevilla.

Via terrena

The *Viae terrenae* were plain roads of leveled earth. These were mere tracks worn down by the feet of humans and animals, and possibly by wheeled carriages.

Via glareata

The *Viae glareatae* were earthed roads with a graveled surface or a gravel subsurface and paving on top. Livy speaks of the censors of his time as being the first to contract for paving the streets of Rome with flint stones, for laying gravel on the roads outside the city, and for forming raised footpaths at the sides.[1034] In these roads, the surface was hardened with gravel, and although pavements were introduced shortly afterwards, the blocks were allowed to rest merely on a bed of small stones.[1035,1036] An example of this type is found on the Praenestine Way. Another example is found near the Via Latina.

Via munita

The best sources of information as regards the construction of a regulation *via munita* are:

1. The many existing remains of *viae publicae*. These are often sufficiently well preserved to show that the rules of construction were, as far as local material allowed, minutely adhered to in practice.
2. The directions for making pavements given by Vitruvius. The *pavement* and the *via munita* were identical in construction, except as regards the top layer, or surface. This consisted, in the former case, of marble or mosaic, and, in the latter, of blocks of stone or lava.

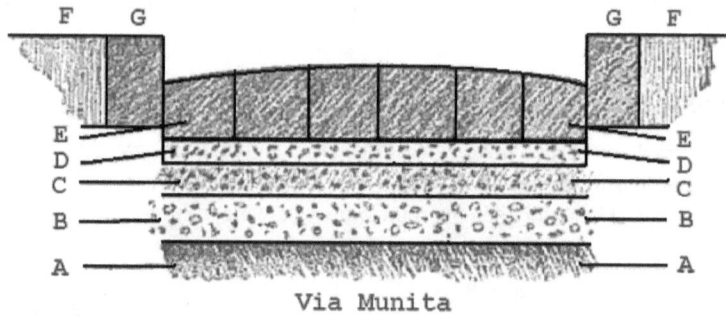

Figure 128: *The general appearance of such a metalled road and footway is shown in an existing street of Pompeii. (A). Native earth, leveled and, if necessary, rammed tight.(B). Statumen: stones of a size to fill the hand.(C). Audits: rubble or concrete of broken stones and lime.(D). Nucleus: kernel or bedding of fine cement made of pounded potshards and lime.(E). Dorsum or agger viae: the elliptical surface or crown of the road (media stratae eminentia) made of polygonal blocks of silex (basaltic lava) or rectangular blocks of saxum qitadratum (travertine, peperino, or other stone of the country). The upper surface was designed to cast off rain or water like the shell of a tortoise. The lower surfaces of the separate stones, here shown as flat, were sometimes cut to a point or edge in order to grasp the nucleus, or next layer, more firmly.(F). Crepido, margo or semita: raised footway, or sidewalk, on each side of the via.(G). Umbones or edge-stones.*

3. A passage in Statius describing the repairs of the Via Domitiana, a branch road of the Via Appia, leading to Neapolis.

After the civil engineer looked over the site of the proposed road and determined roughly where it should go, the agrimensores went to work surveying the road bed. They used two main devices, the rod and a device called a *groma*, which helped them obtain right angles. The *gromatici*, the Roman equivalent of rod men, placed rods and put down a line called the *rigor*. As they did not possess anything like a transit, a civil engineering surveyor tried to achieve straightness by looking along the rods and commanding the *gromatici* to move them as required. Using the *gromae* they then laid out a grid on the plan of the road.

The *libratores* then began their work using ploughs and, sometimes with the help of legionaries, with spades excavated the road bed down to bed rock or at least to the firmest ground they could find. The excavation was called the *fossa*, the Latin word for ditch. The depth varied according to terrain.

The method varied according to geographic locality, materials available and terrain, but the plan, or ideal at which the engineer aimed was always the same. The roadbed was layered. The road was constructed by filling the ditch. This was done by layering rock over other stones.

Into the ditch was dumped large amounts of rubble, gravel and stone, whatever fill was available. Sometimes a layer of sand was put down, if it could be found. When it came to within 1 yd (1 m) or so of the surface it was covered with gravel and tamped down, a process called *pavire*, or *pavimentare*. The flat surface was then the *pavimentum*. It could be used as the road, or additional layers could be constructed. A *statumen* or "foundation" of flat stones set in cement might support the additional layers.

The final steps utilized lime-based concrete, which the Romans had discovered. They seem to have mixed the mortar and the stones in the ditch. First a small layer of coarse concrete, the *rudus*, then a little layer of fine concrete, the nucleus, went onto the pavement or *statumen*. Into or onto the nucleus went a course of polygonal or square paving stones, called the *summa crusta*. The *crusta* was crowned for drainage.

An example is found in an early basalt road by the Temple of Saturn on the Clivus Capitolinus. It had travertine paving, polygonal basalt blocks, concrete bedding (substituted for the gravel), and a rain-water gutter.[1037]

Obstacle crossings

Romans preferred to engineer solutions to obstacles rather than circumvent them. Outcroppings of stone, ravines, or hilly or mountainous terrain called for cuttings and tunnels. An example of this is found on the Roman road from Cazanes near the Iron Gates. This road was half carved into the rock, about 5 ft. to 5 ft. 9 in. (1.5 to 1.75 m), the rest of the road, above the Danube, was made from wooden structure, projecting out of the cliff. The road functioned as a towpath, making the Danube navigable. Tabula Traiana memorial plaque in Serbia is all that remains of the now-submerged road.

Bridges and causeways

Roman bridges, built by ancient Romans, were the first large and lasting bridges built. River crossings were achieved by bridges, or *pontes*. Single slabs went over rills. A bridge could be of wood, stone, or both. Wooden bridges were constructed on pilings sunk into the river, or on stone piers. Larger or more permanent bridges required arches. These larger bridges were built with stone and had the arch as its basic structure (see arch bridge). Most also used concrete, which the Romans were the first to use for bridges. Roman bridges were so well constructed that a number remain in use today.

Figure 129: *The remains of Emperor Trajan's route along the Danube (see Roman Serbia)*

Figure 130: *Roman auxiliary infantry crossing a river, probably the Danube, on a pontoon bridge during the emperor Trajan's Dacian Wars (101–106)*

Causeways were built over marshy ground. The road was first marked out with pilings. Between them were sunk large quantities of stone so as to raise the causeway to more than 5 feet (1.5 metres) above the marsh. In the provinces, the Romans often did not bother with a stone causeway, but used log roads (*pontes longi*).

Military and citizen utilization

The public road system of the Romans was thoroughly military in its aims and spirit. It was designed to unite and consolidate the conquests of the Roman people, whether within or without the limits of Italy proper. A legion on the march brought its own baggage train (*impedimenta*) and constructed its own camp (*castra*) every evening at the side of the road.

Milestones and markers

Milestones divided the via Appia even before 250 BC into numbered miles, and most *viae* after 124 BC. The modern word "mile" derives from the Latin *milia passuum*, "one thousand paces", which amounted to 4,841 feet (1,476 metres). A milestone, or *miliarium*, was a circular column on a solid rectangular base, set for more than 2 feet (0.61 metres) into the ground, standing 5 feet (1.5 metres) tall, 20 inches (51 centimetres) in diameter, and weighing more than 2 tons. At the base was inscribed the number of the mile relative to the road it was on. In a panel at eye-height was the distance to the Roman Forum and various other information about the officials who made or repaired the road and when. These miliaria are valuable historical documents now. Their inscriptions are collected in the volume XVII of the *Corpus Inscriptionum Latinarum*.

Examples of Roman Milestones

Figure 131: *Rome, Campidoglio: the Miliarium (milestone), point of departure of the consular roads by Lalupa*

Figure 132: *Turda, Romania: 1993 copy of the Milliarium of Aiton, dating from 108 and showing the construction of the road from Potaissa to Napoca built by Cohors I Hispanorum miliaria in Roman Dacia, by demand of the Emperor Trajan*

Figure 133: *Remains of the miliarium aureum in the Roman Forum*

Figure 134: *A provincial Roman milestone, at Alto Rabagão, Portugal (road from Bracara Augusta to Asturias)*

The Romans had a preference for standardization wherever possible, so Augustus, after becoming permanent commissioner of roads in 20 BC, set up the *miliarium aureum* ("golden milestone") near the Temple of Saturn. All roads were considered to begin from this gilded bronze monument. On it were listed all the major cities in the empire and distances to them. Constantine called it the *umbilicus Romae* ("navel of Rome"), and built a similar—although more complex—monument in Constantinople, the Milion.

Milestones permitted distances and locations to be known and recorded exactly. It was not long before historians began to refer to the milestone at which an event occurred.

Itinerary maps and charts

Combined topographical and road-maps may have existed as specialty items in some Roman libraries, but they were expensive, hard to copy and not in general use. Travelers wishing to plan a journey could consult an *itinerarium*, which in its most basic form was a simple list of cities and towns along a given road, and the distances between them.[1038] It was only a short step from lists to a master list, or a schematic route-planner in which roads and their branches were represented more or less in parallel, as in the *Tabula Peutingeriana*. From this master list, parts could be copied and sold on the streets. The

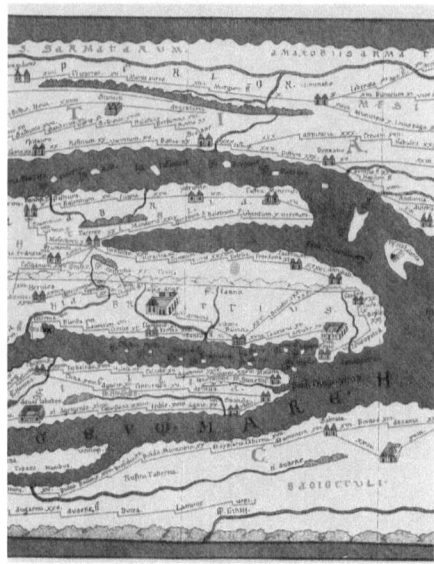

Figure 135: *Tabula Peutingeriana' (Southern Italy centered).*

most thorough used different symbols for cities, way stations, water courses, and so on. The Roman government from time to time would produce a master road-itinerary. The first known were commissioned in 44 BC by Julius Caesar and Mark Antony. Three Greek geographers, Zenodoxus, Theodotus and Polyclitus, were hired to survey the system and compile a master itinerary; the task required over 25 years and the resulting stone-engraved master itinerary was set up near the Pantheon. Travelers and itinerary sellers could make copies from it.

Vehicles and transportation

Outside the cities, Romans were avid riders and rode on or drove quite a number of vehicle types, some of which are mentioned here. Carts driven by oxen were used. Horse-drawn carts could travel up to 40 to 50 kilometres (25 to 31 mi) per day,[1039] pedestrians 20 to 25 kilometres (12 to 16 mi). For purposes of description, Roman vehicles can be divided into the car, the coach, and the cart. Cars were used to transport one or two individuals, coaches were used to transport parties, and carts to transport cargo.

Of the cars, the most popular was the *carrus*, a standard chariot form descending to the Romans from a greater antiquity. The top was open, the front closed. One survives in the Vatican. It carried a driver and a passenger. A *carrus* with

Figure 136: *Roman carriage (reconstruction)*

two horses was a *biga*; three horses, a *triga*; and four horses a *quadriga*. The tyres were of iron. When not in use, its wheels were removed for easier storage.

A more luxurious version, the *carpentum*, transported women and officials. It had an arched overhead covering of cloth and was drawn by mules. A lighter version, the *cisium*, equivalent to a gig, was open above and in front and had a seat. Drawn by one or two mules or horses, it was used for cab work, the cab drivers being called *cisiani*. The builder was a *cisarius*.

Of the coaches, the mainstay was the *raeda* or *reda*, which had four wheels. The high sides formed a sort of box in which seats were placed, with a notch on each side for entry. It carried several people with baggage up to the legal limit of 1000 Roman *librae* (pounds), modern equivalent 328 kilograms (723 pounds). It was drawn by teams of oxen, horses or mules. A cloth top could be put on for weather, in which case it resembled a covered wagon.

The *raeda* was probably the main vehicle for travel on the roads. *Raedae meritoriae* were hired coaches. The *fiscalis raeda* was a government coach. The driver and the builder were both referred to as a *raedarius*.

Of the carts, the main one was the *plaustrum* or *plostrum*. This was simply a platform of boards attached to wheels and a cross-tree. The wheels, or *tympana*, were solid and were several centimetres (inches) thick. The sides could be built up with boards or rails. A large wicker basket was sometimes placed on it. A two-wheel version existed along with the normal four-wheel type called the *plaustrum maius*.

The military used a standard wagon. Their transportation service was the *cursus clabularis*, after the standard wagon, called a *carrus clabularius*, *clabularis*, *clavularis*, or *clabulare*. It transported the *impedimenta* (baggage) of a military column.

Way stations and traveler inns

Non-military officials and people on official business had no legion at their service and the government maintained way stations, or *mansiones* ("staying places"), for their use. Passports were required for identification. *Mansiones* were located about 25 to 30 kilometres (16 to 19 mi) apart. There the official traveller found a complete *villa* dedicated to his use. Often a permanent military camp or a town grew up around the *mansio*. For non-official travelers in need of refreshment, a private system of "inns" or *cauponae* were placed near the *mansiones*. They performed the same functions but were somewhat disreputable, as they were frequented by thieves and prostitutes. Graffiti decorate the walls of the few whose ruins have been found.

Genteel travelers needed something better than *cauponae*. In the early days of the *viae*, when little unofficial provision existed, houses placed near the road were required by law to offer hospitality on demand. Frequented houses no doubt became the first *tabernae*, which were hostels, rather than the "taverns" we know today. As Rome grew, so did its *tabernae*, becoming more luxurious and acquiring good or bad reputations as the case may be. One of the best hotels was the *Tabernae Caediciae* at Sinuessa on the Via Appia. It had a large storage room containing barrels of wine, cheese and ham. Many cities of today grew up around a *taberna* complex, such as Rheinzabern in the Rhineland, and Saverne in Alsace.

A third system of way stations serviced vehicles and animals: the *mutationes* ("changing stations"). They were located every 20 to 30 kilometres (12 to 19 mi). In these complexes, the driver could purchase the services of wheelwrights, cartwrights, and *equarii medici*, or veterinarians. Using these stations in chariot relays, the emperor Tiberius hastened 296 kilometres (184 mi) in 24 hours to join his brother, Drusus Germanicus,[1040,1041] who was dying of gangrene as a result of a fall from a horse.

Roman roads

Figure 137: *The Roman empire in the time of Hadrian (ruled 117–138), showing the network of main Roman roads.*

Post offices and services

Two postal services were available under the empire, one public and one private. The Cursus publicus, founded by Augustus, carried the mail of officials by relay throughout the Roman road system. The vehicle for carrying mail was a *cisium* with a box, but for special delivery, a horse and rider was faster. On average, a relay of horses could carry a letter 80 kilometres (50 mi)[1042] in a day. The postman wore a characteristic leather hat, the *petanus*. The postal service was a somewhat dangerous occupation, as postmen were a target for bandits and enemies of Rome. Private mail of the well-to-do was carried by *tabellarii*, an organization of slaves available for a price.

Locations

There are many examples of roads that still follow the route of Roman roads.

Italian areas

Major roads

- Via Aemilia, from Rimini (Ariminum) to Placentia

Figure 138: *Italian and Sicilian roads in the time of ancient Rome.*

- Via Appia, the Appian way (312 BC), from Rome to Apulia
- Via Aurelia (241 BC), from Rome to France
- Via Cassia, from Rome to Tuscany
- Via Flaminia (220 BC), from Rome to Rimini (Ariminum)
- Via Raetia, from Verona north across the Brenner Pass
- Via Salaria, from Rome to the Adriatic Sea (in the Marches)

Others

- Via Aemilia Scauri (109 BC)
- Via Aquillia, branches off the Appia at Capua to the sea at Vibo
- Via Amerina, from Rome to Amelia and Perusia
- Via Canalis, from Udine, Gemona and Val Canale to Villach in Carinthia and then over Alps to Salzburg or Vienna
- Via Claudia Julia Augusta (13 BC)
- Via Claudia Nova (47 AD)
- Via Clodia, from Rome to Tuscany forming a system with the Cassia
- Via Domitiana, coast road from Naples to Formia
- Via Flavia, from Trieste (Tergeste) to Dalmatia
- Via Gemina, from Aquileia and Trieste through the Karst to Materija, Obrov, Lipa and Klana, from where, near Rijeka, descending towards Trsat (Tersatica) to continue along the Dalmatian coast

- Via Julia Augusta (8 BC), exits Aquileia
- Via Labicana, southeast from Rome, forming a system with the Praenestina
- Via Ostiensis, from Rome to Ostia
- Via Postumia (148 BC), from Aquileia through Verona across the Apennines to Genoa
- Via Popilia (132 BC), two distinct roads, one from Capua to Rhegium and the other from Ariminum through the later Veneto region
- Via Praenestina, from Rome to Praeneste
- Via Schlavonia, from Aquileia across northern Istria to Senj and into Dalmatia
- Via Severiana, Terracina to Ostia
- Via Tiburtina, from Rome to Aternum
- Via Traiana Nova (Italy), from Lake Bolsena to the Via Cassia. Known by archaeology only

Other areas

Africa

- Main road: from Sala Colonia to Carthage to Alexandria.
- In Egypt: Via Hadriana
- In Mauretania Tingitana from Tingis southward (see: Roman roads in Morocco)

Albania / Republic of Macedonia / Greece / Turkey

- Via Egnatia (146 BC) connecting Dyrrhachium (on Adriatic Sea) to Byzantium via Thessaloniki

Austria / Serbia / Bulgaria / Turkey

- Via Militaris (Via Diagonalis, Via Singidunum), connecting Middle Europe and Byzantium
- Roman road in Cilicia in south Turkey

France

In France, a Roman road is called *voie romaine* in vernacular language.

- Via Agrippa
- Via Aquitania, from Narbonne, where it connected to the Via Domitia, to the Atlantic Ocean across Toulouse and Bordeaux
- Via Domitia (118 BC), from Nîmes to the Pyrenees, where it joins to the Via Augusta at the Col de Panissars
- *Voie romaine*, extending from Dunkirk to Cassel in Nord Département

Figure 139: *A road in Histria (Sinoe) presumed to be of Roman origin (the rectangular blocks are not true Roman construction)*[1043]

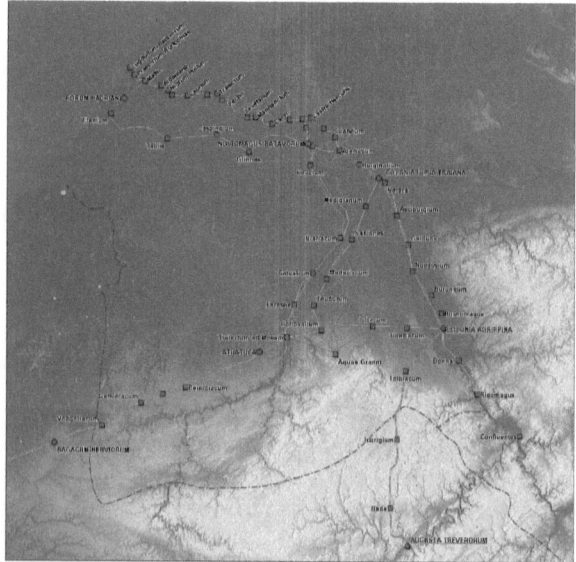

Figure 140: *Major Roman roads in Germania Inferior*

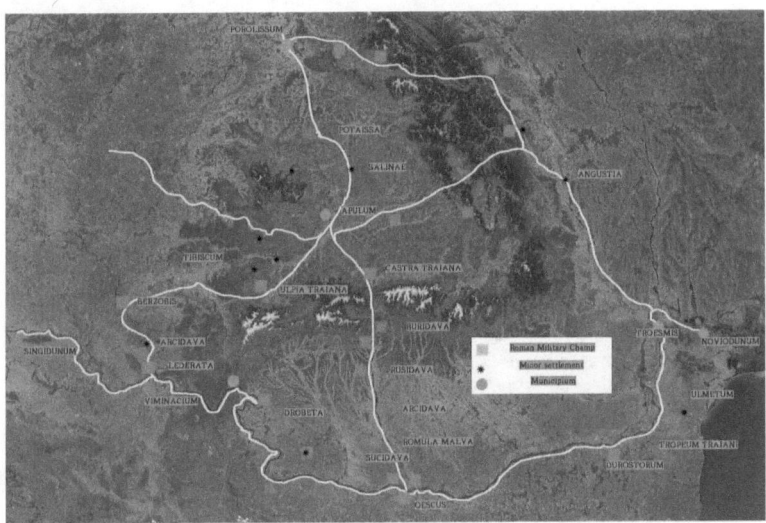

Figure 141: *Roman roads along the Danube*

Germania Inferior (Germany, Belgium, Netherlands)
- Via Belgica (Boulogne-Cologne)
- Lower Limes Germanicus
- Interconnections between Lower Limes Germanicus and Via Belgica

Middle East
- Via Maris
- Via Traiana Nova
- Petra Roman Road 1st century Petra, Jordan

Romania
- Trajan's bridge and Iron Gates road.
- Via Traiana: Porolissum Napoca Potaissa Apulum road.
- Via Pontica: Troesmis Piroboridava Caput Stenarum Apulum Partiscum Lugio

Romania / Bulgaria
- Via Pontica

Figure 142: *Roman roads in Hispania, or Roman Iberia*

Figure 143: *Roman road in the urban fabric of Tarsus, Mersin Province in Turkey*

Spain and Portugal

- Iter ab Emerita Asturicam, from Sevilla to Gijón. Later known as *Vía de la Plata* (*plata* means "silver" in Spanish, but in this case it is a false cognate of an Arabic word *balata*), part of the fan of the Way of Saint James. Now it is the A-66 freeway.
- Via Augusta, from Cádiz to the Pyrénées, where it joins to the Via Domitia at the Coll de Panissars, near La Jonquera. It passes through Valencia, Tarragona (anciently Tarraco), and Barcelona.
- Camiño de Oro, ending in Ourense, capital of the Province of Ourense, passing near the village of Reboledo.

Syria

- Road connecting Antioch and Chalcis.
- Strata Diocletiana, along the Limes Arabicus, going through Palmyra and Damascus, and south to Arabia.

Trans-Alpine roads

These roads connected modern Italy and Germany

- Via Claudia Augusta (47) from Altinum (now Quarto d'Altino) to Augsburg via the Reschen Pass
- Via Mala from Milan to Lindau via the San Bernardino Pass
- Via Decia

Trans-Pyrenean roads

Connecting Hispania and Gallia:

- Ab Asturica Burdigalam

United Kingdom

- Akeman Street
- Camlet Way
- Dere Street
- Ermine Street
- Fen Causeway
- Fosse Way
- King Street
- London-West of England Roman Roads
- Peddars Way
- Pye Road
- Stane Street (Chichester)
- Stane Street (Colchester)
- Stanegate
- Via Devana
- Watling Street

Figure 144: *High Street, a fell in the English Lake District, named after the Roman road which runs over the summit, is the highest Roman road in Britain*

References

General information

<templatestyles src="Template:Refbegin/styles.css" />

- Laurence, Ray (1999). The roads of Roman Italy: mobility and cultural change[1044]. Routledge.
- Von Hagen, Victor W. (1967). The Roads That Led to Rome[1045]. The World Publishing Company, Cleveland and New York.
- Codrington, Thomas (1905). Roman Roads in Britain[1046]. London [etc.]: Society for promoting Christian knowledge.
- Forbes, Urquhart A., and Arnold C. Burmester (1904). Our Roman Highways[1047]. London: F.E. Robinson & co.
- Roby, Henry John (1902). Roman Private Law in the Times of Cicero and of the Antonines[1048]. Cambridge: C.U.P.
- Smith, William, William Wayte, and G. E. Marindin (1890). A Dictionary of Greek and Roman Antiquities[1049]. London: J. Murray. Page 946–954[1050].
- Smith, William (1858). A School Dictionary of Greek and Roman Antiquities[1051]; Abridged from the Larger Dictionary by William Smith, with

Corrections and Improvements by Charles Anthon. N.Y.: [s.n.]. Page 354–355[1052]
- Cresy, Edward (1847). *An Encyclopædia of Civil Engineering, Historical, Theoretical, and Practical*[1053]. London: printed for Longman, Brown, Green, and Longmans, Paternoster-Row.

Primary sources

- Siculus Flaccus, De condicionibus agrorum cap. XIX
- Isidori Hispalensis Episcopi Etymologiarum sive Originum Liber XV, 15–16
- Codex Theodosianus:
  - 8.5 De cursu publico angariis et parangariis;
  - 15.3 De itinere muniendo

- Corpus Iuris Civilis
  - C.12.50 De cursu publico angariis et parangariis
  - D.8.3.0 De servitutibus praediorum rusticorum.
  - D.8.6.2
  - D.43.7 De locis et itineribus publicis
  - D.43.8 Ne quid in loco publico vel itinere fiat.
  - D.43.10 De via publica et si quid in ea factum esse dicatur.
  - D.43.11 De via publica et itinere publico reficiendo.
  - D.43.19 De itinere actuque privato.

Further reading

- Adams, Colin. 2007. *Land transport in Roman Egypt 30 BC–AD 300: A study in administration and economic history.* Oxford: Oxford Univ. Press.
- Coarelli, Filippo. 2007. *Rome and environs: An archaeological guide.* Berkeley: Univ. of California Press.
- Davies, Hugh, E. H. 1998. "Designing Roman roads." *Britannia: Journal of Romano-British and Kindred Studies* 29: 1–16.
- Erdkamp, Peter. *Hunger and the Sword: Warfare and Food Supply in Roman Republican Wars (264–30 B.C.).* Amsterdam: Gieben, 1998.
- Isaac, Benjamin. 1988. "The meaning of 'Limes' and 'Limitanei' in ancient sources." *Journal of Roman Studies* 78: 125–47.
- MacDonald, William L. 1982–1986. *The architecture of the Roman Empire.* 2 vols. Yale Publications in the History of Art 17, 35. New Haven, CT: Yale Univ. Press.
- Meijer, Fik J., and O. Van Nijf. 1992. *Trade, transport and society in the ancient world: A sourcebook.* London: Routledge.
- O'Connor, Colin. 1993. *Roman bridges.* Cambridge, UK: Cambridge Univ. Press.
- Laurence, Ray. 1999. *The roads of Roman Italy. Mobility and cultural change.* London: Routledge.
- Lewis, Michael J. T. 2001. *Surveying instruments of Greece and Rome.* Cambridge, UK: Cambridge Univ. Press.

- Quilici, Lorenzo. 2008. "Land transport, Part 1: Roads and bridges." In *The Oxford handbook of engineering and technology in the classical world*. Edited by John P. Oleson, 551–79. New York: Oxford Univ. Press.
- Talbert, Richard J. A., et al. 2000. *Barrington atlas of the Greek and Roman world*. Princeton, NJ: Princeton Univ. Press.
- Wiseman, T. P. 1970. "Roman Republican road-building." *Papers of the British School at Rome* 38: 122–52.

External links

Library resources about **Roads, Roman**
• Online books[1054] • Resources in your library[1055] • Resources in other libraries[1056]

Maps

<templatestyles src="Template:Refbegin/styles.css" />

- Orbis maps of the Roman world[1057]
- The Antiquity À-la-carte interactive digital atlas of the Ancient Mediterranean World[1058]

General articles

<templatestyles src="Template:Refbegin/styles.css" />

- Roman Roads[1059]
- Omnes Viae: Roman route planner based on Tabula Peutingeriana[1060]
- Viae Romanae[1061]
- Road Map[1062]
- "Viae"—article by William Ramsay[1063]
- Traianus: Technical investigation of Roman public works[1064]

Road descriptions

<templatestyles src="Template:Refbegin/styles.css" />

- Vias Romanas em Portugal (in Portuguese)[1065]
- Itineraires Romains en France (in French)[1066]
- Augustine's Africa[1067]
- Pictures of Roman roads in the province of Raetia (German captions)[1068]

Roman law regarding public and private domain

<templatestyles src="Template:Refbegin/styles.css" />

- Servitutes[1069]

Road construction

<templatestyles src="Template:Refbegin/styles.css" />

- Roman Road Construction[1070]
- Construction of Roman Roads[1071]
- Design and Construction of Roman Roads[1072]
- Roman Road Construction[1073]

Strategy

Strategy of the Roman military

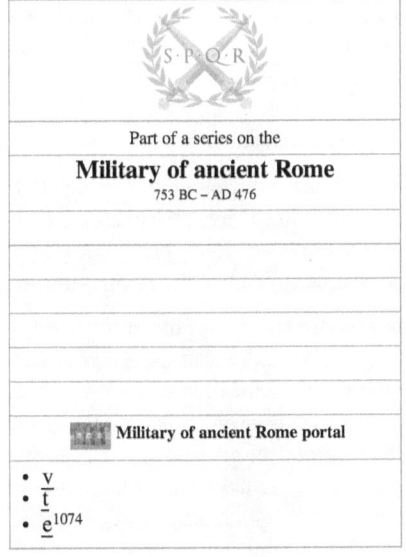

The **strategy of the Roman military** contains its grand strategy (the arrangements made by the state to implement its political goals through a selection of military goals, a process of diplomacy backed by threat of military action, and a dedication to the military of part of its production and resources), operational strategy (the coordination and combination of the military forces and their tactics for the goals of an overarching strategy) and, on a small scale, its military tactics (methods for military engagement in order to defeat the enemy). If a fourth rung of "engagement" is added, then the whole can be seen as a ladder, with each level from the foot upwards representing a decreasing concentration on military engagement. Whereas the purest form of tactics or engagement are those free of political imperative, the purest form of political policy does not involve military engagement. Strategy as a whole is the connection between political policy and the use of force to achieve it.

Grand strategy

In its clearest form, strategy deals solely with military issues: either a threat or an opportunity is recognised, an evaluation is made, and a military stratagem for meeting it is devised. However, as Clausewitz stated, a successful military strategy may be a means to an end, but it is not an end in itself. Where a state has a long term political goal to which it applies military methods and the resources of the state, that state can be said to have a grand strategy. To an extent, all states will have a grand strategy to a certain degree even if it is simply determining which forces to raise as a military, or how to arm them. Whilst early Rome did raise and arm troops, they tended to raise them annually in response to the specific demands of the state during that year. Such a reactive policy, whilst possibly more efficient than the maintenance of a standing army, does not indicate the close ties between long-term political goals and military organization demanded by grand strategy.

Early indications for a Roman grand strategy emerged during the three Punic wars with Carthage, in which Rome was able to influence the course of the war by selecting to ignore the armies of Hannibal threatening its homeland and to invade Africa instead in order to dictate the primary theatre of war.

In the Empire, as the need for and size of the professional army grew, the possibility arose for the expansion of the concept of a grand strategy to encompass the management of the resources of the entire Roman state in the conduct of warfare: great consideration was given in the Empire to diplomacy and the use of the military to achieve political goals, both through warfare and also as a deterrent. The contribution of actual (rather than potential) military force to strategy was largely reduced to operational strategy - the planning and control of large military units. Rome's grand strategy incorporated diplomacy through which Rome might forge alliances or pressure another nation into compliance, as well as the management of the post-war peace.

Strategy of the Roman military

Operational strategy

Vegetius wrote that "every plan... is to be considered, every expedient tried and every method taken before matters are brought to this last extremity [general engagements]... Good officers decline general engagements where the odds are too great, and prefer the employment of stratagem and finesse to destroy the enemy as much as possible... without exposing their own forces.".[1075] However, Vegetius was writing late in the fourth century AD, in the latter years of the Empire. During this period, and for much of the Empire, it can be argued that the Romans did follow a grand strategy calling for limited direct operational engagement. However, earlier in its history, in the Republic and early Empire Rome showed little reluctance to become engaged in direct military engagement, prosecuting offensive operations against numerous adversaries.

When a campaign did go badly wrong, operational strategy varied greatly as the circumstances dictated, from naval actions to sieges, assaults of fortified positions and open battle. However, the preponderance of Roman campaigns exhibit a preference for direct engagement in open battle and, where necessary, the overcoming of fortified positions via military engineering. The Roman army was adept at building fortified camps for protection from enemy attack, but history shows a reluctance to sit in the camp awaiting battle and a history of seeking open battle.

Infantry tactics

Roman armies of the Republic and early empire worked from a set tactical 'handbook', a military tradition of deploying forces that provided for few variations and was ignored or elaborated only on occasion.

Tactical pre-battle maneuvers

Once the legion had deployed on an operation, they would generally march to their objective. There were exceptions when the armies were transported by the Roman navy but even then in most instances this was followed by a march of several days or weeks. The approach to the battlefield was made in several columns, enhancing maneuver. Typically a strong vanguard preceded the main body, and included scouts, cavalry and light troops. A tribune or other officer often accompanied the vanguard to survey the terrain for possible camp locations. Flank and recon elements were also deployed to provide the usual covering security. Behind the vanguard came the main body of heavy infantry. Each legion marched as a distinct formation and was accompanied by its own baggage train.

At the end of a day's march, the Romans would typically establish a strong field camp called a castra, complete with palisade and a deep ditch, providing a basis for supply storage, troop marshalling and defence. Streets were laid out, units designated to take specific places, and guards posted at carefully designed gates. Construction could take between 2 and 5 hours with part of the army laboring, while the rest stood guard, depending on the tactical situation. No other ancient army persisted over such a long period in systematic camp construction like the Romans, even if the army rested for only a single day. This concentration of conservative security in deployment was mirrored both in the measured tactics of engagement for the infantry and by the largely conservative operational strategies employed.

Tactical deployment

The Roman heavy infantry typically was deployed, as the main body, facing the enemy, in three approximately equal lines, with the cavalry or equites on their wings to prevent them being flanked and turned, and light infantry in a screen in front of them to hide maneuvers of the heavy infantry, harass the enemy forces and, in some cases, drive off units such as elephants that would be a great threat to close-order heavy infantry. They were deployed in a quincunx checkered pattern. Alternative tactical formations were adopted occasionally..

Tactical engagement

In the same way that Roman tactical maneuver was measured and cautious, so too was their actual engagement of the enemy. The soldiers were long-term service professionals whose interest lay in receiving a large pension and an allocation of land on retirement from the army, rather than in seeking glory on the battlefield as a warrior. The tactics of engagement largely reflected this, concentrating on maintaining formation order and protecting individual troops

Alternative formations and variations in deployment

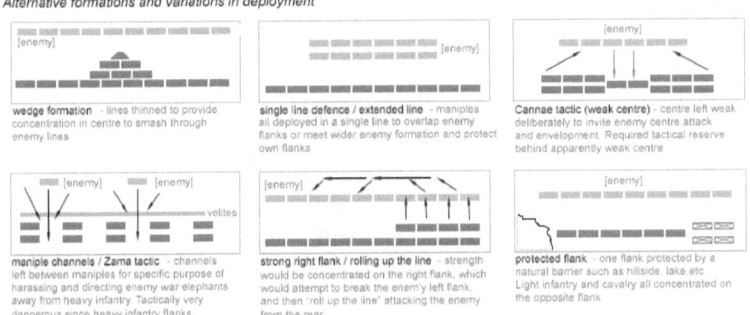

rather than pushing aggressively to destroy the maximum number of enemy troops in a wild charge.

A battle usually opened with light troops skirmishing with the opposition. These light forces then withdrew to the flanks or between the gaps in the central line of heavy infantry. Cavalry might be launched against their opposing numbers or used to screen the central core from envelopment. As the gap between the contenders closed, the heavy infantry typically took the initiative, attacking on the double. The front ranks usually cast their pila, and the following ranks hurled theirs over the heads of the front-line fighters. If a cast pilum did not cause direct death or injury, they were so designed that the hard iron triangular points would stick into enemy shields, bending on their soft metal shafts, weighing down the shields and making them unusable.

After the pila were cast, the soldiers then drew their swords and engaged the enemy. However, rather than charging as might be assumed, great emphasis was placed on the protection gained from sheltering behind the scutum and remaining unexposed, stabbing out from behind the protection of the shield whenever an exposed enemy presented himself. Fresh troops were fed in from the rear, through the "checkboard" arrangement, to relieve the injured and exhausted further ahead.

Many Roman battles, especially during the late empire, were fought with the preparatory bombardment from ballistas and onagers. These war machines, a form of ancient artillery, launched arrows and large stones towards the enemy, proving most effective against close-order formations and structures.

Roman infantry tactics

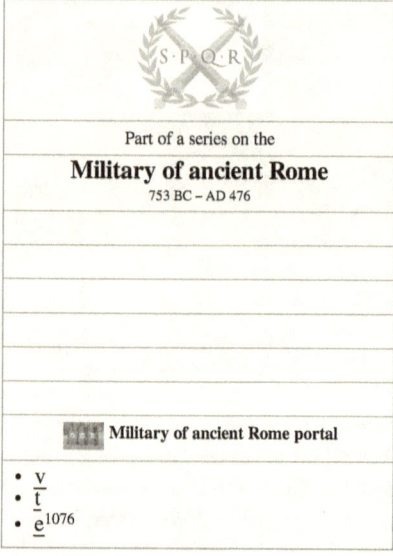

Part of a series on the
Military of ancient Rome
753 BC – AD 476

Military of ancient Rome portal

- v
- t
- e[1076]

Roman infantry tactics refers to the theoretical and historical deployment, formation, and maneuvers of the Roman infantry from the start of the Roman Republic to the fall of the Western Roman Empire. The article first presents a short overview of Roman training. Roman performance against different types of enemies is then analyzed. Finally a summation of what made the Roman tactics and strategy militarily effective through their long history is given below, as is a discussion of how and why this effectiveness eventually disappeared.

The focus below is primarily on Roman tactics - the "how" of their approach to battle, and how it stacked up against a variety of opponents over time. It does not attempt detailed coverage of things like army structure or equipment. Various battles are summarized to illustrate Roman methods with links to detailed articles on individual encounters. For in depth background on the historical structure of the infantry relevant to this article, see Structure of the Roman military. For a history of Rome's military campaigns see Campaign history of the Roman military. For detail on equipment, daily life and specific legions see Roman legion and Roman military personal equipment.

Evolution

Roman military tactics and strategy evolved from that typical of a small tribal host seeking local hegemony, to massive operations encompassing a world empire. This advance was affected by changing trends in Roman political, social and economic life, and that of the larger Mediterranean world, but it was also undergirded by a distinctive "Roman way" of war. This approach included a tendency towards standardization and systematization, practical borrowing, copying and adapting from outsiders, flexibility in tactics and methods, a strong sense of discipline, a ruthless persistence that sought comprehensive victory, and a cohesion brought about by the ideal of Roman citizenship under arms - embodied in the legion.[1077] These elements waxed and waned over time, but they form a distinct basis underlying Rome's rise.

Some key phases of this evolution throughout Rome's military history include:[1078]

- Military forces based primarily on heavy citizen infantry with tribal beginnings and early use of phalanx-type elements (see Military establishment of the Roman kingdom)
- Growing sophistication as Roman hegemony expanded outside Italy into North Africa, Greece and the Middle East (see Military establishment of the Roman Republic)
- Continued refinement, standardization and streamlining in the period associated with Gaius Marius including a broader based incorporation of more citizenry into the army, and more professionalism and permanence in army service
- Continued expansion, flexibility and sophistication from the end of the republic into the time of the Caesars (see Military establishment of the Roman Empire)
- Growing barbarization, turmoil and weakening of the heavy infantry units in favour of cavalry and lighter troops (See *Foederati*)
- Demise of the Western Empire and fragmentation into smaller, weaker local forces. This included the reversal of status of cavalry and infantry in the Eastern Empire. Cataphract forces formed an elite, with infantry being reduced to auxiliaries.

Manpower

Numerous scholarly histories of the Roman military machine note the huge numbers of men that could be mobilized, more than any other Mediterranean power. This bounty of military resources enabled Rome to apply crushing pressure to its enemies, and stay in the field and replace losses, even after suffering setbacks. One historian of the Second Punic War states:

"According to Polybius (2.24), the total number of Roman and allied men capable of bearing arms in 225 exceeded 700,000 infantry and 70,000 cavalry. Brunt adjusted Polybius' figures and estimated that the population of Italy, not including Greeks and Bruttians, exceeded 875,000 free adult males, from whom the Romans could levy troops. Rome not only had the potential to levy vast numbers of troops, but did in fact field large armies in the opening stages of the war. Brunt estimates that Rome mobilized 108,000 men for service in the legions between 218BC and 215BC, while at the height of the war effort (214BC to 212BC) [against Hannibal] Rome was able to mobilize approximately 230,000 men. Against these mighty resources Hannibal led from Spain an army of approximately 50,000 infantry and 9,000 cavalry... Rome's manpower reserves allowed it to absorb staggering losses yet still continue to field large armies. For example, according to Brunt, as many as 50,000 men were lost between 218BC and 215BC, but Rome continued to place between 14 and 25 legions in the field for the duration of the war. Moreover, as will be discussed below, Roman manpower allowed for the adoption of the so-called "Fabian strategy", which proved to be an effective response to Hannibal's apparent battlefield superiority. Put simply, the relative disparity in the number of available troops at the outset of the conflict meant that Hannibal had a much narrower margin for error than the Romans."[1079]

Equipment and training

See Roman military personal equipment and Roman legion for more information on equipment, individual legions and structure

Equipment

Individual weapons, personal equipment and haulage

A legionary typically carried around 27 kilograms (60 pounds) of armour, weapons, and equipment. This load consisted of armour, a sword called a gladius, a shield, two pila (one heavy, one light) and 15 days' food rations. There were also tools for digging and constructing a castra, the legions' fortified base camp. One writer recreates the following as to Caesar's army in Gaul:[1080] Each soldier arranged his heavy pack on a T or Y-shaped rod, borne on his left shoulder. Shields were protected on the march with a hide cover. Each legionary carried about 5 days worth of wheat, pulses or chickpeas, a flask of oil and a mess kit with a dish, cup, and utensil. Personal items might include a dyed horsehair crest for the helmet, a semi-water resistant oiled woolen cloak, socks and breeches for cold weather and a blanket. Entrenchment equipment included a shallow wicker basket for moving earth, a spade and/or pick-axe like dolabra, or turf cutter, and two wooden staves to construct the next camp palisade. All these were arranged in the marching pack toted by each infantryman.

Fighters travelled in groups of eight, and each octet was sometimes assigned a mule. The mule carried a variety of equipment and supplies, including a mill for grinding grain, a small clay oven for baking bread, cooking pots, spare weapons, waterskins, and tents. A Roman century had a complement of 10 mules, each attended by two non-combatants who handled foraging and water supply. A century might be supported by wagons in the rear, each drawn by six mules, and carrying tools, nails, water barrels, extra food and the tent and possessions of the centurion- commanding officer of the unit.

Artillery package

The legion also carried an artillery detachment with 30 pieces of artillery. This consisted of 10 stone-throwing onagers and 20 bolt-shooting ballistas, in addition each of the legion's centuries had its own scorpio bolt thrower (60 total), together with supporting wagons to carry ammunition and spare parts. Bolts were used for targeted fire on human opponents, while stones were used against fortifications or as an area saturation weapon. The catapults were powered by rope and sinew, tightened by ratchet and released, powered by the stored torsion energy. Caesar was to mount these in boats on some operations in Britain, striking fear in the heart of the native opponents according to his writings. His placement of siege engines and bolt throwers in the towers and along the wall of his enclosing fortifications at Alesia were critical to turning back the enormous tide of Gauls. These defensive measures, used in concert with the cavalry charge led by Caesar himself, broke the Gauls and won the battle—and therefore the war—for good. Bolt-throwers like the "scorpion" were mobile and could be deployed in defence of camps, field entrenchments and even in the open field by no more than two or three men.[1081]

Training

Over time the military system changed its equipment and roles, but throughout the course of Roman history, it always remained a disciplined and professional war machine. Soldiers carried out training common to every organized army, from initial muster, arms and weapons drill, formation marching and tactical exercises.

According to Vegetius, during the four-month initial training of a Roman legionary, marching skills were taught before recruits ever handled a weapon; since any formation would be split up by stragglers at the back or soldiers trundling along at differing speeds.[1082] Standards varied over time, but normally recruits were first required to complete 20 Roman miles (29.62 km or

18.405 modern miles) with 20.5 kg in five summer hours (the Roman day was divided into 12 hours regardless of season, as was the night), which was known as "the regular step" or "military pace".[1083] They then progressed to the "faster step" or "full pace" and were required to complete 24 Roman miles (35.544 km or 22.086 modern miles) in five summer hours loaded with 20.5 kilograms (45 lb). The typical conditioning regime also included gymnastics and swimming to build physical strength and fitness.[1084]

After conditioning, the recruits underwent weapons training; this was deemed of such importance that weapons instructors generally received double rations. Legionaries were trained to thrust with their *gladii* because they could defend themselves behind their large shields (*scuta*) while stabbing the enemy. These training exercises began with thrusting a wooden *gladius* and throwing wooden *pila* into a *quintain* (wooden dummy or stake) while wearing full armor. Their wooden swords and *pila* were designed to be twice as heavy as their metal counterparts so that the soldiers could wield a true *gladius* with ease. Next, soldiers progressed to *armatura*, a term for sparring that was also used to describe the similar one-on-one training of gladiators. Unlike earlier training, the wooden weapons used for *armatura* were the same weight as the weapons they emulated. Vegetius notes that roofed halls were built to allow for these drills to continue throughout the winter.

Other training exercises taught the legionary to obey commands and assume battle formations.[1085] At the end of training the legionary had to swear an oath of loyalty to the SPQR (Senatus Populusque Romanus, or the Senate and the Roman People) or later to the emperor. The soldier was then given a diploma and sent off to fight for his living and the glory and honor of Rome.

Organization, leadership and logistics

Command, control and structure

Once the soldier had finished his training he was typically assigned to a legion, the basic mass fighting force. The legion was split into ten sub-units called cohorts, roughly comparable to a modern infantry battalion. The cohorts were further sub-divided into three maniples, which in turn were split into two centuries of about 60-100 men each. The first cohort in a legion was usually the strongest, with the fullest personnel complement and with the most skilled, experienced men. Several legions grouped together made up a distinctive field force or "army". Fighting strength could vary but generally a legion was made up of 4,800 soldiers, 60 centurions, 300 artillerymen, and 100 engineers and artificers, and around 1,600 non-combatants. Each legion was supported by a unit of 300 cavalry, the equites.

Supreme command of either legion or army was by consul or proconsul or a praetor, or in cases of emergency in the Republican era, a dictator. A praetor or a propraetor could only command a single legion and not a consular army, which normally consisted of two legions plus the allies. In the early Republican period it was customary for an army to have dual commands, with different consuls holding the office on alternate days. In later centuries this was phased out in favor of one overall army commander. The legati were officers of senatorial rank who assisted the supreme commander. Tribunes were young men of aristocratic rank who often supervised administrative tasks like camp construction. Centurions (roughly equivalent in rank to today's non-commissioned or junior officers, but functioning as modern captains in field operations) commanded cohorts, maniples and centuries. Specialist groups like engineers and artificers were also used.

Military structure and ranks

An in-depth analysis of ranks, types, and historical units including their evolution over time is beyond the scope of this article. See Structural history of the Roman military and Roman legion for a detailed breakdown. Below is a very basic summary of the legion's structure and ranks.[1086]

Force structure

- Contubernium: "tent unit" of 8 men
- Centuria: 80 men commanded by a centurion
- Cohort: 6 centuries or a total of 480 fighting men. Added to these were officers. The first cohort was double strength in terms of manpower, and generally held the best fighting men
- Legion: made up of 10 cohorts
- Field army: a grouping of several legions and auxiliary cohorts
- Equites: Each legion was supported by 300 cavalry (equites), sub-divided into ten *turmae*
- Auxilia and velites: allied contingents, often providing light infantry and specialist fighting services, like archers, slingers or javelin-men. They were usually formed into the light infantry or velites. Auxilia in the Republican period also formed allied heavy legions to complement Roman citizen formations.
- Non-combatant support: generally the men who tended the mules, forage, watering and sundries of the baggage train.
- 4,500-5,200 men in a legion.

Rank summary

- Consul - elected official with military and civic duties; like a co-president (there were two), but also a major military commander
- *Praetor* - appointed military commander of a legion or grouping of legions, also a government official
- *Legatus legionis* - the legate or overall legion commander, usually filled by a senator
- Tribune - young officers, second in command of the legion. Other lesser tribunes served as junior officers
- Prefect - third in command of the legion. There were various types. The *prefectus equitarius* commanded a unit of cavalry
- *Primus pilus* - commanding centurion for the first cohort - the senior centurion of the entire legion
- Centurion - basic commander of the century. Prestige varied based on the cohort they supervised
- *Decurio* - commander of the cavalry unit or *turma*
- *Aquilifer* - standard bearer of each legion - a position of much prestige
- *Signifer* - one for each century, handled financial matters and decorations
- *Optio* - equivalent to a sergeant, second in command for the centurion
- *Cornicen* - horn blower or signaler
- *Imaginifer* - carried standard bearing the emperor's image
- *Decanus* - equivalent to a corporal, commanded an eight-man tent party
- *Munifex* - basic legionary - the lowest of the trained rank and file
- *Tirones* - new recruit to the legions, a novice

Logistics

Roman logistics were among some of the best in the ancient world over the centuries- from the deployment of purchasing agents to systematically buy provisions during a campaign, to the construction of roads and supply caches, to the rental of shipping if the troops had to move by water. Heavy equipment and material (tents, artillery, extra weapons and equipment, millstones etc.) were moved by pack animal and cart, while troops carried weighty individual packs with them, including staves and shovels for constructing the fortified camps. Typical of all armies, local opportunities were also exploited by troops on the spot, and the fields of peasant farmers unlucky enough to be near the zone of conflict might be stripped to meet army needs. As with most armed forces, an assortment of traders, hucksters, prostitutes and other miscellaneous service providers trailed in the wake of the Roman fighting men.

Battle

Initial preparations and movement for battle

The approach march. Once the legion was deployed on an operation, the marching began. The approach to the battlefield was made in several columns, enhancing maneuverability. Typically a strong vanguard preceded the main body, and included scouts, cavalry and light troops. A tribune or other officer often accompanied the vanguard to survey the terrain for possible camp locations. Flank and reconnaissance elements were also deployed to provide the usual covering security. Behind the vanguard came the main body of heavy infantry. Each legion marched as a distinct formation and was accompanied by its own baggage train. The last legion usually provided the rear force, although several recently raised units might occupy this final echelon.

Construction of fortified camps. Legions on a campaign typically established a strong field camp, complete with palisade and a deep ditch, providing a basis for supply storage, troop marshaling and defense. Camps were recreated each time the army moved, and were constructed with a view to both military necessity and religious symbolism. There were always four gateways, connected by two main criss-crossing streets, with the intersection at a concentration of command tents in the center. Space was also made for an altar and religious gathering area. Everything was standardized, from the positioning of baggage, equipment and specific army units, to the duties of officers who were to set up sentries, pickets and orders for the next day's march. Construction could take between 2 and 5 hours with part of the army laboring, while the rest stood guard, depending on the tactical situation. The shape of the camp was generally rectangular, but could vary based on the terrain or tactical situation. A distance of about 60 meters was left clear between the entrenchments and the first row of troop tents. This gap provided space for marshaling the legionnaires for battle and kept the troop area out of enemy missile range.[1087] No other ancient army persisted over such a long period in systematic camp construction like the Romans, even if the army rested for only a single day.[1088]

Breaking camp and marching. After a regimented breakfast at the allocated time, trumpets were sounded and the camp's tents and huts were dismantled and preparations made for departure. The trumpet then sounded again with the signal for "stand by to march". Mules and wagons of the baggage train would be loaded and units formed up. The camp would then be burned to the ground to prevent its later occupation and use by the enemy. The trumpets would then be sounded for a final time and then the troops were asked three times whether they were ready, to which they were expected to shout together "Ready!", before marching off.[1089]

Intelligence. Good Roman commanders did not hesitate to exploit useful intelligence, particularly where a siege situation or impending clash in the field was developing. Information was gathered from spies, collaborators, diplomats and envoys, and allies. Intercepted messages during the Second Punic War for example were an intelligence coup for the Romans, and enabled them to dispatch two armies to find and destroy Hasdrubal's Carthaginian force, preventing his reinforcement of Hannibal. Commanders also kept an eye on the situation in Rome since political enemies and rivals could use an unsuccessful campaign to inflict painful career and personal damage. During this initial phase the usual field reconnaissance was also conducted - patrols might be sent out, raids mounted to probe for weaknesses, prisoners snatched, and local inhabitants intimidated.[1090]

Morale. If the field of potential battle were near, movement became more careful and more tentative. Several days might be spent in a location studying the terrain and opposition, while the troops were prepared mentally and physically for battle. Pep talks, sacrifices to the gods and the announcements of good omens might be carried out. A number of practical demonstrations might also be undertaken to test enemy reaction as well as to build troop morale. Part of the army might be led out of the camp and drawn up in battle array towards the enemy. If the enemy refused to come out and at least make a demonstration, the commander could claim a morale advantage for his men, contrasting the timidity of the opposition with the resolution of his fighting forces.

Historian Adrian Goldsworthy notes that such tentative pre-battle maneuvering was typical of ancient armies as each side sought to gain maximum advantage before the encounter.[1091] During this period, some ancient writers paint a picture of meetings between opposing commanders for negotiation or general discussion, as with the famous pre-clash conversation between Hannibal and Scipio at Zama. But whatever the truth of these discussions, or the flowery speeches allegedly made, the only encounter that ultimately mattered was battle.

Deployment for combat

Pre-battle maneuver gave the competing commanders a feel for the impending clash, but final outcomes could be unpredictable, even after the start of hostilities. Skirmishing could get out of hand, launching both main forces towards one another. Political considerations, exhaustion of supplies, or even rivalry between commanders for glory could also spark a forward launch, as at the Battle of the Trebia River. The Roman army after the reforms of 107 B.C. was also unique in the ancient world because when lined up opposite an enemy readying for battle it was completely silent except for the orders of officers and the sound of trumpets signaling orders. The reason for this was because the soldiers needed to be able to hear such instruction, the Optios of the Legions would patrol behind the century and anyone who was talking or falling to obey orders immediately was struck with the stick of the optio. This silence also had the unintended consequence of being very intimidating to its enemies because they recognized this took immense discipline to achieve before a battle.

Layout of the triple line

Once the machinery was in motion however, the Roman infantry typically was deployed, as the main body, facing the enemy. During deployment in the Republican era, the maniples were commonly arranged in *triplex acies* (triple battle order): that is, in three ranks, with the hastati in the first rank (that nearest the enemy), the principes in the second rank, and the veteran *triarii* in the third and final rank as barrier troops, or sometimes even further back as a strategic reserve. When in danger of imminent defeat, the first and second lines, the hastati and principes, ordinarily fell back on the *triarii* to reform the line to allow for either a counter-attack or an orderly withdrawal. Because falling back on the *triarii* was an act of desperation, to mention "falling on the triarii" (*"ad triarios rediisse"*) became a common Roman phrase indicating one to be in a desperate situation.[1092]

Within this triplex acies system, contemporary Roman writers talk of the maniples adopting a checkered formation called *quincunx* when deployed for battle but not yet engaged. In the first line, the hastati left modest gaps between each maniple. The second line consisting of principes followed in a similar manner, lining up behind the gaps left by the first line.[1093] This was also done by the third line, standing behind the gaps in the second line. The velites were deployed in front of this line in a continuous, loose-formation line.[1094]

The Roman maneuver was a complex one, filled with the dust of thousands of soldiers wheeling into place, and the shouting of officers moving to and from as they attempted to maintain order. Several thousand men had to be positioned from column into line, with each unit taking its designated place, along with light troops and cavalry. The fortified camps were laid out and organized to facilitate deployment. It might take some time for the final array of the host, but when accomplished the army's grouping of legions represented a formidable fighting force, typically arranged in three lines with a frontage as long as one mile (1.6 km).[1095]

A general three line deployment was to remain over the centuries, although the Marian reforms phased out most divisions based on age and class, standardized weapons and reorganized the legions into bigger maneuver units like cohorts. The overall size of the legion, and length of the soldier's service also increased on a more permanent basis.[1096]

Roman manipular disposition after deployment but prior to engagement

- triarii maniples
- principes maniples
- hastati maniples
- velites skirmishers

ROMAN MANIPULAR FORMATION

ENEMY FORMATION

Roman manipular disposition after velites engagement and retreat

- triarii maniples
- principes maniples
- velites skirmishers
- hastati maniples

ROMAN MANIPULAR FORMATION

ENEMY FORMATION

Maneuvering

As the army approached its enemy, the velites in front would throw their javelins at the enemy and then retreat through the gaps in the lines. This was an important innovation since in other armies of the period skirmishers would have to either retreat through their own army's ranks, causing confusion, or else flee around either flank of their own army. After the velites had retreated through the hastati, the 'posterior' century would march to the left and then forward so that they presented a solid line, creating a solid line of soldiers. The same procedure would be employed as they passed through the second and third ranks or turned to the side to channel down the gap between the first and second rows on route to help guard the legion's flanks.[1097]

At this point, the legion then presented a solid line to the enemy and the legion was in the correct formation for engagement. When the enemy closed, the hastati would charge. If they were losing the fight, the 'posterior' century returned to its position creating gaps again. Then the maniples would fall back through

Alternative formations and variations in deployment

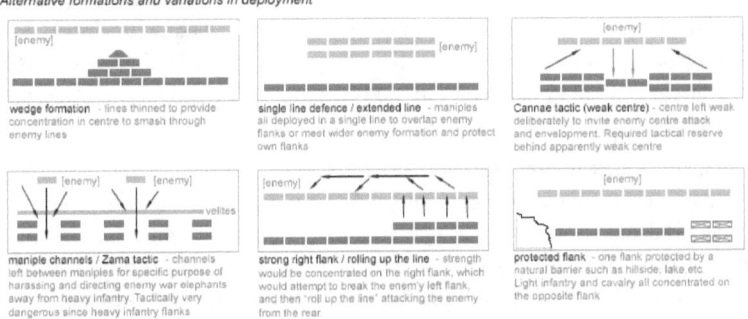

the gaps in the principes, who followed the same procedure to form a battle line and charge. If the principes could not break the enemy, they would retreat behind the *triarii* and the whole army would leave the battlefield in good order. According to some writers, the *triarii* formed a continuous line when they deployed, and their forward movement allowed scattered or discomfited units to rest and reform, to later rejoin the struggle.[1098]

The manipular system allowed engaging every kind of enemy even in rough terrain, because the legion had both flexibility and toughness according to the deployment of its lines. Lack of a strong cavalry corps however, was a major flaw of the Roman forces.

In the later imperial army, the general deployment was very similar, with the cohorts deploying in quincunx pattern. In a reflection of the earlier placement of the veteran *triarii* in the rear, the less experienced cohorts - usually the 2nd, 3rd, 4th, 6th, and 8th - were in the front; the more experienced cohorts - 1st, 5th, 7th, 9th, and 10th - were placed behind.[1099]

Formations

The above is only standard procedure and was often modified; for example, at Zama, Scipio deployed his entire legion in a single line to envelop Hannibal's army just as Hannibal had done at Cannae. A brief summary of alternative formations known to have been used is shown below:

Combat

Hand-to-hand engagement after release of missile weapons: Once the deployment and initial skirmishing described above took place, the main body of heavy infantry closed the gap and attacked on the double. The front ranks usually cast their pila, and the following ranks hurled theirs over the heads of the front-line fighters. After the pila were cast, the soldiers then drew their swords and engaged the enemy. Emphasis was on using the shield to provide maximum body coverage, while attacking with their gladius in thrusts and short cuts, minimizing exposure to the enemy. In the combat that ensued, Roman discipline, heavy shield, armor and training were to give them important advantages.

The acute shock of combat: Some scholars of the Roman infantry maintain that the intense trauma and stress of hand-to-hand combat meant that the contenders did not simply hack at one another continuously until one dropped. Instead, there were short periods of intense, vicious fighting. If indecisive, the contenders might fall back a short distance to recuperate, and then surge forward to renew the struggle. Others behind them would be stepping up into the fray meanwhile, engaging new foes or covering their colleagues. The individual warrior could thus count on temporary relief, rather than endless fighting until death or crippling injury. As the battle progressed, the massive physical and mental stress intensified. The stamina and willpower demanded to make yet one more charge, to make yet one more surge grew even greater. Eventually one side began to break down, and it is then that the greatest slaughter began.

Use of war machines and covering fire: Many Roman battles, especially during the late empire, were fought with the preparatory fire from Ballistas and Onagers. These war machines, a form of ancient artillery, fired arrows and large stones towards the enemy (although many historians question the battlefield effectiveness of such weapons). Following this barrage, the Roman infantry advanced, in four lines, until they came within 30 meters of the enemy, then they halted, hurled their pila and charged. If the first line was repelled by the enemy, another line would rapidly resume the attack. Often this rapid sequence of deadly attacks proved the key to victory. Another common tactic was to taunt the enemy with feigned charges and rapid arrow fire by the *auxiliares equites* (auxiliary cavalry), forcing the enemy into pursuing them, and then leading the enemy into an ambush where they would be counterattacked by Roman heavy infantry and cavalry.

3-line system advantages

Flexibility

Some ancient sources such as Polybius seem to imply that the legions could fight with gaps in their lines. Yet, most sources seem to admit that more usually a line would form into a solid front. Various approaches have been taken to reconcile these possibilities with the ancient writings.[1100] The advantages of gaps are obvious when a formation is on the move- it can more easily flow around obstacles and maneuver and control are enhanced and, as the Romans did in the pre-Marius republic, place baggage between the lines meaning that the cargo cannot be easily captured and that the army can quickly get ready for a battle by using it as cover. After the approach marching was complete, it would be extremely difficult to deploy an unbroken army of men for combat across any but the flattest ground without some sort of intervals. Many ancient armies used gaps of some sort, even the Carthaginians, who typically withdrew their initial skirmishing troops between the spaces before the main event. Even more loosely organized enemies like the Germanic hosts typically charged in distinct groups with small gaps between them, rather than marching up in a neat line.[1101]

Fighting with gaps is thus feasible as writers like Polybius assert. According to those who support the *quincunx* formation view, what made the Roman approach stand out is that their intervals were generally larger and more systematically organized than those of other ancient armies. Each gap was covered by maniples or cohorts from lines farther back. A penetration of any significance could not just slip in unmolested. It would not only be mauled as it fought past the gauntlet of the first line, but would also clash with aggressive units moving up to plug the space.[1102] From a larger standpoint, as the battle waxed and waned, fresh units might be deployed through the intervals to relieve the men of the first line, allowing continual pressure to be brought forward.

Mixing of a continuous front with interval fighting

One scenario for not using gaps is deployment in a limited space, such as the top of a hill or ravine, where extensive spreading out would not be feasible. Another is a particular attack formation, such as the wedge discussed above, or an encirclement as at the battle of Ilipa. Yet another is a closing phase maneuver, when a solid line is constructed to make a last, final push as in the battle of Zama. During the maelstrom of battle it is also possible that as the units merged into line, the general checkerboard spacing became more compressed or even disappeared, and the fighting would see a more or less solid line engaged with the enemy. Thus gaps at the beginning of the struggle might tend to vanish in the closing phases.[1103]

Some historians view the intervals as primarily useful in maneuver. Before the legionaries closed with the enemy each echelon would form a solid line to engage. If things went badly for the first line, it would retreat through the gaps and the second echelon moved up- again forming a continuous front. Should they be discomfited, there still remained the veterans of the *triarii* who let the survivors retreat through the preset gaps. The veterans then formed a continuous front to engage the enemy or provided cover for the retreat of the army as a whole. The same procedure was followed when the *triarii* was phased out - intervals for maneuver, reforming and recovery- solid line to engage.[1104]

Some writers maintain that in Caesar's armies the use of the *quincunx* and its gaps seems to have declined, and his legions generally deployed in three unbroken lines as shown above, with four cohorts in front, and three apiece in the echeloned order. Relief was provided by the second and third lines 'filtering' forward to relieve their comrades in small groups, while the exhausted and wounded eased back from the front.[1105] The Romans still remained flexible however, using gaps and deploying four or sometimes two lines based on the tactical situation.[1106]

Line spacing and combat stamina

Another unique feature of the Roman infantry was the depth of its spacing. Most ancient armies deployed in shallower formations, particularly phalanx-type forces. Phalanxes might deepen their ranks heavily to add both stamina and shock power, but their general approach still favored one massive line, as opposed to the deep three-layer Roman arrangement. The advantage of the Roman system is that it allowed the continual funneling or metering of combat power forward over a longer period—massive, steadily renewed pressure to the front—until the enemy broke. Deployment of the second and third lines required careful consideration by the Roman commander. Deployed too early, and they might get entangled in the frontal fighting and become exhausted. Deployed too late, and they might be swept away in a rout if the first line began to break. Tight control had to be maintained, hence the 3rd line *triarii* were sometimes made to squat or kneel, effectively discouraging premature movement to the front. The Roman commander was thus generally mobile, constantly moving from spot to spot, and often riding back in person to fetch reserves, if there was no time for standard messenger service. The large number of officers in the typical Roman army, and the flexible breakdown into sub-units like cohorts or maniples greatly aided coordination of such moves.[1107]

Whatever the actual formation taken however, the ominous funneling or surge of combat power up to the front remained constant:

> "When the first line as a whole had done its best and become weakened and exhausted by losses, it gave way to the relief of fresh men from the second line who, passing through it gradually, pressed forward one by one, or in single file, and worked their way into the fight in the same way. Meanwhile the tired men of the original first line, when sufficiently rested, reformed and re-entered the fight. This continued until all men of the first and second lines had been engaged. This does not presuppose an actual withdrawal of the first line, but rather a merging, a blending or a coalescing of both lines. Thus the enemy was given no rest and was continually opposed by fresh troops until, exhausted and demoralized, he yielded to repeated attacks."[1108]

Roman infantry tactics

Figure 145: *Roman re-enactors demonstrate a variant of the Roman testudo formation*

Post-deployment commands

Whatever the deployment, the Roman army was marked both by flexibility and strong discipline and cohesion. Different formations were assumed according to different tactical situations.

- *Repellere equites* ("repel horsemen/knights") was the formation used to resist cavalry. The legionaries would assume a square formation, holding their pila as spears in the space between their shields and strung together shoulder to shoulder.
- At the command *iacite pila*, the legionaries hurled their pila at the enemy.
- At the command *cuneum formate*, the infantry formed a wedge to charge and break enemy lines. This formation was used as a shock tactic.
- At the command *contendite vestra sponte*, the legionaries assumed an aggressive stance and attacked every opponent they faced.
- At the command *orbem formate*, the legionaries assumed a circle-like formation with the archers placed in the midst of and behind the legionaries providing missile fire support. This tactic was used mainly when a small number of legionaries had to hold a position and were surrounded by enemies.
- At the command *ciringite frontem*, the legionaries held their position.

Figure 146: *Modern reconstruction of a Scorpio.*

- At the command *frontem allargate*, a scattered formation was adopted.
- At the command *testudinem formate*, the legionaries assumed the *testudo* (tortoise) formation. This was slow moving but almost impenetrable to enemy fire, and thus very effective during sieges and/or when facing off against enemy archers. However the testudo formation didn't allow for effective close combat and therefore it was used when the enemy were far enough away so as the legionaries could get into another formation before being attacked.
- At the command *tecombre*, the legionaries would break the Testudo formation and revert to their previous formation.
- At the command *Agmen formate*, the legionaries assumed a square formation, which was also the typical shape of a century in battle.

Siegecraft and fortifications

Besieging cities.

Oppidum expugnare was the Roman term for besieging cities. It was divided into three phases:

1. In the first phase, engineers (the *cohors fabrorum*) built a fortified camp near the city with walls of circumvallation and at the command 'turres

extruere' built watch towers to prevent the enemy from bringing in reinforcements. Siege towers were built, trenches were dug and traps set all around the city. Also second, exterior line of walls (*contravallation*) was built around the city facing the enemy, as Caesar did at the Battle of Alesia. Sometimes the Romans would mine the enemy's walls.

2. The second phase began with onager and ballista fire to cover the approach of the siege towers, which were full of legionaries ready to assault the wall's defenders. Meanwhile, other cohorts approached the city's wall in testudo formation, bringing up battering rams and ladders to breach the gates and scale the walls.

3. The third phase included opening of the city's main gate by the cohorts which had managed to break through or scale the walls, provided the rams had not knocked the gate open. Once the main gate was opened or the walls breached, the cavalry and other cohorts entered the city to finish off the remaining defenders.

Field fortifications. While strong cities/forts and elaborate sieges to capture them were common throughout the ancient world, the Romans were unique among ancient armies in their extensive use of field fortifications. In campaign after campaign, enormous effort was expended to dig—a job done by the ordinary legionary. His field pack included a shovel, a *dolabra* or pickaxe, and a wicker basket for hauling dirt. Some soldiers also carried a type of turf cutter. With these they dug trenches, built walls and palisades and constructed assault roads. The operations of Julius Caesar at Alesia are well known. The Gallic city was surrounded by massive double walls penning in defenders, and keeping out relieving attackers. A network of camps and forts were included in these works. The inner trench alone was 20 feet (6.1 m) deep, and Caesar diverted a river to fill it with water. The ground was also sown with caltrops of iron barbs at various places to discourage assault. Surprisingly for such an infantry centered battle, Caesar relied heavily on cavalry forces to counter Gallic sorties. Ironically, many of these were from Germanic tribes who had come to terms earlier.[1109]

The power of Roman field camps has been noted earlier, but in other actions, the Romans sometimes used trenches to secure their flanks against envelopment when they were outnumbered, as Caesar did during operations in Belgaic Gaul. In the Brittany region of France, moles and breakwaters were constructed at enormous effort to assault the estuarine strongholds of the Gauls. Internal Roman fighting between Caesar and Pompey also saw the frequent employment of trenches, counter-trenches, dug-in strong points, and other works as the contenders maneuvered against each other in field combat. In the latter stages of the empire, the extensive use of such field fortifications declined as the heavy infantry itself was phased down. Nevertheless, they were an integral part of the relentless Roman rise to dominance over large parts of the ancient world.[1110]

Resource tactics

As with any military organization, training soldiers/armies requires a number of things and could prove to be quite costly in the long run.

The Romans understood this concept very well and realized that training soldiers could include paying for his rations [*food*], his salary, his armor, his armaments [*weapons*], and a soldier's honorarium [*which was paid to those who received honorable discharges*]. With all this in perspective, they realized each individual soldier was a far too valuable resource to waste. They knew the costs they were incurring for each soldier had to be quite similar on their enemy's side. So they developed a tactic that could cause a significant setback or even defeat for their enemy while only creating a limited risk for their own soldiers. This was known as "Resource Tactics." Standing armies run on their stomachs and their equipment, and both require regular supplies. "Resource Tactics" cut off their opponents from resources in one of three ways:

1. Attack resource locations: Once they conquered a territory, the Romans would secure as many resources as they could handle. This allowed them to restock their own supply and prevent the available resources from falling into their opponents' hands.[1111]
2. Intercept supplies while in transit: The Romans would identify their enemies' main supply routes and create a *stopping point*. Once the enemy was stopped, the Romans would ransack the supply, which would drastically reduce the supplies reaching the enemy.
3. Conduct a "siege" [*siege - a military operation in which troops surround a place and cut off all outside access to force surrender*]: The Romans would typically build a wall around the existing city to help control the enemy. This wall would be built out of reach of the archers and would prevent the enemy from escaping. Once the Romans completed the wall, they would use catapults, ballistas and onagers to hurl rocks, spears, and other objects from safe distances. The ongoing siege would eventually cause the city/fort to run out of resources, thus causing the opponents to die off or surrender.

The basic principle behind these tactics was to disrupt their enemies' resources while increasing Roman resources. Without a regular supply of food, water, and other commodities, armies would begin to starve or dehydrate, resulting to low morale or killing of fellow soldiers.

Infantry effectiveness

Roman infantry versus the Macedonian phalanx

Strengths of the Macedonian phalanx. Prior to the rise of Rome, the Macedonian phalanx was the premiere infantry force in the Western World. It had proven itself on the battlefields of Mediterranean Europe, from Sparta to Macedonia, and had met and overcome several strong non-European armies from Persia to Pakistan/Northwest India. Packed into a dense armored mass, and equipped with massive pikes 12 to 21 feet (6.4 m) in length, the phalanx was a formidable force. While defensive configurations were sometimes used, the phalanx was most effective when it was moving forward in attack, either in a frontal charge or in "oblique" or echeloned order against an opposing flank, as the victories of Alexander the Great and Theban innovator Epaminondas attest. When working with other formations—light infantry and cavalry—it was, at its height under Alexander, without peer.[1112]

Weaknesses of the Macedonian phalanx. Nevertheless, the Macedonian phalanx had key weaknesses. It had some maneuverability, but once a clash was joined this decreased, particularly on rough ground. Its "dense pack" approach also made it rigid. Compressed in the heat of battle, its troops could only primarily fight facing forward. The diversity of troops gave the phalanx great flexibility, but this diversity was a double-edged sword, relying on a mix of units that was complicated to control and position. These included not only the usual heavy infantrymen, cavalry and light infantry, but also various elite units, medium armed groups, foreign contingents with their own styles and shock units of war-elephants.[1113] Such "mixed" forces presented additional command and control problems. If properly organized and fighting together a long time under capable leaders, they could be very proficient. The campaigns of Alexander and Pyrrhus (a Hellenic-style formation of mixed contingents) show this. Without such long-term cohesion and leadership, however, their performance was uneven. By the time the Romans were engaging against Hellenistic armies, the Greeks had ceased to use strong flank guards and cavalry contingents, and their system had degenerated into a mere clash of phalanxes. This was the formation overcome by the Romans at Cynoscephalae.

Advantages of Roman infantry. The Romans themselves had retained some aspects of the classical phalanx (not to be confused with the Macedonian phalanx) in their early legions, most notably the final line of fighters in the classic "triple line", the spearmen of the *triarii*. The long pikes of the *triarii* were to eventually disappear, and all hands were uniformly equipped with short sword, shield and pilum, and deployed in the distinctive Roman tactical system, which provided more standardization and cohesion in the long run over the Hellenic type formations.

Phalanxes facing the legion were vulnerable to the more flexible Roman "checkerboard" deployment, which provided each fighting man a good chunk of personal space to engage in close order fighting. The manipular system also allowed entire Roman sub-units to maneuver more widely, freed from the need to always remain tightly packed in rigid formation. The deep three-line deployment of the Romans allowed combat pressure to be steadily applied forward. Most phalanxes favored one huge line several ranks deep. This might do well in the initial stages, but as the battle entangled more and more men, the stacked Roman formation allowed fresh pressure to be imposed over a more extended time. As combat lengthened and the battlefield compressed, the phalanx might thus become exhausted or rendered immobile, while the Romans still had enough left to not only maneuver but to make the final surges forward. Hannibal's deployment at Zama appears to recognize this—hence the Carthaginian also used a deep three-layer approach, sacrificing his first two lower quality lines and holding back his combat-hardened veterans of Italy for the final encounter. Hannibal's arrangement had much to recommend it given his weakness in cavalry and infantry, but he made no provision for one line relieving the other as the Romans did. Each line fought its own lonely battle and the last ultimately perished when the Romans reorganized for a final surge.

The legions also drilled and trained together over a more extended time, and were more uniform and streamlined, (unlike Hannibal's final force and others) enabling even less than brilliant army commanders to maneuver and position their forces proficiently. These qualities, among others, made them more than a match for the phalanx, when they met in combat.

According to Polybius, in his comparison of the phalanx versus the Roman system:

> ".. Whereas the phalanx requires one time and one type of ground.. Its use requires flat and level ground which is unencumbered by any obstacles.. If the enemy refuses to come down to [meet it on level ground].. what purpose can the phalanx serve?.. [Also] the phalanx soldier cannot operate in either smaller units or singly, whereas the Roman formation is highly flexible. Every Roman soldier.. can adapt himself equally well to any place of time and meet an attack from any quarter.. Accordingly since the effective use of parts of the Roman army is so much superior, their plans are much more likely to achieve success."

Versus Pyrrhus

See detailed article Pyrrhus of Epirus

The Greek king Pyrrhus' phalangical system was to prove a tough trial for the Romans. Despite several defeats the Romans inflicted such losses on the

Epirote army that the phrase "Pyrrhic victory" has become a byword for a victory won at a terrible cost. A skillful and experienced commander, Pyrrhus deployed a typically mixed phalanx system, including shock units of war-elephants, and formations of light infantry (peltasts), elite units, and cavalry to support his infantry. Using these he was able to defeat the Romans twice, with a third battle deemed inconclusive or a limited Roman tactical success by many scholars. The battles below (see individual articles for detailed accounts) illustrate the difficulties of fighting against phalanx forces. If well led and deployed (compare Pyrrhus to the fleeing Perseus at Pydna below), they presented a credible infantry alternative to the heavy legion. The Romans however were to learn from their mistakes. In subsequent battles after the Pyrrhic wars, they showed themselves masters of the Hellenic phalanx.

- Battle of Heraclea
- Battle of Asculum
- Battle of Beneventum

Notable triumphs

Battle of Cynoscephalae

In this battle the Macedonian phalanx originally held the high ground but all of its units had not been properly positioned due to earlier skirmishing. Nevertheless, an advance by its left wing drove back the Romans, who counterattacked on the right flank and made some progress against a somewhat disorganized Macedonian left. However the issue was still in doubt, until an unknown tribune (officer) detached 20 maniples from the Roman line and made an encircling attack against the Macedonian rear. This caused the enemy phalanx to collapse, securing a rout for the Romans. The more flexible, streamlined legionary organization had exploited the weaknesses of the densely packed phalanx. Such triumphs secured Roman hegemony in Greece and adjoining lands.

Battle of Pydna

At Pydna the contenders deployed on a relatively flat plain, and the Macedonians had augmented the infantry with a sizeable cavalry contingent. At the hour of decision, the enemy phalanx advanced in formidable array against the Roman line, and made some initial progress. However, the ground it had to advance over was rough, and the powerful phalangial formation lost its tight cohesion. The Romans absorbed the initial shock and came on into the fray, where their more spacious formation and continuously applied pressure proved decisive in hand-to-hand combat on the rough ground. Shield and sword at close quarters on such terrain neutralized the long pike, and supplementary Macedonian weapons (lighter armor and a dagger-like short sword) made an indifferent showing against the skillful and aggressive assault of the heavy Roman infantrymen. The opposition also failed to deploy supporting forces effectively to help the phalanx at its time of dire need. Indeed, the Macedonian commander, Perseus, seeing the situation deteriorating, seems to have fled without even bringing his cavalry into the engagement. The affair was decided in less than two hours, with a comprehensive defeat for the Macedonians.

Other anti-phalanx tactics

"Breaking phalanxes" illustrates more of the Roman army's flexibility. When the Romans faced phalangite armies, the legions often deployed the velites in front of the enemy with the command to *contendite vestra sponte* (attack), presumably with their javelins, to cause confusion and panic in the solid blocks of phalanxes. Meanwhile, auxilia archers were deployed on the wings of the legion in front of the cavalry, in order to defend their withdrawal. These archers were ordered to *eiaculare flammas*, fire incendiary arrows into the enemy. The cohorts then advanced in a wedge formation, supported by the velites' and auxiliaries' fire, and charged into the phalanx at a single point, breaking it, then flanking it with the cavalry to seal the victory. See the Battle of Beneventum for evidence of fire-arrows being used.

Versus Hannibal's Carthage

Tactical superiority of Hannibal's forces. While not a classic phalanx force, Hannibal's army was composed of "mixed" contingents and elements common to Hellenic formations, and it is told that towards the end of his life, Hannibal reportedly named Pyrrhus as the commander of the past that he most admired[1114] Rome however had blunted Pyrrhus' hosts prior to the rise of Hannibal, and given their advantages in organization, discipline, and resource mobilization, why did they not make a better showing in the field against the Carthaginian, who throughout most of his campaign in Italy suffered from numerical inferiority and lack of support from his homeland?

Hannibal's individual genius, the steadiness of his core troops (forged over several years of fighting together in Spain, and later in Italy) and his cavalry arm seem to be the decisive factors. Time after time Hannibal exploited the tendencies of the Romans, particularly their eagerness to close and achieve a decisive victory. The cold, tired, wet legionnaires that slogged out of the Trebia River to form up on the river bank are but one example of how Hannibal forced or manipulated the Romans into fighting on his terms, and on the ground of his own choosing. The later debacles at Lake Trasimene and Cannae, forced the proud Romans to avoid battle, shadowing the Carthaginians from the high ground of the Apennines, unwilling to risk a significant engagement on the plains where the enemy cavalry held sway.

Growing Roman tactical sophistication and ability to adapt overcomes earlier disasters. But while the case of Hannibal underscored that the Romans were far from invincible, it also demonstrated their long-term strengths. Rome had a vast manpower surplus far outnumbering Hannibal that gave them more options and flexibility. They isolated and eventually bottled up the Carthaginians and hastened their withdrawal from Italy with constant maneuver. More importantly, they used their manpower resources to launch an offensive into Spain and Africa. They were willing to absorb the humiliation in Italy and remain on the strategic defensive, but with typical relentless persistence they struck elsewhere, to finally crush their foes.

They also learned from those enemies. The operations of Scipio were an improvement on some of those who had previously faced Hannibal, showing a higher level of advance thinking, preparation and organization. (Compare with Sempronius at the Battle of the Trebia River for example). Scipio's contribution was in part to implement more flexible maneuver of tactical units, instead of the straight-ahead, three-line grind favored by some contemporaries. He also made better use of cavalry, traditionally an arm in which the Romans were lacking. His operations also included pincer movements, a consolidated battle line, and "reverse Cannae" formations and cavalry movements. His victories in Spain and the African campaign demonstrated a new sophistication in Roman warfare and reaffirmed the Roman capacity to adapt, persist and overcome.[1115] See detailed battles:

- Battle of Baecula
- Battle of Ilipa
- Battle of Zama

Roman infantry versus Gallic and the Germanic tribes

Barbarian Armies

Views of the Gallic enemies of Rome have varied widely. Some older histories consider them to be backward savages, ruthlessly destroying the civilization and "grandeur that was Rome." Some modernist views see them in a proto-nationalist light, ancient freedom fighters resisting the iron boot of empire. Often their bravery is celebrated as worthy adversaries of Rome. See the Dying Gaul for an example. The Gallic opposition was also composed of a large number of different peoples and tribes, geographically ranging from the mountains of Switzerland, to the lowlands of France and thus are not easy to categorize. The term "Gaul" has also been used interchangeably to describe Celtic peoples farther afield in Britain adding even more to the diversity of peoples lumped together under this name. From a military standpoint however, they seem to have shared certain general characteristics: tribal polities with a relatively small and lesser elaborated state structure, light weaponry, fairly unsophisticated tactics and organization, a high degree of mobility, and inability to sustain combat power in their field forces over a lengthy period.[1116] Roman sources reflect on the prejudices of their times, but nevertheless testify to the Gauls' fierceness and bravery.

> *'Their chief weapons were long, two-edged swords of soft iron.. For defense they carried small wicker shields. Their armies were undisciplined mobs, greedy for plunder.. Brave to the point of recklessness, they were formidable warriors, and the ferocity of their first assault inspired terror even in the ranks of veteran armies. "*[1117]

Early Gallic victories

Though popular accounts celebrate the legions and an assortment of charismatic commanders quickly vanquishing massive hosts of "wild barbarians",[1118] Rome suffered a number of early defeats against such tribal armies. As early as the Republican period (circa 390–387 BC), they had sacked Rome under Brennus, and had won several other victories such as the Battle of Noreia and the Battle of Arausio. The foremost Gallic triumph in this early period was *'The Day of Allia"*- July 18- when Roman troops were routed and driven into the Allia River. Henceforth, July 18 was considered an unlucky date on the Roman Calendar.[1119]

Some writers suggest that as a result of such debacles, the expanding Roman power began to adjust to this vigorous, fast-moving new enemy.[1120] The Romans began to phase out the monolithic phalanx they formerly fought in, and adopted the more flexible manipular formation. The circular hoplite shield was also enlarged and eventually replaced with the rectangular *scutum* for better protection. The heavy phalanx spear was replaced by the pila, suitable for throwing. Only the veterans of the *triarii* retained the long spear- vestige of the former phalanx. Such early reforms also aided the Romans in their conquest of the rest of Italy over such foes as the Samnites, Latins and Greeks.[1121] As time went on Roman arms saw increasing triumph over the Gallics, particularly in the campaigns of Caesar. In the early imperial period however, Germanic warbands inflicted one of Rome's greatest military defeats, (the Battle of the Teutoburg Forest) which saw the destruction of three imperial legions, and was to place a limit on Roman expansion in the West. And it was these Germanic tribes in part (most having some familiarity with Rome and its culture, and becoming more Romanized themselves) that were to eventually bring about the Roman military's final demise in the West. Ironically, in the final days, the bulk of the fighting was between forces composed mostly of barbarians on either side.[1122]

Tactical performance versus Gallic and Germanic opponents

Gallic and Germanic strengths

Whatever their particular culture, the Gallic and Germanic tribes generally proved themselves to be tough opponents, racking up several victories over their enemies. Some historians show that they sometimes used massed fighting in tightly packed phalanx-type formations with overlapping shields, and employed shield coverage during sieges. In open battle, they sometimes used a triangular "wedge" style formation in attack. Their greatest hope of success lay in 4 factors: (a) numerical superiority, (b) surprising the Romans (via an ambush for example) or in (c) advancing quickly to the fight, or (d) engaging the Romans over heavily covered or difficult terrain where units of the fighting horde could shelter within striking distance until the hour of decision, or if possible, withdraw and regroup between successive charges.[1123]

Most significant Gallic and Germanic victories show two or more of these characteristics. The Battle of the Teutoburg Forest contains all four: numerical superiority, surprise, quick charges to close rapidly, and favorable terrain and environmental conditions (thick forest and pounding rainstorms) that hindered Roman movement and gave the warriors enough cover to conceal their movements and mount successive attacks against the Roman line. Another factor in the Romans' defeat was a treacherous defection by Arminius and his contingent.[1124]

Gallic and Germanic weaknesses

Weaknesses in organization and equipment. Against the fighting men from the legion however, the Gauls, Iberians and Germanic forces faced a daunting task. The barbarians' rudimentary organization and tactics fared poorly against the well-oiled machinery that was the Legion. The fierceness of the Gallic and Germanic charges is often commented upon by some writers, and in certain circumstances they could overwhelm Roman lines. Nevertheless, the in-depth Roman formation allowed adjustments to be made, and the continual application of forward pressure made long-term combat a hazardous proposition for the Gauls.

Flank attacks were always possible, but the legion was flexible enough to pivot to meet this, either through sub-unit maneuver or through deployment of lines farther back. The cavalry screen on the flanks also added another layer of security, as did nightly regrouping in fortified camps. The Gauls and Germans also fought with little or no armor and with weaker shields, putting them at a disadvantage against the legion. Other items of Roman equipment from studded sandals, to body armor, to metal helmets added to Roman advantages. Generally speaking, the Gauls and Germans needed to get into good initial position against the Romans and to overwhelm them in the early phases of the battle. An extended set-piece slogging match between the lightly armed tribesmen and the well-organized heavy legionaries usually spelled doom for the tribal fighters. Caesar's slaughter of the Helvetii near the Saône River is just one example of tribal disadvantage against the well-organized Romans,[1125] as is the victory of Germanicus at the Weser River and Agricola against the Celtic tribesmen of Caledonia (Scotland) circa 84 A.D.[1126]

Weaknesses in logistics. Roman logistics also provided a trump card against Germanic foes as it had against so many previous foes. Tacitus in his *Annals* reports that the Roman commander Germanicus recognized that continued operations in Gaul would require long trains of men and material to come overland, where they would be subject to attack as they traversed the forests and swamps. He therefore opened sea and river routes, moving large quantities of supplies and reinforcements relatively close to the zone of battle, bypassing the dangerous land routes. In addition, the Roman fortified camps provided secure staging areas for offensive, defensive and logistical operations, once their troops were deployed. Assault roads and causeways were constructed on marshy ground to facilitate maneuver, sometimes under direct Gallic attack. These Roman techniques repeatedly defeated their Germanic adversaries.[1127] While Germanic leaders and fighters influenced by Roman methods sometimes adapted them, most tribes did not have the strong organization of the Romans. As German scholar Hans Delbruck notes in his "History of the Art of War":

> *".. the superiority of the Roman art of warfare was based on the army organization.. a system that permitted very large masses of men to be concentrated at a given point, to move in an orderly fashion, to be fed, to be kept together. The Gauls could do none of these things."*[1128]

Gallic and Germanic chariots

The Gallics also demonstrated a high level of tactical prowess in some areas. Gallic chariot warfare for example, showed a high degree of integration and coordination with infantry, and Gallic horse and chariot assaults sometimes threatened Roman forces in the field with annihilation. At the Battle of Sentinum for example, c. 295 BC, the Roman and Campanian cavalry encountered Gallic war-chariots and were routed in confusion—driven back from the Roman infantry by the unexpected appearance of the fast-moving Gallic assault. The discipline of the Roman infantry restored the line however, and a counterattack eventually defeated the Gallic forces and their allies.[1129]

The accounts of Polybius leading up to the Battle of Telamon, c. 225 BC mention chariot warfare, but it was ultimately unsuccessful. The Gauls met comprehensive defeat by the Roman legions under Papus and Regulus. Chariot forces also attacked the legions as they were disembarking from ships during

Caesar's invasion of Britain, but the Roman commander drove off the fast-moving assailants using covering fire (slings, arrows and engines of war) from his ships, and reinforcing his shore party of infantry to charge and drive off the attack. In the open field against Caesar, the Gallic/Celtics apparently deployed chariots with a driver and an infantry fighter armed with javelins. During the clash, the chariots would drop off their warriors to attack the enemy and retire a short distance away, massed in reserve. From this position they could retrieve the assault troops if the engagement was going badly, or apparently pick them up and deploy elsewhere. Caesar's troops were discomfited by one such attack, and he met it by withdrawing into his fortified redoubt. A later Gallic attack against the Roman camp was routed.[1130]

It should be noted also that superb as the Gallic fighters were, chariots were already declining as an effective weapon of war in the ancient world with the rise of mounted cavalry.[1131] At the battle of Mons Grapius in Caledonia (circa 84AD), Celtic chariots made an appearance. However they were no longer used in an offensive role but primarily for pre-battle show - riding back and forth and hurling insults. The main encounter was decided by infantry and mounted cavalry.

Superior tactical organization: victory of Caesar at the Sambre River

Superior Gallic mobility and numbers often troubled Roman arms, whether deployed in decades-long mobile or guerrilla warfare or in a decisive field engagement. The near defeat of Caesar in his Gallic campaign confirms this latter pattern, but also shows the strengths of Roman tactical organization and discipline. At the Battle of the Sabis river, (*see more detailed article*) contingents of the Nervii, Atrebates, Veromandui and Aduatuci tribes massed secretly in the surrounding forests as the main Roman force was busy making camp on the opposite side of the river. Some distance away behind them, slogged two slow moving legions with the baggage train. Engaged in foraging and camp construction the Roman forces were somewhat scattered. As camp building commenced, the barbarian forces launched a ferocious attack, streaming across the shallow water and quickly assaulting the distracted Romans. This incident is discussed in Caesar's *Gallic War Commentaries*.[1132]

So far the situation looked promising for the warrior host. The 4 conditions above were in their favor: (a) numerical superiority, (b) the element of surprise, (c) a quick advance/assault, and (d) favorable terrain that masked their movements until the last minute. Early progress was spectacular as the initial Roman dispositions were driven back. A rout looked possible. Caesar himself rallied sections of his endangered army, impressing resolve upon the troops. With their customary discipline and cohesion, the Romans then began to drive back the barbarian assault. A charge by the Nervi tribe through a gap between the legions however almost turned the tide again, as the onrushing warriors seized the Roman camp and tried to outflank the other army units engaged with the rest of the tribal host. The initial phase of the clash had passed however and a slogging match ensued. The arrival of the two rear legions that had been guarding the baggage reinforced the Roman lines. Led by the 10th Legion, a counterattack was mounted with these reinforcements that broke the back of the barbarian effort and sent the tribesmen reeling in retreat. It was a close run thing, illustrating both the fighting prowess of the tribal forces, and the steady, disciplined cohesion of the Romans. Ultimately, the latter was to prove decisive in Rome's long fought conquest of Gaul.

Persisting logistics strategy: Gallic victory at Gergovia

As noted above, the fierce charge of the Gauls and their individual prowess is frequently acknowledged by several ancient Roman writers.[1133] The Battle of Gergovia however demonstrates that the Gallic were capable of a level of strategic insight and operation beyond merely mustering warriors for an open field clash. Under their war leader Vercingetorix, the Gallics pursued what some modern historians have termed a "persisting" or "logistics strategy" - a mobile approach relying not on direct open field clashes, but avoidance of major battle, "scorched earth" denial of resources, and the isolation and piecemeal destruction of Roman detachments and smaller unit groupings.[1134] When implemented consistently, this strategy saw some success against Roman operations. According to Caesar himself, during the siege of the town of Bourges, the lurking warbands of Gauls were:

> "on the watch for our foraging and grain-gatherer parties, when necessarily scattered far afield he attacked them and inflicted serious losses... This imposed such scarcity upon the army that for several days they were without grain and staved off starvation only by driving cattle from remote villages."[1135]

Caesar countered with a strategy of enticing the Gallic forces out into open battle, or of blockading them into submission.

At the town of Gergovia, resource denial was combined with concentration of superior force, and multiple threats from more than one direction. This caused the opposing Roman forces to divide, and ultimately fail. Gergovia was situated on the high ground of a tall hill, and Vercingetorix carefully drew up the bulk of his force on the slope, positioning allied tribes in designated places. He drilled his men and skirmished daily with the Romans, who had overrun a hilltop position, and had created a small camp some distance from Caesar's larger main camp. A rallying of about 10,000 disenchanted Aeudan tribesmen (engineered by Vercingetorix's agents) created a threat in Caesar's rear, including a threat to a supply convoy promised by the allied Aeudans, and he diverted four legions to meet this danger.¹¹³⁶ This however gave Vercingetorix's forces the chance to concentrate in superior strength against the smaller two-legion force left behind at Gergovia, and desperate fighting ensued. Caesar dealt with the rear threat, turned around and by ruthless forced marching once again consolidated his forces at town. A feint using bogus cavalry by the Romans drew off part of the Gallic assault, and the Romans advanced to capture three more enemy outposts on the slope, and proceeded towards the walls of the stronghold. The diverted Gallic forces returned however and in frantic fighting outside the town walls, the Romans lost 700 men, including 46 centurions.

Caesar commenced a retreat from the town with the victorious Gallic warriors in pursuit. The Roman commander however mobilized his 10th Legion as a blocking force to cover his withdrawal and after some fighting, the tribesmen themselves withdrew back to Gergovia, taking several captured legion standards. The vicious fighting around Gergovia was the first time Caesar had suffered a military reverse, demonstrating the Gallic martial valor noted by the ancient chroniclers. The hard battle is referenced by the Roman historian Plutarch, who writes of the Averni people showing visitors a sword in one of their temples, a weapon that reputedly belonged to Caesar himself. According to Plutarch, the Roman general was shown the sword in the temple at Gergovia some years after the battle, but he refused to reclaim it, saying that it was consecrated, and to leave it where it was.¹¹³⁷

The Gallic were unable to sustain their strategy however, and Vercingetorix was to become trapped in Alesia, facing not divided sections or detachments of the Roman Army but Caesar's full force of approximately 70,000 men (50,000 legionnaires plus numerous additional auxiliary cavalry and infantry). This massive concentration of Romans was able to besiege the fortress in detail and repulse Gallic relief forces, and it fell in little more than a month. Vercingetorix overall persisting logistics policy however, demonstrates a significant level of strategic thinking. As historian A. Goldsworthy (2006) notes: "His [Vercingetorix's] strategy was considerably more sophisticated than that employed by Caesar's earlier opponents.."¹¹³⁸ At Alesia this mobile approach became overly static. The Gauls gave battle at a place where they were inadequately provisioned for an extended siege, and where Caesar could bring his *entire* field force to bear on a single point without them being dissipated, and where his lines of supply were not effectively interdicted.¹¹³⁹ At Gergovia by contrast, Caesar's strength was divided by the appearance of another Gallic force in his rear (the Aeudans)- threatening his sources and lines of supply. Together with a strong defensive anvil, (the town) supported by an offensive hammer (the open field forces), and coupled with previous resource denial pressure over time, the Romans were forced to retreat, and the Gallic secured a victory. As one historian notes about the persisting strategy:

"But before the defeat at Alesia, Vercingetorix's strategy had driven Cesar from central Gaul.. In finding and overwhelming Roman foragers as Fabius had done to Hannibal's men, the Gauls concentrated against weakness to win many small victories. Their strength in cavalry helped them concentrate rapidly, facilitating the application of the combat element in their strategy, though attacking foragers and grain gatherers was also intrinsic to the logistic aspect of their campaign."[1140]

Roman infantry versus mobile and guerilla warfare in Spain

The Iberian zone of struggle. The Gallic-Celtic-Iberian peoples, like many other tribes descended from the general "Celtic" race, put up an obstinate fight against Roman hegemony. Based in what is now Spain and Portugal, they fought continuously, with varying levels of intensity, for almost two centuries, beginning around 218 BC. The initial hegemons of Spain were the Carthaginians who struggled against various tribes to carve out colonies and a commercial empire, primarily in coastal enclaves. Carthaginian defeats by Rome brought struggle against a new imperium. Tribes such as the Celtiberi carried out a strong resistance, a struggle later continued by other groups such as the Lusitani, under Viriathus. The Lusitanian War and the Numantine War are but a few examples of the prolonged conflict, which cut across 20 decades of Roman history. Full conquest was not achieved until the time of Augustus. The vicious long-term fighting made Hispania a place of dread for the Roman soldier. Historian Sir Edward Creasy, in his "The Fifteen Decisive Battles of the World" had this to say about the Iberian conflicts.[1141]

> "The war against the Spaniards, who, of all the nations subdued by the Romans, defended their liberty with the greatest obstinacy... the Romans in both provinces were so often beaten, that nothing was more dreaded by the soldiers at home than to be sent there...

Roman tactics. Rome deployed its standard methods, with greater emphasis on blended units of light troops, cavalry and heavy infantry when confronting the guerrilla or mobile tactics used by the Iberians. Roman fortified camps were also valuable in protecting the troops and providing bases of operation. While combat results were mixed in the open field, the Romans did comparatively well when besieging Iberian cities, systematically eliminating enemy leaders, supply bases and centers of resistance. Destruction of Iberian resources by burning grain fields or demolishing villages also put the native resistance under greater pressure. The operations of Scipio during the Numantine War illustrate these methods, including a crackdown on lax practices and tightening of legionary discipline.[1142]

Other Roman tactics touched on the political sphere such as the "pacification" treaties of Gracchus, and treachery and trickery, as in the massacres of tribal leaders by Lucullus and Galba under guise of negotiation. Rome frequently capitalized on divisions among the tribes. A "divide and conquer" policy was in use, with competing (and sometimes insincere) treaties being negotiated to isolate targeted groups, and allied tribes being used to subdue others.[1143]

Celtic-Iberian tactics. Fighting for their independence and survival, the Iberian tribes used fortified cities or strongpoints to defend against their enemies, and mixed this with mobile warfare in formations ranging from small guerrilla bands, to large units numbering thousands of men. The Celtic/Iberian horsemen in particular appear to be more than a match for those of Rome, a fact proved in earlier years by the key role such allied cavalry played in Hannibal's victories. Favorable mobility and knowledge of the local terrain were to help the tribes immensely. One of the most successful ambushes was pulled off by a chieftain named Carus, who liquidated around 6,000 Romans in a combined cavalry-infantry strike. Another was executed by one Caesarus, who took advantage of a disorderly Roman pursuit under Mummius, to lay a trap that resulted in Roman losses of around 9,000 men. A similar Iberian "turn and fight" gambit is also recorded as being successful against Galba. Roman arms however triumphed over two grinding centuries of conflict. See *"Appian's History of Rome: The Spanish Wars"* for a more detailed discussion of individual battles, leaders and engagements.

Victory through attrition

In their battles against a wide variety of opponents, Rome's ruthless persistence, greater resources and stronger organization wore down their opponents over time.[1144] Rome's massive manpower supply was the foundation of this approach. Opponents could be relentlessly weakened and exhausted over the long run.[1145] In Spain, resources were thrown at the problem until it yielded over 150 years later- a slow, harsh grind of endless marching, constant sieges and fighting, broken treaties, burning villages and enslaved captives. As long as the Roman Senate and its successors were willing to replace and expend more men and material decade after decade, victory could be bought through a strategy of exhaustion.[1146]

The systematic wastage and destruction of enemy economic and human resources was called *vastatio* by the Romans. Crops and animals were destroyed or carried off, and local populaces were massacred or enslaved. Sometimes these tactics were also used to conduct punitive raids on barbarian tribes which had performed raids across the border. In the campaigns of Germanicus, Roman troops in the combat area carried out a "scorched earth" approach against their Germanic foes, devastating the land they depended on for supplies. *'The country was wasted by fire and sword fifty miles round; nor sex nor age found mercy; places sacred and profane had the equal lot of destruction, all razed to the ground..*" (Tacitus, *Annals*). The Roman "grind down" approach is also seen in the Bar Kokba Jewish revolt against the Romans. The Roman commander Severus avoided meeting the hard-fighting Jewish rebels in the open field. Instead he relied on attacking their fortified strongpoints and devastating the zone of conflict in a methodical campaign.[1147] This "attritional" aspect of the Roman approach to combat contrasts with the notion of brilliant generalship or tactics sometimes seen in popular depictions of the Roman infantry.

Some historians note however that Rome often balanced brutal attrition with shrewd diplomacy, as demonstrated by Caesar's harsh treatment of Gallic tribes that opposed him, but his sometimes conciliatory handling of those that submitted. Rome also used a variety of incentives to encourage cooperation by the elites of conquered peoples, co-opting opposition and incorporating them into the structure of the empire. This carrot and stick approach forms an integral part of "the Roman way" of war.[1148]

Roman infantry versus cavalry

Tactical problems of fighting cavalry

Cavalry opponents were one of the toughest challenges faced by the Roman infantry. Combining both missile and shock capability with extensive mobility, cavalry exploited the inherent weakness of the legion—its relatively slow movement and deployment. Defeat by strong cavalry forces is a recurring event in Roman military history. The campaigns of Hannibal illustrate this well, as Numidian and Spanish/Gallic horsemen repeatedly outflanked Roman formations, dealing devastating blows in the sides and rear. Hannibal's great victory at Cannae (considered one of the greatest Roman defeats ever) was primarily an infantry struggle, but the key role was played by his cavalry, as in his other victories.

An even more dramatic demonstration of Roman vulnerability is shown in the numerous wars against Parthian heavy cavalry. The Parthians and their successors used large numbers of fast-moving light riders to harass and skirmish, and delivered the coup de grâce with heavily armored lancers called "cataphracts". Both types of troops used powerful composite bows that shot arrows of sufficient strength to penetrate Roman armor. The cataphracts extended combat power by serving as shock troops, engaging opposing forces with their heavy lances in thundering charges after they had been "softened up" by swarms of arrows. The Parthians also conducted a "scorched earth" policy against the Romans, refusing major set-piece encounters, while luring them deeper on to unfavorable ground, where they would lack water supplies and a secure line of retreat. The debacle of the Battle of Carrhae saw a devastating defeat of Roman arms by the Parthian cavalry.[1149]

Successful tactics

Clues exist in the earlier campaigns of Alexander the Great against mounted Asiatic warriors—engaging the horsemen with strong detachments of light infantry and missile troops, and driving them off with charges by Alexander's heavy cavalry units. The Roman variant, with its large manpower resources, continued the same "combined arms" approach, with a larger role for cavalry as the empire went on. The Eastern half of the Roman Empire, particularly, was ultimately to rely mostly on cavalry forces.

Adjustments of Ventidius. The operations of the Roman commander Publius Ventidius Bassus illustrate three general tactics used by the infantry to fight their mounted foes. These drew on Caesar's veteran legions, and made Ventidius one of the Roman generals to celebrate a triumph against the Parthians. In three separate battles, he not only managed to defeat the Parthian armies and drive them out of Roman territory, but also managed to kill Parthia's three top military commanders during the battles.[1150] The adjustments of Ventidius were as follows:

1. *Increase in firepower.* Ventidius sought to neutralize the Parthian advantage in firepower, by adding his own, and provided his legions with numerous slingers whose furious fire was instrumental in checking the Parthian horsemen during several battles. In subsequent engagements, other Roman commanders increased cavalry units and slingers, with the latter being supplied with leaden bullets which gave more range and killing power.
2. *Securing the high ground and other terrain features.* In his three victories over the horsemen, Ventidius had his infantry secure the high ground, bolstering defensive positions and maneuvers with withering covering fire by the slingers. Seizure of key terrain features also obstructed avenues of attack and provided anchor points that allowed maneuvering detachments to counterattack, or to fall back if unfavorable conditions developed. Against the horsemen, heavy infantry units had to work closely with cavalry and light troops, and be mutually supporting, or they could be quickly isolated and destroyed.
3. *Aggressive operations from a stable base.* During movement against the horsemen, special care had to be taken when crossing a mountain,

ravine or bridge. In such cases, sub-sections of the legion had to be redeployed to provide covering and blocking forces until the army had safely navigated the route.[1151] Once entering the zone of battle, Ventidius generally operated from a defensive base and did not prematurely venture on to flat terrain or allow his forces to lose cohesion as at Carrhae. He let the Parthian forces come to him after taking a strong position, and aggressively counterattacked. In two victories the Parthians were induced to attack the army camp, where they were mauled by the corps of slingers. The legions then counterattacked from this defensive anvil, light and heavy units working together to smash opposition.[1152] In a third triumph, Ventidius dispatched a strong vanguard of cavalry against a Parthian concentration at the Syrian Gates, or narrow pass over Mount Amanus, leading from Cilicia into Syria. As the Parthians moved in for the kill, Ventidius quickly brought up his main force behind the vanguard, defeating his opponents in detail, and killing Pharnapates the Parthian commander. Throughout these maneuvers deadly sling fire was continuous and victory for the Romans was secured.

Combined arms and quick advance. In the later Roman empire, cavalry forces played a larger role, with the infantry in support. The campaign of the Emperor Julian II against the Persians is instructive in this regard. On June 22, 363 a large-scale clash occurred near the town of Maranga. Facing an enemy that threatened to blanket his troops with a hail of arrows, and in danger of envelopment, Julian deployed his force in a crescent formation, and ordered an advance by both infantry and cavalry on the double, thwarting both dangers by closing quickly. The gambit was successful. After a long battle, the Persians withdrew- a tactical victory (albeit a costly one for the Romans according to some historians).[1153] The work of Roman historian Ammianus Marcellinus offers a detailed description of the Persian campaign, including the quick charge by the heavy Roman infantry under Julian.

> 'To prevent the preliminary volleys of the archers from disrupting our ranks he (Julian) advanced at the double and so ruined the effect of their fire... Roman foot in close order made a mighty push and drove the serried ranks of the enemy before them..."

Marcellinus's commentary also sharply contrasts the fighting spirit of the Persian infantrymen with those of Rome, stating that they had "aversion to pitched infantry battles."[1154] In an earlier engagement outside the walls of Ctesiphon, Marcellinus again notes the value of the quick advance by the infantry:

> "both sides fought hand-to-hand with spears and drawn swords; the quicker our men forced themselves into the enemy's line the less they were exposed to danger from arrows."[1155]

Mixed results against major cavalry enemies. Rome's overall record against the Parthians was favourable, although the Parthian horsemen offered stiff resistance, as it was against the horsemen of Hannibal, and some Gallic opponents. Subsequent Roman leaders like Antony invaded Parthian territory but had to withdraw after severe losses. Others like Severus and Trajan saw great success in their invasions of Mesopotamia, defeating Parthian armies through combined arms tactics.. Thus, the battles of Ventidius and Julian show that the Roman infantry, when properly handled and maneuvered, and when working in conjunction with other supporting arms like slingers, could certainly meet the challenge of enemy cavalryman.

Assessment of the Roman infantry

Central factors in Roman success

Some elements that made the Romans an effective military force, both tactically and at higher levels, were:

The Romans were able to copy and adapt the weapons and methods of their opponents more effectively. Some weapons, such as the gladius, were adopted outright by the legionaries. Publius asserts that the *pilum* was of Samnite origin, and the shield was based on Greek design.[1156] In other cases, especially formidable units of enemy forces were invited to serve in the Roman army as auxiliaries after peace was made. In the naval sphere, the Romans followed some of the same methods they used with the infantry, dropping their ineffective designs and copying, adapting and improving on Punic warships, and introducing heavier marine contingents (infantry fighters) on to their ships.[1157]

Roman organization was more flexible than those of many opponents. Compared to the tightly packed spearmen of the phalanx, the Roman heavy infantry, through their training and discipline, and operating in conjunction with light foot and cavalry, could quickly adopt a number of methods and formations depending on the situation. These range from the Testudo formation during siege warfare, to a hollow square against cavalry attack, to mixed units of heavy foot, horse and light infantry against guerrillas in Spain, to the classic "triple line" or checkerboard patterns. Against more sophisticated opponents the Romans also showed great flexibility at times, such as the brilliant adjustments Scipio made against Hannibal at Zama. These included leaving huge gaps in the ranks to trap the charging elephants, and the recall, reposition and consolidation of a single battle line that advanced to the final death struggle against the Carthaginian veterans of Italy.[1158]

Roman discipline, organization and logistical systemization sustained combat effectiveness over a longer period. Notably, the Roman system of *castra*, or fortified camps, allowed the army to stay in the field on favorable ground and be rested and resupplied for battle. Well organized Roman logistics also sustained combat power, from routine resupply and storage, to the construction of military roads, to state run arsenals and weapons factories, to well organized naval convoys that helped stave off defeat by Carthage. The death of a leader generally did not cause the legions to lose heart in battle. Others stepped to the fore and carried on. In the defeat by Hannibal at the River Trebia, 10,000 Romans cut their way through the debacle to safety, maintaining unit cohesion when all around was rout, a testimony to their tactical organization and discipline.

The Romans were more persistent and more willing to absorb and replace losses over time than their opponents. Unlike other civilizations, the Romans kept going relentlessly until typically their enemies had been completely crushed or neutralized. The army acted to implement policy and were not allowed to stop unless they received a command from the emperor or a decree from the senate.

Against the tribal polities of Europe, particularly in Hispania, Roman tenacity and material weight eventually wore down most opposition. The tribes of Europe did not have a state or economic structure able to support lengthy campaigns and therefore could often (but not always) be made to change their minds about opposing Roman hegemony. The defeat in the Teutoburg Forest might seem like an exception, but even here, the Romans were back on the warpath 5 years later with major forces against their Germanic opponents. That there is an obvious limit to endless persistence does not negate the general pattern.

Where the Romans faced another large state structure, such as the Parthian Empire, they found the military road rocky indeed and were sometimes forced to an impasse. Nevertheless, the distinct pattern of Roman tenacity holds. Rome suffered its greatest defeats against sophisticated Carthage, notably at Cannae, and was forced to avoid battle for a lengthy period. Yet in time, it rebuilt its forces on land and at sea, and persisted in the struggle, astonishing the Punics who expected it to sue for peace. Against the Parthians, crushing defeats did not stop the Romans from inflicting serious defeats on the Parthians themselves, for they invaded Parthian territory several times afterwards, and though Parthia proper was never totally conquered, Rome ultimately secured a rough hegemony in the area, and managed to successfully destroy Parthian forces in Mesopotamia on numerous occasions.

Roman leadership was mixed, but over time it was often effective in securing Roman military success. Leadership debacles are common in Roman military history, from the routs against Hannibal, to the demise of the unlucky Crassus against the Parthians. The Roman polity's structuring however produced a steady supply of men willing and able to lead troops in battle- men that were held accountable for defeat or malfeasance. It was not unusual for a losing general to be prosecuted by political enemies in Rome, with some having their property confiscated and barely escaping death. The senatorial oligarchy, for all its political maneuvering, interference and other faults, provided the functions of oversight and audit over military matters, that over the course of time, shaped final results. The record is a mixed one, but whether under boisterous Republic or Imperial emperor, Rome produced enough competent leaders to secure its military dominance for over a millennium. Some of the best leaders come from both eras, including Marius, Sulla, Scipio, Caesar, Trajan and others.

Note should be taken here of the large number of junior officers the Romans typically used to assure coordination and guidance. The initiative of such men played a key part in Roman success. Effective leadership was also bound up with the famous Roman centurions, the backbone of the legionary organization. While not all such men could be considered models of perfection, they commanded substantial respect.

The influence of Roman military and civic culture, as embodied particularly in the heavy infantry legion, gave the Roman military consistent motivation and cohesion. Such culture included but was not limited to: (a) the valuing of Roman citizenship, (b) the broad-based muster of free males into mass infantry units (as opposed to widespread use of foreign contingents, slaves or mercenaries), and (c) loyalty to those fighting units (the Legion) which remained characteristically Roman in outlook and discipline. Citizenship conveyed certain valuable rights in Roman society, and was another element that helped to promote the standardization and integration of the infantry.[1159] The citizen under arms - the legion soldier - was supposed to reflect and practice the Roman ideal of *virtus, pietas, fides*, - self-discipline, respect and faithfulness to engagements. Implementation of such ideals could be mixed according to some writers, but it was "a trilogy [driving] every aspect of military, domestic, economic and social life."[1160] As such it was a strong force for cohesion among Rome's infantrymen.

Rome's massive manpower supply enabled it to stay in the field and continue fighting after defeats and to launch new campaigns. Against Hannibal for example, Rome suffered huge losses, but still vastly outnumbered Hannibal's forces. This meant not only defensive operations under Fabius, but the aggressive deployment of new armies under Scipio to take the battle to the Carthaginians in Africa. Other enemies of Rome came up against this massive manpower reserve and faltered over time - from small tribes, city-states or kingdoms fighting to maintain their independence, to major empires that confronted the Romans. The huge pool of fighting men gave the Romans much more room for error or setbacks, compared to their opponents.[1161]

Decline

Any history of the Roman infantry must grapple with the factors that led to the decline of the heavy legions that once dominated the Western world. Such decline of course is closely linked with the decay of other facets of Rome's economy, society and political scene. Nevertheless, some historians emphasize that the final demise of Rome was due to **military** defeat, however plausible (or implausible) the plethora of theories advanced by some scholars, ranging from declining tax bases, to class struggle, to mass lead poisoning.[1162] Two of the major factors that have occupied scholars of the military will be discussed here: barbarization and the adaptation of a "mobile reserve" strategy. There are a number of controversies in this area with dueling scholars advancing competing theories.

Changes in the legions

To combat the more frequent raids and advances of their hostile neighbors the legions were changed from slow and heavy to much lighter troops, and cavalry was introduced as a serious concept. State controlled factories produced vast quantities of less specialist arms such as chainmail armor and spears as opposed to the gladius and lorica segmentata more prevalent in the early empire. The difference between auxiliaries and legionaries began to become negligible from an equipment point of view. This meant that the new subdivided infantry lost the awesome power that the earlier legions had, meaning that whilst they were more likely to see a battle they were less likely to win it. That legion size was at an all-time low was also a factor. On the other hand, legions in the late empire were used far more flexibly as accounts by authors like Ammianus Marcellinus make clear. Smaller detachments waged more personal and smaller scale, yet intense operations against tribal foes on the Rhine and Danubian frontiers. Instead of vast formations of thousands of troops, smaller units would engage smaller-scale incursions by raiders. Roman horsemen, while fast, were actually much too weak to cope with the very cavalry based invasions of the Huns, Goths, Vandals and Sassanids. Their ineffectiveness was demonstrated at Cannae and Adrianople; in both instances the cavalry was completely destroyed by a vastly more powerful enemy horse. Advances in Roman tactical thinking led to the adoption of eastern-style cataphracts and mass-use of auxiliary forces as cavalry, both of which were used to address previous shortcomings of the Roman army. The later Roman army was more cavalry-orientated than it had been before and as a result detachments were able to be moved around the empire at will, ending the previous doctrine of keeping all forces on the frontiers at the edge of the empire.

"Barbarization" of the heavy infantry

"Barbarization" is a common theme in many works on Rome (See Gibbon, Mommsen, Delbrück, et al.), and thus cannot be excluded from any analysis of its infantry forces. Essentially it is argued that the increasing barbarization of the heavy legions weakened weaponry, training, morale and military effectiveness in the long run. The weapons changes described above are but one example.[1163]

It could be argued that the use of barbarian personnel was nothing new. This is accurate, however such use was clearly governed by "the Roman way." It was the barbarian personnel who had to adapt to Roman standards and organization, not the other way around. In the twilight of the empire, this was not the case. Such practices as permitting the settlement of massive, armed barbarian populations on Roman territory, the watering down of the privilege of citizenship, increasing use of alien contingents, and relaxation or removal of traditionally thorough and severe Roman discipline, organization and control, contributed to the decline of the heavy infantry.[1164]

The settlement of the foederati for example, saw large barbarian contingents ushered on to Roman territory, with their own organization, under their own leaders. Such groupings showed a tendency to neglect "the Roman way" in organization, training, logistics etc., in favor of their own ideas, practices and agendas. These settlements may have bought short-term political peace for imperial elites, but their long-term effect was negative, weakening the traditional strengths of the heavy infantry in discipline, training and deployment. They also seemed to have lessened the incentive for remaining "old Guard" troops to adhere to such strengths, since the barbarians received equal or more favor with less effort. Indeed, such "allied" barbarian contingents were at times to turn on the Romans, devastating wide areas with sack and pillage and even attacking imperial army formations.[1165] Other writers argue that while some ancient Romans did view the world in terms of barbarians versus civilized Romans (epitomized in Hadrian's Wall of separation), the reality of Roman frontiers was a fuzzy set of interlocking zones - political, military, judicial and financial, rather than a neat linear boundary. Changes to the Roman forces that moved away from the old fighting organization order were thus the outcome of several influences, rather than simply the appearance of more, allegedly uncivilized non-Romans.[1166]

The mobile forces approach

The "mobile reserve" strategy, traditionally identified with Constantine I, saw reversal of the traditional "forward" policy of strong frontier fortifications backed by legions stationed near likely zones of conflict. Instead, it is argued that the best troops were pulled back into a type of "mobile reserve" closer to the center that could be deployed to trouble areas throughout the empire. Some scholars claim this was a positive development, (Luttwak, Delbruck, et al.) given growing difficulties with governing the vast empire, where political turmoil and severe financial difficulties had made the old preclusive security system untenable. Some writers such as Luttwak condemn the old style "forward" policy as indicating a "Maginot Line" mentality in the troubled latter centuries of the Empire.[1167]

Disadvantages of the mobile reserve strategy versus the "forward" policy

Ancient writers like Zosimus in the 5th century AD condemned the "reserve" policy as a major weakening of the military force. Other modern scholars (Ferrill et al.) also see the pullback as a strategic mistake, arguing that it left lower quality "second string" limitanei forces to stop an enemy, until the distant mobile reserve arrived. While the drop in quality did not happen immediately, it is argued that over time, the limitanei declined into lightly armed, static watchman type troops that were of dubious value against increasing barbarian marauders on the frontiers. The pullback of the best infantry was based more on political reasons (shoring up the power bases of the emperors and various elites) rather than on military reality. In addition it is claimed, the "forward" policy was not at all a static "Maginot" approach, but that traditional heavy legions and supporting cavalry could still move to a trouble spot by redeploying them from fortifications elsewhere along a particular frontier. Some scholars challenge the notion that a "mobile reserve" in the modern military sense existed in the Roman Empire, and instead argue that the shifts in organization represent a series of field armies deployed in various areas as needed, particularly in the East. Others point to the heavy fiscal difficulties and political turmoil of the later Empire that made it difficult to continue traditional policy.[1168]

Twilight of the hard-core infantry

There are numerous other facets to the controversy, but whatever the school of thought, all agree that the traditional strengths and weaponry of the heavy infantry legion declined from the standards of earlier eras. The 4th century writer Vegetius, in one of the most influential Western military works *De Re Militari*, highlighted this decline as the key factor in military weakness, noting that the core legions always fought as part of an integrated team of cavalry and light foot. In the latter years, this formula that had brought so much success petered out. Caught between the growth of lighter armed/less organized foot soldiers, and the increasing cavalry formations of the mobile forces, the "heavies" as the dominant force, withered on the vine. This does not mean that heavy units disappeared entirely, but that their mass recruitment, formation, organization and deployment as the dominant part of the Roman military was greatly reduced. Ironically, in Rome's final battles (the Western half of the empire) the defeats suffered were substantially inflicted by infantry forces (many fighting dismounted).

Speaking of the decline of the heavy infantry, the Roman historian Vegetius lauded the old fighting units, and lamented how the heavy armor of the early days had been discarded by the weaker, less disciplined, barbarized forces:

> 'Those who find the old arms so burdensome, must either receive wounds upon their naked bodies and die, or what is worse still, run the risk of being made prisoners, or of betraying the country by their flight. Thus, to avoid fatigue, they allow themselves to be butchered shamefully, like cattle.'[1169]

Historian Arther Ferrill notes that even towards the end, some of the old infantry formations were still in use. Such grouping was increasingly ineffective however, without the severe close order discipline, drill and organization of old times. At the Battle of Châlons (circa 451 AD) Attila the Hun rallied his troops by mocking the once vaunted Roman infantry, alleging that they merely huddled under a screen of protective shields in close formation. He ordered his troops to ignore them and to attack the powerful Alans and Visigoths instead. It was a sad commentary on the force that had once dominated Europe, the Mediterranean and much of the Middle East. It is true that at Châlons, the Roman infantry contributed to the victory by seizing part of the battlefield's high ground. Nevertheless, its day had already passed in favor of the mass levies of the barbarian federates.

References

Sources

Primary sources
- Caesar's *Commentarii de Bello Gallico*
- Vegetius's *De Re Militari*
- *Notitia Dignitatum*

Secondary sources

- 'Later Roman Battle Tactics' in C. Koepfer, F.W. Himmler and J. Löffl (eds), *Die römische Armee im Experiment* (Region im Umbruch, Band 6). Frank & Timme, Berlin 2011, 267–286. — An essay on Roman infantry and cavalry tactics from AD 194 to 378.
- Ross Cowan, *Roman Battle Tactics, 109 BC - AD 313*. Osprey, Oxford 2007. — The book clearly explains and illustrates the mechanics of how Roman commanders — at every level — drew up and committed their different types of troops for open-field battles.
- Adrian Goldsworthy (2001), *The Punic Wars*, Cassell — A detailed breakdown of Roman strategy, methods, tactics and those of their opponents. Analyzes strengths and weaknesses of the Roman military and how they were able to beat a sophisticated Carthage
- Arther Ferrill (1986), *The Fall of the Roman Empire: The Military Explanation*, Thames & Hudson — Focuses on military issues leading to the fall of Rome as opposed to a plethora of theories such as overpopulation, shrinking tax bases, "class struggle", etc. Reemphasizes the military factors in Rome's final demise. Compares the "mobile reserve" strategy of later decades o the earlier "forward" policy of keeping the heavy fighting legions near likely combat zones. Ferrill also tackles the weakening effect of "barbarization", particularly on the core heavy infantry legions.

> **"** **"**
> Many historians have argued [...] that the fall of Rome was not primarily a military phenomenon. In fact, it was exactly that. After 410 the emperor in the West could no longer project military power to the frontiers.
>
> —The Fall of the Roman Empire: The Military Explanation, p. 164

- Adrian Goldsworthy (2003), *The Complete Roman Army*, Thames & Hudson — One volume history covering the Roman Army, which was the biggest most important part of its military. Goldsworthy covers the early Republican days down to the final Imperial era demise, tracing changes in tactics, equipment, strategy, organization etc. He notes the details of the military system such as training and battlefield tactics, as well as bigger picture strategy, and changes that impacted Roman arms. He assesses what made the Romans effective, and ineffective in each of the various eras.
- Edward Luttwak (1979), *Grand Strategy of the Roman Empire*, Thames & Hudson — *Prominent advocate* of the mobile or central reserve theory.
- Hans Delbrück (1990), *History of the Art of War: Warfare in Antiquity*, University of Nebraska — *Prominent advocate* of the mobile or central reserve theory. ISBN 0-8032-9199-X

- Xenophon (1988), *Anabasis*, Loeb Classical Library — See this classic work for a detailed discussion of anti-cavalry problems by another heavy infantry formation- the Hellenic phalanx, including the weaknesses of the hollow square formation.

External links
- Later Roman Battle Tactics[1170]
- C hanging Formations and Specialists: Aspects of Later Roman Battle Tactics[1171]

Fortification

Roman military frontiers and fortifications

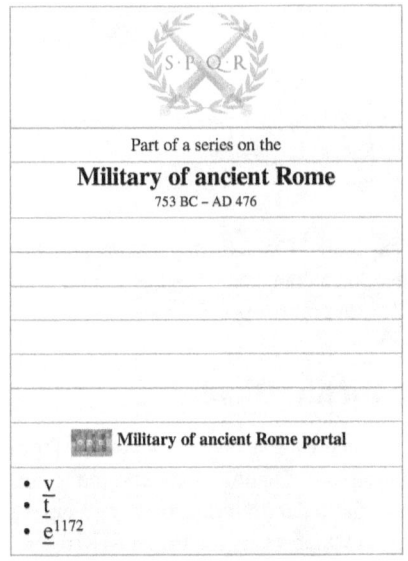

Roman military borders and fortifications were part of a grand strategy of territorial defense in the Roman Empire, although this is a matter of debate. By the early 2nd century, the Roman Empire had reached the peak of its territorial expansion and rather than constantly expanding their borders as earlier in the Empire and Republic, the Romans solidified their position by fortifying their strategic position with a series of fortifications and established lines of defense. Historian Adrian Goldsworthy argues that the Romans had reached the natural limits which their military traditions afforded them conquest over and that beyond the borders of the early-to-mid Empire lay peoples whose military traditions made them militarily unconquerable, despite many Roman

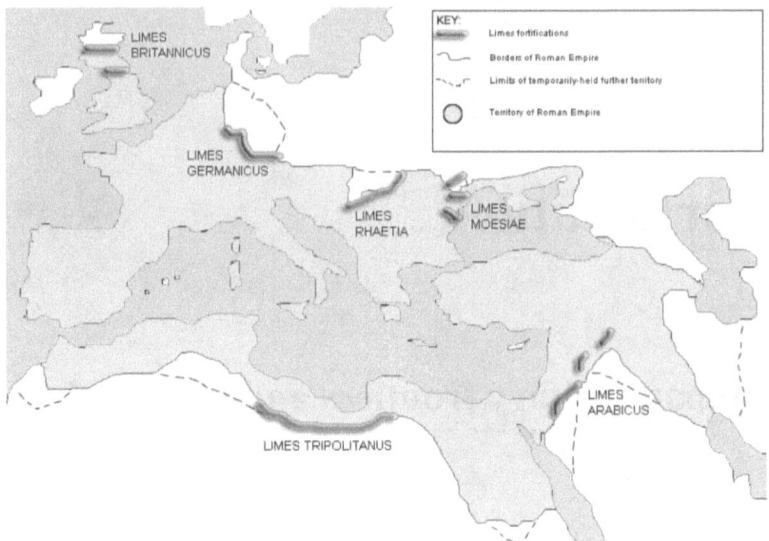

Figure 147: *Map of all the territories once occupied by the Roman Empire, along with locations of limes*

battle victories. In particular, Goldsworthy argues that the cavalry-based warfare of the Parthians, Sarmatians and Persians presented a major challenge to the expansion of Rome's infantry-based armies.

Nature of the fortifications

The borders of the Roman Empire, which fluctuated throughout the empire's history, were a combination of natural frontiers (the Rhine and Danube rivers to the north and east, the Atlantic to the west, and deserts to the south) and man-made fortifications which separated the lands of the empire from the "barbarian" lands beyond.

Individual fortifications had been constructed by the Roman military from as early as the building of Rome's first city walls in the 6th or 7th century BC. However, systematic construction of fortifications around the periphery of the empire on a strategic scale began around 40 AD under Emperor Caligula.Wikipedia:Citation needed However, it was under Hadrian's rule, which began in 117, that the Roman frontier was systematically fortified. He spent half of his 21-year reign touring the empire and advocating for the construction of forts, towers, and walls all across the edges of the empire.[1173] The coherent construction of these fortifications on a strategic scale (*i.e.* to protect the empire as a whole rather than fortifying individual settlements) are known as the *limes*, and continued until around 270.

The *limes* consisted of fortresses for legions or vexillations (e.g. Segedunum) as well as a system of roads for the rapid transit of troops and, in some places, extensive walls. Perhaps the most famous example of these is Hadrian's Wall in Great Britain, which was built across the entire width of the island to protect from attack from tribes located in modern-day Scotland. The so-called *Limes Britannicus* is perhaps the best example of the ultimate *limes* - like the Great Wall of China, it was an attempt to construct a continuous man-made fortification along the length of an entire border, a massive undertaking. However, it is not correct to interpret other *limes* in the same way or to view the *limes* as an impenetrable barrier. Other limes would not have had a continuous man-made fortification for the entirety of their length. In places, a river, desert or natural outcropping of rock could provide the same effect for zero outlay. Also, fortifications as impressive as Hadrian's Wall were not unbreachable: with milecastles some distance apart and patrols infrequent, small enemy forces would have been able to penetrate the defenses easily for small-scale raiding. However, a raiding party would be forced to fight its way through one of the well-defended gates, abandon its loot, such as cattle, thus negating the whole purpose of the raid or be trapped against the wall by the responding legions. Additionally, a large army would have been able to force a crossing of the *limes* using siege equipment. The value of the limes lay not in its absolute impenetrability but, as S. Thomas Parker argues, in its hindrance to the enemy: granting a delay or warning that could be used to summon concentrated Roman forces to the site. The *limes* are therefore perhaps better seen as an instrument allowing a greater economy of force in defense of a border than otherwise would be necessary to provide the same level of defense.

After 270, the maintenance of an impenetrable solid frontier was abandoned by Constantine I in favor of a policy, whether deliberate or forced by circumstance, of "defense in depth". This called for the maintenance of a softer, deeper perimeter area of defense, with concentrated hard points throughout its depth. The idea was that any invading force of a sufficient size could penetrate the initial perimeter but in doing so with any element of surprise or rapid movement would be forced to leave several defended hard points (fortresses) to its rear, hampering its lines of supply and communications, and threatening surrounding of the force.

In the very late Empire the frontiers became even more elastic, with little effort expended in maintaining frontier defense. Instead, armies were concentrated near the heart of the empire, and enemies allowed to penetrate in cases as far inwards as the Italian peninsula before being met in battle.

Figure 148: *Hadrian's Wall viewed from Vercovicium*

Northern borders

Britannia

After conquering much of the modern landmass of Great Britain, the Romans halted their northern expansion at the southern fringe of Caledonia, what is now central Scotland. This left them with a border shared with a people who made repeated raids and insurrections against them. Unlike other borders throughout the empire, there was no natural border to fall back on such as desert or wide river that crossed the whole peninsula, so instead a series of defenses were built in southern to mid-Scotland in order to protect the province of *Britannia* from the Caledonians and later the Picts.

Although the border was not a continuous wall, a series of fortifications known as Gask Ridge in mid-Scotland may well be Rome's earliest fortified land frontier. Constructed in the **70CE** or **80CE**, it was superseded by the later Hadrian's Wall forty years later and then the final Antonine Wall twenty years after that. Rather than representing a series of consecutive advancements, the border should be seen as fluctuating - the Antonine Wall for example was built between 142 and 144, abandoned by 164 and briefly re-occupied in 208.

Although records are scarce, there are indications that the border fluctuated between the various fortifications depending on the local strength of the military.

There is archaeological evidence for widespread burning of fortifications, but it is disputed whether this represents fortifications falling to attack or part of the normal process of the Roman military to destroy their own fortified camps on abandonment so as not to furnish the enemy with a fortified base at their expense.

These northern fortifications are sometimes styled the *Limes Britannicus*. The average garrison of the wall fortifications is thought to have been around 10,000 men. Along with a continuous wall (except in the case of Gask Ridge), there existed a metaled road immediately behind the wall for transport of troops. Along the wall there existed a few large forts for legions or vexillations, as well as a series of milecastles - effectively watchtowers that were unable to defend a stretch of wall against anything but low-scale raiding but were able to signal attack to legionary forts by means of fire signals atop the towers.

In the later Empire, Roman Britannia found itself increasingly vulnerable to external aggression, in parallel to attacks felt across the length of the Empire's borders. However, since Britannia shared no land bridge with continental Europe, the method of attack and thus methods of defense varied from the imperial standard. A series of naval forts was built along the south east coast, initially to combat piracy but later to protect from raiding and the threat of invasion from Saxons that eventually led to the Saxon occupation of Lowland Britain by 600 and is reflected in the name of the fortification system: the Saxon Shore, which extended to the northern coasts of France. Each shore fort both protected against direct attack and also sheltered a small naval sub-fleet of vessels that could patrol the coast against pirates and raiders.

Continental Europe

In continental Europe, the borders were generally well defined, usually following the courses of major rivers such as the Rhine and the Danube. Nevertheless, those were not always the final border lines: the original province of Dacia, in modern Romania, was completely north of the Danube, and the province of *Germania Magna*,Wikipedia:Citation needed which should not be confused with *Germania Inferior* and *Germania Superior*, was the land between the Rhine, the Danube and the Elbe (Although this province was lost three years after its creation as a result of the Battle of Teutoburg Forest). The *limes* that ran across the line of the Rhine-Danube was known as the Limes Germanicus. It consisted of:

- The Lower (Northern) Germanic Limes, which extended from the North Sea at Katwijk in the Netherlands along the Rhine;

Figure 149: *Roman watchtower and beacon on the lower Danube frontier*

- The Upper Germanic Limes (just to be confusing, also called the Rhaetian Limes or simply "the Limes") started from the Rhine at Rheinbrohl (Neuwied (district)) across the Taunus mountains to the river Main (East of Hanau), then along the Main to Miltenberg, and from Osterburken (Neckar-Odenwald-Kreis) south to Lorch (Ostalbkreis) in a nearly perfect straight line of more than 70 km;
- The proper Rhaetian Limes extended east from Lorch to Eining (close to Kelheim) on the Danube. The total length was 568 km (353 mi). It included at least 60 castles and 900 watchtowers.

In *Dacia*, the limes between the Black Sea and the Danube were a mix of the camps and the wall defenses: the *Limes Moesiae* was the conjunction of two, and sometimes three, lines of *vallum*, with a Great Camp and many minor camps spread through the fortifications.

Eastern borders

The eastern borders changed many times, of which the most enduring was the Euphrates river, bordering the Parthian Empire in modern Iran and western Iraq. Rome advanced beyond the Euphrates for a time upon defeating their rivals, the Parthians in 116 AD, when Trajan captured Ctesiphon, and established new provinces in Assyria and Babylonia. Later that year he took the Parthian capital, Susa, and deposed the Parthian King Osroes I. However, the Romans did not Romanize the entire Parthian Empire, leaving Parthamaspates as a puppet king on the throne to rule over former Parthian lands with the exclusion of modern Iraq, which became Assyria and Mesopotamia.

Southern borders

At its greatest extent, the southern borders were the deserts of Arabia and the Sahara, that represented a natural barrier to prevent expansion. The Empire controlled the Mediterranean shores and the mountains opposite. However the Romans attempted twice to occupy effectively the Siwa Oasis (and failed) and controlled the Nile many miles into Africa until the 1st Cataract near the modern border between Egypt and Sudan.

For *Mauretania* there was a single wall with forts on both sides of it. In other places, such as *Syria* and *Arabia Petraea*, there was instead a network of border settlements and forts occupied by the Roman army.

- Limes Arabicus, (called the *Limes Uranus*) was the frontier of the Roman province of Arabia Petraea facing the desert.
- Limes Tripolitanus was the frontier in modern Libya facing the Sahara.

Western borders

The western borders were mainly protected by the Atlantic coast and unfortified.

References

<templatestyles src="Template:Refbegin/styles.css" />

- *Nuovo Atlante Storico De Agostini*, by "Instituto Geografico De Agostini", ISBN 88-415-4230-6 Novara 1995.
- *Corso di storia antica e medievale 1* (seconda edizione) by Augusto Camer and Renato Fabietti ISBN 88-08-24230-7

External links

- Official website of the *Verein Deutsche Limes-Straße* (in German)[1174]
- Limes Tripolitanus[1175]

Appendix

References

[1] //en.wikipedia.org/w/index.php?title=Template:Ancient_Rome_military_sidebar&action=edit
[2] "History of Rome", Book 1.4.
[3] Williamson, G. (tr.), Josephus, *The Jewish War*, 1959, p. 378
[4] Estimates range wildly because census data was imprecise and there is some disagreement over how many federated tribes had settled permanently in Roman lands during the Mid to late Empire.
[5] Gibbon E., *The Decline and Fall of the Roman Empire*, Penguin, 1985, para. 65
[6] Santosuosso, p. 188
[7] Heather, P., *The Fall of the Roman Empire*, Macmillan, 2005, p. 6
[8] Heather, P., *The Fall of the Roman Empire*, Macmillan, 2005, p.6
[9] Heather, P., *The Fall of the Roman Empire*, Macmillan, 2005, p. 64
[10] Caesar is said to have spent "huge portions of the wealth he accumulated in his victorious wars... on celebrating Triumphs... [and] on erecting magnificent buildings". Grant, p. 194
[11] Gibbon, p. 199
[12] Santosuosso, p. 214
[13] Jones, p. 1041
[14] Heather, p. 297
[15] Hadas, M, et al., *Imperial Rome*, in *Great Ages of man: A History of the World's Cultures*, New York, Time-Life Books, 1965
[16] Jones, AHM, *The Later Roman Empire 284-602*, Johns Hopkins University Press, 1964, p.1035
[17] Including the millions of citizens of Rome
[18] Edward Gibbon relates that "the fertile... province of Campania...was [w]ithin sixty years of the death of Constantine... granted [an exemption from tax amounting to] three hundred and fifty thousand... acres of desert and uncultivated land" - Gibbon, p. 376
[19] Santosuosso A., *Soldiers, Emperors and Citizens in the Roman Empire*, Westview, 2001, p. 214
[20] Grant, M., *The History of Rome*, Fabre and Faber, 1993, p. 287
[21] Heather, P., *The Fall of the Roman Empire*, Macmillan, 2005, p. 29
[22] Luttwak, p. 80
[23] Luttwak notes that Roman troops could march roughly 15 miles per day over long distances, while ships could carry them far more economically and at speeds of 27-81 miles per day. - Luttwak, p. 81
[24] Heather, P., *The Fall of the Roman Empire*, Macmillan, 2005, p. 55
[25] Heather, P., *The Fall of the Roman Empire*, Macmillan, 2005, p. 7
[26] Fan Ye, *Xiyu chuan* ("Chapter on the Western Regions"), in *Hou Han shu* (Official history of the Later Han Dynasty), ch. 88.
[27] Luttwak, p. 1
[28] Sims, Lesley: "The Roman Soldier's Handbook", page 17. Published, 2005.
[29] Sims, Lesley: "The Roman Soldier's Handbook", page 38-31. Published, 2005.
[30] Elton, Hugh, 1996, *Warfare in Roman Europe, AD 350-425*, p. 110
[31] In Luttwack, E., *The Grand Strategy of the Roman Empire*, JHUP, 1979, Luttwack states that "Roman weapons, far from being universally more advanced, were frequently inferior to those used by... enemies
[32] //tools.wmflabs.org/ftl/cgi-bin/ftl?st=wp&su=Military+of+ancient+Rome&library=OLBP
[33] //tools.wmflabs.org/ftl/cgi-bin/ftl?st=wp&su=Military+of+ancient+Rome
[34] //tools.wmflabs.org/ftl/cgi-bin/ftl?st=wp&su=Military+of+ancient+Rome&library=0CHOOSE0
[35] http://penelope.uchicago.edu/Thayer/E/Roman/Texts/Polybius/home.html
[36] http://www.gutenberg.org/etext/731
[37] http://www.sheffield.ac.uk/content/1/c6/09/70/25/roman-soldiers.jpg
[38] //en.wikipedia.org/w/index.php?title=Template:Ancient_Rome_military_sidebar&action=edit

[39] *Encyclopædia Britannica*, Eleventh Edition (1911), *The Roman Army*
[40] Goldsworthy, *In the Name of Rome*, p. 18
[41] Mommsen, *The History of Rome*, Volume 1, p. 40
[42] Keppie, *The Making of the Roman Army*, p. 14
[43] Mommsen, *The History of Rome*, Volume 1, p. 22
[44] Grant, *The History of Rome*, p. 22
  * Boak, *A History of Rome to 565 AD*, p. 69
[45] Mommsen, *The History of Rome*, Volume 1, p. 20
[46] Boak, *A History of Rome to 565 AD*, p. 69
[47] Boak, *A History of Rome to 565 AD*, p. 86
[48] Mommsen, *The History of Rome*, Volume 1, p. 65
[49] Livy, *The Rise of Rome*, Book 5, chapter 33
  * Pallottino, *The Etruscans*, p. 68
[50] Livy, *The Rise of Rome*, Book 1, chapter 42
[51] Livy, *The Rise of Rome*, Book 1, chapter 43
[52] Smith, *Service in the Post-Marian Roman Army*, p. 10
[53] Gabba, *Republican Rome, The Army And the Allies*, p. 2
[54] Grant, *The History of Rome*, p. 334
  * Boak, *A History of Rome*, p. 454
[55] Campbell, *The Crisis of Empire*, p. 126
  * Boak, *A History of Rome*, p. 454
[56] Vogt, *The Decline of Rome*, p. 158
[57] Gabba, *Republican Rome, The Army And the Allies*, p. 5
[58] Grant, *The History of Rome*, p. 24
[59] Cornell (1995) 182
[60] Livy
[61] Grant, *The History of Rome*, Faber and Faber, 1979 p. 54
[62] Rome, The Samnite Wars http://history-world.org/samnite_wars.htm
[63] Sekunda, *Early Roman Armies*, p. 40
[64] Boak, *A History of Rome to 565 A.D.*, p. 87
[65] Santosuosso, *Storming the Heavens*, p. 10
[66] Santosuosso, *Storming the Heavens*, p. 18
[67] Polybius, *History*, Book 6
[68] From Maniple to Cohort http://www.strategypage.com/articles/default.asp?target=marius/manipletocohort, Strategy Page
[69] Luttwak, *The Grand Strategy of the Roman Empire*, p. 40
[70] Livy, *The Rise of Rome*, Book 5, ch. 1
[71] Webster, *The Roman Imperial Army*, p. 156
[72] Smith, *Service in the Post-Marian Roman Army*, p. 2
[73] Gabba, *Republican Rome, The Army and The Allies*, p. 7
[74] Gabba, *Republican Rome, The Army and The Allies*, p. 9
[75] Santosuosso, *Storming the Heavens*, p. 11
[76] Webster, *The Roman Imperial Army*, p. 143
[77] Boak, *A History of Rome to 565 A.D.*, p. 189
  * Santosuosso, *Storming the Heavens*, p. 10
[78] Gabba, *Republican Rome, The Army And the Allies*, p. 1
[79] Cary & Scullard, *A History of Rome*, p. 219
[80] Luttwak, *The Grand Strategy of the Roman Empire*, p. 27
[81] Santosuosso, *Storming the Heavens*, p. 16
[82] Tacitus, *Annals*, IV, 5
[83] Luttwak, *The Grand Strategy of the Roman Empire*, p. 16
[84] Santosuosso, *Storming the Heavens*, p. 29
[85] Santosuosso, *Storming the Heavens*, p. 51
[86] Smith, *Service in the Post-Marian Roman Army*, p. 56
[87] Gabba, *Republican Rome, The Army and The Allies*, p. 25
[88] Boak, *A History of Rome*, p. 189

[89] Smith, *Service in the Post-Marian Roman Army*, p. 29
[90] Luttwak, *The Grand Strategy of the Roman Empire*, p. 14
[91] Webster, *The Roman Imperial Army*, p. 116
[92] Luttwak, *The Grand Strategy of the Roman Empire*, p. 15
[93] Smith, *Service in the Post-Marian Roman Army*, p. 27
[94] Webster, *The Roman Imperial Army*, p. 146
[95] Luttwak, *The Grand Strategy of the Roman Empire*, p. 43
[96] Luttwak, *The Grand Strategy of the Roman Empire*, p. 44
[97] Santosuosso, *Storming the Heavens*, p. 67
[98] Smith, *Service in the Post-Marian Roman Army*, p. 57
[99] Smith, *Service in the Post-Marian Roman Army*, p. 71
[100] Boak, *A History of Rome to 565 A.D.*, p. 270
  * Smith, *Service in the Post-Marian Roman Army*, p. 71
[101] Luttwak, *The Grand Strategy of the Roman Empire*, p. 17
  * Grant, *A History of Rome*, p. 209
[102] Santosuosso, *Storming the Heavens*, p. 91
[103] Hassall, *The Army*, p. 325
  * Santosuosso, *Storming the Heavens*, p. 91
[104] Santosuosso, Storming the Heavens, p. 98
[105] Cary & Scullard, *A History of Rome*, p. 338
[106] Gibbon, *The Decline and Fall of the Roman Empire*, Chapter I, p. 36
[107] Mattingly, *An Imperial Possession - Britain in the Roman Empire*, pp. 166–8
[108] Webster, *The Roman Imperial Army*, p. 144
[109] Webster, *The Roman Imperial Army*, p. 152
[110] Webster, *The Roman Imperial Army*, p. 150
[111] Webster, *The Roman Imperial Army*, p. 147
[112] Webster, *The Roman Imperial Army*, p. 165
[113] Hassall, *The High Empire, AD 70–192*, p. 320
[114] Hassall, *The High Empire, AD 70–192*, p. 331
[115] Hassall, *The High Empire, AD 70–192*, p. 331
  * Gibbon, *The Decline and Fall of the Roman Empire*, Chapter I, p. 36
[116] Alfoldi, *The Crisis of the Empire*, p. 211
[117] Luttwak, *The Grand Strategy of the Roman Empire*, p. 124
[118] Luttwak, *The Grand Strategy of the Roman Empire*, pp. 153–154
[119] Alfoldi, *The Crisis of the Empire*, p. 208
[120] Vogt, *The Decline of Rome*, p. 58.
[121] Santosuosso, *Storming the Heavens*, p. 173
[122] Tacitus, *History*, 4, 64
[123] Santosuosso, *Storming the Heavens*, p. 174
[124] Santosuosso, *Storming the Heavens*, p. 175
[125] Luttwak, *The Grand Strategy of the Roman Empire*, p. 122
[126] Luttwak, *The Grand Strategy of the Roman Empire*, p. 123
[127] Alfoldi, *The Crisis of the Empire*, p. 216
[128] Luttwak, *The Grand Strategy of the Roman Empire*, p. 176
[129] Alfoldi, *The Crisis of the Empire*, p. 211
  * Heather, *The Fall of the Roman Empire*, pp. 58–67
[130] Elton, *Warfare in Roman Europe*, p. 94
  Santosuosso, *Storming The Heavens*, p. 190
[131] Southern and Dixon, *The Late Roman Army*, pp. 11–12
[132] Treadgold, *Byzantium and its Army, 284–1081*, p. 56.
[133] Alfoldi, *The Crisis of the Empire*, p. 212
[134] Alfoldi, *The Crisis of the Empire*, p. 219
[135] Vogt, *The Decline of Rome*, p. 178
[136] Treadgold 1995, p. 161.
[137] Strobel 2011, p. 268.
[138] Southern & Dixon, 1996, p. 57.

[139] Treadgold 1995, pp. 97–98.
[140] Southern & Dixon, 1996, p. 36.
[141] Luttwak, *The Grand Strategy of the Roman Empire*, p. 173
[142] Boak, *A History of Rome to 565 AD*. p. 452
  * Vogt, *The Decline of Rome*, p. 177
[143] Vogt, *The Decline of Rome*, p. 177
[144] Campbell, *The Army*, p. 121
[145] Boak, *A History of Rome to 565 AD*. p. 452
  * Grant, *A History of Rome*, p. 333
  * Santosuosso, *Storming the Heavens*, p. 188
[146] Luttwak, *The Grand Strategy of the Roman Empire*, pp. 154, 173
[147] Cary & Scullard, *A History of Rome*, p. 534
[148] Boak, *A History of Rome to 565 AD*. p. 451
[149] Elton, *Warfare in Roman Europe, A.D. 350–425*, pp. 103, 105–106
  * Treadgold, *Byzantium and its Army*, pp. 44–59.
[150] Southern & Dixon, *The Late Roman Army*, pp. 15–38.
[151] Campbell, *The Army*, p. 121
  * Southern & Dixon, *The Late Roman Army*, pp. 11–17
[152] Southern & Dixon, *The Late Roman Army*, pp. 15–20 & 37–38
[153] Boak, *A History of Rome to 565 AD*. p. 451
  * Cary & Scullard, *A History of Rome*, p. 537
  * Vogt, *The Decline of Rome*, p. 25
[154] Gibbon, *The Decline and Fall of the Roman Empire*, Chapter XXXVIII, p. 622
  * Grant, A History of Rome, p. 333
  * Santosuosso, *Storming the Heavens*, p. 229
[155] Vogt, *The Decline of Rome*, p. 59
[156] Alfoldi, *The Crisis of the Empire*, p. 208
  * Boak, *A History of Rome to 565 AD*, p. 451
  * Vogt, *The Decline of Rome*, p. 178
[157] Gibbon, *The Decline and Fall of the Roman Empire*, Chapter VI, p. 188
[158] Luttwak, *The Grand Strategy of the Roman Empire*, p. 171
[159] Boak, *A History of Rome to 565 AD*. p. 453
  * Vogt, *The Decline of Rome*, p. 59
[160] Luttwak, *The Grand Strategy of the Roman Empire*, p. 175
[161] Brian Campbell, *The Crisis of Empire*, p. 123
[162] Cary & Scullard, *A History of Rome*, p. 535
[163] Alfoldi, *The Crisis of the Empire*, p. 209
[164] Alfoldi, *The Crisis of the Empire*, p. 209
  * Luttwak, *The Grand Strategy of the Roman Empire*, p. 175
[165] Alfoldi, *The Crisis of the Empire*, p. 213
[166] Grant, *A History of Rome*, p. 310
[167] Treadgold, *A History of Byzantine State and Society*, 19
[168] Grant, *The History of Rome*, p. 334
[169] Ammianus Marcellinus, *Historiae*, book 31, chapters 3–16.
[170] Santosuosso, *Storming the Heavens*, p. 189
[171] Elton, *Warfare in Roman Europe*, pp. 145–152.
[172] Santosuosso, *Storming the Heavens*, p. 192
[173] Salway. *Roman Britain*, 1981, p 437
[174] Treadgold, *Byzantium and its Army, 284–1081*, pp. 43–59.
[175] Boak, *A History of Rome to 525 AD*, p. 521
[176]
[177] Grant, *A History of Rome*, p. 344
[178] Vogt, *The Decline of Rome*, p. 250
[179] Runciman, *The Fall of Constantinople: 1453*.

[180] Adrian Goldsworthy *The Fall of the West: The Slow Death of the Roman Superpower*, Great Britain, Weidenfeld & Nicolson, paperback edition by Orion Books Ltd, London, 2010. Published in the U.S.A. as *How Rome Fell: Death of a Superpower*.
[181] http://www.thelatinlibrary.com/ammianus.html
[182] http://www.fh-augsburg.de/~harsch/Chronologia/Lspost05/Notitia/not_intr.html
[183] http://penelope.uchicago.edu/Thayer/E/Roman/Texts/Polybius/home.html
[184] http://www.gutenberg.org/etext/731
[185] //en.wikipedia.org/w/index.php?title=Template:Ancient_Rome_military_sidebar&action=edit
[186] The Complete Roman Army, Adrian Goldsworthy Thames & Hudson, 2011
[187] The Roman Army: A Social and Institutional History, Pat Southern, Oxford University Press, 2007
[188] Companion to the Roman Army, Paul Erdkamp, John Wiley & Sons, 31 Mar 2011
[189] Rostovtzeff, Michael. *Rome*. Oxford, England: Oxford University Press, 1960
[190] Vegetius, *The Military Institutions of the Romans* (J. Clark, transl.) Harrisburg Penn.; 1944.
[191] Dando-Collins, Stephen. *Legions of Rome*. New York: St. Martin's Press, 2010.
[192] Southern, Pat. *The Roman Army: A Social and Institutional History*. Oxford, England: Oxford University Press, 2007.
[193] Angold, p. 127
[194] Konstam, p. 141.
[195] W. Treadgold, *A History of the Byzantine State and Society*, 680
[196] https://www.academia.edu/31883463/Augustan_Legionaries
[197] https://www.academia.edu/31575917/Centurion
[198] https://www.academia.edu/31592032/Roman_Warriors_The_Myth_of_the_Military_Machine
[199] https://www.academia.edu/31575918/Head_Hunting_Roman_Cavalry
[200] https://www.academia.edu/31575921/Protecting_the_Emperor_The_Praetorian_Guard
[201] https://www.academia.edu/862755/Did_Diocletian_overhaul_the_Roman_army
[202] https://www.academia.edu/32297118/The_Last_Legion
[203] https://www.imperiumromanum.edu.pl/en/life-of-a-roman-legionary/
[204] //en.wikipedia.org/w/index.php?title=Template:Ancient_Rome_military_sidebar&action=edit
[205] Polybius, *The Histories*, III.39
[206] Some sources call it a civilian award. See the main article.
[207] Polybius, *The Histories*, III.37
[208] *Vita Aureliani*, VII.4.
[209] It is interesting that the soldier in question was a billetee – i.e. not living in one of the Roman Army's permanent cantonments. This suggests that his unit was on detached service – always a recipe for relaxed discipline and undesirable interaction with the civilian population.
[210] *Roman History* 64.3.2
[211] *The Twelve Caesars*, translated by Dennison, (London: Atlantic Books, 2012), p. 207
[212] //en.wikipedia.org/w/index.php?title=Template:Ancient_Rome_military_sidebar&action=edit
[213] http://www.legionx.pl
[214] http://www.livius.org/le-lh/legio/legions.htm
[215] http://www.davros.org/romans/legions.html
[216] https://web.archive.org/web/20080507205724/http://web.utk.edu/~cohprima/
[217] http://bbs.keyhole.com/ubb/ubbthreads.php?ubb=download&Number=977551&filename=Roman%20castra%20from%20Romania.kmz
[218] //en.wikipedia.org/w/index.php?title=Template:Ancient_Rome_military_sidebar&action=edit
[219] Goldsworthy (2000) 44
[220] Goldsworthy (2000) 51
[221] Goldsworthy (2000) 49
[222] Holder (2003) 145
[223] Hassall (2000) 320
[224] Goldsworthy (2000) 74–5
[225] Goldsworthy (2000) 78–9
[226] Goldsworthy (2000) 126
[227] Goldsworthy (2000) 107
[228] Keppie (1996) 372

[229] Keppie (196) 375
[230] Livy *Ab Urbe Condita* XXII.37
[231] G.L. Cheesman, *The Auxilia of the Roman Imperial Army* (Oxford, 1914), 8–9.
[232] Keppie (1996) 373
[233] Keppie (1996) 379
[234] Goldsworthy (2000) 127
[235] Holder (1980) 7
[236] Goldsworthy (2000) 214
[237] Goldsworthy (2003) 27
[238] Holder (1980) 9
[239] Keppie (1996) 382
[240] Holder (1982) 110–3
[241] Tacitus *Annales* IV.5
[242] Goldsworthy (2003) 51
[243] Keppie (1996) 396
[244] Goldsworthy (2000) 119
[245] Holder (1982) 145
[246] Dio LV.29.1
[247] Dio LV.29.2
[248] Dio LV.29.3
[249] Dio LV.29.4
[250] Dio LV.30.1
[251] Dio LV.31.1
[252] Suetonius III.16
[253] Goldsworthy (2003) 64
[254] Dio LV.30.6
[255] Dio LV.30.5
[256] Suetonius III.17
[257] Goldsworthy (2000) 165–6
[258] Keppie (1996) 391
[259] http://www.romanlegions.info *Military Diplomas Online Introduction*
[260] Keppie (1996) 390
[261] Tacitus *Historiae* IV.18
[262] Tacitus *Historiae* IV.12
[263] Birley (2002) 43
[264] Scheidel (2006) 9
[265] Tacitus *Germania* 29.1 and *Historiae* II.28
[266] Dio Cassius LXIX.9.6
[267] Tacitus *Historiae* IV.12
[268] Tacitus *Annales* IV.12
[269] Tacitus *Historiae* IV.13
[270] Tacitus *Historiae* II.5
[271] Tacitus *Historiae* I.64, II.66
[272] Tacitus *Historiae* IV.14
[273] Tacitus *Historiae* IV.13
[274] Tacitus *Historiae* IV.54
[275] Tacitus *Historiae* IV.24, 27
[276] Tacitus *Historiae* IV.15–6
[277] Tacitus *Historiae* IV.16
[278] Tacitus *Historiae* IV.20
[279] Tacitus *Historiae* IV.21, 28
[280] Tacitus *Historiae* IV.33, 66, 67
[281] Tacitus *Historiae*
[282] Tacitus *Historiae* IV.68
[283] Tacitus *Historiae* V
[284] Tacitus *Historiae* V.26

[285] Birley (2002) 44
[286] Tacitus *Agricola* 35-8
[287] *Notitia Dignitatum* Titles IV and V
[288] Mattingly (2006) 132
[289] Roxan (2003); Holder (2006)
[290] Keppie (1996) 394
[291] Mattingly (2006) 168-9
[292] Hassall (2000) 332-4
[293] Goldsworthy (2003) 138
[294] Spaul (2000) 526
[295] Goldsworthy (2000) 152 (map): *Legiones* II and III Italica under Marcus Aurelius (r. 161-80) and I, II and III Parthica under Septimius Severus (r. 197-211).
[296] 25 legions of 5,000 men each
[297] 28 legions of 5,500 each (double-strength 1st cohorts introduced under Domitian (r. 81-96)
[298] Goldsworthy (2000) 152 (map): 33 legions of 5,500 each
[299] Tacitus *Annales* IV.5
[300] Holder (2003) 120
[301] J. C. Spaul *ALA* (1996) 257-60 and *COHORS* 2 (2000) 523-7 identify 4 *alae* and 20-30 *cohortes* raised in the late 2nd/early 3rd centuries
[302] Goldsworthy (2003) 58: 9 cohorts of 480 men each plus German bodyguards
[303] Rankov (1994) 8
[304] Implied by Tacitus *Annales*
[305] Hassall (2000) 320 estimates 380,000
[306] MacMullen *How Big was the Roman Army?* in *KLIO* (1979) 454 estimates 438,000
[307] Assuming 33% drop in nos. due to war/disease
[308] John Lydus *De Mensibus* I.47
[309] Holder (2006) 985; Roxan (2003) 672
[310] Campbell (2005) 212
[311] The Roman Law Library *Constitutio Antoniniana de Civitate*
[312] Goldsworthy (2003) 74
[313] Elton (1996) 148-52
[314] Goldsworthy (2000) 162
[315] D. Ch. Stathakopoulos *Famine and Pestilence in the late Roman and early Byzantine Empire* (2007) 95
[316] Zosimus *New History* 26, 37, 46
[317] MacMullen (1979) 455
[318] Lee (1997) 223
[319] http://www.roman-britain.org list of alae
[320] Dio LXXI
[321] Jones (1964) 620
[322] Goldsworthy (2003) 206
[323] Jones (1964) 610
[324] *Notitia Dignitatum* passim
[325] Goldsworthy (2000) 174
[326] Vegetius III.3
[327] Birley (2002) 46
[328] Arrian *Ars Tactica* 17.3
[329] Hassall (2000) 339
[330] Goldsworthy (2003) 136
[331] Goldsworthy (2003), pp. 52-53
[332] Goldsworthy (2000), p. 52
[333]
[334] Goldsworthy (2003), p. 168
[335] Cheesman (1914)
[336] Davies (1988), pp. 141-143
[337] Goldsworthy (2000), p. 140

[338] Holder (2003), pp. 135, 133
[339] Livy XXXV.12
[340] Rossi (1971), p. 104
[341] Sidnell (2006), p. 172
[342] CAH XII 212
[343] Holder (2003), p. 140
[344] Holder (2003)
[345] Rossi (1971), p. 102
[346]
[347] Mattingly, 2006, 223
[348] Holder, *The Roman Army in Britain* Batsford, 1982.
[349] Dando-Collins, *The Legions of Rome*, pp40, Quercus (2010).
[350] Grant (1985), p. 72
[351] Rossi (1971), p. 104.
[352] Dio Cassius LXXI.16
[353] Starr, *Imperial Roman Navy, 31BC-AD324* Westport, 1975.
[354] Gardiner 2000, p. 80
[355] Morris, *Londinium*, pp44, Book Club Associates, 1982
[356] Based on data in Goldsworthy (2003) 95–5; Holder (1980) 86–96; Elton (1996) 123
[357] Davies (1988) 148
[358] Goldsworthy (2003) 78, 80
[359] Holder (1980) 123
[360] Goldsworthy (2003) 76
[361] Holder (1980) 138
[362] Military Diplomas Online *Introduction*
[363] RMD Vol V Appendix 4 e.g. RMD 127, 128
[364] Mattingly (2006) 190
[365] Holder (1980) 86–8
[366] Heather (2005) 119
[367] Mattingly (2006) 223
[368] http://www.roman-britain.org *List of auxiliary units in Britain*
[369] Goldsworthy (2003) 94
[370] Hassall (2000) 336
[371] Goldsworthy (2003) 95
[372] Based on figs in Goldsworthy (2003) 94; Duncan-Jones (1994) 33–41
[373] Duncan-Jones (1994) 34
[374] Jones (1964) 647
[375] Goldsworthy (2003) 96
[376] Duncan-Jones (1994) 40
[377] Duncan-Jones (1994) 36
[378] Birley (2002) 47
[379] Birley (2002) 47–8; Vindolanda Tablets Online *Introduction: Personnel*
[380] Goldsworthy (2003) 73
[381] Goldsworthy (2003) 72
[382] Dewijver (1992) 120
[383] Goldsworthy (2003) 65–6
[384] Goldsworthy (2000) 165
[385] Holder (1980) Chapter 2
[386] Goldsworthy (2003) 97
[387] Auxiliary unit figures from Holder (2003) 145
[388] Goldsworthy (2000)
[389] http://www.romancoins.info/MilitaryDiploma.html
[390] http://www.romanarmy.net/Auxilia.htm
[391] http://www.roman-britain.org/military/british_cohortes.htm
[392] http://vindolanda.csad.ox.ac.uk
[393] //en.wikipedia.org/w/index.php?title=Template:Ancient_Rome_military_sidebar&action=edit

[394] command of the war against Mithridates VI of Pontus
[395] defeated the Seleucid ruler Antiochus the Great at the Battle of Thermopylae
[396] Battle of Lake Regillus, Roman victory over the Latin League
[397] Roman Senate voted him a naval triumph
[398] entrusted with the defence of Illyricum against the Pompeians
[399] ordered to clear the Mediterranean Sea of piracy, but instead, plundered the provinces he was supposed to protect
[400] first to lead an army outside of the Italian mainland
[401] defeated and captured at the Battle of Tunis
[402] fought and defeated Gaius Scribonius Curio
[403] one of the so-called Thirty Tyrants
[404] twice defeated Andriscus, self-proclaimed pretender to Macedonian throne
[405] defeated the Lusitanians at Ilipa, and subjugated the Boii
[406] hero of the Samnite Wars
[407] instigated his "Fabian strategy" against Hannibal
[408] successful campaign to restore Ptolemy XII of Egypt
[409] led the Roman conquest of Britain
[410] defeated the Sclaveni Slavs near Thessalonica
[411] defeated the rebellion of Boudica
[412] led Roman Army in the Second Macedonian War
[413] defeated the Bessi in Thrace
[414] defeated successively the Gauls, the Volscians, the Samnites, the Etruscans and the Marsians
[415] next Roman general to cross the Rhine after Julius Caesar
[416] //en.wikipedia.org/w/index.php?title=Template:Ancient_Rome_military_sidebar&action=edit
[417] Map of the Roman Fleet http://www2.rgzm.de/Navis/Themes/Flotte/Karten/Image/RoemFlotte.jpg
[418] Livy, *AUC* IX.30; XL.18,26; XLI.1
[419] Goldsworthy (2003), p. 34
[420] Goldsworthy (2000), p. 97
[421] Polybius, *The Histories* http://penelope.uchicago.edu/Thayer/E/Roman/Texts/Polybius/home.html, I.20-21
[422] Webster & Elton (1998), p. 166
[423] Goldsworthy (2003), p. 38
[424] Gruen (1984), p. 359.
[425] D.B. Saddington (2011) [2007]. " the Evolution of the Roman Imperial Fleets https//books.google.co.uk," in Paul Erdkamp (ed), *A Companion to the Roman Army*, 201-217. Malden, Oxford, Chichester: Wiley-Blackwell. Plate 12.2 on p. 204.
[426] Coarelli, Filippo (1987), *I Santuari del Lazio in età repubblicana*. NIS, Rome, pp 35-84.
[427] Connolly (1998), p. 273
[428] Appian, *The Mithridatic Wars*, §92 http://www.livius.org/ap-ark/appian/appian_mithridatic_19.html#§92
[429] Starr (1989), p. 62
[430] Cassius Dio, *Historia Romana*, XXXVI.22 http://penelope.uchicago.edu/Thayer/E/Roman/Texts/Cassius_Dio/36*.html#22
[431] Plutarch, *Life of Pompey*, §24 http://penelope.uchicago.edu/Thayer/E/Roman/Texts/Plutarch/Lives/Pompey*.html#24
[432] Appian, *The Mithridatic Wars*, §93 http://www.livius.org/ap-ark/appian/appian_mithridatic_19.html#§93
[433] Goldsworthy (2007), p. 186
[434] Appian, *The Mithridatic Wars*, §94 http://www.livius.org/ap-ark/appian/appian_mithridatic_19.html#§94
[435] Appian, *The Mithridatic Wars*, §95 http://www.livius.org/ap-ark/appian/appian_mithridatic_19.html#§95- §96 http://www.livius.org/ap-ark/appian/appian_mithridatic_20.html#§96
[436] Caesar, *Commentaries on the Gallic Wars, III.9*
[437] Caesar, *Commentaries on the Gallic Wars, III.13*
[438] Caesar, *Commentaries on the Gallic Wars, III.14*

[439] Caesar, *Commentaries on the Gallic Wars*, III.15
[440] Tacitus, *The Annals* II.6
[441] *Res Gestae* http://penelope.uchicago.edu/Thayer/E/Roman/Texts/Augustus/Res_Gestae/home.html, 26.4
[442] Webster & Elton (1998), pp. 160-161
[443] Webster & Elton (1998), p. 161
[444] Tacitus, *The Histories*, II.12
[445] Tacitus, *The Histories*, II.67
[446] Webster & Elton (1998), p. 164
[447] Tacitus, *The Histories*, IV.16
[448] Tacitus, *The Histories*, IV.79
[449] Tacitus, *The Histories*, V.23-25
[450] Tacitus, *Agricola*, 25; 29
[451] Tacitus, *Agricola*, 10
[452] Tacitus, *Agricola*, 24
[453] Lewis & Runyan (1985), p. 3
[454] Lewis & Runyan (1985), p. 4
[455] Casson (1991), p. 213
[456] *Scriptores Historiae Augustae, Vita Gallienii*, 13.6-7 http://penelope.uchicago.edu/Thayer/E/Roman/Texts/Historia_Augusta/Gallieni_duo*.html#13.6
[457] *Scriptores Historiae Augustae, Vita Gallienii*, 13.8-9 http://penelope.uchicago.edu/Thayer/E/Roman/Texts/Historia_Augusta/Gallieni_duo*.html#13.8
[458] *Scriptores Historiae Augustae, Vita Divi Claudii*, 6.2-4 http://penelope.uchicago.edu/Thayer/E/Roman/Texts/Historia_Augusta/Claudius*.html#6.2; 8.1 http://penelope.uchicago.edu/Thayer/E/Roman/Texts/Historia_Augusta/Claudius*.html#8.1
[459] Zosimus, *Historia Nova*, I.42-45
[460] Eutropius, *Breviarium*, IX.21 http://www.forumromanum.org/literature/eutropius/trans9.html#21
[461] *Panegyrici Latini*, 8.6
[462] *Panegyrici Latini*, 8.12
[463] *Panegyrici Latini*, 6.5; 8.6-8
[464] Eutropius, *Breviarium* 9.22 http://www.forumromanum.org/literature/eutropius/trans9.html#22; Aurelius Victor, *Book of Caesars* 39.42 http://www.thelatinlibrary.com/victor.caes.html#39
[465] Treadgold (1997), p. 145
[466] MacGeorge (2002), pp. 306-307
[467] Lewis & Runyan (1985), pp. 4-8
[468] MacGeorge (2002), p. 307
[469] Casson (1991), p. 188
[470] Starr (1960), p. 75 Table 1
[471] Starr (1960), p. 39
[472] Webster & Elton (1998), pp. 165-166
[473] Starr (1960), pp. 42-43
[474] Wesch-Klein (1998), p. 25
[475] Rodgers (1976), p. 60
[476] Livy, *AUC* XXVI.48; XXXVI.42
[477] Webster & Elton (1998), p. 165
[478]
[479] Pflaum, H.G. (1950). *Les procurateurs équestres sous le Haut-Empire romain*, pp. 50-53 http://www.csun.edu/~hcfll004/equesproc.html
[480] Cassius Dio, *Historia Romana*, L.23.2
[481] Plutarch, *Antony*, 62
[482] Vegetius, *De Re Militari*, IV.33 http://www.thelatinlibrary.com/vegetius4.html
[483] Casson (1995), p. 141
[484] Casson (1995), pp. 357–358; Casson (1991), pp. 190–191
[485] Warry (2004), p. 183

[486] Warry (2004), p. 98
[487] Warry (2004), p. 118
[488] Appian, *The Civil Wars*, V.106 http://penelope.uchicago.edu/Thayer/E/Roman/Texts/Appian/Civil_Wars/5*.html#106 & V.118 http://penelope.uchicago.edu/Thayer/E/Roman/Texts/Appian/Civil_Wars/5*.html#118
[489] Warry (2004), pp. 182–183
[490] Tacitus, *The Annals*, IV.5; Strabo, *Geography*, IV.1.9 http://penelope.uchicago.edu/Thayer/E/Roman/Texts/Strabo/4A*.html
[491] Webster & Elton (1998), p. 158
[492] *Scriptores Historiae Augustae, Vita Commodi*, 17.7 http://penelope.uchicago.edu/Thayer/E/Roman/Texts/Historia_Augusta/Commodus*.html#17
[493] Webster & Elton (1998), p. 159
[494] Cleere (1977), pp. 16; 18-19
[495] Cleere (1977), p. 19
[496] Cleere (1977), p. 16
[497] Webster & Elton (1998), p. 160
[498] Köln-Alteburg http://www.livius.org/cn-cs/cologne/alteburg.html at *livius.org*
[499] Webster & Elton (1998), p. 162
[500] Webster & Elton (1998), pp. 162-165
[501] Webster & Elton (1998), p. 163
[502] Starr (1989), p. 76
[503] Tacitus, *The Histories*, II.83; III.47
[504] Starr (1989), p. 77
[505] Josephus, *The Jewish War*, II.16.4
[506] Codex Theodosianus, X.23.1
[507] *Römisch-Germanisches Zentralmuseum Mainz*: The Fleets and Roman Border Policy http://www2.rgzm.de/Navis/Themes/Flotte/FleetsAndBorder.htm
[508] Pauly-Wissowa, XXII.1300–1301
[509] *Notitia Dignitatum, Pars Occ.*, XXXII. http://www.intratext.com/IXT/LAT0212/_PU.HTM
[510] *Notitia Dignitatum, Pars Occ.*, XXXIII. http://www.intratext.com/IXT/LAT0212/_PV.HTM
[511] *Notitia Dignitatum, Pars Occ.*, XXXIV. http://www.intratext.com/IXT/LAT0212/_PW.HTM
[512] *Notitia Dignitatum, Pars Orient.*, XLI. http://www.intratext.com/IXT/LAT0212/_P26.HTM
[513] *Notitia Dignitatum, Pars Orient.*, XLII. http://www.intratext.com/IXT/LAT0212/_P27.HTM
[514] *Notitia Dignitatum, Pars Orient.*, XL. http://www.intratext.com/IXT/LAT0212/_P25.HTM
[515] *musculus* (meaning "small mouse") was a kind of small ship
[516] *Notitia Dignitatum, Pars Orient.*, XXXIX. http://www.intratext.com/IXT/LAT0212/_P24.HTM
[517] *Notitia Dignitatum, Pars Occ.*, XLII. http://www.intratext.com/IXT/LAT0212/_P13.HTM
[518] Pauly-Wissowa, III.2639 & XXII.1300
[519] *Notitia Dignitatum, Pars Occ.*, XXXVIII. http://www.intratext.com/IXT/LAT0212/_P10.HTM
[520] Lewis & Runyan (1985), p. 6
[521] *Classis Britannica* http://www.roman-britain.org/military/classis.htm#CILxii686 at RomanBritain.org
[522] Pauly-Wissowa, III.2645–2646 & XXII.1300
[523] *Codex Justinianus*, XI.2.4 http://webu2.upmf-grenoble.fr/Haiti/Cours/Ak/Corpus/CJ11.htm#2
[524] *Codex Justinianus*, XI.13.1 http://webu2.upmf-grenoble.fr/Haiti/Cours/Ak/Corpus/CJ11.htm#13
[525] Codex Theodosianus, XIII.5.32
[526] https://books.google.com/?id=4Ls6MczXvBEC
[527] http://ads.ahds.ac.uk/catalogue/adsdata/cbaresrep/pdf/018/01804001.pdf
[528] https://books.google.com/?id=V5TZSAVLIMcC
[529] http://digilander.libero.it/agenziagiornalisti/
[530] http://www.classis-britannica.co.uk/sml/index.htm
[531] http://www.roman-empire.net/army/leg-fleet.html
[532] http://www.historynet.com/the-roman-navy-masters-of-the-mediterranean.htm
[533] http://www.romaeterna.org/galleria/index.html

[534] http://www.romaeterna.org/navigare.html
[535] http://www2.rgzm.de/navis/Musea/Ostia/Fiumicino_English.htm
[536] https://web.archive.org/web/20050831002501/http://nemiship.multiservers.com/
[537] http://www2.rgzm.de/Navis/Themes/Flotte/FleetsAndBorder.htm
[538] http://terraromana.org/navis/Forum/index.php
[539] //en.wikipedia.org/w/index.php?title=Template:Ancient_Rome_military_sidebar&action=edit
[540] Trigger, *Understanding Early Civilizations*, p. 240
[541] Luttwak, *The Grand Strategy of the Roman Empire*, p. 38
[542] Goldsmith, *An Estimate of the Size and Structure of the National Product of the Early Roman Empire*, p. 263
[543] Johnson, *The Dream of Rome*, p. 8
[544] Goldsworthy, *In the Name of Rome*, p. 15
[545] Goldsworthy, *In the Name of Rome*, p. 31
[546] Goldsworthy, *The Punic Wars*, p. 96
[547] Pennell, *Ancient Rome*, first page of Chapter III.
[548] Grant, *The History of Rome*, p. 23
[549] Pennell, *Ancient Rome*, Ch. IX, para. 3
[550] Ronald Syme, following G. M. Hirst, has argued for 64 BC–12 AD. For a presentation on the dates see Livy.
[551] Florus, *Epitome of Roman History*, Book 1, ch. 1
[552] Florus, *Epitome of Roman History*, Book 1, ch. 2
[553] Cassius Dio, *The Roman History*, Vol. 1, VII, 6
[554] Florus, *Epitome of Roman History*, Book 1, ch. 3
[555] Florus, *Epitome of Roman History*, Book 1, ch. 4
[556] Pennell, *Ancient Rome*, Ch. V, para. 1
[557] Grant, *The History of Rome*, p. 21
[558] Livy, *The Rise of Rome*, p. 13
[559] Livy, *The Rise of Rome*, p. 3
[560] Cassius Dio, *The Roman History*, Vol. 1, VII, 9; Livy, *Ab urbe condita*, 1:10–13
[561] Livy, *Ab urbe condita*, 1:35
[562] "The Cholas"" University of Madras"K. A. Nilakanta Sastri
[563] Livy, *Ab urbe condita*, 1:38
[564] Livy, *Ab urbe condita*, 1.42
[565] Livy, *Ab urbe condita*, 1.50–52
[566] *Fasti Triumphales*
[567] Livy *Ab urbe condita* 1.53–55
[568] Livy *Ab urbe condita* 1.55
[569] Livy, *Ab urbe condita*, 1.57
[570] Livy, *Ab urbe condita*, 1.57–60
[571] Grant, *The History of Rome*, p. 33
[572] Grant, *The History of Rome*, p. 32
[573] Livy, *Ab urbe condita*, 2.6–7
[574]
[575] Livy, *Ab urbe condita*, 2.9–13
[576] Florus, *The Epitome of Roman History*, Book 1, ch. 11
[577] Grant, *The History of Rome*, p. 38
[578] Grant, *The History of Rome*, p. 37
[579] Livy, *The Rise of Rome*, p. 89
[580] Grant, *The History of Rome*, p. 41
[581] Florus, *The Epitome of Roman History*, Book 1, ch. 12
[582] Cassius Dio, *The Roman History*, Vol. 1, VII, 17
[583] Cassius Dio, *The Roman History*, Vol. 1, VII, 16
[584] *The Enemies of Rome*, p. 13
[585] Livy, *The Rise of Rome*, p. 96
[586] Grant, *The History of Rome*, p. 42
[587] Cassius Dio, *The Roman History*, Vol. 1, VII, 20

[588] Grant, *The History of Rome*, p. 39
[589] Pennell, *Ancient Rome*, Ch. II
[590] Grant, *The History of Rome*, p. 44
[591] Florus, *The Epitome of Roman History*, Book 1, ch. 13
[592] Pennell, *Ancient Rome*, Ch. IX, para. 2
[593] Livy, *The Rise of Rome*, p. 329
[594] Lane Fox, *The Classical World*, p. 283
[595] Livy, *The Rise of Rome*, p. 330
[596] Appian, *History of Rome*, The Gallic Wars, §1
[597] Pennell, *Ancient Rome*, Ch. IX, para. 4
[598] Pennell, *Ancient Rome*, Ch. IX, para. 23
[599] Florus, *The Epitome of Roman history*, Book 1, ch. 16
[600] Lane Fox, *The Classical World*, p. 282
[601] Pennell, *Ancient Rome*, Ch. IX, para. 8
[602] Grant, *The History of Rome*, p. 48
[603] Pennell, *Ancient Rome*, Ch. IX, para. 13
[604] Grant, *The History of Rome*, p. 49
[605] Pennell, *Ancient Rome*, Ch. IX, para. 14
[606] Grant, *The History of Rome*, p. 52
[607] Lane Fox, *The Classical World*, p. 290
[608] Grant, *The History of Rome*, p. 53
[609] Grant, *The History of Rome*, p. 77
[610] Matyszak, *The Enemies of Rome*, p. 14
[611] Grant, *The History of Rome*, p. 78
[612] Cantor, *Antiquity*, p. 151
[613] Pennell, *Ancient Rome*, Ch. X, para. 6
[614] Florus, *The Epitome of Roman history*, Book 1, ch. 18
[615] Lane Fox, *The Classical World*, p. 304
[616] Lane Fox, *The Classical World*, p. 305
[617] Grant, *The History of Rome*, p. 79
[618] Cassius Dio, *The Roman history*, Vol. 1, VIII, 3
[619] Pennell, *Ancient Rome*, Ch. X, para. 11
[620] Lane Fox, *The Classical World*, p. 306
[621] Lane Fox, *The Classical World*, p. 307
[622] Pennell, *Ancient Rome*, Ch. XI, para. 1
[623] Grant, *The History of Rome*, p. 80
[624] Matyszak, *The Enemies of Rome*, p. 16
[625] Sallust, *The Jugurthine War*, XIX
[626] Cantor, *Antiquity*, p. 152
[627] Goldsworthy, *The Punic Wars*, p. 13
[628] Goldsworthy, *The Punic Wars*, p.68
[629] Cassius Dio, *The Roman History*, Vol. 1, VIII, 8
[630] Pennell, *Ancient Rome*, Ch. XII, para. 14
[631] Lane Fox, *The Classical World*, p. 309
[632] Goldsworthy, *The Punic Wars*, p. 113
[633] Goldsworthy, *The Punic Wars*, p. 84
[634] Goldsworthy, *The Punic Wars*, p. 86
[635] Goldsworthy, *The Punic Wars*, p. 87
[636] Goldsworthy, *The Punic Wars*, p. 88
[637] Lane Fox, *The Classical World*, p. 310
[638] Goldsworthy, *The Punic Wars*, p. 90
[639] Goldsworthy, *The Punic Wars*, p. 128
[640] Florus, *The Epitome of Roman history*, Book 2, ch. 3
[641] Florus, *The Epitome of Roman history*, Book 2, ch. 4
[642] Goldsworthy, *In the Name of Rome*, p. 29
[643] Matyszak, *The Enemies of Rome*, p. 25

[644] Pennell, *Ancient Rome*, Ch. XIII, para. 15
[645] Cantor, *Antiquity*, p. 153
[646] Matyszak, *The Enemies of Rome*, p. 27
[647] Goldsworthy, *In the Name of Rome*, p. 30
[648] Matyszak, *The Enemies of Rome*, p. 29
[649] Matyszak, *The Enemies of Rome*, p. 31
[650] Polybius, *The Histories*, 243
[651] Matyszak, *The Enemies of Rome*, p. 34
[652] Polybius, *The Histories*, 263
[653] Matyszak, *The Enemies of Rome*, p. 36
[654] Matyszak, *The Enemies of Rome*, p. 38
[655] Liddell Hart, *Scipio Africanus*, p. xiii
[656] Matyszak, *The Enemies of Rome*, p. 40
[657] Matyszak, *The Enemies of Rome*, p. 41
[658] Pennell, *Ancient Rome*, Ch. XV, para. 24
[659] Goldsworthy, *The Punic Wars*, p. 338
[660] Goldsworthy, *The Punic Wars*, p. 339
[661] Florus, *The Epitome of Roman history*, Book 2, ch. 15
[662] Cantor, *Antiquity*, p. 154
[663] Goldsworthy, *The Punic Wars*, p. 12
[664] Florus, *The Epitome of Roman history*, Book 2, ch. 17
[665] Grant, *The History of Rome*, p. 122
[666] Pennell, *Ancient Rome*, Ch. XX, para. 2
[667] Matyszak, *The Enemies of Rome*, p. 54
[668] Matyszak, *The Enemies of Rome*, p. 56
[669] Matyszak, *The Enemies of Rome*, p. 57
[670] Pennell, *Ancient Rome*, Ch. XX, para. 4
[671] Matyszak, *The Enemies of Rome*, p. 58
[672] Matyszak, *The Enemies of Rome*, p. 61
[673] Grant, *The History of Rome*, p. 123
[674] Luttwak, *The Grand Strategy of the Roman Empire*, p. 8
[675] Matyszak, *The Enemies of Rome*, p. 47
[676] Grant, *The History of Rome*, p. 115
[677] Grant, *The History of Rome*, p. 116
[678] Matyszak, *The Enemies of Rome*, p. 48
[679] Goldsworthy, *In the Name of Rome*, p. 71
[680] Matyszak, *The Enemies of Rome*, p. 49
[681] Goldsworthy, *In the Name of Rome*, p. 72
[682] Goldsworthy, *In the Name of Rome*, p. 73
[683] Grant, *The History of Rome*, p. 117
[684] Lane Fox, *The Classical World*, p. 325
[685] Matyszak, *The Enemies of Rome*. p. 51
[686] Florus, *The Epitome of Roman history*, Book 2, ch. 9
[687] Florus, *The Epitome of Roman history*, Book 2, ch. 10
[688] Florus, *The Epitome of Roman history*, Book 2, ch. 13
[689] Florus, *The Epitome of Roman history*, Book 2, ch. 16
[690] Pennell, *Ancient Rome*, Ch. XVII, para. 1
[691] Grant, *The History of Rome*, p. 119
[692] Lane Fox, *The Classical World*, p. 326
[693] Grant, *The History of Rome*, p. 120
[694] Goldsworthy, *In the Name of Rome*, p. 75
[695] Goldsworthy, *In the Name of Rome*, p. 92
[696] Lane Fox, *The Classical World*, p. 328
[697] Matyszak, *The Enemies of Rome*, p. 53
[698] Luttwak, *The Grand Strategy of the Roman Empire*, p. 9
[699] Sallust, *The Jugurthine War*, V

[700] Santosuosso, *Storming the Heavens*, p. 29
[701] Sallust, *The Jugurthine War*, XII
[702] Matyszak, *The Enemies of Rome*, p. 64
[703] Matyszak, *The Enemies of Rome*, p. 65
[704] Florus, *The Epitome of Roman history*, Book 3, ch. 1
[705] Sallust, *The Jugurthine War*, XIII
[706] Sallust, *The Jugurthine War*, XVIII
[707] Sallust, *The Jugurthine War*, LII
[708] Matyszak, *The Enemies of Rome*, p. 69
[709] Sallust, *The Jugurthine War*, LXXVI
[710] Sallust, *The Jugurthine War*, XCIV
[711] Sallust, *The Jugurthine War*, CI
[712] Grant, *The History of Rome*, p. 153
[713] Sallust, *The Jugurthine War*, CXIII
[714] Matyszak, *The Enemies of Rome*, p. 71
[715] Grant, *The History of Rome*, p. 152
[716] Appian, *History of Rome*, §6
[717] Matyszak, *The Enemies of Rome*, p. 75
[718] Santosuosso, *Storming the Heavens*, p. 6
[719] Florus, *The Epitome of Roman history*, Book 3, ch. 3
[720] Santosuosso, *Storming the Heavens*, p. 39
[721] Matyszak, *The Enemies of Rome*, p. 77
[722] Appian, Civil Wars, 1, 117
[723] Santosuosso, *Storming the Heavens*, p. 43
[724] Grant, *The History of Rome*, p. 156
[725] Lane Fox, *The Classical World*, p. 351
[726] Cantor, *Antiquity*, p. 167
[727] Santosuosso, *Storming the Heavens*, p. 30
[728] Grant, *The History of Rome*, p. 161
[729] Florus, *The Epitome of Roman history*, Book 3, ch. 5
[730] Matyszak, *The Enemies of Rome*, p. 76
[731] Grant, *The History of Rome*, p. 158
[732] Lane Fox, *The Classical World*, p. 363
[733] Plutarch, *Lives*, Pompey
[734] Grant, *The History of Rome*, p. 165
[735]
[736] Holland, *Rubicon*, p. 170
[737] Cicero, *Pro Lege Manilia*, 12 or De Imperio Cn. Pompei (in favour of the Manilian Law on the command of Pompey), 66 BC.
[738] Plutarch, *Lives*, Caesar
[739] Santosuosso, *Storming the Heavens*, p. 58
[740] Goldsworthy, *In the Name of Rome*, p. 187
[741] Matyszak, *The Enemies of Rome*, p. 117
[742] Goldsworthy, *In the Name of Rome*, p. 191
[743] Florus, *The Epitome of Roman history*, Book 3, ch.10
[744] Cantor, *Antiquity*, p. 162
[745] Santosuosso, *Storming the Heavens*, p. 48
[746] Matyszak, *The Enemies of Rome*, p. 116
[747] Santosuosso, *Storming the Heavens*, p. 59
[748] Goldsworthy, *In the Name of Rome*, p. 201
[749] Santosuosso, *Storming the Heavens*, p. 60
[750] Goldsworthy, *In the Name of Rome*, p. 204
[751] Matyszak, *The Enemies of Rome*, p. 78
[752] Santosuosso, *Storming the Heavens*, p. 62
[753] Goldsworthy, *In the Name of Rome*, p. 212
[754] Cantor, *Antiquity*, p. 168

[755] Matyszak, *The Enemies of Rome*, p. 133
[756] Plutarch, *Lives of the Noble Grecians and Romans*, p. 266
[757] Goldsworthy, *In the Name of Rome*, p. 213
[758] Matyszak, *The Enemies of Rome*, p. 79
[759] Cantor, *Antiquity*, p. 169
[760] Goldsworthy, *In the Name of Rome*, p. 271
[761] Goldsworthy, *In the Name of Rome*, p. 214
[762] Goldsworthy, *In the Name of Rome*, p. 215
[763] Lane Fox, *The Classical World*, p. 398
[764] Holland, *Rubicon*, p. 299
[765] Goldsworthy, *In the Name of Rome*, p. 216
[766] Holland, *Rubicon*, p. 298
[767] Holland, *Rubicon*, p. 303
[768] Lane Fox, *The Classical World*, p. 402
[769] Goldsworthy, *In the Name of Rome*, p. 217
[770] Julius Caesar, *The Civil War*, 81–92
[771] Goldsworthy, *In the Name of Rome*, p. 218
[772] Goldsworthy, *In the Name of Rome*, p. 220
[773] Goldsworthy, *In the Name of Rome*, p. 227
[774] Lane Fox, *The Classical World*, p. 403
[775] Holland, *Rubicon*, p. 312
[776] Lane Fox, *The Classical World*, p. 404
[777] Plutarch, *Life of Crassus*, XXIII–V
[778] Cantor, *Antiquity*, p. 170
[779] Goldsworthy, *In the Name of Rome*, p. 237
[780] Luttwak, *The Grand Strategy of the Roman Empire*, p. 7
[781] Cassius Dio, *The Roman History: The Reign of Augustus*, p. 61
[782] Goldsworthy, *In the Name of Rome*, p. 244
[783] Luttwak, *The Grand Strategy of the Roman Empire*, p. 37
[784] Grant, *The History of Rome*, p. 208
[785] Goldsworthy, *In the Name of Rome*, p. 245
[786] Matyszak, *The Enemies of Rome*, p. 159
[787] Clunn, *In Quest of the Lost Legions*, p. xv
[788] Tacitus, *The Annals*, Book 1, ch. 56
[789] Tacitus, *The Annals*, Book 1, ch. 60
[790] Santosuosso, *Storming the Heavens*, p. 143–144
[791] Goldsworthy, *In the Name of Rome*, p. 248
[792] Goldsworthy, *In the Name of Rome*, p. 260
[793] Churchill, *A History of the English Speaking Peoples*, p. 1
[794] Lane Fox, *The Classical World*, p. 379
[795] Churchill, *A History of the English Speaking Peoples*, p. 4
[796] Churchill, *A History of the English-Speaking Peoples*, p. 5
[797] Tacitus, *Annals* 14.29–39, *Agricola* 14–16
[798] Dio Cassius, *Roman History*, 62.1–12
[799] Churchill, *A History of the English-Speaking Peoples*, p. 6
[800] Churchill, *A History of the English-Speaking Peoples*, p. 7
[801] Welch, *Britannia: The Roman Conquest & Occupation of Britain*, 1963, p. 107
[802] Tacitus, *Annals*, 14.37
[803] Matyszak, *The Enemies of Rome*, p. 189
[804] Fraser, *The Roman Conquest Of Scotland: The Battle Of Mons Graupius AD 84*
[805] Churchill, *A History of the English-Speaking Peoples*, p. 9
[806] Churchill, *A History of the English-Speaking Peoples*, p. 10
[807] Goldsworthy, *In the Name of Rome*, p. 269
[808] Clunn, *In Quest of the Lost Legions*, p. 303
[809] Goldsworthy, *In the Name of Rome*, p. 322
[810] Matyszak, *The Enemies of Rome*, p. 213

[811] Matyszak, *The Enemies of Rome*, p. 215
[812] Matyszak, *The Enemies of Rome*, p. 216
[813] Luttwak, *The Grand Strategy of the Roman Empire*, p. 53
[814] Matyszak, *The Enemies of Rome*, p. 217
[815] Matyszak, *The Enemies of Rome*, p. 219
[816] Luttwak, *The Grand Strategy of the Roman Empire*, p. 54
[817] Goldsworthy, *In the Name of Rome*, p. 329
[818] Matyszak, *The Enemies of Rome*, p. 222
[819] Matyszak, *The Enemies of Rome*, p. 223
[820] Luttwak, *The Grand Strategy of the Roman Empire*, p. 39
[821] Tacitus, *The Annals*, Book 2, ch. 3
[822] Tacitus, *The Histories*, Book 1, ch. 41
[823] Plutarch, *Lives*, Galba
[824] Luttwak, *The Grand Strategy of the Roman Empire*, p. 51
[825] Lane Fox, *The Classical World*, p. 542
[826] Tacitus, *The Histories*, Book 1, ch. 57
[827] Plutarch, *Lives*, Otho
[828] Tacitus, *The Histories*, Book 1, ch. 14–15
[829] Tacitus, *The Histories*, Book 1, ch. 22
[830] Tacitus, *The Histories*, Book 1, ch, 26
[831] Luttwak, *The Grand Strategy of the Roman Empire*, p. 52
[832] Tacitus, *The Histories*, Book 1, ch. 44
[833] Tacitus, *The Histories*, Book 1, ch. 49
[834] Tactitus, *The Histories*, Book 3, ch. 18
[835] Tactitus, *The Histories*, Book 3, ch. 25
[836] Tactitus, *The Histories*, Book 3, ch. 31
[837] Lane Fox, *The Classical World*, p. 543
[838] Goldsworthy, *In the Name of Rome*, p. 294
[839] Matyszak, *The Enemies of Rome*, p. 192
[840] Matyszak, *The Enemies of Rome*, p. 194
[841] Goldsworthy, *In the Name of Rome*, p. 295
[842] Santosuosso, *Storming the Heavens*, p. 146
[843] Luttwak, *The Grand Strategy of the Roman Empire*, p. 3
[844] Goldsworthy, *In the Name of Rome*, p. 292
[845] Grant, *The History of Rome*, p. 273
[846] Grant, *The History of Rome*, p. 279
[847] Luttwak, *The Grand Strategy of the Roman Empire*, p. 128
[848] Luttwak, *The Grand Strategy of the Roman Empire*, p. 146
[849] Grant, *The History of Rome*, p. 282
[850] Luttwak, *The Grand Strategy of the Roman Empire*, p. 150
[851] Luttwak, *The Grand Strategy of the Roman Empire*, p. 147
[852] Jordanes, *The Origins and Deeds of the Goths*, 103
[853] Jordanes, *The Origins and Deeds of the Goths*, 108
[854] Gibbon, *The Decline and Fall of the Roman Empire*, p. 624
[855] Matyszak, *The Enemies of Rome*, p. 270
[856] Grant, *The History of Rome*, p. 322
[857] Jordanes, *The Origins and Deeds of the Goths*, 121
[858] Santosuosso, *Storming the Heavens*, p. 196
[859] Grant, *The History of Rome*, p. 285
[860] Jordanes, *The Origins and Deeds of the Goths*, 110
[861] Goldsworthy, *In the Name of Rome*, p. 344
[862] Goldsworthy, *In the Name of Rome*, p. 345
[863] Ammianus Marcellinus, *Historiae*, book 31.
[864] Jordanes, *The Origins and Deeds of the Goths*, 138.
[865] Gibbon, *The Decline and Fall of the Roman Empire*, p. 534
[866] Grant, *The History of Rome*, p. 284

[867] Luttwak, *The Grand Strategy of the Roman Empire*, p. 149
[868] Grant, *The History of Rome*, p. 280
[869] Matyszak, *The Enemies of Rome*, p. 226
[870] Gibbon, *The Decline and Fall of the Roman Empire*, p. 113
[871] Matyszak, *The Enemies of Rome*, p. 227
[872] Gibbon, *The Decline and Fall of the Roman Empire*, p. 133
[873] Gibbon, *The Decline and Fall of the Roman Empire*, p. 129
[874] Gibbon, *The Decline and Fall of the Roman Empire*, p. 130
[875] Gibbon, *The Decline and Fall of the Roman Empire*, p. 131
[876] Gibbon, *The Decline and Fall of the Roman Empire*, p. 135
[877] Grant, *The History of Rome*, p. 283
[878] Matyszak, *The Enemies of Rome*, p. 234
[879] Luttwak, *The Grand Strategy of the Roman Empire*, p. 151
[880] Matyszak, *The Enemies of Rome*, p. 235
[881] Shapur, *Deeds of the God-Emperor Shapur*
[882] Matyszak, *The Enemies of Rome*, p. 236
[883] Matyszak, *The Enemies of Rome*, p. 237
[884] Goldsworthy, *In the Name of Rome*, p. 358
[885] Procopius, *History of the Wars*, Book 1, Pt 1, Ch. 2
[886] Goldsworthy, *In the Name of Rome*, p. 361
[887] Matyszak, *The Enemies of Rome*, p. 231
[888] Matyszak, *The Enemies of Rome*, p. 285
[889] Jordanes, *The Origins and Deeds of the Goths*, 147
[890] Procopius, *History of the Wars*, Book 3, Pt 1, Ch. 2
[891] Gibbon, *The Decline and Fall of the Roman Empire*, p. 551
[892] Matyszak, *The Enemies of Rome*, p. 260
[893] Gibbon, *The Decline and Fall of the Roman Empire*, p. 563
[894] Jordanes, *The Origins and Deeds of the Goths*, 154
[895] Gibbon, *The Decline and Fall of the Roman Empire*, p. 565
[896] Matyszak, *The Enemies of Rome*, p. 263
[897] Grant, *The History of Rome*, p. 324
[898] Grant, *The History of Rome*, p. 327
[899] Jordanes, *The Origins and Deeds of the Goths*, 156
[900] Matyszak, *The Enemies of Rome*, p. 267
[901] Gibbon, *The Decline and Fall of the Roman Empire*, p. 589
[902] Gibbon, *The Decline and Fall of the Roman Empire*, p. 587
[903] Wood, *In Search of the First Civilizations*, p. 177
[904] Gibbon, *The Decline and Fall of the Roman Empire*, p. 560
[905] Churchill, *A History of the English-Speaking Peoples*, p. 16
[906] Churchill, *A History of the English-Speaking Peoples*, p. 17
[907] Santosuosso, *Storming the Heavens*, p. 187
[908] Jordanes, *History of the Goths*, 207
[909] Matyszak, *The Enemies of Rome*, p. 276
[910] Gibbon, *The Decline and Fall of the Roman Empire*, p. 489
[911] Jordanes, *The Origins and Deeds of the Goths*, 197
[912] Jordanes, *The Origins and Deeds of the Goths*, 222
[913] Gibbon, *The Decline and Fall of the Roman Empire*, ch. 35
[914] Gibbon, *The Decline and Fall of the Roman Empire*, p. 618
[915] Procopius, *History of the Wars*, Book 3, Pt 1, Ch. 4
[916] Jordanes, *The Origins and Deeds of the Goths*, 243
[917] http://penelope.uchicago.edu/Thayer/E/Roman/Texts/Polybius/home.html
[918] http://penelope.uchicago.edu/Thayer/E/Roman/Texts/secondary/BURLAT/home.html
[919] https://web.archive.org/web/20110718205608/http://www.roiw.org/1984/263.pdf
[920] http://www.roiw.org/1984/263.pdf
[921] http://www.gutenberg.org/catalog/world/readfile?fk_files=1226967
[922] https://www.worldcat.org/oclc/676710326

[923] //en.wikipedia.org/w/index.php?title=Template:Ancient_Rome_military_sidebar&action=edit
[924] Bennett, J. *Trajan: Optimus Princeps.* 1997. Fig. 1
[925] http://courses.wcupa.edu/jones/his101/web/t-roman.htm
[926] http://www.roman-emperors.org/battles.htm
[927] https://web.archive.org/web/20070927225625/http://platial.com/panairjdde/map/7743?title=Roman_Battles
[928] //en.wikipedia.org/w/index.php?title=Template:Ancient_Rome_military_sidebar&action=edit
[929] John W. Humphrey, John P. Oleson and Andrew N. Sherwood; *Greek and Roman Technology: A sourcebook*
[930] Keppie 1984: 99
[931] Le Bohec, p. 52
[932] Goldsworthy, p. 144
[933] http://www.unc.edu/courses/rometech/public/content/special/James_Hurst/THE_ROMAN_SWORD_IN_THE_REP.htm
[934] //en.wikipedia.org/w/index.php?title=Template:Ancient_Rome_military_sidebar&action=edit
[935] A 2nd declension neuter noun. According to Lewis & Short, dictionary item linked in External links, General, either the singular or plural was used, castra with a possible meaning of *tents*.
[936] See Vegetius, *Epitoma rei militaris*, 3.8. In Clark's translation, 3.8 is "Rules for Encamping an Army," last paragraph. "Small fort" is *castellum*, which Vegetius explains is the diminutive of *castra*. He conceives of them as fortified outposts to be manned by cavalry protecting a supply route; i.e., a base from which to conduct patrols.
[937] . Included is a discussion about the typologies of Roman fortifications.
[938] The acute ka, or Ḱ, transliterating Macedonian Kje, is used by some writers instead, but the major etymologists, following Pokorny, have continued with the circumflex.
[939] Lewis & Short under External links, General, as well as many uncited Latin dictionaries, make this suggestion.
[940] https://www.academia.edu/865462/A_Camp_in_search_of_a_Campaign_The_reality_of_Hyginus_Roman_army
[941] Flavius Josephus: *The Jewish War.* III.5.1, trans. William Whiston.
[942] Ramsay's classic article, linked under External links, General, below, covers types of camps and camps in general. This Wikipedia article is heavily indebted but not exclusively to it.
[943] See Rebecca H. Jones 2012 *Roman camps in Britain*, Amberley Press, Stroud.
[944] see W.S. Hanson 2009 Building the forts and frontiers, in W.S. Hanson (ed) *The army and frontiers of Rome. Papers offered to David Breeze on the occasion of his sixty-fifth birthday and his retirement from Historic Scotland*, JRA Supplementary Series 74, Portsmouth, Rhode Island, 33-43.
[945] Roman Legionary Fortresses 27BC-378AD, D.B.Campbell, Osprey.
[946] M. C. Bishop, Handbook to Roman Legionary Fortresses, Pen & Sword, Hbk 208 pp
[947] See Hanson and Friel (1995) under External links, Forts and fortifications, below.
[948] Book VI Section 19 *The Roman Military System* pages 313-368 in Thayer's Loeb's Polybius under Primary sources below..
[949] An extensive lexicon at the *Romans in Britain* site, linked under External links, General, below, matches military terms of all periods of ancient Rome to English equivalents.
[950] Bell (2001) linked in External links, General, favors the view that the Greeks either influenced the Romans directly in the choice of the quadrangular plan or influenced the Etruscans, who influenced the Romans. The Greek theory certainly does not exclude an Indo-European origin.
[951] Smith (1875) under External links, Forts and fortifications. The *sudes* were not just simple stakes. Three or four branches were left on for interlocking.
[952] *Cardo* is the hinge line of a door and therefore is any main axis. In surveying it was the line drawn across (at 90° using a groma) the east-west *decumanus*, which was the first line drawn based on the position of the sun at sunrise. The *via principalis* would certainly be a cardo.
[953] *Decumana* (feminine of *decumanus*) derives most likely from *decima manus*, "tenth part" or "tenfold." As tenfold, it meant "immense." As tenth part, it also meant "across", such as a cross-path or cross-boundary. In surveying it was the first line drawn, after noting the position of the sun at sunrise in order to know exactly where east was; the *cardo* was then drawn across it at right angles. This was necessary, because the ancient Romans did not have the compass to

determine the position of the magnetic north. The connection between tenth and across remains obscure. The presence of numbered streets makes it less likely that the *via decumana* was "cross street" than that it was "10th street."

[954] The term *legatus* had other meanings in other contexts, such as governor or ambassador.

[955] Sims, Lesley: "Roman Soldier's Handbook", page 55-56. Usborne Publishing Ltd, 2004.

[956] Spain was especially heavily colonized by veterans, who Romanized the language and the architecture. Refer to Miranda (2002) under External links, Camp life, below.

[957] Roby under Secondary sources below.

[958] Vegetius Book I, linked in Primary sources below.

[959] Verboven, pages 15-17, under External links, Camp life. The author states estimates of coinage passing hands at various locations. A soldier received pay less deductions for expenses. He could borrow from or invest with the first bankers, the *argentarii* or *negotiatores nummularii*, whose business was to supply the legion with money for a percentage.

[960] A link to the Vindolanda tablets database with introductions, descriptions and bibliography is given under Primary sources below.

[961] See *The Tombstone of Anicius Ingenuus*, a medicus ordinarius, under Primary sources below.

[962] Scheidel page 14 under External links, Camp life.

[963] Scheidel pages 2-8 under External links, Camp life.

[964] Duncan B. Campbell, "Women in Roman forts: Residents, visitors or barred from entry?", Ancient Warfare, vol. IV (2010), issue 6, pp. 48-53, cf. p. 50

[965] Verboven describes the process. A veteran with a certain skill continued it as a contractor for the army. For example, a *gladiarius* or maker of swords, became a *negotiator gladiarius*, a supplier of swords. There were a large number of such names: the *negotiatores vestiarii* for clothing, *frumentarii* for grain, *salsari leguminari* for the salted vegetable concession, and so on.

[966] Forman, Joan: "The Romans", page15. Macdonald educational. 1975

[967] http://vindolanda.csad.ox.ac.uk/tablets/TVII-2-5.shtml

[968] http://www.thelatinlibrary.com/hyginus/hyginus6.shtml

[969] http://penelope.uchicago.edu/Thayer/E/Roman/Texts/Polybius/6*.html

[970] http://www.legionxxiv.org/diploma160ad.htm

[971] https://web.archive.org/web/20060825045351/http://museums.ncl.ac.uk/archive/old_fotm/old_fotmo98/

[972] http://museums.ncl.ac.uk/archive/old_fotm/old_fotmo98/

[973] https://web.archive.org/web/20060618184027/http://museums.ncl.ac.uk/archive/arma/contents/text/technica/veg1.htm

[974] http://museums.ncl.ac.uk/archive/arma/contents/text/technica/veg1.htm

[975] http://www.digitalattic.org/home/war/vegetius/

[976] https://books.google.com/?id=hRIAAAAAYAAJ&pg=PA453&lpg=PA453&dq=vigilia+roman+military+watch

[977] http://www.fsgfort.com/

[978] http://www.roman-empire.net/army/army-pictures.html

[979] http://cac-scec.ca/concours_essais/01Bell.html

[980] http://www.perseus.tufts.edu/cgi-bin/ptext?doc=Perseus%3Atext%3A1999.04.0059%3Aentry%3D%237013

[981] http://penelope.uchicago.edu/Thayer/E/Roman/Texts/secondary/SMIGRA*/Castra.html

[982] http://www.roman-britain.org/military/military_intro.htm

[983] https://web.archive.org/web/20060622110221/http://www.romans-in-britain.org.uk/glo_military_glossary_a.htm

[984] http://www.roman-britain.org/places/bearsden.htm

[985] http://ads.ahds.ac.uk/catalogue/adsdata/PSAS_2002/pdf/vol_125/125_499_519.pdf

[986] http://www.roman-britain.org/places/brandon_camp.htm

[987] http://www.livius.org/ha-hd/haltern/haltern.html

[988] http://www.roman-britain.org/places/nidum.htm

[989] http://www.roman-britain.org/places/pinnata-castra.htm

[990] https://web.archive.org/web/20060612234608/http://exeter.gov.uk/timetrail/02_romanfortress/growth.asp

[991] http://www.exeter.gov.uk/timetrail/02_romanfortress/growth.asp

[992] http://penelope.uchicago.edu/Thayer/E/Roman/Texts/secondary/SMIGRA*/Vallum.html
[993] http://www.eduvinet.de/tribus/roemlag/sache/rl.htm
[994] https://web.archive.org/web/20080724192753/http://www.bulgariancastles.com/bulgariancastles/en/fortress-sostra-en
[995] http://bulgariancastles.com/bulgariancastles/en/fortress-sostra-en
[996] https://web.archive.org/web/20060913152621/http://www.history.ucla.edu/undergrad/pat/journal2002/miranda.pdf
[997] http://www.history.ucla.edu/undergrad/pat/journal2002/miranda.pdf
[998] http://www.princeton.edu/~pswpc/pdfs/scheidel/110509.pdf
[999] http://www.ancienthistory.ugent.be/history/en/Verboven_Good_for_business.pdf
[1000] //en.wikipedia.org/w/index.php?title=Template:Ancient_Rome_military_sidebar&action=edit
[1001] Goldsworthy 2000: 144
[1002] Keppie 1984: 99
[1003] Le Bohec 1994: 138
[1004] Catapulta at LegionXXIV http://www.legionxxiv.org/catapulta/
[1005] Werner Soedel, Vernard Foley: "Ancient Catapults", *Scientific American*, Vol. 240, No. 3 (March 1979), p.120-128 (121ff.)
[1006] Le Bohec 1994: p. 138
[1007] Le Bohec 1994: p. 49
[1008] Garrison 1997.
[1009] Goldsworthy 2000: 191
[1010] Siege weapons at roman-empire.net http://www.roman-empire.net/army/leg-siege.html
[1011] Goldsworthy 2000: p. 145
[1012] Gilliver 1999: p. 140
[1013] Le Bohec 1994: p. 139
[1014] Gilliver 1999: pp. 134-135
[1015] Gilliver 1999: p. 138
[1016] Gilliver 1999: pp. 136-137.
[1017] Gilliver 1999: 138
[1018] Gilliver 1999: 140
[1019] Histories. Polybius. Evelyn S. Shuckburgh. translator. London, New York. Macmillan. 1889. Reprint Bloomington 1962.http://www.perseus.tufts.edu/hopper/text?doc=Plb.+1.22&fromdoc=Perseus%3Atext%3A1999.01.0234
[1020] //en.wikipedia.org/w/index.php?title=Template:Ancient_Rome_military_sidebar&action=edit
[1021] https://books.google.com/books?id=v86gAAAAMAAJ&pg=PP5&dq=Mirabilia+Urbis+Rom%C3%A6
[1022] Kaszynski, William. *The American Highway: The History and Culture of Roads in the United States*. Jefferson, N.C.: McFarland, 2000. Page 9 https://books.google.com/books?id=Dzv2oZM5_38C&pg=PA9
[1023] Corbishley, Mike: "The Roman World", page 50. Warwick Press, 1986.
[1024]
[1025] Gabriel, Richard A. *The Great Armies of Antiquity*. Westport, Conn: Praeger, 2002. Page 9 https://books.google.com/books?id=y1ngxn_xTOIC&pg=PA9.
[1026] Michael Grant, *History of Rome* (New York: Charles Scribner, 1978), 264.
[1027] Quilici, Lorenzo (2008): "Land Transport, Part 1: Roads and Bridges", in: Oleson, John Peter (ed.): *The Oxford Handbook of Engineering and Technology in the Classical World*, Oxford University Press, New York, , pp. 551–579 (552)
[1028]
[1029] Timothy Darvill, *Oxford Archaeological Guides: England* (2002) pp. 297–298
[1030] The ten men who judge lawsuits.
[1031] Subordinate officers under the aediles, whose duty it was to look after those streets of Rome which were outside the city walls.
[1032] also, *glarea strata*
[1033] also *lapide quadrato strata* or *sílice strata*

[1034] Graham, Alexander. Roman Africa; An Outline of the History of the Roman Occupation of North Africa, Based Chiefly Upon Inscriptions and Monumental Remains in That Country. London: Longmans, Green, and co, 1902. Page 66 https://books.google.com/books?id=PT1CAAAAIAAJ&pg=PA66.
[1035]
[1036] Ancient Roman Street re-emerges close to Colleferro http://www.thinkarchaeology.net/42/ancient-roman-street-colleferro/archaeology-italy/#more-42. thinkarchaeology.net. October 10, 2007.
[1037] Middleton, J. H. *The Remains of Ancient Rome*. London: A. and C. Black, 1892. Page 251 https://books.google.com/books?id=k35LLSdsA78C&pg=RA1-PA251.
[1038] Jaś Elsner, "The *Itinerarium Burdigalense*: politics and salvation in the geography of Constantine's Empire", *Journal of Roman Studies*, (2000), pp. 181–195, p. 184.
[1039] *Travel in the Ancient World*, Lionel Casson, p. 189
[1040] Naturalis Historia http://la.wikisource.org/wiki/Naturalis_Historia/Liber_VII by Gaius Plinius Secundus, Liber VII, 84.
[1041] The General History of the Highways https://books.google.com/books?id=pW9bAAAAQAAJ by Nicolas Bergier, page 156.
[1042] C.W.J.Eliot, New Evidence for the Speed of the Roman Imperial Post. Phoenix 9, 2, 1955, 76ff.
[1043] The Archaeological Site of Histria http://archweb.cimec.ro/Arheologie/web-histria/4imagini/imagini_eng.htm, archweb.cimec.ro.
[1044] https://books.google.com/books?id=sUhT_AcJyYEC
[1045] https://books.google.com/books?id=6qRAAAAAIAAJ
[1046] https://books.google.com/books?id=zDaWWTxnVNQC
[1047] https://books.google.com/books?id=UVMDAAAAMAAJ
[1048] https://books.google.com/books?id=9wsxAAAAIAAJ
[1049] https://books.google.com/books?id=3uYtAAAAIAAJ
[1050] https://books.google.com/books?id=NngPAAAAYAAJ&pg=PA946
[1051] https://books.google.com/books?id=Vs5QKRNq5_0C
[1052] https://books.google.com/books?id=Vs5QKRNq5_0C&pg=PA354
[1053] https://books.google.com/books?id=MUMOAAAAYAAJ
[1054] //tools.wmflabs.org/ftl/cgi-bin/ftl?st=wp&su=Roman+roads&library=OLBP
[1055] //tools.wmflabs.org/ftl/cgi-bin/ftl?st=wp&su=Roman+roads
[1056] //tools.wmflabs.org/ftl/cgi-bin/ftl?st=wp&su=Roman+roads&library=0CHOOSE0
[1057] http://orbis.stanford.edu/#
[1058] http://awmc.unc.edu/awmc/applications/alacarte/#
[1059] http://www.unrv.com/culture/roman-roads.php
[1060] http://www.omnesviae.org/
[1061] http://www.csun.edu/~hcfll004/viaeromanae.html
[1062] http://www.historylink102.com/Rome/roman-roads.htm
[1063] http://penelope.uchicago.edu/Thayer/E/Roman/Texts/secondary/SMIGRA*/Viae.html
[1064] https://web.archive.org/web/20080528061612/http://traianus.rediris.es/
[1065] http://viasromanas.planetaclix.pt
[1066] http://perso.wanadoo.fr/itineraires-romains-en-france/default.htm
[1067] https://web.archive.org/web/20051208013907/http://ccat.sas.upenn.edu/jod/augustine/routes.html
[1068] http://www.kaluwi.de/Roemerstrassen.html
[1069] http://penelope.uchicago.edu/Thayer/E/Roman/Texts/secondary/SMIGRA*/Servitutes.html
[1070] https://web.archive.org/web/20141006212211/http://www.brrp.bham.ac.uk/construction/construction.html
[1071] http://www.battleoffulford.org.uk/ev_roman_rd_constrct.htm
[1072] http://eeg.geoscienceworld.org/cgi/content/abstract/3/1/123
[1073] http://www.unrv.com/culture/roman-road-construction.php
[1074] //en.wikipedia.org/w/index.php?title=Template:Ancient_Rome_military_sidebar&action=edit
[1075] Vegetius, *The Military Institutions of the Romans*, Greenwood, 1985, p. 87
[1076] //en.wikipedia.org/w/index.php?title=Template:Ancient_Rome_military_sidebar&action=edit
[1077] John Warry, *Warfare in the Ancient World*, (St. Martin's, 1980), pp. 70-193

[1078] Adrian Goldsworthy, *In the Name of Rome: The Men Who Won the Roman Empire*, Weidenfeld & Nicolson, 2003 pp. 18-117
[1079] Michael Fronda (2010) Between Rome and Carthage: Southern Italy during the Second Punic War. p 38
[1080] Colleen McCullough, (2003) Caesar, p 303-417
[1081] Rome at war. (2005) Gilliver et al. Osprey, p 63-97
[1082] http://www.roman-empire.net/army/training.html
[1083] http://www.therthdimension.org/AncientRome/Roman_Army/Training/training.htm
[1084] Adrian Goldsworthy, *The Complete Roman Army*, Thames & Hudson, 2003, pp. 72-186
[1085] Goldsworthy, *The Complete Roman Army*, op. cit
[1086] Albert Harkness, *The Military System of the Romans*, University Press of the Pacific, 2004, pp. 53-89
[1087] Pierre Grimal, *The Civilization of Rome*, op. cit
[1088] John Warry, *Warfare in the ancient World*, (St. Martin's, 1980), pp. 70-183
[1089] Williamson, G. A., (tr), Josephus, *The Jewish War*, Penguin Books, 1959, p. 378-179
[1090]
[1091] Adrian Goldsworthy, *The Punic Wars*, (Cassell 2001) p. 50-69
[1092] Warry, *Warfare in the Ancient World*, op. cit
[1093] Taylor, Michael J. 2014 "Roman Infantry Tactics in the Mid-Republic: A Reevaluation." *Historia* 63, 301–322.
[1094] See Polybius, *The Histories* for original commentary– *The Histories* or *The Rise of the Roman Empire* by Polybius: ** At Perseus Project: English & Greek version http://www.perseus.tufts.edu/cgi-bin/ptext?lookup=Plb.+toc
[1095] Goldsworthy, *The Punic Wars*, op. cit
[1096] Wake, T., "The Roman Army After Marius' Reforms", 28 February 2006. http://romans.etrusia.co.uk/roman_army_print
[1097] Harkness, *The Roman Military System*, op. cit
[1098] Pierre Brimal, *The Civilization of Rome*, Simon and Schuster: 1963, Chap 5: *The Conquerors*, pg 162-196
[1099] Warry, op. cit.
[1100] Adrian Goldsworthy, *The Roman Army at War, 100 BC- AD200*, (Oxford, 1996), pp. 179-80
[1101] Goldsworthy, *The Punic Wars*, op. cit.
[1102] Goldsworthy, 1996, pp. 138-40
[1103] Lt. Col. S.G. Brady, *The Military Affairs of Ancient Rome and Roman Art of War in Caesar's Time*, The Military Service Publishing Company: 1947- url: http://www.digitalattic.org/home/war/romanarmy/
[1104] Nardo, *The Roman Army*, p23-29
[1105] Brady, op. cit, See also Warry, pg 169-170
[1106] John Warry, *Warfare in the Ancient World*, p. 169-170
[1107] Goldsworthy, *The Punic Wars*, pp.53-62
[1108] Lt. Col. S.G. Brady, *The Military Affairs of Ancient Rome and Roman Art of War in Caesar's Time*, The Military Service Publishing Company: 1947- url: http://www.digitalattic.org/home/war/romanarmy/
[1109] Warry, pp. 159-172
[1110] Warry, pp. 115-169
[1111] http://romanmilitary.net/strategy/resource
[1112] Polybius, *Histories* pp. 511-12
[1113] John Warry, Warfare in the ancient World, (St. Martin's, 1980), pp. 70-86
[1114] Goldsworthy, *The Punic Wars*
[1115] Goldsworthy, *The Complete Roman Army*, op. cit.
[1116] Hans Delbrück, *Warfare in Antiquity*
[1117] Don Nardo, *The Roman Army: Instrument of Power*, Lucent Books: 2004, 22-23
[1118] The opening scene of the 2000 US movie *Gladiator*, showing Germanic barbarians being vanquished, was shown to senior American officers before the 2003 US attack on Iraq as a motivational tool- reported in Michael R. Gordon and Bernard E. Trainor, *Cobra II: The Inside Story of the Invasion and Occupation of Iraq*, (Pantheon Books, 2006) p. 164

[1119] Don Nardo, *The Roman Army*: pp. 22-23
[1120] Nardo, op. cit
[1121] Nardo, *The Roman Army*, pp. 23-30
[1122] Arther Ferrill, *The Fall of the Roman Empire: The Military Explanation*
[1123] Hans Delbrück, *History of the Art of War*, Vols. I & II. University of Nebraska Press (1990) [1920-21].
[1124] *Encyclopædia Britannica*, Macropedia, 1974 ed, "Germans, Ancient"
[1125] Nardo, pg 74
[1126] Nardo, pg. 90
[1127] Tacitus, *Annals* - Book II - "War with the Germans", THE REIGN OF TIBERIUS, OUT OF THE FIRST SIX ANNALS OF TACITUS; WITH HIS ACCOUNT OF GERMANY, AND LIFE OF AGRICOLA, TRANSLATED BY THOMAS GORDON, 1917. url: https://www.gutenberg.org/dirs/etext05/7rtib10.txt
[1128] Hans Delbrück, *History of the Art of War*, (Vol. I, p. 510), University of Nebraska Press (1990) [1920-21].
[1129] DENISON, GEORGE T. *A History of Cavalry. From the earliest Times, with Lessons for the Future*. London Macmillan and Co. 1877, 1913, pp 62-89 (In public domain- see Google Books
[1130] Gaius Julius Caesar, *Commentaries on the Gallic War*, translated by W.A. McDevitte and W.S. Bohn. New York: Harper & Brothers, 1869. url: http://www.forumromanum.org/literature/caesar/gallic_e4.html#32
[1131] Chariots: Warfare with Attitude http://www.gallica.co.uk/celts/chariot.htm
[1132] *Caesar's Commentaries (THE WAR IN GAUL - THE CIVIL WAR) https://www.gutenberg.org/etext/10657* English translation by W. A. MACDEVITT, introduction by THOMAS DE QUINCEY (1915) – At Gutenberg Project
[1133] Theodore Dodge. 1892. Cæsar: a history of the art of war among the Romans Down to the End of the Roman Empire. 2 vol. Houghton-Mifflin
[1134] Archer Jones. 2001. The art of war in the Western world. University of Illinois Press. pp. 68-89
[1135] Jones, art of war..68-89
[1136] Stephen Dando-Collins (2002). Caesar's legion: the epic saga of Julius Caesar's elite tenth legion. Wiley. pp. 50–69
[1137] Dando-Collins. Caesar's legions. 52-68
[1138] Adrian Goldsworthy. *Caesar: Life of a Colossus*. Yale University Press, 2006, pp. 3291-359
[1139] Stephen Dando-Collins (2002). Caesar's legion: the epic saga of Julius Caesar's elite tenth legion. Wiley. pp. 50–69
[1140] Dando-Collins. Caesar's legions. 52–68
[1141] The Fifteen Decisive Battles Of The World http://www.arthurwendover.com/arthurs/history/tfdbt10.html: From Marathon To Waterloo by Sir Edward Creasy, M.A., 1851
[1142] *History of Rome: The Spanish Wars*, by Appian, circa 165 A.D. http://www.livius.org/ap-ark/appian/appian_spain_00.html
[1143] Appian, op. cit.
[1144] John Warry, Warfare in the classical world, University of Oklahoma Press
[1145] Fronda, 2010. Between Rome and Carthage.. p38
[1146] Robert Asprey, *War in the Shadows: The Guerrilla in History*, Vol 1, Doubleday, 1975, p 21-30
[1147] Richard Gottheil, Samuel Krauss, "Bar-Kokba and The Bar-Kokba War", *The Jewish Encyclopedia*, 2002, See also *Hist. Rom.* lxix. ch. 12-14 of Dio Cassius for details on the massive Jewish Revolt.
[1148] Archer Jones, *The Art of War in the Western World*, University of Illinois Press: 1987, pp. 34-92, 267-381
[1149] Denison, *History of Cavalry*, op. cit
[1150] Denison, op. cit
[1151] Xenophon, *Anabasis*, Loeb's Classical Library, 1998). See this classic work for a detailed discussion of anti-cavalry problems by another heavy infantry formation- the Hellenic phalanx, including the weaknesses of the hollow square formation
[1152] A history of Persia, Volume 1. 1915. By Sir Percy Molesworth Sykes. pg 385-386

[1153] Arther Ferrill, *The Fall of the Roman Empire: The Military Explanation*, (Thames & Hudson, 1986) p. 114-157
[1154] Marcellinus, Ammianus, *The Later Roman Empire*, translated by Hamilton, W. (Penguin, 1987). See also Chris Cornuelle, An Overview of the Sassanian Persian Military, (n.d.) retrieved from May 2008 from Iran Chamber Society http://www.iranchamber.com/history/articles/overview_sassanian_persian_military2.php
[1155] Marcellinus, op. cit.
[1156] Grimal, op. cit
[1157] Goldsworthy, The Punic Wars, 98-162
[1158] Goldsworthy, op. cit
[1159] Grimal, *The Civilization of Rome*, p. 98-102
[1160] Grimal, p. 104
[1161] Michael Fronda (2010) Between Rome and Carthage.. p. 38
[1162] Arther Ferrill, *The Fall of the Roman Empire*, pp. 43-190
[1163] Arther Ferrill, *The Fall of the Roman Empire: The Military Explanation*, op. cit.
[1164] Ferrill, *Fall of the Roman Empire 43-190*
[1165] Ferrill, *Fall of the Roman Empire.. 43-190*
[1166] Hugh Elton, 2012, Frontiers of the Roman Empire, pg 36-131
[1167] Edward Luttwak, *Grand Strategy of the Roman Empire*, (The Johns Hopkins University Press 1979)
[1168] Ferrill, op. cit
[1169] Quoted in Denison, p. 92
[1170] https://www.academia.edu/32352832/Later_Roman_Battle_Tactics
[1171] https://www.academia.edu/31904706/Changing_Formations_and_Specialists_Aspects_of_Later_Roman_Battle_Tactics
[1172] //en.wikipedia.org/w/index.php?title=Template:Ancient_Rome_military_sidebar&action=edit
[1173] Curry, Andrew. "Roman Frontiers." *National Geographic* Sept 2012: 106-127. Print
[1174] http://www.limesstrasse.de/
[1175] http://www.livius.org/li-ln/limes/tripolitanus.html

Article Sources and Contributors

The sources listed for each article provide more detailed licensing information including the copyright status, the copyright owner, and the license conditions.

Military of ancient Rome *Source:* https://en.wikipedia.org/w/index.php?oldid=852352219 *License:* Creative Commons Attribution-Share Alike 3.0 *Contributors:* Abce2, Acroterion, AddWittyNameHere, Allens, Allthefoxes, Alphapeta, Amortias, Anaxial, Andy M. Wang, Art LaPella, Arunsingh16, Bgwhite, Bob Burkhardt, Bongwarrior, Botteville, BrettAllen, Bubbles349, CAPTAIN RAJU, Cannolis, Casscassac4, Charmonnm5, Chris the speller, ClueBot NG, Crovata, CyberWarfare, Cyclist1954, Cynwolfe, DatGuy, DavidLeighEllis, Davidiad, Degen Earthfast, Depaderico, Deuger, Donner60, Doug Weller, DuncanHill, Edgar181, Ermahgerd9, EvergreenFir, Excirial, EyeTruth, Falcon8765, Favonian, Fdewaele, Finnusertop, Flyer22 Reborn, Gaia Octavia Agrippa, Gilliam, Giraffedata, GodenDaeg, Gossamers, Green547, GregMT08, GregNGM, Guest2625, GünniX, HMSSolent, Hairhorn, Headbomb, Historywwii, I dream of horses, Iridescent, Italia2006, JSquish, Jamesx12345, Jan1nad, Jean-Pierrie, Jez99, Jim1138, Jmcleod27, John of Reading, Johnbod, Julietdeltalima, K6ka, KH-1, Krakkos, Larsobrien, Lucas100101, LuigiPortaro29, Maebribri, Marius Gaius Scipio, Mark Arsten, Materialscientist, Mdanaher, Mike Rosoft, Millis21, Mogism, Monsterkid1011, Numbermaniac, Onel5969, Oshwah, PayceBRuhhh, PericlesofAthens, Pinethicket, Pipetricker, PlyrStar93, QuartierLatin1968, Rjwilmsi, Satellizer, Serols, Shellwood, Snow Blizzard, Steve Quinn, Thanatos666, ThePulleySystem, TwoTwoHello, Uhai, Webclient101, WereSpielChequers, Widr, Wiki13, YBG, Yogurldyl, Zanfar, Zedshort, 229 anonymous edits 1

Structural history of the Roman military *Source:* https://en.wikipedia.org/w/index.php?oldid=849783232 *License:* Creative Commons Attribution-Share Alike 3.0 *Contributors:* A little insignificant, Adobber, Aeonx, Alaney2k, Alansohn, Altenmann, Alþykkr, Ananiujitha, Antesignani, Art LaPella, BD2412, BRahn, Barliner, Batmanand, Before My Ken, Between My Ken, Beyond My Ken, Bgwhite, Bill Thayer, Blain Toddi, Brandmeister, Brandmeister (old), Brighterorange, Britzingen, CarloMartinelli, Chris the speller, ClueBot NG, Colonies Chris, Commander Shepard, David0811, DavidLeighEllis, Dawn Bard, Deipnosophista, Dejvid, DocWatson42, DrKay, Dujdjdjm, Dylantv, ENScroggs, East718, Eckenroad, Edgerunner76, EraNavigator, Erkan Yilmaz, Error, Ettrig, Feminist, Filipo, Filippof, Furius, Gadget850, Galoubet, Gene Nygaard, Glloq, Godfreywiki, HansHermans, Haploidavey, Harol035, Harryboyles, Hmains, Hongooi, InformationvsInjustice, Infrogmation, Italia2006, J.delanoy, Jacob Haller, Jay32183, John R. Summers, Johnbod, Jojhutton, Justinsane15, Knife-in-the-drawer, Krakkos, KylieTastic, LilHelpa, Llywrch, LtNOWIS, Lucid Time, Maañón, Maria Sieglinda von Nudeldorf, Miami33139, Michael Devore, Michal Manjura, Mnjorgensen, Moonraker12, Mr Stephen, Mrand, Muhends, Niceguyedc, Nick-D, Norm mit, NousEssayons, Nydas, Omnipaedista, Orcoteuthis, Oreo Priest, Pandacomics, Patton123, Paul S, PericlesofAthens, Piledhigheranddeeper, Pmanderson, PocklingtonDan, Poderi, QueenCake, Rich Farmbrough, Rjdeadly, Rjwilmsi, RobertG, Rosenknospe, Rrburke, Russ3Z, S@bre, SCOTTPAT64, Sadads, Sailko, SandyGeorgia, Sardanaphalus, SchreiberBike, SciMedKnowledge, Sdornan, Semperf, Shem1805, Smalljim, Snorkels, Ssolbergj, Tal'Mahe'Rah, Tassedethe, Tgpedersen, The Dark Side, The Quixotic Potato, TheDJ, Trafford09, Tsob, Untitledmind72, Urselius, Wandalstouring, Wareh, Weirdfungi, Welsh, Widgetdog, Widr, WolfmanSF, Woody, Yannismarou, Yarnalgo, Yomangani, Yosy, Zeta1127,89thLegion, 88 anonymous edits 21

Roman army *Source:* https://en.wikipedia.org/w/index.php?oldid=852832032 *License:* Creative Commons Attribution-Share Alike 3.0 *Contributors:* A. Parrot, A.amitkumar, Acabashi, Alaani, Alexander Domanda, Amaury, Amayaza, BD2412, Babitaarora, Barjimoa, Bertaut, Bgwhite, Bhny, Bob Burkhardt, CAPTACH, CLCStudent, Candlelight0115, Centibyte, Classicwiki, ClueBot NG, CodeTalker, Cosiek, Cplakidas, DVdm, Dan Koehl, Darthkenobi0, David.moreno72, Dcirovic, Dieale19, Discospinster, DocWatson42, Dr.K., Dspradau, DuckeggAlex, Dw122339, Earthforc31, Eddin Bikas, Ehrenkater, EraNavigator, Escape Orbit, Eteethan, Fishie2mh, Flappychappy, Frosty, Gilliam, Gossamers, Halflang, Haploidavey, Hello71, HickoryOughtShirt?4, Historynerd1738, I dream of horses, Iazyges, Iridescent, Italia2006, Jim1138, JohnEntwistle, Josve05a, Katieh5584, Klbrain, Kleuske, Lewmiddwiki, LilHelpa, LindsayH, Llywrch, LogAntiLog, Maddog123456yuiop, Magioladitis, Marek69, Marius∼enwiki, Materialscientist, Medium69, Meters, Misterwolfson2, MusikAnimal, My Chemistry romantic, Neuroforever, NewEnglandYankee, Niamhbutts, Omnipaedista, Oshwah, PCock, PENNYROYALS, PericlesofAthens, Philip Trueman, Picture Master, Pinethicket, RA0808, Redzemp, Remitonova, Rjdeadly, SCOTTPAT64, Seaphoto, Septrillion, Shellwood, SimmeD, Simplexity22, SireWonton, Sjö, Smalljim, Soetermans, Sonicwave32, Stconrad, Sweepy, Tanay Toshnwial, Temmie5687, TerryAlex, TheTruth1453, Thejobro115, Tony Fox, Trappist the monk, Urselius, Viator, Widr, Willc1991, XXx promlg360noscoper xXX, Xherin, Yaris678, Zingarese, శ్రీధర్ బాబు, 215 anonymous edits 47

List of Roman army unit types *Source:* https://en.wikipedia.org/w/index.php?oldid=843486360 *License:* Creative Commons Attribution-Share Alike 3.0 *Contributors:* *Treker, Agentjoerg, Alansohn, Anna Lincoln, Arado, Art LaPella, Bobo192, Bolman Deal, Bouette, Bucephalus the great, C777, Chiconspiracy, Chris the speller, Cianain54, ClueBot NG, Cnwilliams, Corpx, Cp111, Cplakidas, CristianChirita, DferDaisy, Download, DrRC, DragonHawk, Dterry3po, Ecthelion83, Epbr123, Erkan Yilmaz, Frans Fowler, Furrykef, Gaia Octavia Agrippa, Gaius Octavius Princeps, Gilliam, Girolamo Savonarola, GreatWhiteNortherner, Green547, Husond, IPSOS, Itelinee, J.delanoy, JamesBWatson, John Cline, Kai Su?, Kbar1, Kingpin13, KipCujo, Kometman, Kurola, LilHelpa, Limideen, MSTVD, MarcoAurelio, Martylunsford, Materialscientist, Matthew Yeager, Modgamers, Mogism, Moskstraumen33, MrDolomite, Myman129, NawlinWiki, Ndss, Niceguyedc, O not, Oktoberface, Omnipaedista, Pajfarmor, Panarjedde, Pjbjas, PocklingtonDan, Polylerus, Praefectuscohortis, Prolog, RaiderAspect, Riotrocket8676, Rjwilmsi, Rmmalizia, RobotG, Rrostrom, Rsocol, Rymich13, SMC, Sam Korn, Sardanaphalus, Saturnian, Sciurinæ, Shlomke, Sigehelmus, Sion8, Ssolbergj, StAnselm, Steerpike, Taywrizzle 2007, Technopat, Thecheesykid, Thomas Paine1776, Tide rolls, Tramp2012, Tyler, VoABot II, Whipster, Widr, WikipedianMarlith, Wildnox, Woohookitty, XPTO, Yelir55, Yosy, ZappaOMati, Zephyrus67, Zeta1127,89thLegion, Zidel333, 200 anonymous edits 66

Roman military decorations and punishments *Source:* https://en.wikipedia.org/w/index.php?oldid=845185406 *License:* Creative Commons Attribution-Share Alike 3.0 *Contributors:* 72, AlephGamma, Anarkitekt, Aohayou, Articcat50, Bchaosf, Broadhat, ClueBot NG, Coffeeassured, Colin 8, Cplakidas, Cynwolfe, Daonguyen95, David N Brown, Davidiad, Dewritech, Discospinster, Elen of the Roads, Eugenitor, Falcon8765, Fluffernutter, Furrykef, Gilliam, HappyJake, Iridescent, J.delanoy, Jmootz20, JorisEnter, Keenan Pepper, Khazar2, Klemen Kocjancic, Liam.ross, LilHelpa, Llywrch, Me, Myself, and I are Here, Moe Epsilon, Mogism, Moreschi, Murphy321, MusikAnimal, Nazgul02, Neutrality, Niceguyedc, PapalAuthoritah, Per82, Peter Flass, Peti610botH, Peyre, Philip Trueman, Pinheadedobject, Pjbjas, PlyrStar93, PocklingtonDan, QuiteUnusual, Richard Keatinge, RileyBugz, Robert Prummel, Rodarmor, Rrburke, Rubbish computer, ST47, Sardanaphalus, Satellizer, Ssolbergj, The Red, Tri-l, Ushau97, VaneWimsey, Wasbeer, Welsh, Widr, Zaravakos, צבי, דניאל 108 anonymous edits 71

List of Roman legions *Source:* https://en.wikipedia.org/w/index.php?oldid=851854443 *License:* Creative Commons Attribution-Share Alike 3.0 *Contributors:* 2ravens, Ajdebre, Allmightyduck, Amaury, Andrein, Anonimu, Apteva, AshLin, Attilios, BD2412, Barsoomian, Bart172, Baseballbaker23, Basemetal, Bgwhite, Brandmeister (old), CaesarGermanicus, Chajim, ChrisGualtieri, Chunterkap, ClueBot NG, Cplakidas, Danny lost, Davidson.r1, Degen Earthfast, Dhyun2, Djwilms, DocWatson42, Donner60, Ealdgyth, Enok, EraNavigator, Fgjesijyliuyflut, France3470, FueGo, Future Perfect at Sunrise, GELongstreet, Gilliam, GraemeLeggett, Green547, Gun Powder Ma, Hellbus, Hmains, Iazyges, Icairns, InformationvsInjustice, Italia2006, Jasonanaggie, Jayron32, Jbribeiro1, Jimmy Pitt, JoshuaRessel, Kauffner, Kenturion, Legbatterij-Argonautica, Leolaursen, LuxNevada, Matthead, Maximajorian Viridio, Midas02, Mogism, Moswento, Norm mit, Numisantica, OJOM, OlEnglish, Omnipaedista, Paxsimius, Peaceguy123456789, Philipjelley, Pinethicket, Purple XS2, QuartierLatin1968, R'n'B, R.D.H. (Ghost In The Machine), RayAYang, Rich Farmbrough, Rjdeadly, Rolgiati, Rowanashton, Sardanaphalus, Saturnian, SchreiberBike, SheriffIsInTown, Skäpperöd, Smoothmoniker, SoWhy, Spinningspark, Squids and Chips, Ssolbergj, Stone, Thewolfchild, Tokyotown8, Vincentlaji, Wbm1058, Widr, Wiki13, Woohookitty, XPTO, Yosy, Zozo2kx, 132 anonymous edits 77

Auxilia *Source:* https://en.wikipedia.org/w/index.php?oldid=845176481 *License:* Creative Commons Attribution-Share Alike 3.0 *Contributors:* Akitlosz, Alexrexpvt, Ananiujitha, Andrein, AussenzioDrauco, Avicennasis, BD2412, Bahnheckl, BeatrixBelibaste, Biglovinb, Brutaldeluxe, Buistr, Capricorn42, Claritas, Closedmouth, ClueBot NG, CommonsDelinker, Cplakidas, Daizus, Dbachmann, Decurion, Degen Earthfast, DferDaisy, Dis80786, Edward, EraNavigator, Flamarande, FoCuSandLeArN, Foxhunt king, Freeman501, Gadget850, Gaius Cornelius, GenQuest, Glevum, GoingBatty, Gyrobo, Halibutt, Hmains, Iazyges, Italia2006, Jim1138, Joshualouie711, Joy, Jrogerswm, Khazar2, Kt38138, Kumioko, Lapost, Lilaac, Marcus Cyron, Mediatus, Mikeblas, Morgan9060, No Swan So Fine, Notuncurious, Ogress, Oisinsimpson, P Aculeius, Paxsimius, PericlesofAthens, Porsenna1, Prinsgezinde, Punisher-HellHound, QueenCake, R'n'B, RafaAzevedo, Rbyteisbst, Rich Farmbrough, Rjdeadly, Rjwilmsi, Rrburke, Russ3Z, SchreiberBike, SheriffIsInTown, Spudtater, StAnselm, Thecritiqu, Theleftorium, Thirdright, TorpetLegionary, Tpbradbury, Tri-l, Usernameunique, Wandalstouring, Widr, ZH2010, ZxxZxxZ, ÄDA - DÄP, 87 anonymous edits 90

List of Roman generals *Source:* https://en.wikipedia.org/w/index.php?oldid=853550354 *License:* Creative Commons Attribution-Share Alike 3.0 *Contributors:* Andresbarba24, Arthur Rubin, Asparagus, Babbittd, Bender235, Bgwhite, Blain Toddi, Byzantine writer, Chaleyer61, ClueBot NG, Codohu, Colonies Chris, Cynwolfe, Dan149, DeadEyeArrow, Egsan Bacon, Euryalus, Excirial, Fdewaele, Fixer88, Flamarande, FoCuSandLeArN, Gog the Mild, GraemeLeggett, GuyHimGuy, Hohum, Hugo999, HumphreyW, Iazyges, Italia2006, JaGa, Jco5611, Joyous!, Jp858, Kappa, Kevinmon, Levdr1, LilHelpa, LindsayH, Llywrch, Longballer3, Lugia2453, MacStep, Mikmo∼enwiki, Mrld, Nolandda, NotWith, Omnipaedista, P Aculeius, PocklingtonDan, Qzd, R'n'B, Rmhermen, Robert Carmichael, Rockpocket, Rrburke, Sami1991, Serols, Spicemix, Terraflorin, Thắng L.Đ.Q., Tomaxer, Wexcan, Widr, Wikibiohistory, Wikipelli, Woohookitty, XPTO, Zsh, 64 anonymous edits 127

Roman navy *Source:* https://en.wikipedia.org/w/index.php?oldid=837970519 *License:* Creative Commons Attribution-Share Alike 3.0 *Contributors:* Agamemnus, Arch dude, Arthena, AstaBOTh15, Atdheu, BD2412, Baddu676, Bahudhara, Bejnar, Bender235, Billyondrums, Blingbo, Bongwarrior, Brien.watson, Byblios, CAPTAIN RAJU, Caravaggista, Citation bot 1, ClueBot NG, Colonies Chris, CommonsDelinker, Cplakidas, Cuddy Wifter, Cynwolfe, Deor, Discospinster, Disdero, Dr. Dan, Dynasteria, Dyolf77, Edward C Piercy, Eustachiusz, Eyesnore, FelixLeclerc001, Fixer88, Flyer22 Reborn, GFlusitania, GiW, Gioto, Grafen, HamburgerRadio, Haploidavey, Harsh 2580, Hmains, Hydro, IMCUMIN4U12, Iazyges, Italia2006, J.delanoy, J04n, JJMC89, JaconaFrere, JamesBWatson, Jayjg, Jim1138, John "Hannibal" Smith, Joy, Khazar2, Kurt Leyman, Levdr1, Lightmouse, LlywelynII, LolChavista, MacDaddy9823, Magioladitis, MarcoTolo, Marcocapelle, Mathglot, Matthew Stannard, Mike Rosoft, Mikeo, Mild Bill Hiccup, Miyagawa, Mkpumphrey,

Mojo Hand, NMDR, Narayan89, Natg 19, Neptune's Trident, No Swan So Fine, Nono64, Notuncurious, Paste, Paxsimius, PericlesofAthens, Peter Isotalo, Philip Trueman, Picture Master, QueenCake, R'n'B, RenamedUser01302013, Rich Farmbrough, Richard Keatinge, Rjwilmsi, Ronhjones, Russ3Z, Ryanmarty72, SchreiberBike, Senjuto, Shamrock31, ShelfSkewed, Silesianus, Simplexity22, SkiDragon, Sluzzelin, Stifle, SvenLittkowski, Terraflorin, The High Fin Sperm Whale, The Monarch, TheCormac, Timmay911, Tramp2012, Trappist the monk, Tri-l, Ulric1313, Vanished User 8a9b4725f8376, WikiMasterGhibif, Wikichangeryoullhateme, William Avery, Woohookitty, Yaris678, Zeta1127,89thLegion, Zundark, Филель22, [illegible], 115 anonymous edits 135

Campaign history of the Roman military *Source:* https://en.wikipedia.org/w/index.php?oldid=849780973 *License:* Creative Commons Attribution-Share Alike 3.0 *Contributors:* AdamBMorgan, Alarics, AlexiusHoratius, Alphalurion, Alvestrand, Antiqueight, Aregakn, Ashmedai 119, BD2412, Bajjer21, Bearcat, Bender235, Beyond My Ken, Botteville, Brandmeister, Breandandalton, CAPTAIN RAJU, CD-Host, Calidius, Catgut, Chewings72, Chris the speller, Citation bot 1, ClueBot NG, ColRad85, CommonsDelinker, Cplakidas, Cranston lamont, D-Notice, Damianmx, Davidiad, Dejvid, Delusion23, DemocraticLuntz, Deor, Der Golem, Dewritech, Diannaa, Discospinster, Dj777cool, Djma12, Download, Dpwkbw, DrKay, Edward, Egsan Bacon, Epbr123, Eustachiusz, Fidelojimba, Filos96, Flamarande, Fornadan, Gambori, Gareth Griffith-Jones, George Ponderevo, Gilliam, Graham87, Grandiose, Heqwm2, Hmains, Hmainsbot1, Huangdi, Hyrudagon, I Feel Tired, Iazyges, Iblardi, InformationvsInjustice, Iohannes Animosus, Irb, Ism schism, Italia2006, J.delanoy, JaconaFrere, Javierfv1212, Jbribeiro1, Jimbo Cymru, Jimp, Jmullaly, Joeblow179350, John of Reading, Johnor, KarlFrei, Kfitzgib, Khazar2, KiwiBiggles, Krakkos, LarryMorseDCOhio, Lightmouse, Like tears in rain, Lilac Soul, Llywrch, LuxNevada, MadameArsenic, Markussep, Mdotley, Mike Tizzle4, Miranche, MusikAnimal, NeilN, Nenya17, Nev1, Niceguyedc, Nicknack009, Nikkimaria, Notuncurious, NuclearWarfare, Od Mishehu, Onel5969, Oshwah, P Aculeius, P. S. Burton, PatGallacher, PericlesofAthens, Piledhigheranddeeper, Plastikspork, Redtigerxyz, Rividian, Rjwilmsi, Rogerb67, Rrburke, Rror, ScottJ, Ser Amantio di Nicolao, Sfan00 IMG, ShelfSkewed, Sillyfolkboy, Slon02, Sluzzelin, Smalljim, Snarkibartfast, StAnselm, StjJackson, Suruena, Sémhur, Tataryn, Thecutestkitty, Thắng L.Đ.Q., TiltuM, Tiptoety, Tpbradbury, Urg writer, Versus22, Washburnmav, Wiae, WilliamThweatt, Winteremrald, Yamaguchi先生 , Yngvadottir, Yoyoni123, YukioSanjo, Zedshort, Zppix, Zzuuzz, [illegible], 122 anonymous edits 165

List of Roman wars and battles *Source:* https://en.wikipedia.org/w/index.php?oldid=852783787 *License:* Creative Commons Attribution-Share Alike 3.0 *Contributors:* Academic Challenger, Adapad, Aitias, Akhenaten0, Alexkin, Anaxial, Arjayay, Averysoda, BD2412, Bamyers99, Belligero, Bencherlite, Bgwhite, Byblios, CAPTAIN RAJU, Camajulissa, Chewings72, Chuckiesdad, Ciphers, ClueBot NG, Cplakidas, Damianmx, Danski454, David.moreno72, Dcirovic, Dimadick, Discospinster, Dw122339, DéRahier, Epicgenius, EuroCarGT, Favonian, Fdewaele, Flyer22 Reborn, FoCuSandLeArN, Gilliam, Green547, Happy puff, Helenabella, Hyrudagon, I dream of horses, IW.HG, Iazyges, Jacob Haller, John of Reading, Joshwill, Jth11399, K6ka, Katharineamy, Kirrages, Kuru, Lophostrix, LouisAragon, Ludde23, MarcusBritish, Maxipuchi, Melody Concerto, MicroMagus, Mike Rosoft, Mikemoral, Mojo Hand, Mr Stephen, MusikAnimal, Natg 19, Navops47, Oatley2112, OcarinaOfTime, P Aculeius, Panarjedde, ParisianBlade, Passengerpigeon, Peluba, Philippians220, Pizza12341, PleaseConsider, PocklingtonDan, Prestonlust, Pronoia, Pruy0001, QuickWittedHare, Rami R, RedMC, Rich Farmbrough, Rknasc, SOCL, Sardanaphalus, Serols, Shellwood, Shey32, Sindala, Sjö, Skysmith, Ssolbergj, Theinstantmatrix, Urg writer, Wessexranger, Zntrip, 183 anonymous edits 206

Technological history of the Roman military *Source:* https://en.wikipedia.org/w/index.php?oldid=779365713 *License:* Creative Commons Attribution-Share Alike 3.0 *Contributors:* Aldis90, Allens, BD2412, ChrisCork, Cynwolfe, Da fett, Dimadick, Glevum, Godfollower4ever, Improbcat, James.f.caulfield, Nankai, Omnipaedista, Ozone77, Panarjedde, Peterlewis, Philip Trueman, PocklingtonDan, RafaelG, Rjwilmsi, Rmky87, Sardanaphalus, Snapperman2, Some jerk on the Internet, Ssolbergj, Stevv, The-Pope, Tommy2010, Vedexent, Wandalstouring, Yelir55, 25 anonymous edits 231

Castra *Source:* https://en.wikipedia.org/w/index.php?oldid=846163282 *License:* Creative Commons Attribution-Share Alike 3.0 *Contributors:* 72, AdamBMorgan, Aisteco, Allens, Andreas Kaganov, Anrnusna, Attilios, BD2412, BOTarate, Barticus88, Bazuz, Bender235, Bennoed, Bermicourt, BlueDevil, Bota47, Botteville, Bporopat, Bunet1981, Capmo, Chavanarchy, Chris the speller, Ciroa, Citation bot 1, Closedmouth, ClueBot NG, Codrinb, ColorOfSuffering, ComfyKem, CommonsDelinker, Corpx, Cplakidas, CrniBombarder!!!, Cymrogogoch, Cynwolfe, D A R C 12345, Da Joe, Davidiad, Dbachmann, Dcirovic, EEye, Ehrenkater, EndoSTEEL, Erutuon, Espoo, Fryslan0109, Funnyfarmofdoom, GinAndChronically, Gioto, Gun Powder Ma, Hughey, Iazyges, Iridescent, J04n, Jamelan, JamesBWatson, Johnbod, JoniFili, Ken Gallager, Kirriemuir, Kleo73, Kushboy, Lateg, Laurel Lodged, Lielais Rolands~enwiki, Lightmouse, LilHelpa, Lizia7, LombardBeige, Loraof, Mathiasrex, Mediatus, Michaeldsuarez, Mike hayes, MjMenuet111, Mndata, Mr Stephen, Muhandes, Naraht, Nasakev, Neddyseagoon, Nephsam, Nev1, Nick Number, Nihiltres, Noetica, Nortonius, Ogress, Omnipaedista, Orijentolog, Panarjedde, Perspicaris, Petercorless, Picapica, PocklingtonDan, Prari, Qst, Rambler24, Rich Farmbrough, Rjdeadly, Rjwilmsi, Rrburke, Rubenescio, Sardanaphalus, Shgür Datsügen, Sintaku, Sir Ian Richmond, Sitehut, Snowmanradio, Ssolbergj, Stamptrader, Steinsplitter, THEN WHO WAS PHONE?, Theelf29, Timurite, Trappist the monk, Tri-l, Versus22, W S Hanson, WRK, Wcoole, Wieralee, Wilson44691, Woohookitty, Yamaguchi先生 , Yomanhi6, Zoeperkoe, 102 anonymous edits 235

Roman siege engines *Source:* https://en.wikipedia.org/w/index.php?oldid=815892682 *License:* Creative Commons Attribution-Share Alike 3.0 *Contributors:* 07UNCBean, Alessandro57, Allen3, Attilios, Baranxtu, Bilsonius, Caltas, Cgeislerwyo, Citation bot 1, ClueBot NG, Cplakidas, David.moreno72, Davidiad, Discospinster, Edward321, Epbr123, Fabrictramp, Floppyweiner, Folantin, Fraggle81, Gaius Cornelius, George Ponderevo, Gilliam, Gioto, Glloq, Gogo Dodo, Granite07, Gun Powder Ma, Herpderp89, Hmains, Imperial fodder, Ixfd64, Jaeger5432, Jalo, John, Junglerot56, KTo288, Katieh5584, Khazar2, LegesRomanorum, LouisAlain, Ludwigs2, Mairi, Marek69, Materialscientist, Melaen, Michaelas10, Mild Bill Hiccup, Neddyseagoon, Nev1, Niceguyedc, Nicknack009, No Guru, No1Knows, Omnipaedista, Oshwah, Peterlewis, Picture Master, PocklingtonDan, R'n'B, Rich Farmbrough, Rjwilmsi, Sardanaphalus, Saturnian, Sfan00 IMG, SquidSK, Squids and Chips, Ssolbergj, Stephan Schulz, Telecineguy, Trex2001, Ugog Nizdast, Verdatum, VoABot II, WOSlinker, West.andrew.g, Widr, Wrathkind, Yintan, Zedshort, Zeta1127,89thLegion, 108 anonymous edits 259

List of Roman triumphal arches *Source:* https://en.wikipedia.org/w/index.php?oldid=842167853 *License:* Creative Commons Attribution-Share Alike 3.0 *Contributors:* 5telios, A.Savin, A3BDFAD9EC0B, AmateurEditor, Attilios, Bhludzin, Bjankuloski06en~enwiki, Brandmeister, BrownHairedGirl, Bschoawsb, ChrisO~enwiki, ClueBot NG, Coldeel~enwiki, Colonies Chris, CommonsDelinker, Coolcat39, Cplakidas, Davidiad, Denisarona, Dom De Felice, Eupator, FAM1885, Fredwords, Furius, Gun Powder Ma, Hiberniantears, Hmains, Hmainsbot1, J36miles, JDHaidar, Jeancey, JeffW, Lemnaminor, LilHelpa, Luk, Magioladitis, Manushand, Maxim, Mrawsome12345, Neddyseagoon, Petri Krohn, PocklingtonDan, Prioryman, Pudelek, R'n'B, Radagast83, Rococo1700, Rwxrwxrwx, STBotD, Sailko, Sardanaphalus, Sheila1988, Ssolbergj, Theartofthemuses, Thoughtfortheday, Thucydidian, TorpetLegionary, Vieque, Vvven, Woohookitty, Xwejnusgozo, Zeelenman, 44 anonymous edits 273

Roman roads *Source:* https://en.wikipedia.org/w/index.php?oldid=850991666 *License:* Creative Commons Attribution-Share Alike 3.0 *Contributors:* A930913, Abelmoschus Esculentus, Acroterion, Adam9007, Adirlanz, Alexander Domanda, Amintly, Ansh666, Arjayay, Armetrek, Avoided, Bender235, Bigman122356, Bisonosib, Boggyman32, Bryceandjayden21, CEpley, Chevvin, Chris the speller, Classicw, Classicwiki, Clean Copy, ClueBot NG, Crystallizedcarbon, Datbubblegumdoe, Davidbena, Davidiad, Dcirovic, Doncram, Donner60, EDitMe, Ehrenkater, El cid, el campeador, Emmo827, FT2, Farmall b, Fixer88, Flyer22 Reborn, Fpr155, Gadget850, Gilliam, Haploidavey, Haydenmcdonald946, HazelAB, Hello71, I dream of horses, IronGargoyle, Italia2006, J 1982, JDHaidar, JWNoctis, Jjjjjjdddddd, Jlewi233, John Abbe, John of Reading, Johnbod, Johnmarkh, Julesd, Kingtigertank1233, Kiore, Klbrain, Ks0stm, KylieTastic, LilHelpa, Llywrch, Magioladitis, MainlyTwelve, Marek69, Materialscientist, Mean as custard, Meeka1147, Morel, MusikAnimal, My Chemistry romantic, Mygodfrey, Nedim Ardoğa, Nondirectional, North Shoreman, Omnipaedista, Onel5969, Optakeover, Oshwah, Paul August, Philg88, Pinethicket, Pippus7, Polyglot, Pratyya Ghosh, PrimeHunter, Quinto Simmaco, RA0808, Recon56, Reddi, Riventree, Rrburke, Russ3Z, SFK2, SUXMYDIK11, Serols, Shellwood, SireWonton, Skywatcher68, Slightsmile, TYelliot, Tassedethe, ToBeFree, Tom.Reding, Tony Mach, TorpetLegionary, Tropicalkitty, Vipinhari, W4L0CK, Webclient101, Whatyoucare, Widr, Wikisaurus, Wopi Dog, WyattAlex, Xyzspaniel, Yinf, Zjenius, [illegible] 224 anonymous edits 279

Strategy of the Roman military *Source:* https://en.wikipedia.org/w/index.php?oldid=839454029 *License:* Creative Commons Attribution-Share Alike 3.0 *Contributors:* Acabashi, Anaxial, Andrewman327, Artaxus, Billybob31st, Bobo192, BroMaster00123, Bsadowski1, Chris the speller, ClueBot NG, DVdm, Dewritech, Discospinster, Dylan620, Ejail, Elbbom, Ettrig, EuroCarGT, Eyesnore, Fences and windows, GJo, Gaius Cornelius, Giver9, Hut 8.5, J04n, Jsc83, KTo288, Kinetic37, L33th4x0rguy, Lowellian, Materialscientist, Mcfar54, Narsil, Natuur12, Nowa, Omnipaedista, Onkelschark, Padenton, Panarjedde, PocklingtonDan, Rjwilmsi, Sardanaphalus, Shadowjams, SkerHawx, Ssolbergj, Tide rolls, VoABot II, Xeolyte, אריה ה., 95 anonymous edits 311

Roman infantry tactics *Source:* https://en.wikipedia.org/w/index.php?oldid=852351997 *License:* Creative Commons Attribution-Share Alike 3.0 *Contributors:* A D Monroe III, Alex Cohn, Atvica, Avoided, Bananastalktome, Bender235, Berean Hunter, Bgwhite, Big smoke1, Bongwarrior, Brufnus, Buffbills7701, Bullseye30, CapitalR, Cartermassey, Charlezanyman, Chris the speller, ChuMao, Citation bot 1, ClueBot NG, Cranberry Products, Dannickjesscatiain, Dcirovic, DemocraticLuntz, Dexippus12, Digital inf3rno, Dimadick, Dobermanji, Doctor Sapiens, Donner60, DuncanHill, EPsi, Egsan Bacon, Excirial, Eyesnore, Flyer22 Reborn, Furrykef, Gareth Griffith-Jones, General Ization, Gevans13, Ginsuloft, Grandpallama, Green547, Guandr, HaiDeaf, Halflang, Hamiltondaniel, HickoryOughtShirt?4, I dream of horses, IdreamofJeanie, Intranetusa, Iridescent, Italia2006, Ito123456789, J4eo124, JesseRafe, Jim1138, Jodosma, Kage Acheron, Kris159, KylieTastic, Lacrimosus, Lifeislifey, Linguisticgeek, Magioladitis, Marcocapelle, MarkR1717, Materialscientist, Mathonius, Maurice Carbonaro, Metalello, Midas02, Mogism, Monterey Bay, Mr. Stradivarius, MrChupon, Natg 19, Ngebendi, Nick Number, Nicknack009, Noformation, OJJ, Omnipaedista, Oshwah, P.Henrich Jochen, Paul August, Penbat, Peter Isotalo, Philip Trueman, Pourhouse, Primergrey, Prof. H . Khelman, Racerx11, Rbyteisbst, Rhododendrites, Rich Farmbrough, Rocketrod1960, Rrburke, ScottyBerg, Serbchingo, Serols, Shellwood, Sir Charms a Lot, Sjö, Slightsmile, Srednuas Lenoroc, Stesmo, Sɛvɪnti farv, TYelliot, Ubiquity, Valery Staricov, Whoop whoop pull up, Wiae, Widr, WorldWarTwoEditor, Xenoskin, Yakushima, Yintan, ZxxZxxZ, 251 anonymous edits 316

Roman military frontiers and fortifications *Source:* https://en.wikipedia.org/w/index.php?oldid=837585421 *License:* Creative Commons Attribution-Share Alike 3.0 *Contributors:* Adecastick, Ananiujitha, Angusmclellan, Bermicourt, Blaylockjam10, ClueBot NG, Cplakidas, Cymru.lass, Dc76, Dewritech, DrDaveHPP, Droll, Epolk, Firsfron, Flyer22 Reborn, Fryslan0109, Frze, Fuhghettaboutit, Gioto, GreatWhiteNortherner, Gun Powder Ma, Hiberniantears, Hmains, Hmainsbot1, Iridescent, Jairogyro, Jmlk17, Johnbod, Jza84, Laurel Lodged, Magioladitis, Mogism, Omnipaedista, Panarjedde, PocklingtonDan, R'n'B, RJFJR, RadiX, RedMC, Rhndevu02, Rmky87, S (usurped also), Sander123, Sardanaphalus, Serols, Ssolbergj, Steve Quinn, THEN WHO WAS PHONE?, Thefuguestate, Walgamanus, WolframWolf40, Woohookitty, ZxxZxxZ, 31 anonymous edits 361

Image Sources, Licenses and Contributors

The sources listed for each image provide more detailed licensing information including the copyright status, the copyright owner, and the license conditions.

Image *Source:* https://en.wikipedia.org/w/index.php?title=File:Roman_Military_banner.svg *License:* Creative Commons Attribution-Sharealike 3.0 *Contributors:* Sonarpulse 1
Image *Source:* https://en.wikipedia.org/w/index.php?title=File:Scutum_1.jpg *License:* Creative Commons Attribution-ShareAlike 3.0 Unported *Contributors:* User:MatthiasKabel 1
Figure 1 *Source:* https://en.wikipedia.org/w/index.php?title=File:Cornicen_on_Trajan's_column.JPG *License:* Public Domain *Contributors:* User:Gaius Cornelius 3
Figure 2 *Source:* https://en.wikipedia.org/w/index.php?title=File:Column_of_Marcus_Aurelius_-_detail3.jpg *License:* Creative Commons Attribution 3.0 *Contributors:* Barosaurus Lentus 4
Figure 3 *Source:* https://en.wikipedia.org/w/index.php?title=File:7antoninianii.jpg *License:* Public Domain *Contributors:* 1989, Circeus, Lotje, Saperaud~commonswiki 6
Figure 4 *Source:* https://en.wikipedia.org/w/index.php?title=File:Roman_Legions_camps_-_AD_80.png *License:* Creative Commons Sharealike 1.0 *Contributors:* Bibi Saint-Pol, Botteville, Codrinb, Flamarande~commonswiki, It Is Me Here, Karlfk, Nev1, Panairjdde~commonswiki, 8 anonymous edits 8
Figure 5 *Source:* https://en.wikipedia.org/w/index.php?title=File:Vista_general_de_Masada.jpg *License:* Public Domain *Contributors:* Original uploader was אסף.צ at he.wikipedia 10
Figure 6 *Source:* https://en.wikipedia.org/w/index.php?title=File:Grande_Ludovisi_Altemps_Inv8574.jpg *License:* Public Domain *Contributors:* User:Jastrow 11
Figure 7 *Source:* https://en.wikipedia.org/w/index.php?title=File:Roman_Balista_on_trajan_column.jpg *License:* GNU Free Documentation License *Contributors:* CristianChirita, G.dallorto, MGA73bot2, MatthiasKabel, Иван Дулин 12
Figure 8 *Source:* https://en.wikipedia.org/w/index.php?title=File:Roman_Empire_125_political_map.svg *License:* Creative Commons Attribution-Sharealike 3.0 *Contributors:* User:Andrein, with the assistance of EraNavigator 14
Figure 9 *Source:* https://en.wikipedia.org/w/index.php?title=File:Hospital_at_Novaesium_near_Dusseldorft._Wellcome_L0005983.jpg *Contributors:* DenghiùComm, Fæ, Zeromonk, Иван Дулин 15
Figure 10 *Source:* https://en.wikipedia.org/w/index.php?title=File:Roman-legions-212-AD-Centrici-site-Keilo-Jack.jpg *License:* Creative Commons Attribution-Sharealike 3.0 *Contributors:* User:Jack Keilo 18
Image *Source:* https://en.wikipedia.org/w/index.php?title=File:Wikisource-logo.svg *License:* Creative Commons Attribution-Sharealike 3.0 *Contributors:* ChrisiPK, Guillom, INeverCry, Jarekt, JuTa, Leyo, Lokal Profil, MichaelMaggs, NielsF, Rei-artur, Rocket000, Romaine, Steinsplitter 20
Image *Source:* https://en.wikipedia.org/w/index.php?title=File:Cscr-featured.svg *License:* GNU Lesser General Public License *Contributors:* Anomie 21
Figure 11 *Source:* https://en.wikipedia.org/w/index.php?title=File:Helmed_Hoplite_Sparta.JPG *License:* GNU Free Documentation License *Contributors:* de:Benutzer:Ticinese 24
Figure 12 *Source:* https://en.wikipedia.org/w/index.php?title=File:Altar_Domitius_Ahenobarbus_Louvre_n3bis.jpg *License:* Public Domain *Contributors:* User:Jastrow 26
Figure 13 *Source:* https://en.wikipedia.org/w/index.php?title=File:Marius_Glyptothek_Munich_319.jpg *License:* Public Domain *Contributors:* Albertomos, Bibi Saint-Pol, DIREKTOR, G.dallorto, Jbribeiro1, Lparsp, Shakko, Sprachpfleger, TheVovaNik, 4 anonymous edits 30
Figure 14 *Source:* https://en.wikipedia.org/w/index.php?title=File:2005-12-28_Berlin_Pergamon_museum_(16).jpg *License:* Creative Commons Attribution-ShareAlike 3.0 Unported *Contributors:* Magnus Manske 33
Figure 15 *Source:* https://en.wikipedia.org/w/index.php?title=File:Roman_soldiers_with_marching_packs_02.JPG *License:* Public Domain *Contributors:* User:Gaius Cornelius 35
Figure 16 *Source:* https://en.wikipedia.org/w/index.php?title=File:Sarcofago_dio_portonaccio,_03.JPG *License:* Creative Commons Attribution-Sharealike 3.0 *Contributors:* User:Folegandros 36
Figure 17 *Source:* https://en.wikipedia.org/w/index.php?title=File:Grande_Ludovisi_Altemps_Inv8574.jpg *License:* Public Domain *Contributors:* User:Jastrow 37
Figure 18 *Source:* https://en.wikipedia.org/w/index.php?title=File:Knight-Iran.JPG *License:* Public domain *Contributors:* Zereshk 38
Figure 19 *Source:* https://en.wikipedia.org/w/index.php?title=File:Constantine_arch_troops.jpg *License:* Public Domain *Contributors:* Filipo, G.dallorto, Sailko, Varano 40
Figure 20 *Source:* https://en.wikipedia.org/w/index.php?title=File:Greatpalacemosaic.jpg *License:* Public Domain *Contributors:* User:Ghirlandajo 44
Figure 21 *Source:* https://en.wikipedia.org/w/index.php?title=File:Solidus_Julian-transparent.png *License:* GNU Free Documentation License *Contributors:* Medium69, OgreBot 2 48
Figure 22 *Source:* https://en.wikipedia.org/w/index.php?title=File:Roman_Legionaries-MGR_Lyon-IMG_1050.JPG *License:* Creative Commons Attribution-Sharealike 2.0 *Contributors:* User:Rama/use_my_images 50
Figure 23 *Source:* https://en.wikipedia.org/w/index.php?title=File:0418_Befreiung_einer_belagerten_Stadt_Bodemuseum_anagoria.JPG *License:* Creative Commons Attribution 3.0 *Contributors:* Anagoria 52
Figure 24 *Source:* https://en.wikipedia.org/w/index.php?title=File:Altar_Domitius_Ahenobarbus_Louvre_n3bis.jpg *License:* Public Domain *Contributors:* User:Jastrow 55
Figure 25 *Source:* https//en.wikipedia.org *Contributors:* User:Neuroforever 58
Figure 26 *Source:* https://en.wikipedia.org/w/index.php?title=File:Roman_military_clothes_National_Military_Museum_Bucharest_Romania.jpg *License:* Creative Commons Attribution-Sharealike 2.0 *Contributors:* Elkost, FlickreviewR, OttawaAC 59
Figure 27 *Source:* https://en.wikipedia.org/w/index.php?title=File:Lens_-_Inauguration_du_Louvre-Lens_le_4_décembre_2012,_la_Galerie_du_Temps,_n°_058.JPG *License:* GNU Free Documentation License *Contributors:* Historien spécialiste du bassin minier du Nord-Pas-de-Calais JÄNNICK Jérémy 59
Figure 28 *Source:* https//en.wikipedia.org *License:* Attribution *Contributors:* Giovanni Dall'Orto 60
Figure 29 *Source:* https://en.wikipedia.org/w/index.php?title=File:Column_of_Marcus_Aurelius_-_detail1.jpg *License:* Creative Commons Attribution 3.0 *Contributors:* Barosaurus Lentus 60
Figure 30 *Source:* https://en.wikipedia.org/w/index.php?title=File:Jean_II_Comnene.jpg *Contributors:* File:Comnenus_mosaics_Hagia_Sophia.jpg: Photographer: Myrabella derivative work: Myrabella 64
Figure 31 *Source:* https://en.wikipedia.org/w/index.php?title=File:Roman_coins_sestertius_Nero_countermark_X_Legion_Gemina.jpg *License:* Creative Commons Attribution-Sharealike 3.0 *Contributors:* Numisantica 78
Figure 32 *Source:* https://en.wikipedia.org/w/index.php?title=File:Roman_Empire_125.png *License:* Creative Commons Attribution-Sharealike 3.0 *Contributors:* User:Andrein 80
Figure 33 *Source:* https://en.wikipedia.org/w/index.php?title=File:Scutum_Iovianorum_seniorum.svg *License:* GNU Free Documentation License *Contributors:* Panairjdde (FlagUploader) 87
Figure 34 *Source:* https://en.wikipedia.org/w/index.php?title=File:Engineering_corps_traian_s_column_river_crossing.jpg *License:* GNU Free Documentation License *Contributors:* CristianChirita 91
Figure 35 *Source:* https://en.wikipedia.org/w/index.php?title=File:Arte_etrusca,_urna_cineraria_in_terracotta_con_policromia_forse_autentica,_150_ac_ca._02.JPG *License:* Creative Commons Attribution 3.0 *Contributors:* User:Sailko 92
Figure 36 *Source:* https://en.wikipedia.org/w/index.php?title=File:Slingers_on_Trajan's_Column.JPG *License:* Public Domain *Contributors:* User:Gaius Cornelius 94
Figure 37 *Source:* https://en.wikipedia.org/w/index.php?title=File:Roman_helmet.jpg *License:* Creative Commons Attribution-Sharealike 3.0,2.5,2.0,1.0 *Contributors:* User:Michel wal 98
Figure 38 *Source:* https://en.wikipedia.org/w/index.php?title=File:Germania_70.svg *License:* GNU Free Documentation License *Contributors:* BotMultichillT, Filipo, Furfur, Hannolans, Hans Erren, JuJu939, QuartierLatin1968, 2 anonymous edits 100
Figure 39 *Source:* https://en.wikipedia.org/w/index.php?title=File:Grave_for_Titus_Flavius_Bassus_Römisch-Germanisches_Museum_Cologne.jpg *License:* Creative Commons Attribution-ShareAlike 3.0 Unported *Contributors:* Marcus Cyron = User:Kenwilliams 103
Figure 40 *Source:* https://en.wikipedia.org/w/index.php?title=File:Spatha_end_of_second_century_1.jpg *License:* Creative Commons Attribution-ShareAlike 3.0 Unported *Contributors:* User:MatthiasKabel 104

Figure 41 *Source:* https://en.wikipedia.org/w/index.php?title=File:Roman_cavalry_-_Big_Game_Hunt_mosaic_-_Villa_Romana_del_Casale_-_Italy_2015.JPG *Contributors:* © José Luiz Bernardes Ribeiro 108

Figure 42 *Source:* https://en.wikipedia.org/w/index.php?title=File:028_Conrad_Cichorius,_Die_Reliefs_der_Traianssäule,_Tafel_XXVIII.jpg *Contributors:* Gun Powder Ma, Jusjih, Thib Phil 111

Figure 43 *Source:* https://en.wikipedia.org/w/index.php?title=File:086_Conrad_Cichorius,_Die_Reliefs_der_Traianssäule,_Tafel_LXXXVI.jpg *Contributors:* Gun Powder Ma, Jusjih, Soerfm 112

Figure 44 *Source:* https://en.wikipedia.org/w/index.php?title=File:047_Conrad_Cichorius,_Die_Reliefs_der_Traianssäule,_Tafel_XLVII_(Ausschnitt_03).jpg *Contributors:* Gun Powder Ma, Jusjih, Wheeke 112

Figure 45 *Source:* https://en.wikipedia.org/w/index.php?title=File:CohMont1.jpg *License:* GNU Free Documentation License *Contributors:* El bes with help from: Leg XIII Gemina et Coh I It C R, Exercitus Pannonia Superior, Gesellschaft für römische Geschicht 117

Figure 46 *Source:* https://en.wikipedia.org/w/index.php?title=File:Grabstein_Titus_Calidius_Carnuntum.jpg *License:* Creative Commons Attribution-ShareAlike 3.0 Unported *Contributors:* User:MatthiasKabel 121

Figure 47 *Source:* https://en.wikipedia.org/w/index.php?title=File:Roman_Empire_125.png *License:* Creative Commons Attribution-Sharealike 3.0 *Contributors:* User:Andrein 126

Figure 48 *Source:* https://en.wikipedia.org/w/index.php?title=File:Quinquereme-and-corvus.jpg *License:* Creative Commons Attribution 3.0 *Contributors:* Lutatius 138

Figure 49 *Source:* https://en.wikipedia.org/w/index.php?title=File:As_Publius_Cornelius_Lentulus_Marcellinus.jpg *License:* Public Domain *Contributors:* Carlomorino, DenghiùComm, Yuri Che 139

Figure 50 *Source:* https://en.wikipedia.org/w/index.php?title=File:D473-birème_romaine-Liv2-ch10.png *License:* Public Domain *Contributors:* DenghiùComm, Garitan, PericlesofAthens, Vieux têtard, Иван Дулин 141

Figure 51 *Source:* https://en.wikipedia.org/w/index.php?title=File:Hw-pompey.jpg *License:* Public Domain *Contributors:* G.dallorto, Jmabel, Makthorpe, Paddy, Sailko, Tacsipacsi, Xenophon, 2 anonymous edits 142

Figure 52 *Source:* https://en.wikipedia.org/w/index.php?title=File:Pompey_by_Nasidius.jpg *License:* GNU Free Documentation License *Contributors:* CNG 144

Figure 53 *Source:* https://en.wikipedia.org/w/index.php?title=File:Castro_Battle_of_Actium.jpg *License:* Public Domain *Contributors:* Alonso de Mendoza, Boo-Boo Baroo, BotMultichill, Bukk, Caravaggista, Cplakidas, Martin H., Mattes, Shakko, Sswelm, Sterntreter, W!B:, 1 anonymous edits . 144

Figure 54 *Source:* https://en.wikipedia.org/w/index.php?title=File:058_Conrad_Cichorius,_Die_Reliefs_der_Traianssäule,_Tafel_LVIII.jpg *Contributors:* Eleassar, Gun Powder Ma, Hedwig in Washington, Jusjih, Stegop 147

Figure 55 *Source:* https://en.wikipedia.org/w/index.php?title=File:Mosaïque_d'Ulysse_et_les_sirènes.jpg *License:* Public Domain *Contributors:* Giorces derivative work: Habib M'henni 147

Figure 56 *Source:* https://en.wikipedia.org/w/index.php?title=File:Denarius_Mark_Anthony-32BC-legIII.jpg *License:* GNU Free Documentation License *Contributors:* Carlomorino, CatMan61, G.dallorto, MGA73bot2, Panairjdde~commonswiki, Paradoctor, Saperaud~commonswiki, Warburg, 1 anonymous edits 150

Figure 57 *Source:* https://en.wikipedia.org/w/index.php?title=File:Trireme_1.jpg *License:* Creative Commons Attribution-Sharealike 2.0 *Contributors:* Rama 153

Figure 58 *Source:* https://en.wikipedia.org/w/index.php?title=File:Roemerschiff1.jpg *License:* GNU Free Documentation License *Contributors:* Martin Bahmann 154

Figure 59 *Source:* https://en.wikipedia.org/w/index.php?title=File:Ballistae_on_roman_ship.JPG *License:* Public Domain *Contributors:* User:Gaius Cornelius 155

Figure 60 *Source:* https://en.wikipedia.org/w/index.php?title=File:Roman_harbors_and_fleets_Augustus-Severus.png *License:* Public Domain *Contributors:* Roman_Empire_with_provinces_in_210_AD.png: Mandrak derivative work: Cristiano64 (talk) 156

Figure 61 *Source:* https://en.wikipedia.org/w/index.php?title=File:Limes4.png *License:* Creative Commons Attribution-Sharealike 3.0,2.5,2.0,1.0 *Contributors:* Ziegelbrenner & Mediatus 159

Figure 62 *Source:* https://en.wikipedia.org/w/index.php?title=File:Limes5.png *License:* Creative Commons Attribution-Sharealike 3.0,2.5,2.0,1.0 *Contributors:* Ziegelbrenner 160

Figure 63 *Source:* https://en.wikipedia.org/w/index.php?title=File:Litus_Saxonicum.png *License:* Public Domain *Contributors:* Cplakidas ... 161

Figure 64 *Source:* https://en.wikipedia.org/w/index.php?title=File:Poussin_RapeSabineLouvre.jpg *License:* Public Domain *Contributors:* Auntof6, Chewie, Hsarrazin, JuTa, Kilom691, Mattes, Mel22, Urbourbo, 1 anonymous edits 167

Figure 65 *Source:* https://en.wikipedia.org/w/index.php?title=File:Etruscan_civilization_map.png *License:* Creative Commons Attribution-ShareAlike 3.0 Unported *Contributors:* NormanEinstein 170

Figure 66 *Source:* https://en.wikipedia.org/w/index.php?title=File:Pietra_bismantova.jpg *License:* GNU Free Documentation License *Contributors:* BotMultichill, MGA73bot2, Mac9, Paolo da Reggio~commonswiki, 2 anonymous edits 172

Figure 67 *Source:* https://en.wikipedia.org/w/index.php?title=File:Roman_conquest_of_Italy.PNG *License:* Public domain *Contributors:* Javierfv1212 172

Figure 68 *Source:* https://en.wikipedia.org/w/index.php?title=File:Pyrrhic_War_Italy_en.svg *License:* GNU Free Documentation License *Contributors:* Piom, translation by Pamela Butler 174

Figure 69 *Source:* https://en.wikipedia.org/w/index.php?title=File:Map_of_Rome_and_Carthage_at_the_start_of_the_Second_Punic_War.svg *License:* Creative Commons Attribution-Sharealike 3.0 *Contributors:* Rome_carthage_218.jpg: William Robert Shepherd derivative work: Grandiose 176

Figure 70 *Source:* https://en.wikipedia.org/w/index.php?title=File:Macedonia_and_the_Aegean_World_c.200.png *License:* Public domain *Contributors:* AnonMoos, Athaenara, Citypeek, Cplakidas, Filipo, Icesea, Karlfk, MGA73bot2, Megistias, PericlesofAthens, Razorbliss, Zykasaa, 2 anonymous edits 180

Figure 71 *Source:* https://en.wikipedia.org/w/index.php?title=File:Caesar_campaigns_gaul-en.svg *License:* Creative Commons Attribution-Sharealike 2.5 *Contributors:* User:Historicair, User:Sémhur 185

Figure 72 *Source:* https://en.wikipedia.org/w/index.php?title=File:RomanEmpire_117.svg *Contributors:* Amadscientist, Amphipolis, AnonMoos, Basvb, Begoon, BotMultichill, Codrinb, Cplakidas, EliasAlucard~commonswiki, File Upload Bot (Magnus Manske), Frank C. Müller, Fschoenm, Furfur, Geagea, JoKalliauer, KillOrDie, Malus Catulus, Nachosan, Nima Farid, OgreBot 2, Sidonius, Sprachpfleger, Tacsipacsi, TcfkaPanairjdde, 5 anonymous edits 189

Figure 73 *Source:* https://en.wikipedia.org/w/index.php?title=File:Alemanni_expansion.png *License:* Public Domain *Contributors:* Alexander.stohr, Bibi Saint-Pol, BokicaK, Bullenwächter, Cristiano64, Dbachmann, Gryffindor, MGA73bot2, Michiel1972, OwenBlacker, Roland zh, W-j-s, 9 anonymous edits 193

Image *Source:* https://en.wikipedia.org/w/index.php?title=File:GothicInvasions250-251-en.svg *License:* Creative Commons Attribution-Sharealike 3.0 *Contributors:* User:Dipa1965 194

Image *Source:* https://en.wikipedia.org/w/index.php?title=File:GothicInvasions_267-269-en.svg *License:* Creative Commons Attribution-Sharealike 3.0 *Contributors:* User:Dipa1965 194

Figure 74 *Source:* https://en.wikipedia.org/w/index.php?title=File:Gaul_IVth_century_AD.svg *License:* Creative Commons Attribution-Sharealike 3.0 *Contributors:* Codrinb, Edelseider, Mu, Niedźwiadek78, OgreBot 2, ZH2010, 1 anonymous edits 195

Figure 75 *Source:* https://en.wikipedia.org/w/index.php?title=File:Raphael-Constantine_at_Milvian_Bridge.jpg *License:* Public Domain *Contributors:* Bukk, Flamarande~commonswiki, G.dallorto, Jcb, Jusjih, Sailko, Shakko, Spider, 1 anonymous edits 196

Figure 76 *Source:* https://en.wikipedia.org/w/index.php?title=File:476eur.jpg *License:* Public Domain *Contributors:* 1989, Electionworld, JuTa, Julieta39, Roke~commonswiki, Ruthven, Ulamm, ZH2010, 1 anonymous edits 200

Figure 77 *Source:* https://en.wikipedia.org/w/index.php?title=File:628px-Western_and_Eastern_Roman_Empires_476AD(3).PNG *License:* Creative Commons Attribution-ShareAlike 3.0 Unported *Contributors:* User:Bigdaddy1204, User:Geuiwogbil 200

Figure 78 *Source:* https://en.wikipedia.org/w/index.php?title=File:Rome_in_753_BC.png *License:* GNU Free Documentation License *Contributors:* Roma_Romolo_753aC_png.png: Cristiano64 derivative work: Richardprins (talk) 207

Figure 79 *Source:* https://en.wikipedia.org/w/index.php?title=File:Siège_de_Porsenna.GIF *License:* Creative Commons Attribution-Sharealike 3.0,2.5,2.0,1.0 *Contributors:* Coldeel 207

Figure 80 *Source:* https://en.wikipedia.org/w/index.php?title=File:Roman_conquest_of_Italy.PNG *License:* Public domain *Contributors:* Javierfv1212 210

Figure 81 *Source:* https://en.wikipedia.org/w/index.php?title=File:Expansion_of_Rome,_2nd_century_BC_Only.png *Contributors:* User:Eitan96 213

Figure 82 *Source:* https://en.wikipedia.org/w/index.php?title=File:Expansion_of_Rome,_2nd_century_BC.gif *License:* Public Domain *Contributors:* Bibi Saint-Pol, Flamarande~commonswiki, Gryffindor, JMCC1, Karlfk, Kenmayer, Kirill Lokshin, Ras67, 4 anonymous edits 216

Figure 83 *Source:* https://en.wikipedia.org/w/index.php?title=File:1stMithritadicwar89BC-pt.svg *License:* Creative Commons Zero *Contributors:* User:Renato de carvalho ferreira 216

Figure 84 *Source:* https://en.wikipedia.org/w/index.php?title=File:RomanRepublic40BC.jpg *License:* Public Domain *Contributors:* Tataryn77 219

Figure 85 *Source:* https://en.wikipedia.org/w/index.php?title=File:Augusto_30aC_-_6dC_55%CS_jpg.JPG *License:* GNU Free Documentation License *Contributors:* Cristiano64 221

Figure 86 *Source:* https://en.wikipedia.org/w/index.php?title=File:Roman_Empire_Trajan_117AD.png *License:* Creative Commons Attribution-Sharealike 3.0 *Contributors:* User:Tataryn ... 223
Figure 87 *Source:* https://en.wikipedia.org/w/index.php?title=File:Map_of_Ancient_Rome_271_AD.svg *License:* Creative Commons Attribution-Sharealike 2.5 *Contributors:* Blank map of South Europe and North Africa.svg: historicair 23:27, 8 August 2007 (UTC) ... 224
Figure 88 *Source:* https://en.wikipedia.org/w/index.php?title=File:Tetrarchy_map3.jpg *License:* GNU Free Documentation License *Contributors:* Coppermine Photo Gallery ... 226
Figure 89 *Source:* https://en.wikipedia.org/w/index.php?title=File:ConstantineEmpire.png *License:* Creative Commons Attribution-Sharealike 3.0 *Contributors:* User:Tataryn ... 226
Figure 90 *Source:* https://en.wikipedia.org/w/index.php?title=File:Invasions_of_the_Roman_Empire_1.png *License:* Creative Commons Attribution-Sharealike 2.5 *Contributors:* User:MapMaster ... 228
Figure 91 *Source:* https://en.wikipedia.org/w/index.php?title=File:Pont_du_gard.jpg *License:* GNU Free Documentation License *Contributors:* Bernard bill5∼commonswiki, ClemRutter, Cyr∼commonswiki, Hazhk, MGA73bot2, 3 anonymous edits ... 233
Figure 92 *Source:* https://en.wikipedia.org/w/index.php?title=File:Panorámica_de_Las_Médulas.jpg *License:* Creative Commons Attribution-ShareAlike 3.0 Unported *Contributors:* Rafael Ibáñez Fernández ... 234
Figure 93 *Source:* https://en.wikipedia.org/w/index.php?title=File:Templeborough_Roman_Fort_visualised_3D_flythrough_-_Rotherham.webm *Contributors:* Morio, PatHadley, Richard Nevell (WMUK), Sixflashphoto, 1 anonymous edits ... 236
Figure 94 *Source:* https://en.wikipedia.org/w/index.php?title=File:Castra1.png *License:* GNU Free Documentation License *Contributors:* BotMultichill, BotMultichillT, DieBuche, Gbarta, Hartmann Linge, Linguae, Longbow4u, MGA73bot2, Matt314, Poyekhali, Redtony, 1 anonymous edits ... 239
Figure 95 *Source:* https://en.wikipedia.org/w/index.php?title=File:Kastell_Theilenhofen_Iciniacum_(English).png *License:* Creative Commons Attribution-Sharealike 3.0 *Contributors:* Mediatus ... 240
Figure 96 *Source:* https://en.wikipedia.org/w/index.php?title=File:Arbeia_Roman_Fort_reconstructed_gateway.jpg *Contributors:* Chris McKenna (user:Thryduulf) ... 241
Figure 97 *Source:* https://en.wikipedia.org/w/index.php?title=File:Holzwachturm_am_rätischen_Limes_(Rekonstruktion)_-_Wp12_77.jpg *License:* Creative Commons Attribution-Sharealike 3.0,2.5,2.0,1.0 *Contributors:* Haselburg-müller ... 242
Figure 98 *Source:* https://en.wikipedia.org/w/index.php?title=File:Porta_Praetoria_Kastell_Pfünz.jpg *License:* Creative Commons Attribution-ShareAlike 3.0 Unported *Contributors:* Mediatus ... 242
Figure 99 *Source:* https://en.wikipedia.org/w/index.php?title=File:Masada_Roman_Ruins_by_David_Shankbone.jpg *License:* GNU Free Documentation License *Contributors:* David Shankbone ... 243
Figure 100 *Source:* https://en.wikipedia.org/w/index.php?title=File:Ostkastell_Welzheim.jpg *License:* Creative Commons Attribution-Sharealike 3.0 *Contributors:* Mediatus ... 244
Figure 101 *Source:* https://en.wikipedia.org/w/index.php?title=File:Susa_PortaSavoia.jpg *License:* Creative Commons Attribution-Sharealike 3.0 *Contributors:* Alessandro Vecchi ... 244
Figure 102 *Source:* https://en.wikipedia.org/w/index.php?title=File:Weißenburg_Porta_decumana2.jpg *License:* Creative Commons Attribution-Sharealike 3.0 *Contributors:* Mediatus ... 245
Figure 103 *Source:* https://en.wikipedia.org/w/index.php?title=File:DevaMinervaPlan(bq).jpg *License:* Creative Commons Attribution-Share Alike *Contributors:* Łukasz Nurczyński ... 246
Figure 104 *Source:* https://en.wikipedia.org/w/index.php?title=File:Arbeia_Roman_Fort_grannaries.jpg *Contributors:* Chris McKenna (user:Thryduulf) ... 247
Figure 105 *Source:* https://en.wikipedia.org/w/index.php?title=File:Roman_Onager.jpg *License:* Public Domain *Contributors:* Apocheir, Avron, DieBuche, Foil Fencer, Hossmann∼commonswiki, JMCC1, Konto na chwilę, Medium69, Picture Master, Sindala, The RedBurn, Wieralee, 2 anonymous edits ... 248
Figure 106 *Source:* https://en.wikipedia.org/w/index.php?title=File:2006_0602TurdaPotaissa0122.jpg *License:* Creative Commons Attribution 2.5 *Contributors:* © ... 249
Figure 107 *Source:* https://en.wikipedia.org/w/index.php?title=File:Arbeia_Roman_Fort_reconstructed_barracks.jpg *Contributors:* Chris McKenna (user:Thryduulf) ... 250
Figure 108 *Source:* https://en.wikipedia.org/w/index.php?title=File:Granary_at_Housesteads_Roman_Fort.jpg *License:* GNU Free Documentation License *Contributors:* uploaded to Wikipedia by Fryslan0109 ... 252
Figure 109 *Source:* https://en.wikipedia.org/w/index.php?title=File:Cohen_0008.jpg *License:* GNU Free Documentation License *Contributors:* Alixpeeke, Amada44, Carlomorino, DenghiùComm, Fallschirmjäger, G.dallorto, JuTa, Luigi Chiesa, MGA73bot2 ... 254
Figure 110 *Source:* https://en.wikipedia.org/w/index.php?title=File:Hadrians_Wall_05.JPG *License:* Public domain *Contributors:* Fschoenm, Mediatus, OgreBot 2, Wilson44691 ... 255
Image *Source:* https://en.wikipedia.org/w/index.php?title=File:Commons-logo.svg *License:* logo *Contributors:* Anomie, Callanecc, CambridgeBayWeather, Jo-Jo Eumerus, RHaworth ... 257
Figure 111 *Source:* https://en.wikipedia.org/w/index.php?title=File:Young_Folks'_History_of_Rome_illus216.png *License:* Public Domain *Contributors:* Yonge, Charlotte Mary, (1823-1901) ... 260
Figure 112 *Source:* https://en.wikipedia.org/w/index.php?title=File:Roman_siege_machines.gif *License:* Public Domain *Contributors:* The Air War college ... 261
Figure 113 *Source:* https://en.wikipedia.org/w/index.php?title=File:Young_Folks'_History_of_Rome_illus103.png *License:* Public Domain *Contributors:* Yonge, Charlotte Mary, (1823-1901) ... 262
Figure 114 *Source:* https://en.wikipedia.org/w/index.php?title=File:Bal_BBC1.jpg *License:* Public Domain *Contributors:* Vissarion ... 262
Figure 115 *Source:* https://en.wikipedia.org/w/index.php?title=File:Ballista.gif *License:* Public Domain *Contributors:* BLueFiSH.as, Quibik, Shauni, 1 anonymous edits ... 263
Figure 116 *Source:* https://en.wikipedia.org/w/index.php?title=File:047_Conrad_Cichorius,_Die_Reliefs_der_Traianssäule,_Tafel_XLVII_(Ausschnitt_02).jpg *Contributors:* Gun Powder Ma, Jusjih ... 264
Figure 117 *Source:* https://en.wikipedia.org/w/index.php?title=File:Ballista_(PSF).png *Contributors:* Crowsnest, JMCC1, KTo288, Look2See1, Macesito, Magnus Manske, Picture Master, Wieralee, WikipediaMaster ... 265
Figure 118 *Source:* https://en.wikipedia.org/w/index.php?title=File:Roman_Onager.jpg *License:* Public Domain *Contributors:* Apocheir, Avron, DieBuche, Foil Fencer, Hossmann∼commonswiki, JMCC1, Konto na chwilę, Medium69, Picture Master, Sindala, The RedBurn, Wieralee, 2 anonymous edits ... 266
Figure 119 *Source:* https://en.wikipedia.org/w/index.php?title=File:Balliste.jpg *License:* Creative Commons Attribution-ShareAlike 3.0 Unported *Contributors:* User:MatthiasKabel ... 267
Figure 120 *Source:* https://en.wikipedia.org/w/index.php?title=File:Meyers_b1_s0808_b1.png *License:* Public Domain *Contributors:* Bohème, Classiccardinal, Mapmarks, Picture Master, Wieralee ... 268
Figure 121 *Source:* https://en.wikipedia.org/w/index.php?title=File:Murbräcka_med_skjul,_Nordisk_familjebok.png *License:* Public Domain *Contributors:* Martin Fickelscherer ... 268
Figure 122 *Source:* https://en.wikipedia.org/w/index.php?title=File:MasadaRamp.jpg *License:* GNU Free Documentation License *Contributors:* Avron, BotAdventures, File Upload Bot (Magnus Manske), Liftarn, MGA73bot2, OgreBot 2, Pieter Kuiper, Reinhard Dietrich ... 269
Figure 123 *Source:* https://en.wikipedia.org/w/index.php?title=File:Young_Folks'_History_of_Rome_illus106.png *License:* Public Domain *Contributors:* Yonge, Charlotte Mary, (1823-1901) ... 270
Image *Source:* https://en.wikipedia.org/w/index.php?title=File:Djemila,_Algeria.jpg *License:* Creative Commons Attribution-ShareAlike 3.0 Unported *Contributors:* Paebi ... 273
Image *Source:* https://en.wikipedia.org/w/index.php?title=File:Tébessa-Porte_Caracala.jpg *License:* Public Domain *Contributors:* Zalitahar ... 273
Image *Source:* https://en.wikipedia.org/w/index.php?title=File:Arc_de_triomphe_de_Trajan.jpg *License:* Creative Commons Attribution-Sharealike 2.0 *Contributors:* Yves Jalabert ... 274
Image *Source:* https://en.wikipedia.org/w/index.php?title=File:Heidentor_(by_Pudelek).JPG *License:* Creative Commons Attribution-Sharealike 3.0 *Contributors:* Pudelek (Marcin Szala) ... 274
Image *Source:* https://en.wikipedia.org/w/index.php?title=File:Croatia_Pula_Arch_of_the_Sergii_2014-10-11_12-22-20.jpg *Contributors:* user:Berthold Werner ... 274
Image *Source:* https://en.wikipedia.org/w/index.php?title=File:Arc_de_Campanus_et_thermes_nationaux.JPG *License:* Creative Commons Attribution-Sharealike 3.0 *Contributors:* Florian Pépellin ... 274
Image *Source:* https://en.wikipedia.org/w/index.php?title=File:Porte_Noire_Besançon.jpg *License:* Creative Commons Attribution-ShareAlike 3.0 Unported *Contributors:* myself ... 274
Image *Source:* https://en.wikipedia.org/w/index.php?title=File:Carpentras_-_Arc_Romain.JPG *License:* Public Domain *Contributors:* Véronique PAGNIER ... 274
Image *Source:* https://en.wikipedia.org/w/index.php?title=File:Arc_de_Triomphe_d'Orange.jpg *License:* Public domain *Contributors:* DenghiùComm, File Upload Bot (Magnus Manske), Foroa, Funfood, MGA73bot2, OgreBot 2, Tiefkuehlfan ... 274
Image *Source:* https://en.wikipedia.org/w/index.php?title=File:Porte_de_Mars,_Reims(1).jpg *License:* GNU Free Documentation License *Contributors:* Magnus Manske ... 274

Image *Source:* https://en.wikipedia.org/w/index.php?title=File:Pont_Flavien,_Bouches-du-Rhône,_France._Pic_02.jpg *License:* Creative Commons Attribution 2.0 *Contributors:* maarjaara ... 274
Image *Source:* https://en.wikipedia.org/w/index.php?title=File:Glanum-triomphal_arch-arc_de_triomphe.jpg *License:* Public Domain *Contributors:* Greudin ... 274
Image *Source:* https://en.wikipedia.org/w/index.php?title=File:Arc_de_Germanicus.JPG *License:* Creative Commons Attribution-Sharealike 2.5 *Contributors:* Propre travail ... 274
Image *Source:* https://en.wikipedia.org/w/index.php?title=File:Attica_06-13_Athens_24_Arch_of_Hadrian.jpg *Contributors:* A.Savin ... 274
Image *Source:* https://en.wikipedia.org/w/index.php?title=File:Arch_of_Galerius.jpg *License:* Creative Commons Attribution 2.0 *Contributors:* George Groutas from Idalion, Cyprus ... 274
Image *Source:* https://en.wikipedia.org/w/index.php?title=File:29AnconaTraiano.jpg *License:* Creative Commons Attribution-Sharealike 3.0 *Contributors:* MarkusMark ... 274
Image *Source:* https://en.wikipedia.org/w/index.php?title=File:Arco_Augusto_Aosta.jpg *License:* Creative Commons Attribution-Sharealike 3.0,2.5,2.0,1.0 *Contributors:* Agnello ... 274
Image *Source:* https://en.wikipedia.org/w/index.php?title=File:Arco_trionfale_di_marcantonio.jpg *Contributors:* User:FAM1885 ... 275
Image *Source:* https://en.wikipedia.org/w/index.php?title=File:Benevento-Arch_of_Trajan_from_North.jpg *License:* Creative Commons Attribution-Sharealike 2.0 *Contributors:* Alatius, Albedo-ukr, Decan, DenghiùComm, G.dallorto, Nonopoly, 1 anonymous edits ... 275
Image *Source:* https://en.wikipedia.org/w/index.php?title=File:CanosaDiPugliaArcoTraiano.jpg *License:* Public Domain *Contributors:* MM . 275
Image *Source:* https://en.wikipedia.org/w/index.php?title=File:Fano,_arco_di_augusto_04.JPG *License:* GNU Free Documentation License *Contributors:* User:Sailko, user:sailko ... 275
Image *Source:* https://en.wikipedia.org/w/index.php?title=File:S03_06_01_024_image_3140.jpg *License:* Public Domain *Contributors:* DenghiùComm, Lalupa, Theartofthemuses ... 275
Image *Source:* https://en.wikipedia.org/w/index.php?title=File:Arco_d'Augusto_Rimini.JPG *License:* Public Domain *Contributors:* Tobabi1 . 275
Image *Source:* https://en.wikipedia.org/w/index.php?title=File:RomeConstantine'sArch03.jpg *License:* GNU Free Documentation License *Contributors:* User:Alexander Z. ... 275
Image *Source:* https://en.wikipedia.org/w/index.php?title=File:Appia_antica_2-7-05_003.jpg *License:* Public Domain *Contributors:* Nick ... 275
Image *Source:* https://en.wikipedia.org/w/index.php?title=File:Arco_di_Gallieno_o_Porta_Esquilina_-_lato_interno_-_Panairjdde.jpg *License:* Creative Commons Sharealike 1.0 *Contributors:* FlagUploader (User:Panairjdde) ... 275
Image *Source:* https://en.wikipedia.org/w/index.php?title=File:RomeForumRomanumArchofSeptimiusSeverus01.jpg *License:* GNU Free Documentation License *Contributors:* Alexander Z., FoeNyx, G.dallorto, Geofrog, MGA73bot2, Mac9, Marcok, Olivier, Wknight94 ... 275
Image *Source:* https://en.wikipedia.org/w/index.php?title=File:Arc_de_titus_frontal.jpg *License:* Public Domain *Contributors:* FoeNyx, G.dallorto, Geofrog, Greudin, Longbow4u, Mac9, Olivier, Stan Shebs ... 275
Image *Source:* https://en.wikipedia.org/w/index.php?title=File:RomaArcoGianoCostantino1.JPG *License:* Public Domain *Contributors:* User:MM 275
Image *Source:* https://en.wikipedia.org/w/index.php?title=File:RomaViaFlaminiaArcoMalborghetto4.jpg *License:* Public Domain *Contributors:* MM ... 275
Image *Source:* https://en.wikipedia.org/w/index.php?title=File:Ehrenbogen_arco_di_adriano.jpg *License:* GNU Free Documentation License *Contributors:* Stanley-goodspeed at de.wikipedia ... 275
Image *Source:* https://en.wikipedia.org/w/index.php?title=File:Spoleto005.jpg *License:* Creative Commons Attribution 3.0 *Contributors:* JoJan 276
Image *Source:* https://en.wikipedia.org/w/index.php?title=File:Arco_di_Augusto-Susa.jpg *License:* Creative Commons Attribution-Sharealike 3.0 *Contributors:* Duvilar (Lorenzo Rossetti) ... 276
Image *Source:* https://en.wikipedia.org/w/index.php?title=File:Arcoromano.jpg *License:* GNU Free Documentation License *Contributors:* Zinn 276
Image *Source:* https://en.wikipedia.org/w/index.php?title=File:Arco_Gavi.jpg *License:* Creative Commons Attribution-Sharealike 3.0 *Contributors:* Lo Scaligero ... 276
Image *Source:* https://en.wikipedia.org/w/index.php?title=File:Hadrian_Arc_Pan-2.jpg *License:* Creative Commons Attribution 3.0 *Contributors:* Askii ... 276
Image *Source:* https://en.wikipedia.org/w/index.php?title=File:Tyre_Triumphal_Arch.jpg *License:* Creative Commons Attribution-Sharealike 2.5 *Contributors:* Bontenbal, Cybjorg~commonswiki, DenghiùComm, G.dallorto, Heretiq, Olivier, Pazuzu, 1 anonymous edits ... 276
Image *Source:* https://en.wikipedia.org/w/index.php?title=File:Leptis_Magna_Arch_of_Septimus_Severus.jpg *License:* Public Domain *Contributors:* Daviegunn ... 276
Image *Source:* https://en.wikipedia.org/w/index.php?title=File:Marcus_Aurelius_Arch_Tripoli_Libya.jpg *License:* Creative Commons Attribution 2.0 *Contributors:* Daniel and Kate Pett ... 276
Image *Source:* https://en.wikipedia.org/w/index.php?title=File:Triumphal_Arch_in_Volubilis.jpg *License:* Creative Commons Attribution 2.0 *Contributors:* BotAdventures, FlickrLickr, FlickreviewR, G.dallorto, High Contrast, MGA73bot2, 1 anonymous edits ... 276
Image *Source:* https://en.wikipedia.org/w/index.php?title=File:Arco_romano_de_Cabanes.jpg *License:* Creative Commons Attribution-Share Alike *Contributors:* Andrés Lozano Bojadós ... 276
Image *Source:* https://en.wikipedia.org/w/index.php?title=File:Arco_de_Medinaceli_(cara_norte).jpg *License:* Creative Commons Attribution-Share Alike *Contributors:* Rastrojo (D•ES) ... 276
Image *Source:* https://en.wikipedia.org/w/index.php?title=File:Spain.Catalonia.Roda.de.Bara.Arc.Bera.jpg *License:* Creative Commons Attribution-ShareAlike 3.0 Unported *Contributors:* User:Yearofthedragon ... 276
Image *Source:* https://en.wikipedia.org/w/index.php?title=File:Arch_latakia1.jpg *License:* GNU Free Documentation License *Contributors:* Allamlatakia (talk) (Uploads) ... 276
Image *Source:* https://en.wikipedia.org/w/index.php?title=File:Dougga_10.jpg *License:* Creative Commons Attribution-Sharealike 3.0,2.5,2.0,1.0 *Contributors:* Bernard Gagnon ... 277
Image *Source:* https://en.wikipedia.org/w/index.php?title=File:Arc_septime_severe_dougga.jpg *License:* Creative Commons Attribution-Sharealike 3.0,2.5,2.0,1.0 *Contributors:* Pradigue ... 277
Image *Source:* https://en.wikipedia.org/w/index.php?title=File:Sbeitla_10.jpg *License:* Creative Commons Attribution-Sharealike 3.0,2.5,2.0,1.0 *Contributors:* Bernard Gagnon ... 277
Image *Source:* https://en.wikipedia.org/w/index.php?title=File:Anazarbus_klikya_city_south_gate.jpg *License:* Creative Commons Attribution-Sharealike 3.0,2.5,2.0,1.0 *Contributors:* DenghiùComm, File Upload Bot (Magnus Manske), Freta, OgreBot 2, Svens Welt ... 277
Image *Source:* https://en.wikipedia.org/w/index.php?title=File:Hadrianus_gate.jpg *License:* Creative Commons Attribution-Sharealike 2.0 *Contributors:* Alexandrin, AnRo0002, FlickreviewR, Freta, G.dallorto, Nosferattü, Sunrise1, 2 anonymous edits ... 277
Image *Source:* https://en.wikipedia.org/w/index.php?title=File:Arch_of_August.png *License:* Public Domain *Contributors:* Christian Hülsen . 277
Image *Source:* https://en.wikipedia.org/w/index.php?title=File:Piranesi-1018.jpg *Contributors:* Bkmd, DenghiùComm ... 277
Image *Source:* https://en.wikipedia.org/w/index.php?title=File:NERONE-RIC_I_393-2580351_ARCHTRIUMPH.jpg *License:* GNU Free Documentation License *Contributors:* Cristiano64 ... 278
Image *Source:* https://en.wikipedia.org/w/index.php?title=File:Arch_of_Portugal_reconsruction.png *License:* Public Domain *Contributors:* GifTagger ... 278
Image *Source:* https://en.wikipedia.org/w/index.php?title=File:Palmyra_-_Monumental_Arch.jpg *License:* Creative Commons Attribution-Sharealike 3.0,2.5,2.0,1.0 *Contributors:* Bernard Gagnon ... 278
Image *Source:* https://en.wikipedia.org/w/index.php?title=File:Forum_Theodosius_Istanbul_March_2008_(15).JPG *License:* Creative Commons Attribution-Share Alike *Contributors:* Gryffindor ... 278
Figure 124 *Source:* https://en.wikipedia.org/w/index.php?title=File:PompeiiStreet.jpg *License:* GNU Free Documentation License *Contributors:* Paul Vlaar ... 280
Figure 125 *Source:* https://en.wikipedia.org/w/index.php?title=File:Carved_steps_along_Ancient_Roman_Road.jpg *Contributors:* User:Davidbena 281
Figure 126 *Source:* https://en.wikipedia.org/w/index.php?title=File:Aeclanum_(Ancient_Roman_Street).jpg *License:* Creative Commons Attribution-Share Alike *Contributors:* Дэя-Бøяг ... 282
Figure 127 *Source:* https://en.wikipedia.org/w/index.php?title=File:Metopa_Columna_lui_Traian_Constructie_drum.jpg *License:* GNU Free Documentation License *Contributors:* AxelHH, CristianChirita, G.dallorto, MGA73bot2, MatthiasKabel, The Patriot Woodworker, Thib Phil, Иван Дулин 288
Figure 128 *Source:* https://en.wikipedia.org/w/index.php?title=File:Via_Munita.png *License:* Public Domain *Contributors:* Smith, William, William Wayte, and G. E. Marindin ... 290
Figure 129 *Source:* https://en.wikipedia.org/w/index.php?title=File:Tabula_Traiana.jpg *License:* GNU Free Documentation License *Contributors:* Rlichtefeld ... 292
Figure 130 *Source:* https://en.wikipedia.org/w/index.php?title=File:Engineering_corps_traian_s_column_river_crossing.jpg *License:* GNU Free Documentation License *Contributors:* CristianChirita ... 292
Figure 131 *Source:* https://en.wikipedia.org/w/index.php?title=File:Campidoglio_-_il_miliarium.JPG *License:* Public Domain *Contributors:* user:Lalupa ... 293

Figure 132 *Source:* https://en.wikipedia.org/w/index.php?title=File:Milliarum_of_Aiton,_modern_copy_erected_in_Turda,_Romania_in_1993.jpg *License:* Public Domain *Contributors:* User:CristianChirita 294
Figure 133 *Source:* https://en.wikipedia.org/w/index.php?title=File:RomaForoRomanoMiliariumAureum01.JPG *License:* GNU Free Documentation License *Contributors:* Blackcat, Flamarande~commonswiki, G.dallorto, Jbribeiro1, Jean-Louis Hens, LX, Leyo, Longbow4u, MGA73bot2, Pmontaldo, SPQRobin, 1 anonymous edits 294
Figure 134 *Source:* https://en.wikipedia.org/w/index.php?title=File:Roman_milestone_rabagao_portugal.jpg *License:* Public Domain *Contributors:* BBird 295
Figure 135 *Source:* https://en.wikipedia.org/w/index.php?title=File:Part_of_Tabula_Peutingeriana.jpg *License:* Public Domain *Contributors:* unkwon 296
Figure 136 *Source:* https://en.wikipedia.org/w/index.php?title=File:Römischer_Reisewagen.JPG *License:* Creative Commons Attribution 2.5 *Contributors:* Nicolas von Kospoth (Triggerhappy) 297
Figure 137 *Source:* https://en.wikipedia.org/w/index.php?title=File:Roman_Empire_125_general_map_(Red_roads).svg *Contributors:* User:DS28 299
Figure 138 *Source:* https://en.wikipedia.org/w/index.php?title=File:The_Ancient_Roads_of_Italy_and_Sicily_nopng.svg *License:* Public Domain *Contributors:* Agamemnus 300
Figure 139 *Source:* https://en.wikipedia.org/w/index.php?title=File:2006_0814Histria_Road_Market20060416.jpg *License:* GNU Free Documentation License *Contributors:* 1989, Badseed, CristianChirita, MGA73bot2, Scientus, 1 anonymous edits 302
Figure 140 *Source:* https://en.wikipedia.org/w/index.php?title=File:Germania_inferior_roads_towns.png *License:* Creative Commons Attribution-Sharealike 3.0,2.5,2.0,1.0 *Contributors:* Hans Erren 302
Figure 141 *Source:* https://en.wikipedia.org/w/index.php?title=File:BALKANS_ROMAN_ROADS_cropped.jpg *License:* Public Domain *Contributors:* Work of NASA + CristianChirita (released into public domain, see Image:BALKANS_ROMAN_ROADS_.jpg) + own work 303
Figure 142 *Source:* https://en.wikipedia.org/w/index.php?title=File:Hispania_roads.svg *License:* Creative Commons Attribution-Sharealike 3.0,2.5,2.0,1.0 *Contributors:* Redtony 304
Figure 143 *Source:* https://en.wikipedia.org/w/index.php?title=File:Roman_road_in_Tarsus,_Mersin_Province.jpg *License:* Creative Commons Attribution-Sharealike 3.0 *Contributors:* User:Nedim Ardoğa 304
Figure 144 *Source:* https://en.wikipedia.org/w/index.php?title=File:High_Street_and_Small_Water_from_Harter_Fell.jpg *License:* GNU Free Documentation License *Contributors:* Personal Photo taken by Mick Knapton at en.wikipedia 306
Image *Source:* https://en.wikipedia.org/w/index.php?title=File:Policy-to-engagement_en.svg *License:* Creative Commons Attribution-Sharealike 3.0 *Contributors:* GJo 313
Image *Source:* https://en.wikipedia.org/w/index.php?title=File:Mpl-frm-variations.png *License:* Public Domain *Contributors:* PocklingtonDan, Sdrtirs, 2 anonymous edits 315
Image *Source:* https://en.wikipedia.org/w/index.php?title=File:Rom-mnpl-1.png *License:* Public Domain *Contributors:* PocklingtonDan 326
Image *Source:* https://en.wikipedia.org/w/index.php?title=File:Rom-mnpl-2.png *License:* Public Domain *Contributors:* PocklingtonDan 326
Figure 145 *Source:* https://en.wikipedia.org/w/index.php?title=File:Reenact_testudo.jpg *License:* Public domain *Contributors:* Athaenara, Common Good, File Upload Bot (Magnus Manske), OgreBot 2, 1 anonymous edits 331
Figure 146 *Source:* https://en.wikipedia.org/w/index.php?title=File:Balliste.jpg *License:* Creative Commons Attribution-ShareAlike 3.0 Unported *Contributors:* User:MatthiasKabel 332
Figure 147 *Source:* https://en.wikipedia.org/w/index.php?title=File:Limes_and_borders.gif *License:* Public domain *Contributors:* Abafttours, Auntof6, Caligatus, Carolmooredc, File Upload Bot (Magnus Manske), Geagea, Joanbanjo, Laerol, OgreBot 2, PANONIAN 362
Figure 148 *Source:* https://en.wikipedia.org/w/index.php?title=File:Hadrians_Wall_from_Housesteads1.jpg *License:* Public domain *Contributors:* Beyond My Ken, Fschoenm, Mediatus, OgreBot 2, Verica Atrebatum 364
Figure 149 *Source:* https://en.wikipedia.org/w/index.php?title=File:004_Conrad_Cichorius,_Die_Reliefs_der_Traianssäule,_Tafel_IV_(Ausschnitt_02).jpg *Contributors:* CristianChirita, Gun Powder Ma, Jusjih 366

License

Creative Commons Attribution-Share Alike 3.0
//creativecommons.org/licenses/by-sa/3.0/

Index

Ab Asturica Burdigalam, 305
Abila (Decapolis), 82
Ab urbe condita (book), 377, 378
Ab urbe condita libri (Livy), 166, 380
Accensi, 28, 69
Accusative case, 237
Achaea, 181
Achaean League, 181, 214
Achaean War, 181, 215
Actarius, 66
Adiutor, 66
Adrian Goldsworthy, 20, 45, 46, 204, 361, 373
Adrianople, 354
Adriatic, 139
Adriatic Sea, 300, 301
Adsidui, 24, 25, 29
Aeclanum, 282
Aedile, 285, 287
Aegean sea, 148, 158
Aegidius, 128, 229
Aegyptus, 80
Aelius Gallus, 145
Aeneator, 66
Aequi, 169, 170, 208
Aetolian League, 140, 180
Aetolian War, 181, 214
Africa proconsularis, 80
Africa Province, 43
Africa (Roman province), 2, 113
Agrimensor, 66, 290
A.H.M. Jones, 63
Aix-les-Bains, 274
Akeman Street, 305
Alae, 109
Alamanni, 194, 227
Alans, 45, 195, 228, 357
Alaric I, 201, 228
Alaris (Roman military), 66
Ala (Roman allied military unit), 49, 55, 93
Ala (Roman cavalry unit), 95
Ala (Roman military), 31, 66
Alba Iulia, 84
Albania, 139, 301
Alban war with Rome, 168

Albert Harkness, 204
Alemanni, 50, 225, 227
Alesia (city), 266
Alexander Severus, 197, 198
Alexander the Great, 335
Alexandria, 82, 85, 146, 157, 162, 301
Alexandrian War, 132
Algeria, 113, 273, 274
Al Khums, 276
Allectus, 85
Allobroges, 182
Alpine regiments of the Roman army, 103, 117
Alpine regiments of the Roman auxilia, 121
Alsace, 298
Altar of Domitius Ahenobarbus, 26, 55
Altinum, 202, 305
Ambrosius Aurelianus, 229
Amelia, Umbria, 300
Ameriola, 168
Amida (Roman city), 227
Ammaedara, 82
Ammianus Marcellinus, 45
Anatolia, 53, 65, 114, 184
Anazarbus, 277
Ancient Carthage, 174–176, 178, 289
Ancient China, 11
Ancient Corinth, 181
Ancient Germanic, 115
Ancient Greece, 19, 174
Ancient Greek, 48
Ancient Greeks, 171
Ancient Italic peoples, 175
Ancient Rome, 9, 11, 21, 47, 135, 165, 206, 287
Ancient trackway, 280
Ancona, 274
Ancus Marcius, 166
Ancyra, 214
Anderitum, 157
Andrew Alfoldi, 46
Andriscus, 181, 214, 377
Anesthesia, 16
Anglo-Saxons, 229
Anicetus (pirate), 146

Annals (Tacitus), 374
Antalya, 277
Antemnae, 168
Anthemius, 150
Antioch, 199, 305
Antiochus III the Great, 175, 181, 214
Antiochus the Great, 377
Antonine Plague, 107
Antonine Wall, 364
Antoninus Pius, 151, 254
Antonio Santosuosso, 4, 20, 36, 46, 205
Antonius Primus, 222
Aosta, 274
Apamea (Syria), 82
Apennine Mountains, 301
Apiolae, 168
Apocryphal, 166
Apollo, 84
Apollodorus of Damascus, 270
Appian, 347, 377, 379
Appian Way, 279
Appius Claudius, 212
Appius Claudius Caudex, 129
Apulia, 300
Apulum (castra), 303
Aqueduct (bridge), 232
Aqueduct (watercourse), 232, 233
Aquila (Roman), 84, 85
Aquileia, 161, 301
Aquilifer, 66
Aquincum, 82
Aquino, Italy, 275
Arab conquests, 52
Arabian peninsula, 145
Arabia Petraea, 80, 87, 367
Arabia (Roman province), 305
Arbeia, 247
Arbogast (general), 227
Arc de Berà, 276
Arch, 232, 291
Arch bridge, 291
Archery, 65, 338
Archimedean screw, 233
Archimedes, 140
Architecti, 66
Arch of Alexander Severus, 277
Arch of Arcadius, Honorius and Theodosius, 277
Arch of Augustus (Aosta), 274
Arch of Augustus (Fano), 275
Arch of Augustus (Rimini), 275
Arch of Augustus, Rome, 277
Arch of Augustus (Susa), 276
Arch of Cabanes, 276
Arch of Campanus, 274
Arch of Caracalla (Djémila), 273

Arch of Caracalla (Thebeste), 273
Arch of Carpentras, 274
Arch of Claudius (British victory), 277
Arch of Constantine, 40, 275
Arch of Drusus, 275
Arch of Galerius and Rotunda, 274
Arch of Gallienus, 275
Arch of Germanicus, 274
Arch of Glanum, 274
Arch of Gratian, Valentinian and Theodosius, 277
Arch of Hadrian (Athens), 274
Arch of Hadrian (Capua), 275
Arch of Hadrian (Jerash), 276
Arch of Janus, 275
Arch of Lentulus and Crispinus, 277
Arch of Malborghetto, 275
Arch of Marcus Aurelius, 276
Arch of Mark Antony, 275
Arch of Nero, 278
Arch of Octavius, 278
Arch of Pietas, 278
Arch of Portugal, 278
Arch of Septimius Severus, 275
Arch of the Sergii, 274
Arch of Tiberius, 278
Arch of Titus, 275
Arch of Titus (Circus Maximus), 278
Arch of Trajan (Ancona), 274
Arch of Trajan (Benevento), 275
Arch of Trajan (Canosa), 275
Arch of Trajan (Timgad), 274
Archontopouloi, 65
Arco dei Gavi, Verona, 276
Arco di Riccardo, 276
Arcus Novus, 278
Ardashir I, 192
Ardea, Lazio, 169
Arelate, 161
Argentorate, 83
Ariminum, 301
Ariovistus, 218
Aristotle, 23
Armenia, 190, 198
Armicustos, 66
Armilla (military decoration), 74
Arminius, 95, 96, 133, 188, 221, 341
Armor, 341
Arnold Hugh Martin Jones, 20, 46, 204
Arnold J. Toynbee, 6
Arquites, 23
Arrian, 109, 125, 128, 375
Arrow, 338
Arruns Tarquinius (Egerius), 168
Arsenal, 352
Artaxata, 221

Arther Ferrill, 204
Arthur Boak, 46
Artillery, 260, 322, 328
Arverni, 182
As (coin), 28
Asia Minor, 62, 64, 140, 183
As (Roman coin), 139
Assault of Placentia, 191
Assyria, 366
Assyria (Roman province), 366
Asturias, 179
Aternum, 301
Athens, 138, 148, 217, 274
Atlantic, 362
Attalus II, 214
Attila, 229
Attila the Hun, 45, 229, 357
Augsburg, 305
Augur, 246
Augustus, 2, 14, 32, 51, 57, 72, 77, 79, 82–85, 93, 136, 145, 157, 187, 188, 220, 239, 279, 286, 295, 299, 346
Aulus Atilius Calatinus, 128
Aulus Caecina Alienus, 129
Aulus Didius Gallus, 129
Aulus Gabinius, 130
Aulus Plautius, 132, 221
Aulus Postumius Albus Regillensis, 208
Aurelian, 195, 225
Aurelius Victor, 378
Aureolus, 128
Aureus, 253
Aurunci, 170, 208
Auspice, 246
Austria, 274
Autokrator, 72
Auxilia, 22, 51, 57, **90**, 222, 235
Auxilia deployment in the 2nd century, 105
Auxilia palatina, 107
Auxiliaries (Roman military), 3, 29, 53, 63, 151
Avidius Cassius, 192
Axle, 266

Babylonia, 192, 366
Bacon, 17
Bahram V, 199
Balearic Islands, 49, 55, 94, 114
Balearics, 31
Balearic slinger, 111
Balkans, 238
Ballista, 10, 12, 13, 155, 232, 234, 261, 315, 319, 328, 333
Ballistae, 31, 39
Ballistarius, 66
Baquates, 196

Barbarian, 7, 36, 51, 62, 136, 343, 362
Barbarians, 391
Barbatio, 128
Barbegal, 232
Barcelona, 251, 305
Barcid, 177
Barcids, 178
Bardo Museum, 147
Bar Kokhba revolt, 223
Bar Kokhbas revolt, 192
Barley, 76
Barnes & Noble Books, 46
Barracks, 249
Barrier troops, 325
Basileus, 72
Bastarnae, 42, 181
Bastinado, 75
Batavian rebellion, 83, 146
Batavians, 191
Batavi (Germanic tribe), 99
Baths of Diocletian, 232
Batna City, 82
Battering ram, 272
Battle of Abrittus, 83, 194, 225
Battle of Actium, 101, 136, 145, 157, 188, 220
Battle of Adamclisi, 222
Battle of Adrianople, 43, 89, 196, 227
Battle of Adrianople (324), 198, 227
Battle of Adys, 177, 211
Battle of Ager Falernus, 211
Battle of Agrigentum, 176, 210
Battle of Alesia, 10, 171, 186, 218, 266, 319, 333
Battle of Amida, 199, 227
Battle of Ancyra, 214
Battle of Antioch (218), 197, 224
Battle of Antium, 208
Battle of Aquae Sextiae, 183, 215
Battle of Aquilonia, 209
Battle of Arausio, 171, 182, 215, 340
Battle of Argentovaria, 196, 227
Battle of Aricia, 170, 208
Battle of Arles, 202
Battle of Arretium, 209
Battle of Artaxata, 218
Battle of Asculum, 210, 337
Battle of Asculum (209 BC), 177, 212
Battle of Asculum (279 BC), 129
Battle of Asculum (89 BC), 183, 215
Battle of Augusta Treverorum, 191
Battle of Ausculum, 174
Battle of Badon, 229
Battle of Baecula, 177, 212, 339
Battle of Bagbrades, 178, 212
Battle of Barbalissos, 199
Battle of Bedriacum, 222

Battle of Beneventum (275 BC), 175, 210, 337, 338
Battle of Beroa, 194
Battle of Beth Horon (66), 192, 222
Battle of Bibracte, 185, 218
Battle of Bovianum, 173, 209
Battle of Burdigala, 215
Battle of Cabira, 217
Battle of Caer Caradoc, 189, 221
Battle of Callicinus, 181, 214
Battle of Callinicum (296), 224
Battle of Camerinum, 173, 209
Battle of Campania, 218
Battle of Campania II, 218
Battle of Camulodunum, 222
Battle of Cannae, 93, 177, 182, 211, 327, 338
Battle of Cap Bon (468), 228
Battle of Cape Ecnomus, 138, 177, 210
Battle of Carmona, 212
Battle of Carnuntum, 223
Battle of Carrhae, 186, 187, 192, 218, 349
Battle of Carteia, 212
Battle of Carthage (238), 198, 224
Battle of Carthage (c.149 BC), 178, 215
Battle of Castra Vetera, 191
Battle of Chaeronea (86 BC), 184, 217
Battle of Châlons, 357
Battle of Chalons (273), 198
Battle of Châlons (274), 224
Battle of Chios (201 BC), 140
Battle of Chrysopolis, 198, 227
Battle of Cibalae, 198, 225
Battle of Cirta (104 BC), 182
Battle of Cissa, 211
Battle of Clastidium, 171, 213
Battle of Colline Gate (477 BC), 208
Battle of Corbio, 170, 208
Battle of Corinth (146 BC), 181, 215
Battle of Cremona (200 BC), 171, 213
Battle of Crotona, 212
Battle of Ctesiphon (363), 199, 227
Battle of Cynoscephalae, 141, 180, 213
Battle of Cyzicus (193), 197, 223
Battle of Drepana, 139, 211
Battle of Dyrrhachium (1081), 64
Battle of Dyrrhachium (48 BC), 187, 219
Battle of Ebro River, 140, 211
Battle of Edessa, 83, 199, 224
Battle of Emesa, 225
Battle of Faesulae, 171, 213
Battle of Fano, 195, 225
Battle of Fanum Fortunae, 195
Battle of Faventia (82 BC), 217
Battle of Fidentia (82 BC), 217
Battle of Forum Gallorum, 187, 220
Battle of Forum Julii, 222
Battle of Fucine Lake, 183, 215
Battle of Gergovia, 344
Battle of Grumentum, 212
Battle of Gythium, 181, 214
Battle of Harzhorn, 224
Battle of Heraclea, 174, 209, 337
Battle of Herdonia, 212
Battle of Histria, 190
Battle of Ilerda, 187, 219
Battle of Ilipa, 178, 212, 329, 339
Battle of Immae, 225
Battle of Issus (194), 197, 223
Battle of Korakesion, 184
Battle of Lake Benacus, 195, 225
Battle of Lake Regillus, 170, 208, 377
Battle of Lake Trasimene, 177, 211
Battle of Lake Trasimeno, 338
Battle of Lake Vadimo (283 BC), 171, 209
Battle of Lake Vadimo (310 BC), 209
Battle of Laugaricio, 223
Battle of Lautulae, 173, 209
Battle of Levounion, 64
Battle of Lilybaeum, 140, 211
Battle of Lingones, 196, 225
Battle of Locus Castorum, 191
Battle of Longula, 208
Battle of Lugdunum, 197, 223
Battle of Magnesia, 181, 214
Battle of Mainz (406), 228
Battle of Manlian Pass, 214
Battle of Manzikert, 53, 64
Battle of Mardia, 198, 225
Battle of Masada, 222
Battle of Mediolanum, 225
Battle of Milvian Bridge, 198, 225
Battle of Misikhe, 199
Battle of Mona, 189
Battle of Mons Graupius, 189, 221
Battle of Mons Seleucus, 198, 227
Battle of Mount Algidus, 170, 208
Battle of Mount Gaurus, 173, 209
Battle of Mount Olympus, 214
Battle of Mount Tifata, 217
Battle of Mount Venus (144 BC), 179
Battle of Mount Venus (146 BC), 179
Battle of Mount Vesuvius, 218
Battle of Mulucha, 182
Battle of Munda, 187, 219
Battle of Mursa Major, 198, 227
Battle of Mutina, 187, 220
Battle of Mutina 193 BCE, 214
Battle of Mutina (194 BC), 171
Battle of Mutina I, 218
Battle of Mylae, 138, 176, 210
Battle of Myonessus, 141, 181, 214
Battle of Naissus, 149, 195, 225

Battle of Narbonne (436), 202, 228
Battle of Naulochus, 83, 144, 188, 220
Battle of Nicaea, 197, 223
Battle of Nisibis (217), 224
Battle of Noreia, 182, 215, 340
Battle of Numistro, 177, 212
Battle of Octodurus, 218
Battle of Orchomenus, 184, 217
Battle of Orleans (463), 229
Battle of Panormus, 211
Battle of Pavia (271), 195, 225
Battle of Perugia, 188, 220
Battle of Pharsalus, 187, 219
Battle of Philippi, 188
Battle of Philippopolis (250), 194, 225
Battle of Picenum, 218
Battle of Pistoria, 218
Battle of Placentia (194 BC), 214
Battle of Placentia (271), 195, 225
Battle of Pollentia, 201, 228
Battle of Pometia, 206
Battle of Populonia, 173, 209
Battle of Pydna, 181, 214
Battle of Pydna (148 BC), 181, 214
Battle of Ravenna (432), 228
Battle of Reims (356), 196, 227
Battle of Resaena, 199, 224
Battle of Rhandeia, 222
Battle of Ruspina, 187, 219
Battle of Sacriporto, 217
Battle of Salamis, 154
Battle of Samarra, 199
Battle of Sarmisegetusa, 222
Battle of Scotch Corner, 221
Battle of Sentinum, 173, 209, 342
Battle of Silva Arsia, 208
Battle of Singara, 227
Battle of Soissons (486), 229
Battle of Solicinium, 196, 227
Battle of Strasbourg, 196, 227
Battle of Suessula, 173, 209
Battle of Sulci, 138, 210
Battle of Suthul, 182
Battle of Tapae (101), 190
Battle of Tapae 88, 190
Battle of Telamon, 171, 213, 342
Battle of Tenedos, 142
Battle of Teutoburg Forest, 365
Battle of Thala, 182
Battle of Thapsus, 187, 219
Battle of the Aegates Islands, 139, 177, 211
Battle of the Allia, 49, 171, 182, 208, 340
Battle of the Aous (198 BC), 180, 213
Battle of the Arar, 185, 218
Battle of the Asio River (82 BC), 217
Battle of the Axona, 186, 218

Battle of the Baetis River, 217
Battle of the Bagradas River (49 BC), 219
Battle of the Catalaunian Plains, 202, 229
Battle of the Caudine Forks, 173, 209
Battle of the Colline Gate (82 BC), 183, 217
Battle of the Cremera, 170, 208
Battle of the Eurymedon (190 BC), 141, 181, 214
Battle of the Frigidus, 198, 227
Battle of the Guadalquivir (206 BC), 212
Battle of the Hellespont, 149, 198, 227
Battle of the Lipari Islands, 138, 176, 210
Battle of the Lupia River, 220
Battle of the Lycus, 184, 218
Battle of the Margus, 198, 224
Battle of the Medway, 189, 221
Battle of the Metaurus, 177, 212
Battle of the Muthul, 182, 215
Battle of the Nervasos Mountains, 228
Battle of the Nile (47 BC), 219
Battle of the Port of Carthage, 215
Battle of the Rhone River, 215
Battle of Thermopylae (191 BC), 181, 214, 377
Battle of the Sabis, 186, 218, 343
Battle of the Save, 198, 227
Battle of the Silarus, 177, 212
Battle of the Siler River, 218
Battle of Thessalonica (380), 227
Battle of the Temple of Hope, 208
Battle of the Teutoburg Forest, 84, 85, 96, 133, 145, 188, 221, 340, 341
Battle of the Ticinus, 177, 211
Battle of the Trebia, 93, 177, 211, 324, 339
Battle of the Upper Baetis, 212
Battle of the Utus, 229
Battle of the Weser River, 189, 221
Battle of the Willows, 227
Battle of Thurii, 174
Battle of Thyatira, 198, 227
Battle of Ticinum, 195
Battle of Tifernum, 209
Battle of Tigranocerta, 217
Battle of Tribola, 179
Battle of Trifanum, 173, 209
Battle of Tunis, 177, 211, 377
Battle of Turin (312), 198, 225
Battle of Tyndaris, 138, 177, 210
Battle of Tzirallum, 198, 225
Battle of Veii, 208
Battle of Veii (480 BC), 208
Battle of Vellica, 220
Battle of Vercellae, 171, 183, 215
Battle of Verona (251), 198
Battle of Verona (312), 198, 225
Battle of Verona (402), 201, 228
Battle of Vesuvius, 173, 209

Battle of Vindonissa, 196, 225
Battle of Watling Street, 84, 109, 189, 222
Battle of Zama, 93, 140, 178, 213, 324, 327, 329, 336, 339
Battle of Zela, 220
Bavares, 196
Bavaria, 245
BBC Books, 205
Beit Gubrin, 281
Belfort, 218
Belgae, 218
Belgrade, 82, 158
Beneficiarius, 66
Benevento, 275
Berber mythology, 113
Berber people, 96, 113
Berlin, 33
Besançon, 274
Bessi, 377
Betuwe, 146
Bezabde, 82
B. H. Liddell Hart, 204
BH Liddell Hart, 178
Biga (chariot), 297
Bireme, 141
Bithynia, 184
Black Death, 65
Black Sea, 146, 158, 190
Blackwell Publishing, 163
Boar, 83
Boarding (attack), 138, 155
Boii, 214, 377
Bolsena, 301
Bonifacius, 43, 128, 228
Bonn, 81, 101
Bonosus (usurper), 128
Bordeaux, 301
Borders of the Roman Empire, 362
Boris Johnson, 204
Bosnia (region), 97
Bosporus, 158
Bostra, 82
Boudica, 84, 109, 377
Boudicas uprising, 222
Boulogne-sur-Mer, 157
Bow (weapon), 266
Brass, 232
Breastplate, 25
Brenner Pass, 300
Brennus, 340
Brennus (4th century BC), 171
Breuci, 97
Bridge, 232
Bridle path, 279
Britannia, 2, 99
British Isles, 148

British Museum, 233
Brittannia, 339
Brittany, 333
Bronze, 232
Bruce Trigger, 205
Bructeri, 189, 193
Brython, 265
Buccina, 252
Bucinator, 66
Buckler, 28
Budapest, 82
Bulgaria, 301, 303
Burgundians, 201
Burgus, 242
Burnum, 85
Burrium, 85
Busra, 82
Byzantine, 45
Byzantine army, 45, 52, 62
Byzantine civil war of 1341–1347, 65
Byzantine Empire, 44, 65, 136, 202, 317
Byzantine navy, 136, 150
Byzantium, 148, 158, 227, 301

Cádiz, 305
Caerleon, 82
Caesar Augustus, 183
Caesars Civil War, 219
Caesars invasions of Britain, 143, 189
Caesar (title), 72, 149, 225, 227, 317
Calaici, 185
Caledonia, 364
Caledonians, 146
Calidia (gens), 121
Caliga, 116
Caligula, 84, 85, 189, 238, 287, 362
Cambridge University Press, 205
Cameria, 168
Camiño de Oro, 305
Camlet Way, 305
Campaign against the pirates, 143
Campaign history of the Roman military, 2, 53, **165**, 316
Campania, 137
Camp crown, 72
Camp of Diocletian, 88
Camulodunum, 85
Cananefates, 101, 146
Cannae, 354
Canosa di Puglia, 275
Cantabri, 220
Cantabria, 179
Cantabrian Wars, 95, 96, 179, 220
Canton (administrative division), 284
Caparcotna, 83
Capitoline Museums, 278

Capitoline Wolf, 82
Cappadocia, 81
Capricorn (astrology), 79, 81
Capsarior, 66
Capture of Antium, 170
Capture of Fidenae, 170
Capture of Neapolis, 173
Capua, 275, 300, 301
Caput, 303
Caracalla, 58, 73, 106, 192, 197
Caratacus, 132, 221
Carausian Revolt, 149
Carausius, 149
Carburization, 231
Carburizing, 13
Cardiff, 233
Cardo, 243
Carinthia, 300
Carinthia (state), 117
Carinus, 198, 224
Carnuntum, 84, 121, 160, 274
Carpentras, 274
Carpentum, 297
Carpetani, 179
Carpians, 42, 194, 196
Carriage, 297
Carrus clabularius, 298
Cart, 296
Carthage, 28, 56, 137, 271, 301, 312, 352
Carthaginians, 329
Carus, 199
Caspian Sea, 190
Cassius Dio, 76, 197, 377, 378
Castellón de la Plana, 276
Castellum, 235
Castigatio, 76
Castle, 251
Castra, 86, **235**, 293, 314, 318, 351
Castra Albana, 82
Castra Vetera, 83–85
Castres, 251
Castro (surname), 238
Castrum, 157
Cataphract, 65, 192, 317, 348
Cataphracti, 31
Cataphracts, 111
Catapult, 155, 266
Catapults, 263
Category:Articles contradicting other articles, 41
Category:Military of ancient Rome, 1, 21, 47, 71, 77, 90, 127, 135, 165, 206, 231, 235, 259, 273, 311, 316, 361
Catiline, 218
Catiline Conspiracy, 218
Caucasian Iberia, 146, 184

Caucasus, 81, 148
Causarius, 66
Causeway, 293
Cavalry, 317, 333, 338
Cazanes, 291
Celeusta, 151
Celt, 339
Celtiberi, 346
Celtiberians, 178, 214
Celtic tribes, 221
Celts, 171
Centaur, 81
Centenarii, 152
Central Belt, 364
Centum and satem languages, 237
Centumcellae, 157
Centuria, 54, 70, 150, 235, 247, 256, 263, 320
Centuriae, 61
Centurion, 61, 67, 70, 95, 109, 121, 151, 253, 353
Centuriones, 151
Centurion (Roman army), 321
Cestius Gallus, 130, 222
Chain mail, 26
Chalcis, 305
Chalon-sur-Saône, 160
Chapter 16, 379
Charax, Crimea, 146
Chariot, 265, 296, 342
Chatti, 189, 193
Chauci, 145, 146, 189
Cheese, 17
Cherchell, 158
Chersonesos Taurica, 146
Cherusci, 189, 193
Chester, 85, 246, 251
Chios, 140
Christianity, 62
Cicero, 286
Cilicia, 32, 142, 184
Cilician pirates, 142
Cimbri, 182, 215
Cimbrian War, 182, 215
Circumflex, 236
Circumvallation, 10, 332
Cisalpine Gaul, 29, 213
Cisarius, 297
Cisiani, 297
Cisium, 297
Civic crown, 71
Civil engineer, 290
Civil war, 166
Civil wars of the Tetrarchy, 225
Clabulare, 298
Clabularis, 298
Clades Lolliana, 188, 220

Classes, 25
Classis Africana Commodiana Herculea, 157
Classis Alexandrina, 157
Classis Anderetianorum, 160
Classis Ararica, 160
Classis barcariorum, 160
Classis Britannica, 149, 157
Classis Comensis, 160
Classis Flavia Moesica, 158
Classis fluminis Rhodani, 161
Classis Germanica, 101, 152, 157
Classis Mauretanica, 158
Classis Misenatis, 160
Classis Misenensis, 153, 157
Classis nova Libyca, 158
Classis Pannonica, 158
Classis Perinthia, 158
Classis Pontica, 158
Classis Ravennas, 157, 162
Classis Ravennatis, 160
Classis Sambrica, 161
Classis Syriaca, 158
Classis Venetum, 161
Claudius, 84, 96, 98, 151, 152, 190, 221, 285, 287
Claudius Gothicus, 107
Claudius II, 149, 195, 225
Claudius Pompeianus, 129
Clausewitz, 312
Clavularis, 298
Claw of Archimedes, 140
Cleopatra, 145
Cleopatra VII of Egypt, 188, 220
Clibanarii, 31, 111
Client state, 190
Client states, 8, 190
Clinicus, 67
Clivus Capitolinus, 285, 291
Clodius Albinus, 197, 223
Clovis I, 229
Clusium, 170, 171
Cnaeus Domitius Corbulo, 189
Codex Justinianus, 379
Codex Theodosianus, 307, 379
Cognomen, 72, 157
Cohors equitata, 95
Cohors I Hispanorum miliaria, 294
Cohortes urbanae, 32
Cohort (military unit), 31, 49, 51, 57, 61, 70, 95, 109, 235, 255, 320
Colchester, 251
Colchis, 184
Col de Panissars, 301
Collatia, 168
Coll de Panissars, 305
Cologne, 157

Colonel, 122
Column of Marcus Aurelius, 4, 60
Comagena, 159
Combat readiness, 18
Comitatenses, 40, 51, 107
Comitatensis, 88
Comitia Centuriata, 49
Commentarii, 265
Commentarii de Bello Gallico, 186, 265, 357
Commissioner, 282
Commodus, 116, 157, 197
Commons:Castra, 257
Compass, 387
Composite bow, 114
Concrete, 232, 291
Conflict with ancient Rome, 169
Conscription, 62, 91, 117
Constantine I, 41, 78, 88, 98, 107, 149, 198, 356, 363
Constantine I (emperor), 225, 295
Constantine III (Western Roman Emperor), 43
Constantine the Great, 199, 225
Constantinople, 65, 295
Constantius Chlorus, 149, 225
Constantius Gallus, 134
Constantius II, 198, 227
Constantius III, 43
Constitutio Antoniniana, 106
Consul, 2
Contravallation, 333
Contubernia, 31
Contubernium, 69, 70, 248
Copper, 233
Cora (Ancient Latin town), 206
Corbulo, 287
Corduroy road, 282, 293
Corinth, 149
Coriolanus, 279
Cornelius Fuscus, 130, 222
Cornelius Nepos, 237
Cornicen, 67
Corniculum (ancient Latin town), 168
Cornu (horn), 252
Corporal, 120
Corpus Inscriptionum Latinarum, 293
Corpus Iuris Civilis, 307
Corselet, 60
Corvus (boarding device), 138
Corvus (weapon), 13, 176
Council for British Archaeology, 162
Crassus, 218, 219, 352
Crete, 31, 49, 94, 114, 142, 149
Crimea, 158
Crisis of the Third Century, 6, 106, 136, 148, 197, 224
Crispus, 149, 227

Critolaus, 215
Croatia, 274
Crossbow, 263, 267
Crossing of the Rhine, 161
Crustumerium, 168
Ctesiphon, 192, 222, 366
Cumae, 144
Cumans, 64
Cunei, 40
Curia, 23
Cursus clabularis, 298
Cursus honorum, 61
Cursus publicus, 299
Cynoscephalae, 335
Cyrenaica, 158
Cyrene, Libya, 82, 96
Cyzicus, 158

Dacia, 81, 87, 148, 190, 222, 365, 366
Dacians, 83, 104, 195
Dacia ripensis, 159
Dalmatae, 97
Dalmatia, 95, 98
Dalmatia (Roman province), 81, 161, 300
Damascus, 305
Danube, 61, 64, 91, 97, 136, 148, 280, 291, 303, 362, 365
Danube River, 43
David Mattingly (author), 46
De Architectura, 263, 269
Debasement, 6
Decanus, 67, 69, 70
Decebalus, 104, 190, 222
Decemviri, 286
Decimation (Roman Army), 76, 82
Decimus Junius Brutus Albinus, 128
Decimus Junius Brutus Callaicus, 128
Decius, 198, 225
Decline of the Roman Empire, 166, 200
Decumanus Maximus, 246
Decurio, 95, 109
Decurion (military), 67, 121
Defence-in-depth (Roman military), 53, 63
Defense in depth, 363
Deiotarus, 85
Delbruck, 356
Delphi, 137
Demetrias, 140
Demetrius of Pharos, 139
De Munitionibus Castrorum, 238, 240
Denarii, 119
Denarius, 144, 150
Dentheletae, 103
De Re Militari, 356, 357, 378
Dere Street, 305
Deva Victrix, 85, 246

Dexippus, 129
Diadem (personal wear), 48
Diadochi, 152
Dio Cassius, 125, 283, 374, 376
Diocletian, 41, 51, 61, 62, 78, 87, 98, 107, 149, 198, 199, 224
Dionysius of Halicarnassus, 23, 49, 279
Discens, 67
District, 284
Djémila, 273
Doctor (Roman military), 67
Dolabra, 319, 333
Dolaucothi, 233
Dominate, 77
Domitian, 81, 103, 119, 190, 287, 375
Domitians Dacian War, 222
Donativum, 119
Don River, Russia, 146
Dorsal consonant, 236
Dougga, 277
Dover, 157
Draconarius, 67
Draw bridges, 270
Dromedarii, 113
Druidism, 62
Duncan Campbell (ancient historian), 257, 258
Duoviri, 286
Duplicarius, 116, 120
Durostorum, 84
Durrës, 301
Duumviri navales, 137
Dux, 67, 74, 159
Dying Gaul, 339

Early Imperial campaigns in Germania, 188
Early Roman army, 48, 55
East, 387
Eastern Roman Empire, 47, 200
East Roman army, 51, 62
Ebro River, 211
Eburacum, 83
Edelweiss, 117
Edict of Caracalla, 51
Edward Gibbon, 3, 20, 46, 197, 355, 369
Edward Luttwak, 12, 20, 46, 204
Egypt, 2, 145, 301
Egyptians, 135
Egypt (Roman province), 2
Elagabalus, 197, 224
Elbe, 96, 145, 365
Eleazar ben Simon, 222
Elephant, 79
Elio Lo Cascio, 259

Èmegara, 60

Emilio Gabba, 46
Empire, 14, 317
Empire of Trebizond, 65
Ems (river), 145
Encyclopædia Britannica, 370
Encyclopædia Britannica Eleventh Edition, 20
Engineers, 321
England, 2, 251
English Channel, 32, 143, 196
English language, 235
En masse, 43
Enns (city), 82, 159
Epaminondas, 335
Epirote, 337
Epirus, 174
Equestrian order, 61
Equestrian rank, 287
Equestrian (Roman), 28, 93, 152
Equites, 25, 27, 56, 168, 253
Equites cataphractarii, 39, 111
Equites Dalmatae, 113
Equites legionis, 31
Equites Maurorum, 113
Equites singulares Augusti, 67
Ermine Street, 305
Es:Adherbal (Segunda Guerra Púnica), 212
Es:Cayo Lucio Marcio Séptimo, 212
Es:Hannón (206 a. C.), 212
Esprit de corps, 5
Etruscan civilisation, 167
Etruscan civilization, 92, 166, 174, 208, 209, 232, 240, 289, 377
Etruscans, 23, 137, 169, 208
Etruscan warfare, 48
Etymology, 236
Eugenius, 227
Euphrates, 148, 280, 366
Europe, 251
Eutropius (historian), 149, 378
Evergetism, 284
Evocatus, 67
Evolution, 317
Expansionist, 166
Exploratores, 32

Faber and Faber, 20, 46, 204
Fabia (gens), 208
Fabian strategy, 377
Fabius Valens, 130
Fall of Constantinople, 45, 66
Fall of the Western Roman Empire, 1, 21, 47, 71, 77, 90, 127, 135, 136, 165, 206, 228, 231, 235, 259, 273, 311, 316, 361
Fano, 275
Fasti Triumphales, 168, 169, 380
Faustinus, 277

Faustus (II) Cornelius Sulla, 133
Feces, 17
Fectio, 242
Fell, 306
Fen Causeway, 305
Ferentina, 169
Ficulea (ancient Latin town), 168
Field hospital, 15
Figurehead (object), 154
Final War of the Roman Republic, 136, 220
First Battle of Avignon (121 BC), 182
First Battle of Bedriacum, 191
First Battle of Capua, 177, 212
First Battle of Clusium (82 BC), 217
First Battle of Nola, 211
First Battle of Philippi, 220
First Celtiberian War, 214
First Dacian War, 222
First Illyrian War, 211
First Jewish–Roman War, 2, 84, 222
First Jewish-Roman War, 146
First Macedonian War, 140, 180, 213
First Mithridatic War, 142, 151, 184, 215, 217
First Numantine War, 179
First Punic War, 23, 136, 137, 155, 166, 176, 210, 271
First Samnite War, 171
First Samnite War (343 to 341 BC), 129, 208
First Servile War, 215
First Triumvirate, 186, 218
First war with Rome, 168
Fiscalis raeda, 297
Fish, 17
Five Good Emperors, 148
Flagrum, 76
Flavian dynasty, 103, 152, 158
Flavius Aetius, 43, 130, 228
Flavius Aëtius, 202
Flavius Valila Theodosius, 134
Flogging, 75
Florus, 190
Flying wedge, 331
Foederati, 4, 39, 106, 115, 317, 355
Foederatii, 42
Foedus Cassianum, 54
Foraging, 17
Formation (military), 338
Fortification, 238
Fortuna, 84
Fortuna (mythology), 141
Forum of Theodosius, 278
Forum (Roman), 245
Fosse Way, 305
Foundation of the Tetrarchy, 277

Founding of Rome, 1, 21, 47, 71, 77, 90, 127, 135, 165, 166, 206, 231, 235, 259, 273, 311, 316, 361
Fourth Macedonian War, 214
France, 232, 251, 274
Frankish realm, 229
Franks, 45, 196, 227, 228
Freedmen, 152
Freeway, 305
Fréjus, 156
Frisia, 148
Frisii, 101, 145, 189, 191
Fritigern, 227
Frontinus, 232, 235
Frumentarii, 67
Fullofaudes, 130
Fulvia, 188
Funerary urn, 92
Fustuarium, 75

Gabii, 169
Gaius Antistius Vetus (consul 6 BC), 220
Gaius Antonius, 128
Gaius Asinius Pollio (consul 40 BC), 128
Gaius Atilius Regulus Serranus, 211
Gaius Avidius Cassius, 192
Gaius Calpurnius Piso (consul 67 BC), 129
Gaius Carrinas (consul 43 BC), 129
Gaius Carrinas (general), 129, 217
Gaius Cassius Longinus, 129, 143, 188, 220
Gaius Claudius Glaber, 218
Gaius Claudius Nero, 129, 177, 212
Gaius Duilius, 130, 138
Gaius Flaminius, 130, 211
Gaius Flavius Fimbria, 130
Gaius Gracchus, 283
Gaius Horatius Pulvillus, 208
Gaius Julius Caesar the Elder, 130
Gaius Julius Civilis, 100, 129, 146, 191
Gaius Laelius, 131, 212
Gaius Lutatius Catulus, 131, 139
Gaius Marcius Censorinus (general), 217
Gaius Marcius Coriolanus, 129
Gaius Marcius Rutilus, 131
Gaius Marius, 29, 30, 57, 78, 131, 215, 317
Gaius Marius the Younger, 131, 217
Gaius Norbanus, 132
Gaius Norbanus Balbus, 217
Gaius Norbanus Flaccus, 132
Gaius Octavius (praetor 61 BC), 132
Gaius Salvius Liberalis (history), 130
Gaius Scribonius Curio, 133, 283, 377
Gaius Servilius Ahala, 133
Gaius Sosius, 133
Gaius Suetonius Paulinus, 133
Gaius Terentius Varro, 134

Gaius Valerius Flaccus (consul), 134
Galatia, 30, 81, 96, 214
Galatian War, 214
Galba, 76, 81, 83, 101, 191, 347
Galen, 16, 17
Galerius, 199, 224
Galilee, 83
Galley slave, 150
Gallia, 305
Gallia Aquitania, 80
Gallia Belgica, 95, 102
Gallia Narbonensis, 222
Gallic War, 177
Gallic Wars, 93, 143, 185, 218, 265
Gallienus, 39, 69, 86, 149, 195, 198, 225
Gallienus usurpers, 198
Gallo-Roman culture, 229
Garamantes, 128
Gask Ridge, 364
Gaul, 9, 42, 220, 229, 265, 279, 333
Gauls, 93, 110, 171, 214
Gaziantep, 83
Geiseric, 149, 229
Gelderland, 99, 100
Gellius Publicola, 218
Gemona, 300
General contractor, 282
Genitive case, 237
Genoa, 301
George Patrick Welch, 205
Gepids, 149, 196
Gérard Chaliand, 203
Germania, 9, 110, 145
Germania Inferior, 81, 95, 99, 191, 302, 303, 365
Germania Magna, 365
Germania Superior, 81, 95, 365
Germanic peoples, 36, 87, 148, 182, 220
Germanic tribes, 36, 133
Germanicus, 97, 130, 146, 189, 221
Germanic Wars, 165
Germany, 242, 245
Gig (carriage), 297
Gijón, 305
Giulio Romano, 196
Gjirokastër, 238
Gladiator, 320
Gladius, 9, 13, 27, 320, 328, 351
Glanum, 50
G. M. Hirst, 380
Gnaeus Cornelius Lentulus Clodianus, 129, 218
Gnaeus Cornelius Scipio Calvus, 212
Gnaeus Domitius Ahenobarbus (consul 122 BC), 129

Gnaeus Domitius Ahenobarbus (consul 32 BC), 129
Gnaeus Domitius Calvinus, 129
Gnaeus Domitius Corbulo, 129, 146, 190, 221
Gnaeus Fulvius Centumalus Maximus, 212
Gnaeus Hosidius Geta, 130
Gnaeus Julius Agricola, 146, 221
Gnaeus Mallius Maximus, 131, 215
Gnaeus Manlius Cincinnatus, 208
Gnaeus Manlius Vulso, 214
Gnaeus Octavius (consul 87 BC), 132
Gnaeus Papirius Carbo, 132, 217
Gnaeus Papirius Carbo (consul 113 BC), 215
Gnaeus Pompeius Magnus, 186
Gnaeus Pompeius (son of Pompey the Great), 132
Gnaeus Servilius Geminus, 133
Gold, 233
Gold mine, 233
Gordian II, 198, 224
Gordian III, 198, 199, 224
Gothic society and forces in the 3rd and 4th Centuries, 194
Gothic War (376-382), 227
Goths, 43, 44, 194–196, 225, 227, 228
Gradus deiectio, 77
Grain supply to the city of Rome, 143, 157
Graltinus Maximus Aurelius, 128
Grand strategy, 12, 311, 361
Grappling hook, 155
Grass crown, 71, 129
Gratianus, 227
Great Britain, 363, 364
Great Illyrian Revolt, 96
Great Wall of China, 363
Greece, 175, 179, 274, 301
Greek birth, Roman acquisition, 290
Greek language, 238
Greeks, 135
Greek technology, 232
Greuthungi, 149
Groma surveying, 240, 290, 387
Gromatici, 290
Guadalquivir, 212
Gubernator, 151
Guerrilla, 347
Guerrilla war, 179
Gundobad, 130
Gutenberg:10701, 205
Gutenberg:14809, 203
Gutenberg:18047, 203
Gutenberg:731, 204
Gutenberg:7990, 203
Gutenberg Project, 392

Hadrian, 3, 35, 61, 80, 105, 286, 299, 362

Hadrians Gate, 277
Hadrians Wall, 62, 83, 107, 189, 255, 280, 363, 364
Halyard, 143
Han dynasty, 11
Hannibal, 56, 93, 140, 166, 178, 213, 214, 312, 324, 327
Hannibal Barca, 177
Hans Delbrück, 355, 358
Hard palate, 236
Harpax, 155
Harvard University Press, 19, 45, 203
Hasdrubal, 211
Hasdrubal Barca, 177, 212
Hasdrubal (Barcid), 324
Hasdrubal Gisco, 178, 212
Hasta pura, 74
Hastati, 27, 67, 256, 325
Hastatus Posterior, 67
Hastatus Prior, 67
Hastiliarius, 67
Heavy infantry, 29, 50, 92
Heidentor, 274
Heligoland, 145
Hellenistic, 56, 140
Hellenistic civilization, 259
Hellenistic period, 136
Helvetii, 185, 215, 218
Hemiolia, 152
Henry John Roby, 257
Henry William Frederick Saggs, 205
Heraclius, 72
Hercules, 82, 85, 154
Herculians, 89
Herennius Etruscus, 225
Hermunduri, 189
Hero, 103
Heruli, 148, 149, 194
Hexareme, 152
Hiero II of Syracuse, 94
Hierosolyma, 83
Hispania, 31, 43, 95, 178, 211, 212, 304, 305, 346, 352
Hispania Tarraconensis, 81
Hispanophone, 238
Historia Augusta, 75, 149
History, 157, 252
History of Anatolia, 166
History of Italy during Roman times, 165
Histria (Sinoe), 302
Hod Hill, 15
Honesta missio, 74, 116, 151, 254
Honorius (emperor), 201
Hoplite, 24, 25
Hoplites, 54
Horse archer, 31, 91, 192

Howard Hayes Scullard, 33
Howard Scullard, 46
Hugh Elton, 13, 46
Hun, 165
Huns, 195, 228
Hydraulic cement, 232
Hydraulic mining, 233

Iatros, 151
Iazyges, 196
Iberian peninsula, 128, 175, 178, 212
Iberians, 110, 346
Icknield Way, 280, 283
Ilipa, 377
Illyria, 36, 139
Illyrian revolt, 51
Illyrians, 180
Illyrian War, 181
Illyrian Wars, 139
Illyricum (Roman province), 43, 95, 377
Imaginifer, 67
Immortals (Byzantine), 65
Immunes, 66, 67, 69, 151
Imperator, 72, 79, 247
Imperator Destinatus, 73
Imperial Roman army, 2, 91
Imperium, 73, 143
Inchtuthil, 15, 85
Indo-European languages, 236
Infantry, 316
Infantry square, 331, 332
Infection, 16
International Phonetic Alphabet, 236
International Standard Book Number, 19, 20, 45–47, 52, 162, 163, 202–205, 257, 259, 272, 358, 367
Inuus, 238
Iran, 2, 366
Iraq, 366
Iron, 232
Iron Age, 231
Iron-Age, 23
Iron Gates, 158, 291, 303
Irregular units, 106
Isaccea, 158
Isca Augusta, 82
Isidore of Sevilla, 289
Isidore of Seville, 307
Isis, 154
ISO 9, 236
Israel, 146
Istanbul, 278
Istrians, 181
Istrian War, 181
Italian peninsula, 165, 174
Italia (Roman province), 81, 88, 89, 182

Italic languages, 236
Italic peoples, 91
Italy, 176, 238, 274–278
Iter ab Emerita Asturicam, 305
Itinerarium, 295
Itinerary of Antoninus, 279
Iudaea Province, 81, 191
Iudaea (Roman province), 96
Iuthungi, 196

Jacques Amyot, 203
James Burke (science historian), 6
James Earle Fraser (historian), 204
Jaś Elsner, 390
Jerash, 276
Jerome, 44
Jerusalem, 83, 281
Jewish revolt against Gallus, 134
John Bagnall Bury, 203
John Carew Rolfe, 203
John Dryden, 203
John II Komnenos, 64
John Peter Oleson, 389
John Selby Watson, 203
Johns Hopkins University Press, 20, 46, 204
Jordan, 276, 303
Jordanes, 202
Jordan River, 158
Josephus, 2, 158, 256, 269, 270, 379
Joseph Vogt, 47
Jotapata, 269, 270
Journal of Roman Studies, 390
Jovians, 87, 89
Juba I of Numidia, 219
Jugurtha, 182, 215
Jugurthine War, 215
Julian (emperor), 16
Julian the Apostate, 48, 161, 199, 227, 350
Julio-Claudian dynasty, 91
Julius Caesar, 32, 50, 79–84, 131, 143, 185, 186, 218, 259, 265, 279, 286, 296, 330, 333
Julius Caesar Drusus, 130
Julius Pokorny, 236
Junior officers (principales), 68
Jupiter (mythology), 85, 154

Ḱ, 387

Ka (Cyrillic), 236
Kaiseraugst, 89
K. A. Nilakanta Sastri, 380
Karpathos, 162
Karst, 300
Kilogram, 264
Kingdom of Aksum, 11

Kingdom of Armenia (antiquity), 190, 223
Kingdom of Pergamon, 140, 180
Kingdom of Pontus, 183, 217, 219, 220, 377
Kingdom of Sicily, 64
Kingdom of Soissons, 229
King of Italy, 229
Kings Highway (ancient), 283
King Street (Roman road), 305
Kitos War, 192, 223
Kje, 387
Klana, 300
Kneel, 330
Komnenian army, 65
Komnenian Byzantine army, 53, 63
Komnenian period, 63
Komnenos, 53
Kontos (weapon), 111
Kos, 143, 151
Kostolac, 83

LacusCurtius, 19, 45, 203
La Jonquera, 305
Lake Como, 160
Lake Constance, 145
Lake District, 306
Lake Neuchâtel, 160
Lambaesis, 82
Lancaster, England, 251
Landowner, 282
Largest naval battle in history, 138
Lars Porsenna, 170
Las Medulas, 233
Latakia, 276
Latakia Tetraporticus, 276
Late Roman army, 62, 64, 107, 159
Later Roman army, 51
Latin, 26, 171, 235, 236, 271, 279
Latin language, 47, 91, 135
Latin League, 169, 377
Latins (Italic tribe), 28, 31, 54, 170
Latin War, 173, 209
Latin War (498–493 BC), 208
Latium, 1
Laureys a Castro, 144
Lavinium, 170
Lawrence Keppie, 46
Laws and traditions, 288
Lebanon, 276
Legatus, 67, 321
Legatus Augusti pro praetore, 61
Legatus legionis, 70, 122, 322
Legend, 167
Legio I Adiutrix, 81, 146
Legio I Armeniaca, 88
Legio I Flavia Pacis, 88
Legio I Germanica, 79, 81

Legio II Adiutrix, 82, 146
Legio II Armeniaca, 89
Legio II Augusta, 79, 82, 101
Legio II Flavia Constantia, 89
Legio II Flavia Virtutis, 89
Legio II Herculia, 89, 160
Legio III Augusta, 82
Legio III Cyrenaica, 79, 82
Legio III Diocletiana, 89
Legio III Flavia Salutis, 89
Legio III Gallica, 79, 82
Legio III Isaura, 89
Legio III Italica, 82
Legio III Parthica, 82
Legio II Isaura, 89
Legio II Italica, 82, 160
Legio I Iovia, 88
Legio II Parthica, 82
Legio I Isaura Sagittaria, 88
Legio I Italica, 81
Legio II Traiana Fortis, 82
Legio I Macriana liberatrix, 81
Legio I Maximiana, 89
Legio I Minervia, 81
Legio I Parthica, 81
Legio IV Flavia Felix, 82
Legio IV Italica, 89
Legio IV Macedonica, 79, 83
Legio IV Martia, 89
Legio IV Scythica, 79, 83
Legio IX Hispana, 79, 83
Legionaries, 290
Legionary, 3, 67
Legio V Alaudae, 79, 83, 102, 222
Legio VI Ferrata, 79, 83
Legio VI Herculia, 89
Legio VI Hispana, 83
Legio VII Claudia, 79, 83
Legio VII Gemina, 79, 83
Legio VIII Augusta, 79, 83
Legio V Iovia, 89
Legio VI Victrix, 79, 83
Legio V Macedonica, 83
Legio X Equestris, 76, 79, 84
Legio X Fretensis, 79, 83, 158
Legio X Gemina, 84, 100, 160
Legio XI, 80
Legio XI Claudia, 84
Legio XII Fulminata, 80, 84
Legio XIII Gemina, 80, 84
Legio XIV Gemina, 80, 84, 101, 146, 160
Legio XIX, 85
Legio XV Apollinaris, 84, 121
Legio XVI Flavia Firma, 84
Legio XVI Gallica, 84
Legio XVII, 84

Legio XVIII, 80, 85
Legio XV Primigenia, 84, 102
Legio XXII Deiotariana, 85
Legio XXII Primigenia, 85, 158
Legio XXI Rapax, 85
Legio XX Valeria Victrix, 85
Legio XXX Classica, 80
Legio XXX Ulpia Victrix, 85
León, Spain, 83
Leptis Magna, 162, 276
Lex Gabinia, 143
Lex Iulia Municipalis, 281
Lex Julia, 183
Lex Julia Municipalis, 286
Lex Plautia Papiria, 183
Lex Viaria, 283
Liberatores, 187
Liberators civil war, 220
Libratore, 290
Liburnian (ship), 152
Libya, 276
Licinius, 149, 198, 225
Lictor, 287
Light cavalry, 91, 115
Light infantry, 109
Ligurian War, 177
Lime mortar, 291
Limes, 35, 88, 193, 363
Limes Arabicus, 305, 367
Limes Britannicus, 363
Limes Germanicus, 161, 303, 365
Limes Moesiae, 366
Limes Tripolitanus, 367
Limitanei, 40, 88, 107
Lindau, 305
Lingones, 102
Lipa, Beltinci, 300
List of castra, 235
List of post-Roman triumphal arches, 273
List of Roman army unit types, **66**, 271, 272
List of Roman generals, **127**
List of Roman legions, **77**, 239
List of Roman triumphal arches, **273**
List of Roman wars and battles, **206**
Litorius, 131
Little Brown, 204
Livy, 19, 23, 45, 49, 166, 167, 279, 374, 377, 378, 380
Locations, 280
Loeb Classical Library, 203
Logistics, 322
Londinium, 149
London, 35
London-West of England Roman Roads, 305
Lorica segmentata, 59, 109
Louvre Museum, 167

Luceres, 23
Lucilius Bassus, 128
Lucius Aemilius Barbula, 128
Lucius Aemilius Mamercus, 208
Lucius Aemilius Paullus Macedonicus, 214
Lucius Aemilius Paulus Macedonicus, 128
Lucius Aemilius Regillus, 214
Lucius Antonius (brother of Mark Antony), 128
Lucius Artorius Castus, 128
Lucius Caecilius Metellus Denter, 131
Lucius Caesennius Paetus, 222
Lucius Calpurnius Piso (consul 15 BC), 132
Lucius Cassius Longinus (consul 107 BC), 215
Lucius Clodius Macer, 81, 129
Lucius Cornelius Balbus (minor), 128
Lucius Cornelius Cinna, 129
Lucius Cornelius Lentulus, 129
Lucius Cornelius Scipio Barbatus, 129, 209
Lucius Cornelius Sisenna, 133
Lucius Cornelius Sulla, 32, 183, 184, 217
Lucius Cornelius Sulla Felix, 217
Lucius Flavius Silva, 133
Lucius Gellius Publicola, 130
Lucius Hostilius Mancinus (consul 145 BC), 215
Lucius Julius Caesar (consul 90 BC), 131
Lucius Junius Brutus, 131, 169, 208
Lucius Licinius Lucullus (consul 151 BC), 131, 179
Lucius Licinius Lucullus (consul 74 BC), 184
Lucius Lucullus, 217
Lucius Manlius Vulso Longus, 131, 139, 211
Lucius Mummius, 215
Lucius Mummius Achaicus, 131, 181
Lucius Opimius, 132
Lucius Papirius Cursor, 132, 209
Lucius Pinarius, 131
Lucius Porcius Cato, 215
Lucius Postumius Albinus (consul 234 BC), 132
Lucius Quincius, 217
Lucius Quinctius Cincinnatus, 133, 208
Lucius Tarquinius Priscus, 168
Lucius Tarquinius Superbus, 208
Lucius Valerius Flaccus, 134
Lucius Verus, 192
Lucullus, 131, 142, 184, 347
Ludovisi Battle sarcophagus, 11, 37
Luentinum, 233
Lugio, 303
Lupercal, 79
Lusitani, 178, 185, 346
Lusitania, 95, 191
Lusitanians, 377
Lusitanian War, 178, 214, 346

417

Lusius Quietus, 133
Lympne, 157

Macedon, 141, 179, 335, 377
Macedonia (ancient kingdom), 32
Macedonian wars, 175
Macedonia (Roman province), 81
Macmillan Publishers, 20, 46, 204
Macrinus, 197, 224
Maghreb, 113
Maginot Line, 356
Magister militum, 88, 227
Magister Peditum, 88, 160
Magistrate, 284
Magistratus, 137, 287
Magistri pagorum, 286
Magna Grecia, 174
Magnentius, 198, 227
Magnetic north, 388
Magnus Maximus, 227
Main (river), 158
Mainz, 83–85, 154
Majorian, 150
Malatya, 84
Mancetter, 84, 251
Manchester, 251
Mancipes, 287
Mangonel, 264, 267
Maniple (military unit), 26, 49, 70, 92, 256, 320
Mani (prophet), 11
Manius Acilius Glabrio (consul 191 BC), 128, 181, 214
Manius Acilius Glabrio (consul 67 BC), 128
Manius Aquillius (129 BC), 128
Manius Valerius Maximus Corvinus Messalla, 134
Mansio, 298
Marches, 300
Marcius Turbo, 131
Marcomanni, 82, 189, 194
Marcomannic Wars, 115, 148, 193, 223
Marcus Aemilius Lepidus (consul AD 6), 131
Marcus Aemilius Lepidus (triumvir), 80, 84, 128, 188, 283
Marcus Aemilius Scaurus (praetor 56 BC), 128
Marcus Agrippa, 144
Marcus Antonius, 184
Marcus Antonius Creticus, 128, 143, 184
Marcus Antonius Orator, 128
Marcus Antonius Primus, 132
Marcus Atilius Regulus, 128, 138, 177
Marcus Aurelius, 82, 107, 115, 148, 278, 375
Marcus Brutus, 188, 220
Marcus Calpurnius Bibulus, 129

Marcus Claudius Marcellus, 129, 140, 177, 211, 213
Marcus Crassus, 76, 218
Marcus Fabius Vibulanus, 208
Marcus Fulvius Flaccus (consul 125 BC), 130
Marcus Fulvius Flaccus (consul 264 BC), 130
Marcus Fulvius Nobilior, 130
Marcus Furius Camillus, 25, 130
Marcus Junius Brutus the Younger, 32
Marcus Junius Silanus (consul 109 BC), 215
Marcus Licinius Crassus, 79, 131, 186
Marcus Livius Salinator, 131, 177
Marcus Lollius, 131
Marcus Lollius Paulinus, 220
Marcus Perperna, 132
Marcus Perperna Vento, 132
Marcus Popillius Laenas, 132
Marcus Popillius Laenas (consul 173 BC), 132
Marcus Pupius Piso Frugi Calpurnianus, 132
Marcus Roscius Coelius, 133
Marcus Salvius Otho, 191
Marcus Sergius, 133
Marcus Terentius Varro Lucullus, 134, 217
Marcus Valerius Corvus, 134, 209
Marcus Valerius Laevinus, 140
Marcus Valerius Maximianus, 131
Marcus Valerius Messalla Corvinus, 85, 134
Marcus Vipsanius Agrippa, 134, 220
Mare Nostrum, 136, 141
Marian reforms, 29, 30, 57, 69, 78, 131, 325
Marines (military), 150
Marinus (Roman), 150
Mark Antony, 79, 80, 82, 83, 128, 143, 145, 150, 187, 188, 220, 283, 296
Mark Hassall, 46
Marsala, 241
Marseilles, 161
Marsi, 189, 193
Marsian, 377
Mars (mythology), 2, 154
Martigny, 218
Masada, 10, 243, 263, 269, 270
Masinissa, 93
Massimo Pallottino, 46
Materija, 300
Mauretania, 81, 96, 99
Mauretania Caesariensis, 113
Mauretania Tingitana, 301
Mauri people, 130
Max Cary, 46
Maxentius, 198, 225
Maximian, 149
Maximinus II, 149, 198, 225
Maximinus Thrax, 37, 197, 224
Medicine in ancient Rome, 16, 18
Medinaceli, 276

Mediolanum, 202
Mediolanum Santonum, 274
Mediterranean, 231
Mediterranean Basin, 166, 174
Mediterranean Sea, 166
Medullia, 168
Melitene, 84
Mercenaries, 29
Mercenary, 53, 94
Mersin Province, 304
Mesopotamia, 198, 366
Metellus Scipio, 187
Michael Grant (author), 20, 46, 167, 204
Michael Wood (historian), 205
Middle Ages, 41, 267, 287
Middle Europe, 301
Milan, 39, 161, 305
Mile, 279
Milecastle, 365
Milestone, 293, 295
Miliarium aureum, 295
Milion, 295
Military, 31, 317
Military diploma, 320
Military establishment of the Roman Empire, 317
Military establishment of the Roman kingdom, 317
Military establishment of the Roman Republic, 317
Military history, 165
Military history of ancient Rome, 279
Military history of Italy, 92
Military intelligence, 324
Military medical corps, 68
Military of ancient Rome, 1, **1**, 21, 47, 71, 77, 90, 127, 135, 165, 206, 231, 235, 259, 273, 311, 316, 361
Military service, 254
Military settlements, 238
Military tactics, 311, 317
Military tribune, 69
Milites, 68
Militia, 183
Militiae mutatio, 77
Milliarium of Aiton, 294
Minerva, 81, 154
Mining (military), 271, 333
Mirabilia Urbis Romae, 277, 278
Mirebeau-sur-Bèze, 83
Misenum, 156, 162
Mithraism, 62
Mithridates of Armenia, 221
Mithridates the Great, 183
Mithridates VI of Pontus, 142, 217, 377
Mithridatic Wars, 142, 377

Modern Age, 287
Moesia, 81, 96, 97, 158, 190, 191
Moesia I, 159
Moesia II, 160
Moesia Superior, 98
Moguntiacum, 81, 83–85
Mole (architecture), 333
Mommsen, 355
Monarch, 72
Monumental Arch of Palmyra, 278
Morocco, 113, 276
Mosaic, 108
Mucianus, 131
Mule, 323
Mummius, 347
Munerum indictio, 77
Mural crown, 72
Mursa, 159
Muscularii, 160
Museo Pio-Clementino, 141
Mutina, 187, 220
M. Valerius Laevinus, 134
Mystery cult, 62

Nabis, 214
Napoca (ancient city), 294
Narbonne, 301
Narseh, 224
National Military Museum, Romania, 59
National Museum of Wales, 233
Naturalis Historia, 232
Nauclarii, 160
Nautae, 151
Naval boarding, 271
Naval crown, 71
Naval tactics in the Age of Galleys, 138
Naval warfare, 166
Navarch, 151
Navis actuaria, 153
Navis lusoria, 154
Near East, 165
Neptune (mythology), 80, 84
Nereid, 60
Nero, 78, 81, 99, 146, 190
Nero Claudius Drusus, 130, 145, 157, 220, 298
Nerva–Antonine dynasty, 287
Nervii, 343
Netherlands, 99
Neuss, 84
New World, 17, 251
Nicolas Poussin, 167
Nicopolis, 82
Nijmegen, 83, 100
Nile, 367
Nile Delta, 157
Nîmes, 301

419

Nisibis, 81
Nomentum, 168
Non-commissioned officer, 61, 68
Noricum, 81, 89, 96, 103
Norman Cantor, 203
Normans, 64
North Africa, 165, 175
North Sea, 145, 149, 157
Notitia Dignitatum, 4, 87, 88, 90, 107, 149, 159, 357, 375
Novae, 81, 83
Numantia, 179, 214
Numantine War, 214, 346
Numa Pompilius, 166
Numeri (Roman troops), 38
Numerus (Roman military unit), 50, 68
Numidia, 31, 93, 96, 182, 215
Numidian, 49, 348
Numidian cavalry, 55, 93, 113

Oak, 143
Obrov, 300
Oceanus, 154
OCLC, 205
Octavian, 278
Octavianus, 283
Odaenathus, 132
Odoacer, 202, 229
Odrysian kingdom, 97
Oea, 276
Oescus, 83
Oise River, 160
Omen, 324
Onager, 266
Onager (siege weapon), 10, 248, 261, 264, 315, 319, 328, 333
Operational strategy, 311
Oppidum Ubiorum, 85
Optimates, 217
Optio, 68, 70, 121, 151
Orange, France, 274
Orkney Islands, 148
Oscan language, 236
Osroes I, 366
Ostia Antica, 142, 157
Ostia Antica (archaeological site), 162, 301
Otho, 146, 222

Ötztal Alps, 305

Ovation, 74
Oxford Classical Dictionary, 90
Oxford University Press, 19, 45, 163, 203

Pace (length), 293
Palaiologan Byzantine army, 53, 65

Palaiologos, 53, 65
Palatal consonant, 236
Palatalization (sound change), 237
Palatina, 87
Palatine Hill, 167
Palatini (Roman military), 40, 88, 102, 107
Paleolinguistics, 236
Palestrina, 141
Palisade, 323
Palmyra, 88, 225, 278, 305
Panegyrici Latini, 378
Pannonia, 81, 87, 96, 98, 111
Pannonia I, 159
Pannonia II, 159
Pannonian revolt, 188
Pannonians, 97
Pannonia Valeria, 159
Pantheon, Rome, 232, 296
Papus, 342
Parthamaspates, 366
Parthamaspates of Parthia, 192
Parthia, 2, 13, 111, 190, 219, 222, 224, 352, 366
Parthian Empire, 11, 186, 192, 348, 362, 366
Parthians, 86
Passports, 298
Patavium, 202
Pater Patriae, 73
Patrician (ancient Rome), 48
Pat Southern, 47
Pauly-Wissowa, 379
Peace of Nisibis (299), 199
Pecheneg, 64
Pechenegs, 64
Pecunaria multa, 75
Pedanius Dioscorides, 17
Peddars Way, 305
Peditatus, 68
Pedites, 68
Pegasus, 82
Peltasts, 337
Penguin Books, 20, 46, 202–204
Pentacontarchos, 151
Peregrinus (Roman), 51, 57, 91, 117, 150
Pergamon Museum, 33
Pergamum, 214, 261
Perinthus, 158
Perseus of Macedon, 181, 214, 337
Perseus Project, 391
Persia, 350
Persian Gulf, 148
Perusia, 300
Perusine War, 220
Pescennius Niger, 192, 197, 223
Petavonium, 84
Peter Connolly, 20

Peter Heather, 5, 9, 20, 46, 204
Petra, 303
Petra Roman Road, 303
Petronell, 84
Petronell-Carnuntum, 274
Pevensey, 157
Phalangite, 338
Phalanx, 49
Phalanx formation, 54, 55, 330, 335, 338
Phalera (military decoration), 74
Pharnaces II, 220
Pharsalus, 32
Phi Alpha Theta, 258
Philip Matyszak, 20, 46, 197, 205
Philip the Arab, 198
Philip V of Macedon, 139, 179, 213
Philological, 23
Philopoemen, 214
Phoenicia, 175
Physical trauma, 328
Piacenza, 299
Picts, 148, 364
Pike (weapon), 27, 337
Piling, 291
Pilum, 9, 27, 315, 318, 320, 327
Pilumni, 23
Pilus Posterior, 68
Pilus Prior, 68
Pirates, 184
Piroboridava, 303
Plague of Cyprian, 107
Plate armour, 59
Plaustrum, 297
Plaustrum maius, 298
Plebeian Council, 143
Pliny the Elder, 232, 233, 235
Plostrum, 297
Plough, 290
Plutarch, 142, 187, 377, 378
Pöchlarn, 159
Poetovio, 84
Politician, 127
Polybius, 19, 23, 27, 45, 49, 137, 203, 240, 256, 271, 328, 342
Polybolos, 232, 268
Polychrome, 92
Polyclitus (geographer), 296
Pompei, 275
Pompeii, 280
Pompeius Strabo, 132
Pompey, 32, 79, 132, 143, 184, 219, 377
Pompeys campaign in Iberia and Albania, 184
Pompeys Georgian campaign, 218
Pompey the Great, 184, 218
Pomponius, 286
Pomponius Secundus, 132

Pont du Gard, 232
Pont Flavien, 274
Pontifex Maximus, 73
Pontus (region), 146, 148, 158
Pope, 73
Populares, 217
Porsena, 279
Portal:Military of ancient Rome, 1, 21, 47, 71, 77, 90, 127, 135, 165, 206, 231, 235, 259, 273, 311, 316, 361
Port and starboard, 271
Porte Mars, 274
Porte Noire, 274
Port of Mainz, 162
Portonaccio sarcophagus, 36
Portugal, 178
Portus, 162
Portus Julius, 144, 157, 162
Portus Lemanis, 157
Potaissa, 83, 249, 294
Poultry, 17
Pound (weight), 264
Po Valley, 161
Power projection, 8
Practices and terminology, 281
Praefectus, 61, 109
Praefectus Castrorum, 68, 70
Praefectus Cohortis, 68
Praefectus legionis agens vice legati, 68
Praefectus praetorio, 61
Praeneste, 141, 301
Praenestine Way, 289
Praenomen, 72
Praetor, 54, 143, 151, 179, 243, 321
Praetores classici, 137
Praetorian Guard, 32, 35, 41, 53, 59, 68, 88
Praetorian prefecture of Illyricum, 225
Praetorium, 243
Praetor peregrinus, 286
Primus inter pares, 73
Primus Ordinis, 68
Primus Pilus, 68, 70, 151
Princeps, 73, 183
Princeps Posterior, 68
Princeps Prior, 68
Princeps Senatus, 73
Principate, 62, 77, 91, 110, 156
Principes, 27, 68, 325
Priscus, 150
Proceedings of the Society of Antiquaries of Scotland, 258
Proconsul, 78, 179, 243, 321
Procopius (usurper), 227
Procuratores ducenarii, 152
Procurator (Roman), 152
Project Gutenberg, 203–205

421

Proletarii, 25
Promagistrate, 151
Promoti, 39
Pronoia, 53, 65
Propontis, 158
Propraetor, 321
Proreta, 151
Prostitute, 322
Protectores Augusti Nostri, 68
Proto-Italic language, 236
Proxy war, 180
Pseudocomitatensis, 88
Ptolemaic Egypt, 145, 153
Ptolemais, Cyrenaica, 158
Ptolemy XIII, 219
Ptolemy XII of Egypt, 377
Publius Attius Varus, 128
Publius Claudius Pulcher, 129, 211
Publius Cornelius Dolabella (consul 283 BC), 132
Publius Cornelius Lentulus Spinther, 129
Publius Cornelius Scipio, 129, 177, 211, 212
Publius Cornelius Scipio Nasica, 129
Publius Cornelius Sulla, 134
Publius Decius Mus (279 BC), 129
Publius Decius Mus (312 BC), 129
Publius Decius Mus (340 BC), 129
Publius Decius Mus (consul 340 BC), 209
Publius Flavius Vegetius Renatus, 108, 257, 263
Publius Licinius Crassus Dives Mucianus, 131
Publius Ostorius Scapula, 132
Publius Petronius Turpilianus, 132
Publius Quinctilius Varus, 98, 133, 188, 190, 221
Publius Rutilius Lupus (consul 90 BC), 133
Publius Rutilius Rufus, 133
Publius Servilius Priscus Structus, 208
Publius Sulpicius Galba Maximus, 134
Publius Sulpicius Rufus, 134
Publius Valerius Laevinus, 134
Publius Ventidius Bassus, 128, 349
Pugio, 110
Pula, 274
Pulley, 271
Punic, 137
Punic Wars, 28, 97, 175, 178, 312
Puppet state, 366
Puteoli, 157
Pye Road, 305
Pyrenees, 301
Pyrénées, 305
Pyrrhic victory, 175, 337
Pyrrhic War, 209
Pyrrhus of Epirus, 129, 166, 174, 209, 335, 336

Quadi, 194, 223
Quadriga, 297
Quadrireme, 152
Quaestionarius, 68
Quaestor, 245, 285
Quality and combat capability, 99
Quarto dAltino, 305
Quattuorvir, 285, 286
Quiberon Bay, 143
Quincunx, 314, 325
Quinquegentanei, 196
Quinquereme, 137, 152
Quintus Aemilius, 133
Quintus Caecilius Metellus Macedonicus, 129, 181, 215
Quintus Caecilius Metellus Pius, 217
Quintus Fabius Maximus, 209
Quintus Fabius Maximus Aemilianus, 179
Quintus Fabius Maximus Rullianus, 130
Quintus Fabius Maximus Verrusosus, 130
Quintus Fabius Vibulanus, 208
Quintus Fufius Calenus, 130
Quintus Fulvius Flaccus, 130
Quintus Fulvius Flaccus (consul 179 BC), 130
Quintus Fulvius Flaccus (consul 179 BCE), 214
Quintus Ligarius, 131
Quintus Lollius Urbicus, 131
Quintus Lutatius Catulus, 131
Quintus Pedius, 133
Quintus Petillius Cerialis, 102, 132, 146
Quintus Salvidienus Rufus, 133
Quintus Sertorius, 133, 217
Quintus Servilius Caepio, 133
Quintus Servilius Caepio the Younger, 133
Quintus Tullius Cicero, 129

Raeda, 297
Raedae meritoriae, 297
Raetia, 81, 96, 158, 191
Ramming, 143
Ramnians, 23
Ram (ship), 154
Ransom, 143
Rape of the Sabine Women, 167
Raphana, 82–84
Rapid reaction force, 9
Ras al-Ayn, al-Hasakah, 82
Ratchet (device), 264
Raubwirtschaft, 6
Ravenna, 156, 157, 161, 162, 201
Raymond W Goldsmith, 204
Reconnaissance, 324
Recruitment, 14
Red Sea, 146
Reduction in rank, 77
Regensburg, 82, 158

Regulus, 342
Reims, 274
Relief, 4, 52, 55, 60, 92, 141
Relief depicting a Roman legionary (Berlin SK 887), 33
Republic, 317, 353
Republic of Macedonia, 301
Resaena, 82
Res Gestae Divi Augusti, 145
Retentus, 68
Revolt of Saturninus, 157
Revolt of the Batavi, 79, 81, 84
Rhaetian Limes, 242
Rhegium, 301
Rheinzabern, 298
Rhine, 42, 61, 136, 145, 154, 158, 280, 362, 365
Rhineland, 227
Rhine river, 157
Rhodes, 140, 180
Rhoemetalces I, 97
Rhône River, 161
Ribchester, 251
Richard Edwin Smith, 47
Richborough, 157, 278
Ricimer, 133
Rijeka, 300
Rimini, 275, 299, 300
Rio Tinto (river), 233
River delta, 99
River Nestos, 149
Road, 279
Robert Franklin Pennell, 205
Robin Lane Fox, 20, 204
Roda de Barà, 276
Roman aqueduct, 249
Roman architecture, 273
Roman arch (Medinaceli), 276
Roman armor, 320
Roman Army, 3, 20, 21, **47**, 66, 111, 127, 136, 316
Roman army of the late Republic, 50
Roman army of the mid-Republic, 49, 55, 70, 114
Roman bridge, 291
Roman Britain, 32, 33, 81, 166, 189, 246
Roman cavalry, 53, 91, 108
Roman censor, 72, 283
Roman citizen, 117, 150
Roman citizens, 51, 57
Roman citizenship, 50, 91, 100, 151, 317
Roman civil war of 350–351, 227
Roman civil wars, 143
Roman colony, 51
Roman commerce, 279

Roman conquest of Britain, 101, 146, 186, 189, 221, 265, 377
Roman conquest of Italy, 174
Roman consul, 29, 72, 93, 151, 208, 243, 321
Roman Consuls, 56
Roman Dacia, 104, 249, 294
Roman Dictator, 321
Roman emperor, 51, 320
Roman Empire, 6, 8, 11, 14, 19, 47, 62, 110, 136, 165, 206, 235, 264, 271, 273, 279, 349, 361
Roman Empire vs Parthia, 190
Roman equestrian order, 24
Roman-Etruscan Wars, 208
Roman Forum, 293
Roman–Latin wars, 206
Roman–Parthian War of 161–166, 223
Roman–Parthian War of 58–63, 221
Roman–Persian Wars, 227
Roman–Volscian wars, 208
Roman-Gallic wars, 171, 213
Roman Gaul, 160
Roman Governor, 67
Roman governors of Germania Inferior, 101
Roman horsemen, 354
Romania, 249, 294, 303, 365
Roman infantry tactics, 53, **316**
Roman invasion of Britain, 157, 221
Romanization, 366
Roman Kingdom, 23, 24, 47, 48, 54, 206
Roman knight, 95
Roman law, 269
Roman legion, 4, 8, 22, 29, 50, 53, 54, 57, 60, 63, 70, 77, 91, 92, 133, 135, 145, 235, 268, 293, 316–318, 320, 321, 365
Roman legionary, 9
Roman legions, 128
Roman magistrate, 151
Roman military, 165, 362
Roman military confederation, 93
Roman military decorations and punishments, 53, **71**
Roman military diploma, 99
Roman military frontiers and fortifications, **361**
Roman military personal equipment, 53, 316, 318
Roman Navy, 9, 21, 106, **135**, 247, 271
Roman numerals, 78
Romano-British, 229
Romano-Germanic Museum, 103
Roman-Parthian War of 58–63, 190
Roman-Parthian Wars, 218
Roman-Persian Wars, 222
Roman province, 61, 87
Roman province of Africa, 301

423

Roman Republic, 2, 6, 47, 54, 78, 91, 136, 206, 231, 235, 260, 261, 273, 279, 316
Roman Republican civil wars, 183
Roman road in Cilicia, 301
Roman roads, **279**
Roman roads in Morocco, 301
Roman-Seleucid War, 214
Roman Senate, 78, 93, 287, 377
Roman Serbia, 292
Roman Servile Wars, 183
Roman siege engines, **259**
Roman-Spartan War, 181, 213
Roman Syria, 305
Roman-Syrian War, 141, 175
Roman triumph, 6, 74, 168, 377
Roman tuba, 252
Roman usurper, 183
Rome, 176, 182, 232, 275, 277, 278
Romulus, 166
Romulus and Remus, 79
Romulus Augustulus, 150, 229
Romulus Augustus, 201, 202
Ronald Syme, 380
Rope, 267
Rorarii, 28, 54, 69
Roxolani, 85
Royal Marines, 5
Royal Road, 283
Rubicon, 84
Rutuli, 169
Rutupiae, 82, 157

Sabalus, 130
Sabine, 171
Sabines, 168–170
Sack of Camulodunum, 189
Sack of Eleusis, 194
Sack of Londinium, 189
Sack of Moguntiacum, 201
Sack of Rome (410), 201, 228
Sack of Rome (455), 136, 229
Sack of Segobriga, 179
Sack of Treviri, 201
Sack of Verulamium, 189
Sacramentum (oath), 75
Sagittarii, 69, 94, 113
S:Agricola, 378
Sagum, 243
Saguntum, 177, 178
Saint-Chamas, 274
Saintes, Charente-Maritime, 274
Saint Patrick, 255
Saint-Rémy-de-Provence, 274
Sala Colonia, 301
Salararius, 69
Salian Franks, 42, 229

Salona, 97
Salzburg, 300
Samnites, 171, 174, 209, 217
Samnite Wars, 55, 92, 377
Samnium, 26, 49, 171, 377
Samosata, 84
Samsat, 84
San Bernardino Pass, 305
Sanitary sewer, 287
Saône, 160
Sappers, 271
Sardinia, 210
Sarmatian, 85, 111
Sarmatians, 42, 111, 115, 194, 195, 362
Sarmizegethusa, 190
Sasanian Empire, 87, 224
Sassanian Empire, 362
Sassanid, 38, 227
Sassanid Empire, 193, 198
Satala, 84
Sava, 158
Saverne, 298
Saxons, 148
Saxon Shore, 157, 161, 365
Sbeitla, 277
Scholae, 41
Scholae Palatinae, 69, 88
Scientific American, 389
Scientific transliteration of Cyrillic, 236
Scipio Aemilianus, 179, 215
Scipio Aemilianus Africanus, 73, 129, 214
Scipio Africanus, 140, 212, 324, 339
Scipio Africanus Major, 178, 212–214
Scipio Africanus Minor, 215
Scipio Asiaticus, 129, 214
Sclaveni, 377
Scorpio (dart-thrower), 69, 261
Scorpionarius, 69
Scorpio (weapon), 319
Scotland, 2, 146, 148
Scutarii, 39
Scutum (shield), 26, 91, 315, 320
Scythia Minor, 88, 160
Sea of Galilee, 146, 158
Second Battle of Avignon (121 BC), 182
Second Battle of Bedriacum, 191, 222
Second Battle of Capua, 212
Second Battle of Clusium (82 BC), 217
Second Battle of Herdonia, 177, 212
Second Battle of Nepheris (147 BC), 215
Second Battle of Nola, 211
Second Battle of Philippi, 220
Second Battle of Tapae, 222
Second-class citizen, 117
Second Dacian War, 222
Second Illyrian War, 211

Second Macedonian War, 140, 180, 213, 377
Second Mithridatic War, 184, 217
Second Numantine War, 179
Second Punic War, 55, 93, 140, 177, 178, 182, 211, 324
Second Samnite War, 26, 28, 173, 209
Second Servile War, 215
Second Triumvirate, 143, 188
Second War with Barack obama.2C under Tullus Hostilius, 206
Second War with Fidenae and Veii.2C under Tullus Hostilius, 168
Secret service, 67
Segedunum, 363
Seine, 160
Sejanus, 133
Selene, 60
Seleucia Pieria, 158
Seleucid Empire, 141, 181, 377
Senones, 171
Septimius Severus, 51, 73, 81, 82, 105, 148, 192, 197, 223, 268, 287, 375
Septimus Severus, 223
Serbia, 82, 83, 291, 301
Sergeant, 120
Sergeant-major, 121
Sertorian War, 217
Servian constitution, 24
Servius Sulpicius Galba (consul 144 BC), 134, 179
Servius Sulpicius Galba (praetor 54 BC), 130
Servius Tullius, 24, 54, 168
Sesterces, 152
Severan dynasty, 148
Sevilla, 305
Sexagenarii, 152
Sextus Julius Severus, 133
Sextus Pompeius, 132, 143, 188, 220
Sextus Tarquinius, 169
S:From the Founding of the City, 19, 45
Shapur I, 199, 224
Shapur II, 199
Shapur II of Persia, 227
Shetland Islands, 148
Shock troops, 331
Sicilian revolt, 143, 220
Sicily, 137, 175, 176, 210
Sickle, 17
Siculus Flaccus, 282, 307
Sidewalk, 285
Sidonius Apollinaris, 150, 202
Siege, 17
Siege engine, 268
Siege engines, 259
Siege of Aquileia, 194
Siege of Aracillum (25 BC), 220

Siege of Athens and Piraeus (87 BC - 86 BC), 217
Siege of Avaricum, 186
Siege of Cyzicus, 217
Siege of Erisone, 179
Siege of Jerusalem (66), 192
Siege of Jerusalem (70), 192
Siege of Lilybaeum, 211
Siege of Masada, 192
Siege of Massilia, 187
Siege of Numantia, 179, 214
Siege of Pirisabora, 199
Siege of Sarmizethusa, 190
Siege of Syracuse (214–212 BC), 140
Siege of Veii, 170
Siege tower, 272
Siege towers, 10, 267
Siege warfare, 259, 351
Signifer, 69
Silistra, 84
Singidunum, 82, 158
Sinjar, 81
Sinuessa, 298
Siraces, 221
Sirmium, 48, 160
Siwa Oasis, 367
Slave, 353
Sling (weapon), 25, 94, 266
Smallpox, 107
Social contract, 22
Social War (90–88 BC), 215
Social War (91–88 BC), 8, 25, 31, 50, 57, 69, 93, 183
Socii, 28, 31, 49, 55, 69
Socii navales, 137, 141
Soft palate, 236
Solidus (coin), 48, 253
Somme River, 161
Sortie, 52
Southern Europe, 165
Southern France, 50
Southern Illinois University Press, 203
Spade, 290
Spain, 178, 233, 238, 251, 276
Spanish colonization of the Americas, 251
Spanish naming customs, 238
Sparta, 148, 181, 214, 335
Spartacus, 76, 218
Sparti (municipality), 24
Spatha, 104, 110
Speculatores, 32, 69, 247
Spoke, 266
Spoleto, 276
SPQR, 2, 75, 320
Springald, 260
Spring (device), 267

425

Spurius Postumius Albinus, 209
Squatting position, 330
Staff (military), 61
Stanegate, 305
Stane Street (Chichester), 305
Stane Street (Colchester), 305
Statius, 290
Staurakios the eunuch, 133
Stenarum, 303
Steven Runciman, 46
S:The Annals (Tacitus), 19, 45
Stilicho, 133, 201, 228
Strabo, 379
Strait of Otranto, 83
Strasbourg, 83
Strata Diocletiana, 305
Strategic reserve, 8
Strategy, 317
Strategy of the Roman military, **311**
Structural history of the Roman military, **21**, 53, 321
Structure of the Roman military, 316
Subsistence agriculture, 119
Sudis (stake), 241
Suebi, 228
Suebians, 201
Suessa Pometia, 169, 206
Suetonius, 97, 125
Suetonius Paullinus, 222
Sugambri, 188
Suing for peace, 173
Sulla, 79, 142, 184
Sullas first civil war, 217
Sullas second civil war, 217
Summit (topography), 306
Sunrise, 387
Susa, 366
Susa (Italy), 276
Susa, Piedmont, 244
Svishtov, 81
Syagrius, 134, 229
Syncretism, 62
Syntagma (linguistics), 237
Syphax, 178, 212
Syracuse, Sicily, 94, 138
Syria, 114, 276, 278
Syria (Roman province), 81, 101, 158, 191, 367
Szeged, 303
Szőny, 81

Tablifer, 69
Tabula Peutingeriana, 295, 296
Tabula Traiana, 291
Tacfarinas, 82
Tacitus, 19, 36, 45, 96, 125, 374, 378, 379

Tadcaster, 251
Tagma (military), 52, 64
Taifali, 196
Talent (measurement), 262
Taranto, 137, 174
Tarquinia (gens), 208
Tarquinii, 208
Tarquinius Priscus, 24, 167
Tarquinius Superbus, 24, 169
Tarraco, 211
Tarragona, 305
Tarsus, Mersin, 304
Taurisci, 103
Taurus (astrology), 79
Tax per head, 119
Tébessa, 273
Technological history of the Roman military, **231**
Tel Aviv, 146
Template:Ancient Rome military sidebar, 1, 21, 47, 71, 77, 90, 127, 135, 165, 206, 231, 235, 259, 273, 311, 316, 361
Template talk:Ancient Rome military sidebar, 1, 21, 47, 71, 77, 90, 127, 135, 165, 206, 231, 235, 259, 273, 311, 316, 361
Temple of Jupiter Optimus Maximus, 169
Temple of Saturn, 291, 295
Tencteri, 188, 193
Tendon, 264
Tent, 237
Terracina, 301
Terracotta, 92
Tervingi, 149
Tesserarius, 69
Testudo formation, 331–333, 351
Tetrarchy, 149, 199
Tetricus I, 198, 224
Teuta, 139
Teutons, 182, 215
Thames and Hudson, 20, 46, 204, 205
The Battle of the Milvian Bridge (Giulio Romano), 196
Thebes, Egypt, 82, 89
The defeat of Cornelius Fuscus, 79
The Fifteen Decisive Battles of the World, 346
The Latin Library, 45
Theme (Byzantine administrative unit), 62
Theme (Byzantine district), 52, 64
Theodolite, 290
Theodoric I, 228
Theodor Mommsen, 23, 46
Theodosius I, 198, 227
Theodotus (geographer), 296
The Pometian revolt, 206
The Ridgeway, 280
Thervings, 227

Thessalonica, 149, 377
Thessaloniki, 274, 301
Theveste, 273
Third Battle of Nola, 212
Third Illyrian War, 214
Third Macedonian War, 141, 181, 214
Third Mithridatic War, 143, 184, 217, 218
Third Punic War, 141, 178, 215
Third Samnite War, 173
Third Samnite War (298 to 290 BC), 209
Third Servile War, 183, 218
Thirty Tyrants (Roman), 377
Thomas North, 203
Thrace, 44, 99, 114, 148, 158, 377
Thracia, 158
Thracians, 110
Throwing spear, 27
Thurii, 132
Tiberius, 97, 145, 287, 298
Tiberius Claudius Paulinus, 132
Tiberius Gracchus Major, 133
Tiberius Julius Cotys I, 221
Tiberius Nero, 132
Tiberius Sempronius Gracchus (consul 215 and 213 BC), 133
Tiberius Sempronius Gracchus (consul 238 BC), 133
Tiberius Sempronius Longus (consul 194 BCE), 133
Tiberius Sempronius Longus (consul 218 BC), 133, 211
Ticinum, 202
Tigranes II of Armenia, 217
Tigranocerta, 221
Tigris, 148
Tigurini, 185
Timgad, 274
Tingis, 301
Tingitania, 43
Tirones, 69
Tisza, 148
Tities (roman tribe), 23
Titus, 103, 287
Titus Aebutius Elva, 128
Titus Didius, 129
Titus Labienus, 187, 219
Titus Larcius, 131
Titus Livius, 1
Titus Manlius Torquatus (235 BC), 131
Titus Manlius Torquatus (consul 347 BC), 131, 209
Titus Quinctius Capitolinus Barbatus, 208
Titus Quinctius Flamininus, 133, 180, 213
Titus Vinius, 134
Tom Holland (author), 204
Tony Clunn, 204, 384

Torc, 74, 123
Torsion (mechanics), 266
Toulouse, 301
Trabzon, 158
Train (military), 322
Trajan, 18, 34, 82, 85, 87, 91, 123, 148, 166, 189, 190, 222, 287, 294, 366
Trajanic, 40
Trajans bridge, 303
Trajans Column, 3, 91, 94, 111, 147, 264
Trajans Dacian Wars, 91, 111, 147, 154, 166
Transalpine Gaul, 32
Transylvania, 222
Treaty of Tempea, 181
Trebbia River, 352
Trebonianus Gallus, 148
Trebonius, 134
Trebuchet, 264
Treveri, 102
Triarii, 27, 69, 256, 325
Tribune, 73, 99, 109, 245, 256
Tribunes, 321
Tribuni militum angusticlavii, 69
Tribunus Laticlavius, 69
Tribunus militum, 61
Tribute, 166
Trier, 102
Trierarch, 151
Trierarchi, 151
Trieste, 276, 300
Triga (chariot), 297
Tripoli, 276
Trireme, 137, 152
Triumphal arch, 273, 276, 278
Triumphal arches, 277
Triumphal Arch of Orange, 274
Triumvir, 184, 188, 220
Triumvirate, 183
Troesmis, 83, 303
Trsat, 300
Trumpet, 323
Tubicen, 69
Tullus Hostilius, 166
Tungri, 101
Tunisia, 2, 147, 277
Turda, 83, 294
Turdetania, 179
Turkey, 277, 278, 301, 304
Turkish people, 53
Turma, 70, 95, 256
Tuscany, 300
Tusculum, 170
Twelve Tables, 280
Tyre, Lebanon, 276

Udine, 300

Ulpian, 282
Ulpia Noviomagus Batavorum, 84
Umbilicus Romae, 295
Umbrian language, 236
Unified Empire under Attila, 11
Unit cohesion, 352
United Kingdom, 278
University of California Press, 162, 203
Urbanae, 69
Ursicinus (Roman general), 134
Usipetes, 188
Usipi, 193
Usurper, 63
Uttoxeter, 251

Val Canale, 300
Valencia (city in Spain), 305
Valens, 43, 196, 198, 227
Valens (usurper), 134
Valentinian I, 227
Valentinian III, 202
Valerian (emperor), 199, 224
Vallum, 241
Vandal Kingdom, 136
Vandals, 161, 165, 196, 201, 228
Varangian Guard, 53
Varangians, 65
Vardariotai, 65
Vatican Museums, 141
Vegetable, 17
Vegetius, 125, 149, 153, 160, 270, 271, 313, 319, 320, 356, 357, 373, 378
Veii, 168, 170, 208
Velar consonant, 236
Velites, 27, 54, 69, 326, 338
Velleius Paterculus, 37
Venator (gladiator type), 69
Veneti (Gaul), 128, 143
Veneto, 301
Vercingetorix, 186, 218, 344
Vercovicium, 364
Verona, 300, 301
Verona, Italy, 276
Vespasian, 79, 82, 84, 85, 101, 103, 146, 157, 158, 191, 222, 287
Veteran, 14, 30, 254
Veterinarius, 68, 120
Vexillarius, 69
Vexillatio, 70
Vexillation, 365
Vexillationes, 35
Vexillum, 69, 74, 120
Via Aemilia, 299
Via Aemilia Scauri, 300
Via Agrippa, 301
Via Amerina, 300

Via Appia, 283, 293, 298, 300
Via Aquillia, 300
Via Aquitania, 301
Via Augusta, 301, 305
Via Aurelia, 300
Via Belgica, 303
Via Canalis, 300
Via Cassia, 283, 300, 301
Via Claudia Augusta, 305
Via Claudia Julia Augusta, 300
Via Claudia Nova, 300
Via Clodia, 300
Via Decia, 305
Via de la Plata, 305
Via Devana, 305
Via Domitia, 301, 305
Via Domiziana, 290, 300
Via Egnatia, 301
Via Flaminia, 283, 300
Via Flavia, 300
Via Gabina, 279
Via Gemina, 300
Via Hadriana, 301
Via Julia Augusta, 301
Via Labicana, 279, 301
Via Latina, 279, 289
Via Mala, 305
Via Maris, 303
Via Militaris, 301
Via Nomentana, 279
Via Ostiense, 301
Via Pontica, 303
Via Popilia, 301
Via Postumia, 301
Via Praenestina, 301
Via Raetia, 300
Via Salaria, 279, 300
Via Schlavonia, 301
Via Severiana, 301
Via Tiburtina, 301
Viaticum, 116
Via Traiana Nova, 303
Via Traiana Nova (Italy), 301
Vibo, 300
Victor Davis Hanson, 204
Victoria and Albert Museum, 35, 94
Victory titles, 72
Vicus (Rome), 284
Vienna, 84, 300
Vigintisexviri, 286
Vigintiviri, 286
Villa, 298
Villach, 300
Villa Romana del Casale, 108
Viminacium, 83, 159
Vindobona, 84

Vindolanda, 253
Vindonissa, 84, 85
Viriathus, 179, 346
Virius Lupus, 197
Viroconium, 85
Visigoths, 45, 201, 228, 357
Vita Aureliani, 76
Vitellius, 146, 191, 222
Vitruvius, 232, 235, 263, 269, 289
Voie romaine (Nord), 301
Völkerwanderung, 136
Vologases I, 190
Vologases IV, 223
Volsci, 169, 170, 208
Volscian, 377
Volubilis, 276

Wales, 2, 233
Walter Scheidel, 259
War elephant, 174
War-elephant, 335
Warrant officer, 121
Warren Treadgold, 39, 47
War with Clusium in 508 BC, 170
War with Fidenae and Veii under Romulus, 168, 206
War withk Tarquinius Priscus, 206
War with Rome under Tarquinius Priscus, 168
War with Rome under Tarquinius Superbus, 169, 208
War with Tarquinius Priscus, 168
War with the Latins and Sabines after the Rape of the Sabine Women, 168, 206
War with Tullus Hostilius, 168, 206
War with Veii and Tarquinii.2C after the overthrow of the monarchy in 509 BC, 170
War with Veii and the Etruscans.2C under Servius Tullius, 168, 206
Watermill, 232
Watling Street, 305
Way of Saint James, 305
Weidenfeld & Nicolson, 204
Weißenburg in Bayern, 245
Weser, 145
Western Europe, 165
Western Roman Empire, 21, 52, 62, 149, 165, 317
Wheat, 76
Wikipedia:Citation needed, 53, 75, 246, 362, 365
Wikipedia:Cleanup, 286
Wikipedia:Link rot, 20
Wikipedia:Please clarify, 25, 40, 41, 49, 284, 286
Wikipedia:Verifiability, 106
Wikisource, 19, 20, 45, 202, 203, 256

Wikisource:Commentaries on the Civil War, 202
Wikisource:Epitome of Roman History, 203
Wikisource:From the Founding of the City, 203
Wikisource:History of the Wars, 203
Wikisource:Lives (Dryden translation), 203
Wikisource:The African War, 203
Wikisource:The Alexandrian War, 203
Wikisource:The Annals (Tacitus), 203
Wikisource:The Histories (Tacitus), 203
Wikisource:The Spanish War, 203
Wikisource:The War of the Jews, 256
Wikt:crossroads, 284
William Smith (lexicographer), 258
William Whiston, 256
Winch, 264
Windisch, 85
Windlass, 267
Winston Churchill, 204
Witcham Gravel helmet, 98
World Heritage Site, 238
WP:LIBRARY, 19, 308
Wroxeter, 84

Xanten, 83–85, 102
Xanthippus of Carthage, 177
XII Fulminata, 80

Yale University Press, 205
Yann Le Bohec, 272
Yazdegerd II, 199
Year of the Five Emperors, 223
Year of the Four Emperors, 101, 146, 157, 222
Yemen, 145
York, 83
Yverdon-les-Bains, 160

Zemun, 158
Zenobia, 225
Zenodoxus (geographer), 296
Zeugma, Commagene, 83
Zosimus, 356, 375, 378
Zuiderzee, 157

www.ingramcontent.com/pod-product-compliance
Lightning Source LLC
Chambersburg PA
CBHW030516230426
43665CB00010B/633